American Literary Scholarship 1993

American Literary Scholarship
An Annual 1993

Edited by Gary Scharnhorst

Essays by David M. Robinson, Leland S. Person, Jr.,
Benjamin F. Fisher, John Wenke, Tom Quirk,
Robert L. Gale, George Kearns, Cleo McNelly Kearns,
Alexander J. Marshall, III, Albert J. DeFazio III, William J.
Scheick, Lawrence I. Berkove, Jo Ann Middleton, Catherine
Calloway, Jerome Klinkowitz, Timothy Materer, Lorenzo
Thomas, James J. Martine, Gary Lee Stonum, Daniel Royot,
Algerina Neri, Keiko Beppu, Jan Nordby Gretlund,
Elisabeth Herion-Sarafidis, and Hans Skei

Duke University Press   Durham and London 1995

© 1995 Duke University Press

All rights reserved

LC 65-19450   ISBN 0-8223-1628-5

Printed in the United States of America

on acid-free paper ∞

Contents

Foreword

As a first-time editor of *American Literary Scholarship,* I inherit the responsibility of compiling it (in alternating years with David J. Nordloh) from its founders, James Woodress and J. Albert Robbins. Having completed the task for the first time, I appreciate more than ever their stewardship as editors of the annual during its first 27 years of existence. First published in 1965, *ALS* has prospered over the years, whatever the ebb and flow of critical fashion. If, as I am sometimes reminded, every term in its title may be "problematized," I am confident, too, that literary theorists, critics, and biographers all continue to find in it a valuable reference tool.

This 31st edition of the annual retains the same basic organization of its predecessors, though it is hardly identical to them in all details. Contributed by James Martine, Timothy Materer, Lorenzo Thomas, and Daniel Royot respectively, the chapters on "Drama," "Poetry: 1900 to the 1940s," "Poetry: The 1940s to the Present," and "French Contributions" reappear in *ALS* after a brief hiatus. Robert Gale, a regular contributor of the "Henry James" chapter to *ALS* throughout the 1970s and 1980s, returns for one year in the same role. Lawrence I. Berkove contributes "19th-Century Literature," the last such chapter before its parameters are redrawn. Gary Lee Stonum shifts from the Whitman-Dickinson chapter to "Themes, Topics, Criticism," and Keiko Beppu takes her turn at "Japanese Contributions." Because of health problems from which she is now recuperating, Martha Nell Smith was unable to contribute the "Whitman and Dickinson" chapter this year and has agreed to cover two years of relevant scholarship in *ALS 1994.*

More changes are in line for *ALS 1994.* The chapter on "19th-Century Literature," in recent years one of the most daunting to prepare given the proliferation of scholarship on the period, will be reconfigured into separate chapters divided chronologically. We bid farewell to several departing contributors with sincere thanks for their hard work: Gale, Berkove, George Kearns, Cleo McNelly Kearns, and Alexander Marshall, III. Several scholars new to *ALS* will join the roster of contributors next year, including Greg W. Zacharias of Creighton University ("James"), Michael Coyle of Colgate University and Laura Cowan of the University of Maine ("Pound and Eliot"), Philip Cohen of the University of Texas at Arlington ("Faulkner"), and Laura Skandera-Trombley of SUNY-Potsdam ("Late-19th-Century Literature"). Hiroko Sato will continue her alternation with Keiko Beppu on "Japanese Contributions." *ALS 1994* will be edited by David Nordloh, and authors are invited to forward offprints and review copies of books to him at the Department of English, Indiana University, Bloomington, IN 47405.

More so than most editorial projects, as I have learned, *American Literary Scholarship* is a genuinely collaborative effort. I am indebted not only to each of the many contributors but to the staff of the MLA Center for Bibliographic Services, under the direction of Terence Ford, for again supplying a preprint of the *International Bibliography* for use by *ALS* contributors; to Dean Bill Gordon of the College of Arts and Sciences, University of New Mexico, for his generous support; and to Jami Hacker for her capable assistance. I am particularly indebted to Pam Morrison and Bob Mirandon of the Duke University Press, new friends who have tolerated my idiosyncrasies and corrected my most glaring mistakes.

Gary Scharnhorst
University of New Mexico

Key to Abbreviations

Festschriften, Essay Collections, and Books Discussed in More Than One Chapter

Aging and Gender in Literature / Anne M. Wyatt-Brown and Janice Rossen, eds., *Aging and Gender in Literature: Studies in Creativity* (Virginia)

Alice Walker and Zora Neale Hurston / Lillie P. Howard, ed., *Alice Walker and Zora Neale Hurston: The Common Bond* (Greenwood)

Almost Common People / Michael Zuckerman, *Almost Common People: Oblique Biographies in the American Grain* (Calif.)

American Culture Between the Wars / Walter Kalaidjian, *American Culture between the Wars: Revisionary Modernism and Postmodern Critique* (Columbia)

American Iconology / David C. Miller, ed., *American Iconology: New Approaches to Nineteenth-Century Art and Literature* (Yale)

American Salons / Robert M. Crunden, *American Salons: Encounters with European Modernism, 1885–1917* (Oxford)

Angels of Reality / David Michael Hertz, *Angels of Reality: Emersonian Unfoldings in Wright, Stevens, and Ives* (So. Ill.)

Anxious Power / Carol J. Singley and Susan Elizabeth Sweeney, eds., *Anxious Power: Reading, Writing, and Ambivalence in Narrative by Women* (SUNY)

Authority and Speech / Louise K. Barnett, *Authority and Speech: Language, Society, and Self in the American Novel* (Georgia)

The Birth-Mark / Susan Howe, *The Birth-Mark: Unsettling the Wilderness in American Literary History* (Wesleyan)

Black and White Strangers / Kenneth W. Warren, *Black and White Strangers: Race and American Literary Realism* (Chicago)

By the Sweat of the Brow / Nicholas K. Bromell, *By the Sweat of the Brow: Literature and Labor in Antebellum America* (Chicago)

Cambridge Guide to American Theatre / Don B. Wilmeth and Tice L. Miller, eds., *Cambridge Guide to American Theatre* (Cambridge)

Child Brides and Intruders / Carol Wershoven, *Child Brides and Intruders* (Bowling Green)

Columbia History of American Poetry / Jay Parini, ed., *The Columbia History of American Poetry* (Columbia)

Coordinates of Anglo-American Romanticism / Richard E. Brantley, *Coordinates of Anglo-American Romanticism: Wesley, Edwards, Carlyle, and Emerson* (Florida)

The Coupling Convention / Ann duCille, *The Coupling Convention: Sex, Text, and Tradition in Black Women's Fiction* (Oxford)

Culture and Commerce / Andrew Levy, *The Culture and Commerce of the American Short Story* (Cambridge)

Cultures of Letters / Richard Brodhead, *Cultures of Letters: Scenes of Reading and Writing in Nineteenth-Century America* (Chicago)

Deadly Musings / Michael Kowalewski, *Deadly Musings: Violence and Verbal Form in American Fiction* (Princeton)

Discovering Difference / Christoph Lohmann, ed., *Discovering Difference: Contemporary Essays in American Culture* (Indiana)

(Dis)Forming the American Canon / Ronald A. T. Judy, *(Dis)Forming the American Canon: African-Arabic Slave Narratives and the Vernacular* (Minnesota)

Dreaming Revolution / Scott Bradfield, *Dreaming Revolution: Transgression in the Development of American Romance* (Iowa)

Ethnic Passages / Thomas J. Ferraro, *Ethnic Passages: Literary Immigrants in Twentieth-Century America* (Chicago)

Exploring the Midwestern Literary Imagination / Marcia Noe, ed., *Exploring the Midwestern Literary Imagination: Essays in Honor of David D. Anderson* (Whitston)

Faulkner, His Contemporaries, and His Posterity / Waldemar Zacharasiewicz, ed., *Faulkner, His Contemporaries, and His Posterity* (Franke)

Female Tradition / Carol Manning, ed., *The Female Tradition in Southern Letters* (Illinois)

Feminine Sense in Southern Memoir / Will Brantley, *Feminine Sense in Southern Memoir: Smith, Glasgow, Welty, Hellman, Porter, and Hurston* (Miss.)

Fictions of Form in American Poetry / Stephen Cushman, *Fictions of Form in American Poetry* (Princeton)

A Fictive People / Ronald J. Zboray, *A Fictive People: Antebellum Economic Development and the American Reading Public* (Oxford)

Frontier Gothic / David Mogen, Scott P. Sanders, and Joanne B. Karpinski, eds., *Frontier Gothic: Terror and Wonder at the Frontier in American Literature* (Fairleigh Dickinson)

The Ghost of Meter / Annie Finch, *The Ghost of Meter: Culture and Prosody in American Free Verse* (Michigan)

Gothic (Re)Visions / Susan Wolstenholme, *Gothic (Re)Visions: Writing Women as Readers* (SUNY)

Having It Both Ways / Forrest G. Robinson, *Having It Both Ways: Self-Subversion in Western Popular Novels* (New Mexico)

Imagining Paris / J. Gerald Kennedy, *Imagining Paris: Exile Writing and American Identity* (Yale)

Invalid Women / Diane Price Herndl, *Invalid Women: Figuring Feminine Illness in American Fiction and Culture, 1840–1940* (No. Car.)

Lost in the Customhouse / Jerome Loving, *Lost in the Customhouse: Authorship in the American Renaissance* (Iowa)

Love and Theft / Eric Lott, *Love and Theft: Blackface Minstrelsy and the American Working Class* (Oxford)

Maupassant and the American Short Story / Richard Fusco, *Maupassant and the American Short Story: The Influence of Form at the Turn of the Century* (Penn. State)

Melville and Melville Studies in Japan / Kenazburo Ohashi, ed., *Melville and Melville Studies in Japan* (Greenwood)

Modernism, Mass Culture, and Professionalism / Thomas Strychacz, *Modernism, Mass Culture, and Professionalism* (Cambridge)

Monstrous Imagination / Marie-Helene Huet, *Monstrous Imagination* (Harvard)

Mules and Dragons / Mary E. Young, *Mules and Dragons: Popular Culture Images in the Selected Writings of African-American and Chinese-American Women Writers* (Greenwood)

Myth of New Orleans / Violet Harrington Bryan, *The Myth of New Orleans in Literature: Dialogues of Race and Gender* (Tennessee)

Narrative Discovery / Bruce Greenfield, *Narrative Discovery: The Romantic Explorer in American Literature, 1780–1855* (Columbia, 1992)

New England Humor / Cameron C. Nickels, *New England Humor: From the Revolutionary War to the Civil War* (Tennessee)

The New England Milton / K. P. Van Anglen, *The New England Milton: Literary Reception and Cultural Authority in the Early Republic* (Penn. State)

The Nineteenth-Century American Short Story / Douglas Tallack, *The Nineteenth-Century American Short Story: Language, Form, and Ideology* (Routledge)

Nobody's Home / Arnold Weinstein, *Nobody's Home: Speech, Self, and Place in American Fiction from Hawthorne to DeLillo* (Oxford)

Old West–New West / Barbara Howard Meldrum, ed., *Old West–New West: Centennial Essays* (Idaho)

Oratorial Culture in Nineteenth-Century America / Gregory Clark and S. Michael Halloran, eds., *Oratorial Culture in Nineteenth-Century America: Transformations in the Theory and Practice of Rhetoric* (So. Ill.)

Over Her Dead Body / Elisabeth Bronfen, *Over Her Dead Body: Death, Femininity, and the Aesthetic* (Routledge)

Palimpsest / George Bornstein and Ralph G. Williams, eds., *Palimpsest: Editorial Theory in the Humanities* (Michigan)

Pilgrims to the Wild / John P. O'Grady, *Pilgrims to the Wild: Everett Ruess, Henry David Tho-

reau, John Muir, Clarence King, and Mary Austin (Utah)

Pillars of Salt, Monuments of Grace / David A. Cohen, *Pillars of Salt, Monuments of Grace: New England Crime Literature and the Origins of American Popular Culture, 1674–1860* (Oxford)

Plight in Common / Elzbieta H. Olesky, *Plight in Common: Hawthorne and Percy* (Peter Lang)

Poe, King, and Other Contemporaries / J. Lasley Dameron, *Edgar Allan Poe, Stephen King, and Other Contemporaries* (Odense)

The Problem of American Realism / Michael Davitt Bell, *The Problem of American Realism: Studies in the Cultural History of a Literary Idea* (Chicago)

Readers in History / James L. Machor, ed., *Readers in History: Nineteenth-Century American Literature and the Contexts of Response* (Hopkins)

The Regenerate Lyric / Elisa New, *The Regenerate Lyric: Theology and Innovation in American Poetry* (Cambridge)

Representative Words / Thomas Gustafson, *Representative Words: Politics, Literature, and the American Language, 1776–1865* (Cambridge, 1992)

Resistant Essays / Jesse Bier, *Resistant Essays* (Univ. Press)

Reverse Tradition / Robert Kiely, *Reverse Tradition: Postmodern Fictions and the Nineteenth Century Novel* (Harvard)

Rewriting the South / Lothar Hönnighausen and Valeria Gennaro Lerda, eds., *Rewriting the South: History and Fiction* (Franke)

The Rites of Assent / Sacvan Bercovitch, *The Rites of Assent: Transformations in the Symbolic Construction of America* (Routledge)

Sacred Estrangement / Peter A. Dorsey, *Sacred Estrangement: The Rhetoric of Conversion in Modern American Autobiography* (Penn. State)

Significance of Sibling Relationships in Literature / Jo Anna Stephens Mink and Janet Doubler Ward, eds., *The Significance of Sibling Relationships in Literature* (Bowling Green)

Six Literary Lives / Reed Whittemore, *Six Literary Lives: The Shared Impiety of Adams, London, Sinclair, Williams, Dos Passos, and Tate* (Missouri)

Splintered Worlds / Robert M. Greenberg, *Splintered Worlds: Fragmentation and the Ideal of Diversity in the Work of Emerson, Melville, Whitman, and Dickinson* (Northeastern)

Subjectivity, Identity, and the Body / Sidonie Smith, *Subjectivity, Identity, and the Body: Women's Autobiographical Practices in the Twentieth Century* (Indiana)

Summoning / Ellen Spolsky, ed., *Summoning: Ideas of the Covenant and Interpretive Theory* (SUNY)

Sweet Home / Charles Scruggs, *Sweet Home: Invisible Cities in the Afro-American Novel* (Hopkins)

To Wake the Nations / Eric J. Sundquist, *To Wake the Nations: Race in the Making of American Literature* (Harvard)

Upstaging Big Daddy / Ellen Donkin

and Susan Clement, eds., *Upstaging Big Daddy: Directing Theater as if Gender and Race Matter* (Michigan)

Women and the Journey / Bonnie Frederick and Susan H. McLeod, eds., *Women and the Journey: The Female Travel Experience* (Washington State)

Women and World War I / Dorothy Goldman, ed., *Women and World War I: The Written Response* (St. Martin's)

Wretched Exotic / Katherine Joslin and Alan Price, eds., *Wretched Exotic: Essays on Edith Wharton and Europe* (Peter Lang)

Periodicals, Annuals, and Series

AAR / *African American Review*
ABSt / *A/B: Auto/Biography Studies*
AI / *American Imago*
AIQ / *American Indian Quarterly*
AL / *American Literature*
ALR / *American Literary Realism, 1870–1910*
AmDram / *American Drama*
American Journal of Legal History
AmerS / *American Studies*
AmerSS / *American Studies in Scandinavia*
AmLH / *American Literary History*
AmPer / *American Periodicals*
ANQ: A Quarterly Journal of Short Articles, Notes, and Reviews
APR / *American Poetry Review*
AQ / *American Quarterly*
ArAA / *Arbeiten aus Anglistik und Amerikanistik*
ARLR / *American Renaissance Literary Report*

ArQ / *Arizona Quarterly*
ASch / *American Scholar*
Atlantic
ATQ / *American Transcendental Quarterly*
BB / *Bulletin of Bibliography*
Bestia / *Bestia: Yearbook of the Beast Fable Society*
Biography / *Biography: An Interdisciplinary Quarterly*
BJA / *British Journal of Aesthetics*
BoundaryII / *Boundary 2: An International Journal of Literature and Culture*
BSWWS / Boise State University Western Writers Series
Caliban (Toulouse Le Mirail)
CanL / *Canadian Literature*
Catholic Historical Review
CEA / *CEA Critic*
CLAJ / *College Language Association Journal*
CLS / *Comparative Literature Studies*
Clues: A Journal of Detection
CML / *Classical and Modern Literature*
CollL / *College Literature*
CompD / *Comparative Drama*
ConL / *Contemporary Literature*
Connecticut Review
CQ / *Cambridge Quarterly*
CRevAS / *Canadian Review of American Studies*
Crit / *Critique: Studies in Modern Fiction*
CritI / *Critical Inquiry*
Criticism: A Quarterly for Literature and the Arts
Critique of Anthropology
CS / *Concord Saunterer*
Culture
Cycnos (Univ. de Nice)

Differences: A Journal of Feminist Cultural Studies
EA / *Etudes Anglaises*
EAL / *Early American Literature*
EAS / *Essays in Arts and Sciences*
Eastern Buddhist
ECent / *The Eighteenth Century: Theory and Interpretation*
ECF / *Eighteenth Century Fiction*
ECS / *Eighteen-Century Studies*
EdN / *Editors' Notes*
EGN / *Ellen Glasgow Newsletter*
EigoS / *Eigo Seinen* (Tokyo)
EIHC / *Essex Institute Historical Collections*
ELH [formerly *Journal of English Literary History*]
ELN / *English Language Notes*
ELWIU / *Essays in Literature* (Western Ill. Univ.)
EONR / *Eugene O'Neill Review*
ES / *English Studies*
ESP / *Emerson Society Papers*
ESQ: *A Journal of the American Renaissance*
EWhR / *Edith Wharton Review*
Expl / *Explicator*
Extrapolation: A Journal of Science Fiction and Fantasy
Fitzgerald Newsletter
FJ / *Faulkner Journal*
FNS / *Frank Norris Studies*
Frontiers
GaHR / *Georgia Historical Review*
GaR / *Georgia Review*
GNR / *Germanic Notes and Reviews*
GR / *Germanic Review*
HEI / *History of European Ideas*
HJR / *Henry James Review*
HK / *Heritage of the Great Plains*
HLB / *Harvard Library Bulletin*
HN / *Hemingway Review*

Horisont (Malmoe, Sweden)
HSE / *Hungarian Studies in English* (Debrecen)
HTR / *Harvard Theological Review*
HudR / *Hudson Review*
IdSUJAL / *Idaho State University Journal of Arts and Letters*
IEB / *Illinois English Bulletin*
InMH / *Indiana Magazine of History*
IowaR / *Iowa Review*
ISLE: *Interdisciplinary Studies in Literature and Environment*
JAAC / *Journal of Aesthetics and Art Criticism*
JACult / *Journal of American Culture*
JADT / *Journal of American Drama and Theatre*
JAmS / *Journal of American Studies*
JBE / *Journal of Business Ethics*
JEGP / *Journal of English and German Philology*
JEP / *Journal of Evolutionary Psychology*
JHI / *Journal of the History of Ideas*
JHS / *Journal of the History of Sexuality*
JMS / *Journal of Men's Studies*
JNT / *Journal of Narrative Technique*
Journal of Psychohistory
Journal of Religious Ethics
Journal of Rheumatology
JPRS / *Journal of Pre-Raphaelite Studies*
JSH / *Journal of Social History*
JSSE / *Journal of the Short Story in English* (Angers, France)
JSW / *Journal of the Southwest*
Judaism
JW / *Journal of the West*
JWIL / *Journal of West Indian Literature*
K&K / *Kultur og Klasse*

Kalki

KR / *Kenyon Review*

LaEJ / *Louisiana English Journal*

L&M / *Literature and Medicine*

LAmer / *Letterature d'America: Rivista Trimestale*

Lang&Lit / *Language and Literature*

LangQ / *The Language Quarterly*

L&P / *Literature and Psychology*

LATR / *Latin American Theatre Review*

Legacy: A Journal of Nineteenth-Century American Women Writers

LHY / *Literary Half-Yearly*

Linea d'Ombra

Ling&L / *Lingua e Literatura: Revista dos Departamentos de Letras de Faculdade de Filosofia, Letras e Ciencas Humanas da Universidade de Sao Paulo*

MD / *Modern Drama*

MELUS: The Journal of the Society for the Study of Multi-Ethnic Literature of the United States

Menckeniana: A Quarterly Review

MFS / *Modern Fiction Studies*

MHM / *Maryland Historical Magazine*

MHR / *Missouri Historical Review*

MiltonQ / *Milton Quarterly*

MissQ / *Mississippi Quarterly*

MissR / *Missouri Review*

MLQ / *Modern Language Quarterly*

MLR / *Modern Language Review*

MLS / *Modern Language Studies*

ModA / *Modern Age: A Quarterly Review*

Monatshefte

Mosaic: A Journal for the Interdisciplinary Study of Literature

MP / *Modern Philology*

MQ / *Midwest Quarterly: A Journal of*

Contemporary Thought (Pittsburg, Kans.)

MR / *Massachusetts Review*

MSEx / *Melville Society Extracts*

MTJ / *Mark Twain Journal*

N&Q / *Notes and Queries*

Narrative

NCF / *Nineteenth-Century Literature*

NConL / *Notes on Contemporary Literature*

NCS / *Nineteenth-Century Studies*

Neophil / *Neophilologus* (Groningen, Netherlands)

NEQ / *New England Quarterly*

NewC / *The New Criterion*

NewComp / *New Comparison: A Journal of Comparative and General Literary Studies*

Newport History

NHR / *Nathaniel Hawthorne Review*

NJH / *New Jersey History*

NLH / *New Literary History: A Journal of Theory and Interpretation*

Novel: A Forum on Fiction

NYTBR / *New York Times Book Review*

Obsidian / *Obsidian II: Black Literature in Review*

OL / *Orbis Litterarum: International Review of Literary Studies*

PAAS / *Proceedings of the American Antiquarian Society*

Paideuma: A Journal Devoted to Ezra Pound Scholarship

PAPA / *Publications of the Arkansas Philological Society*

PAPS / *Proceedings of the American Philosophical Society*

P&R / *Philosophy and Rhetoric*

ParisR / *Paris Review*

PennE / *Pennsylvania English*

Playbill: The National Theatre Magazine

PLL / *Papers on Language and Literature*

PMLA: *Publications of the Modern Language Assn.*

PMPA / *Publications of the Missouri Philological Assn.*

PoeS / *Poe Studies*

Poesia

Polysemes (Univ. de Paris III)

PQ / *Philological Quarterly*

PR / *Partisan Review*

Pre/Text: *A Journal of Rhetorical Theory*

Prologue

Prospects: *An Annual Journal of American Cultural Studies*

PSt / *Prose Studies*

PULC / *Princeton University Library Chronicle*

RALS / *Resources for American Literary Study*

Raritan, A Quarterly Review

RCF / *Review of Contemporary Fiction*

REALB / REAL: *The Yearbook of Research in English and American Literature*

Renascence: *Essays on Value in Literature*

RFEA / *Revue Française d'Etudes Américaines*

RFR / *Robert Frost Review*

RhetRev / *Rhetoric Review*

RSAJ / RSA Journal: *Rivista de Studi Nord-Americani*

SAD / *Studies in American Drama, 1945–Present*

SAF / *Studies in American Fiction*

Sagetrieb: *A Journal Devoted to Poets in the Pound–H.D.–Williams Tradition*

SAIL / *Studies in American Indian Literature*

SAJL / *Studies in American Jewish Literature*

SALit / *Chu-Shikoku Studies in American Literature*

SAQ / *South Atlantic Quarterly*

SAR / *Studies in the American Renaissance*

SCR / *South Carolina Review*

SCRev / South Central Review: *The Journal of the South Central Modern Language Assn.*

SCS / *Stephen Crane Studies*

SDR / *South Dakota Review*

SELit / *Studies in English Literature* (Tokyo)

ShakB / *Shakespeare Bulletin*

Shenandoah

Short Story

Signs: *A Journal of Women in Culture and Society*

Simms Review

SlavR / Slavic Review: *American Quarterly of Soviet and East European Studies*

SLJ / *Southern Literary Journal*

SNNTS / *Studies in the Novel* (North Texas State Univ.)

SoAR / *South Atlantic Review*

SoQ / *Southern Quarterly*

SoR / *Southern Review*

Soundings: *An Interdisciplinary Journal*

SPR: *Student Press Review*

SSF / *Studies in Short Fiction*

StAH / *Studies in American Humor*

StQ / *Steinbeck Quarterly*

Studies in English Literature and Linguistics (Taipei, Taiwan)

StWF / *Studies in Weird Fiction*

Style

SVEC / *Studies on Voltaire and the Eighteenth Century*

SWR / *Southwest Review*

TCL / *Twentieth-Century Literature*
TDR / *The Drama Review*
Teaching Philosophy
TexP / *Textual Practice*
Thalia: Studies in Literary Humor
Theater
Theatre Week
ThS / *Theatre Studies*
TJ / *Theatre Journal*
TPQ / *Text and Performance Quarterly*
TSLL / *Texas Studies in Language and Literature*
TWA / *Transactions of the Wisconsin Academy of Science*
TWN / *Thomas Wolfe Review*
UTQ / *University of Toronto Quarterly*
VLang / *Visible Language*
VMHB / *Virginia Magazine of History and Biography*
W&D / *Works and Days: Essays in the Socio-Historical Dimensions of Literature and the Arts*
WAL / *Western American Literature*
W&Lang / *Women & Language*
WCPMN / *Willa Cather Pioneer Memorial Newsletter*
WHR / *Western Humanities Review*
Wide Angle
WilsonQ / *Wilson Quarterly*
WMQ / *William and Mary Quarterly*
WS / *Women's Studies*
WSJour / *Wallace Stevens Journal*
WVUPP / *West Virginia University Philological Papers*
YJC / *The Yale Journal of Criticism: Interpretation in the Humanities*
YULG / *Yale University Library Gazette*

Publishers

Aarhus / Aarhus, Denmark: Universitetsforlag

Addison-Wesley / Redding, Mass.: Addison-Wesley Publishing Co.
Alabama / Tuscaloosa: Univ. of Alabama Press
Almqvist and Wiksell / Stockholm: Almqvist and Wiksell
American Philosophical Society / Philadelphia: American Philosophical Society
American Studies Research Centre / Hyderabad, India: American Studies Research Centre
Amistad / New York: Amistad (dist. by Penguin USA)
Andrews & McMeel (Kansas City, Mo.)
Arizona / Tucson: Univ. of Arizona Press
Arkansas / Fayetteville: Univ. of Arkansas Press
Atlantic Monthly / New York: Atlantic Monthly Press
Bamberger / Flint, Mich.: Bamberger Books
Big Fish / San Francisco: Big Fish Books
Black Ice / Boulder: Black Ice Press
Bologna / University of Bologna Press
Borgo / San Bernardino, Calif.: Borgo Press
Bowling Green / Bowling Green, Ohio: Bowling Green State Univ. Popular Press
Bulzoni / Rome: Bulzoni Editore
Calif. / Berkeley: Univ. of California Press
Cambridge / New York: Cambridge Univ. Press
Camden House / Columbia, S.C.: Camden House
Carroll / New York: Carroll & Graf (dist. by Publishers Group West)

Caxton / Dallas: Caxton's Modern Arts Press

Center for Learning / Villa Maria, Penn.: The Center for Learning

Center for Mark Twain Studies / Elmira College for Mark Twain Studies at Quarry Farm

Chicago / Chicago: Univ. of Chicago Press

Chicago Review / Chicago: Chicago Review Press

Chronicle Books / San Francisco: Chronicle Books (div. of Chronicle Publishing)

Clarendon / Oxford: Clarendon Press

Columbia / New York: Columbia Univ. Press

Conch Cats / Key West: Conch Cats

Continuum / New York: Continuum Publishing Co. (dist. by Harper & Row Pubs.)

Copper Canyon / Port Townsend, Wash.: Copper Canyon Press

Cornell / Ithaca, N.Y.: Cornell Univ. Press

Dalkey Archive / Elmwood Park, Ill.: Dalkey Archive Press

Delaware / Newark: Univ. of Delaware Press (dist. by Associated Univ. Presses)

Duke / Durham, N.C.: Duke Univ. Press

Dutton / New York: E. P. Dutton

Edward Arnold / London: Edward Arnold

Einaudi / Turin: Einaudi

Everyman / London: Everyman

Fairleigh Dickinson / Teaneck, N.J.: Fairleigh Dickinson Univ. Press (dist. by Associated Univ. Presses)

Florida / Gainesville: Univ. of Florida Press

Fordham / New York: Fordham Univ. Press

Francke / Tübingen: A. Francke Verlag GmbH

Gale / Detroit: Gale Research (subs. of International Thompson Publishing)

Garland / New York: Garland Publishing

Georgia / Athens: Univ. of Georgia Press

Graywolf / St. Paul: Graywolf Press

Greenwood / Westport, Conn.: Greenwood Press

Grove / New York: Grove Press (dist. by Random House)

Hall / Boston: G. K. Hall & Co. (div. of Macmillan Publishing Co.)

Harcourt / San Diego, Calif.: Harcourt Brace Jovanovich

Harvard / Cambridge: Harvard Univ. Press

Hermitage Antiquarian Bookshop / Denver: Hermitage Antiquarian Bookshop

Holt / New York: Henry Holt and Co. (subs. of Verlagsgruppe Georg Von Holszbrinck)

Hopkins / Baltimore: Johns Hopkins Univ. Press

Hyperion / New York: Hyperion

Idaho / Moscow: Univ. of Idaho Press

Illinois / Champaign: Univ. of Illinois Press

Indiana / Bloomington: Indiana Univ. Press

Iowa / Iowa City: Univ. of Iowa Press

Island / Washington, D.C.: Island Press

Kansas / Lawrence: Univ. Press of Kansas

Kenhyusha (Tokyo)

Kentucky / Lexington: Univ. Press of Kentucky

Knopf / New York: Alfred A. Knopf, Inc. (subs. of Random House)

Library of America / New York: Library of America (dist. by Viking Penguin)

Longman / White Plains, N.Y.: Longman

LSU / Baton Rouge: Louisiana State Univ. Press

Manchester / Manchester: Manchester Univ. Press (dist. by St. Martin's Press, subs. of Macmillan Publishing Co.)

Marsilio / Venice: Marsilio

Mass. / Amherst: Univ. of Massachusetts Press

McGill-Queens: Toronto: McGill-Queens Univ. Press (imprint of Univ. of Toronto Press)

Mellen / Lewiston, N.Y.: Edwin Mellen Press

MHS / Boston: Massachusetts Historical Society

Michigan / Ann Arbor: Univ. of Michigan Press

Minnesota / Minneapolis: Univ. of Minnesota Press

Miss. / Jackson: Univ. Press of Mississippi

Missouri / Columbia: Univ. of Missouri Press

Nanundo (Tokyo)

NBM / New York: NBM

NCUP / Formerly College & University Press

Nebraska / Lincoln: Univ. of Nebraska Press

New Directions / New York: New Directions Publishing Corp. (dist. by W. W. Norton and Co.)

New Mexico / Albuquerque: Univ. of New Mexico Press

Newton Compton / Rome: Newton Compton

No. Car. / Chapel Hill: Univ. of North Carolina Press

No. Ill. / DeKalb: Northern Illinois Univ. Press

North American / Golden, Colo.: North American Press

Northeastern / Boston: Northeastern Univ. Press

Northwestern / Evanston, Ill.: Northwestern Univ. Press

Norwegian American Historical Assn. / Northfield, Minn.: NAH Assn.

NYU / New York: New York Univ. Press

Odense / Odense Univ. Press

Okla. / Norman: Univ. of Oklahoma Press

Overlook / New York: Overlook Press (dist. by Viking Penguin)

Oxford / New York: Oxford Univ. Press

Pencraft / Alexandria, Va.: Pencraft International

Penguin / New York: Penguin Books

Penn. / Philadelphia: Univ. of Pennsylvania Press

Penn. State / University Park: Pennsylvania State Univ. Press

Persea / New York: Persea Books

Peter Lang / New York: Peter Lang Publishing, Inc. (subs. of Verlag Peter Lang AG [Switzerland])

Pineapple / Sarasota: Pineapple

Poe Society / Baltimore: Edgar Allan Poe Society

Prentice Hall / Englewood Cliffs, N.J.: Prentice Hall

Princeton / Princeton, N.J.: Princeton Univ. Press

PUB / Presses universitaires de Bordeaux

PUL / Presses universitaires de Lyon

PUM / Presses universitaires du Mans

PUN / Presses universitaires de Nancy

PUR / Presses universitaires de Reims

Putnam / New York: G. P. Putnam's Sons

PUV / Presses universitaires de Vincennes

Random House / New York: Random House

Rejl / Los Angeles: David Rejl

Rodopi / Amsterdam: Editions Rodopi BV

Routledge / New York: Routledge, Chapman & Hall

Rutgers / New Brunswick, N.J.: Rutgers Univ. Press

Sairyusha (Tokyo)

Scarecrow / Metuchen, N.J.: Scarecrow Press, Inc. (subs. of Grolier Educational Corp.)

So. Car. / Columbia: Univ. of South Carolina Press

So. Ill. / Carbondale: Southern Illinois Univ. Press

Stanford / Stanford, Calif.: Stanford Univ. Press

State House / Austin: State House Press

Sterne / Amiens: Sterne Editions

St. Martin's / New York: St. Martin's Press (subs. of Macmillan Publishing Co.)

Summa / Birmingham: Summa Pubs.

SUNY / Albany: State Univ. of New York Press

Susquehanna / Selinsgrove, Pa.: Susquehanna Univ. Press (dist. by Associated Univ. Presses)

Swallow / Athens, Ohio: Swallow Press

TCU / Fort Worth: TCU Press

Temple / Philadelphia: Temple Univ. Press

Tennessee / Knoxville: Univ. of Tennessee Press

Texas / Austin: Univ. of Texas Press

Theatre Communications / New York: Theatre Communications Group

Twayne / New York: Twayne Publishers (imprint of G. K. Hall and Co., div. of Macmillan Publishing Co.)

UBC / Vancouver, B.C.: UBC Press

Union / Schenectady, N.Y.: Union College Press

Univ. Press / Lanham, Md.: University Press of America

Utah / Salt Lake City: Univ. of Utah Press

Viking / New York: Viking Penguin

Villard / New York: Villard Books

Virginia / Charlottesville: Univ. Press of Virginia

Washington State / Pullman: Washington State Univ. Press

Wayne State / Detroit: Wayne State Univ. Press

Whitston / Troy, N.Y.: Whitston Publishing Co.

Wilfrid Laurier / Waterloo, Ont.: Wilfrid Laurier Univ. Press

Wisconsin / Madison: Univ. of Wisconsin Press

Yale / New Haven, Conn.: Yale Univ. Press

Part I

Emerson, Thoreau, Fuller, and
Transcendentalism

David M. Robinson

This busy year of scholarship on Transcendentalism brought several new
scholarly editions, contributions to the continuing discussion of Emerson's context and influence, and a variety of new essays on Thoreau and
Fuller. We also saw the first *Margaret Fuller Society Newsletter,* marking
the formation of a scholarly group dedicated to the study of Fuller's life
and works, the revival of *The Concord Saunterer,* a journal published by
the Thoreau Society, and the first issue of *ISLE: Interdisciplinary Studies
in Literature and Environment.*

i Scholarly Editions

Ronald A. Bosco's edition of the second volume of *The Topical Notebooks
of Ralph Waldo Emerson* (Missouri) includes five notebooks dating from
the middle 1850s to the late 1870s—"Orientalist," "RT" (Rhetoric), "LI"
(Literature), "PY" (Theory of Poetry), and "PH" (Philosophy)—composed of translation drafts, literary excerpts, and remembered conversational remarks that provide insight into "Emerson's methodology—his
actual practice—of reading and writing." The "Orientalist" notebook is
of particular value to students of Emerson's poetry, showing his en-
thralled apprenticeship to Saadi; the "Rhetoric" and "Poetry" notebooks
enhance our sense of Emerson's later aesthetic theory, which continued
to develop beyond "The Poet," as Bosco has elsewhere demonstrated (see
ALS 1989, p. 10). These notebooks are, as Bosco writes, affirmations of
"the authority with which intellect, memory, and imagination may
overcome the anarchy of material culture."

Bradley P. Dean has collected and edited four of Thoreau's unpublished later natural history texts in *Faith in a Seed: The Dispersion of
Seeds and Other Late Natural History Writings* (Island). The longest and

most complete of these texts, "The Dispersion of Seeds," edited primarily from Thoreau's manuscript in the Berg Collection of the New York Public Library, is a study of seed dispersal and forest regeneration that arises from Thoreau's project of observing and recording the natural phenomena of the Concord area. Dean's volume also includes "Wild Fruits," the beginning of what Thoreau had hoped would be a book-length work on the cycle of the ripening of fruit around Concord, and two other fragments, "Weeds and Grasses" and "Forest Trees," probably intended for inclusion in "The Dispersion of Seeds." Dean provides a clear reading text of each work, and he includes extensive and helpful explanatory and textual notes. These texts, Dean explains, show Thoreau's commitment to make "science and literature mutually enriching, rather than mutually exclusive, pursuits." The volume includes a foreword by Gary Paul Nabhan and an informative introductory essay by Robert D. Richardson, Jr., on Thoreau's later assumptions about natural history. Dean has also brought to light an exchange of letters between Thoreau, Horace Greeley, and E. G. Waters on seed dispersion and the spontaneous generation of plants published in 1861 in the *New-York Weekly Tribune* ("Henry D. Thoreau and Horace Greeley Exchange Letters on the 'Spontaneous Generation of Plants'" [*NEQ* 66: 630–38]). In "Confucius at Walden Pond: Thoreau's Unpublished Confucian Translations" (*SAR*, pp. 275–303) Hongbo Tan has edited Thoreau's translation of selections from M. J. Pauthier's *Confucius et Mencius* (1841), the source of the Confucian quotations and references in *Walden*. Tan's informative history of the transmission of the Confucian texts sketches Thoreau's interest in their emphasis on "the priority of self-improvement," and it establishes 1843 as the "most likely" date of Thoreau's translations.

Although Jones Very has been frequently acknowledged as one of the most interesting and accomplished American poets of the nineteenth century, scholars who would study him have been confronted with a textual morass of incomplete and unreliable editions of his poems. Helen R. Deese has corrected this situation and done an enormous service to future scholars with *Jones Very: The Complete Poems* (Georgia), an edition that will be the starting point for all future work on Very and will, I believe, stimulate new interest in his work. Deese's critical un-modernized edition, based on individual copy text decisions for each of Very's poems, includes extensive historical and textual notes, a description of the manuscripts, and a discussion of the publication history of the poems. Deese believes that Very's poetic reputation will rest on the poems written from 1838 until 1840 during a period of mystical excitement, many of which were not published until William I. Bartlett's 1942 biography and are still not well known. Surprisingly, even Emerson, who championed Very and was fascinated by his mystical fervor, did not include many of these poems in his 1839 edition of *Essays and Poems*, presenting instead a "toned down and cleaned up" version of the poet.

Nancy Craig Simmons's edition of *The Selected Letters of Mary Moody Emerson* (Georgia) will prove an invaluable resource, not only for scholars of Emerson and Transcendentalism, but for those interested in the question of women's authorship in the 19th century. The volume contains the texts of 334 of some 900 of Mary Emerson's surviving letters, with notations on her revisions and informative annotations for each letter. Simmons has arranged the letters in six chronological groupings, with a helpful introduction on Emerson's life at that period. Simmons persuasively presents Emerson as a writer who was "transforming the minor genre of letter writing into a major vehicle for free discussion." Readers may initially be interested in the letters to Ralph Waldo Emerson and his brothers, but they will, I think, find that the letters have an integrity and frame of reference that reaches further. Simmons has also compiled a useful supplement to the edition, "A Calendar of the Letters of Mary Moody Emerson" (*SAR*, pp. 1–41), which lists each of the nine hundred extant letters chronologically, providing its date and place of composition, its recipient, and the letter's current location.

Larry A. Carlson's edition of "Bronson Alcott's 'Journal for 1838' (Part One)" (*SAR*, pp. 161–244) provides Alcott's record of this exceedingly rich period in the Transcendentalist movement, centering on the pain with which Alcott struggled to reformulate his sense of vocation as his Temple School failed, and, with Emerson's encouragement, began to shift his energies to his manuscript *Psyche*. Alcott's personality is revealed here as a fascinating mixture of shrewd discernment and self-pitying naïveté, and the *Journals* from this period help us understand him, and something of the atmosphere of the Transcendentalist ferment at its high point in 1838. In "The Temple School Journals of George and Martha Kuhn" (*SAR*, pp. 55–145) Alfred G. Litton and Joel Myerson provide a view of Alcott's teaching practices from a student's perspective, with the journals themselves evidence of his focus on the child's inner resources as the foundation of education. Greta D. Little and Joel Myerson have edited *Three Children's Novels by Christopher Pearse Cranch* (Georgia), which includes *The Last of the Huggermuggers: A Giant Story* (1856), *Kobboltozo: A Sequel to The Last of the Huggermuggers* (1857), and the previously unpublished *The Legend of Doctor Theophilus; or, the Enchanted Clothes*. The volume also contains Cranch's illustrations, and a detailed introduction on the publication history of the books, enhancing our knowledge of Cranch's activities in the 1850s and 1860s.

ii Emerson

a. **Intellectual Contexts**   The reading of Emerson as a founder of pragmatism has been the most important direction of Emerson studies in the past several years, with Richard Poirier (see *ALS 1987*, p. 8, and *ALS 1992*, p. 6) and Cornel West (*ALS 1989*, pp. 3–4) envisioning Emerson as a crucial precursor to William James and other philosophical and literary pragmatists. Two new books focus on the pragmatic direction of Emerson's development. David Jacobson's *Emerson's Pragmatic Vision: The Dance of the Eye* (Penn. State) portrays Emerson as having undergone something of a postmodernist crisis of faith in wrestling with epistemological uncertainty in the early 1840s. Jacobson traces Emerson's abandonment of an early "humanist synthesis," with its "desire that nature should be *for* man, that human beings should be the end of nature," for an "antihumanism" in which humanity is radically displaced, and "nature's onwardness can no longer imply a teleological development." This break from humanism can be traced to "The Method of Nature" and is extended in "Experience," in which "experience replaces nature as the object of Emerson's inquiry." Jacobson's insightful readings center on Emerson's increasing preoccupation with the theme of illusion and his depiction of "sheer and radical solitude." Emerson's later works deemphasize "the turn inward to an abstract reflection on the source of action," transferring concern and value to "the everyday practices of life," a shift that connects him with "the tradition of American pragmatism." My study of Emerson's later writings, *Emerson and the Conduct of Life: Pragmatism and Ethical Purpose in the Later Work* (Cambridge), traces Emerson's evolution from mystic to pragmatist, emphasizing his increasing concern with social relations, political issues, and questions of ethical conduct. The period that we associate with Emerson's articulation of a mystical idealism, the late 1830s and early 1840s, is also marked by an increasingly tense recognition of the evaporation of his ecstatic consciousness and a deepening dialogue with skepticism. Emerson's social and ethical orientation, though submerged in the middle and late 1830s, begins to grow in response to his loss of ecstatic vision and informs generally overlooked essays such as "Friendship" and "Compensation." This pragmatism emerges more insistently in "Experience," an essay that records his search for new philosophical grounding. Emerson's turn to ethics as an answer to a fading mysticism was reinforced by his journey to England in the late 1840s, which immersed him in both social density and technological modernity, and by the highly charged American political atmosphere of the 1850s, a scene that he entered with two addresses on the Fugitive Slave Law, among his most rhetorically accomplished works. Two important and largely overlooked later volumes, *The Conduct of Life* and *Society and Solitude*, are evidence that this period should not be read, in Stephen E. Whicher's terms, as an "acquiescence," but rather as Emerson's complex and tough-minded attempt to work out the ethical and practical implications of his earlier idealism.

Several works offered new perspectives on the cultural and intellectual contexts of Emerson's thought. Lawrence Buell's *Ralph Waldo Emerson: A Collection of Critical Essays* (Prentice Hall) is a useful collection that traces the development and parameters of Emerson's modern reputation. Buell's "Emerson in His Cultural Context" (pp. 48–60), a new essay in the volume, discusses the paradoxical mixture of provincialism and cosmopolitanism in Emerson's intellectual practice, linking it to "Emerson's immediate cultural context: the culture of Unitarian liberalism." Noting that Emerson shares this orientation with William Ellery Channing, Buell posits that "a certain self-decentering that had been built into liberal Congregationalist culture from the start," the reflection of "a 'postcolonial' condition" that characterizes the origins of American literary culture. In *Coordinates of Anglo-American Romanticism,* Richard E. Brantley describes the "simultaneously rational and sensationalist reliance on experience" that is the common intellectual ground of Wesley and Edwards, and in a later generation, Carlyle and Emerson. Brantley argues that Emerson's development was guided by "key Lockean tenets," and in an extended treatment of *Nature* he traces the Lockean "emphasis on perception" characteristic of the English empiricist tradition. In *Splintered Worlds,* Robert M. Greenberg figures Emerson as one of four representative authors for whom "variety replaced uniformity, difference replaced universality, natural dynamism replaced fixed forms, and spontaneity replaced mechanical rules," a shift that responded to "the splintering historical scene" of antebellum America. Greenberg effectively calls attention to the "fragmentary sense of self that Emerson diligently describes alongside the unitary sense of self he regularly espouses," proposing that his emphasis on "shooting the gulf" of experience was a response "to the problem of multiplicity and disjunction" that characterize modern life. Thomas Gustafson's *Representative Words* also makes persuasive connections between antebellum American literature and its social and political contexts. Gustafson finds that "early hopes Americans had for the reform of the English language in America . . . gave way in the mid-nineteenth century to increasing fears of its corruption," and that the nation's political degeneracy was fundamentally connected with "the misuse and misunderstanding of words." Gustafson sees Emerson as one of a long line of American writers who see that "their mission is to sustain faith in the word." The project of *Nature*, Emerson's "guidebook to reform," was to recover "the original relation of language to nature." In his *The Rites of Assent*, Sacvan Bercovitch includes a revised version of his important earlier essay on Emerson and the ideology of liberal individualism (see *ALS 1990*, p. 5). Bercovitch reads Emerson in the context of the work of Pierre Leroux and is concerned to explore the extent to which Emerson's espousal of individualism undercuts his ability to be a critic of American culture. In "Educating the 'Immortal Pupil': Emerson's Identity Politics and the Question of Freedom in the Age of Reform" (*Prospects* 13: 29–49) Stephen P. Knadler examines Emerson's theory of education in the context of 19th-century educational reforms exemplified in the work of Horace Mann. Emerson concurred with Mann's view of education as the process through which the individual constructed a social identity, but he also emphasized the incorporation of standards of taste and beauty in an educational project of "self-creation." Glen M. Johnson's "Ralph Waldo Emerson on Isaac Hecker: A Manuscript with Commentary" (*Catholic Historical Review* 79: 54–64) provides the text of Emerson's previously unpublished account of an 1863 meeting with Isaac Hecker and an incisive analysis of Emerson's two intellectual encounters with Hecker, a representative of Catholicism. Johnson notes a harshness in Emerson's attitude after the 1863 meeting that is in large part caused by Hecker's role in the conversion of Anna Barker Ward.

In "Emerson's Beautiful Estate," an elegantly written chapter in his *Lost in the Customhouse*, Jerome Loving reconsiders the way that "Experience" marks Emerson's departure from the "unacceptable idealism" of his earlier work. Loving understands that the love Emerson had felt for his first wife, Ellen, was in some sense reborn in his love of Waldo, each relationship producing a joy beyond the reach of the explanatory powers of language. "Experience" is, for Loving, not only the recording of Emerson's loss, but a crucial testament to the limitations of both language and the "ideology of Transcendentalism" which had interfused Emerson's art in the late 1830s. John G. Rudy offers another illuminating essay on "Experience" in "Engaging the Void: Emerson's Essay on Experience and the Zen Experience of Self-Emptying" (*Eastern Buddhist* 26, i: 101–25). Rudy explains how the essay "articulates a path to the Zen condition of enlightened selflessness," and he traces the parallels between the Buddhist conception of the delusion of "self-existence" and Emerson's opening sense of the instability of perception and identity. Emerson's representation of perception accords with the Zen emphasis on "a preconceptual, prelingual ground of mutual identity for all things" in which consciousness is "an ever-opening field of acceptance."

Gib Prettyman's "'Working After His Thought': The Signification of Industry in Emerson's *The Conduct of Life*" (*ATQ* 7: 45–63) investigates Emerson's sense of his social vocation, describing *The Conduct of Life* as part of his effort to salvage certain values of "middle-class life under industrial rationalism." Emerson revised the Franklinian connection of "work and moral progress" by stressing "intellectual work rather than manual labor," thus offering an idealized representation of the "progressive self-determination" of "entrepreneurs and other industrial idealists." In "Landscapes of Commodity: Nature as Economy in Emerson's Poems" (*ESQ* 38 [1992]: 265–91) Duane Coltharp proposes a materialist reading of Emerson's poetry, arguing that it reveals both Emerson's intention "to think seriously about social, political, and economic issues" and "his equal and opposite impulse to evade them." By projecting both "poetic rebellion and capitalist mystification" onto the same landscapes, Emerson "conflates poetry and social praxis by confusing opposition and complicity," a confusion that Emerson is, in some respects, happy to promote, instinctively knowing that such mystification "will keep the dialectic always on the move." Eduardo Cadava ("The Nature of War in Emerson's 'Boston Hymn,'" *ArQ* 49, iii: 21–58) analyzes Emerson's fusion of Puritan typology with abolitionist political assumptions in "Boston Hymn." The authority of Emerson's representation of emancipation, Cadava believes, is enhanced by his use of natural metaphors, and his association of recent political turns with "the history and meaning of America." In "Thoreau as Napoleon; or a Note on Emerson's Big,

Little, and Good Endians" (*ESP* 4, i: 1–4) Nancy Craig Simmons sheds new light on Emerson's journal entries of 1849 and 1877 in which he pairs the subjects of his *Representative Men* with his contemporary acquaintances.

b. Literary and Philosophical Influence The recent explorations of Emerson's connections with pragmatism by no means exhaust the question of his influence. Elisa New's *The Regenerate Lyric* challenges the theory of an Emersonian visionary lineage in American poetry by describing a neo-Calvinist tradition of lyric poetry conditioned by a desire for "regeneracy" rather than Emersonian "originality." New insists that poetic acts are theological ones, and she characterizes the lyric poem as a work of "verbal choice" under severe restraint rather than a celebration of possibility and multiplicity. New argues that "Emersonianism . . . builds a religion out of the notion of poetic license, but in so doing saps the poem of what makes it a poem: the limitation all licenses press." Such poetics yielded, in Emerson's case, poems that are "unnervingly undistinguished," leaving a theoretical legacy that was, for poets like Dickinson, Frost, Crane, and even Whitman, more a burden to cast off than an enabling vision. New is a cogent thinker and a strikingly effective prose stylist, and her book should reopen the question of Emerson's poetic legacy. I did not find that she granted Emerson's lyric achievement in the essays—"My singing . . . is for the most part in prose," as Emerson claimed. Genre was for all the Transcendentalists a very fluid concept. But even if you are not wholly persuaded by New's thesis, her trenchant reading of the American poetic tradition is thought-provoking and illuminating. Cary Wolfe's *The Limits of American Literary Ideology in Pound and Emerson* (Cambridge) is a significant addition to the political critique of Emersonian individualism, as articulated earlier by Quentin Anderson and Sacvan Bercovitch. Wolfe sees Pound as "the inheritor of a very American lineage of individualist cultural practice" theorized by Emerson and transmitted through the mediation of Henry and William James. This tradition, with its Lockean figuration of the self in terms of private property, served to validate "self-reliance and the 'influence of private character' " over class-conscious political practice, thus inevitably undercutting the critique of capitalist production that is incipient in the early work of both Emerson and Pound. Emerson's connections with modernism were approached differently in David Michael Hertz's *Angels* *of Reality,* which traces the influence of Emerson on Frank Lloyd Wright, Wallace Stevens, and Charles Ives. Hertz emphasizes the early, direct exposure of all three artists to Emerson, and he finds in each an Emersonian disposition to a strong-willed and individualistic experimentalism, motivated by a shared artistic ideal of natural organicism. Their careers can be read as "searches for the practical truths" that often led them to "visionary and grandiose" efforts whose pragmatic results were mixed. For Ives and Wright, who did not work in Emerson's literary medium, the "absorption" of Emersonian ideas was "more direct and uninhibited" than for Stevens, "a doubting student of Emerson." In "Living in the Iron Mills: A Tempering of Nineteenth-Century America's Orphic Poet" (*JACult* 16, i: 67–72) J. F. Buckley reads Rebecca Harding Davis's *Life in the Iron Mills* as a critique of Emerson's figure of the "Orphic poet" through a demonstration that modern industrial labor can pose inherent limits to individuals of a poetic sensibility. Brian A. Bremen's "Du Bois, Emerson, and the 'Fate' of Black Folk" (*ALR* 24, iii [1992]: 80–88) explores the "intertextual relations" between Emerson's "Fate" and Du Bois's *The Souls of Black Folk* by describing Du Bois's reformulation of Emerson's concept of "the double consciousness." Noting that both texts treat fate and race as intertwined categories, Bremen argues that Du Bois attempts "to make the fate of both races hang upon the mutual 'revelation' of each other's worth." Marilyn Vogler Urion considers "Emerson's Presence in Rilke's Imagery: Shadows of Early Influence" (*Monatshefte* 85: 153–69), demonstrating how "Circles" and "The Poet" influenced Rilke's composition of "Notizen zur Melodie der Dinge." Urion notes the similarity of Emerson's and Rilke's views of the "physical component" and the "melodic essence" that comprise all things. Readers of Stanley Cavell's recent work on Emerson (see *ALS 1988,* p. 4; *ALS 1989,* p. 9; and *ALS 1990,* pp. 5–6) will be interested in the exchange between Stephen Melville ("Oblique and Ordinary: Stanley Cavell's Engagements of Emerson," *AmLH* 5: 172–92) and Joseph G. Kronick ("Telling the Difference: Stanley Cavell's Resistance to Theory," *AmLH* 5: 193–200). Melville effectively explains the philosophical context of Cavell's work, arguing that his construction of "reading" is in some senses an answer to the problem of linguistic undecidability. Kronick maintains that Cavell "has little to offer critical theory," and he argues that he "turn[s] Emerson's essays into self-positing enactments of their own possibility," thereby preserving reading as a guarantor of epistemological stability.

iii Thoreau

a. *Walden:* New Readings   *Walden* was accorded much critical attention this past year, led by Alan D. Hodder's splendid analysis of Thoreau's use of Eastern religious sources: "'Et Oriente Lux': Thoreau's
Ecstasies and the Hindu Texts" (*HTR* 86: 403–38). Hodder elucidates
the historical context of Thoreau's interest in Hinduism, which helped
him to comprehend and articulate the "experiences of 'ecstasy' with
which he had long been familiar." While Oriental texts were not the
source of Thoreau's ecstatic experience, they were "an indispensable
vehicle for his comprehension and representation of them." In particular, Hindu sources were instrumental in Thoreau's representation of
Walden Pond as a mirror in which vision served as a means of "self-
displacement and autoreflection," important components of his meditative and ecstatic experience. Hodder's essay sets a new standard for
scholarly acumen and informed judgment in the evaluation of the
impact of Oriental texts on the Transcendentalists. My essay "'Unchronicled Nations': Agrarian Purpose and Thoreau's Ecological Knowing" (*NCF* 48: 326–40) explores the tension between Thoreau's interest
in conducting an agrarian experiment at Walden and his distrust of the
demands and methods of farming as he saw it practiced around Concord. This tension is provisionally resolved in Thoreau's description of
field labor in "The Bean-Field," during which he uncovered "the ashes of
unchronicled nations who in primeval years lived under these heavens."
This discovery sacralizes Thoreau's labor, placing ordinary work within a
much richer context of human endeavor across time and cultures. In
"Re-Creating *Walden*: Thoreau's Economy of Work and Play" (*AL* 65:
673–701) William Gleason thoughtfully reconsiders Thoreau's treatment of the Irish immigrants in *Walden*, arguing that the influx of new
laborers initially "alarmed Thoreau" by "accelerating the separation of
work time from play time, which Thoreau was so anxious to undo."
Even though Thoreau's sympathy for the Irish increased in the early
1850s, the disdain expressed in "Baker Farm" remained largely unrevised
because of the chapter's important rhetorical signal of Thoreau's "intro-
spective reaffirmation" of his ideals. In "Thoreau, Extravagance, and the
Economy of Nature" (*AmLH* 5: 30–50) Richard Grusin analyzes "The
Bean-Field" along with "Wild Apples" and "Autumnal Tints," noting
Thoreau's resistance to "the idea that nature's economy can best be
understood on the analogy of the capitalist marketplace." Grusin stresses

Thoreau's comprehension "that nature's economy is extravagant," more analogous to an economy of "gift exchange" that Pierre Bourdieu finds in "archaic economies of expenditure" than modern economies of thrift. Ron Balthazor's "To Play Life: Thoreau's Fabulous Reality" (*ATQ* 7: 159–70) analyzes the epistemological complexity of the final paragraphs of "Where I Lived and What I Lived For," in which Thoreau's quest "to name a transcendent reality" is undermined because language "persistently fails him." Thoreau, however, continues the quest, "making the meaningful meaningless, and instilling and drenching meaningless itself with meaning." David Strong's "The Significance of the Loss of Things: Walden Pond as 'Thing'" (*Soundings* 75 [1992]: 147–74) approaches *Walden* through Heidegger's discourse on the power of "things" to gather the world into meaningful connections. Strong argues that Thoreau represents Walden Pond as a world-focusing thing, which can "actively appeal and call out to us, move or animate us." Jim Lewis's "A Response to *Walden*" (*JAmS* 27: 237–43) is a meditation on the importance of the reader's "keeping *Walden* open," or entering a relationship with the text that parallels Thoreau's creative and metamorphic approach to his experiment at Walden Pond and his account of it.

The first issue of *ISLE* included a cluster of four essays on "Ecology, Feminism, and Thoreau," each of which concentrates on *Walden*. These articles reveal some disagreement about the extent to which Thoreau can be appropriated by feminist thought. Two essays explore what Louise Westling terms the "gender dynamic embedded in the rich dialogic texture of *Walden*." In "Thoreau's Ambivalence Toward Mother Nature" (pp. 145–50) Westling notes that Thoreau depicted Walden as a "feminine 'other'" that was "beautiful and magnetic," but also "somehow horrifying in its material being, subject to decay like the body." His gendered representation of the landscape also entailed a "masculine ethic of heroic assertion and exploitation," part of a long-standing attitude in Western culture that legitimized both sexist repression and the exploitation of natural resources. Leigh Kirkland ("Sexual Chaos in Walden Pond," pp. 131–36) argues that Thoreau's relationship with the pond is "metonymic of the relationship between women and men, especially as it existed in the 19th century." By describing the pond in terms of "an idealized and therefore unobtainable Woman," Thoreau sexualizes his desire "to merge, 'to get wet inwardly & deeply' in the water of Walden." This desire is thwarted, however, by his own temperament and 19th-century conventions, leaving Thoreau "unable to complete the immersion plot he initiates" and thus "unable to accept the multiplicity inherent in organicism." Two other essays present *Walden* as a more politically relevant text. Leonard M. Scigaj and Nancy Craig Simmons ("Ecofeminist Cosmology in Thoreau's *Walden*," pp. 121–29) answer Carolyn Merchant's dismissal of Thoreau's "ineffectual romanticism" by stressing his "biocentric vision of life beyond dualism, hierarchy, and anthropocentric domination of nature," tenets that are "congruent with the central tenets of contemporary ecofeminism." Laura Dassow Walls ("*Walden* as Feminist Manifesto," pp. 137–44) contends that the female reader can locate herself within the text of *Walden* and therein find a feminist empowerment. *Walden* "elaborately strips away the artifacts of social existence," thus turning "the basis for gender conventions into rubble." Walls finds a "gender fluidity" in the text, a "symphony of 'he' and 'she,' " in which "Thoreau is either and both," enacting that role through an "ethic of interaction rather than dominance," and dramatizing values of "sympathy," "sensual contact," and "cooperation." Walls's persuasive analysis of *Walden* in feminist terms is an important contribution to an assessment of the book's continuing relevance.

b. Other Biographical and Critical Works The relationship of Emerson and Thoreau, a subject of much recent revision and investigation, was analyzed in two insightful essays. In "The Stalk of the Lotus: Concord's Most Famous Friendship" (*CS* n.s. 1: 3–10) Robert D. Richardson, Jr., offers discerning analysis of what brought the men together and what kept them apart, describing them as "modern stoics, interested in self-rule and autonomy." The nature of their relationship was conditioned by a shared commitment to similar ideas and values, but since autonomy was key among these ideas and values, they were "cursed by the resulting, inevitable, unbridgeable need to stand apart." Jerome Loving's chapter on "Thoreau's Quarrel with Emerson" in *Lost in the Customhouse* emphasizes the Walden experiment as a crucial period of independent self-reformulation for Thoreau, an attempt "to re-order his life in the wake of Emerson's influence," and to memorialize his lost brother, John. Thoreau's remaking of his Walden experience in the construction of the text restored in him a firm sense of particularity and the present moment, freeing him from the Emersonian urge toward "the restoration of the Whole in the mind of God." This process of intellectual maturation was also advanced by the Katahdin excursion, which taught Thoreau that nature can "support more than 'one order of understandings.'" John McWilliams describes their differing views of the "Revolutionary mythology" of the Lexington and Concord battle ("Lexington, Concord, and the 'Hinge of the Future,'" *AmLH* 5: 1–29), characterizing Emerson's "Concord Hymn" and "Historical Discourse at Concord" as pieces that, while investing a certain "sanctity" in the Revolutionary battles, complicate any simple patriotic mythology. Thoreau, however, will not offer even a doubtful patriotism, representing the battles through a "derisive mock epic" in the battle of the ants.

Cliff Tolliver's "The Re-creation of Contemplation: Walton's *Angler* in Thoreau's *Week*" (*ESQ* 38 [1992]: 293–313) notes the "basic narrative similarity" of the two works, illustrating how Thoreau's first major digression in *A Week* "may almost be denominated a recasting of *The Compleat Angler* in miniature." Tolliver's line on Walton's influence also extends to a discussion of Thoreau's borrowing the "device of elucidating human nature by examining fish" and his valuation of "contemplative digression over narrative action." Ian Marshall examines Thoreau's love of another form of recreation in "Winter Tracings and Transcendental Leaps: Henry Thoreau's Skating" (*PLL* 29: 459–74), explaining how skating extended Thoreau's winter excursions into nature and served as a metaphor of intellectual and spiritual activity. Linda Frost examines Thoreau's evolving awareness of the historical situation of the Penobscot Indians in his Maine narratives ("'The Red Face of Man,' the Penobscot Indian, and a Conflict of Interest in Thoreau's *Maine Woods*," *ESQ* 39: 21–47). His initial romantic tendency to figure the Indian through the "opposition between nature and culture" was reinforced by his inability to understand his guide Joe Aitteon's Penobscot language. This dichotomy becomes hard for Thoreau to sustain, however, in "The Allegash and East Branch," where he comes to appreciate Joe Polis's literacy and concern for the educational advancement of Indians, thus developing a more realistic sense of the interdependence of the two cultures. In "'Captain of a Huckleberry Party': Thoreau and a New England Ritual of Summer" (*CS* n.s. 1: 13–20) Wesley T. Mott reminds us that after Thoreau's night in the Concord jail, he joined a huckleberry party and thus took part in "virtually a ritual of summer in New England," one described in Leonard Withington's popular and nostalgic account of the ritual. Thoreau scholars who are also interested in the larger tradition of nature writing in America will want to consult John P. O'Grady's *Pilgrims to the Wild* (Utah), which emphasizes Thoreau's "sauntering" as a means to "a disciplined unlearning" that "leads not to nihilism but to wisdom."

c. Literary and Cultural Reputation   Investigation of the creation of Thoreau's modern reputation has been one of the liveliest strands of recent Transcendentalist scholarship. Gary Scharnhorst makes an important contribution to this discourse in *Henry David Thoreau: A Case Study in Canonization* (Camden House), a historical account of the shifting concerns and judgments of Thoreau's readers since the first reviews of his work. Scharnhorst provides a close-grained and informative account of five phases of Thoreau's "canonization," beginning with the editorial and promotional efforts of James T. Fields in the 1860s and Bliss Perry at the turn of the century. While these efforts helped to secure Thoreau's literary stature, they by no means settled the basis of his importance, and Scharnhorst traces the fundamental division in modern Thoreau criticism between those who have advocated Thoreau's stylistic and aesthetic accomplishment, and those who have viewed him principally as a social philosopher and activist. As Scharnhorst demonstrates, this fundamental division has persisted into our theory-preoccupied era.

Thoreau's World and Ours: A Natural Legacy, ed. Edmund A. Schofield and Robert C. Baron (North American), is the record of the 1991 Thoreau Society Jubilee, a rich volume that brings together forty essays in seven major groupings, ranging from literary history and biography to ecological studies of the Walden Woods. A complete account of the volume is impossible, but I will note here sections and essays of particular significance to literary scholars. I urge all Thoreauvians to consult this book. The volume includes a cluster of three essays on "Civil Disobedience" (pp. 5–34) by Barry Kritzberg, Richard M. Lebeaux, and Jack Schwartzman; a section on Thoreau and music (pp. 79–101), with contributions by Walter Harding, Stuart Feder, and Edmund Schofield; essays on Thoreau in Worcester, Massachusetts (pp. 141–49), by Albert B. Southwick and Milton Meltzer; and essays by various hands on the ecology of Walden Woods (pp. 155–297) and the American nature writing tradition (pp. 304–92). In an essay of particular significance, "The Availability of Thoreau's Texts and Manuscripts from 1862 to the Present" (pp. 107–20), Elizabeth Hall Witherell offers a detailed account of the transmission and preservation of Thoreau's manuscripts, drawing in part on letters from Henry Salt to several of Thoreau's earliest American biographers and critics. Joseph J. Moldenhauer's "Highlights of the Last Fifty Years of Thoreau Criticism" (pp. 121–25) offers a useful overview of modern critical treatments of Thoreau, and Richard M. Lebeaux ("From Canby to Richardson: The Last Half-Century of Thoreau Biography," pp. 126–36) surveys the modern biographical work on Thoreau. Thoreau scholars will also be interested in Austin Meredith's description of "'The Artist of Kouroo' Project at the University of Minnesota" (pp. 393–94), the creation of a "hypertext multimedia textbase" of Thoreau's work.

As Dean's edition of *Faith in a Seed* (see above) indicates, Thoreau's interest in the scientific discourse of his day is one of the most important emerging directions in recent Thoreau studies. *Thoreau's World and Ours* includes a cluster of four essays on Thoreau and science that stand as the book's most important section. A. Hunter Dupree's "Thoreau as Scientist: American Science in the 1850s" (pp. 42–47) surveys the effect of botanical developments of the 1850s on Thoreau, noting his drift away from Goethean science to the more empirical and professionalized modern discipline. In "The Coleridgean Influence on Thoreau's Science" (pp. 48–54) Robert Sattelmeyer presents a discerning explanation of the influence of Coleridge and the German school of *Naturphilosophie* on Thoreau's scientific intelligence. Sattelmeyer shows how these principles were propounded in the work of Louis Agassiz, and he traces Thoreau's eventual divergence from Agassiz through a "reversal of the anthropocentrism of this entire school." In "Seeing New Worlds: Thoreau and Humboldtian Science" (pp. 55–63) Laura Dassow Walls illustrates how Humboldt provided Thoreau a scientific alternative to the school of *Naturphilosophie,* based on an "Empirical Holism" that emphasized the particulars of nature rather than the "Rational Holism" characteristic of Coleridgean science with its emphasis on idealistic truth. William Rossi's "Thoreau as a Philosophical Naturalist-Writer" (pp. 64–73) explores the apparent conflict between Thoreau's sense of himself as a Transcendentalist and his growing interest in empirical science. Rossi suggests that Thoreau did not see these as mutually exclusive identities because of his sophisticated understanding of the active role of perception in scientific observation. He was committed not only to the gathering of observations and data, but also to a rigorous reflection on the process and method of scientific epistemology.

iv Fuller and the Transcendentalist Movement

a. Fuller Margaret Fuller's growing critical stature has brought much attention to *Summer on the Lakes,* a book now seen to be crucially centered on issues of gender and race. In "Under the Sign of Gender:

Margaret Fuller's *Summer on the Lakes*" (*Women and the Journey*, pp. 67–83) Joan Burbick cogently reads *Summer on the Lakes* as a text in which Fuller struggles, without any clear breakthrough into theoretical consistency, with the related questions of gender, class, and race, as she finds the prevailing cultural assumptions problematized by "the disorienting conditions of the frontier." Burbick thus resists Annette Kolodny's argument that Fuller comes to see gender as a category that transcends class and racial divisions, and she cautions against the tendency to read the book "as a developmental step toward *Woman in the Nineteenth Century*." She describes the text instead as a site of puzzlement and intellectual struggle, in which we can discern both Fuller's Eurocentric cultural assumptions and her sympathetic observations of the oppression of frontier women and Native Americans. Such tensions are also the focus of Christina Zwarg's "Footnoting the Sublime: Margaret Fuller on Black Hawk's Trail" (*AmLH* 5: 616–42), which traces Fuller's cognizance of "a troubling conflict between her growing faith in the limitless opportunities that might open for women and her sense of the deadly limit that had already been imposed upon Native Americans." Zwarg sees Fuller both assenting to "the discourse of the 'vanishing American'" and resisting it through the strategic interposition of a wide range of contemporary cultural texts, interventions in her narrative that have previously been regarded as digressions. Nicole Tonkovich ("Traveling in the West, Writing in the Library: Margaret Fuller's *Summer on the Lakes*," *Legacy* 10: 79–102) reminds us that Fuller composed her book "in the Harvard library, where she was the first woman to use its collections." Like Burbick and Zwarg, Tonkovich finds divided purpose in the text, and she focuses on the "authorial anxiety" that is revealed as Fuller "both contested and reproduced the power arrangements the library represented." While Fuller ultimately "reinscribes the Indians in terms and hierarchies already established by the library's historians and ethnographers," she was able to voice some measure of resistance through "parody, playfulness, and the creation of multiple and fictive versions of the authorial 'self.'" Sharon Stout Brause ("Wit in Margaret Fuller's *Summer on the Lakes*," *PMPA* 18: 18–25) discusses the effectiveness of Fuller's use of humor and wit, noting in particular her satiric observations of the "crudely pragmatic Americans" she encountered.

Christina Zwarg's instructive "Reading Before Marx: Margaret Fuller and the *New-York Daily Tribune*" (*Readers in History*, pp. 228–58) is an important addition to her recent series of articles which trace Fuller's developing feminism and its relation to her broadening view of political agency (see also *ALS 1989*, pp. 9–10; *ALS 1990*, p. 16; and *ALS 1991*, p. 16). Zwarg explains Fuller's view of "reading as an important site for significant social change" through a careful examination of her *Tribune* articles of 1844–46, arguing with persuasive detail that Fuller brought an already well-developed political sensitivity to the Italian scene, having evolved a "theory of cultural interaction that anticipates Gramsci's notion of hegemonic transformation." In " 'With Ready Eye': Margaret Fuller and Lesbianism in Nineteenth-Century American Literature" (*AL* 65: 1–18) Mary E. Wood argues that Fuller "fails to maintain a consistent, unidirectional narrative voice—gendered as male" in *Woman in the Nineteenth Century*, thus resisting "the gendering and the heterosexuality of narrative itself." Working from Teresa De Lauretis's theory of the engendering quality of narrative, Wood reads Fuller's text as a deconstruction of "gendered narrativity" through its disruptions of "the traditional male-generated, heterosexual movement of narrative."

Donna Dickenson's *Margaret Fuller: Writing a Woman's Life* (St. Martin's) begins with an examination of "the process of mythologising Fuller into obscurity after her death," building on Sandra M. Gilbert and Susan Gubar's depiction of the sense of threat within the male literary establishment to explain the distorted representation of Fuller in the *Memoirs* and later 19th-century works. Dickenson stresses the largely overlooked influence of Fuller's mother, and she describes Fuller's developing years in New England, including her teaching, her conducting of Conversations, and her editorship of the *Dial*, as a "period of waiting" that would be superseded by her later life in New York and Italy. *Woman in the Nineteenth Century* was a key sign of her emergence, a text that built from, but ultimately transcended, 19th-century norms of "the cult of True Womanhood."

b. The Transcendentalist Movement   K. P. Van Anglen's *The New England Milton* is the most comprehensive study to date on Milton's reception in New England culture. Van Anglen traces the Unitarian reconstruction of the great Puritan poet into an icon of religious liberalism, led by William Ellery Channing's influential reassessment; extensive analysis is provided of the continuing appropriation of Milton by the Transcendentalists. Van Anglen argues that the liberal reading of Milton reflected the tension between Arminian and antinomian elements of New England culture, the former mirroring a concern for cultural authority and continuity, and the latter a dissenting or rebellious rejection of the claims of cultural authority. Although Milton gave representation to the antinomian sensibility in *Paradise Lost*, it rarely overcame the Arminian concern for cultural continuity. *Walden* and "Ktaadn," however, offer moments when the "antinomian structure of feeling" became "close to dominant." In *American Transcendentalism and Asian Religions* (Oxford) Arthur Versluis surveys the impact of Asian religious ideas on the Transcendentalist movement, beginning with Emerson's sympathetic "assimilation" of Asian religious concepts, and concluding with the attempts of later thinkers influenced by the Free Religion movement to formulate a theory of progress toward a universal religion. Versluis includes discussions of Emerson, Thoreau, and Alcott's appropriation of Asian religions, Melville and Brownson's dissent to this appropriation, and the treatment of Asian religious ideas in Transcendentalist and American general-interest periodicals. Most valuable is his discussion of the lesser-known thinkers of the Free Religion movement, whose studies of Asian religions were motivated by the hope that "there is a religion dawning that will take the place of Christianity and the other traditions as a single world religion."

Frank Carpenter's "Paradise Held: William Ellery Channing and the Legacy of Oakland" (*Newport History* 65, iii: 91–124) is an informative account of the Gibbs-Channing family's struggle over an estate that included the country home Oakland, Channing's summer "place of refuge" during his ministry at the Federal Street Church, and the place where he did much significant writing. Elisabeth Hurth's "The 'Uses' of the 'Literary' Jesus: Ernest Renan's *Life of Jesus* in New England" (*ESQ* 38 [1992]: 315–37) astutely traces the reception of Renan's " 'humanized' life of Jesus" in New England liberal circles, noting both the popular appeal of Renan's sentimental portrait, and the resistance to aspects of the work that ran counter to evidentialist premises affirming "the traditional supernatural view of the Scriptures." Hurth also notes several "literary lives of Jesus which were consciously modelled after its example," including Harriet Beecher Stowe's *Footsteps of the Master* and Elizabeth Stuart Phelps's *Story of Jesus Christ*.

In "Bronson Alcott and Jacob Böhme" (*SAR*, pp. 153–59) Arthur Versluis notes Alcott's lifelong fascination with the work of Böhme and his English followers, demonstrating how both Böhme's language and mystical concepts can help us decipher, to some extent at least, Alcott's notoriously obscure "Orphic Sayings." Guy R. Woodall's "Convers

Francis and the Concordians: Emerson, Alcott, and Others" (*CS* n.s. 1: 23–58) investigates Francis's many connections with Concord, recording his frequent preaching there and describing his friendships with Emerson and Samuel and Sarah Ripley. Joan Goodwin ("Sarah Alden Ripley, Another Concord Botanist," *CS* n.s. 1: 77–86) sketches Sarah Ripley's life and personality, emphasizing the interest in botany that she shared with Thoreau. In "Ellery Channing: The Turning Point" (*CS* n.s. 1: 89–94) Harmon Smith uses manuscript letters in the Massachusetts Historical Society to describe the impact of Ellen Fuller Channing's death on her husband Ellery.

Oregon State University

2 Hawthorne

Leland S. Person, Jr.

Even by recent standards the gushing out of interesting *Scarlet Letter* criticism in 1993 astonishes—with *The Scarlet Letter* shutting out *The House of the Seven Gables*, 19–0. Highlighting a solid year's work dominated by New Historicist approaches are T. Walter Herbert's book on the Hawthornes as a conflicted middle-class family, G. R. Thompson's narratological analysis of Hawthorne's Provincial Tales, John Dolis's postmodern analysis of Hawthorne's "vision," and provocative essays by Eric Savoy, Claudia Johnson, Jay Grossman, Michael T. Gilmore (all on *Scarlet Letter*), Manfred Mackenzie (on *Blithedale*), David Leverenz (on selected tales), Cindy Weinstein (on "The Birth-mark"), and Lesley Ginsberg (on *Wonder Book*). *The Nathaniel Hawthorne Review* again features several worthwhile articles—a sign that the journal continues to exploit its new, more scholarly format.

i Bibliography, Biography, and Reference Guides

The year's most provocative study is Herbert's. *Dearest Beloved: The Hawthornes and the Making of the Middle-Class Family* (Calif.) is a psychocultural family biography and New Historicist exposé of the "torments intrinsic to the domestic ideal" that dominated 19th-century life—and one of the most extreme views of Hawthorne and the Hawthorne marriage that we are ever likely to see. Words such as hate, malice, cruelty, disgust, dread, obsession, fixation, terror, monstrosity, self-loathing, and revenge create a gothic family portrait, "teeming with covert sexual politics," in which the parents' unresolved childhood traumas visit themselves upon their three children.

Herbert keys each of four sections to one of the major romances and ingeniously interprets the conversation between life and art that such juxtaposition establishes. *The Blithedale Romance*, for example, reflects Hawthorne's effort to resolve the gender conflicts that his marriage intensified. Embodying "true" manhood and womanhood in Hollingsworth and Priscilla, as he and Sophia projected the same cultural ideals onto each other, Hawthorne uses this fictional relation to "advance a radical criticism of the domestic ideal"—and thus, indirectly, of his own marriage. Rereading family relations in *Seven Gables*, Herbert confirms Hawthorne's conservatism—reconfigured as a "parable of the transition to a domestic family ideology": a family grounded in the mutual love of a "self-sufficient man and a 'true woman.'" In a 100-page section on the Hawthornes' "Marital Politics" and its influence on *The Scarlet Letter*, the novel "meditates" on the Hawthornes' "paradise of domesticity" in which the "disjointed double family" represented by Hester, Arthur, Chillingworth, and Pearl suggests the double family romance—joyful domestic surface, agonized underworld—that the Hawthornes typified.

Herbert's best section involves *The Marble Faun*, the climactic family romance because of the psychic forces and characters that surfaced during the Hawthornes' Roman visit. Una's governess and doctor (Franco), as well as the sculptor Louisa Lander and Margaret Fuller, "play out a congregation of stories" and a crisis that "disables the language by which 'the family'—both the Hawthorne family and the middle-class family—understood itself." The Cenci legend offers a key paradigm, evoking the incest and patricide that lurk within the Hawthorne household. Hence, Hawthorne's revulsion/desire for Una and her sexual independence/submissiveness stage an "erotic drama" that test the meanings of manhood and womanhood. Herbert's psychological analyses throughout *Dearest Beloved* are rich, well-reasoned, and almost always keyed to textual evidence—and complex enough to provide fertile and contested ground for many future scholars to work.

In "*Memories of Hawthorne*: Rose Hawthorne Lathrop's Auto/Biography" (*ABSt* 8: 1–15) Patricia Dunlavy Valenti offers an interesting postscript to her 1991 biography, fixing on Rose's need to inscribe her own "identity theme" upon her father's experience and to write her own interdependent story. In "Hawthorne's Love Letters: The Threshold World of Sophia Peabody" (*ATQ* 7: 127–39) Julie M. Norko argues the common position that Hawthorne "creates Sophia" as a "threshold [figure] between the heavenly and the earthly" who empowers a "fuller conception of himself."

David Cody usefully surveys and summarizes the consistently prolific

Japanese scholarship in "Hawthorne in Japan: Some Recent Studies, 1975–1991" (*EIHC* 129: 297–342).

ii Critical Books

Where Herbert's Hawthorne seems passive—a blank mind on which culture writes—G. R. Thompson's "Hawthorne" in *The Art of Authorial Presence: Hawthorne's Provincial Tales* (Duke) is a crafty manipulator of narrative voice and "authorial presence." Central to Hawthorne's "narrative aesthetics" is the "complex nature of the foregrounded narrator as figured 'author' and his intricate relation to the structure of narrator-narratee transactions."

Except for his fascinating final chapter on Hawthorne's dismantled "Story Teller" sequence, Thompson limits himself to eight early tales, which he (re)constructs as Hawthorne's *Provincial Tales:* four "dreamvision sketches" ("The Hollow of the Three Hills," "The Wives of the Dead," "An Old Woman's Tale," "Alice Doane's Appeal") and four historical tales ("The Gray Champion," "Roger Malvin's Burial," "The Gentle Boy," "My Kinsman, Major Molineux"). All feature the mediating figure of the "Story Teller," who enables Hawthorne to experiment metafictionally and especially to subvert genre conventions. In "The Gray Champion," for example, Thompson shows Hawthorne ironically intertwining the question of the gray champion's "ontological reality" with the narrators' "aesthetic and philosophical struggle" to " 'tell' " the story. In "The Gentle Boy," Thompson shows how the "historical truth of the Puritan-Quaker conflict is entangled in moral-psychological perspectivism"—as the product of author/reader, narrator/narratee transactions. Hawthorne criticizes both Puritans and Quakers, Thompson argues, but the narrative emerges not in balanced criticism but in the "contestatory gap between opposing constructs." By focusing new attention on the narrator's commentary, Thompson usefully reinforces and somewhat extends ironic readings of the tale. "My Kinsman, Major Molineux" serves Thompson as an important example of Hawthorne's metafictionality. Although his reading of this oft-discussed tale is not particularly new, he does provide, by carefully analyzing the framing devices, one of the best analyses I know of *how* Hawthorne achieves his notorious ambiguity, and his idea that "shrewd" readers *and* Robin Molineux both "undergo a kind of parallel manipulation via the narratival structuring of the text" is inspired.

Thompson concludes with "Alice Doane's Appeal," the "most highly metafictional and aggressively author-foregrounding" narrative among the *Provincial Tales*. Countering psychoanalytic approaches emphasizing the incestuous "interior" story, he stresses the "problematic relationship of fictive 'author' to text, audience, and genre" and the "self-reflexive aesthetic-philosophical question of narrative itself." Unnecessarily long-winded though it is, Thompson's book makes a worthwhile contribution to Hawthorne studies by refocusing attention on the formalistic complexities of the fiction and encouraging renewed appreciation for Hawthorne's aesthetic sophistication and control.

Marked by ingenious wordplay and indebted theoretically to Derrida, Lacan, Heidegger, and Merleau-Ponty, John Dolis's *The Style of Hawthorne's Gaze: Regarding Subjectivity* (Alabama) focuses on the visually deconstructive aspect of Hawthorne's imagination—a metamorphic gaze that offers a "counter-visual response" to the prevailing "technological prejudice for transparency." Focusing almost exclusively on the novels, especially *The Scarlet Letter* ("Ethan Brand" does warrant a be-wildering and fascinating analysis), Dolis offers a kaleidoscopic account of Hawthorne's "metamorphic reality" and the situational subjectivity it engenders. Hawthorne consistently honors the "reciprocity between subject and object" by destabilizing the subject-object dichotomy, representing "variable figure-ground relations," and re-creating the "way in which corporeality itself strikes the subject in its affective being"—a phenomenon Dolis illustrates in a brilliant analysis of the brookside scene in *The Scarlet Letter*, for example. Turning the conventional thumbscrew on Hawthorne's scientists (Aylmer, Rappaccini, et al.) as gazers who refuse the other's gaze, Dolis provocatively contrasts Dimmesdale and Coverdale. While Dimmesdale's "evasive glance signals his awareness of the other" and leads to "sympathetic union" (an arguable proposition), Coverdale's voyeurism suggests a "failure to find 'completion' in the gaze of the other" and thus alienation from his own subjectivity. Dolis's book will exasperate some readers for its exhibitionism, and for all its emphasis on reciprocity in Hawthorne it resists reading in many places. But at his critical best—explaining Hawthorne's visual style, negotiating the relation among Hawthorne, Pearl, letters, and *The Scarlet Letter*, or citing/siting connections between Pearl and Donatello, letter and faun—Dolis deserves an extended look.

Nancy Bunge's *Nathaniel Hawthorne: A Study of the Short Fiction* (Twayne) makes a negligible scholarly contribution. Bunge cites more criticism from the 1950s and 1960s than from more recent decades, and she adopts a simplistic moral-psychological approach to themes she finds unambiguously stated in key passages. Devoting 80 pages to superficial critical summaries of a third of Hawthorne's tales, Bunge fills another 80 pages with very brief excerpts from Hawthorne's letters, notebooks, and prefaces and from previously published criticism by Richard Harter Fogle, Nina Baym, Michael Colacurcio, and Gloria Erlich (whose name she misspells).

iii General Essays

In "Hawthorne's Moral Theaters and the Post-Puritan Stage" (*SAR*, pp. 255–73) Kurt Eisen insightfully traces Hawthorne's ambivalence toward the theatrical—his "post-Puritan sense of the stage's dangerous stimulation of the mind" versus his "aesthetic of sympathy." Examples include "Passages from a Relinquished Work," "Fancy's Show Box," "Alice Doane's Appeal," and *The Blithedale Romance*. Eric Fretz does what his title suggests in "Stylized Processions and the Carnivalesque in Nathaniel Hawthorne's Fiction: A Selected Sampling" (*NHR* 19, i: 11–17). He cites the usual scenes in "The May-Pole of Merry Mount," *The Scarlet Letter*, and *The Marble Faun* and concludes that character transformations promised by carnival do not occur. In an unwitting parody of Leslie Fiedler, marked by hyperbole and many references to "man," Carol Wershoven analyzes Priscilla, Phoebe, and Hilda (*Child Brides and Intruders*, pp. 17–34) as American "darlings"—helpless "child brides" who make "typical American unions" with "dominant males."

iv Essays on the Novels

a. *The Scarlet Letter* As noted, criticism of Hawthorne's first major novel abounded. Most remarkable—the number of first-rate critical studies. Eric Savoy, for example, gives the critical screw an interesting new turn in " 'Filial Duty': Reading the Patriarchal Body in 'The Custom House' " (*SNNTS* 25: 397–417). Hawthorne's preface is "a protracted and rhetorically complex meditation on the gendered, historically determined subjectivity of the male author," Savoy claims. Through the trope of prosopopoeia Hawthorne affiliates himself with (dead) patriarchal authority, assumes a "patriarchal agenda," and reinscribes an "exemplary tale of Puritan misogyny" that subverts Hester's anticipated "feminist utopia" by employing "terrorist strategies" of scarification. A smart new reading of "The Custom-House." Sandra Tomc, "'The Sanctity of the Priesthood': Hawthorne's 'Custom-House'" (*ESQ* 39: 161–84), usefully cites the "radical discrepancy" between Hawthorne's authorial self-portraits in "The Old Manse" and "The Custom-House" to show his struggle to adapt in the latter to authorship as private, commercial enterprise.

Claudia Durst Johnson, "Impotence and Omnipotence in *The Scarlet Letter*" (*NEQ* 66: 594–612), provocatively examines male self-representation in the novel, which becomes a "tale shaped by impotence." Johnson sees the narrator of "The Custom-House" playing out a "convoluted drama of his own literary dysfunction through the sexuality of his fictional characters," and she links Chillingworth and Dimmesdale to literary and legal precedents involving impotent men. Dimmesdale plays the key role in this drama as surrogate impotent for Hawthorne's narrator, but both characters discover "self-potency" by drama's end.

Accounting for the recurring image of the "black man" in *The Scarlet Letter*, Jay Grossman, in his neo-Marxist "'A' is for Abolition?: Race, Authorship, *The Scarlet Letter*" (*TexP* 7: 13–30), reveals a novel "implicated" in "antebellum discourses of miscegenation." With Sherlock Holmesian perspicacity, Grossman shakes the word "black" out of the text and repeatedly demonstrates that "black fruit" can "blossom darkly." In a metacritical twist, he also accounts for the black man's invisibility in recent historical criticism of *The Scarlet Letter* (especially Jonathan Arac's and Jean Fagin Yellin's), which closes off particularized racial readings of the textual evidence in favor of more universal, allegorical interpretations.

In an adroit Foucauldian study, "Authorizing the Body: Scientific Medicine and *The Scarlet Letter*" (*L&M* 12, ii: 139–60), Stephanie P. Browner historicizes the competition in the novel among religious, legal, medical, and literary authorities. Hawthorne pointedly critiques medicine, scathingly condemning the positivist "clinical gaze" (popularized in Paris, reflected in Chillingworth) that reduces bodies to a statistically constructed generic body. Ultimately, Hawthorne represents the body, especially Hester's female body, as "unpredictable and idiosyncratic"— unknowable by medical observation.

Michael T. Gilmore's "Hawthorne and the Making of the Middle Class" (*Discovering Difference*, pp. 88–104) complements Herbert's section on *The Scarlet Letter* by stressing socioeconomic spheres rather than sexual mores. Racking up insights with every sentence, Gilmore discovers a text that "organizes itself as an instantiation of middle-class experience." Hester and Arthur epitomize an upwardly and downwardly mobile middle class, he suggests, even as their instabilities (especially their "transvestism") destabilize gendered class lines.

Jerome Loving's Lawrentian thesis in "Hawthorne's Awakening in the Customhouse" (*Lost in the Customhouse*, pp. 19–34) depends on Hawthorne's writing "The Custom-House" preface before he wrote the last three chapters of the novel. That is, by reviving his "social sense" in the preface, Hawthorne betrayed Hester's Ahab-like "self-consecrated-self" and thus failed to write "the true ending of the novel," in which she celebrates her—and his—"solitary self."

If readers feel seduced by such a Loving-ly subversive, romantic reading of *The Scarlet Letter*, they might read Stephen Railton's "The Address of *The Scarlet Letter*" (*Readers in History*, pp. 138–63). Historicizing his reader-response approach, Railton insightfully uses *Uncle Tom's Cabin* to establish the crucial role audience plays in Hawthorne's rhetorical strategy to challenge his readers. Hawthorne's Puritans, he argues, comprise a surrogate Victorian audience whose "terrible" example encourages the real audience to be more tolerant even as Hawthorne demonstrates that "the law must be obeyed." Cynthia Bernstein also examines the internal audience in "Reading *The Scarlet Letter* Against Hawthorne's Fictional Interpretive Communities" (*Lang&Lit* 18: 1–20), but the essay is much more rudimentary than Railton's.

Louise K. Barnett has slightly revised and updated her seminal 1983 article on "Speech and Society" in *The Scarlet Letter* (*Authority and Speech*, pp. 43–58), taking issue with such critics as Millicent Bell and Evan Carton in arguing Hawthorne's "confidence in the resources of language to communicate meaning." Nancy Tenfelde Clasby, "Being True: *Logos* in *The Scarlet Letter*" (*Renascence* 45: 247–57), ignores a lot of relevant scholarship in arguing somewhat similarly that Hawthorne turns the word into deed and flesh. Hester and Dimmesdale climactically synthesize *logos* and *mythos*, she claims (cf. Derrida), and thus achieve "full revelation." This is head vs. heart, "to-the-dogs-with-the-*logos*" criticism with a lingua-Christian twist.

In contrast, Samuel Kimball's Derridean "Countersigning Aristotle: The Amimetic Challenge of *The Scarlet Letter*" (*ATQ* 7: 141–58) argues that the scarlet letter "disrupts the disclosure of truth" via its "*a*mimetic" character. Although not original, Kimball's deconstruction of *The Scarlet*

Letter is the clearest and most cogent I have seen. Sylvie Mathé also researches indeterminacies in an overlong essay, "The Reader May Not Choose: Oxymoron as Central Figure in Hawthorne's Strategy of Immunity From Choice in *The Scarlet Letter*" (*Style* 26 [1992]: 604–35). Focused on Hawthorne's "shifty" narrator and "reading contract," Mathé shows how he forecloses on the "multiple-choices" he seems to offer his readers—particularly by using oxymorons. Rather than promoting undecidability, multiple choice sponsors multiple meanings.

Dipping into Cotton Mather's *Magnalia Christi Americana* for a source in "Dimmesdale and His Bachelorhood: 'Priestly Celibacy' in *The Scarlet Letter*" (*SAF* 21: 103–10), Carol M. Bensick discovers Thomas Parker of Newbury, whose bachelorhood became a serious issue for none other than John Wilson, who rebuked him for not marrying. A nice piece of detective work in itself, but Bensick goes on to show how Parker's association of marriage with infidelity and apostasy could have inspired Dimmesdale, a sexual hypocrite who professed celibacy while indulging in sexual fantasies and encouraging them in his female parishioners. In "'Subtle, but remorseful hypocrite': Dimmesdale's Moral Character" (*SNNTS* 25: 257–71) Kenneth D. Pimple offers a new take on the forest scene in arguing that, instead of being seduced by Hester, Dimmesdale talks her into talking him into fleeing with her. Pimple artfully analyzes both semantic and pragmatic aspects of Dimmesdale's speech to establish the minister's "manipulative doubletalk."

Carol Wershoven, "Hester as First Rebel" (*Child Brides and Intruders*, pp. 161–76), rehearses familiar points about Hester's rebelliousness in a largely expository reading. In another superficial essay, "'Apples of the Thoughts and Fancies': Nature as Narrator in *The Scarlet Letter*" (*ATQ* 7: 307–19), Janice B. Daniel shows how Hawthorne personifies nature as an additional, more benevolent narrative "voice." In "*Adam Blair* and *The Scarlet Letter*" (*NHR* 19, ii: 1–10) Will and Mimosa Stephenson re-sift the evidence of Hawthorne's reliance on John Lockhart's 1822 novel and, relying mainly on character parallels, conclude that Hawthorne "wrote in active dialogue with it." Finally, John L. Idol, Jr., and Sterling Eisiminger describe the first operatic performances of the novel, including George Parsons Lathrop's version, in "*The Scarlet Letter* as Opera: The First Settings" (*NHR* 19, ii: 11–16).

b. *The Blithedale Romance* Richard Brodhead's brilliant cultural-historical article (see *ALS 1989*, p. 28), "Veiled Ladies: Toward a History of

Antebellum Entertainment," appears slightly revised in his *Cultures of Letters* (pp. 48–68). The Everyman edition of *Blithedale*, based on the Ohio State text, features a snappy introduction by Malcolm Bradbury (emphasizing the novel's satiric Utopianism and Coverdale's unreliability), a handy chronology of Hawthorne and of his "times," and very brief excerpts of previous criticism.

Manfred Mackenzie's fascinating "postcolonial" reading of *Blithedale* highlights the year's critical activity. In "Colonization and Decolonization in *The Blithedale Romance*" (*UTQ* 62: 504–21) Mackenzie deliberately supplements Lauren Berlant's *The Anatomy of National Fantasy* (see *ALS 1991*, pp. 23–24), which he finds essentially nationalistic (*A*-colonial, as it were), and argues for *Blithedale* as a "fiction of colonization," "primary Manicheanism," and "dedoublement" (cf. Frantz Fanon). Mackenzie concludes that Hawthorne distances himself sufficiently from Coverdale to write a form of "counter-discourse" that resists a colonizing impulse. Mackenzie's essay has broad implications for Hawthorne studies and points a way that many other scholars may wish to follow.

Two gendered readings of *Blithedale* help us understand Zenobia's role in this androcentric text. Laura Tanner's "Speaking with 'Hands at our Throats': The Struggle for Artistic Voice in *The Blithedale Romance*" (*SAF* 21: 1–19) demonstrates how Hawthorne subtly undermines Coverdale's artistic values and narrative authority—his attempt to silence Zenobia—and privileges Zenobia's subversive creative power. Somewhat similarly, in "Spectating the spectator, re(ad)dressing the (ad)dressor" (*ATQ* 7: 321–33), Minaz Jooma uses "gaze" theory to analyze Zenobia's "double vision"—as observer and observed—and especially her creative role as a signifying woman whose self-conscious constructions of "woman" destabilize Coverdale's traditional male gaze.

c. *The Marble Faun* In a neat historical essay worth comparing to John McWilliams's (see below), Robert H. Byer in "Words, Monuments, Beholders: The Visual Arts in Hawthorne's *The Marble Faun*" (*American Iconology*, pp. 163–85) compares Hawthorne's "pedagogy of monumental beholding" with two contemporaneous modes—the monumental oration (e.g., Daniel Webster's at Bunker Hill) and the stereoscope—in order to show the loss of monumental authority in American culture.

Two comparative studies, pivoting critically in opposite directions from the text, place *The Marble Faun* in conversation with others. Looking backward for influence in "*Villette* and *The Marble Faun*"

(*SNNTS* 25: 272–90), Jack C. Wills finds enough parallels—use of confession, specters, carnival scenes, art, double love stories, growth through suffering, and more—to suspect that Hawthorne borrowed from Brontë's novel. Looking forward in "The Reader without a Country: Nathaniel Hawthorne's *The Marble Faun* after Nabokov" (*Reverse Tradition*, pp. 152–75), Robert Kiely emphasizes Hawthorne's mischievous, Nabokovian gamesmanship toward his readers and highlights the novel's numerous interpretive, house-of-mirrors-like puzzles.

v Essays on Tales and Sketches

New Essays on Hawthorne's Major Tales, ed. Millicent Bell (Cambridge), highlights the year's work on the short fiction, even though the contributors understandably ignore many of Hawthorne's arguably "major" tales. Bell's "Introduction" (pp. 1–35) provides a comprehensively researched account of Hawthorne's career as American short-story writer. Neither Michael Colacurcio nor Carol M. Bensick, on the other hand, contributes as many "new" insights into the short fiction as this series would seem to promise, although their essays represent intelligent rehearsals of previously published ideas. In "'Certain Circumstances': Hawthorne and the Interest of History" (pp. 37–66) Colacurcio wittily and effectively argues the case for "particularist" historical scholarship (as opposed to "universalist" psychoanalysis) and for historical readings of "My Kinsman, Major Molineux," "Roger Malvin's Burial," and "Young Goodman Brown." Bensick's "World Lit Hawthorne: Re-Allegorizing 'Rappaccini's Daughter'" (pp. 67–82) doubles back on her earlier *La Nouvelle Beatrice* to allege Dantean and other literary-historical allusions and to argue against John N. Miller's ridicule of such critical treatments of the tale in his 1991 article. Rita Gollin in "Ethan Brand's Homecoming" (pp. 83–100) deftly links Ethan's obsessive, albeit circular, home-seeking to Hawthorne's own return to his Salem home. Gollin emphasizes circular imagery in arguing that "Ethan Brand," like many other tales, reflects Hawthorne's anxious, ironic regard for "home" and "homecomings." The "newest" essay in the volume belongs to David Leverenz, whose "Historicizing Hell in Hawthorne's Tales" (pp. 101–32) bridges the scholarly gap between Colacurcio's Hawthorne-as-pedant and G. R. Thompson's Hawthorne-as-metafictionist approach to the tales. With characteristic wit, Leverenz historicizes Hawthorne's narrative voice as a "thick ventriloquism," a double-edged tongue of flame, as it were, that mocks his culture's progressive liberalism in such tales as "My Kinsman, Major Molineux," "Wakefield," "Young Goodman Brown," "The Celestial Railroad," and "Earth's Holocaust." A truly "new" and brilliant essay. Another smart essay is Edgar A. Dryden's "Through a Glass Darkly: 'The Minister's Black Veil' as Parable" (pp. 133–50). Like Thompson, Dryden focuses on the theoretically minded Hawthorne who works self-consciously with generic conventions and expectations—in this case, the parable. Dryden's generic focus through the biblical parable of Moses and the veil (upon his return from the wilderness) extends J. Hillis Miller's deconstructive reading of 1988.

Although ignored by the new essayists, "The Birth-mark" sparked more critical interest than any other tale or sketch this year. Especially notable is Cindy Weinstein's "The Invisible Hand Made Visible: 'The Birth-mark'" (*NCF* 48: 44–73), which employs C. B. Macpherson's theory of marketplace individualism to historicize what she calls Hawthorne's "economics of allegory." Siting a circulatory concept of identity-formation in Georgiana's body, Weinstein cogently unpacks the relation between bodies, literature, and labor. The key: erasing/excising traces of the hand of labor (especially the labor of allegory) in a workplace that increasingly fragmented workers' bodies. In "'(Super)'Natural' Invalidism: Male Writers and the Mind/Body Problem" (*Invalid Women,* pp. 75–109) Diane Price Herndl briefly treats "The Birth-mark" and "Rappaccini's Daughter" (along with *Blithedale*) in relation to 19th-century medical discourse. While Hawthorne searches for a "new union of mind and body," she argues, he cannot finally resist medical definitions of separatism, and he visits the result on the bodies of women characters. Elisabeth Bronfen (*Over Her Dead Body*, pp. 126–30) covers similar ground, with a Lacanian twist, but she ignores all relevant criticism and reinvents a lot of "others'" ideas. The same blithe spirit marks her discussion of Zenobia and her "excesses" in *The Blithedale Romance* (pp. 241–49). Also unoriginal, Liz Rosenberg's "'The Best That Earth Could Offer': 'The Birth-mark,' A Newlywed's Story" (*SSF* 30: 145–51) simply labels Aylmer a newlywed (like Hawthorne) and Georgiana's death "the ultimate divorce." Far more original and intriguing, in "Resisting the Birth Mark: Subverting Hawthorne in a Feminist Theory Play" (*Upstaging Big Daddy,* pp. 121–32) Gayle Austin describes writing, staging (at Georgia State University), and deconstructing "The Birth-mark" by interrupting the narrative with short feminist theoretical texts (especially Judith Fetterley's).

In "American Literature's Declaration of Independence: Stanley Cavell, Nathaniel Hawthorne, and the Covenant of Consent" (*Summoning*, pp. 211–28) Emily Miller Budick continues her Cavellian analysis of Hawthorne's fiction by focusing on "My Kinsman, Major Molineux." Citing Cavell as a reader-responsible alternative to deconstruction and New Historicism, Budick argues that he and Hawthorne respect their readers' autonomy while encouraging them to "consent" to a relationship, or covenant, with the "other." "Hawthorne's story is filled with moments typified by consensual understandings of reality," she argues, and it promotes "the value of negotiated relations."

Worth reading in tandem with Thompson's book, Douglas Tallack's older-fashioned "Generic Discontinuities in the Stories of Nathaniel Hawthorne" (*The Nineteenth-Century American Short Story*, pp. 107–39) derives Hawthorne's tales, interestingly enough, from Anne Hutchinson, who inaugurated an "aesthetic which looked to the self, rather than to collective, authorizing institutions." Tallack's best point: that various generic requirements (i.e., of legends, fantasies, fragments, biographies, parables, fables) compete and cooperate in many Hawthorne tales. In "Endicott and the Red Cross" and "The Minister's Black Veil," for example, story competes generically with history, symbolic insight with linear narrative time. In " 'A Thick and Darksome Veil': The Rhetoric of Hawthorne's Sketches" (*NCF* 48: 310–25) Thomas R. Moore analyzes representative sentences in "Monsieur du Miroir," "The Old Apple-Dealer," and "The Haunted Mind" to show that Hawthorne subverts the "clear"-style principles of Hugh Blair's *Lectures on Rhetoric and Belles Lettres*. Moore thus restyles Hawthorne's well-known ambiguity as a "rhetoric of subversion."

More meditative than analytical, Arnold Weinstein's "Hawthorne's 'Wakefield' and the Art of Self-Possession" (*Nobody's Home*, pp. 13–26) links Wakefield himself to Odysseus, Leopold Bloom, Proust's Marcel, Kafka's Josef K., and others. He substantiates his extravagant claims for the tale in a Borgesian meditation on "self-enactment": a man discovering presence by observing his own absence. One of the most compelling essays we have on "Wakefield." In "Hawthorne's Black Veil: From Image to Icon" (*CEA* 55, iii: 79–87) Samuel Coale takes off from Hillis Miller's 1991 study to examine the psychoreligious *process* by which an object becomes an idol or icon representing the congregation's "most Puritan and personal fears." David D. Joplin extends John F. Birk's 1991 study (see *ALS 1992*, p. 95) in " 'May-Pole of Merry Mount': Hawthorne's 'L'Allegro' and 'Il Penseroso' " (*SSF* 30: 185–92) by arguing that Merry Mount "stands as a structural inversion" of the poems, with emphasis on the "negative mirth" of "Il Penseroso." Stephen Orton, "De-centered Symbols in 'Endicott and the Red Cross' " (*SSF* 30: 565–74), also examines inversions and doublings in an insightful deconstructive reading of symbolism that "embodies the *lack* of the thing signified."

"The Prophetic Pictures" exemplifies male "hermaphroditic dreams of parental singularity" for Marie-Helene Huet in "The Artist's Studio" (*Monstrous Imagination*, pp. 163–74). Hawthorne's artist appropriates the "feminine" in his art, but by representing and then causing Elinor's attempted murder he demonstrates that such appropriative art is a "monstrous project." In "Democrats Abroad: Continental Literature and the American Bard in the *United States Magazine and Democratic Review*" (*AmPer* 3: 75–99) Joshua David Scholnick highlights the first publication of "Rappaccini's Daughter," complete with "Aubépine's" preface, as Hawthorne's contribution to the magazine's efforts to create an American culture in relation to Continental literature.

vi **Essays on Other Works**

Richly analyzing commemorations of Lexington and Concord, John McWilliams in "Lexington, Concord, and the 'Hinge of the Future' " (*AmLH* 5: 1–29) contrasts Hawthorne's *Septimius Felton* with other writings that validated the "patriots' collective identity as oppressed farmers and homespun martyr-heroes." Instead, Hawthorne "wholly inverts the treasured assumptions of patriotic history."

In an informative essay, "The Two Lives of Franklin Pierce: Hawthorne, Political Culture, and the Literary Market" (*AmLH* 5: 203–30), Scott E. Casper examines Hawthorne's campaign biography in relation to a "publishing war" between Ticknor, Reed, and Fields and the rival publishers of David W. Bartlett's biography. Although Bartlett's was more innovative, interpolating dialogue from Pierce's Bowdoin years and his closing argument from an 1850 murder trial and thus linking him to popular sentimental and sensational literature, Hawthorne's enabled Pierce to ride on Hawthorne's better-known coattails and to benefit from Ticknor's fierce effort to suppress Bartlett's book.

Lesley Ginsberg also invokes the Pierce biography in " 'The Willing

Captive': Narrative Seduction and the Ideology of Love in Hawthorne's *A Wonder Book for Boys and Girls*" (*AL* 65: 255–73), an ingenious reading of "The Chimaera" as a "psychodrama" of seduction that promotes a pro-bondage ideology through a "willing captive" myth. In "History and the Literary Imagination in Hawthorne's 'Chiefly About War-Matters'" (*ES* 74: 352–59) Charles H. Adams argues that, in his narrator (a "Peaceable Man"), Hawthorne created an ironic portrait of his own artistry and his romancer's limitations in coming to grips with historical crisis.

In "What Happened to Hawthorne?: Metaphor versus Narrative in the Unfinished Romances" (*Raritan* 12, iv: 94–108) James Barszcz discovers a protomodernist Hawthorne by making literary virtues out of alleged defects. "Precisely in their confusion," Barszcz claims, the unfinished romances attack a "destructive hunger" for continuities of class, individual and family identity, and narrative form. As an alternative to completed narrative forms, Hawthorne fell back, like Emerson, on metaphor, the "precipitates of the active mind's apprehension of the world."

vii Hawthorne and Others

Citing "strong psychological and spiritual affinities" between the two writers in *Plight in Common*, Elzbieta H. Oleksy compares *The Scarlet Letter* and *The Moviegoer*, *The House of the Seven Gables* and *Lancelot*, *The Marble Faun* and *The Second Coming*. Most interestingly for Hawthorne scholars, she sees Hawthorne as a "precursor" of literary existentialism. The Kierkegaardian "structure" of Hester's experience may seem overly schematic, but the parallels that Oleksy finds shed fresh light on the chapters (3, 13, 18, 19, 21, 23, 24) that comprise Hester's story. In an uneven biblical-mythic-Freudian reading, Oleksy considers *The House of the Seven Gables* an "apocalyptic" narrative, while French philosopher Gabriel Marcel's "personalist philosophy" helps her plot character transformations in *The Marble Faun*—culminating in a "double communion," *syneidesis*. In a meticulously researched essay, "A Long Incubation before a Renaissance: Hawthorne's Introduction into Meiji Japan" (*EIHC* 129: 269–98), Fumio Ano describes Hawthorne's significant literary impact on Japan during the 1868–1912 Meiji period—including *Peter Parley's Universal History* in 1867 and translations of such tales as "David Swan" and "Fancy's Show Box" in *Women's Magazine* in 1889.

Carol M. Bensick, "Hawthorne and His Bunyan" (*NHR* 19, i: 1–10), considers Hawthorne's choosing excerpts from Bunyan's *The Life and Death of Mr. Badman* for inclusion in *The American Magazine of Useful and Entertaining Knowledge* (1836), an attempt to illustrate the moral and intellectual transition from a medieval to a modern worldview.

Southern Illinois University

3 Poe

Benjamin F. Fisher

Poe's stature seems to be in no way diminishing; diversity and controversy maintain keynote status in this year's scholarship as enhancements to continued scholarly excitement. Predictably, the tales receive greatest attention. Bibliographical work is more prevalent than it has been for some time, and source studies occupy many devotees. Biographical issues also continue to be compelling interests. Poe's attitudes toward women constitute another recurrent critical pursuit.

i Bibliographical, Textual, and Biographical Work

Scott Peeples provides useful, annotated citations in "International Poe Bibliography, 1989–1991" (*PoeS* 25 [1992]: 10–36). Chester W. Tropp's *Victorian Yellowbacks & Paperbacks, 1849–1905*. Volume I: *George Routledge* (Hermitage Antiquarian Bookshop, pp. 20, 325, 351, 365, 442, 445, 448, 505) handily cites Poe titles brought out in cheap form by a popular Victorian firm. "Correcting the Poe Canon: Beverley Tucker's Anecdote on Gibbon and Fox" (*NCL* 48: 89–92) is Terence Whalen's conclusive demonstration that Tucker wrote a piece long thought to be Poe's. Conversely, John A. Hodgson in "Decoding Poe: Poe, W. Tyler, and Cryptography" (*JEGP* 92: 523–34) argues convincingly against Poe's authorship of the Tyler cryptograph in *Graham's* for December 1841. Hodgson thus poses challenges to Louis A. Renza (see *ALS 1985*, p. 50) and Shawn Rosenheim (see *ALS 1989*, p. 42). In "Thomas Cottrell Clarke's Poe Collection: New Documents" (*PoeS* 25 [1992]: 1–5) Richard Kopley and Michael Singer draw on letters, reminiscences, and Gill's 1877 biography to indicate what Clarke materials are on record—and what, speculatively, they wish might yet come to light.

We may shift our attention to scholarship that mingles the bibliographical and biographical by way of James Kibler's " 'Poe's Poetry': A

New Simms Essay"—from the Charleston, South Carolina, *Southern Patriot*, 10 November 1845—which deals with Poe the poet (and his "music"), critic, personality, and Boston Lyceum lecturer (*Simms Review* 1, ii: 20–24). Poe himself had reprinted Simms's piece in the *Broadway Journal*, 22 November 1845, pp. 309–10. Katherine Hemple Prown's far-ranging claims regarding Poe's Boston appearance as a "watershed event" for his ideas about his failure in popular writing, his uncertainties about mass audience, his role as critic, and his antiwoman mind-set are challenged by Kent Ljungquist in "The Cavalier and the Syren: Edgar Allan Poe, Cornelia Wells Walter, and the Boston Lyceum Incident" and follow-up letters to the editor (*NEQ* 66: 110–23, 465–68). Ljungquist's responses to Prown (whose name he misspells), especially those concerning Griswold and on Poe and women, are sensible rejoinders; they also open doors to further exploration of Poe's attitudes toward women. I might add that on the woman issue Prown should have cited more texts by Poe than "Berenice" and "The Philosophy of Composition." Two of his poems about women, "The Assignation," and "Eleonora," throw different lights on his attitudes (cf. J. Gerald Kennedy, below). Prown also ignores Poe's favorable estimates of women authors, as well as pertinent scholarship by Burton R. Pollin on Poe and Fuller. Misspelling of Longfellow's "Pröem" in Prown's essay should not go unnoticed; he would have cared.

Arguing zealously for "Poe's Authorship of Three Long Critical and Autobiographical Articles of 1843 Now Authenticated" (*ARLR* 7: 139–71) Burton R. Pollin reprints and copiously annotates pieces in the Philadelphia *Saturday Museum*, a mammoth weekly, as unquestionably Poe's: a hatchet notice of Griswold's *Poets and Poetry of America*; a demolition of the March *Graham's* and Griswold, its editor; and a well-known, but generally unavailable biography of Poe himself. This last, usually cited as the work of Henry B. Hirst though understood to be based on notes provided by Poe, is presented in facsimile. Imperfections in the text, however, necessitate another, better rendering. The authorship must also remain questionable because, whatever his limitations in verse might have been, Hirst, *pace* Pollin, could write good prose—for example, in essays on autography and on P. P. Cooke in the *Illustrated Monthly Magazine*. Moreover, Poe credited Hirst with excellent knowledge about prosody. Many of the expressions or words found in the three *Museum* essays—for example, "humbug," "rigmarole," or "Sissy," were not uniquely Poe's, as Pollin implies. Furthermore, as Dwight Thomas (in his 1978 dissertation and pertinent parts of *The Poe Log* [1987]) and other Poe scholars sift the evidence, there is as much likelihood for Hirst as writer of items one and three as for Poe. The late T. O. Mabbott's notes at the University of Iowa indicate that the biography might well appear in a "complete" edition, but not without a caveat as to authorship. Poe had earlier importuned F. W. Thomas to write the sketch, but Thomas returned Poe's memoranda. Thus, as I see it, authorship, particularly for items one and three, remains unsettled. Hirst may have had as many reasons for savaging Griswold as Poe, and Griswold's inclusion of Hirst in a later edition of *Poets and Poetry of America* might have aimed at forestalling further attacks from him. Pollin's list of other likely Poe attributions in the *Saturday Museum* is interesting, but it awaits documentary proof to make it more than inferential, as do several other claims in this essay, which, as they appear, are as much speculative as authenticating.

An 1899 recollection of Poe is given placement and clarification as a document for Poe biography by John E. Reilly in "Robert D'Unger and His Reminiscences of Edgar Allan Poe in Baltimore" (*MHM* 88: 60–72). Reilly publishes the full text of D'Unger's letter of 29 October 1899 to Chevalier Elmer Robert Reynolds, of Washington, D.C., responding to Reynolds's query for information about Poe. D'Unger's portrait of Poe during 1846–49 is not flattering, except to state that Poe worked hard. According to D'Unger, he also drank hard, preserved a generally aloof mien, and had predilections for talking about the supernatural. D'Unger's statement that Poe's sympathy and pity were reserved for women alone makes significant reading in line with the Prown-Ljungquist-Kennedy opinions already mentioned.

Editing *New Essays on Poe's Major Tales,* Kenneth Silverman leads off with a condensation of his recent biography as part of the "Introduction" (Cambridge, pp. 1–26). Emphasizing Poe's life in his art does not give just dues to literary origins for, say, death or sensational elements in his writings, although the examination of Poe's theory and practice in imaginative writing, in which certain nonbiographical inspirations are mentioned, compensates for the heavily psychoanalytic slant.

ii Books, Parts of Books

John T. Irwin in *The Mystery to a Solution* (Hopkins) addresses the analytic detective story, engages us with links between Poe and Borges (in the main), and shapes his book rather like a great detective story. Irwin analyzes motifs of doublings (a salient feature in analytic detective fiction), incest, revenge, mathematics history and theory, along with French Revolutionary political concerns, and quincuncial symbolism, pointing out where several or all these matters intersect in coming to bear on Poe and Poe's impact (sometimes via Faulkner) on Borges. Irwin offers new interpretations of Poe's ratiocinative tales, noting how Dupin figures into two signal artistic successes ("Murders" and "The Purloined Letter") and one failure ("Marie Roget"). Doubling Poe's methods, Borges turned out two successes and one failure in his detective-fiction ventures. Irwin reasonably blends a T. O. Mabbott methodology with recent theoretical approaches, especially (and fittingly) those of Lacan, Derrida, and Johnson in this labyrinthine book—through which he guides us to a freedom of renewed, expanded thinking about Poe's and Borges's detective literature. Irwin's enthusiasm for his topic sparks like excitement in a reader. This book has been well worth its long gestation. For brief comments on Poe's use of chess or its motifs in "Murders" and "The Purloined Letter," in ways that prefigure Borges's uses of such material in *The Garden of Forking Paths,* Irwin's "The False Artaxerxes: Borges and the Dream of Chess" (*NLH* 24: 425–45) is worth reading. One should also consult Burton R. Pollin's "The Presence of Poe in Borges's Reviews in *El Hogar*" (*PoeS* 25 [1992]: 39), which cites previously unavailable items from a Buenos Aires newspaper.

Richard Fusco's shorter study of Poe and detective fiction, *Fin de Millénaire* (Poe Society), is rewarding in several respects. Noting how often devotees of crime fiction overemphasize the sleuthing excellence in the Dupin tales (usually excluding "Marie Roget" from their enthusiasms), Fusco holds up "The Gold-Bug" as particularly "vital in understanding Poe's notions about ratiocination" (p. 1). The Poesque descent into later crime-fiction writers is also thoughtfully considered. Related topics occur in Manju Jaidka's "Let's Play FOOJY: The Politics of Detective Fiction" (*Clues* 14, i: 69–86), which notes how near-perfection in Dupin and other fictional sleuths creates "admiration [rather] than sympathy" among readers, and Rose May Verrico's "Detective Fiction and the Quest Hero" (*Clues* 14, i: 135–53), an analysis of superman traits in Dupin and his progeny.

In *Rituals of Dis-Integration* (Garland, pp. xv, 8, 144, 178–79, 208, 213) Edwin F. Block, Jr., reasonably outlines Poe's place in the "Victorian psychomythic tale," that is, short fiction that emphasizes psychological tensions more than had earlier Gothic productions. Persuasive as he is, Block will probably take heat because of his seeming minimalizing of early Gothic. Nonetheless, he shows how, along with others like Hawthorne, Gautier, and Mermeé, Poe transmuted horror fiction into art. Family circumstances, especially those that couple characters and psychological substance with architecture (notably in "Usher") and damaging silences ("The Tell-Tale Heart"), descend from Poe and other earlier Gothicists into writings by Henry James, Arthur Machen, Violet Paget, Walter Pater, Arthur Symons, W. B. Yeats, and R. L. Stevenson.

Poe the magazinist, as he stands among creators of short fiction, is Andrew Levy's subject in chapter 1 of *Culture and Commerce.* Though he never made much money from his short stories, Poe advocated and practiced techniques that led to the short story's establishment as a major type of American creative writing. The 1842 review of Hawthorne set forth Poe's ideals about the short story; his plans for an ideal literary magazine indicate how he intended to secure a market among high- and middle-brow readers for such wares. Poe the magazine fictionist is also, principally, the subject in chapter 4 of Michael Kowalewski's *Deadly Musings* (pp. 82–104), although *Pym* is also included under the rubric of brutality that, for Kowalewski, permeates Poe's fiction. That violence mingled with comedy, couched in heterogeneous styles, peppers Poe's fiction is no news. Critiques of "How to Write a Blackwood Article," "A Predicament," and "Hop-Frog" lend strength to this analysis that, unfortunately, is often undercut by lengthy summaries of previous criticism (and the works), reference to Robert, not John T., Irwin as author of *American Hieroglyphics,* and to serialized *Pym* as commencing in 1838 (pp. 96, 267).

Just so, nothing new or startling informs the Foucault and Derrida theories brought to bear on *Pym,* "Usher," and the Dupin tales in chapter 4 of Scott Bradfield's *Dreaming Revolution,* but development of points about William Godwin and Poe made long ago by Burton Pollin is worth notice. Bradfield discerns interesting connections between Poe's characters and Caleb Williams; all pursue "universal secrets [but] Poe's characters simultaneously vanish into them" (p. 69). Further possibilities in these kinships loom. Jerome Loving's *Lost in the Customhouse* better serves *Pym,* "Murders," and "The Imp of the Perverse," with sidelights on many other Poe works (chapter 4). In Loving's analytic survey of American dreamers, *Pym* involves recurrent premature burials and re-births that culminate in the Pym-Peters disappearance into polar "whiteness," which signifies "Poe's subsequent pages and Pym's missing chapters" (p. 60). The novel was intended to admit of no definite conclusion. Likewise, Dupin remains in darkness, "where the crime is motiveless and thus without a destiny of 'proper ending'" (p. 71). Poe's women, too, "always seem to be vanishing as in a dream" (p. 70). Loving's anti-New Historicist, anti-deconstructive, but nonetheless judicious, stance will doubtless elicit debate.

iii Poems

Jeffrey Meyers's account of Poe's work in verse (*Columbia History of American Poetry*) offers no startling interpretations throughout its generally balanced outlook. The death of a beautiful woman theme in Poe's poems is highlighted, as are his affinities with other 19th-century poets (notably Coleridge, Shelley, and Tennyson) and his impact on 20th-century American poets (e.g., Eliot, Auden, and Wilbur). His lyric propensities are also well treated. Meyers's placement of "The Raven" among other key Romantic poems is a useful corrective to those who dwell on its horrors as if they were aberrations in poetic tradition. Poe's relationships with literary women of his time are also brushed skilfully into the larger portrait. The paradox of Poe the writer of dramatic poems (and tales) producing less sophisticated drama, in *Politian*, a pseudo-Elizabethan verse-play, may be information useful to nonspecialists, although the staging of this play may have been more feasible and attractive than Meyers suggests; see T. O. Mabbott's historical commentary in his edition of *Poems* (1969). Better editing might have eliminated another ambiguity, that of *The Raven and Other Poems* (1845) being Poe's "fourth and final volume" (p. 184)—of verse, yes, but not within the canon entire. "Ulalume" first appeared in December 1847, not 1848 (p. 196). Additional worthwhile comment appears elsewhere in the *Columbia History*. Time's revenges have caught up with Poe in the Longfellow chapter, notably in Dana Gioia's designation of *Pym* as not quite a masterpiece (although this observation is balanced by generosity toward Poe the critic, pp. 85, 80). Poe, Gothicism, women, and art enter meaningfully into the discussion of Dickinson's poetry (pp. 132–33). Poe's influences on 20th-century poets are also showcased, as they are in Elisa New's *The Regenerate Lyric,* most notably in the chapters on Emerson (whose poems, New thinks, give less pleasure than Poe's or Bryant's), Dickinson, Whitman, and Hart Crane. Faustian and Gothic elements in Poe's works are especially noteworthy.

iv Tales

Timothy H. Scherman's charting of Poe's strategies to get "Tales of the Folio Club" published—"The Authority Effect: Poe and the Politics of Reputation in the Pre-Industry of American Publishing" (*ArQ* 49, iii: 1–19)—gives us little new information on those tales proper (and could have incorporated additional scholarship on Poe's aims and intents therein) or on Poe's multiple audiences. More useful is Scherman's placement of Poe's review of Fay's *Norman Leslie* and Poe's follow-up submission of the Folio Club manuscript to Harpers, which had published Fay's novel.

Essays in Silverman, mentioned above, range chronologically from the late 1830s to 1846. Without fail, someone will quibble over "major" status for eight tales alone, but the contributors offer provocative readings of what they address. J. Gerald Kennedy's "Poe's 'Liegia' and the Problem of Dying Women" (pp. 113–29) extends ideas expressed in his *Poe, Death and the Life of Writing* (1987), and supplements feminist readings in its considerations of Poe's works about women. Kennedy concludes that the narrator never comprehends the nature of his feelings toward his two wives, deliberately rejecting Rowena because he felt rejected by Ligeia, and that the "plot [in his Gothic abbey] is ultimately a plot against Woman, an attack on the female loveliness he cannot live without." Such idolatry "must end in despair and anger" (pp. 126–27). Inclusion of "The Assignation" and "Eleonora" imparts a completeness to Kennedy's Poe-Woman perspective that is often wanting in others' theories.

Louise J. Kaplan's "The Perverse Strategy in 'The Fall of the House of Usher,'" excepting the confusion in title/dates for *Tales of the Grotesque and Arabesque* or the 1845 *Tales* (p. 48), views the famous tale as one in which the aesthetically idealizing Roderick fetishizes (entombs) Madeline's body to escape its "unwelcome and frightening reality" (p. 53), only to have it perversely round upon him. Morally at odds, the narrator responds to Roderick in terms of a "personal quest for the sublime" (p. 55), all the while holding too unyieldingly to a conventional morality, which Roderick has left behind as he tries by means of his art to evade incest lures. The narrator's arranging details to suit his own illusions is as perverse as his friend's pursuits, however, and thereby he intensifies the aura of Gothic fear that pervades the Ushers and their environs. Kaplan's interpretation reinforces those of Darrel Abel (1949), the cluster of essays in *Ruined Eden of the Present* (see *ALS 1981*, p. 47), and Robert Hoggard

(see *ALS 1989*, p. 44). Close in its import to Kaplan is Leila S. May's
" 'Sympathies of a Scarcely Intelligible Nature': The Brother-Sister Bond
in Poe's 'Fall of the House of Usher' " (*SSF* 30: 387–96). To May, Poe in
this tale probes Victorian concepts of family, especially those involving
feminine desire and the anxieties it fostered in brother-sister relationships. At the time, live (emotional) "burial" of the sister was the inevitable outcome.

In "Detecting Truth: The World of the Dupin Tales" (pp. 65–91)
David Van Leer dwells overlong on familiar thought about Poe's ratiocinative pieces and their legacies to detective fiction, in order to offer
feminist readings of the Dupin chronicles. Van Leer's hypothesis that
"Marie Roget" has been neglected because readers "fear the social reality"
in gender-class elements it incorporates offers a new angle on what, for
many, is simply dullness spun out to great length. Irwin and Fusco, cited
above, offer ideas of greater substance about the Dupin chronicles.

Christopher Benfey's "Poe and the Unreadable: 'The Black Cat' and
'The Tell-Tale Heart' " (pp. 27–44) scrutinizes inaccessibilities between
one mind and another as manifest in the designated tales. Anxieties
about sexuality, love, and isolation—which, at their extremes, "lead to
disaster" (p. 43)—inform these pieces. Benfey's view dovetails in many
ways with those of Kaplan and Kennedy. Fred Madden cautiously
submits that Poe, if not directly influenced by Hoffmann, certainly
reveals affinities with the European's handling of the uncanny. "Poe's
'The Black Cat' and Freud's 'The Uncanny' " (*L&P* 39, i: 52–62) proposes that technique in this tale permits readers to find both super-
naturalism and psychological plausibility. Tests of limits of a rational
mind are inherent, too. Madden also thinks that Poe's knowledge of
German was probably greater than many others have allowed.

Finally, David S. Reynolds draws in much criticism, but it enhances
his own stimulating evaluation of another warhorse in "Poe's Art of
Transformation: 'The Cask of Amontillado' in Its Cultural Context"
(pp. 93–112). Showing how Poe took familiar materials (e. g., live burial)
from terror fiction, from outlooks on Catholicism, Freemasonry, and
alcoholism, and went on to impart new life to them by dint of exquisite
construction, zesty wordplay, and psychological ambiguities, Reynolds
produces what will surely become "must" reading for enthusiasts and
novices alike in illuminating "Cask" as it does.

v Pym, Eureka

Surprises may await readers of Bruce Greenfield's *Narrating Discovery* (pp. 165–87) because he teams Poe with Thoreau as writers of travel literature; he sees *Pym* as embodying all conventions of formal travel-discovery narrative. Like Block above, Greenfield provides observations about family relationships as they affected Pym. Greenfield's declaration that Poe was "not an Emersonian transcendentalist, confident in the fundamental correspondence between natural and spiritual facts" (p. 180), will also land him far down the coast from one circle of Poe devotees (although Greenfield's differentiation is sensible). For Greenfield, Poe is, rather, like Melville in showing how destructive some of his protagonist's explorations can be (p. 187).

Beverly A. Hume's "Poe's Mad Narrator in *Eureka*" (*EAS* 22: 51–65) unfolds a negative Romantic slant within Poe's book that questions the "bizarre metaphysics" in other Poe works (p. 51). Hume challenges much other scholarship, in much the same manner as Loving (mentioned above) does for his subjects. Hume sees the primary narrator in *Eureka* as a madman unique among Poe's insane narrators, one who holds out startlingly atypical views of relationships between the human mind and the universe (rejecting contemporaneous, widely accepted Newtonian mathematical interpretations). This critique dovetails neatly with Benfey's.

vi Sources, Influences, Miscellaneous

Don G. Smith's explanatorily titled "Shelley's *Frankenstein*: A Possible Source for Poe's 'MS. Found in a Bottle'" (*PoeS* 25 [1992]: 37) persuasively and readably establishes parallels. Narayana Chandran's equally solid "Poe's Use of *Macbeth* in 'The Masque of the Red Death'" (*PLL* 29: 236–40) increases our knowledge of Poe's literary backgrounds, lengthens the numbers of Shakespearean parallels marshaled by Burton R. Pollin, and supplements Richard Wilbur and Kermit Vanderbilt (see *ALS 1985*, p. 46). Chandran's essay is not restricted to listing parallels; the perceptive criticism fleshes them out. In "Poe's 'Diddling': Still Another Possible Source and Date of Composition" (*PoeS* 25 [1992]: 6–9) John E. Reilly brings forth "a flesh-and-blood Jeremy Diddler"—the Baltimore-Philadelphia mountebank known as David Theodosius Hynes, Dr. Hind, Colonel John Benton—as exposed in the Philadelphia *Public Ledger* for 9 August 1838 (which quotes the *Baltimore Sun* of 7

August). Reilly supplements and challenges work on record by Burton R. Pollin, Alexander Hammond, and Claude Richard. Nathan Cervo's "Poe's 'The Cask of Amontillado'" (*Expl* 51: 155–56) convincingly links Montresor's motto to that of the Scottish Order of the Thistle. The St. Andrew figure in the order's insignia is one which, like Fortunato, is "crossed out" or eliminated. Fortunato also appears as a Merry Andrew, or quack, figure. Terse as it is, Cervo's essay unravels another subtle dimension in Poe's tale.

Turning to Poe's influence and image, in "Preuss and Stoddard on Poe" (*PoeS* 25 [1992]: 38–39) John E. Reilly enlarges his own earlier treatment of the Poe-Preuss relationship as he supplements and corrects J. Gerald Kennedy (see *ALS 1990*, p. 53). Poe's influences in style and characterization on Maupassant, Bierce, and others receive full credit in relevant sections of Richard Fusco's *Maupassant and the American Short Story*. Jules Verne's ideas about and derivations from Poe's works, most notably perhaps in his adaptation of *Pym,* have long been remarked. Now, further connections are plausibly made in David Meakin's "Like Poles Attracting: Intertextual Magnetism in Poe, Verne, and Gracq" (*MLR* 88: 600–11), which calls attention to the attraction-repulsion in views of Poe and his texts, especially as they filtered through Verne to Julien Gracq's novel *Le Rivage des Syrtes* (1952). The impact of *Politian* and of Poe's psychological makeup on Robert Penn Warren is soundly demonstrated in Stephen E. Ryan's "World Enough and Time: A Refutation of Poe's History as Tragedy" (*SoQ* 31, iv: 86–94). Warren's Jeremiah Beaumont also recalls Montresor in "Cask," who murders for honor. Poe and the Poesque in popular fiction are adroitly sketched in Lee Server's *Danger Is My Business: An Illustrated History of the Fabulous Pulp Magazines* (Chronicle Books, pp. 18, 34, 38, 41). Jacob Clark Henneberger, founder of *Weird Tales* (1923) and a lifelong Poe fan, naturally promoted fantasy fiction à la Poe; no wonder that H. P. Lovecraft and Robert Bloch were numbered among his admired contributors. Poesque influences on theme, style, and characterization in works by Stephen King, Thomas Harris, and Arthur C. Clarke occupy J. Lasley Dameron in *Poe, King, and Other Contemporaries.* Oddly, Dameron omits mention of my 1986 study of the Poe-King (and John Dickson Carr) similarities (see *ALS 1986*, p. 45). Good companion reading, for Poe's role in detective fiction, may be found in *The Fine Art of Murder,* ed. Ed Gorman et al. (Carroll, pp. 3, 10, 61, 153, 265, 269, 366).

University of Mississippi

4 Melville

John Wenke

A new edition of the letters and major studies of Melville's Civil War, his rhetoric and humor, and *Clarel's* theology highlight an impressive year's work. Important new studies also examine Melville and science; the influence of Dante, Shakespeare, and Milton; the presence of homoeroticism in *Pierre;* and the historical ramifications of racial conflict in *Benito Cereno.*

i Editions

The Northwestern-Newberry edition weighs in with volume 14, *Correspondence*, ed. and annotated by Lynn Horth. She revises and augments Merrell R. Davis and William H. Gilman's *The Letters of Herman Melville* (1960), printing 313 letters by Melville and in a separate sequence 88 written to him. The letters "provide only a spotty chronicle of Melville's outer, and intermittent revelations of his inner, life." Indeed, most of the letters are functional and business-like. They are not designed to reveal. To counter the lacunae, Horth provides in chronological sequence entries "for letters both by and to Melville for which no full text has been located but for which some evidence survives." Explanatory headnotes and textual endnotes engage biographical, historical, and genetic concerns, addressing the related imperatives of a reading and scholarly text. Horth adds 52 letters to those printed by Davis and Gilman, with 29 of them more recent discoveries. In juxtaposing found texts with information on lost texts, Horth erects a sturdy scaffold that contains the fullest record to date, while directing the way toward new findings. The editorial appendix includes a compact and illuminating historical note and a meticulous note on the text. Scholars will find the calendar of Melville's correspondence a valuable reference. For readers familiar with

Davis and Gilman, this edition honors their great work by extending it; for new readers, the *Correspondence* will provide fascinating glimpses into a tight Melville circle.

ii Biographical Contexts

A collection of new, revised, and reprinted essays that achieves provocative dialectical cohesiveness, Philip Young's three-part *The Private Melville* (Penn. State) suggests and uncovers secrets that insinuate themselves into Melville's work. Three essays on "Family Matters" combine creative sleuthing, literary criticism, and genealogical excavation. "History of a Secret Sister" explores the mystery associated with Ann Middleton Allen, the "A.M.A." who seems to have been Allan Melvill's unacknowledged daughter. Young updates Henry A. Murray's discoveries and links this putative half-sister to her literary counterpart in the "remarkably autobiographical" *Pierre*. In "Melvills, and the Heroine of *Pierre*" Young finds in cousin Priscilla Melvill's letters evidence of her influence in the creation of Isabel. Four essays in "Tales of the Berkshire Bishopric" consider stories "that depend heavily on 'private jokes' and thus have secret meaning." The "hidden meanings" in such tales as "Cock-a-Doodle-Doo!" and "I and My Chimney," Young contends, "challenged and slipped past the guardians of Victorian taste." Two essays in "Fathers and Sons" respectively consider Ahab's baffling speech in "The Candles" and "Daniel Orme" as a fictional self-portrait.

Stanton Garner's *The Civil War World of Herman Melville* (Kansas) transverses the "deadly space between" the national cataclysm and its pervasive presence within the expansive but close circle of Melville's family, friends, and acquaintances. In this masterwork of biographical and historical reconstruction, Garner tells the griping tale of Melville's consumed relation and literary response to the Civil War. In dramatizing the personal and political milieu out of which *Battle-Pieces* evolves, Garner treats the poems not in their order of composition but as responses to the originating events and individuals that inspired them. The result is a book both panoramic and focused. Far from being aloof, Melville lived the war with day-to-day intensity, following the shifting fortunes of Union and Confederate forces, seeing in the sundered Union germinous seeds of a problematical future. His life within the war informs the creation of the verse. At one point he rides with Union forces searching for the elusive guerrilla John Singleton Mosby. The result of

Melville's direct experience of war is "The Scout Toward Aldie," which Garner sees as a "small-scale version of *Moby-Dick*. . . . In place of the infinite sea, the travelers wend through the eerie forest, as ambiguous in its tangled fertility and its peril as the whiteness of the whale." In a book replete with treasures too numerous to specify, Garner presents Melville's attraction to and repulsion from the new technology of mass slaughter; the downward declension of Guert Gansevoort's career; Melville's admiration for General George McClellan; Hawthorne's gloomy retreat from life; Melville's meeting with General Grant; the most complete account anywhere of the background to "The House-Top" in the 1863 New York Draft Riots. Hershel Parker (with Edward Daunias) also fills out our understanding of Melville's circle. In "Sarah Morewood's Last Drive, as Told in Caroline S. Whitmarsh's 'A Representative Woman'" (*MSEx* 93: 1–4) Parker reveals Morewood to be a more complex figure than the lively socialite depicted in biographies.

iii General

In *Melville and Repose: The Rhetoric of Humor in the American Renaissance* (Oxford) John Bryant undertakes a major reevaluation of Melville's aesthetics. The result is our most ranging and informative study of the ontological and rhetorical dimensions of humor. Melville assimilates and transfigures multiple resources, essentially balancing "the integrative mode of geniality and the more subversive rhetoric of deceit." Melville pursues a "*tense repose:* tense because of its probing toward Being and yet reposeful because of its containment of our anguish over the futility of the quest." Bryant describes Melville's reconstruction of the "moral picturesque" and its affiliation with America's "comic debate," an intermittently genial and satirical tradition that fuses a host of British and American voices. America's "rhetoric of deceit" engages epistemological implications of narrative reliability. After examining Poe and T. B. Thorpe, Bryant claims that Melville tentatively resolves or magnifies the debate with the "cosmopolitan figure of 'the genial misanthrope.'" In Part Two, "Rhetoric and Repose," Bryant provides close discussions of *Typee, Moby-Dick,* and *The Confidence-Man.* In *Typee,* Tommo "contains satiric impulses and excessive self-involvement within good-natured humor." His conflicting voices betray Melville's "immediate anxiety of addressing his first audience." By analyzing the first British and American editions, Bryant discusses expurgations and smuggled subversions: "Whenever Melville compressed social outrage within an amiable frame, his words were not cut. Satiric eruptions against Western powers and mores, however, prompted excisions." Chapters on *Moby-Dick* explore Ishmael's comic and lyrical qualities and Ahab's personality and rhetoric. Bryant demythologizes Ahab into a self-deluding over-reacher, a "trickster relying upon false wit and the false logic of an imperfect transcendentalism." In two chapters on *The Confidence-Man* Bryant explores what happens as the Ishmael voice settles for silence. *Melville and Repose* manages to unify the unnecessary bifurcation between old and New Historicism. Bryant takes the bad word called intention and reveals how it participates within the dynamism of social forces.

Two essays respectively consider language and iconography as reflections of Melville's modernity. Andrew Delbanco in "Melville's Sacramental Style" (*Raritan* 12, iii: 69–91) finds Melville divided "between a reverential solemnity . . . and an antic fury." This "boundless versatility" refigures literary antecedents into startling combinations. He discovers "modernity" within the extravagances of his style, repudiating testament and formula in favor of form-breaking and improvisation. Basem L. Ra'ad's "Palm and Apple: Melville's Metaphor of the Trees" (*MSEx* 92: 9–10) briefly discusses how these trees function in *Typee, Mardi,* the 1856 *Journal,* and *Clarel.* The palm evokes "primal simplicity and timelessness," while the apple tree constitutes a complex emblem of fractured modern experience.

Richard Dean Smith in *Melville's Science: "Devilish Tantalization of the Gods!"* (Garland) delineates Melville's explorations into phenomena, especially his uses of natural history, taxonomy, anatomy, biology, cosmology, and paleontology. In this intriguing encyclopedic study, Smith examines novels, stories and poems, tracking Melville's sources and allusions, his adaptations of ancient and modern science, and his interest in the conflict between religious and evolutionary theory. Melville is concerned mostly with "literary effect, not necessarily scientific credibility." David Kirby's *Herman Melville* (Continuum) links the life and work through the figure of the picaro: "There is a sound biographical basis for the presence in Melville's work of both a fondness for and a suspicion of rootlessness . . . and . . . permanence." Within this useful but (seemingly) under-researched introduction, one occasionally finds breezy distinctions and weak generalities. Kirby identifies narratives that are "rhetorical and windy" and "plotty and linear. . . . [T]he largely rhetorical Melville wrote most of *Mardi* and nearly all of *Pierre* and *The Confidence-Man*; the largely plotty one wrote *Typee*, *Omoo*, and *Redburn*." He gives a sketchy chronology, listing the publication of *The Piazza Tales* rather than the original dates of specific stories. There is also some distortion of fact: "As [Melville] lay on his deathbed, he wrote one of the finest short fictions of his or any time." Similarly it is a mistake to contend that a "draft of 'Billy Budd' was not completed until 1891." By then Melville had embarked on at least four fair-copy inscriptions, though each led him to further (unfinished) revision.

Melville and Melville Studies in Japan collects 11 essays by notable Japanese scholars. In "Melville in Japan: Reception among Writers and Critics" (pp. 3–20) Kenzaburo Ohashi surveys Melville's influence on writers and intellectuals. Masayuki Sakamoto in "Melville's 'Transcendentalism' in the Context of His Time" (pp. 99–121) reconsiders Melville's ambivalent feelings toward Emerson and his circle as well as Transcendental complexes in *Mardi* and *Moby-Dick*. Masao Tsunematsu in "Japanese Scholarship on Herman Melville: A Bibliographical Essay" . (pp. 221–43) offers an illuminating chronological survey that includes translations.

iv Source, Influence, and Affinity

A profusion of fine studies engage new and old resources, demonstrating Melville's creative responses to ancient, Renaissance, and contemporary authors. Michele Ronnik in "Melville's Classical Library" (*MSEx* 94: 6–11) collates 85 specific classical sources into such handy categories as Greek Authors, Latin Authors, and Histories. Three scholars illuminate Melville's responses to Dante, Shakespeare, and Milton. Lea Bertani Vozar Newman's excellent "Melville's Copy of Dante: Evidence of New Connections Between the *Commedia* and *Mardi*" (*SAR*, pp. 305–36) examines the markings and notes in the recently discovered copy of Dante. She discusses allusions, parallels, and echoes in *Mardi*: "In structuring a work of mixed genres, in exploring new philosophical and theological concepts, and in utilizing vision-oriented imagery and diction that allowed free rein to his imaginative powers, Melville capitalized on his reading of Cary's translation." Along with identifying connections between the *Kostanza* and *Commedia*, Newman explains Dante's presence within the Maramma, "Dreams," and Serenia chapters. Babbalanja's vision in chapter 188 marks "the most intensely realized of Melville's Dantean creations in *Mardi.*" Julian Markels's lively and learned *Melville and the Politics of Identity: From King Lear to Moby-Dick* (Illinois) depicts Melville's response to Shakespeare's political vision as it shapes "a correspondingly theoretical vision of America's constitutive politics." Melville found in *Lear* a conflict between benign "aristocratic feudalism" and predatory, self-destructive democracy. Ahab emerges here as a usurper, Melville's Edmond, seeking to overturn established hierarchies. On the contrary, "Cordelia and Ishmael represent an alternative possibility of personal identity and cosmic fair play." In this reading, the rational Anglican Richard Hooker collides with the combative power politics of Thomas Hobbes. Markels positions Melville in relation to his contemporaries' responses to Shakespeare: thus Melville re-creates *Lear* within the ideological context of America's political revolution. Ahab's association with Calvinist and Hobbesian complexes counterpoints Ishmael's reconfiguration of Locke's politics and epistemology.

Two essays consider the Milton marginalia. Daniel Göske in "Melville's Milton" (*PULC* 54: 296–302) summarizes the numerous markings in the two-volume Hilliard edition of *The Poetical Works of John Milton* (1836), now in the Princeton holdings. Göske explores Melville's "private debate" carried on over a lifetime of reading. In her excellent "Surmising the Infidel: Interpreting Melville's Annotations on Milton's Poetry" (*MiltonQ* 26, iv [1992]: 103–13), Robin Sandra Grey argues that the markings are "sparing but sufficient" for deriving a "distinct, composite interpretation of Milton's poetic and theological agendas." Melville's Milton seems "much darker, more doubting . . . than the Anglican editor of Melville's . . . edition." This heretical Milton possesses a "Samson-like, embittered, and impious" quality. Melville responds to a "'*twist* in Milton'"—Melville's phrase—"that insists upon desecrating the sacred truths already mysteriously desecrated by God." According to Grey, Melville projects on Milton the very drama played out between defiant Ahab and skeptical Ishmael.

James Kirkland's "A New Source for the 'Trepan' Scenes in Melville's *Mardi*" (*ELN* 30, iv: 39–47) identifies Melville's application of a well-traveled folktale. Samoa's "trepaning" surgical operation—the replacement of skull part with coconut—derives from "a cycle of international folktales known collectively as 'The Three Doctors.'" Melville heard some version of the tale and adapted it: "the result is one of the finest sustained comic episodes in all his fiction—a satire on human pretension and gullibility masquerading as an ethnographic account." In "Melville and Scoresby on Whiteness" (*ES* 74: 96–104) J. Lasley Dameron updates and extends our knowledge of Melville's debt in *Moby-Dick* to William Scoresby, Jr.'s *An Account of the Arctic Regions* and *Journal of a Voyage to the Northern Whale-Fishery*. Among Melville's cetological sources, only Scoresby combines "emotive intensity and pictorial imagery, especially the bizarre effects of the polar landscape upon the human consciousness." Jonathan Hall's "The Non-correspondent Breeze: Melville's Rewriting of Wordsworth in *Pierre*" (*ESQ* 39: 1–19) finds in the novel an expression of Melville's problematical engagement with Romanticism. In opposition to "Wordsworth's invocation of a welcoming and answering Nature" *Pierre* offers a "black comedy of self-disintegration that reduces Nature to a mirror of consciousness with no meaning of its own." Even if Hall might see *Pierre* as too much an argument with Wordsworth, this rich and well-written essay deftly engages Melville's complex critique of Romantic thought. Daniel Reagan in "Charles Knight's *London* in Melville's *Israel Potter*" (*ESQ* 38 [1992]: 189–205) makes an incontrovertible case for Knight's influence on the final sections of *Israel Potter*. Melville adapts figures of speech, reconceives passages, and applies factual information, thereby deriving "imaginative solutions to rhetorical, thematic, and formal problems."

Scholars continue to explore Melville's relation to the visual arts. James Duban, in "Transatlantic Counterparts: The Diptych and Social Inquiry in Melville's 'Poor Man's Pudding and Rich Man's Crumbs'" (*NEQ* 66: 274–86), identifies probable sources for the story's pictorial form in Charles Lock Eastlake and a 31 January 1850 editorial in the *Christian Inquirer:* "In using the diptych form . . . Melville was drawing on a well-established pictorial tradition, but he bent that tradition to serve the ends of plaintive social commentary." Daniel Göske's "Dark Satyrs, White Enthusiasts: Hawthorne's and Melville's Variations on 'St. Michael and the Dragon'" (*PULC* 54: 207–24) plausibly identifies the immediate source of *Benito Cereno*'s symbolic stern-piece in Anna Jameson's "interpretation of Raphael's painting of *St. Michael and the Dragon*" as discussed in her *Sacred and Legendary Art* (1850). It is not clear when or where Melville might have read Jameson, though editions were in print and readily available. In "Dürer 'At the Hostelry': Melville's Misogynist Iconography" (*MSEx* 95: 1–8) Dennis Berthold argues that Melville's verbal portrait of Albrecht Dürer was drawn "primarily from popular illustrations." Melville identified with Dürer as an artist held captive within a frustrating marriage. Berthold convincingly links his two subjects with images of John the Baptist, Samson, and Milton. Robert K. Wallace in "Melville's Prints: The Reese Collection" (*HLB* 4, iii: 7–42) analyzes the literary implications of 44 engravings from Melville's collection that were purchased in 1991 by William Reese of New Haven, Connecticut. For example, "*Beatrix Cenci* provides documentation for a pictorial interest that Melville expressed in *Pierre*, the 1856–57 *Journal*, and *Clarel*." Wallace inventories these prints into such categories as "Continental Masters" and "Late Eighteenth-Century Topographical Views."

v Early Works

In "Melville's First Five Poems?" (*MSEx* 92: 13–16) Warren F. Broderick prints newspaper verse published between September 1838 and April 1839 and proposes Melville as possible author. Peter A. Obuchowski's "Melville's First Short Story: A Parody of Poe" (SAF 21: 97–102) claims "Fragments from a Writing Desk" satirizes "the idealization of women in popular romantic fiction." This early work is not a fledgling's failure but a successful parody of Poe's overheated prose in "Ligeia." Obuchowski overstates how "Fragments" reflects the "temperamental and artistic bias for satire that will characterize Melville's genius." In "Herman Melville as Sex Symbol" (*Profils Americains: Herman Melville*, ed. Phillippe Jaworski [Montpellier: Université Paul-Valéry, 1992], pp. 7–23) Hershel Parker examines how early reviewers of *Typee* and *Omoo* were titillated or appalled by the books' sexual content. As Melville's "most famous character" during his lifetime, Fayaway focused the hail of attraction and detraction and led to Melville himself becoming a subject of "intense sexual speculation." Michel Imbert in "*Typee*: The Primitive Masquerade" (*Profils Americains*, pp. 43–57) explores the interplay of "treachery and trust" in relation to Tommo's transfiguration of Christian typology, his depictions of cannibalism, and his fears of tattooing and death. *Typee's* drama of confidence and distrust prefigures *Benito Cereno* and *The Confidence-Man*. In "'born-free-and-equal': Benign Cliché and Narrative Imperialism in Melville's *Mardi*" (*SNNTS* 25: 16–27) Michael C. Berthold proposes that "forms of captivity" provide a nexus "for negotiating the novel's abundances and sprawl." He considers political clichés in the "Vivenza" episode as well as Taji's appropriation of Yillah.

The nature of work focuses explorations of *Mardi* and *Redburn*. In

"The Calm Before the Storm: Laboring Through *Mardi*" (*AL* 65: 239–52) Cindy Weinstein examines intersections among work, leisure, and literary production. Somehow Melville's expansive narrative "seemed to threaten the middle-class construction of American identity because [allegory's] two-dimensional characters reminded readers and reviewers that working-class Americans were increasingly being deprived of agency and identity by the repetitious nature of their work." In this view *Mardi* invites metanarrational flights. Melville's putative intention is "to reconceptualize a textual economy that incorporates signs of authorial labor into the finished artifact." Nicholas K. Bromell's "The Erotics of Labor in Melville's *Redburn*" in *By the Sweat of the Brow* (pp. 61–79) also fuses manual labor with literary labors. The tale of Redburn's "Franklinesque" experiences points to problems of artistic representation: the "feminized free-play of the imagination is at once essential to his identity as an artist and incompatible with the disciplined work, and . . . degraded erotic life of the common sailor." Bromell invests Melville with a rarefied purpose: "To make authorial work compatible with manual labor by dissolving both in an alembic of acceptable desire is the primary aim, and the unfulfilled hope, of *Redburn*." Mark Niemeyer in "Redburn and the Suppression of Patrician Fantasy" (*Profils Americains*, pp. 63–79) focuses on the oppression of the workers by monied bosses. He explores "the dynamics of wealth and power" as it emerges in Redburn's experiences of "the frustrations of poverty . . . and the hope for wealth and standing." In this narrative of "conflicting ideologies," Melville's own unfulfilled yearning for patrician privilege keeps the narrator from taking "any true political stand." Social concerns also inform Sally Greene's "Who But 'Some Howard': Redburn's Search for Charity" (*MSEx* 93: 5–8). On two occasions the narrator alludes to John Howard, an 18th-century English philanthropist and prison reformer, who functions as an impossible model and ideal. The distance between Howard's success and Redburn's "powerlessness seems to reflect Melville's own skepticism toward charitable and philanthropic movements."

Michael J. Crawford's "*White Jacket* and the Navy in Which Melville Served" (*MSEx* 94: 1–5) examines the veracity of Melville's portrait of the antebellum navy, focusing on "religion, medicine, and the education of officers." Despite some caricature, "Melville's critique . . . almost always rings true." In "Order and Disorder: Perversion, Subversion and Salvation in Melville's *White-Jacket; or, The World in a Man-of-War*" (*Profils Americains*, pp. 81–89) Dominique Marçais explores the hierarchies of power and discipline as they undermine and even parody the ethical framework of Christianity. A natural aristocracy appears in such transgressive figures as Mad Jack and Jack Chase.

vi Moby-Dick

According to John Staud's " 'What's in a Name?' The *Pequod* and Melville's Heretical Politics" (*ESQ* 38 [1992]: 339–59), the ship's "dual etymology" includes the extinct Massachusetts tribe and the book of Jeremiah. Melville thereby "enriches the political symbolism . . . by extending the typology of disfavor and rebellion established through the names of Ishmael and Ahab." By linking the *Pequod* with "a Babylonian tribe singled out for punishment," Staud explains the relationship between Ishmael, Ahab, America's violation of Covenant Theology, and Melville's inversion of the jeremiad. Jerome Loving's "Melville's High on the Seas" (*Lost in the Customhouse,* pp. 35–52) examines the "dialectic of the Leviathan" in relation to its incessant restarting of "the voyage of the self into the unknown . . . *Moby-Dick* begins every time it ends with the awakening of the orphan in a coffin." In this rich mediation on language and myth, Loving illuminates Ishmael's ongoing search for origins as well as his attempt to defeat confusion, failure, and blankness through his reconstitution of "the remembered life." Similarly, in "Metaphysical Otherness: Reading the Wonder of Ishmael's Telling," pp. 40–63 in *Liminal Readings: Forms of Otherness in Melville, Joyce and Murdoch* (St. Martin's) David Scott Arnold concentrates on Ishmael's "imagination of wonder" and his "radical openness to experience" as he reconstructs his journey toward an ambiguous "otherness" and possible "self-transcendence." Robert M. Greenberg, on the contrary, concentrates on the recalcitrance of brute phenomena and "the sense of epistemological fragmentation." His "Multiplicity and Uncertainty in Melville's *Moby-Dick*" (*Splintered Worlds,* pp. 82–118) focuses on the cetology materials and Melville's attempt to "dramatize a suprahuman perspective about the manifold interactions of mind and matter." Greenberg considers the relationship of nature and Christianity, evolution and Calvinism.

Susan Weiner's "Melville at the Movies: New Images of *Moby-Dick*" (*JACult* 16, ii: 85–90) offers one of the most interesting arguments of the year. She examines the importation of *Moby-Dick* into three contemporary films: Woody Allen's *Zelig* (1983), Michael Lehmann's *Heathers* (1988), and Jon Avnet's *Fried Green Tomatoes* (1991): "In a dazzling reversal of fortune, a complex artifact of high culture has transcended that category to become a popular icon." In *Zelig,* for example, Melville's book is critiqued as unapproachably complex, though it becomes ironically assimilated through repeated evocation. In *Fried Green Tomatoes,* Melville's book "literally takes the place of the Bible." The substitution allows a godly minister to avoid perjury by swearing at trial on his own copy of Ishmael's good book.

Gordon Poole in "Stubb Diddles the Rose-Bud: Melville's Dirty Joke" (*MSEx* 92: 11–13) elaborates on Melville's wordplay. Arimichi Makino's "A Bird in an Out-of-Joint Time: Captain Ahab in *Moby-Dick*" (*Melville Studies in Japan,* pp. 41–67) examines how bird imagery evokes Melville's "doubts about Platonic idealism." Toshio Yagi's "*Moby-Dick* as a Mosaic" (*Melville Studies in Japan,* pp. 69–98) engages the text as "a process as well as a structure, a diachrony as well as a synchrony, a construction as well as a deconstruction, a harmony as well as a chaos."

vii From *Pierre* to *The Confidence-Man*

a. *Pierre* Sacvan Bercovitch's illuminating "*Pierre,* or the Ambiguities of American Literary History" in *The Rites of Assent* (pp. 246–306) places the novel within contemporaneous contexts. Bercovitch closely reads Melville's dedication to Mount Greylock as possessing "all the problems that readers have traditionally complained of in *Pierre*: excess, cliché, pasteboard dramatics, unexplained reversals of meaning." The dedication leads him into discussions of the following concerns: the novel as parody; its psychological dramatization of agency and intention; and Melville's transfiguration of sources, allusions, and analogies. Through this complex amalgam, *Pierre* "registers the *shock* of modernism." The narrative dramatizes "the traps of cultural symbology: a meta-history of continuing revolution." In "The Literary Interaction Between Hawthorne and Melville After *Moby-Dick*" (*Melville Studies in Japan,* pp. 21–40) Ginsaku Sugiura compares *The Blithedale Romance* and *Pierre* as literary experiments.

Two studies on *Pierre* engage its problematical explorations of male and female sexuality. T. Walker Herbert in "Willie Nelson and Herman Melville on Manhood: *Pierre* and 'The Red-Headed Stranger'" (*TSLL* 35: 421–39) discusses the dynamics of male isolation, phallic power, and murder. Linking novel and song is the diminution of women into figurines. James Creech's *Closet Writing/Gay Reading: The Case of Melville's*

Pierre (Chicago) applies queer theory to ostensibly homoerotic elements of Melville's work. He seeks "to open literary closets and examine their contents, all the while analyzing the theoretical fallout." He initially argues against claims that *Billy Budd* is essentially unknowable, favoring possible sociohistorical complexes that can be shown and known, particularly Claggart's conflicted homoeroticism. Early chapters ground the attempt to "out" Melville from his tropological closet. Pointing out "hidden sexual concerns" allows Creech to "'re-queer' the censored text . . . putting homosexuality back into its rightful place." Creech views *Pierre* as a "camp" text, invisible to those who are not prepared to see it. Melville's double language produces "not a revelation but a discriminating effect of recognition and collusion." Heterosexual incest here constitutes a displacement of Pierre's desire for homosexual incest: via "transgender encoding" Isabel becomes a gothicized stand-in for a homosexual lover. Isabel "is desirable only insofar as she *is* the image of his father at last made flesh."

b. The Short Fiction   In his deconstructive "Not Unoriginal: Herman Melville's Short Stories" (*The Nineteenth-Century American Short Story*, pp. 140–80) Douglas Tallack explores formal and rhetorical strategies. In "Bartleby," Tallack disputes the Romantic and Modernist aesthetic that seeks to stabilize the lawyer's fragmentary experience of the pale one into a fixed meaning. The tale's putative ironic perspective is not part of the narrator's intent. In "'Truth Is Voiceless': Speech and Silence in Melville's Later Fiction" (*Authority and Speech*, pp. 71–98) Louise K. Barnett explores Melville's preoccupation with evoking experiences "too horrible or incomprehensible." She discusses such figures as Bartleby, the lawyer, Hunilla, Delano, and Babo.

Sheila Post-Lauria in "Canonical Texts and Context: The Example of Herman Melville's 'Bartleby, the Scrivener: A Story of Wall Street'" (*CollL* 20: 196–205) incisively reveals how placing the tale within "its socio-literary context" enhances pedagogical possibilities. Post-Lauria associates "Bartleby" with Melville's astute understanding of the literary marketplace, especially his decision to place the tale before the "more intellectual, politically liberal" audience associated with *Putnam's Monthly*. She successfully develops the complex notion that "the author employs a sentimental style as a methodological weapon against itself and, in doing so, reinforces *Putnam's* editorial stance." Arnold Weinstein's "Melville: Knowing Bartleby" (*Nobody's Home*, pp. 27–43) explains how critical interpretations tell more about psychosociological theories of self and identity than they do about the scrivener. Winifred Morgan in " 'Bartleby' and the Failure of Conventional Virtue" (*Renascence* 45: 257–71) traces the narrator's emotional and moral growth toward "a rattled modern insecurity." In "Bartleby, the Perfect Pupil" (*ATQ* 7: 65–75) John M. Green provides the latest unsatisfactory Gestalt: "Bartleby is presented as the product of nineteenth-century educational theory—particularly that of Horace Mann." Green takes us inside Bartleby's psyche: "Perhaps a bit autistic or somewhat schizophrenic, the scrivener seems to be one of those people who believe everything they're told or taught." The office is perforce a classroom: "Bartleby learns . . . that he has been hoaxed . . . by society in general and its education system in particular; his reaction is to invent the sit-down strike." Marc D. Baldwin's "Herman Melville's 'The Lightning-Rod Man': Discourse of the Deal" (*JSSE* 21: 9–18) examines the "rhetorical design" of the players' repartee.

A number of fine studies consider Melville's explosive accounts of racial conflict. In "Radical Configurations of History in the Era of American Slavery" (*AL* 65: 523–47) Russ Castronovo sees "The Bell-Tower" as an allegory of American slavery, especially as it details the contradictory doubleness of freedom and repression. He repositions this Poesque Gothic tale within its antebellum moment and deftly explains its "ironic historiography." Eric J. Sundquist in "Melville, Delany, and New World Slavery" (*To Wake the Nations*, pp. 135–221) argues that *Benito Cereno* depicts "the superimposition of critical historical moments." The 1790s slave rebellion in Santo Domingo associates Cereno's ship with the legacy of American and French Revolutions. Sundquist analyzes Melville's replications—the fictional redactions of symbolic forms, the multiple narrative voices, the past as present, the North as South—as offering multilayered (and withering) critiques of Delano's self-satisfied "racialism." With tautology as "the governing figure of Melville's narrative method," Sundquist shows how apparent opposites conflate: slavery becomes rebellion; innocence becomes guilt; communalism becomes isolation. The shaving scene "comprehends the power of tautology." This essay depicts Melville's pervasive subversion of Western/colonial ideology, especially as manifested in Africanization, "a force of African resistance to New World slavery." In Terry J. Martin's "The Idea of Nature in *Benito Cereno*" (*SSF* 30: 161–68) nature seems in Delano's mind a benevolent domain of stable relations; the narrative, however, reveals the dislocating power of chaos, ambiguity, and entropy.

c. *Israel Potter* and *The Confidence-Man*   Bill Christophersen's "Israel Potter: Melville's 'Citizen of the Universe'" (*SAF* 21: 21–35) stands among this year's most accomplished essays. Christophersen examines Melville's conflation of typological and historical figures. The narrator "holds up America's self-assumed Election as an ironic frame. . . . Melville's purpose is to scrutinize America's actual identity while deposing her inflated self-image." In the book's second half, historical forces subvert typological claims. At the end, Melville reactivates typological resonances to show the sham of Israel Potter's exodus to the American Canaan. According to Kazuko Fukuoka in "*Israel Potter* and Its Ideological Contamination" (*Melville Studies in Japan*, pp. 123–40), Melville navigates between fidelity to his sources and the dictates of his imagination.

Gustaaf Van Cromphout in "*The Confidence-Man*: Melville and the Problem of the Other" (*SAF* 21: 37–50) explores the narrative's relation to Plato and Descartes and finds the pervasive epistemological concerns a reflection of "other-mind skepticism." With characters persistently failing to overcome the implacable other, human interaction becomes a spectacle. Radical skepticism emerges within the narrator's interpolated tales and discussions of the ongoing fiction. Marc Dolan in "Four Faces of *The Confidence-Man*: An Academic Blind Man's Zoo" (*ESQ* 39: 133–60) attempts "to uncover an elusive coherence" among diverse methodological approaches. This intrepid and illuminating account offers four "'mini-readings,' four brief speculations on the novel's setting, plot, theme, and mode." Joseph Urbas in "Truth in *The Confidence-Man*: The Trickster as Pragmatist" (*Profils Americains*, pp. 115–26) explores Melville's critique of "'foundationalist' thinking. Proof can always be counterfeited." Urbas reveals Mr. Roberts and William Cream as problematical pragmatists. Keiko Beppu in "A Sweet Charity for Melville the Confidence Man" (*Melville Studies in Japan*, pp. 141–56) considers how charity devolves from caritas into negotiations for cash.

viii Late Works

In Edward W. Goggin's "Confusion and Resolution in 'The Scout Toward Aldie'" (*MSEx* 92: 5–9) Melville's war poem depicts "a dark wood of dreams and nightmare without a Vergil for our guide." The shadowy figure of Mosby embodies moral relativism rather than fixed dichotomies. Stan Goldman's *Melville's Protest Theism: The Hidden and*

Silent God in Clarel (No. Ill.) clearly illuminates the poem's recalcitrant theological center. Goldman's notion of "protest theism"—"a paradoxical combination and coalescence of both protest and love"—depends on seeing Melville's sensibility not in terms of "nihilistic" skepticism or protomodernist angst but as "biblically rooted, nonsectarian, nondogmatic." The Books of Job, Psalms, Ecclesiastes, Jeremiah, Lamentations, and the Gospels provide intertextual resources for *Clarel.* Goldman proceeds with an effective and economical topical organization. Chapters explore the epistemological implications of Melville's silent, hidden God; the various speakers' lamentations, disillusionments, and struggles with faith and doubt, especially insofar as Jacob and Job offer types of the "God-wrestler"; and the dialectical presence of four narrative voices—the intrusive-auctorial, the participant, the reverent, and the divine-immanent. Shizuo Suyama's "The Imagination of Death: An Essay on *Clarel*" (*Melville Studies in Japan,* pp. 157–68) views death as fact and motif with special attention to Nathan, Mortmain, and Ruth. Kiyotoshi Murakami in "Beyond 'the Talismanic Secret': Some Aspects of Melville's Later Poetry" (*Melville Studies in Japan,* pp. 169–93) offers a wide-ranging discussion of such complexes as innate depravity and the endless quest, comparing early prose treatments with verse renderings.

Billy Budd continues to incite new disputations on old arguments. Peter Shaw's "The Fate of a Story" (*ASch* 62: 591–600) makes another rousing case for Melville's unequivocal support of Vere. Shaw lambastes anti-Vere forces of the 1980s (and by implication the 1950s) who find "that Vere's application of the law is arbitrary and unnecessary, that it springs from twisted psychological motives." Lacking "commonsensical understanding," they simply impose pseudo-liberal (but actually dogmatic) cultural and political ideologies. Pro-Vere forces are here known as "commonsense critics." Shaw repudiates ironist contentions that Melville knew Vere was wrong about late 18th-century law, and he dismisses all talk of the narrator's unreliability. Ultimately, "*Billy Budd* is about the tragic possibilities inherent in society's invocation of its ultimate power over life and death when faced with an external threat to its existence."

Four readings of *Billy Budd* conclude this year's studies. Brett Zimmerman's "Astronomical Imagery and Symbolic Antitheses in Melville's *Billy Budd*" (*EAS* 22: 1–17) trots out the testament-of-acceptance argument. He explores the antithesis between height and depth. Billy is a Christ figure and associated with the sun, Aldebaran, and Taurus, while

Claggart the Satan figure is associated with the full moon and Scorpio. Arthur Efron's worthwhile but belabored "Melville's Conjectures into Innocence: Chapter 22 of *Billy Budd, Sailor (an Inside Narrative)*" (*REALB*, pp. 34–98) considers the closeted interview between Billy and Vere. The narrator fails to bring into "a compatible relation" his legal concerns for naval discipline and the intricacies of ontological innocence. Jonathan A. Yoder in "The Protagonists' Rainbow in *Billy Budd*: Critical Trimming of Truth's Ragged Edges" (*ATQ* 7: 97–117) views Claggart as more than a fixed archetypal construct. He and Billy, the argument goes, "have much in common—their sexuality, their inability to cope with emotions, and their tendency to resort to force when under stress." Finally, Kiyofumi Tsubaki's "Dynamism in *Billy Budd*" (*Melville Studies in Japan*, pp. 195–219) mounts a formal examination of "the motif of movement and motion, the symbolic meanings of the parts of the ship, and the idea of balance between opposing forces."

Salisbury State University

6 Mark Twain

Tom Quirk

For reasons that I cannot fathom, this year seems to be a year to pause, take stock, and place things in some sort of critical and historical perspective. *The Mark Twain Encyclopedia*—certainly the year's most important Twain publication—accomplishes this end by example; it represents a massive cooperative effort that goes some way toward forging, however provisionally, a critical and scholarly consensus. Four separate collections of essays mingle the old, the recent, and the new. By bringing these several critical perspectives into active conversation with one another and with contemporary critical discourse, the editors implicitly challenge "cutting edge" mentality. And the authors of several essays make compelling arguments by means of thorough and often astute surveys of stuff so mundane and ready at hand as past responses to Twain or a history of critical practice. I suspect that this stock-taking is nothing more than coincidence. However, if, instead of a consensus-building effort, some sort of standoff is in the making, I hope no one gets hurt; as a friend once remarked to me, "Cutting edge is the weapon of choice in my neighborhood."

i Editions

In 1972 *Roughing It* (Calif.) was the first volume of the Works of Mark Twain to be published by the Mark Twain Project. For Hamlin Hill, who reviewed the book for *ALS*, its appearance was both welcome and somewhat problematic. Among the difficulties Hill had with the edition were the basis on which normalization of spelling was justified, the elimination of the illustrations from the first American edition and, necessarily, those clauses referring to them, and the whole difficult business of satisfactorily determining an author's intention. The editors of the 1993 revised edition have addressed these problems and, particularly with regard to the vexed question of authorial intention, answered them in more intricate if not finally conclusive ways than anyone might have anticipated. In any event, though one might wish that other volumes (*A Tramp Abroad,* for example) had made their first appearance before revised editions were issued, this is a good addition to the texts already published. The notes are full and instructive; the stages of composition and revision are described through an intricate system of adjustment of Twain's apparent method of calculating the number of pages in the manuscript; the supplementary materials, including maps, are helpful; and the original illustrations are a happy addition to most any Twain text.

ii Biography and Reference

The "starchy boys" in the title of Edgar M. Branch's *Mark Twain and the Starchy Boys* (Center for Mark Twain Studies, 1992) are those riverboat pilots of the Western Boatman's Benevolent Association whose tough-minded independence, mutual concern, and demonstrated courage of conviction Twain admired and whom he honored in the closing chapters of "Old Times on the Mississippi." Contrary to those who find the WBBA to be represented in "Old Times" as a deadening and decadent force in the piloting profession, Branch, in a richly textured and highly readable piece of scholarship, demonstrates Twain's lifelong affection for the organization and the reasons for his feelings. Branch gives a far more complete history of the combination than has existed—the economic and social conditions that brought it into being, and its governing principles and objectives. He establishes that, apart from his creative touches of exaggeration for dramatic or comic effect, Twain's account of the association is substantially accurate. The story Branch tells is not one of the classic struggle between management and labor; even the most partisan members of the association conceded that organizing against the vested interests of owners and captains was "wrong." Instead, their efforts were spent in ensuring safety on the river—that pilots were well-trained, capable, and of good character, which meant among other things (cf. the *Exxon Valdez*) publicizing the names of pilots who were known alcoholics; and that information about the conditions of the river was reliable and current. By this account, the WBBA constituted something of a meritocracy, and it is largely on this basis that Branch in his concluding chapter describes certain speculative but illuminating parallels between the combination and the values and social organization that Hank Morgan unevenly fosters in *A Connecticut Yankee in King Arthur's Court*. I hasten to add that Branch does not impose a cheerily nostalgic reading on Twain's novel; the same sort of weakening of political solidarity and the corruption that eventuated in the demise of the WBBA may also have contributed to the pessimism of the book and to the disastrous failure of Hank's progressive vision.

Paul Baender provides an extended gloss on his 1966 essay "Alias MacFarlane: A Revision of Mark Twain Biography" in "Alias MacFarlane: Who in L was 'L.'?" (*RALS* 19: 22–34). Baender originally argued that, in the 1890s, Twain used the name of a man he claimed to have known in Cincinnati in the 1850s as a persona through whom he might voice his own dissident opinions. Regretting that he did not construct his argument in the original essay in a way that might have prevented what he terms the Nominalist and Realist reactions, Baender here presents an object lesson in the mustering and assessment of evidence. Specifically, he contests both those who maintain that MacFarlane was a real acquaintance and those who see him as a rhetorical invention. Baender also challenges Branch's attribution of a letter signed "L." as Clemens's own; he reprints a similar letter published in the same journal a few days later and signed "Larkin."

In " 'Wicked Moments': Mark Twain in Brockville, Ontario, 1885" (Brockville Museum *Monitor* 8, i: 2–3) Taylor Roberts gives an account of Twain and George Washington Cable's visit to that city on their reading tour. We learn, among other things, that a reporter heard Twain, though he was not an orthodox Christian, remark on fast trains, "I don't think I ever feel as wicked as when I'm going around a curve at sixty miles an hour." Alan Gribben's review-essay, "Mark Twain's Ladies" (*MissQ* 46: 667–72), nicely summarizes *Mark Twain's Aquarium* (1991), ed. John Cooley, and Resa Willis's *Mark and Livy* (1992) and places them within the contexts of Twain biography. Specifically, he measures their contributions against the biographies of Hamlin Hill and Justin Kaplan, and he indicates the profitable directions in which Twain biography is heading. The *Union Catalog of Letters to Clemens,* ed. Paul Machlis (Calif., 1992), lists more than 18,000 letters to or about Clemens. This reference work serves as a valuable resource and a companion volume to *A Union Catalog of Clemens Letters* (1986).

Several years in the making, and with 180 contributors and 740 entries, *The Mark Twain Encyclopedia* (Garland) will be welcomed by a considerable portion of the Twain establishment. The diligence, judgment, and goodwill of the editors, J. R. LeMaster and James Wilson, and the cooperation of an array of scholars have resulted in a volume that will prove highly informative and valuable. A wealth of biographical information is to be found here, as well as entries on individual works, fictional characters, Twain's relatives and friends, historical and political events, important concepts, and much more. Each entry is cross-referenced to related topics and is followed by an informed if not exhaustive bibliography. (Everett Emerson in a recent number of the *Mark Twain Circular* suggests a number of titles that ought to be added to the bibliographies of several entries.) As is to be expected in an editorial project that, on principle, sought to preserve a diversity of critical methodologies and did not wish to "interfere with the voices (styles) or distinctive approaches" of the contributors, the work is uneven, lacking at times a sense of continuity or proportion. For the same reason, however, there are many delightful surprises—several of the entries have the quality and authority of well-crafted essays. I will not be so rash as to praise some pieces over others, but, on balance, this encyclopedia will likely please most users.

Still, as good as it is, *The Mark Twain Encyclopedia* is probably, even now, in need of a revision and updating, not only because critical reassessments of Twain are ongoing, but because an army of scholars exists with an ample venue for publishing biographical and bibliographical discoveries. The unfortunate corollary to the unearthing of new Twain materials is that forgeries abound and must be weeded out; one highly readable account of this peril is Ronald Wesley Hoag's "All that Glitters Is Not Mark Twain: The Strange Case of the Riverdale '3' " (*MTJ* 29, ii [1991]: 1–9). The Mark Twain Project is only the most visible institution that, with each successive volume, regularly publishes new information and corrects misapprehensions; there are also three Twain newsletters—the *Mark Twain Circular,* the *Mark Twain Society Bulletin,* and *The Twainian* (which has only recently resumed publication)—the on-line *Mark Twain Forum,* and the *Mark Twain Journal.* Little wonder that, however comprehensive, a Twain encyclopedia will never be exhaustive or definitive. A revised edition is not forthcoming anytime soon, I think, and in the meantime this encyclopedia will serve admirably.

iii General Interpretations

Two welcome collections appeared this year. Hamlin Hill prepared a selection of Walter Blair's essays in *Essays on American Humor: Blair Through the Ages* (Wisconsin), and David E. Sloane edited *Mark Twain's Humor: Critical Essays* (Garland).

The collection of Blair essays is divided into four sections: "The Big Picture" (which includes essays on Southern humor, 19th-century American humorists, and a "continuum" of American humor); "Essays on American Humor" (which includes essays on Davy Crockett, E. B. White, Mike Fink, and others); "Essays on Mark Twain" (which reprints, among others, essays on *Tom Sawyer,* the Blue-Jay yarn, the familiar "When Was *Huckleberry Finn* Written?" and the not so familiar "Was *Huckleberry Finn* Written?"); and, finally, "Practice What You Teach: A Short Story" (Blair's own tall tale, "The Ugliest Man in the World"). The volume is punctuated with Blair's cartoons of himself as Mike Fink Blair, Johnny Appleseed Blair, and other comic self-deflations. These essays serve to remind us how various a man he was, and Hill's introduction and brief "Suggestions for Additional Reading" notes how important he has been to the study of American humor and to Mark Twain.

In *Mark Twain's Humor* Sloane has gathered a rich and useful collection of some 34 essays, chapters, and contemporary reviews. The book is divided into three parts. The first treats Twain's growth as a comedian; the second, the comedian as a writer transformed into a major author; and the last deals with the comedian as a cultural representative. More than an aspect of Twain's significance, humor was his trump card, a fact that too often seems to get lost in more solemn critical appraisals. Many of the selections and nearly all of the authors will be familiar—Henry Nash Smith, Leslie Fiedler, James Cox, and many others. The predictability of some of the offerings should not subtract from one's good opinion of the book, however. The selections are judicious, the organizing principle is coherent, and the selected bibliography is unusually full. Three essays have not been published before and therefore deserve some comment.

Michael Kiskis and Laura E. Skandera-Trombley challenge prevailing notions about Twain's biography and criticism, though they do so from rather different perspectives. For Kiskis in "Coming Back to Humor: The Comic Voice in Mark Twain's Autobiography" (pp. 541–69), Twain's adventure in autobiography late in his life renewed and reawakened his humorous resources. Beginning in 1906, Twain's dictated and rambling story of his life called forth his old storytelling powers and helped to integrate a personality that had suffered so many losses. Skandera-Trombley notes in her "'The Mysterious Stranger': Absence of the Female in Mark Twain Biography" (pp. 571–91) that, for most Twain biographers and critics, women are curiously absent or so amorphously treated as to be "interchangeable." In fact, however, women were always important to Clemens's intellectual life and creative resources, and his family gave him "access to a feminine consciousness that enabled him to create a unique brand of fiction." When Olivia died in 1904, "the linchpin of his connection to the feminine consciousness was gone" and "the happiest days and most productive times of his life were over." Finally, Suzanne Weil in "Reconstructing the 'Imagination-Mill': The Mystery of Mark Twain's Late Works" (pp. 505–39) observes that the pronounced technical and creative differences in Twain's late work have more often been treated "like a disease in need of a cure than a question in need of an answer." As part of her answer, Weil postulates 1894 as the "catastrophe" year for Clemens, the time when he had to face reality and, subsequently, to abandon the "good-bad-boy pose" he had adopted in his life as well as in his art. As a consequence, he became more experimental in his fiction and more absolute in his division of good and evil, and he created characters who had transcendent powers but were alienated from community.

Two collections of essays on Twain were published in India this year. In *Mark Twain: An Anthology of Recent Criticism* (Pencraft), editor Prafulla C. Kar gathers a group of previously published essays by American critics, with three new pieces by Indian critics. Kar's own Mark Twain in His Time" (pp. 7–16) argues that Twain's "primary concern as a writer was to unmask the prevailing myths about America" and that he was willing to challenge the "white mythology" of order through comic anarchy. Dilip Kumar Das in "Language, Ideology and Style in Mark Twain" (pp. 60–71) conducts a Bakhtinian reading of *Huckleberry Finn*: the novel attempts to subvert the dominant discourse through "the artful use of the stylistic features of heteroglossia and the carnivalesque"; in this sense the novel is a "classic instance" of language subverting its own authority and semantic codes. Biyot K. Tripathy's "The Ending of *Huck Finn*" (pp. 167–81) maintains that the evasion episode, mostly at the level of imagery, exceeds the savagery of the opening chapters and that Jim becomes the mythic victim, freed only into another form of slavery. Only

Huck escapes the tyranny of institutions and is able to "create values out of exploring life rather than living according to those in existence."

Mark Twain and Nineteenth Century American Literature, ed. E. Nageswara Rao (American Studies Research Centre), is a collection of 16 relatively brief essays, half of which deal with Twain. K. Narayana Chandran's "And Thereby Hangs a Tale: A Reading of Mark Twain's 'A Cat-Tale'" (pp. 1–7) views Twain's story as a performative text that makes and unmakes itself in the telling. "A Cat-Tale" enacts simultaneously a child's and an adult's game, the first providing the pleasure of belief in the narrator's lies, the second providing the "pain of theorizing" a narrative that systematically violates conventions. In "'Perpetuated Piracy': Mark Twain's Attitude toward Monarchy" (pp. 8–16) E. Nageswara Rao surveys Twain's lifelong contempt for monarchy as it is revealed in his fiction and notebooks, and he emphasizes Twain's conviction that monarchy is a form of criminal piracy. S. D. Kapoor's "Some Thoughts on Mark Twain's *Autobiography*" (pp. 17–26) explores the central "issues" of Clemens's autobiography: self, community, success, and the sense of despair that dominates the narrative. Because he could find no right or sustaining relation between self, success, and community, his contemplation of his life and times eventuated in despair. In "Mark Twain's *What Is Man?*—An Indian View" (pp. 27–36) S. Ramaswamy places Twain's philosophical dialogue within the context of Indian philosophy. Without positing an Indian influence on Twain's thinking, Ramaswamy details striking parallels between *What Is Man?* and the Vedantic point of view. Siddiq Ali in "Mark Twain and Black Humor: A Reading of *The Mysterious Stranger*" (pp. 37–43) notes the similarity in technique and vision between Twain and later black humorists such as Barth and Heller, but he observes that, in the last analysis, Twain is not so bleak because he "retains a faith in some kind of humanism." A. N. Dwivedi's "Mark Twain's Humor and *Huckleberry Finn*" (pp. 44–54) distinguishes between wit and humor and offers a brief survey of early 19th-century American humor in preparation for an appreciation of the achievement of *Huck Finn* as "the full emergence and flowering of native American humor." P. Marudanayagam, surveying Leslie Fiedler's career in criticism and fiction in "The Theme of Interethnic Male Bonding: Twain and Fiedler" (pp. 72–78), contends that Fiedler's "achievement as a critic is built on his initial saturation in Mark Twain." Finally, Mohamed Elias in "Rudyard Kipling's Works in Mark Twain's Library" (pp. 128–34) observes that Twain's enthusiasm for Kipling may in part derive from Twain's own influence on Kipling. That is, *Kim* owes something to *Huckleberry Finn,* and thus Twain is responsive to the transformation of his own earlier work. Moreover, Twain's reference to "Mogli" in *The Mysterious Stranger* manuscripts indicates a debt to Kipling and an intention to elaborate on incidents in India and with great sympathy for the victims of imperialism.

In *Mark Twain and Shakespeare: A Cultural Legacy* (Univ. Press) Anthony J. Berret gives a comprehensive account of Twain's use and deliberate misuse of Shakespeare, his debts to and disavowals of the Bard. The book is organized simply but effectively. After a beginning chapter entitled "Biography" in which Clemens's involvement in the Bacon/Shakespeare controversy in *Is Shakespeare Dead?* is recapitulated, Berret offers chapters titled "Comedy," "History," and "Tragedy." The comic uses of Shakespeare were of two sorts—"rhetorical buffoonery" and literary burlesque—and, here as elsewhere, Berret places Twain's appropriations within the context of other humorists who similarly indulged in parodies and burlesques of Shakespeare's language and dramatic incident. In "History," Berret traces Twain's use of Shakespeare to give an authentic air to his historical tales for young folk. Naturally enough, *The Prince and the Pauper* is the text that best illustrates this sort of use. In the final section, "Tragedy," the author notes that Twain was working on his burlesque of *Hamlet* when he was writing *Tom Sawyer,* and he further observes that this play has figured in any number of bildungsromane since Fielding's *Tom Jones.* But Berret finds even more substantial echoes and parallels of *Hamlet* in *Huckleberry Finn* and a few scattered ones in *A Connecticut Yankee* and *Joan of Arc.* Some of the influences Berret detects are questionable, but his treatment acquires persuasive force as the instances multiply.

"Mark Twain in Midwestern Eyes," Leland Krauth's contribution to *Exploring the Midwestern Literary Imagination* (pp. 27–41), offers an illuminating if somewhat familiar picture of Twain as the seminal Midwestern writer. Without once using the threadbare phrase "anxiety of influence," Krauth still manages to offer a brief but instructive survey of three generations of Midwestern writers' opinions of Twain. As the quintessential Midwestern author, one who smuggled that point of view over the middle border and, for many, made it stand for larger democratic sympathies, Twain was at the same time limited in his own perspectives by the provinciality of Midwestern America. For his contemporaries, Twain was a vivid social historian, earnest moralist, and product of the frontier. Sinclair Lewis and Edgar Lee Masters later found him a victim of a village mentality, too attracted to gross materialism and overly bound by convention. For Sherwood Anderson, Twain was also constricted by his environment, but he was still "among the two or three really great American artists." Interestingly, Krauth concludes his survey with two brothers who grew up in the village of Hope, Illinois—Carl and Mark Van Doren. As Columbia University professors, the Van Dorens established and authorized their early affection for Twain in anthologies, literary histories, and magazines.

Sander L. Gilman in his densely documented essay "Mark Twain and the Diseases of the Jews" (*AL* 65: 94–115) offers a comparison of Twain's attitudes toward the Jews in *Innocents Abroad* and the essay "Concerning the Jews," written 30 years later. In the earlier portrayal, Gilman believes, Twain depicted the Jews as a diseased race whose afflictions may mirror an inherited condition that reflected the essence of an unredeemed people. In an engrossing digression he surveys European and American debate about the Jew as a racial type and then returns to an examination of the later essay, in which he detects an only slightly more enlightened writer: "Twain's rhethoric about physical disease has been transformed into rhetoric about psychological predisposition, which was as far as he was able to go in rethinking the meaning of the diseases of the Jews." Gilman provides a rich historical context to frame his argument, but how decisively that context applies to Twain is debatable since Gilman's conclusions and assumptions about Twain are more often asserted than argued.

iv Individual Works Through 1884

Michael Hobbs in "Mark Twain's Infernal Transcendentalism: The Lake Episodes in *Roughing It*" (*ALR* 26, i: 13–25) discerns in the scenes at Lakes Tahoe, Mono, and Kilauea a conflation of the doubled "I" of the narration—the tenderfoot's romanticism fusing momentarily with the veteran's realism. These moments are at once transcendent and disturbingly chaotic, describing as they do scenes of terrible beauty and representing a "collision between the tenderfoot's sacred vision and the veteran's infernal imagination." Hobbs further argues that the imaginative continuity of these episodes contributes to the book's structural unity. Earl Briden's note, " 'The Great Landslide Case': A Mark Twain Debt to a Musty Old Book?' " (*N&Q* 40: 479–81), proposes Sir Richard Baker's

Chronicle of the Kings of England, which Twain discovered in 1864, as a source for the 1870 version of the tale that would eventually find its way into chapter 34 of *Roughing It.* Baker's volume contains an account of an earthquake in Queen Elizabeth's time that carried a tract of virtually intact land more than 150 feet.

In "Tangled Webs: Lies, Capitalist Expansion, and the Dissolution of the Subject in *The Gilded Age*" (*ArQ* 49, iii: 59–92) Ellen J. Goldner offers a provocative, if somewhat denatured, reading of the novel; she sees it as reflecting the shift of subjectivity under the auspices of a global capitalism that, by fostering a worldwide economic interdependence, distances the causes of events from those the individual views and responds to. One consequence of this shift in *The Gilded Age* is that it dramatizes a "crisis in representation" that subverts in advance the realist program it sponsors and "threatens the text's own ideology of populism and individualism." The North, because it is closer to the sources of wealth and political influence, may produce a conventional "hero" like Philip Sterling, but Colonel Sellers becomes a confidence man who is himself duped and whose tall tales in part derive from the attempt to attract capital investment. His tales disclose an economic interdependency that dissolves any claim on a separable and responsible identity.

It is nice to see that *Tom Sawyer* is enjoying attention as something more than a "prequel" to *Huckleberry Finn.* Oxford issued an edition of the novel with a worthwhile introduction by Lee Clark Mitchell. John D. Evans, in an ingeniously simple format, has produced *A Tom Sawyer Companion: An Autobiographical Guided Tour with Mark Twain* (Univ. Press). Synopses of the various episodes in the novel are followed, in bold print, by quoted passages that have their roots in Twain's purported experience, and passages from the *Autobiography* or other sources establish the connection between the fiction and its autobiographical analogue. Evans, properly, does not intrude upon this sourcebook except to clarify certain passages or materials. In "Tom Sawyer's Masculinity" (*ArQ* 49, iv: 33–59) Glenn Hendler provides an interesting account of how the "bad-boy" book constructs an audience (adult men) who identify with the condition of the protagonists (young boys) by misrecognizing the youth's condition as its own. This intricate process of "*interpellation*" does the cultural work of sustaining a masculinity that violently excludes women and of affirming a "heterosexualized" male identity. The exemplary text that illustrates this process is, of course, *Tom Sawyer,* but Hendler takes instructive bypaths through discussions of Howells's *A*

Boy's Town and Charles Dudley Warner's *Being a Boy* as a way of making more generalized conclusions about the genre.

Critical Essays on The Adventures of Tom Sawyer, ed. Gary Scharnhorst (Hall), reprints 25 contemporary notices of *Tom Sawyer*, which, as the editor notes, is "more than twice the total number of notices [the novel] hitherto is known to have received." It also reprints a nice sampling of criticism from 1960 to the present. The final essay, written for this collection, is Henry Wonham's "Undoing Romance: The Contest for Narrative Authority in *The Adventures of Tom Sawyer*" (pp. 228–41). Without replicating it, Wonham's piece extends the argument he had developed in *Mark Twain and the Art of the Tall Tale* (see *ALS 1992*, p. 83)—namely, that Tom, the yarn spinner, vies with the narrator, the romancer, for narrative authority in the book. Tom's tall tales provide an "ironic counterbalance" to the narrator's performance without discrediting it, and the result is that the novel "manages to be a romantic adventure without committing itself to the assumptions endorsed and defended by its romantically inclined narrator." Scharnhorst's introduction nicely frames the history and terms of the critical debate over *Tom Sawyer* and reaffirms the novel's cultural importance.

v Adventures of Huckleberry Finn

Two books on *Huckleberry Finn* appeared this year: my own *Coming to Grips with Huckleberry Finn: Essays on a Book, a Boy, and a Man* (Missouri) and Shelley Fisher Fishkin's *Was Huck Black? Mark Twain and African-American Voices* (Oxford).

My volume is a collection of six essays, some previously published. To quote my prefatory summary: "I have inquired into the genesis of composition of the book; I have tried to measure the author's imaginative involvement with his young hero by studying the novels in the context of Twain's autobiographical writings; I have speculated on the compositional, as opposed to the narrative, conclusion of the novel as a way of throwing certain cross-lights on the vexed question of the evasion episode; I have examined the special and curious relation *Huckleberry Finn* bears to nineteenth-century realism; I have contemplated a double legacy Twain and his novel bequeathed to later American writers; and, finally, I have, in rather antic fashion, measured the book against current ideological opinion."

Despite its provocative title, *Was Huck Black?* is grounded in an assumption no one would seriously question: As Twain "'mixed up' black voices with white ones, the flavors 'swapped around' deliciously. American taste in literature would never be the same." Such a swapping of linguistic juices was inevitable, particularly in the South, and was acknowledged even in the 19th century; and it is likewise common to argue that the publication of *Huckleberry Finn* marks a significant moment in American literary history. Fishkin is also on uncontested ground when she maintains that Twain had a better ear than most for the richness of African American dialect. Her argument becomes more problematic, however, when she discusses, without ever deciding, whether Twain's appropriation of black voices in his fiction was conscious or unconscious; and she places an unusually heavy burden of proof on the slight sketch "Sociable Jimmy" and Clemens's childhood acquaintance with the slave "Jerry" as constituting "compelling" evidence for her belief that Huck was in part modeled after African Americans Twain had known. Nevertheless, Fishkin's remarkably full and well-documented bibliography, along with the responses of African American writers (some of whom she interviewed) to Twain and his work, is in itself valuable.

Readers may appreciate Fishkin's scholarship and still remain unpersuaded by her arguments. It is sufficient to say that *Was Huck Black?* will convince those who are convinced by it. I am rather more certain that her subject matter deserves greater and more expansive attention; for no one would seriously object to the notion that Anglo-American and African American voices (along with many others) have managed to cohabit on far easier terms than have their speakers. A thorough investigation of this phenomenon, informed by a linguistic sophistication that might satisfy practicing dialecticians as well as decoders of discourse, and applied to a wider range of texts and writers, is surely in order. Fishkin may have taken an important first step.

Harry G. Segal in "Life Without Father: The Role of the Paternal in the Opening Chapters of *Huckleberry Finn*" (*JAmS* 27: 19–33) applies what he terms "psychoformalism" to the novel's opening chapters as a way of shedding light on the conclusion. By insisting that sequels are by nature Oedipal struggles with the previous texts on which they are built and whose features are extended and altered as forms of competition and rivalry, Segal sees *Huck Finn* as dramatizing the repressed content of *Tom Sawyer*. Specifically, Huck challenges Twain as the author of the novel in which he first appears, and his encounters with a series of would-be fathers prefigure the appearance of Pap, the real and dreaded father whom Huck would avoid. The final chapters, by this view, represent an attempt to return to the more benign habitation of *Tom Sawyer* as a way "to evade feelings conjured by its sequel." By combining psychological surmise with far-fetched bits of literary decoding, "psychoformalism" appears to benefit from the worst of both worlds. At any rate, I am unpersuaded—to cite only one example—that the two halves of the potato Jim proposes to use to disguise a counterfeit coin symbolize the symbiotic relation of "self" and "other" and predict Huck's life with Pap in the cabin.

Yet another essay that focuses on Pap is Elizabeth Prioleau's " 'That Abused Child of Mine': Huck Finn as a Child of an Alcoholic" (*EAS* 22: 85–98). Prioleau finds that Huck displays the most salient characteristics of the "COA" and that understanding Huck's symptoms challenges what she calls the "standard apple pie versions of Huck." Perhaps. But everywhere there is a drunk in the novel (and they are everywhere) there, too, is a father figure that retards Huck's emotional growth. By this reading, Jim is Huck's "therapist," one who can function effectively only on the raft. Among other questionable assertions, the author maintains that, in killing the drunken Boggs, Sherburn acts out Huck's patricidal wishes and that when Huck tells Aunt Sally that "his steamboat ran aground, blew a cylinder, and killed a nigger," we are to understand that Huck's "own curative project has foundered; his therapist died."

Kelly Anspaugh in "The Innocent Eye? E. W. Kemble's Illustrations to *Adventures of Huckleberry Finn*" (*ALR* 25, ii: 16–30) argues that Twain's dissatisfaction with the illustrator's first batch of drawings, because they were too coarse, indicates that for the purpose of the novel's subscription sales Twain wanted the illustrations to serve as an ameliorative counterpoint to the text. Anspaugh further argues that Kemble, as illustrator, likewise wished to preserve the coarseness of the first drawings by presenting, in visually ambiguous terms, pictures of innocence that are on second glance not so innocent—deliberate representations of phallic symbols, drawings that suggest masturbation and urination, and other suggestively bawdy pictures for this "boy's book."

Susan Derwin in "Impossible Commands: Reading *Adventures of Huckleberry Finn*" (*NCF* 47: 437–54) launches her ingenious interpretation of the novel by contemplating the author's notice at the beginning of the book and by pointing out that, Twain's prohibitions to the reader notwithstanding, one's attempts to make sense of the plot also involves, ipso facto, a moral-making enterprise. In other words, the novel "explores the interplay between morality and sense making, conscience and cognition." It does this through "the (moral) process of identification." Identification here means not only the reader's identification with Huck and others, but also a fictional character's identification with other characters. This process is itself forever complicated and modified by the projective and narcissistic; Huck simultaneously represents Jim to himself and "constructs a flattering self-image" as Jim's would-be savior. Derwin's essay is itself often insightful, but the evidence adduced to make the case is frequently strained. We are to understand that Tom's "*me-yow!*" as a signal to Huck really means "me" and "you" and thus underscores Huck's alienation. And Derwin further speculates that Pap may have been killed by a one-legged black man who, "in his haste to escape, left behind his prosthesis." How hasty a one-legged man without his prosthesis can be is not answered.

Peter Shaw in "The Genteel Fate of *Huckleberry Finn*" (*PR* 60: 434–49), like Derwin, though from a very different perspective, explores through *Huck* the moral possibilities of literature itself. His method is to survey critical assessment of the novel from the early 1950s to the present. Beginning with the familiar trio of Leo Marx, Eliot, and Trilling, Shaw discerns in the tendencies of critical evaluation since that time a common denominator—that, by so construing the novel as racist or nonracist, as an antebellum romance or a Reconstruction allegory, or otherwise managing the text to suit the critic's historical moment and no doubt socially enlightened prepossessions, critics have taken the safe path of moral rectitude and condescension in a way that, ironically, links them with the dreaded Genteel Tradition. He further observes that this same self-righteous attitude obscures whatever moral vision the novel might actually impart. Shaw picks his way through a selected but still considerable number of critics and critical positions in short compass, and this Tinker-to-Evers-to-Chance sort of argument works well enough, I suppose. Whether it justifies conclusions such as the following is more doubtful: "To set side by side virtually any discussion of *Huckleberry Finn* from the 1950s with most of the criticism written after the late 1960s is to witness a distinct loss of sophistication about how literature works."

Jerome Loving also argues in his own reading of *Huckleberry Finn* and *Pudd'nhead Wilson* (see below) that criticism is fundamentally a record of our reshaping of stories to suit our own current interests, political and other, but his call to a return to literature and, by his own example, to a "lost" literary sophistication is somewhat less jaundiced. Another book, complementary in its outlook to Shaw's perspective, though more gently argued, is Howard Fulweiler's *"Here a Captive Heart Busted": Studies in the Sentimental Journey of Modern Literature* (Fordham). Fulweiler is not principally interested in American literary texts, but his book is peppered with comments on *Huckleberry Finn* and, as the title indicates, this novel is central to his thesis that modern literature, like Jim in the Phelps cabin, has been held prisoner by a false sentimentality.

It is no accident that Shaw begins his survey of the critics of *Huckleberry Finn* with Leo Marx, because Marx placed the evasion episode in an interpretive limelight that has not dimmed since. Gary Henrickson's "Biographers' Twain, Critics' Twain, Which of the Twain Wrote the 'Evasion?' " (*SLJ* 26, i: 14—29) also takes inventory of criticism for the last 40 years. Between 1950 and 1991 there were 80 publications defending the ending of the novel. In the decade of the 1980s alone there were 29 articles defending it, and Henrickson gives a whirlwind tour through the various arguments. The conclusion one ought to draw from the recurring publication of essays on the evasion is that this question is an urgent and meaningful one that critics would like to solve. Sadly and predictably, however, as Henrickson also shows by his survey, only a handful of those critics cited, much less actively engaged with, any of the more recent biographical and primary materials published during the same period, nor did they demonstrate acquaintance with or much interest in Twain's compositional habits or his creative limitations. Instead, they cited other critics.

If Shaw is right that there has been a discernible loss of literary sophistication during the last few decades, Henrickson may have come closer to the reason for it. For Henrickson's survey indicates that many of those who would have a say about the ending of *Huckleberry Finn* have no demonstrated interest in settling the question. But there are other implications of his study. No one to my knowledge has established whether the evasion episode is in fact a problem (that is, an interpretive issue that may be framed in a way that makes it susceptible of solution or consensual understanding). It may be merely a conundrum that provides the opportunity to show off one's own critical acrobatics. Would the resolution of the controversy make any practical difference in how we read the book or redefine the place of the novel within the context of American literary tradition? And if it is a problem, whose problem is it?

Huck's? Twain's? The reader's? The critic's? The evidence suggests that it is the critic's problem, and if this is so, might not this debate be better conducted through E-mail instead of in the pages of literary journals? Ah, Huck! How many trees have died for your sins?

vi Individual Works After 1884

Lewis O. Saum in "Colonel Donan, Mark Twain, and a Campaign That Failed" (*MHR* 87: 131–49) offers Peter Donan, one of the original Marion Rangers and a well-known Missouri journalist, as something of a goad to Twain's extenuation of his desertion during the Civil War and as an additional prototype for the character Peterson Dunlap in "The Private History of a Campaign That Failed." Donan had referred disparagingly to Twain's desertion at a public banquet in 1877 and was "besieged" by reporters wanting to know if the remark were true. Only a few months later, Twain gave his own account of his war experience, which Donan viewed as a direct response to his remarks. In 1885 in "The Campaign That Failed," Saum argues, Twain returned fire by drawing the affected and ridiculous figure of Peterson Dunlap as a satirical portrait not only of John L. Robards (the commonly accepted prototype) but of Donan as well.

One of the more interesting essays this year is Helena Maragou's "Game-Playing and Fantasy in Twain's *A Connecticut Yankee*" (*ALR* 26, i: 26–39). Conceding that no clear correspondence between Twain's intention in the novel and a realization of the ideological motives in the narrative can be shown, Maragou admits the book's artistic failure while locating its continuing capacity to fascinate readers in a "semantic flux" that is integral to its theme: "what makes this novel interesting to us is Twain's treatment of the nature of reality and illusion, of the role of language, fiction, and myth." Because Hank Morgan's entrance into the world of Camelot involves a constant disruption of mimetic and rational structures, whatever his ideological and moral motives, Morgan's ethical perceptions are framed and thus thwarted by fantasy and game-playing. The protagonist cannot function as a moral intelligence in the narrative because he himself is "half-way into the world of illusion and dream." As such, *A Connecticut Yankee* is perforce an "amoral" fable that cannot "function as a coherent social statement" but can be read as a sometimes brilliant exploration of the nature of human experience.

Lewis Lawson in "Samuel L. Clemens: Gnosis in Camelot" (*ModA* 36:

47–62) takes a somewhat dimmer and far more eccentric view of Morgan's function in the novel. Lawson makes much of the reference to Columbus in *A Connecticut Yankee* and maintains that, like Columbus, Hank Morgan is a "millienialist," one who is a true Gnostic and something of an Antichrist. Bypaths into the interpretation of Columbus as millienialist, Joachim of Floris, and the detection of several echoes of the Book of Revelation in the novel are interesting in themselves. But it is difficult to go the distance with an author who maintains, among other things, that Morgan is a satanic con man (a "Devil quoting scripture for his own purposes") who may not even be an American and whose tale of Camelot is actually a hoax designed to dupe. Through some artful divagations and ingenious reasoning, Lawson is able to shed considerable darkness on an otherwise obscure text.

Joe D. Thomas's "A Ball of Twain-Told Yarn" (pp. 63–70) in *The Arthurian Myth of Quest and Magic*, ed. William E. Tanner (Caxton), offers a somewhat rambling "reading" of *A Connecticut Yankee* that is nevertheless cordial and astutely sensible. His principal concern is to measure the shifting relation between Twain and his protagonist. Thomas detects a certain "voice-over" throughout the text, one that must be Twain's, since it is too unlike Morgan's, but one which reminds us that Hank's vision of progress and civilization cannot be exactly equated with the Yankee's. And Clemens, himself an "adopted, never quite assimilated Yankee of Connecticut," if he is satirizing anything, is satirizing the "glorification of an unsatisfactory past."

Eric Sundquist's "Mark Twain and Homer Plessy," which first appeared in *Representations* in 1988, is reprinted in a somewhat altered form in *To Wake the Nations* (pp. 225–70). An already impressive if highly speculative essay on the relation of *Pudd'nhead Wilson* to the case of Homer Plessy that was initiated in 1893 and reached its legal conclusion in the Supreme Court ruling of *Plessy* v. *Ferguson* in 1896 is enhanced by the fuller argument of the book and the cross-connections Sundquist makes between Twain and, among others, Melville, Charles Chesnutt, and W. E. B. Du Bois. In contrast, Jerome Loving challenges New Historicist assumptions throughout *Lost in the Customhouse* as well as in his chapter, "Twain's Cigar-Store Indians" (pp. 125–40). With regard to Twain, at least, his readings of *Huckleberry Finn* and *Pudd'nhead Wilson* are complementary to Sundquist's in the sense that both place matters of race at the center of Twain's imaginative concerns. For Loving, however, the very nature of American authorship in the 19th century requires a retelling of imagined experience and dramatizes a desire to be reborn into an innocent condition free from the same burdens that the author depicts; literary texts are not a record of the national life and do not purport to solve real problems by means of something so manifestly unreal as storytelling. Criticism, Loving contends, reshapes the telling to accord with the critic's historically conditioned interests, but of Twain's texts we have only the telling. Within this precinct, Loving argues, it goes without saying that Twain cannot render the black experience except as it is filtered through his own afflicted white conscience, and he could not educate a white audience unless he also conformed to some extent with conventional expectations. For both Sundquist and Loving, the end of Reconstruction in 1877 is significant to our understanding of Twain's works. Jim is a "slave" throughout *Huck Finn,* though he is in fact free for most of the book. According to Loving, Jim's servitude appeals to a white reader's sense of pathos, while the "happy ending" of the book assuages a troubled conscience. And the theme of racism that so dominates *Pudd'nhead Wilson* is seen largely as a "white" problem. Roxy's point of view, whatever it might have been, would have subverted Twain's humor and upstaged his detective story.

In "The Sources of Nat Parson's Tale in *Tom Sawyer Abroad*" (*ANQ* 6: 18–20) Earl Briden corrects the note in the Iowa-California edition of the novella that identifies the source for the opening chapter's Nat Parson's episode as a reworking of the Horace Greeley incident in *Roughing It.* The story of a postmaster who carries a letter to Washington, D.C., and whose legs fall through the broken bottom of a hack derives from three separate but more immediate sources: a notebook entry from 1892, a stray passage about a postmaster from *Life on the Mississippi,* and a description of another postmaster in *Tom Sawyer.*

Peter Messent's "Colonial Discourse in Twain's *Following the Equator*" (*EAS* 22: 67–83) is framed by Toni Morrison's argument in *Playing in the Dark* that a ghost of an African American presence haunts American literature. Thus, the subliminal subject of *Following the Equator* is American race relations, and throughout there is a "self-reflexive" indictment of the United States as he condemns colonial practices abroad. But Twain is caught between his desire to condemn imperialism and his inability to see beyond fixed Western conceptions of other cultures, and thus the "divided nature of Twain's racial discourse." Given these limitations, it is to Twain's credit that he was able to "seriously challenge prevailing colonialist orthodoxies."

In a well-documented and instructive survey of Twain's late political writings, Hunt Hawkins in "Mark Twain's Anti-Imperialism" (*ALR* 25, ii: 31–45) challenges Philip Foner's contention that the author's philosophical pessimism did not interfere with his social criticism. To the contrary, Hawkins asserts, Twain's strident social criticisms are "undercut by his pessimism regarding human nature." Since a human being cannot originate a single thought and stands in need of some authority figure to worship or envy, the same villains Twain isolates for our contempt are in fact products of a vile and servile human nature.

University of Missouri-Columbia

7 Henry James

Robert L. Gale

Hefting this Jamesian yoke one more time, I note that forward-looking criticism continues to vie with old-fashioned criticism of James, who, though some think otherwise, will surely never be "demystified." Criticism reviewed here varies in quality, even as quantity and space are problems. For example, if I adequately covered *A Companion to Henry James Studies* and the 1993 *Henry James Review* available to date, I would have room for little else.

i Editions, Reference Works, Biographical Studies

A big event is *The Correspondence of William James, Volume 2, William and Henry 1885–1896*, ed. Ignas K. Skrupskeles and Elizabeth M. Berkeley (Virginia). Richard A. Hocks commented well on volume 1 of the three-volume series in *ALS 1992*. Volume 2, with 102 letters from Henry James, 161 from William, and an introduction by Daniel Mark Fogel, concerns the brothers' disappointment at the critical reception of their father's *Literary Remains* (1884), ed. William James; Robertson James's instability; Henry's devotion to Alice while she was in England (1884–92) and their responses to her privately printed diary (1894); Henry's increasing loneliness and William's Lake Chocorua summer home (from 1886); and what Fogel calls "the diverse academic, literary, and social worlds in which William and Henry James operated" and "their feelings about place and nationality." While William commented on Henry's style (too much "*curliness*," etc.), Henry sidestepped William's *The Principles of Psychology* (1890) and misstepped in admiring his own *Guy Domville* (1891). Other letters are in Fred Kaplan's "'So Atrocious a World': Selections from the Unpublished Letters of Henry James" (*MissR* 16, ii: 147–68). Kaplan says that World War I gave the lie to many of James's sophisticated, pro-European works and his behavior and embittered James. In chronological order and overdocumented, Kaplan publishes parts of 17 letters (some previously published, despite Kaplan's subtitle) from James, five to him, and two *New York Times* pieces on James's response to the war, including his becoming a British subject.

Rayburn S. Moore's edition of *The Correspondence of Henry James and the House of Macmillan, 1877–1914: "All the Links in the Chain"* (LSU) is the finest work of its sort this year and goes well with his edition of the James/Edmund Gosse correspondence (*ALS 1988*, pp. 95–96). An introduction traces James's friendship with Frederick Macmillan, his main correspondent in the firm, which published 27 of his titles and three editions of his works. The 318 letters, more than 290 of which appear in full here for the first time, are excellently annotated, cross-referenced, and indexed. They reveal James as a unique combination of self-deprecating critic, sound businessman, and sociable friend, and they show Macmillan as canny but generous.

The Library of America continues to provide well-printed, low-priced works by James, among works of other Americans. Added this year are James's *Collected Travel Writings: Great Britain and America: English Hours, The American Scene, Other Travels* and his *Collected Travel Writings: The Continent: A Little Tour in France, Italian Hours, Other Travels*—both expertly edited by Richard Howard.

Jacqueline E. M. Latham in "Henry James Senior's Mrs. Chichester" (*HJR* 14: 132–40) fills us in concerning Sophia Ford Chichester, the woman who recommended Swedenborg to James's father, and also concerning her sister Georgiana Ford Welch and their mystic-socialist friend, James Pierrepont Greaves. But why in the *Henry James [Junior] Review*? Alice James is analyzed by Kristin Boudreau in "'A Barnum Monstrosity': Alice James and the Spectacle of Sympathy" (*AL* 65: 53–67) as one whose "career [was so] intent upon its own demise" that she developed "a certain authority with respect to the workings of sympathy." In "Some Notes on the Master's Birthdays" (*HJR* 14: 129–31) Leon Edel mentions a few celebrations (not birthdays)—1943 (Bryn Mawr), 1966 (*New York Herald Tribune*), 1976 (Westminster Abbey)—and then rambles on about James, feminism, gender, sex, etc.

The best long essay of the year on James, I say, is Suzi Naiburg's "A Challenge to Apollonian Mastery: A New Reading of Henry James's 'Most Appalling Yet Most Admirable' Nightmare," pp. 217–42 in *The Dream and the Text: Essays on Literature and Language*, ed. Carol Schreier

Rupprecht (SUNY). Convoluted like Apollo's python as depicted in Eugène Delacroix's *Apollo Slaying Python,* which Naiburg aptly analyzes, her essay argues that James's famous dream—triggered by memories of his 1855 visit to the Galerie d'Apollon in the Louvre—of what James calls in his 1913 autobiographical volume "the awful agent" outside his door that 1910 morning should be reinterpreted. Anyone, including James, seeking creative "mastery," à la Apollo, over aspects of life should accept the Dionysian "appalling other" not as inimical but as a completing, a "complement." For example, Alice Staverton in doing so with respect to Spencer Brydon's Dionysian "other" in "The Jolly Corner" was wiser than would-be Apollonian Spencer.

ii Sources, Influences, Parallels

A beautiful parallel study is Susan Winnett's *Terrible Sociability: The Text of Manners in Laclos, Goethe, and James* (Stanford). Winnett theorizes that "the gestures constituting the code that good society calls good manners conceal what it would be a breach of manners to acknowledge in good society." Hence, Christopher Newman's failure with proper Parisians in *The American.* Winnett continues: "Manners encode the unspoken in a society and the unspeakable in the human heart in a discourse that both maintains the proprieties and allows desire to speak through them." After discussing "the code of mondanité" in Choderlos de Laclos's *Les Liaisons dangereuses* and Johann Wolfgang von Goethe's *Die Wahlverwandtschaften,* Winnett analyzes the concealing/revealing sociability of the six principal characters in *The Golden Bowl.*

Kenneth W. Warren in *Black and White Strangers* thrusts James into a surprising position. After surveying his attitudes toward African Americans, mostly in "The Point of View," "The Real Thing," and *The American Scene,* Warren addresses the problem of late 19th-century realists' limitations in presenting, solving, or avoiding aesthetic, social, and political problems vis-à-vis racism. He links *The Bostonians* to Harriet Beecher Stowe's *Uncle Tom's Cabin* as comparably effective rebukes against Southern racism. Peculiar is Warren's reading of sooty but white-handed Spencer Brydon's alter ego in "The Jolly Corner" as a black.

The indefatigable Adeline R. Tintner offers this year *The Lust of the Eyes: Henry James and Twelve Artists* (LSU), a lavishly illustrated and documented book in which she shows how James droolingly grasps landscapes, paintings, and statues, squeezes out their vital juices, and drips them into his fictional productions. She relates "The Siege of London" to Thomas Couture's *Les Romains de la décadence* (thorough), *The Reverberator* to nymph statues by Jean Goujon and Germain Pilon (exciting), "A London Life" to some William Hogarth paintings (helpful), *The Tragic Muse* to Jean-Léon Gérôme's painting of the French actress Rachel (brilliant), "The Chaperon" to Giambellino's *Virgin and Child* painting (skillful), "The Private Life" to some Lord Frederick Leighton works (forced), *The Ambassadors* to a Hals Holbein portrait of two ambassadors (ingenious but forced), *The Wings of the Dove* to Bronzino's *Lucrezia Pancitichi* (fine), *Roderick Hudson* to both Pinturicchio (unconvincing) and Honoré Daumier (eloquent), seven works by James to Pietro Longhi (spectacular), and *The Outcry* to Jan Vermeer (strong).

Adrienne Auslander Munich in "What Lily Knew: Virginity in the 1890s," p. 153–57 in *Virginal Sexuality and Textuality in Victorian Literature,* ed. Lloyd Davis (SUNY), separates sweetly lily-like, unknowingly virginal *jeunes filles en fleur* from stinkingly lily-like, "knowing virgins." She demonstrates that Oscar Wilde's Salomé signals a reluctant change in late 19th-century artistic treatments of knowing virgins. Examples in James are Maisie Farange in *What Maisie Knew* and the governess in "The Turn of the Screw." Both suffer from "virginal anxiety," and each has an unconsummatable, "free floating," self-unflowering love for another. Yes, phallicating lilies fester.

Answering "Yes" to "Is It All Right to Read Trollope?" (*ASch* 62: 447–51) Louise Weinberg opines that Anthony Trollope, whom she reveres, is wrongly defined as "middlebrow," but that unlike Trollope's fiction, James's has grandeur and builds to "interpersonal anguish" and "creepy revelation." William Macnaughton shows in "Edith Wharton's 'Bad Heroine': Sophy Viner in *The Reef*" (*SNNTS* 25: 214–25) how Wharton continued the tradition of the fictive "bad heroine," that is, the unmoneyed woman of beauty and wit. Example? Kate Croy of *The Wings of the Dove*. Roger Gard's "Old Novels in Modern Rome" (*Spectator,* 11 Sept., pp. 33–34) subjectively contrasts items in Rome and emotions evoked by them in Nathaniel Hawthorne's *The Marble Faun* and James's *Roderick Hudson* with present-day equivalents. Poignant lines in "The Ballad of Fenimore Woolson and Henry James" by X. J. Kennedy (*HudR* 46: 294–99) suggest that the suicide of Woolson, who ultimately thought "the sum of it all is ill," caused James to feel "the breath of an unseen beast" in an oneiric jungle.

James and Conrad are linked in Barry Stempfl's "Mapping Conjecture in Henry James and Joseph Conrad: A Stylistic Approach" (*HJR* 14: 99–114). By combining concepts concerning "conjecture" in Charles Sanders Peirce and Hans Vaihinger with insights from psychoanalysts following Helene Deutsch, Stempfl offers "a new approach to stylistic analysis that enables us to follow in greater detail the metaconjectural meditation encoded in James and Conrad." Stempfl applies all this, *cum* jargon, to the vigil scene in *The Portrait of a Lady* and the "river revelation" scene in *The Ambassadors,* and a "discovery" action in Conrad's "The End of the Tether"; summarizes some " 'as if' locutions"; and tentatively formulates some "abductive [i.e., Peircean conjectural] syllogisms." Along come examples of "the pertinence of anti-conjecture" from James's "The Beast in the Jungle" and *The Sacred Fount* and Conrad's *The Secret Agent.* Supported by both conjectural and anticonjectural imagery, Stempfl warns of the totally obvious dangers of conjecture.

Thomas Strychacz connects James, Dreiser, Dos Passos, and Nathanael West in *Modernism, Mass Culture, and Professionalism* as examples of modernist writers who are caught up in the ideas and art forms of mass culture but who at the same time try to separate their own style and content from those of mass culture—by making their writings difficult. They succeed when they are understood mainly by a coterie, but they also hope to be social authorities. Strychacz finds his Jamesian evidence in *The Reverberator* and *The Sacred Fount.*

Two essays link James and H. G. Wells. Virginia Allen's "The Ethos of English Departments: Henry James and H. G. Wells, Continued" (*Extrapolation* 34: 305–28) concludes her 1992 *Extrapolation* essay (see *ALS 1992,* p. 101) by deploring the canonization of James and the exclusion of Wells in English studies. She downgrades the "Harvardizing" of such studies and kites the value of science fiction, her pet. Next, Cynthia Ozick contrasts the literary James and the journalistic Wells in " 'It Takes a Great Deal of History to Produce a Little Literature' " (*P&R* 60: 195–200), so as to denigrate the present and also to wax cocky.

iii Critical Books

The year's most scrupulously abstruse book is Merle A. Williams's *Henry James and the Philosophical Novel: Being and Seeing* (Cambridge). Williams sees James as a philosophical novelist because his "novels enact a predominantly phenomenological approach to human phenomena [à la Maurice Merleau-Ponty], but one tempered by . . . reservations [à la Jacques Derrida], and interspersed with deconstructive digressions." Williams begins with a survey of previous phenomenological pronouncements on what it means for humans to be "condemned to meaning" and a survey of literary criticism relevant to James as analyst-interpreter of this condemnation. She considers evidence mainly from five novels. In *What Maisie Knew,* "[t]he dynamics of Maisie's perceptive faculty produce not only the fearless visionary redemption of an Ida or the heavily qualified recognition of a Mrs. Wix's dubious strengths, but a series of provisional estimates of individuals or situations, which are constantly subject to criticism or restructuration." *The Ambassadors* "displays . . . the subtle articulation of his [James's] later, strongly philosophical method, for it dramatizes the evolution of an entire process [in Lambert Strether] of judging" and reinterpreting social surfaces, depths, and mores in ambiguous opposition. In *The Wings of the Dove* James "provides a compelling analysis of the rewards and pressures of social life, the possibilities for self-fulfilment and the risks of personal pain or disfigurement." *The Spoils of Poynton* "throws a sharp light on several of his [James's] leading philosophical preoccupations," which include exploration, discovery, friendship, struggle, and moral and aesthetic grading. Finally, Williams images "the interaction" of the four major characters in *The Golden Bowl* as "a subtle web of language which . . . envelops their thoughts and responses, while . . . creating, undermining and transforming the entire universe of personal involvement." Among other comments in Williams's concluding chapter: "For James . . . ambiguity and an engaging multiplicity of meanings are two faces of a single philosophical coin."

Edwin Sill Fussell in *The Catholic Side of Henry James* (Cambridge) says that he might have called the book *The Literary Catholicizing of Henry James,* concerned as it is with James's "representation in narrative [or] dramatic . . . form, of identifiably Roman Catholic rites, sacraments, beliefs, practices, and fictive personages, for aesthetic reasons. . . ." Fussell relates salient 19th-century American literature to Catholicism, surveys James vis-à-vis Protestantism, Catholicism, and death, and discusses his several narratives of conversion and nonconversion to Catholicism. Fussell gets down to cases with "Gabrielle de Bergerac," "The Altar of the Dead," "The Great Good Place," and "The Birthplace"; treats *ménages Catholiques* in "De Grey: A Romance," *Guy Domville,* and especially *The Golden Bowl;* and considers "noninterpretability" in *The*

Europeans, The Portrait of a Lady, The Princess Casamassima, The Spoils of Poynton, The Awkward Age, The Ambassadors, and *The Wings of the Dove.* Fussell's organization is "analytic, thematic, formal, critical," but where possible it is also chronological. The result is logical and refreshingly skip-about; also tactful, genial, often humorous, and sparkling with perceptions and connections. Fussell has faithfully studied his James, about whose self-adjurations in the *Notebooks* he startlingly says that "it is tempting . . . to say that he writes to himself as if that second self were God," such is "the divinization of art." At last "[i]t is reductive and foolish to read James as altogether secular. His texts are more serious than that, more ambivalent, more heroic, more desperate, more helpless."

The most useful book this year is *A Companion to Henry James Studies,* ed. Daniel Mark Fogel (Greenwood). He dragooned 20 of the best Jamesians, of various critical persuasions and interests, to write 20 essays, all for this volume. The authors are Maqbool Aziz, Jean Frantz Blackall, Charles Caramello, Susan Carlson, Sarah B. Daugherty, Virginia C. Fowler, James W. Gargano, Richard A. Hocks, Carol Holly, Thomas M. Leitch, Bonney MacDonald, Darshan Singh Maini, Anthony J. Mazzella, Lyall H. Powers, John Carlos Rowe, Daniel R. Schwarz, Mary Doyle Springer, Adeline R. Tintner, James W. Tuttleton, and Philip M. Weinstein. Their essays reflect the whole rainbow of Jamesian scholarship. The three parts of the tome shade into one another. In Part I, the subjects are a survey of James criticism, James the critic, his theory of fiction, his Prefaces, and James and schools of criticism. Part II covers James's long fiction—early, middle, experimental, and late—and tales, then James and four European peers (Dostoyevsky, Flaubert, Proust, and Tolstoy), James and feminism, James and museum art, and his revisions. Part III concerns James's nonfictional writings: Notebooks, letters, *English Hours,* dramas, autobiographical volumes, and *The American Scene.* Appendix 1 lists James's 68 "principal" book publications in chronological order, sometimes with brief commentary. Appendix 2 is a "lightly annotated" list of 144 "landmark" critical works on James. The bibliography of works cited lists about 700 items. It seems useless to comment on the best features of this *Companion,* and it would be ungracious as well. Every essay is first-rate. The contributors have proved themselves to be team players in a matchless endeavor. Those familiar with their work can match contributors and subjects of many of the chapters and go on from there.

The most impenetrable book this year is Mary Cross's *Henry James: The Contingencies of Style* (St. Martin's). From her first five pages:

"James's . . . syntax . . . takes grammar to the limit and outplays its codes; . . . it usurps word order and complacencies of grammar, revolutionising the way meaning could be disseminated over a text." "James's sentences . . . push . . . meaning just out of reach . . . in a dynamic of . . . change and supplement." "The literary language James developed . . . depicts in all its overdeterminedness a struggle with the waywardness of language, and dramatises . . . his own doomed quest for truth and inclusiveness." And "the style he developed . . . reflects . . . his attempt to overcome some of the problems deconstruction has now revealed as inherent to language." And "the language of fiction, as fiction, has no ultimate referent . . . in the real world. . . . " Neo-Jamesians, take up your Cross.

In her introduction, Vivian R. Pollak, editor of *New Essays on* Daisy Miller *and* The Turn of the Screw (Cambridge, pp. 1–33), touches on James's "mother-deprived," freedom-seeking, socially restricted heroines, as well as his sister Alice, to show his "empathy with . . . women who seek to outwit their cultural fates." This book is part of "The American Novel Series," although neither work treated is a novel (see *vi* below).

In *Henry James and the Morality of Fiction* (Peter Lang) Greg W. Zacharias collects four essays he published in 1990, on *Roderick Hudson, Washington Square, The Awkward Age,* and *The Golden Bowl* (see *ALS 1990,* pp. 122–24, 126), and adds two original essays, on *The Bostonians* and *The Princess Casamassima.* His thesis is that in the James canon "the moral is so closely bound to the aesthetic and to the social that if one admits James's interest in the aesthetic, one should also admit his interest in the social and thus in the moral." Zacharias examines Jamesian moral insights generated by "recurrent tropes" in some nonfictional works as well as in the above-listed novels. He suggests that central relationships in these novels involve the age-old mentor/novice conflict and "power" used therein for good or ill. He relates the symbolic significance of such relationships to similar but more explicit items in James's nonfictional writings. The ultimate message of the Master concerns living more fully and considerately.

iv Criticism, General Essays

Malcolm Kelsall in *The Great Good Place: The Country House and English Literature* (Columbia) links country estates in *The Portrait of a Lady, The Princess Casamassima,* and *The Spoils of Poynton,* with such estates appearing in British literature. He pays James the compliment of taking his title from James's story "The Great Good Place." Alex Zwerdling in "The European Capitals of American Culture" (*WilsonQ* 17, i: 126–36) includes James among other American expatriates of his era and later who created, mostly in London and Paris, a new American literature which non-Americans could and did appreciate.

Jonathan Freedman in "Trilling, James, and the Uses of Cultural Criticism" (*HJR* 14: 141–50) discusses the uses of "cultural criticism" found in James in the service of society as it "generates" "forms of representation" to "speak its norms, fears, and hopes." James "uniquely . . . created a rhetoric and erected a stance for the American cultural critic." Freedman focuses on Lionel Trilling, "a crucial . . . American Jewish intellectual," who "reconstructs James as a proleptic version of himself": both engaged in "the social project" of conquering class restrictions through literary endeavor. Freedman comments tellingly on anti-Semitism, James, and Trilling.

Leland S. Person, Jr., in "James's Homo-Aesthetics: Deploying Desire in the Tales of Writers and Artists" (*HJR* 14: 188–203) contends that "as James examines the relation between male authors and their audience . . . [in "The Author of Beltraffio," "The Middle Years," and "The Death of the Lion"], he consistently imagines enabling and empowering male readers, who enjoy an intimate, closeted relationship with the Master writers whose work they admire." Fine, but see what follows. Dencombe's "fingering" his text becomes a "metaphor . . . of masturbation and homosexual penetration"; when the "voyeuristic" narrator sees Neil Paraday's new manuscript, "his . . . desiring gaze transforms Paraday and text into father and mother and the creative transaction between them into a scene of insemination"; etc.

In the process of reviewing four recent books on James, Ruth Bernard Yeazell in "Demystifying the Master" (*AmLH* 5: 314–25) urges us to be "skeptical of claims to aesthetic detachment and autonomy" in James, among others.

v Criticism: Individual Novels

Cheryl B. Torsney argues in "Henry James, Charles Sanders Peirce, and the Fat Capon: Homoerotic Desire in The *American*" (*HJR* 14: 166–78) that James and Peirce tried being a "homoerotic couple" in Paris in 1875–76, that their relationship is echoed when Christopher Newman in *The*

American becomes the wanted object of the Rev. Benjamin Babcock, and that the minister's frustrated love is "fetishized" when Newman sends Babcock an ivory statuette representing a monk with a capon peeping through his gown.

Ian F. A. Bell's *Washington Square: Styles of Money* (Twayne) is an upscale study guide to *Washington Square*. Bell places the novel in its historical context, regards it as important for showing James trying solid Balzacian realism, and summarizes its critical reception. Bell shows how it depicts the social effects of contemporary commercial practices, discusses how James's handling of "time and space" exposes Manhattan— indeed, American—social and financial turbulence in the 1830s and 1840s, and regards the gold-bracketed mirror Morris Townsend glances at as symbolic of "gilt" and "guilt." Bell sees Austin Sloper's aphorisms as evidence of bourgeois "abstraction and paralysis," balances his "poor" daughter's bright dresses against her "quietude" and "immobility," too tolerantly finds Townsend's performance "natural," given his circumstances, and analyzes the main characters' manners and "fibs."

Two essays concern *The Portrait of a Lady*. Evoking George Poulet and Paul de Man, Jonathan Warren takes too much time in "Imminence and Immanence, Isabel Archer's Temporal Predicament in *The Portrait of a Lady*" (*HJR* 14: 1–16) to distinguish between the Isabel as "an icon of imminence confounded by stasis" (and one ever reluctant to prove her "vast potential") and the Isabel who (once she "realizes Osmond's and Merle's duplicitous history") adopts "a radically imminent posture" by promising Pansy she will return to her. In "An 'attendance upon . . . gentlemen': The BBC Video Adaptation of *The Portrait of a Lady*" (*HJR* 14: 179–87) Anthony J. Mazzella contrasts the novel with three screen adaptations of it—the 1968 BBC telecast by Jack Pulman and James Cellan Jones, the four-hour 1991 home video edition of the telecast, and the shortened 1988 "special limited viewing in Dallas" of the video—and concludes that Ralph Touchett is too central on screen; laments the omission of Isabel Archer's vigil scene; and says that the 1972 Pulman-Jones adaptation of *The Golden Bowl* was better partly because it used the voice-over technique.

Two essays also concern *The Bostonians*. In "Basil, Olive, and Verena: *The Bostonians* and the Problem of Politics" (*ArQ* 49, i: 49–72) Anthony Scott sees *The Bostonians* as representing "the social and personal identities of women as political issues"—all this "to . . . understand James' relation to feminism," which here is "public and contestatory," and which drags in family, marriage, and gender-identity concerns. Scott counters biased readings by contending that James "systematically destabilizes all the terms—political, narrative, and sexual"—deployed in the novel. Scott shows that the terms "power, possession, and sexual identity" are relevant also in works of the major phase, during which time feminism became unanswerably incoherent for James. Kristin Boudreau in "Narrative Sympathy in *The Bostonians*" (*HJR* 14: 17–33) theorizes that James was tempted to "heal," that is, revise, the novel to "heal his relationship with his [indifferent if not hostile] audience" and thus heal himself. Although he did not revise and include it in his New York Edition, he did seem to acknowledge adverse criticism of early serialized installments when he "doctored his text in order to create . . . sympathetic readers" of later installments. William James and reviewers responded by preferring those later chapters. Boudreau suggests that James first saw *The Bostonians* as an ironic tale of American social conditions but later made it into a melodramatic romance.

Sheila Teahan offers two essays this year. First, she demonstrates in "*What Maisie Knew* and the Improper Third Person" (*SAF* 21: 127–40) that, despite prefatory and notebook commentary that Maisie Farange is his point of view and consciousness, James has his adult third-person narrator expand her infantile vocabulary and thus, with the outrageous help of "first-person narratorial intrusions," create "the knowledge it [his novel] appears [merely] to reflect." Second, in "The Abyss of Language in *The Wings of the Dove*" (*HJR* 14: 204–14) Teahan shows that Milly Theale is both the thematic exemplar of Christian love and the cause of the breakdown of the "love" of Merton Densher and Kate Croy. More subtly, that "break . . . mirrors a similar break . . . between theme and causation in the novel." Teahan neatly inserts explications of several chiastic images—shipbreak and siren, line and curve, turn, broken sentence, snapping coil, two-faced coin—used to bridge fissures in James's text. A shorter essay on *The Wings of the Dove* is "Milly Theale's London" (*HJR* 14: 215–22) by Chris Brown, who locates all places mentioned in the novel, pinpoints where possible "unplaced" offices of Sir Luke Strett and Merton Densher's digs, and pushes all geotopographic implications to their figurative borders.

In her introduction to a new edition of *The Awkward Age* (Knopf) Cynthia Ozick theorizes that James reveals that "he knows too much, and much more than we, or he, can possibly take in," only in post-1895 works, including *The Awkward Age*. Ozick makes much of three events in James's life—Woolson's suicide (1894), the private printing of Alice James's diary (1894), and the failure of *Guy Domville* (1895). Ozick turns up the sociable carpet of *The Awkward Age* to reveal the lice, calling them "shards and particles of James's chronicle of crisis."

The Ambassadors is never under the rug. It would wrap a puzzle in a figurative carpet to spin comments on Olga McDonald Meidner's criticism in "'What Strether Knew': 'The Novel' as Art Form" (*BJA* 93: 152–61). She feels that Ruth Bernard Yeazell in *Language and Knowledge in the Late Novels of Henry James* (see *ALS 1976*, p. 100) and Maud Ellmann in "'The Intimate Difference': Power and Representation in *The Ambassadors*" (see *ALS 1985*, p. 112) "show an indifference to theory" because in commenting on *The Ambassadors* they seem to "forget . . . that Lambert Strether is not a man . . . but a piece of narrative fiction." But did they forget? Richard Salmon in "The Secret of the Spectacle: Epistemology and Commodity Display in *The Ambassadors*" (*HJR* 14: 43–54) "explore[s] the ways in which the cultural forms of commodity display and advertising shape Jamesian epistemology in *The Ambassadors*." Advertising becomes a theme in the novel, as commodities are strategically represented. Strether visually consumes things in Paris. Books are "a paradigm of Strether's [sexual and] hermeneutic desire."

Two essays concern *The Golden Bowl*. In "Object Lessons: Reading the Museum in *The Golden Bowl*," pp. 199–229 in *Famous Last Words: Changes in Gender and Narrative Closure* (Virginia) Stephen D. Arata relates the novel to late 19th-century "fine-arts museums"—now with originals not copies, and stressing aesthetics not data—and the "commodification" of women and art; and he sees Maggie, who quits liking the Prince's arty aura, as rejecting the new museum ideology to preserve a kind of marriage tableau (Maggie *cum* Prince and Adam *cum* Charlotte, no longer Prince *cum* Charlotte or Adam *cum* Maggie). Thus, Maggie becomes more tableau curator than artist but happily also more than a collectible. Hugh Stevens, after assembling introductory sex/gender buzz-fuzz from Sigmund Freud et al., asserts in his "Sexuality and the Aesthetic in *The Golden Bowl*" (*HJR* 14: 55–71) that Maggie, initially virginal and passive, assumes "agency," tightens her sexual bond with husband, and banishes too loving daddy and too successful rival to a fantasy place of "primal femaleness," that is, America. But Maggie does so by dissipating "savage sexuality" through an aesthetically pleasing adherence to the genteel lie that her marriage is dandy.

Susan S. Williams in "The Tell-Tale Representation: James and *The*

Sense of the Past" (*HJR* 14: 72–86) suggests that *"The Sense of the Past . . .* marks a return to a recurrent theme in his work, that of the portrait as a revelatory force"; provides "the end point of James's career-long interest in portraits"; and details "his interest . . . [in] the dialectic between intimacy and distance" underlining the ability of portraits to represent character. Among much else, Williams discusses James's attitude toward the past as both aid and prison, and toward portraits as time-stoppers both permitting and inhibiting consciousness of the past.

vi   Criticism: Tales

Two essays concern "The Last of the Valerii." In "Swept Away: Henry James, Margaret Fuller, and 'The Last of the Valerii,'" pp. 32–53 in *Readers in History,* John Carlos Rowe notes that James first thought of Margaret Fuller as a laughable Transcendental failure because of too much "masculine will," but that he later saw her as a potent inspiration for the queenly, majestic Juno statue excavated by Fuller-like Martha's husband Count Valerio. Digging psychologically not biographically, Suzi Naiburg in "Archaic Depths in Henry James's 'The Last of the Valerii'" (*HJR* 14: 151–65) interprets the unearthing of Juno as a warning to the callow when they poke around in the "depths of the psyche." She ponders Valerio's paganism, his statue as a Juno rather than a Venus, the "dwarfish" excavator's Jungian wisdom, and Juno's broken hand. The tale "demonstrates the necessity of establishing a conscious relation to such primitive drives and archaic depths lest they produce obsessions."

Kenneth Graham and Robert Weisbuch treat "Daisy Miller" in *New Essays on* Daisy Miller *and* The Turn of the Screw (see *iii* above). To Graham in *"Daisy Miller*: Dynamics of an Enigma" (pp. 35–63), the story embodies the Jamesian principle of "the obsessive building of expressive shapes and words around an enigma that cannot yield itself to direct expression or to direct knowledge." We learn about Daisy through a detailed painterly foreground and background and through her brother, Randolph, her parasol and fan, etc. The pictorial here "contradict[s] the purely verbal," including "the dialogue's cleverly theatrical deployment of question-and-answer . . . persiflage" swirling about Daisy. In Weisbuch's "Winterbourne and the Doom of Manhood in *Daisy Miller*" (pp. 65–89) Winterbourne, the pseudoaristocratic, noncompetitive expatriate, is flaccidized by notions of propriety and is hence unable to match Daisy's innocent Yankee git-up. Outstanding is Weisbuch's aside that Daisy's "sharp, hard[-voiced]" brother, a kind of "walk-ing penis," is Winterbourne's most prominent alter ego. (I dream that Christopher Pearse Cranch caricatured Randolph for Ralph Waldo Emerson's *Dial*.)

Here comes more on sex. Helen Hoy in "Homotextual Duplicity in Henry James's 'The Pupil'" (*HJR* 14: 34–42) says she is going to have fun by reading "The Pupil" as a homotext, widely defined as a work "in which attention to issues of same-sex orientation proves meaningful, profitable, or provocative." So she discusses the "revealing and con-cealing . . . 'transformational' movement between deep structure and surface structure" in "The Pupil." Morgan Moreen is ill and only 11 years old at first. The Moreens are enigmatic and thus are "texts to be trans-lated." Should we think the badly clothed Morgan will be viewed as Pemberton's pederasty victim? Is the tutor's attitude toward Mrs. Moreen misogynistic? As the Moreen family disintegrates, Hoy sees "the homo-text code . . . deconstruct itself disconcertingly." Morgan's death prevents the half-desired "cohabitation" of tutor and pupil and therefore may be read "as a tortuous gesture in the direction of re-establishing the . . . threatened cover story."

Adam Bresnick's "The Artist That Was Used Up: Henry James's 'The Private Life'" (*HJR* 14: 87–98) postulates that "if James's aesthetic theory depends on a notion of disinterest that in turn presupposes a coherent, singular artistic subject, the artists in James's aesthetic allegories find themselves fundamentally split by an imaginary identification with their artwork that problemizes the notion of 'the real,' just as it throws a wrench into the ostensibly unproblematic ethical function of art." Bres-nick analyzes plot elements, discusses "the uncanny" encounter of the narrator and Clare Vawdrey's spinoff self writing in his dark room. The narrator wonders whether Vawdrey is an example of a profound artist— "simultaneously . . . most total and . . . least substantial," partly a "conduit" to present nature as art, and partly so superhuman that his body needs a "doubling that in turn allegorizes his genius." The story itself gets doubled as Alpine realism and allegorical fantasy, with Lord Mellifont "the artist as public performer" and Vawdrey as "private."

Three more turns around "The Turn of the Screw." Millicent Bell and David McWhirter treat it in *New Essays on* Daisy Miller *and* The Turn of the Screw (see *iii* above). Bell in "Class, Sex, and the Victorian Gov-erness: James's *The Turn of the Screw*" (pp. 91–119), finding "reason . . . to set this story in the frame of . . . the 'governess novel,'" surveys both the plight of English governesses in the 1840s and 1850s, and also in a few providential and silver-fork governess novels of the era. In James's story, "the Master and Quint and Miles are one and the Governess, Miss Jessel, and Flora are also one," because "James saw the ambiguity in masculine and class hegemony and saw the Governess . . . as a sympathetic . . . person . . . made dangerous to her society by her 'status incongruity' and her nostalgia for the lost security of the class into which she had been born." McWhirter begins his "In the 'Other House' of Fiction: Writing, Authority, and Femininity in *The Turn of the Screw*" (pp. 121–48) by praising previous critical efforts "to resolve . . . discomforting uncertainties" and "defuse . . . ambiguity" attending the story. Then he contrasts "writer" (expansive, explosive, feminine) and "author" (controlling, limiting, masculine, ergo authoritative) and argues that James concedes his overworked governess narrative authority so as "to express and explore his own ambiguous, embarrassing sexual position." Richard Sawyer in " 'What's your title?'—*The Turn of the Screw*" (*SSF* 30: 53–61) argues that its prologue manipulates us into accepting "The Turn of the Screw" as a ghost story. But the title may imply that we should see the governess as an inquisitorial turner of thumbscrews to save the souls of her charges. Sawyer loads James's three uses of "turn . . . turn . . . " with significance. Like a victim of the Inquisition, Miles at the end confesses, names his source of evil, dies, and is saved.

James, Arnold Weinstein says, pervades his *Nobody's Home*; however, Weinstein only glances at "The Turn of the Screw," "The Beast in the Jungle," and "The Jolly Corner" in discussing "language as the field in which . . . freedom is deployed," while adducing much evidence from elsewhere to show what is obvious enough, that "time and space" are freedom's enemies.

"James's Stories and His Characters: A Reading of 'The Beast in the Jungle' and 'The Bench of Desolation' " (*CQ* 22: 43–59) by James Griffiths scarcely concerns the two named stories. The thesis seems to be that *James* does not fully tell stories about his characters because he does not accord his characters the ability to tell the whole truth when *they* tell their stories.

vii Criticism: Nonfiction

In "Mr. James in Motion" (*NYTBR* 12 Dec., pp. 1, 32–33, 37–38) William F. Buckley, Jr., reviews the two volumes in the Library of

America devoted to James's travel books (see *i* above); notes that various locales seen by James are "described and probed by a belletrist with a mighty, enchanted caduceus in hand"; and says that James presents preferences for certain countries, places, and people without being either "an epicurean or a snob" but sometimes is "too much" of "a bloody genius." James Buzard in "A Continent of Pictures: Reflections on the 'Europe' of Nineteenth-Century Tourists" (*PMLA* 108: 30–44) finds hints in James's 1870s travel essays of unease because his typical "Europe-leaning American" finds too much harmonizing culture in Europe at critical variance from monotonous work and social values back home.

Stanley Tick is positive in his "Positives and Negatives: Henry James vs. Photography" (*NCS* 7: 69–101) about James's negative attitude toward the art and use of photography. Tick downgrades most of the photographs by Alvin Langdon Coburn for the New York Edition. James, who allegedly hamstrung Coburn by restrictive orders, opined that illustrations should be " 'mere optical symbols or echoes, expressions of no particular thing in the text . . . .' " Tick calls the photographs "indifferent," "poor," "commonplace," "bland," "vague," "inexpressive," "toneless," "remote," "modest," "undramatic," "generalized," "uninteresting," "unindividualized," "run-of-the-mill," "dull," "insignificant," "lifeless," and "unremarkable." We get his point but can still disagree. In the process, Tick rebuts earlier laudatory comments by Charles Higgins (see *ALS 1982*, p. 119) and Ralph Bogardus (*ALS 1985*, pp. 109–10) on the photographs.

W. R. Martin and Warren U. Ober in "The 'Inexhaustible Sensibility' of Henry James's Deathbed Dictations" (*Neophil* 77: 163–65) relate James's last dictations to his admiration for Napoleon and Honoré de Balzac, and show the dying artist as still "struggling to create fiction" via creative recollection of memories, history, and snippets from literature. This piece gets my vote as the best short essay on James in 1993. What a finely etched, exemplary gem.

University of Pittsburgh

8   Pound and Eliot

George Kearns and Cleo McNelly Kearns

The Pound studies that draw particular attention this year are Vincent Sherry's consistently interesting *Pound, Lewis, and Radical Modernism,* along with the collection of 19 essays gathered in *Ezra Pound and Europe* (Rodopi), ed. Richard Taylor and Claus Melchior, a selection from papers given at the Fourteenth International Ezra Pound Conference held at Brunnenburg, Italy, in 1991. The outstanding Eliot contribution is Ronald Schuchard's edition of the Clark Lectures. Several of the year's books and essays treat Pound and Eliot and are discussed under both authors.

i Pound

a. Text, Biography, and Bibliography   The most important previously unavailable text is Pound's version of Motokiyo's Noh play *Takasago,* included in Ira B. Nadel's ed. of *The Letters of Ezra Pound to Alice Corbin Henderson* (Texas, pp. 110–17). It is of interest not only for the "pine of Takasago" in Canto 4, but because at an early stage in projecting the *Cantos* Pound thought the theme of his poem was to be "roughly the theme" of Motokiyo's play. Relevant information is supplied in Nadel's introduction (pp. xxii–xxiv). Another newly found text reveals a collaboration between one of the oddest couples in modern letters, Pound and Vita Sackville-West: a short masque, "The Banquet," presented in 1916 for a wartime charity with Pound taking one of the roles, surrounded by titled ladies. Sackville-West concocted the scenario, Pound the dialogue. The inconsequential text and its history are in Archie Henderson, "Pound, the War, and 'The Banquet'" (*Paideuma* 22, i–ii: 57–69). Other trivia include two short poems and a brief satiric verse included in a letter to Henderson (pp. 145–47) and a college humor squib on Yeats's Irishisms in A. Walton Litz and Omar Pound's "An Unpublished Poem of 1909" (*Paideuma* 22, i–ii: 9–10).

Pound's correspondence with Henderson, the associate editor of *Poetry,* is of great interest, made more so by Nadel's generously detailed introduction and notes. Most of the 78 letters date from 1912–17, and to read them gives the pleasant illusion of being present as Pound presided, a busy self-appointed minister, over modernist writing. The directness of his letters to Henderson, whom he respected as editor and poet in her own right, is remarkable. These are letters between peers (as contrasted, say, with Pound's patronizing blasts at Harriet Monroe); Henderson appears as a woman of notable intelligence and independence of mind. Another woman who could talk back to him was Olivia Rossetti Agresti, of the Pre-Raphaelite Rossettis, who lived in Italy most of her life, whose interests in economics and Fascism created a bond with the poet that was both professional and personal, and whose extensive correspondence with Pound touched on almost all of his political, religious, and economic concerns. The letters, with a sketch of Agresti's life, are amply surveyed in Demetres Tryphonopolous's "Ezra Pound and Olivia Rossetti Agresti: Their Correspondence" (*Ezra Pound and Europe,* pp. 93–104). Pound's ambivalent thoughts about Hitler are noted and sharply countered by Agresti, for whom Hitler was a "homicidal maniac"; the poet admired the dictator's "extraordinary flashes of lucidity," yet found him "Crazy as a coot, as Mus/noted on first meeting him." James Generoso's "I Reckon You Pass, Mr. Wuddwudd" allows only a sketchy view of Pound's 1933–37 correspondence with the American historian William E. Woodward (*Paideuma* 22, i–ii: 35–55).

Ira B. Nadel's detailed account of the young poet's first travels in Europe, between the ages of 13 and 26, " 'Nothing but a Nomad': Ezra Pound in Europe (1898–1911)," while interesting as biography, is more interesting for Nadel's skill at showing how impressions from the travels left traces in Pound's work for the rest of his life (*Ezra Pound and Europe,* pp. 19–31). Mary de Rachewiltz tells stories of her father as book collector, and of the vicissitudes of his books before and after his death; she provides a list of his books that remain at Brunnenburg in "Ezra Pound's Library: What Remains" (*Ezra Pound and Europe,* pp. 1–18).

b. General Studies Vincent Sherry has the gift of never writing an uninteresting page in *Pound, Lewis, and Radical Modernism* (Oxford). It is impossible in a brief note to capture the richness of this lucidly, gracefully written book, which, among other things, is surely the most thorough and original study of the influence of Wyndham Lewis on Pound. Yet it has larger implications than for Pound/Lewis: it is an important contribution to the history of literary modernism and political aesthetics. Sherry has identified a discourse that runs from the later-18th century well into the 20th, in which hearing and sight, the musical and the visual, are set in opposition. "Whereas the democratic ear merges," leading to "mob bonding," the "aristocratic eye divides," as the eye "achieves the distinctions on which clear conceptual intelligence relies," thus providing "the emblem and instrument of a ruling intellectual elite." One is reminded of how silly and groundless a discourse can be, yet how tenacious, spreading like kudzu. Sherry puts it more politely, as he traces the permutations of the discourse, its variations reminding us that the writers who employed it "all are offering an imaginative hermeneutic of the senses, not the findings of hard science." It is more than an imaginative hermeneutic for Sherry, rather an extraordinarily useful one for fresh, illuminating readings of Pound's poetry and prose. Chapter 1, "From the Continent to England, 1889–1925," develops the tale of sound/sight *idéologie*, with interesting comments on the nature of ideology itself, as it passes through such writers as Sorel, Benda, and Gourmont to arrive at Anglo-American modernism. Chapter 2 discusses Pound's work from 1908 to 1920, chapter 4 from 1924 to 1939. Discussions in other chapters include imagism, vorticism and symbolism, and original readings of "The Coming of War: Actaeon," Cantos 4–6; *Mauberley* (with important contributions to the endless debates about "Envoi" and "Medallion"); and Cantos 29–30, read through Lewis. An epilogue comments on Pound's later years and the "waning influence of the single force that gave at least an impression of stability to his social sensibility: the aesthetic. [His] jeremiads are, in a full sense of the word, artless. That history will betray *clercs* who intrude into politics is a truth Lewis grasped with masterful despair in the 1930s—its recognition perhaps the best influence the Enemy could have exerted on his old friend."

Demetres P. Tryphonopolous has been Leon Surette's student and research assistant. Both have now published books on Pound's involvement with the occult, each refers generously to the work of the other, and their research is perforce overlapping. Tryphonopolous's *The Celestial Tradition: A Study of Pound's* The Cantos (Wilfrid Laurier) remains the more strictly informative, while Surette's *The Birth of Modernism: Ezra Pound, T. S. Eliot, W. B. Yeats, and the Occult* (McGill-Queens) is wider-ranging, more speculative, and, because of its grander claims, more problematical. Most of the "occult" writers cited have been mentioned or even extensively studied in relation to Pound, but the larger story of the complex crossings in what Surette calls a "babble of occult and mystical speculators and revisers of history" has never been assembled with the sweep of these volumes. Surette and Tryphonopolous take us into such various hermeticisms as gnosticism, the Cabala, the Rosicrucians, Swedenborg, and theosophy; through the thought and practices of many of Pound's associates, among them H. D., Olivia and Dorothy Shakespear, Yeats, G. R. S. Mead, Allen Upward, the Orage of the *New Age,* and Gurdjieff; and to figures behind the "traditions" such as Péladan, Schuré, and Gabriele Rossetti. While it is true that critics have often been embarrassed by, or have downplayed the surround of the occult in Pound, it is an understandable exaggeration for writers so steeped in this research to claim that so little attention has been given it. With these volumes at hand, it certainly can no longer be ignored, although this mass of information will remain open to interpretation. Tryphonopolous sees the *Cantos* "as palingenesis," a poem "intended to be read as are the Hermetic writings on rebirth," to produce an initiation of the reader. Like the Hermetic texts, the *Cantos* "have an outer or exoteric form whose 'meaning' is for general consumption; but the poem can also be understood by the initiates or illuminated souls who are in possession of *gnosis* as an inner or esoteric revelation." He gives particular attention to Cantos 17, 27, 47, 90, and 91, often with useful readings, especially of G. R. S. Mead's theory of the "subtle body" as it surfaces in Canto 91. Surette, in addition to extensive claims for the occult tradition in the *Cantos,* offers a chapter on "Nietzsche, Wagner and Myth." Some of his claims are hard to accept, such as those concerning relations between the occult and Social Credit, and Pound's editing of *The Waste Land.*

Gail McDonald's *Learning to Be Modern: Pound, Eliot, and the American University* (Clarendon) is an alert, thoroughly researched study of all aspects of Pound's relations with education: his own schooling; his very brief tenure as an academic; his scorn for university education in his time as he understood it; and his lifelong effort to educate all who would listen in what he thought they should know. McDonald keeps her eye scrupulously on her subject, and she avoids making any large-scale claims about culture, history, or modernism. Modesty is hardly the mark of Cary Wolfe's supremely confident demonstration of sophisticated theoretical left discourse, *The Limits of American Literary Ideology in Pound and*

Emerson (Cambridge). Wolfe makes gestures at distancing himself from cruder forms of Marxist analysis, yet familiar bêtes noirs remain—the transcendent, the organic, the privileging of "nature" to suppress the value of labor, politically disabling ethical idealism, reactionary populism, etc. Individualism is the central enemy, as Pound's "cultural project" reproduces Emersonian ideology "in striking detail." The "central organizing structure of the economic and ideological totality of Pound's and Emerson's America [is] private property," and "the liberal subject, constituted as it is by the structure and logic of private property, is not pluralist but antisocial to its very core." The answer to "structures of oppression and alienation lay not in collective economic transformation but rather within the individual who could somehow escape his or her economic determinations by holding fast to the vital realm of culture." Pound does not stand a chance in this arena, where he is billed as "nothing if not middle-class," a defender of the "economic epicenter of his own class interest," whose ideograms are "totalizing"; imagism is a call for a "modernist cultural self-reliance" (although no single imagist poem is mentioned, nor its pernicious effects demonstrated).

c. Relation to Other Writers   In "The Hooking of Distant Antennae: Ez Po & Kit-Kat" (*Ezra Pound and Europe*, pp. 119–29) John Solt reviews Pound's long association, from 1936 until his years of silence, with the avant-garde Japanese poet and man-about-culture, Kitasono Katue, who became his principal source of information about Japan. Solt reviews Pound's considerable reputation in Japan in the 1930s, and he examines some of his struggles with the Chinese and Japanese languages. Unfortunately, he says little about "Kit-Kat," his thought, politics, or art. Ernesto Livorno's "Ezra Pound and Giuseppi Ungaretti: Between Haiku and Futurism" (*Ezra Pound and Europe*, pp. 131–44) shows that the poets' "earlier poetic and critical production reveals astounding similarities, which make of Ungaretti a poet not so alien to the Imagist-Vorticist Pound," largely through their common interest in Japanese verse and in the poetics of the fragment. Pound's extensive influence on the work of a contemporary British poet-critic is examined in Avril Horner, "The 'Intelligence at Bay': Ezra Pound and Geoffrey Hill" (*Paideuma* 22, i–ii: 243–54).

d. The Shorter Poems and Translations   Attempts to solve the problem of how to read the lyrics which end the two major parts of *Mauberley*,

"Envoi" and "Medallion," appear endless, as if Pound had unintentionally left us with a critical *aporia*. Helen V. Emmitt's contribution to
the debate, informed by a feminist sensibility, is among the more suggestive. In " 'Make Strong Old Dreams': Ezra Pound and European Aesthet-
icism" (*Ezra Pound and Europe*, pp. 191–206) Emmitt contests Ronald
Bush's claim that the poem ends "on a note that affirms the erotic and
redemptive claims of art," for the "medallion is a purely aesthetic *objet
d'art*, not even a real portrait of a real woman but a version of another
version of Venus." A valuable close reading of another much-debated
section of *Mauberley* is Pamela E. Hurley's "Ezra Pound's 'Yeux Glau-
ques' " (*Paideuma* 22, i–ii: 191–200). In his article on Pound and Ungaretti already noted, Ernesto Livorno offers what is surely the most careful reading we have of "Heather" from *Lustra*, as he examines the use of
"petals" in "In a Station of the Metro" and other early poems. Through a
study of the original sonnet and its intertextuality, G. Schmidt in "Rome/
From the French of Joachim Du Bellay: A European Perspective" (*Ezra
Pound in Europe*, pp. 61–67) looks at the creative misreadings of Pound's
translation.

e. The *Cantos* So many essays on the *Cantos* are concerned with
sources, ideology, and the history of their composition that Frank Lentricchia's "Ezra Pound's American Book of Wonders" (*SAQ* 92: 387–415)
is refreshing. Written for an audience probably not too familiar with the
Cantos, it is an excellent essay for students, corrective as it is of cruder
readings. Lentricchia thinks Pound feared that he lacked the essential
virtù of strong poets, that he had no originality, so the figure "Ezra
Pound" appears in the poem as "a generous capacity for reception, a
subjectivity virtually transparent . . . a mirror for others." There is no
unified vision, no single narrative, no stable foundation of concepts, and
so forth, making the work a failure "by the measure of the ambitious
desire of culture-making that moved [its] writing," yet for its failures "we
should probably be grateful." Lentricchia's undoubtedly problematic
thesis leads to a description of the poem as "an indescribable mixture
whose ingredients of anti-Semitism and fascism are not of the essence
because, in this experiment, nothing is of the essence." The essay contains many fine observations, for example, that the real subject of *Drafts
and Fragments* is "desire become palpable." Another approach to poetics
is John Xiros Cooper's "Music as Symbol and Structure in Pound's *Pisan
Cantos* and Eliot's *Four Quartets*" (*Ezra Pound and Europe*, pp. 177–

89). Cooper employs Adorno's theories of music and his opposition of Schoenberg/Stravinsky, finding Pound on the more of-the-age Schoenbergian school, "musicat[ing] verbal space within which a radical poetics continuously renews itself," demonstrating that "in every historical moment, no matter how fragmented, future possibilities can be glimpsed." Poor Eliot comes off as Stravinsky in this binary, "the terminal point of a mastery without issue, restoration of the obsolete, namely, a matured form of the Catholic aesthetic infantilism of the 1890s." Take or leave the comparison, the remarks on the poetics of the Pisans are valuable. More theoretical, a surprisingly convincing approach to the *Cantos* as poetry is Sylvan Esh's "Pound and Jakobson: The Metaphorical Principle in *The Cantos*" (*Paideuma* 22, i–ii: 129–43). Arguing against those who find the poem primarily metonymic, Esh makes an interesting case for the "ideogrammic method [as] the metaphoric impulse at its most expansive."

Building on the work of Peter Stoicheff, Ronald Bush, with extensive work in the archives, gives what sounds like the last word, if there can be such, on the history of the writing, editing, and transmission of the "at least six different versions of *Drafts and Fragments* and conclusion to the Cantos" in "'Unstill, ever turning': The Composition of Ezra Pound's Drafts and Fragments" (*Ezra Pound and Europe*, pp. 223–42). Massimo Mandolini Pesaresi, learned in Italian traditions, sets aside ideology to defend the Italian Cantos as poetry in "Pound's Admirable Presenza in the Italian Language: Cantos LXXII and LXXIII" (*Ezra Pound and Europe*, pp. 215–21). Backgrounds for obscure references are given in Omar Pound's "Canto 113: Tweddell, Men Against Death and Paul de Kruif" (*Paideuma* 22, i–ii: 173–79) and Colin McDowell's "'In the Minor Key of an Epoch': Georges Herbiet," mentioned in Cantos 80 and 105 (*Paideuma* 22, iii: 93–100).

ii Eliot

a. Text, Biography, and Bibliography Eliot felt strongly that his 1926 Clark Lectures should not be published in their unrevised form. Unavailable except in manuscript at the Houghton and King's College libraries, the lectures unfold a coherent theory of Metaphysical poetry and shed great light on Eliot's personal and poetic development. The taboo overcome, they are now available as *The Varieties of Metaphysical Poetry* (Harcourt), meticulously edited by Ronald Schuchard. Schuchard suggests that their publication "will have as much impact on our revaluation of [Eliot's] critical mind as did the facsimile edition of *The Waste Land* (1971) on our comprehension of his poetic mind," and he is no doubt correct. Although much scholarly work on Eliot's criticism and poetry does take these lectures into account, it is still a surprising and salutary experience to encounter them again, for they are important both for the light they shed on Eliot's mind and for their illuminating perspective on a crux in English literary history.

Eliot was not the first to rediscover the Metaphysicals, but he was quick to seize on them and to advance a critical theory in their regard. Indeed, he took the occasion of a review of Grierson's anthology, *Metaphysical Lyrics and Poems of the Seventeenth Century*, to formulate his oft-cited dictum that in the 17th century a "dissociation of sensibility" had set in which—much to the detriment of the poetry, culture, and spirituality of their time—undid the brilliant work of the school of Donne in "transmuting ideas into sensations, of transforming an observation into a state of mind." This dictum cast a long shadow in Eliot criticism, and it continued to circulate long after he had developed a far more nuanced view of the devolution of literary sensibility in the West. The Clark Lectures represent his effort to support and qualify this initial insight by developing a theory of poetry based on the significant literary groupings of Dante and the troubadours for the Middle Ages, Donne and the Metaphysicals proper for the 16th century, and Baudelaire, Laforgue, and Tristan Corbière for the 19th. (All of these were poets with whom Eliot elsewhere more or less explicitly associated his own work.) Eliot reads these groupings of poets over and against the various theories and manuals of meditation and religious discipline of their respective times, showing the reciprocal relationship between poetic method and spiritual practice. Schuchard generously provides the notes and annotations which open up this world of intertextualities to the interested reader, along with much literary history, including documentation of the strong impact made on Eliot by the publication of Mario Praz's *Secentismo e marinismo in Inghilterra*, a copy of which Eliot received for review while he was working on the lectures.

b. General Studies   Gail McDonald's *Learning to Be Modern* has been mentioned with regard to Pound; she documents Eliot's continued direct involvement with and impact on the university, which, of course, was stronger than Pound's. She offers an informed view of the young Eliot's experience of formal education, and she provides a context for his later views on culture and society. She may, however, miss some of the tensions that cross and crisscross the relationship between poet and university, especially with regard to Eliot's decision to leave the American academy behind and become an avant-garde poet in England. The provincial, constrained, and genteel academic ethos which helped to prompt this decision is probably better conveyed by the philosopher George Santayana (who preceded Eliot in leaving Harvard for Europe) and even by portions of the novels of Henry James than by a review of more sober sources from within the pale. One misses here the sense of just how desperately Eliot wanted to *get out of there.*

Leon Surette's *The Birth of Modernism* attempts to restore to the literary history of modernism a lost dimension: the profound involvement of many if not most of its major figures with the occult. Surette has devoted much research to this study, which uses the term occult with deliberation, although it ranges rather widely in its pursuit. In dealing with Eliot, Surette seeks to restore to his work that part of its matrix which lies in quasitheosophical ideas. Although Eliot's skepticism, his reserve, and his philosophical critique of occult speculation (not to mention his humor on the subject) make him a figure more resistant to this overall project than Surette acknowledges, he does indicate some of Eliot's running interests that have not received their due. Surette's insistence on an occult provenance for, among other things, *The Waste Land* is perhaps overdone, but if it leads to the insight that "sexual encounters" in that poem "exemplify the loss of sanctity suffered by eros rather more clearly than they exemplify a sexual dysfunction," then the sense of strain sometimes generated by this overly recherché study can yield at least some good fruit.

c. Relation to Other Writers After a brief intoxication with Henri Bergson in his early twenties, Eliot almost immediately took a more critical stance toward Bergson's philosophy. M. A. P. Habib's " 'Bergson Resartus' and T. S. Eliot's Manuscript" (*JHI* 54: 255–76) deals with Bergson's influence on Eliot during this early period of quick surrender and recovery. Habib paraphrases and clarifies the philosophical argument contra Bergson which Eliot advances in one of his unpublished papers and provides an intellectual and cultural context for his encounter with Bergsonian thought. Having taken Eliot's formal philosophical position into account, Habib is then able to make a persuasive case for the continued influence of Bergson on Eliot's poetry, even after the prose had taken a critical turn. This is territory already explored by Donald J. Childs (see below and *ALS 1992*, p. 126), but both critics' views are worth reading.

Two of the essays in *Ezra Pound and Europe* (Rodopi) bear on Eliot in relation to Pound: A. D. Moody's "*Bel Esprit* and the Malatesta Cantos: A Post-*Waste Land* Conjunction of Pound and Eliot" (pp. 79–91) and John Xiros Cooper's "Music and Symbol and Structure in Pound's *Pisan Cantos* and Eliot's *Four Quartets*" (pp. 177–89). Moody's exemplary research into Pound's and Eliot's discussions over a scheme for supporting writers (Eliot among them) reveals their differences in matters ranging from literary politics to attitudes toward death. Moody suggests that Eliot's resistance to what he saw as an "undignified" solicitation of charity and violation of privacy on his behalf, together with the challenge to Pound offered by the antithetical but powerful poetry of *The Waste Land,* allowed Pound to separate "his efforts to organize a renaissance from his attempt to write an epic poem." Eliot here plays midwife to Pound's poem, just as Pound had done for *The Waste Land.* For remarks on Cooper's essay, see the Pound section.

d. The Poems and the Plays   *Words in Time* (Michigan), a new anthology entirely devoted to *Four Quartets,* offers essays by its editor, Edward Lobb, and Denis Donoghue, Lyndall Gordon, Ronald Schuchard, Jewel Spears Brooker, Donald J. Childs, Cleo McNelly Kearns, Michael Levenson, A. Walton Litz, and Louis L. Martz. In "On 'Burnt Norton'" Donoghue discusses the poem with previous canonical readings in mind and much along their lines, but he draws attention to the poem's discursive element and calls for a critical method which will show the poetic possibilities of "discourse." Lobb's "Limitation and Transcendence in 'East Coker'" provides an extended analysis, using the image of the closed room which occurs in much of Eliot's poetry, to explore the difference between solipsism philosophically conceived and solipsism poetically transcended. Gordon's "The American Eliot and 'The Dry Salvages'" returns to the question of Eliot's American roots, which Gordon finds more vital to his poetic achievement than was his European identity. Schuchard in "'If I think, again, of this place': Eliot, Herbert and the Way to 'Little Gidding'" traces the important influence of George Herbert on Eliot. Brooker traces the evolution of Eliot's formal solutions to fragmentation from the construction of a shared reference point in the earlier poem to the indirect emergence of a relational pattern in the later one in "From *The Waste Land* to *Four Quartets:* Evolution of a Method." Childs relates Eliot's pragmatism and his critical interest in mysticism, distinguishing both from Bergsonism, with which they have often been confused, in "Risking Enchantment: The Middle Way between Mysticism and Pragmatism in *Four Quartets*." Kearns's "Negative Theology and Literary Discourse in *Four Quartets:* A Derridean Reading" links Eliot's exploration of the *via negativa* with some rhetorical and conceptual problems in rendering negative or apophatic journeys as analyzed by Derrida. Levenson points out and explores parallels between Eliot's sense of his own discontinuous evolution as a poet and critic, his sense of the way literary history unfolds, and his emerging view of the spiritual life, each entailing loss as well as gain in "The End of Tradition and the Beginning of History." Litz describes the tension between "Repetition and Order in the Wartime *Quartets*" and speculates on their genesis. Martz analyzes the various tones of voice of the *Quartets* from prophetic to intimate, from formal to colloquial in "Origins of Form in *Four Quartets*."

In a prizewinning essay " 'Where are the Eagles and the Trumpets?': The Strange Case of Eliot's Missing Quatrains" (*TCL* 39: 129–52) Nigel Alderman takes up the curious critical problem of Eliot's quatrains of 1917–19. Alderman sees as a revealing test of criticism the relegation of these to minor status, over and against Eliot's own explicit and well-considered positive evaluation. (The quatrains in question include a number of the Sweeney poems.) He points out that academics tend to hate these verses, while practicing poets love them. By deftly applying critical theory to challenge this academic judgment, Alderman attempts not only to do the quatrains justice, but to restore to them—and incidentally to Pound's work along the same lines—what in a phrase cited here Fredric Jameson wonderfully calls the "freshness and virulence of modernizing stylization."

In "Cutting Philomela's Tongue: *The Cocktail Party*'s Cure" (*MD* 36: 396–409) Laura Severin continues the by now well-established vein of *reproof* in Eliot criticism. She argues that by sending such female characters as Celia and Lavinia into exile and silence just when they seek the privileges of speech, Eliot is advocating a return to the repressions of Victorian family life. Severin does not do much with the character of Julia, who does not suit her thesis, but she offers a provocation to criticism that other, more attentive readers may wish to take up.

e. Criticism   Kenneth Asher's "T. S. Eliot and the New Criticism" (*ELWIU* 20: 292–309) places Eliot's uneasy relationship with New Criticism, an enterprise to which his own work was more tangential than might at first appear, in the context of his interest in an alternative presented by Maurras and others. Asher traces this alternative to what he somewhat crudely calls "a reactionary stance traceable in its origin to French anti-revolutionary thought." Eliot would probably have agreed with Asher that the New Criticism, in its attempt to elevate the poem to the status of icon, granted it far more powers than it could readily sustain, especially when its appreciation was largely cut off from a wider tradition of European thought, learning, and debate. To Eliot's own awareness of that wider tradition, the Clark Lectures remain the best witness.

Rutgers University
New Jersey Institute of Technology

9   Faulkner

Alexander J. Marshall, III

Overall, this was a special year for Faulkner criticism, with 93 articles and five book-length studies of respectable quality. However, these impressive numbers are generated by the publication of three *Faulkner Journal* issues (including the double issue on Faulkner and Cultural Studies), the Special Faulkner issue of the *Mississippi Quarterly,* a special *Women's Studies* (Women on Faulkner, Faulkner on Women), and two other book-length collections. While all of this "special" interest is gratifying, it is somewhat disconcerting to see only a handful of essays elsewhere (none, for example, in *AL*). One can only hope that Faulkner studies will continue to thrive even in years without works like *Faulkner, His Contemporaries, and His Posterity* that contains 36 articles, more than a third of all the essays published this year.

i   Bibliography, Editions, Manuscripts, and Biography

The single book-length study in this category is Joel Williamson's *William Faulkner and Southern History* (Oxford), a historian's view of the interrelationships among Faulkner's family, his life, and his work. Most intriguing is the claim that Colonel William C. Falkner had a "shadow family" descended from his slave Emiline Lacy. Williamson argues that Faulkner must have seen the tombstones of the "mulatto Falkners, a stone's throw away from" the monument to his great-grandfather in the Ripley cemetery, but the literary implications are left for others to fully explore. Philip Cohen gives us "'This Hand Holds Genius': Three Unpublished Faulkner Letters" (*MissQ* 47: 479–83) from 1924 concern-

Preparation of this chapter was made possible by a grant from the Walter Williams Craigie Faculty Endowment at Randolph-Macon College.

ing *The Marble Faun,* Sherwood Anderson, and the termination of his career as postmaster. James G. Watson reviews "Faulkner in New Orleans: The 1925 Letters" (*Faulkner, His Contemporaries, and His Posterity,* pp. 196–206), while Violet Harrington Bryan's *Myth of New Orleans* contains a chapter on "The *Double Dealer* Movement and New Orleans as Courtesan in Faulkner's *Mosquitoes* and *Absalom, Absalom!*" (pp. 79–94). Calling New Orleans the "dramatic counterpoint to Yoknapatawpha," Bryan points out that this "sophisticated city of Faulkner's literary apprenticeship, is always associated in his fiction with *modernism*—new philosophical, literary, and artistic trends—and with the courtesan, who was herself of a sophisticated older culture." Finally, the *Faulkner Newsletter* rounds out this year's interest in Faulkner's New Orleans connection by announcing *The Double Dealer*'s rebirth; look for it as a quarterly sponsored by the Pirate's Alley Faulkner Society.

ii Criticism: General

"Faulkner's 'Barn Burning' and O'Connor's 'Everything That Rises Must Converge" (*CLAJ* 36: 371–83) by Michael W. Crocker and Robert C. Evans is useful as a compendium of O'Connor's thoughts on Faulkner's work, though the authors seem correct in playing down the connections between these two particular stories. A more detailed and interesting study of parallels is Margaret D. Bauer's "The Sterile New South: An Intertextual Reading of *Their Eyes Were Watching God* and *Absalom, Absalom!*" (*CLAJ* 36: 384–405). Vivian Wagner examines "Gender, Technology, and Utopia in Faulkner's Airplane Tales" (*ArQ* 49, iv: 79–97) and finds that both "Honor" and *Pylon* "represent moments when mechanical motion is eroticized and made organic, even as organic bodies are made mechanical." Wagner argues that even though these works "buy into the sexism and racism of Modernist technophilia, Faulkner also has fantasies of a different order, which are not entirely reducible to masculinist wish fulfillment and prefascist militarism. At moments in these stories, machines function . . . as the signs and symbols of a liberation from normative gender relations, with airplanes providing a utopian space for articulating this liberation."

Lectures from the 1991 International William Faulkner Symposium have been brought together in *Faulkner, His Contemporaries, and His Posterity,* a collection of generally interesting comparisons of Faulkner and writers who read him or whom he read—or in some cases neither. André

Bleikasten opens up with a look at "Faulkner Among His Peers" (pp. 2–19) such as Proust, Mann, Joyce, Woolf, Kafka, Céline, Beckett, and Nabokov. Lothar Hönnighausen's "The Artist as Decadent Aristocrat or Disturbed Burgher: Looking at Faulkner with the Eyes of a Thomas Mann Reader" (pp. 20–31) compares the two authors' views on artists and siblings affected by familial as well as general decadence. Nicole Moulinoux compares and contrasts personal backgrounds and literary themes in "The Enchantments of Memory: Faulkner and Proust" (pp. 32–40). Ilse Dusoir Lind's comparison, "Faulkner and D. H. Lawrence: A New Legatee" (pp. 56–63), is an avowed attempt "to throw new light upon the nature of the relationship" that has been generally overlooked or ignored. Peter Nicolaisen examines "remarkable parallels" in "Faulkner and Hamsun: The Community of the Soil" (pp. 88–101), while admitting "there is no evidence that [Faulkner] was familiar with" the work of the Norwegian novelist who was much admired as a leading modernist in the 1920s. Mario Materassi compares "Two Southern Gentlemen and Their Unsavory Upstarts: Verga's Mazzaro and Faulkner's Flem Snopes" (pp. 102–09). Winfried Herget's "Julien Green—Faulkner's Franco-Southern Contemporary" (pp. 120–28) really focuses more on Green than on Faulkner. More balanced comparisons are M. Thomas Inge's "Yoknapatawpha on the Don: Faulkner and Sholokhov" (pp. 129–42) and Ekaterina Stetsenko's "W. Faulkner and V. Astafiev: The Problems of Nature and Civilization" (pp. 143–51). Hermann Schlosser looks at "William Faulkner's Influence on Post-War German Literature: Erich Franzen, Wolfgang Koeppen, Alfred Andersch" (pp. 152–60); Igor Maver studies "The Usage of Faulknerian Literary Techniques in Contemporary Slovene Fiction" (pp. 167–73); and Josef Grmela overviews "The Checkered Career of William Faulkner in CzechoSlovakia" (pp. 174–83). Returning to American soil, we have Joseph Blotner's "Nobel Laureate and Poet Laureate: William Faulkner and Robert Penn Warren" (pp. 186–95). John T. Matthews examines the popularity and the influence of Anita Loos's 1925 novel in "Gentlemen Defer Blondes: Faulkner, Anita Loos, and Mass Culture" (pp. 207–21), arguing that "the active process by which Faulkner's art fiction *suppressed* the pressures of contemporary social transformations may be read in his casual attitudes toward popular culture. Those attitudes inform his specific response to Loos's book, and reveal his agreement with the general project of modernism." Furthermore, by "reading Faulkner through Loos"—Matthews focuses on Lena Grove and Eula Varner—"we might also be able to appreciate . . . the mangling and silencing of the Othered voice." Ashley Brown's "Evelyn Scott and Faulkner" (pp. 222–28) examines another popular 1920s novelist who was both influential in the publishing and insightful in her criticism of *The Sound and the Fury*. Stephen Ross's purpose in "Thick-Tongued Fiction: Julia Peterkin and Some Implications of the Dialect Tradition" (pp. 229–44) is "to offer some context from [Faulkner's] contemporary environment that will allow us to better understand Faulkner's black dialect stories." Celso de Oliveira compares "Faulkner and Graciliano Ramos" (pp. 253–59), his contemporary, who "brought a new technical awareness to the Brazilian novel." Philip M. Weinstein examines the implications of " 'Coming unalone': Gesture and Gestation in Faulkner and O'Connor" (pp. 262–75), while Faulkner's influence on a Canadian novelist is the subject of "Faulkner and a Contemporary Feminist Novel: From Faulkner's *The Bear* to Aritha Van Herk's *The Tent Peg*" (pp. 309–16) by Rosella Mamoli Zorzi. In "Remarking Bodies: Divagations of Morrison and Faulkner" (pp. 322–27) Patrick O'Donnell argues that "*Beloved* revisits Faulkner's haunted texts, if we regard 'Faulkner,' for Morrison, not as a name or an 'author' in the intentionalist sense, but as the sign under which certain recognizable fictional strategies are repeated, recontextualized, and, in Sethe's phrase, 'rememoried.' " And "William Faulkner and Gabriel García Márquez: A Fictional Conversation" (pp. 336–48) by François Pitavy compares the Colombian Nobel laureate with the Mississippian he called "my master." Michiko Yoshida analyzes "Kenji Nakagami as Faulkner's Rebellious Heir" (pp. 350–60) in Japanese literature. Jacques Pothier compares what he calls "Southern Modes of Commitment: Faulkner and Rushdie" (pp. 361–71); and Michel Gresset closes this lengthy collection with a look at "Faulkner and the Third World" (pp. 372–82).

iii Criticism: Special Studies

Michael Lahey's study of "Women and Law in Faulkner" (*WS* 22: 517–24) finds that "Faulkner's female characters are most helpless, or most punished for their threat of equality" in that "male-constructed, male-centered . . . institution Faulkner returns to again and again, the law." Jay Watson also focuses on "Faulkner's depiction . . . of the legal vocation and the practice of law; his *Forensic Fictions: The Lawyer Figure in Faulkner* (Georgia) sees legal practice as "extend[ing] from the official space of the courtroom and the professional space of the law office to the farthest reaches of the community." Watson argues that "in the figure of the lawyer Faulkner found his most habitual, and in many ways his most rewarding, authorial surrogate, a fictional alter ego on whom he could project, and through whom explore, numerous and often contradictory aspects of his personal experience, his family background, and his cultural heritage." That meaning-making context is the subject of several essays in *Rewriting the South,* beginning with Richard Gray's "History as Autobiography" (pp. 307–16); following Bakhtin, Gray points out that "someone like Faulkner, say, is the site of a struggle between different voices, different systems of speech and therefore value, and it is necessary to know something about *them* in order to begin to know something about *him*. He exists as a point of intersection between conflicting social and historical forces which enter into identity by means of language." Faulkner understood the "dialogic nature of his involvement with language and culture," at least "intuitively." Lothar Hönnighausen's "Faulkner's Rewriting the Indian Removal" (pp. 335–43) concludes that "Indian violence proceeds not from frustrated outrage at white injustice but as an act of black humor betokening Indian superiority." (Other essays from this collection are discussed under specific titles.) Annick Chapdelaine's "Faulkner in French: Humor Obliterated" (*FJ* 7 [1991–92]: 43–60) examines what can be lost in translation. And Marc D. Baldwin looks at "Faulkner's Cartographic Method: Producing the *Land* through Cognitive Mapping" (*FJ* 7: 193–214).

iv Individual Works to 1929

Michael Zeitlin's "The Passion of Margaret Powers: A Psychoanalytic Reading of *Soldier's Pay*" (*MissQ* 46: 351–72) finds that "Faulkner's first important experimental study of the female character . . . is a uniquely modernist fusion of symbol, myth, and psychopathology." Through Margaret, Faulkner not only "give[s] a certain representational and ontological legitimacy to what the male characters . . . experience as woman's fundamental 'otherness,' " but he also "begin[s] to explore from the 'other' perspective the meaning and consequences of male orders of desire and control." Thomas L. McHaney's "At Play in the Fields of Freud: Faulkner and Misquotation" (*Faulkner, His Contemporaries, and His Posterity,* pp. 64–76) examines verbal slips, omissions, puns, and Latin misquotations in *Soldier's Pay* and *The Sound and the Fury.*

Karen M. Andrews in "Toward a 'Culturalist' Approach to Faulkner Studies: Making Connections in *Flags in the Dust*" (*FJ* 7: 13–26) focuses on Caspey Strothers and argues that his subplot "suggests that Faulkner's texts critique the debilitating and socially constructed categories of identity while being informed and, in certain respects, limited by these same ideologically inflected categories of 'difference.'" Allison Berg examines "The Great War and the War at Home: Gender Battles in *Flags in the Dust* and *The Unvanquished*" (*WS* 22: 441–53), finding that "where there is war, there will be gender trouble."

New Essays on The Sound and the Fury (Cambridge) boosted the usual interest in what its editor, Noel Polk, calls "the quintessential American high modernist text"; Polk's introduction (pp. 1–21) goes on to review the novel's publication and critical history. Dawn Trouard's "Faulkner's Text Which Is Not One" (pp. 23–69) poses a "challenge [to] the book's status as unified text" by reexamining the "overshadowed" and critically misunderstood women: "By recognizing the pervasive presence and importance of the Compson women," Trouard "hope[s] to highlight the traditional resistance to their integration, and to stake out actual fictional territory for them: Benjy's 'Good Friday' will become Caroline Compson's 'Mother's Day.'" Stylistic experimentation is the subject of "'Now I Can Write': Faulkner's Novel of Invention" (pp. 71–97) by Donald Kartiganer, while Richard Godden's "Quentin Compson: Tyrrhenian Vase or Crucible of Race?" (pp. 99–137) looks at "the Southern politics of race and gender." Although Godden claims to correct the limitations of Freudian readings of virginity, incest, and miscegenation by historicizing these issues, his focus on the "more or less 'untold stories' among which Faulkner was raised" and the novel's "linked latencies" suggests that there may not be that much of a distinction between "a universal psychology (Freudian or otherwise)" and "an historically specific regional pathology." Polk completes this casebook with "Trying Not to Say: A Primer on the Language of *The Sound and the Fury*" (pp. 139–75), arguing that "Faulkner uses the mechanics of the English language—grammar, syntax, punctuation, spelling—as a direct objective correlative to the states of each of the narrators' minds." These conventions "sometimes work *against the words themselves* . . . to reveal things that the narrators are incapable of saying or are specifically trying to keep from saying, things that have caused them pain and shame."

"Much Ado About Nothing: Language and Desire in *The Sound and the Fury*" (*MissQ* 46: 373–93), a Lacanian reading by Deborah E. Barker and Ivo Kamps, finds that "None of the three brothers . . . is able to negotiate successfully the mirror stage in which the individual recognizes an external and fictive ego which then functions as the site of the speaking subject." Consequently, they are doomed in their quest for Caddy, "what language and desire chase endlessly but fruitlessly." In "Reading Faulkner Reading Cowley Reading Faulkner: Authority and Gender in the Compson Appendix" (*FJ* 7: 27–41) Susan V. Donaldson points out that "at a time when Faulkner's work was becoming increasingly self-reflexive, the Compson appendix offered a critical commentary not just on Malcolm Cowley's virtual creation of the Yoknapatawpha saga but also on the structures of narrative, authority, and gender defining the text of *The Sound and the Fury*." Karen E. Waldron's "Recovering Eve's Consciousness from *The Sound and the Fury*" (*WS* 22: 469–83) argues that "for Faulkner, whose novels do attempt to join archetype and actuality, the paradox of feminine representation results in a troubling practice: attention to·women ends up obscuring that which it seems to be trying to acknowledge, even celebrate—the existence of feminine difference and its alternative way of knowing." Racial difference and the potential "for human beings to connect across barriers of race" are given a Bakhtinian reading in "Mirroring the Racial 'Other': The Deacon and Quentin Compson in William Faulkner's *The Sound and the Fury*" (*SoR* 29: 30–40) by Cedric Gael Bryant. Ivo Hlavizna compares "Patterns of Failure: William Faulkner's *The Sound and the Fury* and John McGahern's *The Dark*" (*Faulkner, His Contemporaries, and His Posterity*, pp. 161–66). Margaret J. Yonce studies "The Pairing of *The Sound and the Fury* and 'Wild Palms'" (*WS* 22: 507–16); and Margaret Boe Birns's "Demeter as the Letter D: Naming Women in *The Sound and the Fury* and *As I Lay Dying*" (*WS* 22: 533–41) examines the "onomastic community ruled by the letter 'D'": Caddy, Addie, Damuddy, Dilsey, Dewey Dell, and the "duck-shaped woman."

v Individual Works, 1930–1939

Exploring the conflict between content and form in "The Textual Coffin and the Narrative Corpse of *As I Lay Dying*" (*ArQ* 49, i: 99–116) Michael Kaufmann finds that Faulkner seeks "to ease the tension between the modern, printed form of the text and the anecdotal traditional content [by integrating] his print form with his narrative," for example, the italics, blank spaces, and coffin drawing. Karen R. Sass explores Lacanian implications in "At a Loss for Words: Addie and Language in *As I Lay Dying*" (*FJ* 6 [1991]: 9–21); and in "Between the Family and the State: Nomadism and Authority in *As I Lay Dying*" (*FJ* 7: 83–94) Patrick O'Donnell takes an Althusserian look at the "negotiation and legitimation of the family's continuance within the bounds of state authority."

"Alcohol, Faulkner, and *Sanctuary*: Myth and Reality" (*PAPA* 19, ii: 37–51) interest Hum Sue Yin and Larry Young, who argue that even though "Faulkner's characters embrace the alluring, hollow myths associated with alcohol which Faulkner himself believed," those myths are debunked through the portrayal of the "unglamorous consequences of alcohol abuse." Kevin A. Boon's "Temple Defiled: The Brainwashing of Temple Drake in Faulkner's *Sanctuary*" (*FJ* 6: 33–50) attacks our patriarchal tradition of seeing Temple "as complicitous in her own oppression" and compares her situation to that of Patty Hearst. Ulf Kirchdorfer focuses on animal imagery in *"Sanctuary*: Temple as a Parrot" (*FJ* 6: 51–53).

Ellen Goellner's "By Word of Mouth: Narrative Dynamics of Gossip in Faulkner's *Light in August*" (*Narrative* 1: 105–23) examines gossip as "the main mode of communication and storytelling" and "as part of the formal design" of the novel. Goellner argues that Faulkner "uses gossip to direct the centrifugal energies that threaten to pull his story apart." In "The Woman in Faulkner Guiding *Light in August*" (*WS* 22: 543–51) Virginia V. James Hlavsa finds anomalies and "striking differences in the characterizations of women from one chapter to another," differences that exist because "the modernist, Faulkner, made his characters reflect mythic and primitive beliefs and behavior" as inspired by the Book of John and *The Golden Bough*. Faulkner's changing use of the past is the subject of Thomas L. McHaney's "Faulkner's Cosmos and the Incarnation of History" (*Rewriting the South,* pp. 324–34); McHaney "suggest[s] that one of the principles around which Faulkner organized its multivalent story reflected as close and as true a representation as he ever made of social and economic forces in his time and place, his little postage stamp of soil—the upper middle south from 1910 or so up through 1931." In "Watching (Jefferson) Watching: *Light in August* and the Aestheticization of Gender" (*FJ* 7: 95–114) M. J. Burgess argues that Faulkner "repeatedly engages" the relationship between romance and history and "that his writing, while locating in romantic models of identity the source and enablement of the toxic power relations that structure and reflect his culture, is itself driven and enabled by these models." " 'How can he be so nothungry?': Fetishism, Anorexia, and the Disavowal of the

Cultural 'I' in *Light in August*" (*FJ* 7: 175–91) by Pamela A. Boker takes a
psychoanalytic approach to Joe Christmas; and Martin Bidney compares
"*Windy McPherson's Son* and Silent McEachern's Son: Sherwood Anderson and *Light in August*" (*MissQ* 46: 395–406), finding "surprising
parallels in plot and characterization."

Gary Harrington looks at some parallels between Nathanael West and
Faulkner in "*Miss Lonelyhearts* and *Pylon*: The Influence of Anxiety"
(*ANQ* 6: 209–11). *Pylon*'s anticipation of Margaret Atwood's *Surfacing* is
Dieter Meindl's subject in "Between Eliot and Atwood: Faulkner as
Ecologist" (*Faulkner, His Contemporaries, and His Posterity*, pp. 301–08).
And David Yerkes reveals "The Reporter's Name in *Pylon* and Why
That's Important" (*FJ* 6: 3–8).

Utz Riese's Foucauldian study of "Faulkner's *Absalom, Absalom!* and
Kafka's *The Castle*: Ethical Space in Modernity's Discourse of History"
(*Faulkner, His Contemporaries, and His Posterity*, pp. 77–86) argues that
"both authors try to establish an ethical space in their texts as against
the process of historical 'modernization.' They write out many ethical
subject-positions, yet the narrative voice fashions itself by moving freely
between these positions without affirming a particular one." Jadwiga
Maszewska's study of "Functions of the Narrative Method in William
Faulkner's *Absalom, Absalom!* and Louise Erdrich's *Tracks*" (pp. 317–21)
compares the two authors' use of "marginal cultures." Heide Ziegler's
explicit thesis in "Rereading Faulkner Through Parody" (pp. 328–35) "is
that because of his concern for innocence and memory Faulkner's texts
resist parody," a thesis developed by comparing *Absalom, Absalom!* to
John Hawkes's *Adventures in the Alaskan Skin Trade*. In "*Absalom, Absalom!*: 'Fluid Cradle of Events (Time)' " (*FJ* 6: 65–84) Carolyn Norman
Slaughter examines the novel in terms of Bergson's concepts of qualita-
tive change and durational time. Deborah Wilson argues in " 'A Shape to
Fill a Lack': *Absalom, Absalom!* and the Pattern of History" (*FJ* 7: 61–81)
that "for Faulkner, the shape of history in his narratives compensates for
the loss of the patriarchal Old South, restoring authority to men who tell
the stories over and over while the women listen silently from the grave."
Linda Dunleavy takes a similar tack in "Marriage and the Invisibility of
Women in *Absalom, Absalom!*" (*WS* 22: 455–65). Kevin Railey's examination of "Paternalism and Liberalism: Contending Ideologies in *Absalom,
Absalom!*" (*FJ* 7: 115–32) is interesting both for connections between
characters and Southern history and for comments on the interplay of
fiction and history.

In *"The Unvanquished:* Faulkner's Nietzschean Skirmish with the Civil War" (*MissQ* 46: 407–36) John Lowe argues that this undervalued work "is a far more disturbing book than many readers realize. Far from being a costumed romp, it moves from comedy to tragedy in a probing examination of issues that also troubled Nietzsche: the will to power, the excesses of virtue, the relationship of justice and revenge, and the dangers involved in distorted perceptions of history." And June Dwyer studies "Feminization, Masculinization, and the Role of the Woman Patriot in *The Unvanquished"* (*FJ* 6: 55–64).

And finally, in "Signification, Simulation, and Containment in *If I Forget Thee, Jerusalem"* (*FJ* 7: 133–50) Charles Hannon seeks to "identify certain tendencies within Faulkner's late modernist novel [*The Wild Palms*] as prefigurations of postmodernism, which in this instance is defined as a metadiscursive challenge to modernism's basic assumptions."

vi Individual Works, 1940–1949

Eula Varner and Ike's cow are the subjects of "Exquisite Agony: Desire for the Other in Faulkner's *The Hamlet"* (*WS* 22: 485–96) by Holli G. Levitsky; and Sonja Basic's "Parody and Metafiction: *Ulysses* and *The Hamlet"* (*Faulkner, His Contemporaries, and His Posterity,* pp. 41–55) compares these modernist, paradoxical "battlefields in which are confronted tendencies towards referentiality and non-referentiality, transparency and opaqueness, histoire and recit, mimesis and diegesis."

Dan Ford's " 'He Was Talking About Truth': Faulkner in Pursuit of the Old Verities" (*Rewriting the South,* pp. 317–23) is about *Go Down, Moses* and Faulkner's "personalizing the historic South, retelling it and reshaping it." "Toward Self-Possession: Women in *Go Down, Moses"* (*WS* 22: 417–27) by Mary Jane Dickerson draws our attention to "the roles women characters play even in a text whose narrative structures actively suppress their voices." Doreen Fowler examines the implications of "The Nameless Women of Faulkner's *Go Down, Moses"* (*WS* 22: 525–32). In *"Go Down, Moses*: The Collective Action of Redress" (*FJ* 7: 151–74) Carey Wall argues that "Ike McCaslin's action is not at all futile. He and others engage in ritualistic action in *this* world to pass the current of life from their own family and people to the black people whom his family has violated."

vii **Individual Works, 1950–1962**

In "Where Is Yoknapatawpha County? William Faulkner, John Updike, and Postwar America" (*Faulkner, His Contemporaries, and His Posterity,* pp. 284–300) Karl F. Zender puzzles out the implications of Faulkner's "distinguish[ing] between Mississippi as idea and as geographical entity" in *Requiem for a Nun* in order to illuminate "the larger issue of how Faulkner represents—or declines to represent—post-World-War-II America." Warwick Wadlington focuses on *A Fable,* Faulkner's "belated thirties 'strike novel,'" in "Doing What Comes Culturally: Collective Action and the Discourse of Belief in Faulkner and Nathanael West" (pp. 245–52). In "Reconsidering Maggie, Charles, and Gavin in *The Town*" (*MissQ* 47: 463–77) Anne Colclough Little discovers a complex triangle beneath an apparently simple surface: "Through subtle hints that reveal basic flaws in the marriage, incestuous overtones in the attachment of the wife for her brother, and the husband's jealousy and retaliation, Faulkner shows yet another example of a distorted male-female relationship in a Waste Land world." And Marcel Arbeit considers initiation themes in "Coming of Age in Faulkner's *The Reivers* and Padgett Powell's *Edisto*" (*Faulkner, His Contemporaries, and His Posterity,* pp. 276–83).

viii **The Stories**

In "Faulkner's Southern Reflections: The Black on the Back of the Mirror in 'Ad Astra'" (*AAR* 27: 53–57) Reginald Martin finds that the early stories frequently feature "a background narrator who implies that the black characters involved in the plot are at least as important and as good as the white, but because the world values color over content, the characters of color find themselves socially disadvantaged." Consequently, Martin argues, Faulkner's "views of race are posited *a priori* with his sincere readership," thus freeing "the narratives in the novels to concentrate," at least superficially, "on the development of other southern themes." Istvan Geher sees a "kinship of cultural coincidence" between "A Rose for Emily" and Zsigmond Moricz's "Barbarians" in "The Skeleton in the Mythology: A Comparative Interpretation of the American Wild South and the Hungarian Wild East" (*Faulkner, His Contemporaries, and His Posterity,* pp. 110–19). Floyd C. Watkins looks at

"Sacrificial Rituals and Anguish in the Victim's Heart in 'Red Leaves'"
(*SSF* 30: 71–78). In "Trying Emotions: Unpredictable Justice in Faulkner's 'Smoke' and 'Tomorrow'" (*MissQ* 47: 447–62) Michael E. Lahey
contends that "Faulkner seems to challenge the notions that law and
emotion are separable." In fact, Lahey argues, "each has claims and
limiting effects on the other." Leona Toker studies "Rhetoric and Ethical
Ambiguities in 'That Evening Sun'" (*WS* 22: 429–39), while Karen M.
Andrews's "White Women's Complicity and the Taboo: Faulkner's Lay-
ered Critique of the 'Miscegenation Complex'" (*WS* 22: 497–506)
focuses on "Dry September." Susan S. Yunis analyzes "The Narrator of
Faulkner's 'Barn Burning'" (*FJ* 6: 23–31), and Sandra Lee Kleppe argues
that the "Elements of the Carnivalesque in Faulkner's 'Was'" (*MissQ* 46:
437–45) "provide comic relief at the same time as they foreground the
bleak reality of the black population's status in the Old South."

Randolph-Macon College

10   Fitzgerald and Hemingway

Albert J. DeFazio III

What is most provocative this year? J. Gerald Kennedy's study of place, *Imagining Paris,* which examines both Fitzgerald and Hemingway. Most essential? Matthew J. Bruccoli's critical edition of *The Love of* The Last Tycoon: *A Western.* Most surprising? The lack of substantial biographical treatment. Persistent? Debates over Catherine Barkley's character and the waiters' dialogue in "A Clean, Well-Lighted Place." Predictable? The absence of critical editions for Hemingway's works, and essays, both short and long, that seem to have been written in a critical vacuum. Most reliable? The semiannual *Hemingway Review,* ed. Susan Beegel, for its consistently high-caliber articles and reviews; the annual *F. Scott Fitzgerald Society Newsletter,* ed. Ruth Prigozy et al., for its news, reviews, synopses of conference papers, and short articles; and the semiannual *Hemingway Newsletter,* for its announcements (books, grants, openings, calls for articles) and news. Least predictable? The new E-mail listservs for both authors; scholars are only beginning to tap the enormous potential of these tools, facilitated by Jack Jobst. Most refreshing? In Hemingway's case, a healthy influx of newer methodologies, some of them as yet unnamed, that are belatedly ushering studies into a new era and, as ever, revising our perspectives.

i   Text, Letters, the Archives, and Bibliography

A screenplay and a critical edition make this a splendid year for textual studies of Fitzgerald. Among Budd Schulberg's carton of "other people's manuscripts," he discovered Fitzgerald's unproduced screenplay which came into his possession in the "late forties" when Lester Cowan, who commissioned the adaptation, sought his services to retune Fitzgerald's efforts. Schulberg declined. His introduction to *Babylon Revisited: The*

Screenplay (Carroll) recounts his acquaintance with his "unfailingly en-
dearing" friend and collaborator, but he leaves me wishing for more than
his meager eight pages provide. The "Afterword" by Matthew J. Bruccoli
makes clear that Fitzgerald "set different standards for his movie work":
he was bound by the "lousy condition" that the screenplay was to star
Shirley Temple and therefore had to expand the child's role. Nonetheless,
Bruccoli echoes the "Author's Note" found on Fitzgerald's own copy of
the screenplay—"let it stand on its own bottom"—and now, half a
century later, we shall.

The screenplay was Fitzgerald's attempt to finance what would sadly
become his "unfinished masterpiece," The Last Tycoon: *An Unfinished
Novel* (1941), published in a "cosmeticized text" edited by Edmund
Wilson. This year's signal achievement in Fitzgerald scholarship is Bruccoli's edition of *The Love of* The Last Tycoon: *A Western* (Cambridge), a
portable petit archive. Whereas the screenplay is mum about editorial
policy (to date, the best discussion about the minor differences between
the newly published Cowan version and Fitzgerald's copy in the Princeton archives is Alan Margolies's review in the *Fitzgerald Newsletter* 4
[1994]: 16–17), Bruccoli's *Last Tycoon* exemplifies the painstaking clarity
and precision that we have come to expect from his editions. In concert
with the late Fredson Bowers, Bruccoli establishes a *base-text,* in this case
the "latest secretarial drafts for the first seventeen episodes as revised by
Fitzgerald in holograph"; and he clearly articulates his policy for emen-
dation. The shape of the text reveals the complications of editing an
unfinished work. Roughly, the first third, an introduction, contains
maps, photographs, chronologies, facsimiles, a statement of editorial
policy, and a detailed account of the "gestation and composition" of the
novel which draws upon Bruccoli's *"The Last of the Novelists": F. Scott
Fitzgerald and* The Last Tycoon (see *ALS 1977,* p. 163). The critical
edition with an emended clear-text occupies the middle third. The final
third provides a full apparatus—of editorial emendations, authorial revisions, Wilson's alterations, and variants between Scribner's setting copy
and the first printing. Facsimiles of working drafts, included in the
appendixes, are delightful to peruse. The explanatory notes, written for
the "attentive American or British undergraduate," serve as a stark
reminder of such readers' preparedness to engage a half-century-old text.

While scholars of Hemingway have no such editorial enterprise to
celebrate, they can cheer the return to print of *Hemingway at Oak Park
High: The High School Writings of Ernest Hemingway, 1916–1917,* ed.

Cynthia Maziarka and Donald Vogel, Jr. (Oak Park and River Forest High School). Excepting introductions by Michael Reynolds and the school's current principal, the substitution of a few photographs, and the addition of two newspaper articles describing postgraduate visits, the volume essentially reprints Bruccoli's out-of-print *Ernest Hemingway's Apprenticeship, Oak Park 1916–1917* (see *ALS 1971*, p. 123). While Charles Fenton and others have trod the territory of Hemingway's juvenilia in the *Trapeze* and *Tabula,* Bruce Rettman's "He was One of Us: Ernest Hemingway and the High School Press" (*SPR* 68 and 69, iv and i: 6–12) demonstrates continued interest in Hemingway's modest beginnings as a journalist.

Slipping the net last year was a novelty item, *Marlin!* (Big Fish), which reprints Hemingway's "The Great Blue River." Only 1,000 copies of this 6 ½″ square, 83-page volume in blue cloth were issued. It features five new duotone photographs (uncaptioned, circa 1949) by Roberto Herrera Sontolongo and a reprinted portion of Gabriel García Márquez's introduction to Norberto Fuentes's *Hemingway in Cuba.* The handsome volume, which takes its title from a subheading in Hemingway's article, differs only slightly from the original, combining the first two paragraphs and eliminating both the final sentence and 11 photographs by George Leavens.

Barbara Lounsberry turns to the archives for "The Holograph Manuscript of *Green Hills of Africa*" (*HN* 12, ii: 36–45), treating readers to "juicy digs" at Hemingway's contemporaries that he excised before serialization in *Scribner's.* She suggests that the book is "as much about the elusive dimensions of art as it is about Africa," a discovery that Hemingway seems to have made *after* completing the manuscript. More importantly, Lounsberry reveals that Hemingway's intriguing Foreword and the four-part, 13-chapter structure were imposed after the manuscript was completed. She applauds his revisions but laments that his haste to publish left him little time to enhance the work's too-subtle aesthetic dimension.

In his tireless effort to win our trust in the unemended text, David Kerner, in "Hemingway's Attention to 'A Clean, Well-Lighted Place' " (*HN* 13, i: 48–62), brings new evidence to an old dispute about what he describes as "the clearly deliberate ambiguity" in the dialogue between the waiters. We should embrace the unemended text, Kerner reasons, because Hemingway proofread the story "attentively at least four times," which would render unlikely Warren Bennett's claim that Hemingway introduced the error while emending the manuscript (see *ALS 1990*, pp. 170–71, and *ALS 1979*, p. 175). The only thing certain in this controversy is a dagger in the margin of the critical edition, accompanied by a lengthy textual note.

Ann Doyle-Anderson and Neal B. Huston read *La Torre Bianca* (1980) against the background of "The Letters of Adriana Ivancich to Ernest Hemingway" (*HN* 13, i: 63–75) and offer a reassessment of the couple's misunderstood relationship. Whereas Jeffrey Meyers finds *Bianca* a "self-pitying and condescending portrait of their friendship," full of "bitterness about [its effect] on her life," these authors turn to the memoir's sources, particularly Hemingway's letters, and determine that what seems to be a May/December relationship is "complex and resistant to stereotyping." Only 38 of Adriana's letters survive, and most of these were written during 1949–50; however, internal evidence in Hemingway's epistles confirms that the correspondence continued uninterrupted from 1949 until 1955. Her missives indicate that Adriana is neither the schoolgirl nor the sycophant; they reveal her "awareness of her incredible good fortune" at having found a friend who took her artistic endeavors seriously. Far from blaming Hemingway for complicating her life, her letters and memoir characterize him as one who "inspired her and gave her confidence in what they could accomplish together." Carolyn Hughes Crowley reports that the Culinary Archives and Museum of Johnson & Whales University in Providence, Rhode Island, is offering up a single serving of Hemingway ("You Say Your Kitchen's Crowded?" *Washington Post* 20 Oct.: E1). According to Curator Barbara Koch, Hemingway's brief, typed letter dated 21 July 1949 and addressed to Java-Indian Condiment Company in New York requests a booklet of precise Indian recipes for making curries in exchange for a three-cent postage stamp.

Megan Floyd Desnoyers, Stephen Plotkin, and Lisa Middents continue to provide invaluable "News from the Hemingway Collection" (*HN* 12, ii: 114–15; 13, i: 120). This year's acquisitions include letters, notebooks, photographs, and audiotapes relating to Paul and Hadley Hemingway Mower and Ernest Hemingway (1926–71); 11 audiotapes containing Alice Hunt Sokoloff's 1971–72 interview with Hadley (the basis for Sokoloff's *The First Mrs. Hemingway*) and a significant source of Gioia Diliberto's *Hadley* (see *ALS 1992*, p. 146); and an oral history interview by Desnoyers with William Walton. Newly opened are more than 169 letters—most by either Maurice Speiser (counsel from 1932–48) or Mary Welsh Hemingway's parents.

With the gracious assistance of the international body of Hemingway and Fitzgerald scholars, I continue to annotate current bibliographies for the *Hemingway Review* (12, ii: 99–113; 13, i: 113–19) and the *Fitzgerald Newsletter* (3: 16–20).

ii Biography

Excepting Marc Dolan's "The (Hi)story of Their Lives: Mythic Autobiography and 'The Lost Generation'" (*JAmS* 27: 35–56), Stuart B. McIver's touristy jaunt through *Hemingway's Key West* (Pineapple) and (dare I include it?) Mona Kelly and Linda Larson's *Conch Cats at Ernest Hemingway Home and Museum* (Conch Cats), biographers were silent, although next year offers the prospect of new installments of the multivolume works by Michael Reynolds and Peter Griffin and the certainty of another life of Fitzgerald by Jeffrey Meyers. Notable reissues include Bruccoli's revised compendium *Some Sort of Epic Grandeur: The Life of F. Scott Fitzgerald* (Carroll; see *ALS 1981*, p. 171) and Fitzgerald's *The Crack-Up* (New Directions).

Working with three texts responsible for creating the myth of the Lost Generation, Dolan asks "Of what use is autobiography to history?" and, using Cowley's *Exile's Return,* Fitzgerald's *The Crack-Up,* and Hemingway's *A Moveable Feast,* discovers their "mythic testimony": each begins with the weight on the noun, "generation," before coming to the eventual realization of the adjective, "lost"; and each begins by describing a decade that commenced with exhilaration and ended in deflation. "The signified journey of all these narratives is from false perception of cultural homogeneity through an illusive sense of cultural uniqueness that renewed commitment to cultural pluralism." But in order to identify "historically significant patterns," Dolan warns, we must recover more than three stories by privileged men. Portions of McIver's montage are culled from other sources such as James McLendon's *Papa: Hemingway in Key West* (identified in the bibliography but otherwise without note), and despite occasional factual missteps and some curious repetitions, it remains a pleasantly readable account of Hemingway's haunts and habits during his years in the Keys. McIver's brief walking tour originates at Hemingway's home on Whitehead Street. Those curious about why portions of the gorgeous grounds are cordoned need only turn to Kelly and Larson's pamphlet for an explanation: the Home has no litter boxes, and the white chain-link fence prevents visitors from "having an unpleasant experience." Included are brief biographies of the polydactyl namesakes of Jennifer Jones, Marlene Dietrich, and Spencer Tracy; photographs capture the colorful diversity of the grounds.

iii Sources, Influences, Parallels

Save two, the lot of these studies fall to Hemingway, dividing evenly between the stories and the novels. Diane Price Herndl's *Invalid Women* (pp. 201–11) briefly compares Fitzgerald's *Tender is the Night* with works by James, Wharton, Glasgow, and Hawthorne. Unlike his predecessors, Fitzgerald "appropriates the domestic economy but moves it to a male realm," strips women of the "sentimental power" gained in the previous century and exploited by early cinema, and allows the male (doctor) to "become the representative of morality and self sacrifice to community good." Where others posit illness and health as things to be "earned," in Fitzgerald's service economy, one such as Nicole may purchase her well-being at another's expense. In "Notes on the Origin of Gatsby's Guest List" (*Fitzgerald Newsletter* 3: 6–8) Michel Viel pursues striking parallels between the novel and Christopher Anstey's *The New Bath Guide* (1766): whether the guide is actually a source depends, Viel concludes, on our learning more about Fitzgerald's reading.

A pair of studies illuminate potential sources in Hemingway's short fiction. Harold Blythe and Charles Sweet expand our knowledge of Hemingway's fictionalized white hunter in "The Real Philip Percival: The Mordens' View of 'Robert Wilson' " (*HN* 12, ii: 78–82) by publishing excerpts from William and Irene Morden's *Our African Adventure* (1954). While the Mordens' Percival shares Wilson's blue eyes, he differs in his good humor, devotion to his wife, and praise of Irene's grace under pressure. Blythe and Sweet may also have found a likely source for the Macomber story in a tale relayed to the Mordens by Percival. Sean O'Rourke's "Evan Shipman and 'The Gambler, the Nun, and the Radio' " (*HN* 13, i: 86–89) helps to distinguish the "invented" and the "reported" elements of the story and suggests that the author's friend was the model for Cayetano, the stoical gambler.

Authors as diverse as Catullus, Sterne, Rilke, and Lewis Carroll are credited with influencing Hemingway. Resting his case on the overlapping of Catullus's poems and Hemingway's novel, Peter L. Hays in "Catullus and *The Sun Also Rises*" (*HN* 12, ii: 15–23) contends that the author read the ancient's poetry at Pound's urging and incorporated its

themes into his treatment of the Lost Generation. His case is circumstan-
tial and not entirely convincing; the parallels and echoes that he cites
substantiate well-trodden themes. Jake Barnes and Uncle Toby are the
focus of John M. McLellan's "The Unrising Sun: The Theme of Castration in Hemingway and Sterne" (*Studies in English Literature and Linguistics* 18 [1992]: 51–61): wars have left both men physically wounded, but
their "resolution never more to think of sex,—or of aught that belonged
to it" results from their emotional woundings by the femme fatale figures
of Widow Wadman and Brett Ashley. Pursuing still more allusions to
Sterne's novel, Wolfgang E. H. Rudat in "Wounds to Manhood: Hemingway, Jake Barnes, and *Tristram Shandy*" (*JEP* 14, iii and iv: 223–37)
proposes that Hemingway projected into Barnes "castration fears which
had initially been instilled in him by the 'summer girl' experience and
[were] later reinforced by the overbearing behavior of Marcelline for
whom he had been forced to pose as a twin sister." Proceeding from
Hemingway's comment that he admired "The Cornet," Dieter Saalmann
in "Hemingway's *Green Hills of Africa* and Rilke's *The Lay of the Love and
Death of Cornet Christopher Rilke*; Tentative Reflections" (*GNR* 24, ii:
68–71) concedes that while Rilke "indulges in unabashed sentimentality"
and Hemingway "proposed to be uncompromisingly factual," they share
tendencies toward "associative retracings" and "creative pursuit." Kermit
Vanderbilt's "Nick Adams Through the Looking Glass: 'A Way You'll
Never Be'" (*Expl* 51: 104–10) pursues analogies between the story and
Lewis Carroll's *Through the Looking Glass.*

Examining the relationship between Caribbean paintings and an
unfinished novel is Charlene M. Murphy's "Hemingway, Winslow Homer, and *Islands in the Stream*: Influence and Tribute" (*HN* 13, i: 76–85),
which documents how Homer's paintings not only "illustrated" *Islands*
but paralleled central themes—such as the struggle to endure in the face
of impossible circumstances and the paradox of struggle and harmony
between humankind and nature.

Explicating the allusive subtext of a neglected short story, Susan F.
Beegel in "*Howard Pyle's Book of Pirates* and Male Taciturnity in Hemingway's 'A Day's Wait'" (*SSF* 30: 535–41) opens the "deceptively simple"
tale to a new reading that has rich implications for the ongoing debate
about codes of masculine behavior. Beegel avers that the story indicts
"*Book of Pirates* and similar boy's books as poor models for American
manhood and questions the very ideals of masculinity Hemingway is
most thought to valorize." Replacing the "ethos of self-reliance," Hem-

ingway heroizes the domestic and "explores the painful cost of failing to express affection." Probing another neglected story, Richard Allan Davison explicates two allusions to *The Great Gatsby* that sandwich a direct reference, "Did you ever run into Scott Fitzgerald?" in "Hemingway's 'Homage to Switzerland' and F. Scott Fitzgerald" (*HN* 12, ii: 72–77): just as Nick Carraway's ancestor has "sent a substitute to the Civil War," Johnson suggests that the waitress find a replacement so that she can join him "in the night life of Vevey"; and Owl Eyes proclaims Gatsby "a regular Belasco" on discovering real books with uncut pages in the library. Having tweaked Fitzgerald allusively and directly with "Homage" in 1933, notes Davison, perhaps Hemingway felt free to do so again in "Snows." Rudat, in "Hemingway's Revenge on Gertrude Stein: Intertextuality between *A Moveable Feast* and *The Sun Also Rises*" (*JEP* 25, i and ii: 39–50) explains that Hemingway's attempt to satirically "kill" Stein is best understood if one reads *Feast* against the background of *Sun*.

Hemingway's influence attracts a pair of minor contributions. Roydon Salvick's "[Samuel] Selvon's Santiago: An Intertextual Reading of *The Plains of Caroni*" (*JWIL* 5, i and ii [1992]: 97–105) remarks similarities between Balgobin, who has a "traditional Indo-Trinidadian peasant sensibility" and is an exemplar of "obsolescent heroism" and Hemingway's fisherman. In "Re-writing Hemingway: Rachel Ingalls's *Binstead's Safari* [1983]" (*Crit* 34: 165–70) Alan Macdonald observes that Ingalls's novel offers a variation of "The Short Happy Life of Francis Macomber": this time, the wife, Millie Binstead, finds happiness and her husband is left with "pale grasses, nothing else."

Comparing Hemingway with a pair of his predecessors, Susan K. Harris in "Vicious Binaries: Gender and Authorial Paranoia in Dreiser's 'Second Choice,' Howells' 'Editha,' and Hemingway's 'The Short Happy Life of Francis Macomber'" (*CollL* 20, ii: 70–82) employs a feminist perspective to reveal that the three stories "feature marginalized female characters who suffer as a result of their distance from whatever the stories define as the focus of freedom and power." Of the three, Hemingway, who cannot "imagine women as active subjects" (Margot "does not 'do' anything" and "possesses only reactive language"), creates the most insightful and the most paranoid construct of Woman: Margot, the "Hegelian Other to Hemingway's masculinized Self," has "the power to destroy not only men's lives, but their self-constructs."

To what extent does the marketplace shape readers' conceptions of Hemingway's work? Daniel Morris focuses on *Life*'s treatment of *For*

Whom the Bell Tolls (1940) and *The Old Man and the Sea* (1952) in "Hemingway and *Life*: Consuming Revolutions" (*AmPer* 3: 62–74) and determines that the magazine "encouraged visualization of the writing" by focusing on "filmic representation" of his work, linked the author to celebrities, deemphasized his prose style, and presented him as a "sign of the value of American consumerism."

iv Criticism

a. Full-length Studies: Fitzgerald   Fitzgerald's debut novel and his short stories attracted full-length treatments. The better is Jack Hendriksen's This Side of Paradise *as a Bildungsroman* (Peter Lang), which cogently argues that Fitzgerald's first novel is a classical bildungsroman in the tradition of Goethe's *Wilhelm Meisters Lehrjahre* and Joyce's *A Portrait of the Artist as a Young Man*. As Hendriksen's review of the criticism demonstrates, most critics focus on the novel's faults, scarcely articulate its strengths, and overlook the complex process of *Bildung,* wherein Armory internalizes the experiences that allow him to live in society. Challenging James E. Miller's assertion in *F. Scott Fitzgerald: His Art and His Technique* (1964) that *Paradise* embodies the "formless precepts of *saturation*" as defined by H. G. Wells, Hendriksen illustrates that the novel adheres to Henry James's idea of *selection*. He defines his terms with care in discussing the works of Goethe, Compton Mackenzie, and Joyce, providing sufficient detail for the uninitiated without stalling in plot summary. Hendriksen's close reading of *Paradise* reveals Fitzgerald's "progressive structure" (often mistaken for absence of plot): his consistent imagery; his use of characters and events progressively to depict Armory's inner growth; and his use of the ironic point of view, basic to the bildungsroman. Hendriksen's is a solid contribution, useful and accessible to student and teacher alike.

The Price of Paradise: The Magazine Career of F. Scott Fitzgerald (Borgo) by Stephen W. Potts challenges the "critical cliché" that forgives the poor quality of much of Fitzgerald's short stories because he was allegedly limited by the editorial whim of the periodicals for which he wrote. Potts takes readers on a forced march through more than 170 short pieces; he provides details of the author's "relationship with readers and editors of contemporary periodicals"; and he profiles the "contents and editorial parameters" of various popular magazines. By noting similarities between Fitzgerald's work and that of his contemporaries with whom he shared pages in the slicks, Potts is able to claim that "the charge that the *Post*'s standards ruined his artistic career seems . . . less credible than the idea that Fitzgerald exhausted his imagination trying to keep himself on the magazine's payroll." He blames Fitzgerald's mediocrity on his own "personal factors" and concludes that "the author and his apologists do not have editorial strictures to blame." Potts is good at documenting the contents of the periodicals in which Fitzgerald published, but in shifting the blame for mediocrity to "personal factors," he is unnecessarily vague. What is more, he fails to place his observations in the context of recent evaluations of Fitzgerald's short stories such as Bryant Mangum's *A Fortune Yet: Money in the Art of F. Scott Fitzgerald's Short Stories* or John Kuehl's *F. Scott Fitzgerald: A Study of the Short Fiction* (see *ALS 1991*, pp. 156–57). In his too-brief conclusion, he acknowledges Fitzgerald's strengths but scarcely makes good on his promise to place the author's magazine career within the perspective of his life's work.

Last year I overlooked Andrew Hook's *F. Scott Fitzgerald* (Edward Arnold). Suitable for novices, this 97-page guide justifies itself by noting that most of the secondary material focuses on *Gatsby* and, to a lesser extent, *Tender*. His readings of the novels are unobjectionable, if abbreviated, and he regularly identifies the stories in which germs of the major works seemed first to appear. Hook's pseudobiographical approach rehearses much of Bruccoli, Kazin, Mizener, and others and serves as a starting point but not much more. Routledge reissued the book this year, but a copy of it eludes me.

b. Full-length Studies: Hemingway   "What are they teaching these kids in high school?" Witness Patrice Benson's A Farewell to Arms, *Ernest Hemingway: Curriculum Unit* (Center for Learning), which provides a book-by-book study outline and includes lessons on background, structure, geography, vocabulary, as well as suggestions for writing assignments and examinations. While it offers fledgling instructors a set of lesson plans, its sources are dated and sophistication limited.

c. Collections: Fitzgerald   None appeared this year.

d. Collections: Hemingway   Harold Hurley, ed., *Hemingway's Debt to Baseball in* The Old Man and the Sea: *A Collection of Critical Readings*

(Mellen, 1992), gathers seven previously published essays and numerous excerpts from a variety of sources relating *Old Man* to the American game. Hurley adds two original essays: "The Facts Behind the Fiction: The 1950 American League Pennant Race and *The Old Man and the Sea*" (pp. 77–93), which pursues Hemingway's allusions to the American League pennant race during the second full week of September; and "The World of Spirit or the World of Sport?: Figuring the Numbers in *The Old Man and the Sea*" (pp. 103–17), which contends that Hemingway's use of the numbers "eighty-four" and "eighty-five" derives from the novel's chronological association with the events of 1950's "September Stretch." Valuable in that it fields the best studies on baseball and Hemingway, this anthology also poses interesting questions about the availability of the sport as a mythology for serious writers, about the relevance of Santiago's reflections on the *Gran Ligas,* and about the aptness of Hemingway's allusions to baseball.

e. General Essays: Fitzgerald   While J. Gerald Kennedy's "Modernism as Exile: Fitzgerald, Barnes, and the Unreal City," pp. 185–242 in *Imagining Paris,* predominantly focuses on *Tender is the Night* and *Nightwood,* it has broader implications for the study of place in the arena of modernism. Kennedy begins his treatise with a provocative exploration of the concept of place, particularly as it affects our sense of who we are, before turning to chapters on Stein, Hemingway, Miller, Fitzgerald, and Djuna Barnes which "indicate how exile in France affected the career of each writer and how Paris became for each a complex image of the possibilities of metamorphosis." Fitzgerald was not initially taken with Paris; his indifference, Kennedy suggests, was owing to his bourgeois conventionality and excessive drinking. Nonetheless, his experience in the city "where the twentieth century was" produced inexorable changes; foremost he came to realize that the "glamorous lifestyle . . . concealed certain insidious risks": innocence, optimism, sanity, and selfhood were in jeopardy. Fitzgerald's meditation on these dangers made their way into "One Trip Abroad," "Babylon Revisited," and *Tender is the Night.* In the novel, personality became "an unstable and indeterminate nexus of tendencies"; it split, merged, and assimilated; male/female distinctions became fluid; a pattern of gender reversals developed. Paris itself figures only briefly in the novel, but this, writes Kennedy, is precisely Fitzgerald's point: as a "locus of the imagination," it is "a theater of dreams, a scene of fantasy and excess which becomes a terrifying site of violent change." Perhaps because Hemingway's treatment of Paris and place is more extensive, Kennedy's discussion of him, below, strikes me as more inspired.

f. General Essays: Hemingway   The role of place, the nuances of style, and the possibilities of methodology join a trio of articles that keep pace with our current penchant to explore sexuality and identity. In "City of Danger: Hemingway's Paris" (pp. 79–141) Kennedy details the effect that Paris had on the emerging identity of Hemingway, particularly as it manifests itself in *The Sun Also Rises, A Moveable Feast,* and a score of other works. At Sherwood Anderson's behest, Hemingway visited and was captured by the Paris of the "unpretentious lower class . . . where people tolerated personal differences." The metropolis sharpened his perspective, cultivated his nostalgia for the "simpler landscapes of American innocence"; exile allowed him to validate Anderson's claim that he "could write about America abroad because the places that mattered . . . were always fixed in memory." But gaining perspective entailed risks: one could lose one's own identity through assimilation. For Hemingway, especially in retrospect, Paris was the site of his "dramatic metamorphosis," always worth revisiting but scarcely concealing "the precariousness of innocence and happiness" which he both lost and found there. An excellent beginning to a fascinating avenue of inquiry, Kennedy's *Imagining Paris* surely deserves a place on the shelves of serious students.

In one of the year's most interesting general treatments, Michael Kowalewski in "The Purity of Execution in Hemingway's Fiction," pp. 131–61 in *Deadly Musings,* proclaims that until we disarm ourselves of prior notions "of an understated style, aestheticized violence, misogynistic tendencies," and more, "we are unlikely to describe the full range of [Hemingway's] fictional abilities." Linking the "long tradition of disliking Hemingway's work" with his preoccupation with violence, Kowalewski chooses to focus on "its imaginative substance and the formal properties responsible for it." Unwilling to shoot in the "psychiatric open season," launched by critics such as Wyndham Lewis, he foregoes attempts to defend Hemingway's work on the grounds of psychological complexity and convincingly argues that we ought to *listen* more to the prose, for often it is concerned with "riding out a rhythm, with completing a self-enclosed verbal movement," as Nick does in successive paragraphs when he is watching the trout.

In "Hemingway's Gay Blades" (*Differences* 5, ii: 116–39) Robert Scholes and Nancy R. Comley begin with the entry on homosexuality in the glossary of *Death in the Afternoon* and proceed through numerous published and unpublished pieces. These texts document "the subtlety of Hemingway's presentation of a range of sexual attitudes and behaviors," revealing that he was interested in "the complexity of human sexuality" rather than macho excesses which have received so much attention.

Gregory Woods in "The Injured Sex: Hemingway's Voice of Masculine Anxiety," pp. 160–72 in *Textuality and Sexuality: Reading Theories and Practices,* ed. Judith Still and Michael Worton (Manchester), contrasts the styles of Proust and Hemingway. He suggests that "masculine anxiety" manifests itself in reticence and resistance to sentimentality: "To say too much might be to sound queer." Gay voices are uninhibited by such anxieties, Woods claims, prompting him to link the voice of heterosexual masculinity to *closeted* gay men because both are "terrified of indiscretion." Frowning on recent trends within Hemingway circles to perform "image maintenance," Debra A. Moddelmog in "Reconstructing Hemingway's Identity: Sexual Politics, the Author, and the Multicultural Classroom" (*Narrative* 1: 187–206) urges her colleagues to acknowledge that Hemingway's canon "contains numerous instances against acculturation into a homophobic patriarchy" and "provides extensive opportunities for dismantling binary opposition of both gender and sexuality."

g. Essays on Specific Works: Fitzgerald   In a slight exaggeration of the usual trend, *Gatsby* alone garnered a dozen specialized studies this year. Among the more insightful is Zsolt K. Virágos's previously overlooked "The Hazards of Interpretive Overkill: The Myths of Gatsby" (*HSE* 22 [1991]: 49–68), which questions the legitimacy of most of the *myth criticism* of Gatsby wherein a *"very vague resemblance"* is often presented as a "meaningful *correlation.*" His suggestion: "locate the focus of universality in the artifact itself, irrespective of the presence or absence of the mythical substance." Also good are John T. Irwin's observations in "Compensating Visions: *The Great Gatsby*" (*SWR* 77 [1992]: 536–45). He perceives that in *Gatsby,* reaching for the object of desire is more important than grasping it. Gatsby betrays this notion when he weds "his unutterable visions to [Daisy's] perishable breath"; likewise, in telling Gatsby's story, Nick rejects his predilection "to reserve all judgments," leaving him with only "the act of figuration itself" as compensation. Echoing his previous publications, Charles Scribner III in "Gatsby

Illuminated" (*ParisR* 35: 249–53) provides an excerpt of his article illustrating the significance and generation of Francis Cugat's paintings for *Gatsby*'s dust jacket (see *ALS 1991*, pp. 153–54, and *ALS 1992*, p. 144).

Lesser fare includes "J. P. Morgan and Gatsby's Name" (*SAF* 21: 111–15) by Karen Bellenir: James Gatz accomplishes his transformation by submerging himself into "the legend and initials of financier J. P. Morgan," thus becoming "J. Gatz P.," then, for "ease of articulation," Jay Gatsby. Thomas H. Pauly in "Gatsby as Gangster" (*SAF* 21: 225–36) suggests possible criminal models for *Gatsby* and notes that Fitzgerald encourages readers to interpret Gatsby himself not only as a lover but as a gangster. Tony McAdams in *"The Great Gatsby* as a Business Ethics Inquiry" (*JBE* 12: 653–60) details his use of the novel as a provocative ethics experience for undergraduates. And Jeffrey Hart's "Anything Can Happen: Magical Transformation in *The Great Gatsby*" (*SCR* 25, ii: 37–50) explores religious issues, magic, and witchcraft, noting that a "strange sense of transformation pervades the book."

h. Essays on Specific Works: Hemingway   An especially useful crop of articles has been harvested from the range of Hemingway's canon. While a few make minor, or even redundant, contributions, the best bestow new insights to ongoing debates. For example, Joseph M. Flora challenges recent tendencies to view Nick Adams as the implied author of the "novel" *In Our Time,* in "Saving Nick Adams for Another Day" (*SoAR* 58, ii: 61–84). He agrees that Nick is a unifying force in the collection but firmly rejects as limiting the concept of Nick as implied author of every story.

Labor in *Sun* produced tiny fruit. Jesse Bier in "Jake Barnes, Cockroaches, and Trout in *The Sun Also Rises,*" pp. 151–58 in *Resistant Essays,* argues that Jake's impotence "is a psychological and moral condition as well as a physical one." Robert E. Fleming notes another instance of humor in "The Fun Also Rises: A Tribute to Jim Hinkle" (*HN* 13, i: 90–91) by explicating a heretofore submerged joke regarding the phallic nickname of Zizi, "the little Greek portrait painter."

Joining the debate over the heroine of Hemingway's novel of World War I, Charles Hatten in "The Crisis of Masculinity, Reified Desire, and Catherine Barkley in *A Farewell to Arms*" (*JHS* 4: 76–98) nudges readers away from "simple polarities" ("male sexual fantasy" vs. "prime mover" in the love story). Suggesting that we set aside preoccupations with Hemingway's personal development, Hatten situates the discussion of masculine identity in the socioeconomic sphere. As models for masculinity shifted at the turn of the century, Frederic stubbornly holds fast to traditional ideals while simultaneously embracing Catherine, who is the embodiment of "reified desire" (i.e., desire, such as forbidden love, that is "embattled" by efforts to restrict it). Both war and romance fail him, but Catherine provides Frederic with a new model in her "aesthetic version of masculine identity, which stands as compensatory to the very fragility of the masculine identity suggested through Henry's relationship with her." Harkening back to the old polarities (Catherine as idealized/reviled), Jamie Barlowe-Kayes in "Re-Reading Women: The Example of Catherine Barkley" (*HN* 12, ii: 24–35) interprets the heroine as a product of Hemingway's "idealization and objectification" of women, reflecting his own marginalization and trivialization of the sex. The tension between ideal and real also informs Gary Sloan's "*A Farewell to Arms* and the Sunday-School Jesus" (*SNNTS* 24: 449–56). He observes Frederic's inability to live up to "the gentle advocate of an ethic of selflessness," which "produces a recurrent self-loathing and a brooding guilt" because of the eternal rift between aspiration and performance.

Taking on the theme of identity in another country, Thomas Strychacz in "Trophy-Hunting as a Trope of Manhood in Ernest Hemingway's *Green Hills of Africa*" (*HN* 13, i: 36–47) observes that just as manhood is "always subject to the unsettling scrutiny of others," so too are trophies, because they are "subject to circumstances outside the control of any individual." What the narrator of *Green Hills* learns, then, is that "manhood must be signified rather than signifying." The fascination of the story derives from the author's irrepressible urge to be a self-described "damned show-off" while simultaneously subverting the notion that trophy hunting—or popular acclaim—is the measure of a man. With reference to "The Killers" and "Ten Indians," Joseph M. Flora in "'Today is Friday' and the Pattern of *Men Without Women*" (*HN* 13, i: 17–35) pursues the theme of betrayal as it links the three stories that Hemingway wrote on 16 May 1926. The massive betrayal of the crucifixion in combination with his local betrayal of Hadley accounts for his preoccupation with the theme. Jeryl J. Prescott's "Liberty and Just[us]: Gender and Race in Hemingway's *To Have and Have Not*" (*CLAJ* 37: 176–88) explains Hemingway's "use of the feminist rhetoric of rage, economy of stereotype, and metonymic displacement to illuminate perceived gender and ethnic differences within a society that professes to foster equality yet frowns on difference."

Setting aside the issue of Hemingway's veracity in *A Moveable Feast*, in "The Good Writer's Tale: The Fictional Method of Hemingway's 'Scott Fitzgerald'" (*HN* 12, ii: 621–71) Marc Dolan focuses on Hemingway's dichotomous comparisons that articulate the differences between Scott and Ernest. Hemingway distinguished his disciplined "craft" from Fitzgerald's effortless "art."

Rose Marie Burwell in "Hemingway's *Garden of Eden*: Resistance of Things Past and Protecting the Masculine Text" (*TSLL* 35: 198–225) works closely with the substantial portion of the manuscript cut by Scribner's editor Tom Jenks in an attempt to "restore textual coherence by tracing the emergence of Bourne's anxiety through the use of (1) excised portions of the manuscript and (2) information establishing the autobiographical matrix of the novel." Doing so reveals that the novel is about an unhappy childhood, the dichotomous sensibility such a childhood creates, and its perils for a writer. Kathy Willingham observes a critical oversight in "Hemingway's *The Garden of Eden*: Writing with the Body" (*HN* 12, ii: 46–61). The novel, "alone or in tandem with the manuscript," focuses on the relationship between gender and the creative process and questions previous charges of misogyny. Faced with patriarchal dominance of the arts, Catherine Bourne's response prefigures theories articulated by Hélène Cixous. For example, Catherine pursues an alternative medium of expression—her own body—with cutting, bleaching, and blending; and she, along with Marita, practices a female economy, which is unrestricted, unlimited, and expects nothing in return. Throughout, Hemingway presents a sympathetic portrait of the creative woman, celebrating her artistic artistry; in turn, she "enables [David] to see beyond restrictive binaries."

James Phelan in "What Hemingway and a Rhetorical Theory of Narrative Can Do for Each Other: The Example of 'My Old Man'" (*HN* 12, ii: 1–14) acknowledges a spate of recent reevaluations. Is the story an unexceptional adolescent narrative, derivative of Anderson's "I Want to Know Why"? Or is its ending complicated by a Jamesian twist which provides evidence that Joe's disillusionment with his father is unfounded? In a refreshingly lucid marriage of theory and practice, Phelan's analysis accomplishes three things: it deepens our appreciation of the ways in which technique and vision function interdependently as we read; it renders the structuralist's story/discourse distinction a heuristic rather than an absolute; and, most interestingly, it exposes the paradox of the first-person naive narrator who is allegedly enlightened by the tale he tells—if he had really shed his naïveté as he experienced the incident in real time, then should not that new attitude pervade his narrative? It does not in Joe's story.

Less ambitious treatments of the short stories include Paul Civello's "Hemingway's 'Primitivism': Archetypal Patterns in 'Big Two-Hearted River'" (*HN* 13, i: 1–16), which focuses on the mythic level in the story (journey to the center, re-creating the cosmos, regenerating himself) and suggests that Hemingway "pointed toward modern man's redemption through primitive patterns of experience." Quentin E. Martin in "Hemingway's 'The Killers'" (*Expl* 52: 53–57) reveals how the story can be seen as a "concise and dramatic representation of certain aspects of Albert Einstein's theory of relativity and Werner Heisenberg's principle of indeterminacy." J. F. Kobler's "'Soldier's Home' Revisited: A Hemingway *Mea Culpa*" (*SSF* 30: 377–85) contends that Hemingway selected Krebs rather than Nick as narrator to assuage the author's guilt for having created a false image of himself as a war hero without damaging his public reputation. S. Kozikowski et al. in "Hemingway's 'The Short Happy Life of Francis Macomber'" (*Expl* 51: 239–41) suggests that the story expresses the "inadequacy of human creation from which [the characters] can at best only inadequately free themselves." And lastly, Gary Harrington's "Hemingway's 'God Rest You Merry, Gentlemen'" (*Expl* 52: 51–53) considers *The Merchant of Venice* and notes that in this story, at least, Hemingway seems to transcend the purportedly anti-Semitic strain found elsewhere.

The year's single linguistic treatment is Martin Montgomery's "Language, Character and Action: A Linguistic Approach to the Analysis of Character in a Hemingway Short Story," pp. 127–42 in *Techniques of Description: Spoken and Written Discourse*, ed. John M. Sinclair et al. (Routledge), wherein Montgomery seeks to rectify the "comparative neglect of character in the systematic treatment of narratives" by generating a transivity profile of Hemingway's "The Revolutionist." This profile enables Montgomery, unaided by reference to existing criticism of the story, to observe that the story "could be seen as built upon an ironic tension between the expectations of the title and the linguistic choices that accumulate around the pronoun that refers back to it."

i. Miscellaneous We find Hemingway's name in two titles this year. James A. Michener's *Literary Reflections: Michener on Michener, Hemingway, Capote & Others* (State House), which reprints his introduction to

The Dangerous Summer, is "updated" only in that it excises "sixty-two compact paragraphs of erudite description of the bullfight." And E. L. Doctorow's *Jack London, Hemingway, and the Constitution: Selected Essays, 1977–1992* (Random House) reprints "Braver Than We Thought," his superb review of *The Garden of Eden,* here entitled "Ernest Hemingway, R.I.P."

Part II

William J. Scheick

Benjamin Franklin, Thomas Jefferson, and Phillis Wheatley enjoyed a bonanza of critical interest this year. So too did the writings of their contemporaries, particularly works reflecting numerous antithetical features of 18th-century American thought and sentiment. With the notable exception of Mary Rowlandson, who is primarily valued for expressing similar tensions, Puritan authors continue to recede before the tide of current scholarly interest in the cultural representations and contradictions of Enlightenment America.

i   Native Americans and the Colonial Imagination

In *The Ordeal of the Longhouse: The People of the Iroquois League in the Era of European Colonization* (No. Car.) Daniel K. Richter documents how colonizers were perceived by a Native American group who in the 17th century underwent changes resulting from disease, trade, and missionary efforts, and who in the 18th century made adaptations to preserve cultural integrity. The cultural intersection of economic and familial perceptions, particularly differences between matriarchal Cherokee and patriarchal Euro-American notions of individual freedom, social authority, and gender roles, is the subject of Tom Hatley's *Dividing Paths: Cherokees and South Carolinians Through the Era of Revolution* (Oxford); because the women of both cultures shared viewpoints, Hatley speculates, colonial males probably worried that colonial women would desire the sort of autonomy enjoyed by tribal women. The colonizers' perceptions interest José Rabasa, whose *Inventing America: Spanish Historiography and the Formation of Eurocentrism* (Okla.) features 16th-century European iconographical and cartographical images that inscribe the New World as a rhetorical text; whatever is factual in this representation

remains elusively screened behind strategic moves at once subjective and
in effect real.

Concern with perception also informs Rabasa's "Aesthetics of Colonial
Violence: The Massacre of Acoma in Gaspar de Villagrá's *Historia de la
Nueva México*" (*CollL* 20, i: 96–114), which argues that grotesque representations deprive indigenous peoples of dignity and also further the
ideological legitimation of the destruction of these peoples. Relatedly, in
"Accounting for One's Self: The Business of Alterity in Fur Trade Narratives" (*CollL* 20, i: 115–32) Dennis Denisoff observes that when their
European perspectives encountered otherness, company-men experienced a disjunction between their representations of the actual situation
and the point of view of distant readers. That the utopian trope of a
gendered paradise (including the promiscuity of female islanders and the
feminization of nature) served as a paradigm for discourse about the
New World is the topic of "Woman and Arcadia: The Impact of Ancient
Utopian Thought on the Early Image of America" (*JAmS* 27: 1–17) by
Mario Klarea. *Early Images of the Americas: Transfer and Invention,* ed.
Jerry M. Williams and Robert E. Lewis (Arizona), offers 12 essays,
including Angel Delgado-Gomez's contention that early reports of Native Americans depart from the noble savage idea and suggest some
objectivity in viewpoint ("The Earliest European Views of the New
World Natives," pp. 3–20); and Maureen Ahern's study of the use of two
ritual signs as a means of incorporating Native American lands within
the coded space of colonial expectations ("The Cross and the Gourd:
The Appropriation of Ritual Signs in the *Relaciones* of Alvar Núñez
Cabeza de Vaca and Fray Marcos de Niza," pp. 215–44).

Focusing on a 1658 account of the Caribbean islands, Keith A. San-
diford analyzes a rhetorical device, at once customary and devious, that
permits the reporting *subject* and the reported *other* to cross boundaries:
"Rochefort's *History*: The Poetics of Collusion in a Colonizing Narrative" (*PLL* 29: 284–302). In *"Oroonoko*'s Gendered Economics of
Honor/Horror: Reframing Colonial Discourse Studies in the Americas"
(*AL* 65: 415–43) Stephanie Athey and Daniel Cooper Alarcón describe
the subtle rhetoric of the narrator of Aphra Behn's novel; this rhetoric—
featuring the issues of slavery, rape, and dismemberment as well as
implying competition between British, African, and Native American
women—is simultaneously politically immune and politically charged.
Highlighting accounts by Alexander Henry, Samuel Hearne, and Alexander Mackenzie, *Narrating Discovery* (pp. 15–69) presents Bruce Green-

field's detection of rhetorical moments in various documents where nature is used to displace history; these occasions reveal uncertain and conflicted attempts to achieve narrative and ideological coherence (see *ALS 1986*, p. 199). The mutability of one author's identity, which is adrift in the multivalent flux that characterizes his New World experience, interests Juan Bruce-Novoa, whose "Shipwrecked in the Seas of Signification: Cabeza de Vaca's *La Relación* and Chicano Literature" is included in *Reconstructing a Chicano/a Literary Heritage: Hispanic Colonial Literature of the Southwest,* ed. María Herrera-Sobek (Arizona, pp. 3–23).

In *The Intellectual Construction of America: Exceptionalism and Identity from 1492 to 1800* (No. Car.) Jack P. Greene examines the changing definitions of the New World from Columbus through the Revolution to the Republic and concludes that distinctiveness was a major adaptable feature of early and late American identity. But economic determinist Denys Delâge alleges in *Bitter Feast: Amerindians and Europeans in Northeastern North America, 1600–64* (UBC) that the global emergence of a transitional country like England depended on internal financial problems that forced emigration to geographic peripheries which were exploited by means of unequal exchange with indigenous peoples. An entrepreneur especially interested in economic exchange is the subject of *Captain John Smith: Revised Edition* by Everett Emerson (Twayne). And according to Myra Jehlen's "History Before the Fact; or, Captain John Smith's Unfinished Symphony" (*CritI* 19: 677–92), Smith's description of the coronation of Powhaton features lapses, incoherence, and paradox because the future is uncertain, historical causality is an illusion, and all discourse is as limited as is human agency.

ii Early Colonial Poetry

In *Edward Taylor: Fifty Years of Scholarship and Criticism* (Camden House) Jeffrey Hammond provides a stunningly thorough and even-handed review of various concerns of Taylorian studies, while in *Sinful Self, Saintly Self: The Puritan Experience of Poetry* (Georgia) he explores one of these concerns shared by Taylor, Bradstreet, and Wigglesworth. Their verse, Hammond convincingly argues, mediated Scripture and was compositionally completed only when its readers closed with its biblical origin. A metaself is projected in this poetry, a paradigmatic self that struggles beyond sin to an imagined assurance. Taylor's later poems, in particular, dramatize this loss of earthly self for a nearly achieved neobiblical identity as the Bride of Christ of the Canticles. A cure for sinfulness in "Meditation 2.40," Karen Gordon-Grube discloses in "Evidence of Medicinal Cannibalism in Puritan New England: 'Mummy' and Related Remedies in Edward Taylor's 'Dispensatory' " (*EAL* 28: 185–221), is said to include an extract of the poet's dead son; for as a practitioner of Paracelsian medicine Taylor evidently approved the therapeutic consumption of prepared human flesh.

Taylor's verse fared less well in four essays. Contending that alliteration, consonance, and assonance are as important as sense in Taylorian art, Percy G. Adams lists examples in "Edward Taylor's Love Affair with Sounding Language" (*Order in Variety: Essays and Poems in Honor of Donald E. Stanford,* ed. R. W. Crump [Delaware, 1991; pp. 12–31]). Keith Polette's "Taylor's 'The Preface' and Borges's 'John 1: 14' " (*Expl* 51: 151–53) reports that both authors dissolve opposites and boundaries in order to suggest the encounter of the divine through the imagination. Elisa New's " 'Both Great and Small': Adult Proportion and Divine Scale in Edward Taylor's 'Preface' and *The New England Primer*" (*EAL* 28: 120–32) deduces that both works use miniaturization to emphasize the smallness of humanity in the divine scheme; consequently "the child learns to wish what she is not in order to regret what she is." And according to Carol Bensick's censorious "Preaching to the Choir: Some Achievements and Shortcomings of Taylor's *Gods Determinations*" (*EAL* 28: 133–47), the "main charge against" this poem, for which "we ought not to forgive Taylor," "is that it lies," "discriminates," and "teaches . . . gloom." In such an approach there is unfortunately, to paraphrase Shakespeare's Cassio, more of the soldier than of the scholar.

Critical responses are summarized in Francis Murphy's "Anne Bradstreet and Edward Taylor," in *Columbia History of American Poetry* (pp. 1–15). *Elizabeth I: The Competition for Representation* (Oxford, pp. 146–47) includes Susan Frye's brief observation that in a poem by Bradstreet the revered queen is a figure of female complexity construed as both familiar and unfamiliar. Bradstreet's written comments to her children are considered in "Women's Autobiography and the Hermeneutics of Conversion" (*ABSt* 8: 72–90), a preview of *Sacred Estrangement* (pp. 25–41), in which Peter A. Dorsey finds the formulae and extended metaphors of Puritan spiritual relations to be sufficiently flexible to accommodate gender, racial, generic, cultural, and historic variations.

A later colonial poet's uneven, inconsistent, and subjective verse, observes Jane Donahue Eberwein in " '*Harvardine* quil': Benjamin Tompson's Poems on King Philip's War" (*EAL* 28: 1–20), served as a sampler of rhetorical modes designed to stimulate other Harvard authors to respond to New England's crisis. And David S. Shields's "Literature of the Colonial South" (*RALS* 19: 174–222) provides editions of four poems that exemplify the propriety of approaching the Southeastern colonies not as places of cultural integrity, but collectively as regions of cultivated staples where a discourse of unresolved thematic tensions emerged.

iii Rowlandson and Early Colonial Prose

According to June Namias's disappointing *White Captives: Gender and Ethnicity on the American Frontier* (No. Car.), the issue of sexual barriers in captivity narratives includes a concern with religious, political, and cultural threats; and in contrast to the melodramatic frail flower and the powerful amazon in these chronicles, Mary Rowlandson is a survivor in her account, someone who adapts by trying to make sense of her situation. Anthropological contact likewise interests Michelle Burnham in "The Journey Between: Liminality and Dialogism in Mary White Rowlandson's Captivity Narrative" (*EAL* 28: 60–75), which argues that the victim's traumatic experience is not the only explanation for the contradictions of tone and narrative form in her account; these contradictions result from Rowlandson's liminal "subject position," which shifts in its representation of various desires. Pertinently, Lisa Logan's "Mary Rowlandson's Captivity and the 'Place' of the Woman Subject" (*EAL* 28: 255–77) focuses on the contradictory function of Rowlandson's literal and figurative positions in her narrative; on restoration, the former abductee is empowered to speak but is now also made captive to emblematic representation. Several related contradictions in representations of Native Americans are detected by Kathryn Zabelle Derounian-Stodola and James Arthur Lavernier, whose *The Indian Captivity Narrative, 1550–1900* (Twayne) devotes a chapter to Mary Rowlandson's reliance on a mythic pattern (capture, initiation, and return), her use of religious commentary, and her narrative-disrupting expression of survivor guilt.

Captivity narratives figure prominently in *A Mixed Race: Ethnicity in Early America* (Oxford), a respectable anthology edited by Frank Shuffelton. David R. Sewell reads these narratives as a linguistic reclamation of control through managed storytelling that reverses the experience of inverted power relations during the captive's imprisonment (pp. 39–55).

Rosalie Murphy Baum interprets John Williams's impersonally narrated *The Redeemed Captive* as an instance of looking *through* French and Native American ethnicity to see only the tropes already constructed by his culture (pp. 56–76). Benilde Montgomery discusses African American consciousness, especially as reflected in the technique of rupture and repetition in John Marrant's captivity narrative (pp. 105–15). John Sekora points out the influence of popular captivity narratives on the publication of Briton Hammon's slave narrative (pp. 92–104). By way of contrast, captivity and victimization are not the focus of early New England rape narratives, Daniel Williams astutely observes; these accounts present rape as a culmination of a life of sinful corruption, as a product of alien ethnicity or identity, and as a violation of patriarchal privilege, including control over the "property" of the victimized female body (pp. 194–221).

Whereas Shuffelton sorts out the strengths and weaknesses of the reliance on the cultural catalog prescribed by 18th-century anthropological method in Jefferson's comments on Native Americans and African Americans (pp. 257-77), Doreen Alvarez Saar exposes how the prescriptive model of propriety and industry, as the measure of ethnic behavior, cuts across Crèvecoeur's notion of the melting pot (pp. 241–56). The economic considerations advanced by Cotton Mather and William Byrd to subvert beliefs in racial difference, explains Dana D. Nelson in a reprise of her book (see *ALS 1992*, pp. 172–73), fail because their arguments derive from and reinforce the privileged cultural status of these men (pp. 19–38). And the participation of elite Jews in commerce, David S. Shields documents, was facilitated by a cosmopolitanism that also became a threat to Jewish heritage and custom (pp. 143–62).

Colonial Pennsylvania Germans, according to William T. Parsons, tended to stress their differences and mutual interests among themselves (pp. 119–42). In contrast, explains Betsy Erkkila, when Phillis Wheatley spoke as a female victim of slavery, she turned to irony to reverse the implications of Anglo-American racial codes (pp. 225–40). The expression of difference in Native American humor interests Luise van Keuren, who indicates that colonial writers used various representations to express their own resistance to Britain (pp. 77–91). Reviewing American jest books, Robert Secor discloses how dialect in humor differs in relation to varying perceptions of ethnic groups (pp. 163–93).

If early captivity narratives were approved in terms of their acculturation to Puritan practice, explains Constance Post, so likewise were reports on "praying Indians," as exemplified by both Cotton Mather's extensive anti-Catholic annotations to a 1687 letter by his father and his privileged presentation of a sermon by Nishokon: "Old World Order in the New: John Eliot and 'Praying Indians' in Cotton Mather's *Magnalia Christi Americana*" (*NEQ* 66: 416–33). Cotton Mather and Jedidiah Morse used maps, and Franklin referred to streets, as texts that narrate the radical reordering of American experience, explains William Boelhower in "Stories of Foundation, Scenes of Origin" (*AmLH* 5: 391–428). Sacvan Bercovitch's 1972 review of Cotton Mather's career, his 1976 essay on the ends of Puritan rhetoric, and his 1978 study of the typology of America's mission are reprinted in *The Rites of Assent.*

Mather also appears in *Salem Story: Reading the Witch Trials of 1692* (Cambridge), Bernard Rosenthal's remarkable disclosure of facts; Rosenthal documents the ongoing distortion of these facts as a result of the conflicted metaphorical use of the Salem episode as an imaginative cultural landscape where injustice and irrationality have been safely encountered through escapist versions of enlightenment. An issue of *EIHC* (129: 1–118) presents five historical studies on colonial witchcraft, including discussions of the place of women and of print in the Salem episode. And, in a related vein, Michael Clark discerns in the Salem turmoil a disjunction between the authorized word and the unauthorized body: " 'Like Images Made Black with the Lightning': Discourse and the Body in Colonial Witchcraft" (*ECent* 34: 199–220).

The use of typology to suggest that human history is fragmented by occasional divine intervention is the subject of Stephen Carl Arch's "The Edifying History of Edward Johnson's *Wonder-Working Providence*" (*EAL* 28: 42–59), which innovatively traces an emblematic triadic structure in Johnson's effort to record and (with some authorial license) to teach his audience. The design behind Thomas Hooker's use of chiasmus, apostrophe, prosopopeia, sermocinatio, minor characters, subplots, scenes, allusions, and figuration interests Alan D. Hodder, whose "In the Glasse of God's Word: Hooker's Pulpit Rhetoric and the Theater of Conversion" (*NEQ* 66: 67–109) reports that these sermonic techniques were intended to remind hearers that the world is a stage with a divine spectator watching humanity act out a sacred drama.

Some of the complexities informing the dramatic encounter of two religious antagonists are explored in David S. Lovejoy's "Roger Williams and George Fox: The Arrogance of Self-Righteousness" (*NEQ* 66: 199–225). In "Arguments in Milk, Arguments in Blood: Roger Williams,

Persecution, and the Discourse of the Witness" (*MP* 91: 133–60) Anne G. Myles focuses on the symbolic terms of Williams's dissent, specifically his expression of the affliction mutually shared by the feeling body and the social "other" for the soul's sake; his manner of intersecting the literal and the figurative resists the "polluted" orthodox New England vocabulary represented by John Cotton's authorized arguments and, in turn, encourages a language of pure affect.

Descent, rather than dissent, was featured in three articles. Mark A. Peterson's "The Plymouth Church and the Evolution of Puritan Religious Culture" (*NEQ* 66: 570–93) documents John Cotton, Jr.'s role in reversing the decline of the closed separatist community by welcoming newcomers and interacting with the emergent religious culture of New England. The importance of family, church, and community to the Quaker son of John Winthrop is detailed in "A Puritan in the West Indies: The Career of Samuel Winthrop" (*WMQ* 50: 768–86) by Larry D. Gragg. And according to the late Cora E. Lutz, an awareness of heritage, including Edward Taylor as his maternal grandfather, informed "Ezra Stiles's Measure of Himself" (*YULG* 67: 127–37).

Hugh Amory profiles a minor early publisher in "Under the Exchange: The Unprofitable Business of Michael Perry, a Seventeenth-Century Boston Bookseller" (*PAAS* 103: 31–60). Concerning related publications, Linda Schlafer's "The Fable Comes to America . . . Or Does It?" (*Bestia* 5: 73–83) and Marcia Miller's "Verse Fables in Eighteenth-Century Newspapers and Magazines" (*RALS* 19: 275–93) document the increasingly Americanized literary use of animals to influence public opinion on moral and political issues.

iv   Edwards, the Great Awakening, and the New Divinity

Delightful Conviction: Jonathan Edwards and the Rhetoric of Conversion by Stephen R. Yarbrough and John C. Adams (Greenwood) presents the following thesis: since Edwards subverts the structures of belief that reinforce a sense of individual self-determination, he avoids the rational prop of preparationist phases in his emphasis on the meaning and effects of conversion. In *The Works of Jonathan Edwards, Volume 11: Typological Writings* (Yale) Wallace E. Anderson and Mason I. Lowance, Jr., with the assistance of David H. Watters, provide editions of three documents that reveal several tensions between conservative and progressive exegetical methods in interpreting divine communication to humanity. Ann-Janine Morey's *Religion and Sexuality in American Literature* (Cambridge, 1992; pp. 24–25) reports on Edwards's concern with mistaking sexual passion for religious affection. And Linda Munk's *The Trivial Sublime: Theology and American Poetics* (St. Martin's, 1992; pp. 136–62) reprints her essay on the Shekinah in Edwards's writings (see *ALS 1992*, p. 169).

John Wesley's adroit suppression of Edwards's emphasis on Original Sin and his heightening of Edwards's emphasis on the sensation of religious affections are surmised by Richard E. Brantley in *Coordinates of Anglo-American Romanticism*. Also in contrast to Edwards, Nancy Ruttenburg contends in "George Whitefield, Spectacular Conversion, and the Rise of Democratic Personality" (*AmLH* 5: 429–58), Whitefield represented himself as having reconciled humility (self-abasement) and power (self-exaltation); this portrait of a regenerated and revolutionary self, textualized through his sermons, functioned as a model for national selfhood.

Benjamin Franklin, Jonathan Edwards, and the Representation of American Culture, ed. Barbara B. Oberg and Harry S. Stout (Oxford), includes William Breitenbach on what both men shared on the twin subjects of salvation and success (pp. 13–26); A. Owen Aldridge on Enlightenment influences on Edwards's ethics and revivalist influences on Franklin's beliefs (pp. 27–41); Edwin S. Gaustad on the relationship between Edwards's understanding of virtue and Franklin's idea of a moral universe (pp. 42–57); Elizabeth E. Dunn on the contrast between Edwards's essentialism and Franklin's pragmatism (pp. 58–74); Daniel Walker Howe on both men's opposite use of faculty psychology (pp. 75–97); Bruce Kuklick on how neither man is representative of his time (pp. 101–13); Leonard I. Sweet on the ways that melancholic Edwards showed a lighter side similar to Franklin's (pp. 114–33); Ruth H. Bloch on the fact that both transitional men, despite their ambivalence toward women and their opposition to romantic love, set the stage for a different understanding of gender (pp. 134–51); David Levin on the place of plain and clear language (appealing to reason through rhythm, proportion, and parallelism) in the writings of both men (pp. 171–85); J. A. Leo Lemay on the successful use of rhetorical strategies in *Sinners in the Hands of an Angry God* and *Narrative of the Late Massacres* (pp. 186–203); R. C. De Prospo on the need for a "counter-discourse" that makes the works of both men "reader-unfriendly" and thereby intimates "a Power that is actually prior to language" that exposes modern humanism (pp. 204–17).

v Franklin, Jefferson, and the Revolution

Reappraising Benjamin Franklin (Delaware) is a valuable resource in which editor J. A. Leo Lemay addresses the theme of vanity in the *Autobiography* and also presents John C. Van Horne on Franklin's conception of philanthropy (pp. 425–40), Heinz Otto Sibum on the background of his moral algebra (pp. 221–42), Robert D. Arner on his perception of class and context in criticizing intemperance (pp. 52–77), Stephen Fender on his contradictory views on emigration (pp. 335–46; see *ALS 1992*, p. 168), A. Owen Aldridge on his stalwart Deism (pp. 362–71), Esmond Wright on his personal relationship with British negotiators as a factor in the peace treaties with Britain (pp. 154–74), Wayne Craven on his changing image in British and American portraits (pp. 247–71), Ellen G. Miles on his depiction by French artists (pp. 272–89), Claude-Anne Lopez on his successful adaptation to French culture (pp. 143–53), Ellen R. Cohn on his musical talent and relish for traditional music (pp. 290–318), James N. Green on his risky ventures in the publication of original imprints (pp. 98–114), Edwin Wolf 2nd on his library (pp. 319–31), and David Yerkes on his previously misrepresented vocabulary (pp. 396–414). Concerning Franklin's strategies in expression, Jack P. Greene explores his use of the domestic relations model to depict the conflict between England and the colonies (pp. 119–42); J. L. Heilbron contextualizes his scientific use of analogy (pp. 196–220); Ralph Lerner focuses on his management of rhetoric to stimulate thought (pp. 415–24); Barbara B. Oberg stresses his reliance on classical rhetorical devices, double negatives, and self-effacement (pp. 175–92); Jeffrey A. Smith emphasizes his development from aggressive voice to negotiating capitalist (pp. 40–51); Norman S. Grabo demarcates his assumed journalistic voices, from *Spectator*-like artifice to personal approach (pp. 31–39); and Daniel Royot interprets his use of personae as a mode of experimentation with the possibilities of life (pp. 388–95). In his sensationalistic writings on deviant behavior, Ronald A. Bosco contends (pp. 78–97), Franklin appeals to his reader's sense of superiority and provides a mechanism to relieve various social tensions; and in his conflicted *Narrative of the Late Massacres,* Carla Mulford argues (pp. 347–58), Franklin's sympathy for Native Americans as natural equals is substantially compromised by his alignment with the hierarchizing mentality of the Anglo-American community.

The uncertain evidence for attributing authorship to the epistolary rhetoric of the American Commission to France is the subject of Barbara Oberg's "Benjamin Franklin's Correspondence: Whose Intent? What Text? I Don't Know's the Author" (*Palimpsest*, pp. 271–84). Kevin J. Hayes, in "The Board of Trade's '*cruel Sarcasm*': A Neglected Franklin Source" (*EAL* 28: 171–76), identifies the British origin of an allusion pertaining to the transportation of felons to America. And in "Figuring Franklin" (*Benjamin Franklin: An American Genius,* ed. Gianfranca Balestra and Luigi Sampietro [Bulzoni], pp. 175–88) Norman S. Grabo reports that this Founding Father and William Carlos Williams both emphasize details as ends in themselves rather than as vehicles of metaphoric meanings.

The man selected by Franklin to serve as a rector and who was later accused by Franklin of emphasizing the classics to the neglect of instruction in English, is the subject of "An Introduction to William Smith and Rhetoric at the College of Philadelphia" (*PAPS* 134 [1990]: 111–60), in which Dennis Barone provides an edition of Smith's "Lectures in Rhetoric" (1760). Barone's "James Logan, Benjamin Franklin, and True and False Reason: A Note on Franklin's 'Errata'" (*PennE* 18: 13–21) focuses on the place of Logan's manuscript commentary in Franklin's retraction of *Dissertation on Liberty and Necessity.* Barone further reports that although philosophers such as Logan maintained that humanity possesses an innate moral sense, they also taught (antidemocratically) that most people will accept the authority of a select few and thereby preserve the social hierarchy: "Teaching Virtue: The Rhetoric of Moral Discourse in Eighteenth-Century Philadelphia" (*Teaching Philosophy* 16: 105–22). A comprehensive review of the long-standing correlation of civil liberty and rhetoric, political theory and linguistic practice appears in Thomas Gustafson's *Representative Words.*

Frank Lambert's "Subscribing for Profits and Piety: The Friendship of Benjamin Franklin and George Whitefield" (*WMQ* 50: 529–54) focuses on the impersonal marketplace as the common ground for two men of different beliefs but shared interest in promoting the religious revivals through print; one made money, while the other gained souls. Opposition to several of Franklin's views surfaces in *The Storm Gathering: The Penn Family and the American Revolution* (Penn. State, 1992), in which

Lorett Treese also documents the Penns' resistance to British policies likely to harm the imperial economy.

The man who praised Franklin for important discoveries in physics is the subject of an issue of *VMHB* (101: 5–157) devoted to six articles on Thomas Jefferson as architect and reformer. And a related issue of *ECS* contains, among other studies, "Argumentation and Unified Structure in *Notes on the State of Virginia*" (26: 581–94) and *"Notes on the State of Virginia*: Thomas Jefferson's Unintentional Self-Portrait" (26: 635-48). In the first article George Alan Davy discloses Jefferson's reliance on an approved 18th-century hierarchy ranging from description to reasoning; in the second article Gisela Tauber (with no regard to previous commentary) speaks of Jefferson's projection of emotion in his descriptions of nature. Jefferson's positive response to James Macpherson's work and the place of persuasive language in his thought are reported in, respectively, Paul J. de Gategno's " 'The Source of Daily and Exalted Pleasure': Jefferson Reads *The Poems of Ossian*" (*SVEC* 305 [1992]: 1385–86) and John Stephen Martin's "Jefferson, Democracy, and Commonsense Rhetoric" (*SVEC* 305 [1992]: 1382–85).

Peter S. Onuf has both edited *Jeffersonian Legacies* (Virginia), a collection of conference papers by historians reflecting on the relevance of the Jeffersonian heritage, and authored "The Scholar's Jefferson" (*WMQ* 50: 671–99), a substantial overview on how Jefferson's image, as a controversial *text* open to interpretation, has been recast in terms of contemporary moral judgments. A didactic classical model that Jefferson and others found suitable to their vision of the emerging nation is the subject of Roxanne M. Gentilcore's "American Georgic: Vergil in the Literature of the Colonial South" (*CML* 13: 257–70). Lee Quinby indicates that Jefferson's equation of Virginia statehood (civic virtue) and human happiness (personal virtue)—an ethos based on an aesthetics of liberty—provided Americans with a way to resist both colonizing power abroad and normalizing power at home: *Freedom, Foucault, and the Subject of America* (Northeastern, 1991; pp. 17–46). And in *Declaring Independence: Jefferson, Natural Language, and the Culture of Performance* (Stanford) Jay Fliegelman considers the complex dialogic interaction between self-expression and self-effacement in the composition of the Declaration, which was also influenced by (a) the structure of the fugue, (b) the particular design of a swivel chair, (c) the way Jefferson wrote the letter *s*, (d) the claim that *Paradise Lost* was plagiarized, and (e) the belief that blacks cannot blush.

An African American poet whom Jefferson believed demonstrated a deficiency of imagination is the subject of four essays in *Style*: "Style as Protest in the Poetry of Phillis Wheatley" (27: 172–93), James A. Levernier's discussion of the poet's ironic criticism of racism, especially in her elegies; "Phillis Wheatley, Americanization, the Sublime, and the Romance of America" (27: 194–221), Phillip M. Richards's discussion of the poet's appropriation of romance neoclassicism and evangelical Protestantism to rewrite marginality and centrality and to rethink inherited ideologies; "Snatching a Laurel, Wearing a Mask: Phillis Wheatley's Literary Nationalism and the Problem of Style" (27: 222–51), Robert L. Kendrick's discussion of the poet's use of the African tradition of Esu-Elegbara and the European practice of Greek *Metis* to resist the dominant discourse from within; and "Phillis Wheatley's Subversion of Classical Stylistics" (27: 252–70), John C. Shields's discussion of the poet's management of Vergilean example to undermine her inherited classical traditions and the convention of slavery.

Focusing on incompatible dual readings of Wheatley's work in relation to European and African American traditions, Anita Silvers concludes that attempts to assess art entirely on a historical basis are inadequate: "Pure Historicism and the Heritage of Hero(in)es: Who Grows in Phillis Wheatley's Garden?" (*JAAC* 51: 475–82). More appropriate, Walt Nott explains in "From 'uncultivated Barbarian' to 'Poetical Genius': The Public Presence of Phillis Wheatley" (*MELUS* 18, iii: 21–32), is the appreciation of her persona; her self-presentation as someone who has progressed toward civilization participates in the tradition of the "public sphere," a mode of discourse that is designed to attain political power by controlling the emergent popular consensus. The posture of subordination to authority interests Hilene Flanzbaum, whose "Unprecedented Liberties: Re-Reading Phillis Wheatley" (*MELUS* 18, iii: 71–81) focuses on the emancipating place of imagination in the poet's escape from the conditions of bondage.

Frances Smith Foster's *Written by Herself: Literary Production of African American Women, 1746–1892* (Indiana, pp. 23–43) emphasizes the artistic ambition behind Wheatley's verse and the context of Lucy Terry Prince's "Bar's Fight"; both writers continued and developed a tradition. The tradition of scriptural symbolism, used to mask antislavery sentiment, is highlighted in *Jupiter Hammon and the Biblical Beginnings of African-American Literature* (Scarecrow), which presents Sondra O'Neale's critical edition of four poems and three essays.

The phrase "American revolution," Ilan Rachum reports in "From 'American Independence' to the 'American Revolution'" (*JAmS* 27: 73–81), emerged as a popular expression after the Declaration, particularly after its appearance in Paine's 1782 pamphlet letter to Guillaume Raynal. The logic of the man who analogized enslavement and the colonial condition, observes Bruce Woodcock in "Writing the Revolution: Aspects of Thomas Paine's Prose" (*PSt* 15 [1992]: 171–86), is sharpest when it is most aphoristic. And Paine, Jefferson, and Franklin appear in *The Dragon and the Eagle: The Presence of China in the American Enlightenment* (Wayne State), A. Owen Aldridge's comprehensive and fascinating study of the facts, myths, and appropriations evident in responses of early America to the idea of China.

vi The Early National Period

Collusion with an emergent culture of consumption is the subject of Daniel A. Cohen's comprehensive *Pillars of Salt, Monuments of Grace,* which traces the transition of moral authority from ministers to such marketplace professionals as lawyers, journalists, and novelists. As the distinction between fact and fiction eventually blurred in crime literature, so too did the relationship between crime and punishment. Their representation of criminal sexuality, at once vicariously enjoyable and socially dangerous, was especially vendible as a result of the increasing tension between indulgence and restraint experienced by readers in the early republic. Examples of such a representation are identified in both "From Damnation to Dollars: The Motivations of Malefactors in Two Eighteenth-Century American Criminal Narratives" (*SVEC* 303 [1992]: 388–91) and "Victims of Narrative Seduction: The Literary Translations of Elizabeth (and 'Miss Harriot') Wilson" (*EAL* 28: 148–70) by Daniel E. Williams. The second article in particular is an entertaining survey of several versions of a single crime narrative, which between 1786 and 1822 changed from an emphasis on religious conventions featuring divine power to a stress on sentimental conventions featuring female powerlessness; what did not change over time was each version's reflection of marketplace pressures that, in effect, fostered the production of warnings about seduction in texts designed to seduce the reader.

Williams's "Specious Spy: The Narrative Lives—and Lies—of Mr. John Howe" (*ECent* 34: 264–86) reports on the journal, attributed to a man who never existed, that dramatizes an antiauthoritarian smuggler capable of transgressing social, traditional, and narrative boundaries. Contrary readings of Satan's transgression were also evident in early national attempts to find in Milton's work a mythic justification for radical, moderate, or elite interpretations of America. K. P. Van Anglen further discloses in *The New England Milton* that Satan was a boundary-less figure, at times seen as an antinomian hero who defied authoritarian hierarchies, at other times seen as a demonic villain who subverted Arminian prospects.

By assuming various roles that interrogate customary boundaries between opposites, Susan M. Marren explains in "Between Slavery and Freedom: The Transgressive Self in Olaudah Equiano's Autobiography" (*PMLA* 108: 94–105), Equiano's ambiguous narrative persona resists an essentialist interpretation of racial representation and encourages white readers to perceive a more fluid definition of individual and collective identities. In his thoughtful "Word Between Worlds: The Economy of Equiano's *Narrative*" (*AmLH* 5: 459–80) Joseph Fichtelberg agrees that Equiano's autobiographical account of personal freedom and his related attempt to revise the status of Africans demonstrate a subversive ambiguity; but the account is also necessarily distorted by the bourgeois discourse of commodification imposed on its author and suggestive of his inability to break discursive enslavement. Divergent and dialogic formulations of selfhood likewise interest Dana D. Nelson, whose "Reading the Written Selves of Colonial America: Franklin, Occom, Equiano, and Palou/Serra" (*RALS* 19: 246–59) interprets autobiography as a form of cultural negotiation, a means whereby some cultures manage to influence even while they accommodate a dominant culture's paradigm for the formation of selfhood. Of tangential interest, Angelo Costanzo's "African-Caribbean Narrative of British America" (*RALS* 19: 260–74) focuses on the influence of West Indian slave memoirs on the abolitionist movement.

However desirable freedom may appear, conventional perceptions of American personal independence are not always what they seem, Michael Zuckerman argues in *Almost Chosen People,* parts of which appear in both *Reappraising Benjamin Franklin* and *Benjamin Franklin, Jonathan Edwards, and the Representation of American Culture.* In response to the Jacobin revolt of the oppressed people of color on Santo Domingo in 1791, for example, the "conservative" Federalists made the connection to the recently concluded American insurgency against Britain and anticipated a multiracial world; in contrast, the "liberal" Republicans, Jefferson in particular, did not extend their revolutionary principles beyond their own kind and provincial bounds. Franklin, a Federalist generally said to be the epitome of personal autonomy, was actually such a master of postures and personae in both his life and his art that no coherent individuality is discernible; his sense of self, moreover, was grounded not in a personal inner life but in a public performance directed toward the common good. And whereas William Byrd ignored the values of personal autonomy and domestic intimacy in Virginia, he devoted himself to his public life in order to foster a nascent sense of community; in England, where a social milieu was firmly in place, Byrd pursued personal interests.

The personal is depreciated in "Crèvecoeur and the Politics of Authorship in Republican America" (*EAL* 28: 91–119), Grantland S. Rice's reading of *Letters* as an epistolary novel that attempts to idealize the emerging nation but succumbs to both authorial and historical contingencies reinforcing Abbé Raynal's theory of exploitative economic behavior. In the contradictory Nantucket section, Anna Carew-Miller argues in "The Language of Domesticity in Crèvecoeur's *Letters from an American Farmer*" (*EAL* 28: 242–54), a forced correspondence between farming and whaling suggests a resistance to effeminate family life by a threatened masculine identity which is expressed through violent encounters with nature.

Focusing on the connection between gender and ethnicity, Julie Ellison's "Race and Sensibility in the Early Republic: Ann Eliza Bleecker and Sarah Wentworth Morton" (*AL* 65: 445–74) concludes that in Bleecker's work female vulnerability and sorrowful maternity provide occasions for appropriating the racist terror of captivity narratives, whereas in Morton's work glamorization of the Other provides an opportunity for the author's idealistic purview. In " 'Till *Grief* Melodious Grow': The Poems and Letters of Ann Eliza Bleecker" (*EAL* 28: 222–41) Allison Griffen examines how the poet's refusal to adopt the elegiac convention of final consolation served as a means of achieving and sustaining an authorial identity beyond what was typical of her time.

A concern with authorial identity informs "Revelation and the American Republic: Timothy Dwight's Civic Participation" (*JHI* 54: 449–68), in which Marc L. Harris contends that Dwight's union of religious and civil humanist traditions is the result of his commitment to rationalism; this commitment implies a belief in a correspondence between the success of America and the demonstration of the truth of revealed religion. Lack of such narrative integration interests Frank Shuffelton, whose "Endangered History: Character and Narrative in Early American Historical Writing" (*ECent* 34: 221–42) maintains that embedded biographical discourse (concerned with character) is different from and disrupts historical discourse (concerned with event); the contention for authority between these two modes raises questions about the very possibility of narrative.

That during the early republic the pattern of disseminating these histories and other works follows inland waterways as well as the needs of local markets is documented by Ronald J. Zboray, whose *A Fictive People* also deduces from the examples of Mason Locke Weems and his supplier Mather Carey that urban publishers dumped overproduced books in nonurban markets. In spite of its omission of Nathan Fiske's 1790 utopian romance ("An Allegorical Description of a Certain Island"), Edward W. R. Pitcher's *Fiction in American Magazines Before 1800: An Annotated Catalogue* (Union) is an extraordinarily valuable book that might inaugurate a revaluation of late-18th-century American literary activity. Useful, too, is *Humor in American Literature: A Selected Annotated Bibliography* by Don L. F. Nilsen (Garland, 1992).

vii Brown, Rowson, and Contemporaries

Wit contributed to the formation of national identity, Cameron C. Nickels argues in *New England Humor*; the figure of the rustic Yankee, in particular, negotiated the period's ambivalence toward the unsettling encounter of traditional Old World and emergent New World values. Brown's fiction relatedly mirrors an anxiety over the sway of cant, dogma, ideals, Enlightenment theory, and the dark side of the self. Bill Christophersen further observes in *The Apparition in the Glass: Charles Brockden Brown's American Gothic* (Georgia) that the goal of Brown's romances was to awaken America, an adolescent nation unknown to itself and at once repudiating and conserving the past.

Although Brown used the commercially successful didactic tradition of the captivity narrative, Steven Hamelman contends in "Rhapsodist in the Wilderness: Brown's Romantic Quest in *Edgar Huntly*" (*SAF* 21: 171–90) that he embedded in it an allegory of the pursuit of artistic self-realization, despite the threat of madness and death; Brown's literary theories in 1789 prefigure his self-portrait in his 1799 romance. The protagonist of *Edgar Huntly,* Scott Bradfield notes in *Dreaming Revolution* (pp. 15–32), is inspired by the unknown but never finds solutions in a terrain simultaneously geographic and psychological; his narrative regresses rather than progresses. "Charles Brockden Brown and the Frontiers of Discourse" (*Frontier Gothic,* pp. 109–25) presents Elizabeth Jane Wall Hinds's report on how unsettled space serves as an inscrutable and irrational agency that subordinates character in Brown's romances. In "Class, Gender, and Genre: Deconstructing Social Formulas on the Gothic Frontier" (*Frontier Gothic,* pp. 126–39) Pattie Cowell reads Brown and others with an eye to the American departure from the British pattern of reaffirming the social hierarchies that at first seem to be violated in Gothic fiction.

In his introduction to *Arthur Mervyn* (NCUP, 1992), "edited for the modern reader," Frank Gado highlights chapter 4 as the psychological key to Brown's romance about the protagonist's journey toward self-discovery and identity, a journey that requires a resolution of his responses to women. In *Wieland* Pamela Clemit sees, instead, a reflexive first-person narrative that, contrary to William Godwin's early faith in personal judgment, dramatizes the threat of psychic dislocation resulting from unrestrained individualism and the repudiation of institutional strictures: *The Godwinian Novel: The Rational Fictions of Godwin, Brockden Brown, Mary Shelley* (Oxford, pp. 105–38). "Subject Female: Authorizing American Identity" (*AmLH* 5: 481–511) conveys Carroll Smith-Rosenberg's similar view that Brown jumbled together Enlightenment and Romantic ideas, whereas Susanna Rowson jumbled together Enlightenment thought and both derivative attacks on Spanish imperialism and mistaken appropriations of the captivity narrative; their writings, which represent the condition of the new republic, are mutually fractured, antihierarchic, resistant to closure, and incapable of reaffirming order.

That Rowson's frame narrator is a symbolic mother figure of pragmatic rationality whose discourse fails to relieve grief is the topic of Julia Stern's "Working Through the Frame: *Charlotte Temple* and the Poetics of Maternal Melancholia" (*ArQ* 49, iv: 1–32), which notes that the incomplete narrative frame in this novel emblemizes the unfinished cultural work of the new nation. Cultural representation similarly interests David Marshall, whose "Writing Masters and 'Masculine Exercises' in *The Female Quixote*" (*ECF* 5: 105–35) focuses on the episode where a young woman has an affair with her male instructor and where writing symbolizes Charlotte Lennox's sense of female authorship as a form of transgressive cross-dressing.

That changing economic forces furthered growth in 18th-century female literacy and authorship is the subject of Gloria Main's "An Inquiry into When and Why Women Learned to Write in Colonial New England" (*JSH* 24 [1991]: 579–89). As their literacy rapidly expanded, Mary Kelley discloses in " 'Vindicating the Equality of Female Intellect': Women and Authority in the Early Republic" (*Prospects* 17 [1992]: 1–27), women entertained new choices even as their time responded in a contradictory manner to the then pressing issue of female intellect. Hannah Webster Foster's *The Boarding School,* as a source for recovering the late 18th-century conflict between the revolutionary use of instruction to promote female personal development and the reactionary use of instruction to promote female social subordination, is featured in "Gender and Writing Instruction in Early America: Lessons from Didactic Fiction" by Janet Carey Eldred and Peter Mortensen (*RhetRev* 12: 25–53).

In "Signing as Republican Daughters: The Letters of Eliza Southgate and *The Coquette*" (*ECent* 34: 243–63) Irene Fizer describes a shared discourse that negotiates filial duty and personal choice, and that also suggests a potential female role in the public sphere. A standby choice—a short-lived guise of respectable independence and female power expressed during courtship—interests Jane Sellwood, whose " 'A little acid is absolutely necessary': Narrative as Coquette in Frances Brooke's *The History of Emily Montague*" (*CanL* 136: 60–79) examines an epistolary narrative voice that mimics coquetry and also critiques 18th-century codes of sensibility.

Female networks, reading, and Federalist politics figure in Carla J. Mulford's "Political Poetics: Annis Boudinot Stockton and Middle Atlantic Women's Culture" (*NJH* 111: 67–110), which presents an edition of seven poems. A unique female choice is documented in Michael W. Vella's "Theology, Genre, and Gender: The Precarious Place of Hannah Adams in American Literary History" (*EAL* 28: 21–41); Adams's theological and historical writings were resisted by Congregationalists and Federalists, who disapproved of her liberal stance and her transgression of gender boundaries evident in her assumed authority to interpret Scripture. And Sharon M. Harris appends a valuable bibliography to "Early American Women's Self-Creating Acts" (*RALS* 19: 223–45), which features Sarah Osborn and others as authors whose experience of writing encouraged a sense of self different from conventional constructions of female identity.

Here in the words of Benjamin Tompson I take my leave: "If [this] displease not many and satisfie any, its to me a glorious Reward, who am more willing than able to any Service."

University of Texas at Austin

12　19th-Century Literature

Lawrence I. Berkove

A paradoxical pattern has been emerging for some time in 19th-century scholarship. Although the field has been expanding greatly through the recovery from obscurity of authors and works, this new material, after it is listed in bibliographies, has thenceforth been largely ignored, and scholarship has tended to stay with already familiar subjects. So, with a few notable exceptions, although the "canon" is being expanded, much of the recovered material is in danger of being lost again. Whether this is because of the innate inferiority of the material, or to shortcomings of scholarship, or to cruel fate cannot be determined, but I will observe for the record that a great many of what looked like possibly promising leads into new territory are not being followed up.

It is also becoming apparent that despite critics' identification of themselves with one or another theoretical position, in fact so great a latitude has developed in most of these positions that the labels are not always significant. The trend seems to be away from the excessively didactic and jargony essays of the recent past and toward an accommodation with traditional terminology and conventional uses of practical evidence: history, biography, and familiar techniques of close reading. Although some essays, of course, continue to be doctrinaire in their approaches and in their obligatory repetitions of the mantras of their sect, these are now distinctly in the minority. One is reminded of Horace's dictum: "You may expel Nature with a pitchfork, but it will always recur."

i General Studies

Perspectives on the century from various categories of general studies continue to contribute useful information. Art, for example, occasions

Nathalia Wright's edition of *The Correspondence of Washington Allston* (Kentucky). It is of value to antebellum studies because Allston, best known as an artist, had a large list of correspondents, including eminent authors and well-known figures in the United States and in England. In another book on art David C. Miller has collected insightful essays in *American Iconology* that illuminate the interrelationship of the period's art and literature.

Among the American Studies approaches is one essay in Richard W. Fox and T. J. Jackson Lear's *The Power of Culture* (Chicago) devoted to the Beecher-Tilton trial of 1875. Thorstein Veblen's role in the scientific management movement is discussed by Martha Banta in *Taylored Lives: Narrative Productions in the Age of Taylor, Veblen, and Ford* (Chicago). Daniel A. Cohen in *Pillars of Salt, Monuments of Grace* traces in court records and crime literature from 1674 to 1860 New England's change from a Calvinistic society to one more pluralistic and culturally ambivalent. Michael Oriard's *Reading Football: How the Popular Press Created an American Spectacle* (No. Car.) uses football as a mirror of turn-of-the-century culture.

Continuing last year's lead in the republishing of works by William Charvat, the pioneer scholar of publishing, is the paperback reissue of his classic *Literary Publishing in America, 1790–1850* (Mass.). A brief afterword by Michael Winship discusses subsequent scholarship in the field. Following Charvat's path is Ronald J. Zboray, whose *A Fictive People* links elements as various as transportation technology, literacy rates, and the stock bookstore inventories to show how these things collectively created and defined a reading public. The major literary phenomenon of post-Civil War publication is surveyed by Michael Lund's *America's Continuing Story: An Introduction to Serial Fictions, 1850–1900* (Wayne State).

Replacing the yeoman farmer as its literary ideal with the planter-aristocrat explains part of the Old South's siding with the Confederacy, maintains Ritchie Devon Watson, Jr., in *Yeoman Versus Cavalier: The Old Southwest's Fictional Road to Rebellion* (LSU). More commentary on the cavaliers is to be found in Michael D. Clark's " 'More English Than the English': Cavalier and Democrat in Virginia Historical Writing" (*JAmS* 27: 187–206). David Mogen, Scott P. Sanders, and Joanne Karpinski have put together in *Frontier Gothic* a collection of essays reflecting D. H. Lawrence's view that American history is a gothic drama, full of ghosts and demons from the past. Among those relevant to our century, Karpinski's in "The Gothic Underpinnings of Realism in the Local Colorists' No Man's Land" (pp. 140–55) argues that Sarah Orne Jewett and Mary Freeman used gothic elements in their fiction, particularly in describing women dealing with gender-role constraints. Gary Scharnhorst in Charlotte Perkins Gilman's 'The Giant Wisteria': A Hieroglyph of the Female Frontier Gothic" (pp. 156–64) argues that Gilman's heretofore lost 1890 story of murder, ghosts, and unresolved questions is related by its theme of antipatriarchialism to "The Yellow Wall-paper," which was written five months later (pp. 165–74).

John Muir, Clarence King, and Mary Austin are among the authors Sean O'Grady in *Pilgrims to the Wild* (Utah) sees as having had an erotic attachment to the natural world. And the various literary modes and customs by which children were given moral instruction are the subject of Samuel F. Pickering, Jr.'s *Moral Instruction and Fiction for Children, 1749–1820* (Georgia).

America's present concerns about race continue to spur interest into their roots. An updated and expanded edition of Ronald T. Takaki's 1972 book *Violence in the Black Imagination* (Oxford), in addition to its biographical introductions, includes three short novels by African Americans: *The Heroic Slave* by Frederick Douglass, *Blake* by Martin Delany, and *Clotel* by William Wells Brown. The book suggests the literary background for today's feelings of antagonism and violence. Kenneth W. Warren uses the lens of literary realism to look at the same phenomenon in *Black and White Strangers*. A New Historical approach to the way the Civil War is treated informs David W. Blight's " 'What Will Peace Among the Whites Bring?' Reunion and Race in the Struggle Over the Memory of the Civil War in American Culture" (*MR* 34: 393–410). Blackface minstrelsy becomes an unexpectedly sensitive gauge of social change and, ultimately, of America's drift toward the Civil War in Eric Lott's *Love and Theft*. Frances Smith Foster's *Written by Herself: Literary Production by African American Women, 1746–1892* (Indiana) is a valuable literary history of African American women writers. It provides a comprehensive contextual view and some in-depth studies of Jarena Lee, Harriet Jacobs, Elizabeth Keckley, Frances Ellen Watkins Harper, and Octavia Victoria Rogers Albert, among others.

Thoughtful literary analysis of familiar situations in fiction often produces new insights. Although only the first part of Ann duCille's *The Coupling Convention* deals specifically with period authors such as William Wells Brown, Harriet Wilson, and Harriet Jacobs, its fresh and impressive perspective on the subject of marriage has broad ramifications for scholarship on the American novel, feminism, and race relations in general. Michael Kowalewski's *Deadly Musings* treats the subject of violence not so much as an author's view of the world as "the mind's form in addressing it"—that is, as a problem of stylistic handling. Kowalewski arrives at some unexpected conclusions about Cooper, Poe, and Crane by shifting his focus from the violence that appears in their work to the way they "realistically imagined" it. Work is the subject of Nicholas K. Bromell's *By the Sweat of the Brow*, which devotes chapters to Rebecca Harding Davis, Susan Warner, Harriet Beecher Stowe, and Frederick Douglass by way of showing how these writers understood various kinds of work: maternal labor, industrial and agricultural labor, even slave labor, and how they reflected on the complicated relationships between physical labor and their own mental work.

A reader-response collection *Readers in History* exemplifies the breadth of approach possible under a theoretical category. Using Margaret Fuller's review of Frederick Douglass's *Narrative* as the occasion for a lesson in reader-response technique, Steven Mailloux in "Misreading as a Historical Act: Cultural Rhetoric, Bible Politics, and Fuller's 1845 Review of Douglass's *Narrative*" (pp. 3–31) details how, because of their own agenda, proslavery individuals read (and misread) the Bible, Douglass read (and misread) his own experiences, and Fuller read (and misread) his book. Wai-Chee Dimock in "Feminism, New Historicism, and the Reader" (pp. 85–106) uses Gilman's "The Yellow Wall-paper" as the basis first for a feminist reading of the story, then for a New Historical interpretation. Then, with increasingly labyrinthine reasoning and jargony explication, she attempts to deconstruct the opposition between the two positions. The familiar conclusion that an author would try to affect the way his readers read his text is arrived at over a theoretical road by Robert Daly in "Cooper's Allegories of Reading and 'The Wreck of the Past'" (pp. 109–37). Raymond Hedin, in "Probable Readers, Possible Stories: The Limits of Nineteenth-Century Black Narrative" (pp. 180–205) assesses how the awareness of a largely white audience affected black writers. His discussion of Chesnutt is particularly acute. A historical survey of the process by which blacks changed their view of Stowe's novel from favorable to resentful is Marva Banks's accomplishment in "*Uncle Tom's Cabin* and Antebellum Black Response" (pp. 209–27). Reactions from Frederick Douglass, Martin Delany, and William Wells Brown are included. Susan K. Harris's "Responding to the Text(s): Women Readers and the Quest for Higher Education" (pp. 259–82) discusses Augusta Evans, Catherine Beecher, Anna Julia Cooper, Harriet Beecher Stowe, Frances W. Harper, and Elizabeth Stuart Phelps in her description of how powerful an attraction formal, "canonical" education was to women of the century.

American literature itself is the subject of some studies. Michael Davitt Bell's *The Problem of American Realism* is a valuable corrective for those who believe that American realism is a sharply defined phenomenon, conforming to particular theoretical tenets. Like other overarching discussions of literary movements, however, it inevitably gets involved in the interpretive debates concerning specific works by the authors it uses as case studies: Howells, Twain, Henry James, Norris, Crane, and Jewett. Ellen Miller Casey offers a view of the increasing importance of American novels to the English reading public, based on reviewers' comments from the 1870s to the 1890s in a London magazine, in " 'Our Transatlantic Cousins': The Battle over American Analytic Novels in the *Atheneum*" (*SAF* 21: 237–46). Poe, Hawthorne, Harte, Howells, and Norris are among the authors studied in Andrew Levy's *Culture and Commerce,* an interesting and well-researched history of the short story as a distinctly American genre. John Hollander's *American Poetry: The Nineteenth Century* (Library of America) is an excellent and important two-volume selection of minor as well as major poets, with biographical and factual notes and a chronology for each poet. This is an edition all libraries ought to have. Steven Olson enumerates and briefly describes allusions to grasslands in *The Prairie in Nineteenth-Century American Poetry* (Okla.). And in *Fictions of Form in American Poetry* Stephen Cushman studies the uses of, and attitudes toward, form in American poets, including Whitman and Dickinson.

ii Women's Literature (General)

Women's literature continues to generate a great deal of activity. It is one of the major exceptions to my earlier observation about how rediscovered authors are being lost again. Some good consequences have come out of Hawthorne's peevish complaint about the "d——d mob of scribbling women." In *Style and the "Scribbling Women": An Empirical Analysis of Nineteenth-Century American Fiction* (Greenwood) Mary Hiatt has compared the writing styles of male and female authors in such features as sentence length, balance, parts of speech, voice, punctuation, etc.

These objective indices may not be the whole picture, but they do indicate no major stylistic differences attributable to gender. Elaine Showalter's edition of *Daughters of Decadence: Women Writers of the Fin-de-Siècle* (Rutgers) is a useful collection of American and English stories by "decadent" New Woman authors, culled from turn-of-the-century magazines. Marjorie Pryse suggests that regionalism had a special appeal to women authors in " 'Distilling Essences': Regionalism and 'Women's Culture' " (*ALR* 25, ii: 1–15). Lauren Berlant's "The Queen of America Goes to Washington City: Harriet Jacobs, Frances Harper, and Anita Hill" (*AL* 65: 549–74), however, is more an expression of Berlant's opinion about recent politics than a literary study of the two period authors.

Anxious Power rides the thesis that "the pen is a metaphorical penis" and argues that women are victims of male-dominated culture's exclusion of them from reading and writing. Ranging from the 14th century to modern times in both Europe and the Western hemisphere, the book devotes several essays to period authors, the most prominent of whom are Harriet Jacobs, discussed by Debra Humphreys in "Power and Resistance in Harriet Jacobs' *Incidents in the Life of a Slave Girl*" (pp. 143–55), and Caroline Lee Hentz, whose novel *Ernest Linwood* is the main example in Elizabeth L. Barnes's "Mirroring the Mother Text: Histories of Seduction in the American Domestic Novel" (pp. 157–72).

A collection of essays intended to restore neglected authors to deserved attention is *The (Other) American Traditions: Nineteenth-Century Women Writers* (Rutgers), ed. Joyce W. Warren. But jargon and a somewhat tiresome refrain of male-bashing run through too many of its essays in place of substantial proof that the authors and works discussed have intrinsic merit. Jane Tompkins argues in "Susanna Rowson, Father of the American Novel" (pp. 29–38) that Rowson is neglected in contrast to Charles Brockden Brown, whom she greatly outwrote and outsold. Carol J. Singley in "Catherine Maria Sedgwick's *Hope Leslie*" (pp. 39–53) holds that Sedgwick strove to alter basic patriotic myths in the novel and that she is unjustly neglected in comparison to James Fenimore Cooper. Nina Baym in "Reinventing Lydia Sigourney" (pp. 54–72) summarizes Sigourney's writings, especially her pro-Indian histories, and shows that they do not support the opinion of her as conventional and thoroughly domesticated. Warren's "Domesticity and the Economics of Independence: Resistance and Revolution in the Work of Fanny Fern" (pp. 73–

91) maintains that Fern (the pen name of Sara Willis Parton) saw marriage as being "for love, companionship, and for cooperation . . . not for bread and meat and clothes." Frances Smith Foster's "Harriet Jacobs's *Incidents* and the 'Careless Daughters' (and Sons) Who Read It" (pp. 92–107) affirms that Jacobs's autobiography was truthful in its events and its writing. Judith Fetterley in "Only a Story, Not a Romance: Harriet Beecher Stowe's *The Pearl of Orr's Island*" (pp. 108–25) offers a subtle reading of the novel's text as a way to identify and illuminate Stowe's autobiography. Works by Eliza Buckminster Lee, Caroline Kirkland, and Lydia Sigourney are used by Sandra A. Zagarell to represent village communities as microcosms of America in " 'America' as Community in Three Antebellum Village Sketches" (pp. 143–63). Joanna Dobson in "The American Renaissance Reenvisioned" (pp. 164–82) aims at a "truly revisionary history" of the period that will dismantle "hierarchical assumptions that privilege masculine experience over feminine, elite literature over popular, and the culturally dissenting over the culturally embedded." In " 'Doers of the Word': Theorizing African-American Women Writers in the Antebellum North" (pp. 183–202) Carla L. Peterson discusses African American women who sought to achieve "racial uplift." Deborah Carlin reports in " 'What Methods Have Brought Blessing': Discourse of Reform in Philanthropic Literature" (pp. 203–25) that in the many late-period novels about economics, women were largely assigned to manifesting goodwill, charity, and sympathy. She finds, nevertheless, that the literature of women, by recognizing disempowerment and marginality, challenged the idea that inequality was immutable. Josephine Donovan in "Breaking the Sentence: Local-Color Literature and Subjugated Knowledges" (pp. 226–43) states that women local color writers focused on "the colonization of local traditions and life-worlds by translocal homogenizing disciplines." In "The Tradition of American Jewish Women Writers" (pp. 244–62) Diane Lichtenstein maintains that American Jewish women writers began a tradition founded on three principles: womanhood, nationality, and American Jewish womanhood. Other critics in this collection would have profited by reading Susan K. Harris's thoughtful " 'But is it any good?': Evaluating Nineteenth-Century American Women's Fiction" (pp. 263–79), which recognizes that the discovery of new texts imposes an obligation of assessing them, and recommends some considerations for evaluating them as "good" or "bad." And Paul Lauter in "Teaching Nineteenth-

Century Women Writers" (pp. 280–301) advocates a clarifying of "alternative assumptions about literary value rather than assuming the absolute validity of canonical literary standards."

iii Cooper, Irving, and Contemporaries

This seems to have been the year of Cooper. An impressive efflorescence of scholarship, including some excellent studies, is found primarily in two collections of essays. The first is *James Fenimore Cooper: His Country and His Art (No. 8)*, the papers of the 1991 Cooper Conference (English Dept., SUNY—Oneonta). Alan Taylor in "Who Murdered William Cooper?" offers evidence to counter the old legend that Cooper's father was killed by a political opponent. Another interesting view of Cooper's family as background to his novels is John McWilliams's "Revolution and the Historical Novel: Cooper's Transforming of European Tradition." As McWilliams suggests, Cooper was ambivalent about revolution and reform, wanting to believe that the molds of heredity, environment, and upbringing can be altered and, at the same time, doubting it. R. D. Madison finds racist elements in Cooper's works in " 'Gib a Nigger Fair Play': Cooper, Slavery, and the Spirit of the Fair." An ingenious but overwrought claim for the centrality of rhetoric to Cooper's fiction is Laurence Mate's "How Rhetoric Figures in Cooper's Fiction; Or, Epitaph Upon Epitaph." Paul S. D'Ambrosio in "Light Upon the Glimmerglass: Cooper and the American Landscape Painters of Otsego Lake" discusses how Cooper and his artistic counterparts manipulated Lake Otsego, the setting for three of his novels. A thoughtful consideration of two contradictory impulses in Cooper—the well-known emphasis on property rights, and a more subtle, but real, recognition of the negative effects of ownership—is at the heart of George F. Bagby's "The Temptation of Pathfinder: Cooper's Radical Critique of Ownership." Scott Michaelsen's "Cooper's *Monikins:* Contracts, Construction, and Chaos" and Christina Starobin's " *The Monikins*" are two vastly different essays on the same difficult novel. Michaelsen regards it as Cooper's satire of the legal process of "constructing," that is, interpreting law; Starobin regards it as an allegorical criticism of human nature in the guise of an animal fable. Finally, Donald A. Ringe in " *The Bravo:* Social Criticism in the Gothic Mode" proposes that Cooper uses the gothic effect of uncertainty in facing the unknown to prophetically denounce the immorality of a totalitarian state.

The other major collection is W. M. Verhoeven's *James Fenimore Cooper: New Historical and Literary Contexts* (Rodopi). In "James Fenimore Cooper and the American Romance Tradition," using Cooper as a prime example, George Dekker takes issue with Richard Chase's influential claim that the American romance novel was ahistorical, not much interested in social realities. A. Robert Lee's "Making History, Making Fiction: Cooper's *The Spy*" is an appreciation of that work as Cooper's first truly American novel. Robert Lawson-Peebles applies Cooper's view that property is the base of all civilization to a study of his early fictions that attempts to show women as the vital link between property and social improvement in "Property, Marriage, Women, and Fenimore Cooper's First Fictions." Verhoeven's own "Neutralizing the Land: The Myth of Authority: and the Authority of Myth in Fenimore Cooper's *The Spy*" is a somewhat forced reading of "neutral" in the novel's subtitle, "*A Tale of the Neutral Ground*," to explain the emergence of American middle-class ideology. John McWilliams's fine "Revolt in Massachusetts: The Midnight March of Lionel Lincoln" demonstrates Cooper's respect for historical accuracy by showing the little-known *Lionel Lincoln* to be the first novel that commemorated the battles of Lexington, Concord, and Bunker Hill, and the only account of them that was based on a review of historical sources instead of patriotic projection. Donald A. Ringe's "Mode and Meaning in *The Last of the Mohicans*" is an erudite and persuasive analysis of the novel that firmly establishes it as a sophisticated work of serious literature. Ringe directly tackles the conventional criticisms of its stylistic shortcomings and demonstrates Cooper's deliberate use of gothic and mock heroic modes as a means to his end of composing a heroic elegy to all Indian nations. " 'In the Land of His Fathers': Cooper, Land Rights, and the Legitimation of American National Identity" is Susan Scheckel's impressive study of *The Pioneers*. She sees in the novel Cooper's attempt to affirm a stable and morally legitimate relationship of the young nation with the Indian and English past, and she compares and contrasts Cooper with Chief Justice John Marshall, whose contemporary legal decisions reveal him to be wrestling with the same issues, but with less room for maneuvering. John G. Cawelti's "Cooper and the Frontier Myth and Anti-Myth" suggests that Cooper was divided between regarding the frontier as a place where civilized men went to recover their lost potency and as a refuge from the destructiveness of civilization. In "From Leatherstocking to Rocketman: Cooper's Leatherstocking and Pynchon's *Gravity's Rainbow* Reconsidered" Jan

Bakker puts forth an ingenious but forced impressionistic comparison of Cooper's and Pynchon's works. Richard D. Rust presents evidence of Cooper's craftsmanship in verbal patterns, names, and character relationships in "On the Trail of a Craftsman: The Art of *The Pathfinder.*" In "Dis-Placing *Satanstoe*" Theo D'haen argues the importance of names to the novel's plot. Charles H. Adams in "Uniformity and Progress: The Natural History of *The Crater*" claims that Cooper in the novel adapts the uniformitarianism of Lyell's *Geology*—the argument that the causes and effects of change are constants in world history—to his moral purpose of demonstrating that the rise and fall of human society is also a constant.

Donald Darnell's *James Fenimore Cooper: Novelist of Manners* (Delaware) treats manners as a central theme in the Cooper canon. However, he takes an extreme position in his claim that Cooper refuses to satirize his upper-class characters. Dieter Schulz's "Cooper's Knight of Columbus: *Mercedes of Castile* as Chivalric Romance" (*LAmer* 44: 31–46) discusses the motif of chivalry and its history in Cooper's thought in this seldom-read novel. That Cooper's *The Spy* invented or anticipated many of the important conventions of the spy novel genre is the thesis of Bruce A. Rosenberg's "Cooper's *The Spy* and the Popular Spy Novel" (*ATQ* 7: 116–25). In " 'Every Wave Is a Fortune': Nantucket Island and the Making of an American Icon" (*NEQ* 66: 434–47) Nathaniel Philbrick surveys Nantucket history to discover the causes for its being regarded as a symbol of the American spirit, and he applies this survey to help explain why Cooper used its reputation in *The Pilot* and why he returned to it as a model in *The Crater*. A new edition of *The Pioneers* (Everyman) includes an introduction, chronology, and Robert Clark's review of noteworthy criticism. Nan Goodman's "A Clear Showing: The Problem of Fault in James Fenimore Cooper's *The Pioneers*" (*ArQ* 49, ii: 1–22) argues that the novel's central deer-killing incident is also the locus of two competing legal doctrines: "the old law of strict liability and the new law of negligence." Goodman believes the novel demonstrates how the American transition from wilderness to society was eased "by the shift to negligence in the standard of tort liability." This novel is also one of the works considered by Paul Witkowsky in "If Prairies Had Trees: East, West, Environmentalist Fiction, and the Great Plains" (*WAL* 28: 195–207). Comparing Cooper's Natty Bumppo to an environmentalist character in Dan O'Brien's contemporary novel *Spirit of the Hills,* Witkowsky explains their differences by their respective Eastern and Western orientations toward nature.

Irving scholarship is divided this year between regarding him as a romanticist and as an ironist. The former position is represented in Malcolm Bradbury's introduction to a new edition of *The Sketch Book of Geoffrey Crayon, Gent.* (Everyman), which also includes a chronology and a survey of criticism. Richard V. McLamore's "Postcolonial Columbus: Washington Irving and *The Conquest of Granada*" (*NCF* 48: 26–43) argues that the book, far from genteelly romanticizing its subject, uses irony to undermine its pious narrator and the nationalistic and religious arguments he advances. McLamore links this book to Irving's larger criticisms of the casuistry that justifies conquest and usurpation. In " 'Girls Can Take Care of Themselves': Gender and Storytelling in Washington Irving's 'The Legend of Sleepy Hollow' " (*SSF* 30: 175–84), Michael Nelson and Laura Plummer affirm a deep irony in the story: although males appear to be dominant in Sleepy Hollow, the physical setting is feminine and the community's women, by their cultivation of folklore, in fact control not only its belief system, in general, but also, specifically, the means by which masculine interlopers like Ichabod Crane are "figuratively neutered" and driven away.

Interest in William Gilmore Simms escalated this year. His novels *Guy Rivers* and *The Yemassee* (Arkansas) were reprinted with introductions by John Caldwell Guilds, whose excellent biography of Simms appeared last year (*ALS 1992*, p. 184). Charles Watson builds on his previous work in publishing *From Nationalism to Secessionism: The Changing Fiction of William Gilmore Simms* (Greenwood). A new journal, *The Simms Review*, published by the University of Georgia, made its debut and will henceforth encourage scholarship. Among the contributions of its first volume's second number are Deborah Bowden Henson's "Simms' Musical Settings" (pp. 1–19), which documents and discusses a number of parlor song settings of various Simms poems and reproduces some of the scores. A newly discovered essay by Simms defending Poe against the hostile Boston reception in 1845 of his reading of his own poetry is reproduced, with commentary, by James Kibler in " 'Poe's Poetry': A New Simms Essay" (pp. 20–25). This essay is valuable for the light it casts on both authors and their Southern sympathies. David Aiken reproduces the text of Whitman's squeamish 1846 review of Simms's anthology, *The Wigwam and the Cabin* in "Walt Whitman on Simms,

Again" (p. 26). Biographical details are supplied by Frank Coleman's "Simms in Spartanburg" (pp. 27–31), "Simms's Last Days and Words: From Two Unrecorded Obituaries" (p. 32), David Aiken's "John Esten Cooke's Sketch of Simms" (pp. 33–40), and Clyde N. Wilson's "Simms and Melville in 1865: A Note on Garner's *Melville*" (pp. 41–42). In "William Gilmore Simms: Deviant Paradigms of Southern Woman-hood?" (*MissQ* 46: 573–88) Delira Johanyak maintains that Simms encouraged readers to view as deviant intellectual, independent, or masculinized women who sought freedom or knowledge. He did this by arranging their downfalls by seduction, the consequence of their actions, and thus he upheld an ideal of domestic purity dominated by masculine authority.

Among several literary considerations of American Indians are Ian Marshall's "Heteroglossia in Lydia Maria Child's *Hobomok*" (*Legacy* 10: 1–16), a feminist and Bakhtinian reading of this 1824 novel about the Puritans and Indians, emphasizing "a dramatic interplay of voices that more fairly represent the diversity of American culture." Indians are given more of their own voice in Timothy Sweet's "Masculinity and Self-Performance in *The Life of Black Hawk*" (*AL* 65: 475–99). Despite the difficulties of authenticating Black Hawk's voice in the 1833 autobiography that was dictated, translated, and edited, Sweet shows that at least Black Hawk did not mouth approval of the Jacksonian master plan that obliged the Indians to vacate their lands. Another view of Black Hawk, also sympathetic, is presented by Rosemarie K. Bank in "Staging the 'Native': Making History in American Theatre Culture, 1828–1838" (*TJ* 45, iv: 461–86). To assess the influence that real-life Indians had on the formation of their representation on the American stage, Bank selects three Indian chiefs who, in the same decade, were brought to Washington to represent their tribes: Red Jacket of the Senecas, Black Hawk of the Sauks, and John Ross of the Cherokees. She finds them impressive yet different from each other. Red Jacket was seen both nostalgically and as an unreconstructed Indian not resigned to surrendering his tribe's rights; Black Hawk as a vanquished but not submissive warrior; and John Ross as politically sophisticated. On their way to the Capitol, these men were photographed, painted, interviewed, and made the occasion of museum "stagings" of Indian costumes, dances, rituals, etc. In sum, Bank finds theater history a contradiction to Emerson's view that America was a country without a past. Another view of Indians as well as an implicit dissent from this Emersonian overstatement is presented in John

Ernest's "Reading of the Romantic Past: William H. Prescott's *History of the Conquest of Mexico*" (*AmLH* 5: 231–49), which discusses the historian's treatment of divine providence.

iv Popular Writers and Others at Midcentury

Scholarship this year on women and African American authors dominates this category. Harriet Beecher Stowe is among the most popular, given extended treatment by Susan Wolstenholme in *Gothic (Re)Visions*. Within her larger framework of explaining how the gothic structure, because it usually involves both seeing and hiding, affords covers for the coding of women in the text, Wolstenholme in her chapter "Eva's Curl" maintains that a sadomasochistic aspect in *Uncle Tom's Cabin* derives from a lock of Eva's hair. Arnold Weinstein, similarly devoting a chapter, "Ghosting in *Uncle Tom's Cabin*," to Stowe in *Nobody's Home*, praises the novel for its success in enlarging the national will for freedom. Stowe's second novel, *Dred: A Tale of the Great Dismal Swamp*, is the focus of Lisa Whitney's "In the Shadow of *Uncle Tom's Cabin*: Stowe's Vision of Slavery from the Great Dismal Swamp" (*NEQ* 66: 552–69). Whitney finds in this "unsuccessful" novel Stowe's loss of confidence in the efficacy of her sentimental solution to slavery. Stowe, she holds, became aware that the presence of the Underground Railway exacerbated Southern opposition to abolition, but that without it, the chances increased for more bloody slave revolts, such as the one led by Nat Turner. In "The Female Imaginary in Harriet Beecher Stowe's *The Minister's Wooing*" (*NEQ* 66: 179–98) Susan Harris finds in that novel a "counterconsciousness that is both secular and gynocentric" derived from its minor plot about women. From this counterconsciousness Harris projects a female imaginary that can resist the androcentrism "of secular and heterosexual American life." A negative view of Stowe appears in Joshua D. Bellin's "Up to Heaven's Gate, Down in Earth's Dust: The Politics of Judgment in *Uncle Tom's Cabin*" (*AL* 65: 275–95). Bellin charges that Stowe's emphasis on "right feeling" helped unleash the horror of the Civil War by "containing horror" within an overarching moral purpose that released individuals from political responsibility. More specifically, the novel's propagandistic success destroyed doubt about the rightness of the war when it convinced readers that the issues came down to a simple right and wrong.

Studies of women authors continue to make valuable contributions to our ongoing reassessment of antebellum and midcentury life. Women authors expressed a full range of views from the conventional to the unconventional. On the conventional side, not surprisingly, Louisa Alcott's *Little Women* is seen by Richard C. Allen in "When Narrative Fails" (*Journal of Religious Ethics* 21: 1, 27–67) as helping Alcott "succeed" in her depiction of the March family ("success" being defined as creating an ethical identity) because the family shares a common world of "social faith" that corrects, challenges, and encourages growth and moral development. The career of an antisuffrage feminist is outlined by Sherry Lee Linkon in "Saints, Sufferers, and 'Strong-minded Sisters': Antisuffrage Rhetoric in Rose Terry Cooke's Fiction" (*Legacy* 10: 31–46). A deeply religious author is depicted in Lynette Carpenter's "Double Talk: The Power and Glory of Paradox in E. D. E. N. Southworth's *The Hidden Hand*" (*Legacy* 10: 17–30). Carpenter shows Southworth's affirmation of the hidden hand of Christianity's God in the novel's recurrent patterns of doubling, puns, paradoxes, reversals, and disguises. And Mary Kelley's edition of *The Power of Her Sympathy: The Autobiography and Journal of Catharine Maria Sedgwick* (MHS) is a rich portrait of Sedgwick's time, community, opinions, and life. A helpful introduction supplies background to the autobiography and the journal entries.

On the unconventional side, Donna Dickenson's *Margaret Fuller: Writing a Woman's Life* (St. Martin's) tells the story of Fuller as a woman who "sought a positive female identity, refusing to define feminine as the mere negative of masculine" and who still does not conform to the posthumous picture of her drawn by her contemporaries as a monster of unfeminine egotism. In "'With Ready Eye': Margaret Fuller and Lesbianism in Nineteenth-Century American Literature" (*AL* 65: 1–18) Mary E. Wood suggests that despite her normative heterosexual identity, Fuller's writings contain evidence of a possibly lesbian identity struggling to assert itself. Louisa May Alcott, it is now clear, is a much more complicated author than earlier generations supposed. In "Writing and *Little Women*: Alcott's Rhetoric of Subversion" (*ATQ* 7: 25–43) Susan Naomi Bernstein finds a pattern of contradictory attitudes in Jo March's experience with writing. The breakdown of these oppositions, she maintains, uncovers "a rhetoric of subversion that seeks to circumvent the traditional values of nineteenth-century American patriarchal culture." Carolyn Kyler's "Alcott's 'Enigmas': Impersonation and Interpretation" analyzes a little-known story by Alcott that "plays with the boundaries between masculine and feminine, secrecy and openness, visibility and invisibility, and raises questions about gender, impersonation, and power" (*ATQ* 7: 229–45). In "Sex, Wit, and Sentiment: Frances Osgood and the Poetry of Love" (*AL* 65: 631–50) Joanne Dobson offers a penetrating discussion of some unexpectedly witty and sexually teasing private poems by Osgood; she then uses these as a key to unlock the private attitudes in her public poetry. *Gerald Gray's Wife* and *Lily,* two novels analyzing Southern society by Susan Petigru King, have been reprinted by Duke with an introduction by Jane H. Pease and William H. Pease. Jan Bakker's "Twists of Sentiment in Antebellum Southern Romance" (*SLJ* 26, i: 3–13) looks at the fiction of Caroline Lee Hentz. An interesting similarity of views between a woman editor and a woman poet is discovered by Patricia Okker in "Sarah Josepha Hale, Lydia Sigourney, and the Poetic Tradition in Two Nineteenth-Century Women's Magazines" (*AmPer* 3: 32–42). Hale was the editor of the *Ladies' Magazine* and then of *Godey's Lady's Book,* and increasingly over the years she contested the tradition of genteel traits in the poetess and championed women poets in her editorials. Based on her reading of Sigourney's contributions to *Godey's Lady's Book* from 1840–42, Okker finds that Sigourney's poems emphasized women's strength, poetic achievement, and public authority. With the recent republication of *Ruth Hall* and other selected writings, Fanny Fern has been successfully resurrected from obscurity. Nancy A. Walker's *Fanny Fern* (Twayne) is a welcome resource and is certain to be heavily used. Joyce W. Warren is another admirer of Fern, but after surveying the reviews of *Ruth Hall* in her "The Gender of American Individualism: Fanny Fern, the Novel, and the American Dream" (pp. 150–57), in *Politics, Gender, and the Arts* (Susquehanna), ed. Ronald Dotterer and Susan Bowers, Warren concludes bitterly that the American dream was a male myth.

Increasingly, realism is being recognized as having been alive and well long before the Civil War ended. At least three women authors, Caroline Kirkland, Elizabeth Stoddard, and Rebecca Harding Davis, are firmly associated with its earlier appearance. Lori Merish's " 'The Hand of Refined Taste' in the Frontier Landscape: Caroline Kirkland's *A New Home. Who'll Follow?* and the Feminization of American Consumerism" (*AQ* 45: 485–523) suggests that the novel's "unromanticized, meticulous representation of everyday domestic life" constitutes evidence that domestic realism and consumer refinement were twinned material expressions of a woman's touch and feminine presence in the antebellum United States. In "Realism and Beyond: The Imagery of Sex and Sexual

Oppression in Elizabeth Stoddard's 'Lemorne *Versus* Huell' " (*SoAR* 58, i: 33–47) John B. Humma argues that this 1863 story, especially in its sexual metaphors and symbols, was a work of realism antedating Howells and James. Scholarship in Rebecca Harding Davis should get a boost from Jane Atteridge Rose's new TUSAS study, *Rebecca Harding Davis* (Twayne). This pioneer realist receives a perceptive and balanced overview as Rose explains how the promise of "Life in the Iron-Mills" was cut short by Davis's decisions to thenceforth concentrate on quantity rather than quality in order to earn more money for her family and to take the advice of her publisher and her husband on what to say. J. F. Buckley in "Living in the Iron Mills: A Tempering of Nineteenth-Century America's Orphic Poet" (*JACult* 16, i: 67–72) claims that two of Davis's characters in the story appear to be influenced by Emerson's notion of the Orphic poet; both are inspired by transcendental ideals and insights. Although they achieve momentary successes, "in the long run they fail because they and their art are never viewed outside of their culture."

Another influence that is changing our understanding of realism comes from subject matter—for example, the depiction of African Americans. Nancy Bentley in "White Slaves: The Mulatto Hero in Antebellum Fiction" (*AL* 65: 501–22) detects authorial ambivalence about color in the works of Harriet Beecher Stowe, Richard Hildreth, Frederick Douglass, and William Wells Brown when they write about light-skinned mulattoes, because these mulattoes are often seen as divided against themselves, the "white part" being the more spirited about individual freedom and the "black part" more passive. Bentley affirms that Martin Delany's fiction and later works by Douglass and Brown set out to remedy this portrayal by creating heroic characters who were fully African. Another work on Delany is Germain J. Bienvenu's "The People of Delany's *Blake*" (*CLAJ* 36: 406–29), which critically depicts slavery and race relations. Barbara A. White reinforces the autobiographical aspect of Harriet Wilson's novel in " 'Our Nig' and the She-Devil: New Information about Harriet Wilson and the 'Bellmont' Family" (*AL* 65: 19–52). This new biographical material illuminates Wilson's decision not to follow either of the two conventional literary models most readily available to her: the slave novel and the sentimental novel. Once it is realized that Wilson experienced racism in the North—putative abolitionists, as well as members of the family Wilson served, showed signs of it—then it can be appreciated that she felt she had to deal circumspectly with Northern racism lest she hurt the cause of slaves in the South.

White, however, errs in her claim that *Our Nig*, published in 1859, was the first novel by a black in the United States; William Wells Brown's *Clotel* was published in 1853. Another article on the same novel is Eric Gardner's " 'This Attempt of their Sister': Harriet Wilson's *Our Nig* from Printer to Reader" (*NEQ* 66: 226–46). Gardner uses a readership survey and biography to speculate why the novel, on publication, went unnoticed in nearby Boston. Carla Kaplan in "Narrative Contrasts and Emancipatory Readers: *Incidents in the Life of a Slave Girl*" (*YJC* 6, i: 93–119) sees the book as both exposing contracts as undependable guarantees of freedom and, paradoxically, as hoping that freedom would be established through appropriate formalities of law. The paradox is resolved, Kaplan holds, in Jacobs's realization that Northerners were freer than slaves, yet not fully free themselves, and that her readers needed to move toward the goal of personal fulfillment as well as legal rights.

Although white male authors do not have much of a showing in this section, there was at least some activity on them. Stephen P. Knadler's "Francis Parkman's Ethnography of the Brahmin Caste and *The History of the Conspiracy of Pontiac*" (*AL* 65: 215–38) claims that Parkman's accounts of Indians and backwoodsmen were colored by preconceptions derived from his Boston Brahmin values. Parkman, he says, regarded as a fantasy the view of nature as a romantic landscape whose beauty elevates man; rather, Parkman tended to regard nature as a site of uncivilized license and Indians in particular as representing " 'foreign,' irrational and sensual desires that had to be excluded for the efficient running of the State." Kinereth Meyer in "Landscape and Counter-Landscape in the Poetry of William Cullen Bryant" (*NCF* 48: 194–211) holds that Bryant's poetry is part of the continuum of American poetry in its "crafted failure" to reconcile the wilderness as an iconic ideal and as a material commodity. Reid's work in imitation of *Robinson Crusoe* is the subject of Susan Naramore Maher's "Westering Crusoes: Mayne Reid's *The Desert Home* and the Plotting of the American West" (*JSW* 35: 92–105). Maher claims that the West and wild nature in Reid's juvenile novel of 1851 is depicted as being superior to the East and civilization. Why the author George Thompson is not read more often is made clear by Christopher Looby's "George Thompson's 'Romance of the Real': Transgression and Taboo in American Sensation Fiction" (*AL* 65: 651–72). Looby retells the plot of the novel *The House Breaker* and concludes turgidly that whatever appeal it had was more voyeuristic than moral. Harley Erdman's "Caught in the 'Eye of the Eternal': Justice, Race, and the Camera, from *The*

Octoroon to Rodney King" (*TJ* 45: 333–48) is a thought-provoking study of Dion Boucicault's use of photography in his famous play, and a comparison of it to the use made of the videotaped record in Rodney King's 1992 trial. Erdman concludes that the play's claims that the camera is the "eye of the eternal" and cannot make a mistake is shown in the play to be untrue and is equally untrue in our time; a camera record is only as powerful as the jury that judges its use.

v Humor

Too little work continues to be done on this worthy subject, although now that *StAH* is being published again, next year may see an upturn. We are not wholly bereft, however. Many of Walter Blair's best essays from the beginning of his career until his death in 1992 have been collected by Hamlin Hill in *Essays on American Humor: Blair Through the Ages* (Wisconsin). It is still enlightening to read Blair's comments on such humorists as Davy Crockett and George Washington Harris, as well as Mark Twain. Another excellent addition to the lively subject is Cameron C. Nickels's *New England Humor,* a solidly researched and comprehensive treatment that contains fresh material as well as new perspectives; it is sure to become a standard work. William E. Lenz reminds us of the work of William T. Porter in "The Function of Women in Old Southwestern Humor: Re-reading Porter's Big Bear and Quarter Race Collections" (*MissQ* 46: 589–600). And Daniel F. Littlefield, Jr., and Carol A. Petty Hunter have revived the adventures of a humorous Indian dialect character in their edition of Alexander Lawrence Posey's *The Fux Fixico Letters* (Nebraska). A new edition of Johnson J. Hooper's 1845 classic *Adventures of Captain Simon Suggs* (Alabama) is now available in a paperback facsimile of the 1858 edition. A substantial biographical and critical introduction by Johanna Nicol Shields makes use, for the first time, of Hooper family correspondence. My own " 'Hades in Trouble': A Rediscovered Story by Ambrose Bierce" (*ALR* 25, ii: 67–84) is the first addition of an entirely new story to the Bierce canon since 1912. Apparently inadvertently overlooked by Bierce when he compiled his short stories for the *Collected Works,* "Hades in Trouble" is a wickedly clever retelling of *Paradise Lost.* This time, however, Adam and Eve—especially Eve—are the culprits and the fallen angels are the ones to be pitied.

vi Post–Civil War Women Writers

The winds of change that blew across the United States for the second half of the century clearly had an effect on the first generation of postwar women writers. Harriet Prescott Spofford is the subject of " 'A Master-piece' of 'The Educated Eye': Convention, Gaze, and Gender in Spof-ford's 'Her Story' " (*SSF* 30: 511–23). Eva Gold and Thomas H. Fisk find in this telling of the rivalry of two women for the affection of one man an exploration of the fictional oppositions that divide women from each other. Carol E. Schmudde in "Sincerity, Secrecy, and Lies: Helen Hunt Jackson's No Name Novels" (*SAF* 21: 51–66) discovers in two of her anonymous novels, *Mercy Philbrick's History* (1876) and *Hetty's Strange History* (1877), Jackson grappling with the moral problem that even well-intentioned lies can harm the deceiver, the deceived, and their social communities. This struggle, in turn, shortly led to her championing the cause of the Indians, whom she had come to realize were the victims of prolonged official hypocrisy and deceit, and to her publishing both historical reports of the magnitude of these lies and *Ramona*. In "Competing Narratives in Elizabeth Stuart Phelps' *The Story of Avis*" (*ALR* 26, i: 60–75) Jack H. Wilson argues that the protagonist Avis is pulled in contradictory directions by her love for her husband and her love for an artistic vocation. As Wilson sees it, although a feminist text began to develop in the novel, it was canceled by Phelps's deeper conviction that wedded love was, ultimately, the more fulfilling role for a woman. Timothy Morris in "Professional Ethics and Professional Eroticism in Elizabeth Stuart Phelps' *Doctor Zay* (*SAF* 21: 141–52) analyzes the novel to show how the woman doctor becomes, through her professionalism, more appealing to her suitor. "Eroticism," however, seems too strong a term for what happens.

A respectable amount of scholarship on Jewett this year shows that interest in her continues to simmer, if not hit a rolling boil, but Freeman has had an off year. Elizabeth Silverthorne has written a biography, *Sarah Orne Jewett: A Writer's Life* (Overlook). It is readable and has a good selective bibliography, but since it does not go very deeply into the author or her works, it will be most useful as an overview. A psychoana-lytical perspective is the approach taken by Joseph Church in "Transgres-sive Daughters in Sarah Orne Jewett's *Deephaven*" (*ELWIU* 20: 231–50). Marjorie Pryse in "Archives of Female Friendship and the 'Way' Jewett

Wrote" (*NEQ* 66: 47–66) compares the relationship of Jewett's female friends in real life with the friendships between women in her fiction. A religious influence on Jewett's life and works is traced by Josephine Donovan in "Jewett and Swedenborg" (*AL* 65: 731–50). Swedenborgianism was more widespread during the century than is generally realized, and Donovan holds that Jewett decided against openly preaching its doctrines in her fiction but instead internalized it and used Swedenborgian metonymy as a way to express those doctrines. In "Mary Wilkins Freeman and the Taste of Necessity" (*AL* 65: 69–94) Virginia L. Blum criticizes Freeman for being "a woman artist who longs to make of her necessity good taste." Blum argues that even the notion that there is such a thing as a "pure," necessity-free art is a fantasy derived from Kant. She believes that Freeman bought that fantasy, as can be seen from her characters, many of whom are often depicted as scrimping and lingering over mere bites of food, and from her letters, many of which use the apology that her writing might have been better had she not been compelled by need.

Last year's deluge of criticism on Charlotte Perkins Gilman has subsided somewhat this year. Thomas L. Erskine and Connie L. Richards have edited a casebook on Gilman's "The Yellow Wall-paper" (Rutgers). It reprints valuable background essays from Gilman and her former doctor, S. Weir Mitchell, as well as more recent critical articles, but like all other present editions of this celebrated and much-analyzed story, it uses, without explanation, the questionable 1892 magazine text instead of the more accurate handwritten manuscript in the Gilman Papers at Radcliffe College. Precisely because the story has been, as the editors say, a "key feminist text" since 1973, it is baffling why so little attention has been shown to the basic scholarly functions of establishing and using the best possible text for it. Looking at Gilman's famous utopian novel, Minna Doskow in "*Herland:* Utopic in a Different Voice" (pp. 52–63) in *Politics, Gender, and the Arts* observes that in contrast to most male-authored utopias, which concentrate on political, economic, social, or religious structures as the foundation of the state, Gilman founds her utopia on a basic human relationship—motherhood—and one emotion—love. The acrimonious relationship between Gilman and Ambrose Bierce is detailed in Lawrence J. Oliver and Gary Scharnhorst's "Charlotte Perkins Gilman and Ambrose Bierce: The Literary Politics of Gender in Fin-de-Siècle California" (*JW* 32, iii: 52–60). Bierce trod on her bunion, it seems, when he criticized in print a women's press association to which she belonged, and in fact singled her out. Oliver and Scharnhorst print a choice but hitherto unpublished letter from Gilman to Brander Matthews, an influential man of letters in New York, asking him to reproach Bierce. Her reference to Matthews's regard for her father, and to herself as a "defenseless" woman, shine a new light on Gilman. Neither Gilman nor Bierce are seen at their best in their protracted feud, but Oliver and Scharnhorst err when they claim that Bierce "never took on Mark Twain"; he did, in print, and more than once.

Among the articles on authors at the very turn of the century is a profile, "Ruth McEnery Stuart," by Joan Wylie Hall (*Legacy* 10: 47–56). Hall credits Stuart with sympathetic stories of blacks, fine stories of Arkansas whites, and good essays on folklore and Southern fiction. The article includes a selected bibliography and some hints for further research. Maureen Fitzgerald has reprinted and introduced Elizabeth Cady Stanton's 1895 *The Woman's Bible* (Northeastern). This is an important document of feminist theology in which Stanton denied divine authorship of the Bible and saw in it instead a misogynistic usurpation of women's rights. Linda Shott's "Jane Addams and William James on Alternatives to War" (*JHI* 54: 241–54) maintains that although both Addams and William James opposed war and sought alternatives, they were circumscribed by both assumed and actual gender differences of the turn of the century, and their "solutions" reflect this limitation. James urged young men, implicitly from the upper classes, to use masculine and military values to serve mankind by overcoming nature. Addams envisaged extending the traditional feminine value of nurture to include men.

Chopin's position as a leading novelist of the turn of the century is upheld by some strong scholarship. Two new editions of *The Awakening* appeared this year. Joyce Dyer has edited one for Twayne, and Nancy A. Walker the other for the Case Series in Contemporary Criticism (St. Martin's). The Case edition consists of the Seyersted text of the novel with five different approaches to it, each defined, explained, and introduced informatively by the general editor, Ross C. Murfin. Elaine Showalter illustrates a feminist critique with "Tradition and the Female Talent: *The Awakening* as a Solitary Book" (pp. 169–89). A New Historical approach is demonstrated by Margit Stange's "Personal Property: Exchange Value and the Female Self in *The Awakening*" (pp. 201–17). Cynthia Griffin Wolffe's "Thanatos and Eros: Kate Chopin's *The Awak-*

ening" (pp. 233–58) practices a psychoanalytic examination. Deconstruction is represented by Patricia S. Yaeger in "A Language Which Nobody Understood: Emancipatory Strategies in *The Awakening*" (pp. 270–96). And Paula A. Treichler takes a reader-response approach in "The Construction of Ambiguity in *The Awakening:* A Linguistic Analysis" (pp. 308–28). Back in the periodicals, Kathryn Lee Seidel's "'Art Is an Unnatural Act': Mademoiselle Reisz in *The Awakening*" (*MissQ* 46: 199–214) sees Mlle Reisz as a lesbian figure in the novel, signified by her identity as an artist who "dares and defies" convention, as well as by her overtures to Edna: touching, stirring her emotionally with music, and by her attraction. Dieter Schulz in "Notes Toward a *fin-de-siècle* Reading of Kate Chopin's *The Awakening*" (*ALR* 25, iii: 69–76) warns against not giving enough emphasis to Chopin's cosmopolitan absorption of late-period international literary developments. In particular, Schulz warns that attitudes in the novel toward the category of mood and the theme and symbolism of Nature should not be mistaken for Chopin's own. Chopin's sensibility, he says, "was equally close to, but also equally remote from Romanticism and modernism."

vii The Howells Generation

It is good to observe that Howells has been steadily gaining in popularity over the years and that he is recognized as having more substance, complexity, depth, range, and passion than was generally accorded him not so long ago when it was in fashion to deride him for celebrating the "more smiling aspects of life." This enhanced view of Howells is reflected in Gore Vidal's "William Dean Howells," an appreciation reprinted in Vidal's *United States Essays, 1952–1992* (Random House, pp. 193–214). A more scholarly discussion of the extent to which Howells was a social critic is James Woodress's "Howells in the Nineties: Social Critic for All Seasons" (*ALR* 25, iii: 18–26). Attention is paid to Howells's involvement in the social causes of the 1890s and to his attraction to several exponents of socialism: Tolstoy, Gronlund, and Bellamy. John W. Crowley relates Howells's novels to the national mood of temperance in their depiction of alcoholism not as a disease but as a weakness of character in "Paradigms of Addiction in Howells' Novels" (*ALR* 25, iii: 3–17). In "Romancing the Beast: Howells' *The Landlord at Lion's Head*" (*ALR* 25, iii: 42–59) Eric Haralson focuses on the character of Jeff Durgin to discuss Howells's changing attitudes toward sexuality and morality. Joel Jones in "Howells's *The Leatherwood God:* The Model in Method for the American Historical Novel" (*Expl* 51: 96–103) infers from the treatment of the novel's historical character, Dylks, both a fondness of Howells for local color and a "realistic" inclination not to sentimentalize the past. An uncollected ironic poem about cannibals eating a missionary is the dish served up in Gary Scharnhorst's "Howells's 'A South Sea Tragedy': A Recovered Poem" (*Expl* 51: 94–95). Edwin Cady's fascinating "Howells on the River" (*ALR* 25, iii: 27–41) is an impressive essay on the influence on Howells of his own not inconsiderable experience with river steamboating. It is also a major comparison of Howells to Twain that should be of great value to both Twain and Howells scholars. Cady and Louis Budd are also the editors of *On Howells: The Best from* American Literature (Duke), a collection of previously published essays.

It is disappointing to find so little work being done on the realist contemporaries of Howells. Nothing at all this year on Cable and Harris, two authors whose wells are far from dry. Hamlin Garland fared better with two solid articles. Bonney MacDonald in "Eastern Imaginings of the West in Hamlin Garland's 'Up the Coolly' and 'God's Ravens' " (*WAL* 28: 209–30) analyzes the two stories to demonstrate how, for Garland, the closing of the frontier was a mental as well as historical condition. Midwestern characters in these stories establish themselves in the East and find that by overidealizing their youthful memories of home they cannot deal with the reality that faces them on their returns, and that they have lost "the capacity for wonder" that is part of the West. A look at Garland's dramatic inclination is supplied by Keith Newlin in "Melodramatist of the Middle Border: Hamlin Garland's Early Work Reconsidered" (*SAF* 21: 153–69). Newlin describes Garland as being torn between an attraction to melodrama and his realization of its limitations as a vehicle for realism; he further observes that Garland was somewhat melodramatic even in his fiction about the Middle Border, and in the final phase of his career he gave greater expression to his melodramatic bent by writing plays and supporting theater.

viii Crane, Norris, Adams, and the Fin-de-Siècle

The main scholarly event in this category is Stanley Wertheim and Paul M. Sorrentino's *The Crane Log: A Documentary Life of Stephen Crane, 1871–1900* (Hall). An excellent work of scholarship, with its abundance of detailed information it will be an indispensable resource.

Wertheim demonstrates, however, with two additional articles that a good deal of important new biographical material outside the *Log*'s scope remains to be excavated. In "Another Diary of the Reverend Jonathan Townley Crane" (*RALS* 19: 35–49) he reproduces the late Crane scholar John Berryman's transcription of entries from the now lost diary of Crane's father. These saved notes add significantly to the scanty documentation available regarding Crane's childhood. Wertheim summarizes what is presently known about Amy Leslie, one of Crane's lovers, in "Who Was 'Amy Leslie'?" (*SCS* 2: 29–37). Joseph R. McElrath, Jr., continues to turn up new material from periodicals in "Stephen Crane in San Francisco: His Reception in *The Wave*" (*SCS* 2: 2–18), in which comments about Crane are reprinted from the San Francisco magazine from 1895 until 1898. Kevin J. Hayes performs a similar service for England in "Crane Reviews in the *Manchester Guardian*," covering 1895–1904 (*SCS* 2: 38–49). In *The Pluralistic Philosophy of Stephen Crane* (Illinois) Patrick K. Dooley finds Crane in general accord with the end-of-the-century view "that there is no Reality, only realities; no Truth, only truths." In other words, human beings are precluded from objective knowledge by the "irreducible plurality of experiences and the inescapable lens of perspective." Keith Gandal's "Stephen Crane's 'Maggie' and the Modern Soul" (*ELH* 60: 759–85) sees in *Maggie* signs of the overturning of the 19th-century belief in "character" and the rise of a modern psychology of self-esteem based on belligerence. Like the medieval theologians who compounded Adam and Eve's single sin into numerous ones, Katrina Irving has, with the aid of theory and scholarship, multiplied "the threat that Maggie poses" and magnified her tragedy in "Gendered Space, Racialized Space: Nativism, the Immigrant Woman, and Stephen Crane's *Maggie*" (*CollL* 20, iii: 30–43). A new edition of *The Red Badge of Courage* (Everyman) has been issued in paperback with an afterword by Malcolm Bradbury. In "'Nobody Seems to Know Where We Go': Uncertainty, History, and Irony in *The Red Badge of Courage*" (*ALR* 26, i: 1–12) John E. Curran, Jr., holds that in basing the novel on the battle of Chancellorsville, where the Union suffered a disastrous defeat, Crane expands the confusion of the Federal troops to a general statement about the whole war: that Americans blindly muddled through a wretchedly conducted and pointless conflict. John Clendenning calls John Berryman's biography of Crane "substantially a self-portrait" in "Rescue in Berryman's Crane" in *Recovering Crane: Essays on a Poet*, ed. Richard J. Kelly and Alan K. Lathrop (Michigan, pp. 179–87).

Despite Berryman's flawed attempt in the biography to seek his own psychological rescue through his analysis of Crane, with whom he identified closely, Clendenning recognizes the biography as "a work of assiduous scholarship and critical insight." And Donald Vanouse updates Patrick Dooley's 1992 bibliography with "Stephen Crane: An Annotated Bibliography of Articles and Book Chapters Since 1991" (*SCS* 2: 22–26), updating further since 1992 (2: 53–58).

A windfall of scholarship was occasioned by the special issue of *FNS* (no. 15) devoted to supplying the background to Norris's "Perverted Tales," a series of short parodies of contemporary authors he published in the Christmas 1897 issue of *The Wave*. Joseph R. McElrath, Jr.'s " 'The Ricksha That Happened': Norris's Parody of Rudyard Kipling" (pp. 1–4) recognizes Kipling as "an experimental realist par excellence" for Norris's generation, and it sees in the parody evidence of Norris's adulation for the author. Crane was the subject of Stanley Wertheim's "Frank Norris's 'The Green Stone of Unrest' " (pp. 5–8), which identifies *The Red Badge of Courage* as the target of the parody. Wertheim notes that Norris concentrates on such idiosyncrasies of Crane's style as his theatrical use of color, his exotic words and neologisms, the "nervous, elliptical" quality of his prose, and "the often hallucinatory nature of his characters's perceptions." Gary Scharnhorst in "Harte, Norris, and 'The Hero of Tomato Can' " (pp. 8–10) observes that Norris parodied Harte in chapter 21 of *McTeague* as well as in this sketch, but that for all his parody, Norris also imitated Harte. It is a sad commentary on Richard Harding Davis that he has been so completely eclipsed by the rediscovery of his mother's work that this rare mention of him is only the by-product of Douglas K. Burgess's study of "Norris's 'Van Bubbles' Story': Bursting the Bubble of the Davis Mystique" (pp. 10–13). Burgess notes that Davis had developed a sort of formulaic hero, a "gentleman" at once manly and socially proper, who was always successful. It is this stereotype that Norris skillfully skewered. In "The Romantic Realism of Bierce and Norris" (pp. 13–17), I link Norris's "Ambrosia Beer" to Ambrose Bierce's 1888 story "One of the Missing," but I find that the sketch parodies only Biercian style, which Norris outgrew after his youthful story of 1891, "The Jongleur of Taillebois." A more important and lasting influence of Bierce on Norris was, I aver, Bierce's publicly argued (in his journalistic columns, which Norris most likely read) preference for romanticism over realism, which preference Norris assimilated and expressed in his famous essay "A Plea for Romantic Fiction." Benjamin F. Fisher's "Frank Norris

Parodies Anthony Hope" (pp. 17–20) completes the series with his discussion of "I Call on Lady Dotty: From the Polly Parables." Fisher considers the sketch to be a direct parody of Hope's *Dolly Dialogues*, which revolve around the flirtations of a young, wealthy, and idle British upper class, which was itself a lampoon of Victorian extravagance. Ultimately, the lightheartedness of this parody of decadence was replaced by more serious social criticism in Norris's later work.

Apart from this special issue of *FNS*, Norris studies appear in other periodicals. McElrath has contributed two of them. His "Grant Richards's Letters to Frank Norris: Addenda to *Frank Norris: Collected Letters*" (*RALS* 19: 50–57) collects letters from Norris's English publisher that show Norris being victimized by the unctuous Richards. According to McElrath, although Norris "specialized in fictional examinations of the darker recesses of human nature," when it came to business, he ironically "had more in common with the sentimental Victorian idealists whose values had shaped his personal life." In "Frank Norris's 'The Puppets and the Puppy': LeContean Idealism or Naturalistic Skepticism?" (*ALR* 26, i: 50–59) McElrath finds in the 1897 story a key to resolving the question whether Norris was a philosophical idealist or a Zolaesque pessimist. The story, McElrath maintains, lays out the path that Norris follows in his major work: that idealists who look for a benign order in the vast and terrible drama of life delude themselves. Robert C. Leitz III compares Norris's and Jack London's respective treatments of the Arctic in "Jack London in 1900: Besting Norris in the Far North" (*FNS* 16: 6–7). Leonard Cassuto's "Keeping Company with the Old Folks: Unravelling the Edges of McTeague's Deterministic Fabric" (*ALR* 25, ii: 46–55) sees the union of Old Grannis and Miss Baker as a fully realized portrait of free will; he also feels that Norris deserves some recognition as an artist of ambiguity. A somewhat different view of the same plot occurs in Donna M. Campbell's "Frank Norris' 'Drama of a Broken Teacup': The Old Grannis-Miss Baker Plot in *McTeague*" (*ALR* 26, i: 40–49). Campbell views it as an exploration of problems that develop when three late 19th-century movements converge: realism, naturalism, and women's local color writing; she claims that local color led to a dead end and that the future for Norris and American realism was henceforth in Zolaesque naturalism. Charles Kaplan briefly comments on the operatic adaptation of *McTeague* in "*McTeague* Lives! The Opera" (*FNS* 16: 7–8). Robert Funk in "Dreiser's *An American Tragedy*" (*Expl* 51: 232–34) reports that Dreiser makes reference to *McTeague* in chapter 46 of *An American*

Tragedy. In "'If Your View Be Large Enough': Native Growth in *The Octopus*" (*ALR* 25, ii: 56–66) Charles Duncan, defending *The Octopus* from charges that it is either structurally or philosophically inconsistent, ascribes a unifying effect to Norris's use of the experimental technique of "free indirect discourse" in the temporary collapsing of characters' points of view into the narrator's.

Henry Adams was the subject of a valuable collection, with a number of notable essays, *Henry Adams and His World* (American Philosophical Society), ed. David R. Contosta and Robert Muccigrosso. Edward Chalfont leads off with "Lies, Silence, and Truth in the Writings of Henry Adams," which argues that the protagonist of *The Education of Henry Adams* was a fiction, and intended as a fiction, and that to read the work as autobiography is needlessly confusing. An interesting narrative of Henry Adams's involvement as well as his interest in politics is Ari Hoogenboom's "Henry Adams and Politics." Hoogenboom avers that Adams was more successful than he admitted. Contosta's "Henry Adams and the American Century" complements Hoogenboom by stating that Adams anticipated nearly every major shift in the international balance of power in the 20th century. In "Religion as Culture: Henry Adams's *Mont-Saint-Michel and Chartres*" Alfred Kazin advances an iconoclastic but plausible critique of the book in proposing that in it Adams abandoned his own historical standards of factual accuracy to project not so much an appreciation of the power of religion as his own infatuation with mind and culture. Eugenia Kaledin in "Henry Adams's Anthropological Vision as American Identity" maintains that Adams exhibited open-mindedness toward women and toward other cultures: those of American Indians, Buddhists, and South Sea islanders. Paul R. Baker reports on Adams's friendships with architects and artists, especially Henry Hobson Richardson, Stanford White, and Augustus Saint-Gaudens, in "Henry Adams and the American Artists: The Two Mansions." Peter Shaw in "A Dissenting View of John Quincy Adams" reveals Adams, surprisingly, to have been antipathetical toward his grandfather. John Lukacs's "Henry Adams and the European Tradition of the Philosophy of History" is an excellent essay that praises Adams as a historian but pans him as a philosopher of history. This closely reasoned piece is likely to be influential. It is at odds with Contosta's and Hoogenboom's articles, but in accord with Kazin's. Anticlimactically, Earl N. Harbert's "Failure or Success? Our Legacy from Henry Adams" concludes the collection by noting simply that Adams was successful at least in stirring up his readers. One additional view of Adams occurs in Reed Whittemore's *Six Literary Lives*. The common ground of all the writers discussed in this book is the impiety (in the Socratic sense) of their reactions to the 19th-century climate of thought. The book is interesting for its perspective rather than for being a source of new biographical information.

In the area of late-period African American authors Richard H. Brodhead has edited *The Conjure Woman and Other Conjure Tales* by Charles W. Chesnutt (Duke). This edition has had restored to it stories originally intended for the book but eliminated by an editor. Brodhead has also edited *The Journals of Charles W. Chesnutt* (Duke), a selection from the journals of 1874–82. Edward H. Bodie, Jr., corrects an editor's note in "Chesnutt's 'The Goophered Grapevine'" (*Expl* 51: 28–29). *The Collected Poetry of Paul Laurence Dunbar* (Virginia) makes available the "largest and most authoritative"—but still not all-inclusive—gathering of Dunbar's poems. Joanne M. Braxton, as editor, supplies an introduction, a list of textual variants, and a selected bibliography, but no notes. It contains 60 poems not available in the 1913 edition. Blake Allmendinger's "Deadwood Dick: The Black Cowboy as Cultural Timber" comments on the 1907 autobiography of Nat Love, aka "Deadwood Dick" (*JACult* 16, iv: 79–89). Although he was an ex-slave, worked as a cowboy—almost a quarter of Western ranch hands were black—and finished his working career as a Pullman porter, Love failed to see evidence of racism.

It is disappointing that a period so rich and full of vitality as the end of the century receives so little activity outside the major authors. In "'Something Uncanny': The Dream Structure in Ambrose Bierce's 'An Occurrence at Owl Creek Bridge'" (*SSF* 30: 349–58) Peter Stoicheff reduces "Owl Creek" from a work of fiction to an intuited anticipation of later dream models of Freud and the French writer, Louis Maury, and characterizes as a dream a psychosomatic phenomenon that could not have lasted more than a fraction of a second. Richard Wattenberg's "Taming the Frontier Myth: Clyde Fitch's *The Cowboy and the Lady*" (*JACult* 16, ii: 77–84) views Fitch's 1899 play as an example of the "Eastern frontier myth"—a depiction of the West that shows the superiority of civilization over savagery, that is, the ruling elite of the East over the roughnecks of the West. A criticism of Fitch's "realism" is tied by Kim Marra's "Clara Bloodgood (1870–1907), Exemplary Subject of Broadway Gender Tyranny" (*ATQ* 7: 193–216) to the suicide of Clara Bloodgood, Fitch's favorite actress. Marra blames the suicide on "influential agents of patriarchal opinion" who exacerbated her perfectionist anxieties by deeming her inadequate to represent the idealized American Girl stereotype that Fitch promoted in his plays. Another slam at masculine tyranny occurs in Grace Ann Hovet and Theodore R. Hovet's "TABLEAUX VIVANTS: Masculine Vision and Feminine Reflections in Novels by Warner, Alcott, Stowe, and Wharton" (*ATQ* 7: 335–56). The villain of this piece is the "masculine gaze," which constructs "feminine images." As the Hovets see it, Susan Warner's *The Wide, Wide World,* Louisa May Alcott's *Little Women,* and Harriet Beecher Stowe's *My Wife and I* all show women successfully manipulating male stereotypes of them so as to achieve personal liberation, but Edith Wharton's *The House of Mirth* depicts Lily Bart's tragic failure to break the strength of the masculine vision. Among the six novels treated briefly in Elizabeth S. Prioleau's tracing of what she considers a uniquely American literary motif in "The Minister and the Seductress in American Fiction: The Adamic Myth Redux" (*JACult* 16, iv: 1–6) is Harold Frederic's *The Damnation of Theron Ware.* Two articles on Lafcadio Hearn appear in *CLS.* Rolf J. Goebel briefly mentions Hearn as an example in his discussion of attempts by three Westerners to interpret Japan from different perspectives, in "Japan as Western Text: Roland Barthes, Richard Gordon Smith, and Lafcadio Hearn" (30: 188–205). Junko (Hagiwara) Umemoto in "Lafcadio Hearn and Christianity" (30: 388–96) affirms that Hearn's embrace of Buddhism in Japan was more a reaction against Christianity than a true religious conversion. Margaret Guilford-Kardell reprints an 1896 address by Joaquin Miller to a Women's Christian Temperance Union meeting and concludes from it that he was pro-woman in "Joaquin Miller's Charcoal Sketches: Women Compiled, Edited, and Annotated" (*AmPer* 3: 43–50). John G. Geer and Thomas R. Rochon's "William Jennings Bryan on the Yellow Brick Road" (*JACult* 16, iv: 59–63) maintains that L. Frank Baum's *Wizard of Oz* was a populist allegory. Dorothy, who wears *silver* shoes in the novel, supposedly represents Bryan, the Scarecrow represents the farmers, the Tin Woodsman industrial workers, and the Cowardly Lion the Populist party.

Several miscellaneous items close this section. John Muir is treated in Margaret Helmers's "Creating the California Alps" (*TWA* 81: 65–78). Helmers remarks on an intentional duality in Muir's descriptions of the Sierras. To save them from development, he had to make them attractive to readers, but because he worried about tourists he concealed from his readers the wild and terrifying aspects of the mountains that he found most appealing. Tim Fort's "Three Voyages of Discovery: The Columbus Productions of Imre Kiralfy, E. E. Rice, and Steele MacKaye" (*JADT* 5: 5–30) summarizes three attempts in 1892 and 1894 to celebrate the Columbian quincentenary with stage productions. All three were extravaganzas: Kiralfy's *Columbus* featured visual—especially electric—effects; Rice's *1492* emphasized singing, dancing, and comedy, as well as electric novelties; and MacKaye's *World Finder* was actorless but depended on elaborate stage effects, a narrator, and choral backgrounds. The first two plays were successes, but MacKaye's 1894 production was successful only technologically, not dramatically. Charles L. P. Silet puts forth his third addition to his 1977 reference guide to Fuller and Garland in "Henry Blake Fuller: Further Additions and Corrections" (*RALS* 19: 75–93). Clare Virginia Eby in "The Psychology of Desire: Veblen's 'Pecuniary Emulation' and 'Invidious Comparison' in *Sister Carrie* and *An American Tragedy*" (*SAF* 21: 191–208) finds a complementary relationship between Dreiser and Thorstein Veblen. Veblen, she says, alters assumptions of economics about psychology, and Dreiser makes economics central to psychological realism.

University of Michigan—Dearborn

13 Fiction: 1900 to the 1930s

Jo Ann Middleton

With the volume of scholarship this chapter now covers, I am beginning to believe that during the early years of the century every literate person in the United States wrote a book—*and* had it published! Feminist, ethnic, contextual, multicultural, and gender studies are reclaiming such a remarkable number of authors that the margins are becoming central. Cather remains the major figure, with Wharton a close second; Jack London scholars had a wonderful year, and Jean Toomer's critical stock is on the rise. The proliferation of primary sources now accessible to scholars means that the richness and diversity of new work and new discoveries will continue.

i Willa Cather

Those who have long suspected that Willa Cather actually wrote Georgine Milmine's controversial 1909 biography of Mary Baker Eddy, *The Life of Mary Baker G. Eddy and the History of Christian Science* (Nebraska), have been vindicated. In his valuable introductory essay, which relates the book to Cather's style, syntax, and narrative strategy in *One of Ours, A Lost Lady, My Mortal Enemy, Death Comes for the Archbishop,* and *Lucy Gayheart,* David Stouck paraphrases Cather's letters to her father and to Edwin H. Anderson of the New York Public Library that disclose her authorship, then reveals that the "Melmine" manuscript of the book has been found in the Mary Baker Eddy Archives: "Cather's handwriting is not only identifiable in edits for the typesetter but in notes on separate pages," conclusively proving that the book belongs in the Cather canon. One of few Cather texts for which we have a manuscript, this early work "presents an important profile of Cather's developing voice" as well as her "powerful and sympathetic interest in human psychology."

Cather papers do turn up in unexpected places. By accident, Dennis Halac discovered in an archive in Prague five letters from Cather to Thomas G. Masaryk in which she discusses automobiles, style, *Death Comes for the Archbishop, Obscure Destinies,* religion, and the world situation. Paraphrased in "Ever So True: Willa Cather & T. G. Masaryk" (*NewC* 12, iii: 36–40), facsimiles and transcripts of the letters are destined for Red Cloud and the Masaryk Collection at Berkeley.

After more than 50 years of research by John March and seven years of editing and verification by Marilyn Arnold with the help of Debra Lynn Thornton, *A Reader's Companion to the Fiction of Willa Cather* (Greenwood) is in print. Thoroughly fascinating, often delightful, and always informative, with thousands of entries on persons, places, and events—both fictional and real—as well as on quotations, works of art, and music, this compendium represents only half of the original manuscript. (A second volume will cover Cather's essays and poems.) We learn a great deal about the way Cather's mind worked, her interests, and how much she knew. Another work conceived more than 50 years ago, Edward Wagenknecht's *Willa Cather* (Continuum), also appeared this year, with thorough discussions of the uncollected stories that Cather "wished to forget" as well as a complete descriptive appendix of them. Wagenknecht's prose is graceful and clear, his scholarship current and wideranging, and, in a rather masterful touch, his use of the now outdated but gentlemanly "Miss Cather" reminds the reader that his is a contemporary's evaluation. After a consideration of Cather's life, Wagenknecht applies his undiminished and considerable critical expertise to her novels and stories (revising some of his previous statements about the work), then concludes with a penetrating section in which he evenhandedly discusses Cather's intensity, eccentricities, and temperament. Of special note is his rebuttal to "recent writers [who] have seen fit to speak of Miss Cather as a lesbian" that includes a "look at the record" of heterosexual passion in Cather's fiction, a catalog of the men who appealed to her sexually, including two who proposed, and assessments of her relationships with Louise Pound, "a not-uncommon college crush"; Isabelle McClung, "the dearest friend Willa Cather ever had"; and Edith Lewis, "Willa's Girl Friday." Wagenknecht's final appraisal of Cather as essentially a religious writer will probably meet only minor disagreement, but his challenge to anyone who insists on reading the Cather-McClung relationship as lesbian to "try his hand at squaring the circle" seems likely to provoke response. Wagenknecht might be reacting to critics such as Frances W. Kaye, who avers in her *Isolation and Masquerade: Willa Cather's Women* (Peter Lang) that Cather can be read only as a lesbian writer, "to validate and politically support the lesbian and gay readers . . . [and] because so many of the nuances of the work are unintelligible unless we read it as being by and about a lesbian consciousness." Kaye's readings attempt to demonstrate that Cather's distrust of women as a class was at least as powerful as her portrayal of great heroines, and she challenges Sharon O'Brien's less arbitrary conclusions in *Willa Cather: The Emerging Voice* (see *ALS 1988*, pp. 217–19) about Cather's development and her subsequent portrayals of women. O'Brien compares *The Emerging Voice*, a scholarly work, to her forthcoming biography of Cather for a general audience to explore "the narrative contingency of feminist biography" and to demonstrate "the complex interplay of psychological, cultural, and professional dynamics" that influence the production of biography in "Feminist Biography as Shaped Narrative: Telling Willa Cather's Stories" (*ABSt* 8: 258–70).

Several works concern themselves with gender issues. Locating Cather in the "high modernist tradition of American letters" which adopts the figure of the dandy and challenges the "two-sex model," Jessica R. Feldman suggests that Cather creates an art "freed from the opposing categories of the ethical and the aesthetic" by adopting the literary "dandy" of the French tradition to address gender and the conflict between female "sensation" (French aesthetic power) and male "sympathy" (American moral power) in her superb study, *Gender on the Divide: The Dandy in Modernist Literature* (Cornell, pp. 143–79). In "Willa Cather and the Fiction of Female Development," pp. 221–34 in *Anxious Power*, Judith Fetterley argues that the misogyny in Cather's work reveals the cost of Cather's male identification and "her inevitable ambivalence about her development as a writer." Fetterley skillfully demonstrates that *The Professor's House*, a novel of failed male development, unwrites *The Song of the Lark*, a novel of successful female development. Thea records Cather's "wonder [at] the miracle of discovering and having her desire" (Isabelle McClung), and the Professor registers "the devastating effect of losing her primary object of desire." Margaret Morganoth Gullette identifies Cather with "decline novelists" such as Atherton, Dreiser, Fitzgerald, and Wharton, who depicted midlife crises, desperation, and decay among the middle-aged (*Aging and Gender in Literature*, pp. 19–

48). Thea Kronborg began as an exception to the pattern of characters whose fears of aging correlate with their gender and with their creators' anxieties, but when Cather wrote the foreword to the 1932 edition, "she retracted the midlife progress features" and "even denied they were there," suggesting that she had faced the complicated consequences of aging.

Critics seem inclined to follow Reginald Dyck's suggestion in "The Feminist Critique of Willa Cather's Fiction: A Review Essay" (*WS* 22: 263–80) that feminists' psychologically and politically astute readings of Cather's fiction be broadened to include class and ethnicity. Annette Bennington McElhiney does just that in her important essay, "Willa Cather's Use of a Tripartite Narrative Point of View in *My Ántonia*" (*CEA* 56, i: 65–76), which reveals Cather's "identification with women's (Ántonia's) 'outsider,' immigrant experience, not with men's (Jim's) 'insider,' dominant-culture experience." Jim's droning, mythmaking narrative leaves little room for Ántonia's storytelling voice, which illustrates that "the perception of the frontier experience depends on gender, class, and ethnic background," but the "I/editor"—Cather—ultimately controls the story through the dialectic exchange between these two voices and by the omission of summaries or comments to question "the male dominant culture's attitudes about women and the American frontier, with its propensity for silencing women or speaking for them." Ann G. MacDonald suggests techniques to help students probe the technical and philosophical aspects of the narrator-author relationship by comparing the 1918 and the 1926 introductions to the novel in "I Finally Listened to My Students: Taking Another Look at the Introduction to *My Ántonia*" (*IEB* 79 [1992]: 68–72). The new Penguin edition of *My Ántonia,* ed. John J. Murphy, contains Murphy's valuable introduction and notes, both of Cather's introductions, and a letter written by Anna Pavelka. Stephen Fender in *Sea Changes: British Emigration and American Literature* (Cambridge, 1992, pp. 325–33) proposes that *My Ántonia* can be read as "a full account of the emigration experience" where parents decline because they have been uprooted even as their children, born in Nebraska, surpass their contemporaries born of American parents. However, Jim's contradictory story sends him back to the "secure structures of time-tested, traditional civilization"; thus Cather encodes her desire to be seen as the writing equivalent of the plowing immigrants and to reinvent America in the European cultural tradition. Contrary to criticism which dismisses or ignores Cather's exposure to Native American influence, Stephen C. Swinehart's "The Native American Voice in Willa Cather's *The Song of the Lark* and Other Writings" (*HK* 25, ii: 39–49) convincingly traces her changing attitudes toward Native Americans, proposes that she had no intention of writing conventional historical novels, and demonstrates that she incorporated the storytelling strategies of indigenous peoples. In writing *The Song of the Lark* she "came as close as any Anglo-American writer had come in her day to recovering the spiritual energies of the land and its Native American people." Fred Setterberg makes some cogent points about Cather's rendering of the Nebraska landscape in his engaging travelogue and memoir, *The Roads Taken: Travels Through America's Literary Landscapes* (Georgia). Setterberg observes that "Nebraska seems to be one of those places that you leave in order to love"; he suggests that Cather's greatness lies in her ability to remember and depict "both her state's isolation and its solitude, the arbitrariness of sudden death as well as the land's insistent rebirth."

Cather's understanding of the land as a dynamic presence which allows her characters to find their authentic selves is central to Laura Winters's perceptive study, *Willa Cather: Landscape and Exile* (Susquehanna). Often banished from a native or authentic landscape, Cather's characters manage the conditions of exile by transforming secular spaces into sacred spaces where "existence suddenly makes sense." Winters provides a thorough scholarly grounding for eminently readable discussions of the metaphors of cantilever and suspension in *Alexander's Bridge,* the parable of inspiration lost and found in *A Lost Lady,* the pervasiveness of possession in *The Professor's House,* death as exile in *My Mortal Enemy,* movement and stasis in *Death Comes for the Archbishop,* and the condition of exile in *Shadows on the Rock.* In her discerning introduction to the Penguin edition of *O Pioneers!* Blanche H. Gelfant shows how Cather's transformation of the Nebraska landscape, "a seemingly uncultivable literary territory," into art reflects her own inner connection to the land. Gary Brienzo explores Cather's transplantation of the frontier and the "noble pioneer" to another time and landscape in "Making an Aristocratic Frontier: Selective History in Willa Cather's *Shadows on the Rock,*" pp. 154–62 in *Old West-New West.* Focusing on Cather's treatment of Laval and Frontenac, Brienzo skillfully demonstrates that Cather transforms history into fiction in *Shadows on the Rock* by carefully applying her own fictional touches to selected details from historical sources "to create an overlying impression of immutability . . . in the rock of Quebec, her last, most unassailable frontier."

Several fine essays appeared in this year's *Willa Cather Pioneer Memorial Newsletter*. John H. Flannigan's compelling comparison of *Shadows on the Rock* and Mérimée's *Cronique du régne de Charles IX* (1829) in "Cather, Mérimée, and the Problem of Fanaticism in *Shadows on the Rock*" (37: 29–35) demonstrates that Cather, like Mérimée, uses a fictional account of historical events to address "the inability of contemporary readers to perceive the historical process in action." Replete with reproductions from the works of Jan Vermeer and Jan van Eyck, "Dutch Genre Painting and Sacramental Symbolism in *Shadows on the Rock*" (37: 11–14) is Trevor D. Packer's contribution to the growing work on Cather's use of the visual arts. Like these painters, Cather associates a sense of order, tranquility, and peace with the domestic interior of the Auclairs' home and likens this sanctuary to "a chapel in which sacred rites are performed" through the use of religious symbolism. In "The Third Chapter of 'Sampson Speaks to the Master' " (37: 1, 9–10) John J. Murphy, who first noted the impact of impressionism and luminism on Cather in My Ántonia: *The Road Home* (see *ALS 1990*, p. 244), expertly demonstrates that scenes in this novel recall paintings by Millet and Brueghel, that the story of Tansy Dave supplies a counterplot to Nancy's victimization by Martin and to the arousal of the Colbert blood in Henry, and that Cather discloses "Henry's lonely and ongoing struggle to curtail his nature" through passages from *Pilgrim's Progress*. One other essay examines *My Mortal Enemy*. Christine Kephart traces patterns of light and dark in " 'He Turned Off the Lights': A Study of Darkness in *My Mortal Enemy*" (37: 36–39) to find that Cather's "dramatic use of darkness" guides the story of Myra Henshawe to its inevitable conclusion.

One of Ours occupied three critics this year. Timothy R. Cramer likens Claude to Paul of "Paul's Case," both "unhappy young [men] living in the midst of Philistines," in "Claude's Case: A Study of the Homosexual Temperament in Willa Cather's *One of Ours*" (*SDR* 31, iii: 147–60), reading both the story and the novel as expressions of Cather's internalized homophobia. In "Some of His: Cather's Use of Dr. Sweeney's Diary in *One of Ours*" (*WCPMN* 37: 5–9) Rebecca Faber compares Book IV of the novel to Cather's primary source to show that the influenza epidemic aboard the troopship and the description of military life, as well as prototypes for some of Cather's characters, come from information appropriated from Sweeney's notes. Inspired by David McCullough's *Truman* (1992), James Woodress's intriguing and engaging essay,

"A Note on *One of Ours*" (*WCPMN* 37: 1, 4), locates ample validation for Claude Wheeler's character in the pivotal war experiences of our 33rd president. Like Claude, Truman was a dissatisfied farmer when the war broke out, felt like "Galahad after the Grail" when he enlisted, took great delight in France, and, during the Argonne offensive, "showed the same kind of courage that cost Claude Wheeler his life." With his customary wit, Woodress points out that unfortunately for Cather, contemporary critics read her novel with a bias induced by postwar disillusionment; fortunately for the United States, Truman came back.

With considerable skill and insight, three noted Catherians furthered the discussion of Cather's creative methods. Richard C. Harris explores her declaration that J. W. N. Sullivan's *Beethoven: His Spiritual Development* was "the only book she ever read that represents any real, detailed thinking about and analysis of the artistic personality and artistic creativity" in his lucid "Willa Cather, J. W. N. Sullivan, and the Creative Process" (*WCPMN* 37: 17, 21–24). Harris finds that, like Cather, Sullivan believed that passion, expression, synthesis, and arrangement were essential to artistic creation. Bruce P. Baker contends that Cather's attempt to define the nature, role, function, and sacrifice demanded of the artist began much earlier than *The Song of the Lark,* and he applies his expertise to her early stories "Peter" and "Nanette: An Aside" as well as to several columns and letters in "Portrait of the Artist by a Young Woman" (*WCPMN* 37: 40–42). Merrill Maguire Skaggs's charming description of the G. P. Cather house *without* Claude Wheeler's sleeping porch and his father George's house *with* such a porch in "Sleeping in Nebraska: Additional Seminar Reflections" (*WCPMN* 37: 20–21) makes very clear a significant aspect of Cather's creative process. Synchronicity in Cather's descriptions between fiction and the actual tells us that she is talking about her own life as she has experienced it; discrepancy signals the hand of the fiction writer engaged in simplification. A companion piece is "Symbolism of Architectural Styles in Cather's *The Professor's House*" (*IdSUSAL* 27 [1991]: 60–80), Curtis Dahl's thorough, persuasive explication of Cather's use of the varied architectural images throughout *The Professor's House.*

Two essays deal with Cather's stories. In "The Unfinished Picture: Willa Cather's 'The Marriage of Phaedra' " (*SSF* 30: 153–60) Emmy Stark Zitter makes a convincing case for the underappreciated "Marriage of Phaedra" as the most original and revolutionary story in *The Troll Garden.* Linked to Phaedra by her secret power to rebel against patriarchal forces, Lady Treffinger refuses to die and insists on continuing her own life, "a powerful act of revenge for all the caretaking women of *The Troll Garden*," foreshadowing Marian Forrester. Alex Vardamis investigates widely divergent perspectives on men, marriage, and family in his comparative study, "Two Hands: Colette's 'The Hand' and Cather's 'Neighbour Rosicky' " (*WCPMN* 37: 35–36).

Finally, the nine essays in volume 2 of *Cather Studies*, ed. Susan Rosowski, recapitulate the variety of issues covered in this year's scholarship. Loretta Wasserman's evenhanded discussion of Cather's alleged anti-Semitism, changing sympathies, and depiction in fiction of the anti-Semitic prejudices of the dominant culture in "Cather's Semitism" (pp. 1–22) concludes that, aware of Jews as a presence in American life, Cather chose to register that presence in her fiction. John H. Flannigan addresses Cather's ambivalence toward gender in "Issues of Gender and Lesbian Love: Goblins in 'The Garden Lodge' " (pp. 23–40). With the help of Teresa de Lauretis and Jurij Lotman, Ann Fisher-Wirth makes the point that Jim's narrative represents "a perpetual desirous return to the last motherbody from which his life necessarily departed," characterized by repeated fluctuation between enclosure and emergence in "Out of the Mother: Loss in *My Ántonia*" (pp. 41–71). In "This is a Frame-Up: Mother Eve in *The Professor's House*" (pp. 72–91) Jean Schwind examines the centrality of literary and cultural "frame-ups" to *The Professor's House*, a novel in which males clearly misread females in "conceptual frame-ups." Matthias Schubnell analyzes that novel using Spengler's characteristics of civilization in "The Decline of America: Willa Cather's Spenglerian Vision in *The Professor's House*" (pp. 92–117); and Linda Chown makes the case for Cather's "subtle narrative technique" in another neglected novel in " 'It Came Closer than That': Willa Cather's *Lucy Gayheart*" (pp. 118–39). Another essay by Skaggs, "Cather's Use of Parkman's Histories in *Shadows on the Rock*" (pp. 140–55), identifies the second and fourth volumes of Parkman's chronicles as most important to Cather's novel, exhaustively identifying events, incidents, themes, and images that Cather expropriated to anchor her fiction in fact. In "Willa Cather and Alphonse Daudet" (pp. 156–66) James Woodress proposes that Cather may have been convinced by her favorite writer of the disaster that romantic relationships or marriage can be for artists, and he also discusses the writers' literary similarities, differences, and parallels. Unlike the many psychological studies of *My Mortal Enemy*, Robert K.

Miller's "Strains of Blood: Myra Driscoll and the Romance of the Celts" (pp. 169–77) reads the novel as a "triumph of race over individuality."

ii Edith Wharton and Ellen Glasgow

The most newsworthy item in Wharton scholarship this year is Marion Mainwaring's controversial completion of Wharton's last, unfinished novel *The Buccaneers* (Viking), which cleverly joins her own prose to Wharton's in an entertaining, romantic "read." Most noteworthy is Viola Hopkins Winner's splendid scholarly edition of *Fast and Loose & The Buccaneers* (Virginia). Juxtaposing the extant texts of works written 60 years apart, Winner meticulously demonstrates how Wharton came "full circle." Winner includes three reviews of *Fast and Loose,* Wharton's scenario for *The Buccaneers,* as well as comprehensive notes, textual emendations, and a compilation of revisions for both novels in a model of textual scholarship. Adeline R. Tintner has two essays on *The Buccaneers.* "Pre-Raphaelite Painting and Poetry in Edith Wharton's *The Buccaneers* (1938)" (*JPRS* 2, ii: 16–20) illustrates "the remarkable operation" of Wharton's "acute art historical sense" and analyzes her use of real and invented art, as well as poetry, to augment character, theme, and plot. Tintner's "Consuelo Vanderbilt and *The Buccaneers*" (*EWhR* 10, ii: 15–19) reminds us of just how enjoyable literary investigation can be by reviewing the details of "the Marlborough case," tying Wharton herself to the players, then expertly applying the facts of the Vanderbilt-Marlborough scandal to the novel. Now available to scholars is Wharton's lively 1888 travel journal, *The Cruise of the Vanadis* (Sterne, 1992), thanks to the efforts of French scholar Claudine Lesage, who discovered the manuscript in the public library at Hyères.

Wretched Exotic collects 19 essays first occasioned by the Paris Edith Wharton Conference (1991), consistently offering fresh insights and new perspectives. Grouped thematically are essays on Wharton as a resident of France by Shari Benstock ("Landscapes of Desire: Edith Wharton and Europe," pp. 19–42), Susan Goodman ("Edith Wharton's Inner Circle," pp. 43–60), and Millicent Bell ("Edith Wharton in France," pp. 61–73); on Wharton's relationship to her American readers by Kristin Olson Lauer ("Can France Survive This Defender? Contemporary American Reaction to Wharton's Expatriation," pp. 77–96), Robert A. Martin and Linda Wagner-Martin ("The Salons of Wharton's Fiction: Wharton and

Fitzgerald, Hemingway, Faulkner, and Stein," pp. 97–110), and Carol
Wershoven ("Edith Wharton's Discriminations: Eurotrash and European Treasures," pp. 111–26); on Wharton as a European traveler
by Shirley Foster ("Making It Her Own: Edith Wharton's Europe,"
pp. 129–46), Mary Suzanne Schriber ("Edith Wharton and the Dog-
Eared Travel Book," pp. 147–64), Maureen E. St. Laurent ("Pathways to
a Personal Aesthetic: Edith Wharton's Travels in Italy and France,"
pp. 165–80), Brigitte Bailey ("Aesthetics and Ideology in *Italian Backgrounds*," pp. 181–200), and Teresa Gómez Reus ("Mapping the Con-
tours of a Forgotten Land: Edith Wharton and Spain," pp. 201–15); on
Wharton and World War I by Alan Price ("Wharton Mobilizes Artists to
Aid the War Homeless," pp. 219–40) and Judith L. Sensibar (" 'Behind
the Lines' in Edith Wharton's *A Son at the Front*: Re-Writing a Masculinist Tradition," pp. 241–56); on new approaches to Wharton's fiction
by Cynthia Griffin Wolff ("Lily Bart and Masquerade Inscribed in
the Female Mode," pp. 259–94), Julie Olin-Ammentorp ("Wharton
Through a Kristevan Lens: The Maternality of *The Gods Arrive*,"
pp. 295–312), and Susan Elizabeth Sweeney ("Edith Wharton's Case of
Roman Fever," pp. 313–31; and on Wharton as an international reader
and writer by Katherine Joslin (" 'Fleeing the Sewer': Edith Wharton,
George Sand, and Literary Innovation," pp. 335–54), Roger Asselineau
("Edith Wharton—She Thought in French and Wrote in English,"
pp. 355–64), and Helen Killoran ("Edith Wharton's Reading in European Languages and Its Influence on Her Work," pp. 365–88). Killoran's
bibliographical essay includes a complete list of foreign language books
in Wharton's library.

Kathy Miller Hadley seeks to rectify the conception of Wharton as a
"relatively old-fashioned writer," persuasively arguing that Wharton's
narrative strategies link her to American modernism in *The Interstices of
the Tale: Edith Wharton's Narrative Strategies* (Peter Lang). Hadley's
competent readings of *The Reef, The Custom of the Country, The Age of
Innocence, The Mother's Recompense,* and *The Children* demonstrate
Wharton's experiments with narrative form, her pervasive irony, and her
exploration of untold women's stories.

Mollie L. Burleson and Marcia Phillips McGowan each deal with
Wharton's stories about women. Burleson reads *Summer* as a self-
subverting novel in which "dark is light, ascendance is descent, [and]
mirrors reflect what is not reality" to reveal the darker substratum in
Wharton's "coming of age" story, in "Edith Wharton's *Summer:* Through

the Glass Darkly" (*StWF* 13: 19–21); and McGowan's lucid "Female Development as Subtext in Edith Wharton's Final Novels" (*Connecticut Review* 15, ii: 73–80) offers close feminist readings of *Hudson River Bracketed* and *The Gods Arrive* as novels that elaborate "full-scale fantasies about the liberation and gratification of female desire and the unleashing of female power" by allowing Halo Tarrent, an embodiment of the ancient mother-goddess, the possibility of sustaining and enduring human relationships inaccessible to her other female characters.

Wharton's short fiction always generates several items. Andrew Levy in *Culture and Commerce,* pp. 58–76, convincingly identifies Wharton's career as "a significant, even archetypal instance of how Poe's vision took corporeal form on the American landscape." Like Poe, Wharton was a literary entrepreneur who wanted control of the narrative transaction and who sought to make literature a paying profession. Elsa Nettels demonstrates just how Wharton uses letters to reveal her characters' moral natures in "The Muse's Tragedy" and *The Touchstone* in "Texts Within Texts: The Power of Letters in Edith Wharton's Fiction" in *Countercurrents: On the Primacy of Texts in Literary Criticism* (SUNY, 1992, pp. 191–205), ed. Raymond Adolph Prier; and Evelyn E. Fracasso continues her work on Wharton's short fiction with "Images of Imprisonment in Two Tales of Edith Wharton" (*CLAJ* 36: 318–26), in which she examines the early "Mrs. Mainstey's View" and the late "Duration" to establish the longevity of Wharton's "obsession" with imprisonment seen in a variety of techniques, particularly the extravagant use of enclosed space.

Sherrie A. Inness takes a close look at Wharton's depiction of beauty in "An Economy of Beauty: The Beauty System in Edith Wharton's 'The Looking Glass' and 'Permanent Wave'" (*SSF* 30: 135–44) to show how Wharton explored the complicated factors that determine whether or not a woman is judged beautiful. "The Looking Glass" portrays the trap a woman falls into if she bases her self-worth on physical beauty; "Permanent Wave" asserts that a woman's reliance on the beauty system can supplant her relationships with men. Michael L. Ross emphasizes the importance of Rome itself as a psychological metaphor for "the looming violence of the past, the menace of human history, and its cunning corridors" in "Roman Fever," in *Storied Cities: Literary Imaginings of Florence, Venice, and Rome* (Greenwood, pp. 265–67). The Spring 1993 issue of *EWhR* (10, i) takes the art of the short story as its theme and contains essays by Mary Beth Inverso on the dynamics of female performance and male audience in "The Other Two" (pp. 3–6), Helen Killoran on the historical murder mystery in "Kerfol" (pp. 12–17), and Janet Ruth Heller on the underlying theme of emotional alienation in "Afterward" (pp. 18–19). Essays on Wharton and the male imagination can be found in the Fall 1993 number (10, ii). Ludger Brinker discusses attitudes shared by Wharton and Abraham Cahan toward the materialism of American culture (pp. 3–7); David Bratton reads *Twilight Sleep* in juxtaposition to Louis Bromfield's *The Green Bay* (pp. 8–11); and Linda Costanza Cahir remarks on the differences between Wharton's *The Age of Innocence* and Martin Scorsese's film adaptation (pp. 13–14, 19). Here, too, is Alfred Bendixen's annual bibliographical essay (pp. 20–24).

Of Wharton's novels, *The House of Mirth* continues to draw the most critical attention. Wharton believed that "illustrations cheapened the level of good literature," so the new edition of the 1905 Scribner's *The House of Mirth* (St. Martin's), ed. Shari Benstock, does not contain Joshua Reynolds's portrait of Mrs. Lloyd. In addition to the text, the volume includes essays representing contemporary critical perspectives by Lillian S. Robinson (cultural), Wai-chee Dimock (Marxist), Frances Restuccis (feminist), Margot Norris (deconstructionist), and Ellie Ragland Sullivan (psychoanalytic), clear introductions to each, a useful glossary of critical and theoretical terms, and Benstock's essays on biographical and historical contexts and on the novel's critical history, which should generate enthusiasm for her forthcoming Wharton biography.

Two feminist studies contain chapters on *The House of Mirth*. In *Gothic (Re)Visions* (pp. 127–46) Susan Wolstenholme discusses the guilt inherent in Wharton's linking of art, sex, and money in *The House of Mirth*, and she traces the novel's "double-written visual perspective" back through George Eliot and Charlotte Brontë. Diane Price Herndl in *Invalid Women* (pp. 110–49) compares the passive women of *The House of Mirth* and "The Yellow Wallpaper" to demonstrate that both Wharton and Charlotte Perkins Gilman effected a "writing cure" for neurasthenia, "killing the invalid" to free themselves from "a debilitating system of power"; Herndl informs us that Wharton's final image of Lily Bart reproduces in print the most popular genre of turn-of-the-century art: the "death" or "sleep" painting. In *"Tableaux Vivants:* Masculine Vision and Feminine Reflections in Novels by Warner, Alcott, Stowe, and Wharton" (*ATQ* 7: 335–56) Grace Ann Hovet and Theodore R. Hovet trace the popular turn-of-the-century fad of "tableau vivant" through the most widely read female-authored novels of the time (*The Wide, Wide World, Little Women, My Wife and I*, and *The House of Mirth*); all share the perception that male-engendered images of the feminine have power, explore the ways women exploit that power through mask, masquerade, and performance, and suggest "the possibility of a constructivist dialogue" with the male observer. In "Female Doubling: The Other Lily Bart in Edith Wharton's *The House of Mirth*" (*PLL* 29: 371–94) Carol Baker Sapora points out that contemporary readers easily recognized and accepted the doubling convention which Wharton revises and subverts in *The House of Mirth* by making Lily's double a division of her personality rather than a physical duplicate. Janet Gabler-Hover and Kathleen Plate identify "the word which made all clear" as Lily's motto, Beyond!— a "talisman of feminist metaphysics"— in *"The House of Mirth* and Edith Wharton's *'Beyond!'"* (*PQ* 72: 357–78). Irene C. Goldman argues that Wharton uses Rosedale's Jewishness to illuminate economic issues and social hypocrisies in "The *Perfect* Jew and *The House of Mirth:* A Study in Point of View" (*MLS* 23, ii: 25–36). Because he belongs to "a race reputed to be vulgar and economically savvy," Rosedale, a complicated amalgam of Wharton's distaste and sympathy, can speak about subjects taboo to others.

Scholarship on *The Reef* continues to prosper. William R. Macnaughton charges that most critics have tended to "ignore, oversimplify and sentimentalize" Sophy Viner, and he argues in "Edith Wharton's 'Bad Heroine': Sophy Viner in *The Reef*" (*SNNTS* 25: 214–25) that she is not just the narrow victim of George Darrow's selfishness, but a "sensual, ambitious and deceptive" woman who struggles to create a free self within almost naturalistic bounds. Macnaughton notes the significance of Jimmy Brance, who alerts the reader to ponder the ominous implications of Sophy's uncertain values and the problematic future her character foreshadows (*Expl* 51: 227–30). Both of Wharton's characters named with variants of Anna play out the mother-child plot, have quasi-incestuous relationships, and find themselves fundamentally at odds with the values of the culture in which they live, as Nancy Walker points out in "Mothers and Lovers: Edith Wharton's *The Reef* and *The Mother's Recompense,*" pp. 91–97 in *The Anna Book* (Greenwood, 1992), ed. Mickey Pearlman. In her carefully argued "Nature, Culture, and Sexual Economics in Edith Wharton's *The Reef*" (*ALR* 26, i: 76–90) Sherrie A. Inness proposes that we can best read *The Reef* as "an attempt by Wharton to explore her own ambivalent relationship to various environments"; Inness elucidates this thesis by examining Anna's and Sophy's intricate relationships to their spatial environment to show that Wharton used spaces such as Givré and its surroundings as metaphors for the socially constructed division between Nature and Culture. Annette Larson Benerts finds that the spatial qualities evident in Wharton's early historical novel· connect the work to topical concerns of Progressive America and anticipates Wharton's later scrutiny of gender and class issues in "The Spectator Prince: Architecture and Class in Edith Wharton's *The Valley of Decision*" (*EdN* 12: 59–66).

Only one journal article appeared on *The Age of Innocence* this year, Joy L. Davis's "The Rituals of Dining in Edith Wharton's *The Age of Innocence*" (*MQ* 34: 465–80). However, *Ethan Frome* is enjoying a revival, perhaps in part because of director John Madden's film released this year. Marlene Springer's carefully conceived and clearly written *Ethan Frome: A Nightmare of Need* (Twayne) focuses on characterization to uncover the complexities of the novel and links it to Wharton's coming of age as an artist and her personal pain. Wharton expunged the sterility of her own life and explored the tragic limitations of human nature through Ethan's passivity, Zeena's perverse manipulation through illness, and Mattie's maimed spirit. Springer's thought-provoking analysis is supplemented by an informative appendix that discusses Owen Davis's 1936 recasting of the novel as a play and Wharton's reaction to it. Much narrower but equally absorbing is Darryl Hattenhauer's explication of the resonances that Wharton arranges for the red pickle dish (*Expl* 51: 226–27). In *Invalid Women* (pp. 150–83) Herndl pairs *Ethan Frome* with Ellen Glasgow's *Barren Ground* as "relentlessly unhappy fictions" in which illness appears as a weapon of feminine or "divine" retribution and punishment. Both Wharton and Glasgow challenge domestic and medical ideologies which would keep women in the home, and both testify to the competition between women and the stress of housework that denies them peace or serenity and makes their lives "as full of strife as male warfare or business."

Scholarship on Ellen Glasgow includes several essays on rebellious women. Mary Waters points out that the broomsedge in *Barren Ground* represents not only sexual passion, but love, futility, and abandonment, all forces with which Dorinda must struggle (*Expl* 51: 234–35). In "Orphaning as Resistance," pp. 89–107 in *Female Tradition*, Joan Schultz offers Milly Burden and Dorinda Oakley as examples of women who "orphan" themselves by disregarding their oppressive families, stifling societal conventions, and insisting on their right to selfhood. Although Glasgow's life might seem traditional, Beverly Spears sees her as a rebellious woman whose "writing shows her refusal of restrictions"; Spears, examining four novels to make the point in "Ellen Glasgow's Spokesmen" (*CEA* 56, i: 107–16), submits that Glasgow evolved through feminism to "*antisexism*."

Will Brantley heeds Eudora Welty's clues at the end of *One Writer's Beginnings* that link it to Glasgow's autobiography, *The Woman Within*, and he defines the achievement of both works, which center on "the conscious, thinking, reflective, and creative inner self" of the woman writer in *Feminine Sense in Southern Memoir* (pp. 86–132). Another literary detective, Frances W. Saunders, begins with Glasgow's disclosure of a love affair in *The Woman Within* and tracks down the man's identity in "Glasgow's Secret Love: 'Gerald B' or 'William T'?" (*EGN* 31: 1, 3–4).

Two unrelated items are admirably provocative. In "The Narrative Ethos of Glasgow's 'A Point in Morals'" (*EGN* 30: 1, 3–4) William J. Scheick offers a masterful reading of Glasgow's "clever little discussion on the propriety of euthanasia" that clarifies its philosophical grounding in the works of Schopenhauer and Von Hartmann. Dorothy M. Scura's astute cross-genre study, "Ellen Glasgow's *The Battle-Ground:* Civil War Richmond in Fiction and History," pp. 185–96 in *Rewriting the South,* compares Glasgow's treatment of wartime Richmond with Mary Chesnut's diary, Emory Thomas's history, and Shelby Foote's narrative of the Civil War. Glasgow scholars should be aware that *EGN* now accepts short, critical essays in addition to biographical articles, notes on work-in-progress and such wonders as six charming letters from Queen Marie of Romania to Henry Anderson, with photographs, ed. Sara B. Bearss (30: 5–10, 31: 7).

iii Gertrude Stein and H. L. Mencken

Jane Palatini Bowers once again proves in *Gertrude Stein* (St. Martin's) that scholarship does not have to be, in Stein's words, "as clear as mud" to be significant. Stein's abiding interest in genre informs this engaging discussion, which ignores the later, accessible texts to concentrate on those which "address the problems and paradoxes at the heart of language and of literary creation." This gem of an essay could convert the most Stein-resistant among us. Scholars and novices alike will welcome *A Stein Reader* (Northwestern), an impeccably edited chronological collection of Stein's experimental writing, which includes more than 50 familiar and lesser-known works, previously unpublished pieces such as "Article," and the plays, *Reread Another* and *Saints and Singing*. With the exception of selections from *The Making of Americans* and *Stanzas in Meditation*, all are reproduced as Stein wrote them and benefit from editor Ulla E. Dydo's intelligent commentary.

Stein's fascination with language always fascinates her critics. Lynn C. Miller analyzes "Miss Furr and Miss Skeene" to demonstrate that Stein's writing is innately oral in "Writing Is Hearing and Saying: Gertrude Stein on Language and in Performance" (*TPQ* 13: 154–67); and Michaela Giesenkirchen explores metrical patterns, rhythms, and rhyme to justify her thesis that the multilingual dimension of "Accents in Alsace" records the Alsatian "spoken" character in "Where English Speaks More Than One Language: Accents in Gertrude Stein's 'Accents in Alsace'" (*MR* 34: 45–62). On the other hand, Karin M. Cope asks whether homosexuality is really a site of "silence" in Stein's texts and whether the reader must make such silences "speak out" in "'Publicity Is Our Pride': The Passionate Grammar of Gertrude Stein" (*Pre/Text* 13: 123–36), which identifies silence as the explicit theme of "Didn't Nelly and Lilly Love You." And Carolynn Van Dyke compares *Lucy Church Amiably* to two computer texts, relishing the irony that Stein "created one of literature's strongest personalities by merging her consciousness with the undirected flow of words" in "'Bits of Information and Tender Feeling': Gertrude Stein and Computer-Generated Prose" (*TSLL* 35: 168–97).

Stein's personality and personal life perennially intrigue scholars. James Goodwin devotes a chapter (pp. 67–84) of *Autobiography: The Self Made Text* (Twayne) to a discussion of *The Autobiography of Alice B. Toklas* as a modernist objectification of experience and *Everybody's Autobiography* as an impersonal reflection on the value of self in a monetary culture. "'Stein' Is An 'Alice' Is A 'Gertrude Stein'" (*Subjectivity, Identity, and the Body*, pp. 64–82), Sidonie Smith's impressive reading of the *Autobiography*, shows how Stein takes the most common female autobiographical form—"the self-effacing figure of the public figure by his spouse"—and makes it a vehicle through which she can speak of her most uncommon and aggressive sexuality. J. Gerald Kennedy in *Imagining Paris* (pp. 38–78) makes Stein's attachments to Parisian exteriors and interiors central to her identity and her work, particularly *The Autobiography of Alice B. Toklas* and *Paris, France*. "Notes from a Women's Biographer" (*Narrative* 1: 265–72) records Linda Wagner-Martin's thoughtful reflections on the shaping of her biography of the Stein siblings and includes an excerpt from the forthcoming book.

Stein's own "Plutarchan" approach to biography is the subject of Neil Schmitz's "Doing the Fathers: Gertrude Stein on U. S. Grant in *Four in America*" (*AL* 65: 751–60), which explores the function of the governess's story as an ironic comment on patriarch discourse and the juxtaposition of the factual Grant with a "counterfactual religious Grant" as Stein's rendering of the distinctive quality of American leadership. Elliot L. Vanskike charts Stein's efforts to define the threat posed by both history and identity, which she forestalled by writing and the use of a powerful image, in " 'Seeing Everything as Flat': Landscape in Gertrude Stein's *Useful Knowledge* and *The Geographical History of America*" (*TSLL* 35: 151–67).

Two of the four writers who couple Stein with other writers chose Nella Larsen. Beginning with the image of Josephine Baker's body, Debra B. Silverman brilliantly explores "the complicated web of desire and representation" facing any literary rendition of black womanhood by juxtaposing *Three Lives* and Larsen's *Quicksand,* exposing Stein's misreadings of black women and Larsen's challenge to those stereotypes in "Nella Larsen's *Quicksand:* Untangling the Webs of Exoticism" (*AAR* 27: 599–614). Corinne E. Blackmer begins with Stein's and Larsen's slight personal relationship and proceeds to a convincing explanation of the complex lines of influence between the two, showing that Larsen reconfigures the "complex and desiring" of Melanctha Herbert in Clare Kendry and, like Stein, explores the central role that racial visibility and invisibility play in establishing gender roles and sexual identities for both black and white women in "African Masks and the Arts of Passing in Gertrude Stein's 'Melanctha' and Nella Larsen's *Passing*" (*JHS* 4: 230–63). Although he finds some parallels between Stein's writing and Bergson's *durée,* Joseph N. Riddel ultimately concludes that "Stein's 'time' must be examined on a model of language Bergson rejects" in his impressive "Modern Times: Stein, Bergson, and the Ellipses of 'American' Writing" in *The Crisis in Modernism: Bergson and the Vitalist Controversy* (Cambridge, 1992, pp. 330–67), ed. Frederick Burwick and Paul Douglass. Perhaps the freshest look at Stein is Diane Simmons's "The Mother Mirror in Jamaica Kincaid's *Annie John* and Gertrude Stein's *The Good Anna*" in *The Anna Book* (Greenwood, 1992, pp. 99–104), ed. Mickey Pearlman. Simmons suggests that both stories have protagonists whose narcissistic mothers imprinted at birth the identity of the all-giving mother by naming them Anna, invoking "the unquestionable good mother" St. Anne. "Incessant german mother" to her employers even though unmarried and childless, the Good Anna never escapes; even on her deathbed she alternates between sacrifice and control. In a final item Linda S. Watts reminds us that Stein wrote for children. In "Twice Upon a Time: Back Talk, Spinsters, and Re-Verse-als in Gertrude Stein's *The World Is Round (1939)*" (*W&Lang* 16, i: 53–57) Watts reads Stein's innovative response to the formulas of spiritual narrative and the European magic tale as a story of "un-learning the ways of the round world."

After three years of major Mencken mania, there is no bombshell this year. However, Fred Hobson's biography will appear next year, so I anticipate another round of lively debate. Nevertheless, the loyal kept busy. Russell Baker gave the annual Mencken Lecture in Baltimore, "Me and Mencken," reprinted in *Menckeniana* (127: 1–5); Kathleen Parker Cleveland became the first woman to win the *Baltimore Sun's* H. L. Mencken Writing Award; and, as if to take up this year's slack, *Menckeniana* offers a number of substantial essays in addition to Vincent Fitzpatrick's bibliographic checklists (125: 15–16, 127: 9–16, 128: 12–16) and Patrick S. Daly's annotated checklist of reviews of *Ventures into Verse* (127: 6–9). Val Holley's expert textual study of Bernard De Voto's inflammatory 1926 profile of Utah for the *American Mercury* discloses Mencken's changes in "Vexing Utah: Mencken, De Voto, and the Mormons" (125: 1–10). "Playful, outrageous" letters documenting the friendship and storytelling skills of Mencken and producer Philip Goodman are the centerpiece of Jack Saunders's "Philip Goodman and the 'Do You Remember?' Letters" (126: 1–6). Claudia Reicha ("Henry Louis Mencken: The Warmth of the Fire" [128: 1–3]) inquires into the passion for beauty in Mencken's work, and P. J. Wingate enumerates the women Mencken charmed in "Women Understood H. L. Mencken" (128: 7–9). Gail Shivel compares the published fiction of Mencken's wife to Glasgow's, suggesting that these works repay study, capturing as they do her ambivalence toward her native South and American life between the world wars, in "Sara Haardt: Her Neglected Writings of the South" (128: 4–7). Finally, Walter B. Edgar credits Mencken with initiating the movement that preserved and re-created the image of the Carolina lowcountry writers by using a South Carolina poet to savage the South as the "Sahara of the Bozart," making Charlestonians so mad that they formed the influential and incredibly productive Poetry Society, in "The Circle of the Charleston Poetry Society and the Creation of the Image of the Carolina Lowcountry" (*Rewriting the South,* pp. 199–209).

iv Sherwood Anderson, Theodore Dreiser, and Sinclair Lewis

The burgeoning Midwestern literature industry accounts for Anderson's relocation to this section; I take my cue from Leland Krauth, who identifies Twain as the seminal, pervasive figure in the Midwestern imagination and explores the power Twain holds over individual writers such as Anderson, Dreiser, and Lewis in "Mark Twain in Midwestern Eyes," pp. 27–41 in *Exploring the Midwestern Literary Imagination.* The collection also contains a bibliography of David Anderson's work (pp. 209–22) that reminds us just how important he has been to Midwestern literature and 15 essays, two of which deal with Sherwood Anderson. In a superb demonstration of Wolfgang Iser's reader-response theories, William V. Miller validates the integrity of the basic text of "A Death in the Woods" after considering the competing claims of a number of subtexts in "Texts, Subtexts and More Texts: Reconstructing the Narrator's Role in Sherwood Anderson's 'Death in the Woods'" (pp. 86–98). Roger J. Bresnahan finds more differences than likenesses in his comparison of *Winesburg, Ohio* and *A Footnote to Youth,* "José García Villa and Sherwood Anderson: A Study in Influence" (pp. 57–67); both are "character-plotted," but Anderson explored "the place of the central character in community," and Villa's attitude toward his characters is distant and alienated.

Martin Bidney's important essay "*Windy McPherson's Son* and Silent McEachern's Son: Sherwood Anderson and *Light in August*" (*MissQ* 46: 395–406) draws parallels between Anderson's first novel and Faulkner's masterwork. Although the differences between the novels are obvious, the books share specific events, themes of guilt-inducing gossip and hypocritical deception, the psychological struggle of father and son, and the reciprocal mental mirroring of husband and wife. Nancy Bunge in her compelling essay, "Child Abuse and Creativity: A New Look at Sherwood Anderson's Breakdown" (*Journal of Psychohistory* 20: 413–26), takes on the mystery of Anderson's abrupt disappearance and subsequent abandonment of his family, carefully sifting through his journal to offer evidence that the cause of such erratic behavior was a flashback memory of childhood abuse. For those who want to know more about life in

Anderson's Chicago, Ben Hecht's *A Thousand and One Afternoons in Chicago* (Chicago), with 64 of his 1921 character sketches and vignettes for the *Chicago Daily News,* is reprinted.

Winesburg never loses its appeal. In *Nobody's Home* (pp. 91–107) Arnold Weinstein finds in *Winesburg* the central American themes—the making of the self and the making of the world. Anderson's four-page "Paper Pills," perhaps the most remarkable tale he wrote, "explodes the daytime logic of its ostensible subject in order to testify to darker powers of sexual desire and violation." John J. Reist, Jr., cleverly makes his point that Anderson uses both George Willard *and* the town to speak about the universally isolated human condition by employing the figure of an ellipse with the reader equidistant between the two foci in "An Ellipse Becomes a Circle: The Developing Unity of *Winesburg, Ohio*" (*CEA* 55, iii: 26–38). James Ellis points out that "I Want to Know Why" and "The Man Who Became a Woman" dramatize Anderson's understanding that sexuality mysteriously threatens the human spirit of male relationships in "Sherwood Anderson's Fear of Sexuality: Horses, Men, and Homosexuality" (*SSF* 30: 595–601). In "The Heritage of the Fathers in 'The Man Who Became a Woman'" (*JSSE* 21: 29–37) Christopher MacGowan reads Anderson's tale as a drama about storytelling in which Tom and Herman's failures are measured against the presence in the text of two writers whom Anderson admired, Alfred Kreymborg and Theodore Dreiser.

This year's Dreiser scholarship is notable for its variety. Louis J. Zanine's intelligent, gracefully written, and engrossing *Mechanism and Mysticism: The Influence of Science on the Thought and Work of Theodore Dreiser* (Penn.) is a major contribution to Dreiser studies. Never losing sight of Dreiser's interest in science as primarily a religious quest for answers about human purpose and destiny, Zanine begins with the author's rejection of Catholicism and his discovery of evolutionary theory in the writings of Darwin, Huxley, and Spencer, which provided the philosophical framework for the pessimistic naturalism of *Sister Carrie, Jennie Gerhardt,* and *The Financier.* Dreiser's fascination with the mechanistic philosophy of Jacques Loeb provides a context for Zanine's reading of *An American Tragedy* and *The Hand of the Potter;* and his intensive period of scientific and speculative study beginning in 1927, which culminated in a mystical experience, elucidates his book of personal philosophy, the uncompleted *Notes on Life.* Zanine concludes by locating Dreiser's later thought in the wider context of 20th-century intellectual trends. The book has an extensive bibliography and eight wonderful pictures of Dreiser the scientist.

In *The Problem of American Realism* (pp. 149–65), the first of two cultural studies that contain chapters on Dreiser, Michael Davitt Bell painstakingly investigates the specific "effects" achieved by Dreiser's style, ably illuminating the complexity of his relationship to the ideology of naturalism in the 1890s. *Sister Carrie* "achieves something like the transparency for which Howells and Norris longed," because, unlike them, Dreiser was able to reconcile "art" and "humanity"; he fulfilled the ideal of American naturalism because he was immune to naturalist thinking. In *Modernism, Mass Culture, and Professionalism* (pp. 84–116) Thomas Strychacz contends that *An American Tragedy* broaches questions of originality well before Dreiser raised them in the courts, and he argues that not only did Dreiser use the furor surrounding the 1931 movie version of the novel to formulate a new sense of professionalism, but he offended the "decorum of originality" by reworking "the voices, expressive forms, and documents of mass culture," a problem that paradoxically constitutes the novel's originality. According to Robert Funk, Dreiser incorporated several of McTeague's characteristics, including his bird cage, into an inconsequential character in *An American Tragedy* as a tribute to Frank Norris (*Expl* 51: 232–34).

Two other essays begin with questions. Philip L. Gerber asks in "Theodore Dreiser: Changing Trains in Chicago" (*Exploring the Midwestern Literary Imagination*, pp. 70–85) why the 73-year-old writer would choose to travel from Los Angeles to New York by train in wartime, then produces a stunning variety of images of Chicago drawn from Dreiser's work—including the posthumous *The Bulwark*—that illustrate the magical spell the city had for him, supporting the theory that he thought "the trip might be his final opportunity for re-experiencing the thrill he had always felt upon approaching the Midwestern metropolis." Though he admits it will take more than one essay, Louis Filler wonders "what Dreiser actually was," and he begins that inquiry with "Theodore Dreiser and the Anti-Progressive Drive" (*Biography* 16: 249–57), which shows how Dreiser's apparent forthrightness masked his "secret" life.

The recent focus on the "why" rather than the "what" of the problem of desire in Dreiser's characters prompts Clare Virginia Eby's insightful essay, "The Psychology of Desire: Veblen's 'Pecuniary Emulation' and 'Invidious Comparison' in *Sister Carrie* and *An American Tragedy*" (*SAF*

21: 191–208). Crammed with consumer goods, *Sister Carrie* and *An American Tragedy* bring together economic and psychological concerns in a new theory of the self which illustrates a "Veblenian model based on the human tendency to compare one's self economically with others and emulate them in response." Susan K. Harris's feminist reading of Dreiser, Howells, and Hemingway, "Vicious Binaries: Gender and Authorial Paranoia in Dreiser's 'Second Choice,' Howells' 'Editha,' and Hemingway's 'The Short Happy Life of Francis Macomber' " (*CollL* 20, ii: 70–82), reveals the binary infrastructure of their stories in which marginalized female characters suffer as a result of their distance from the locus of freedom and power. Joseph Epstein argues that *Jennie Gerhardt* comes closest of Dreiser's novels to "grasping the true mystery of life," lamenting that it is not taught more in "A Great Good Girl: Dreiser's 'Jennie Gerhardt' " (*NewC* 11, x: 14–20); and Michael Lydon defends Dreiser's "superb English prose," proposing that "it is time to drop the barbs and acknowledge, without reservation, that Theodore Dreiser is an immortal," in "Justice to Theodore Dreiser" (*Atlantic* 272, ii: 98–101).

After last year's successful reception of the Library of America *Sinclair Lewis:* Main Street *and* Babbitt (see *ALS 1992*, p. 232), this year both novels are the focus of Twayne Masterwork Studies. Martin Bucco's Main Street: *The Revolt of Carol Kennicott* (Twayne), the first book-length study of the novel, focuses on Lewis's careful construction. Most ingenious is Bucco's organization of his analysis around the various roles Carol tries out as she moves toward self-realization: prairie princess, saint and savior, American Madame Bovary, good wife and mother. As Bucco demonstrates, Carol's story of "aspiration, struggle, revolt, and compromise," so shattering in its own day, has become "the common currency of modern life." Proclaiming that Lewis was a "trailblazer in human anthropology," Frank A. Salamone also analyzes the parallels between the process of cultural discourse and group identity that Lewis dramatizes in *Main Street* and those reproduced by the American enclave in Nigeria in "The Reproduction of *Main Street:* The American Diplomatic Corps in Nigeria" (*Mosaic* 26, iv: 87–102). Glen A. Love's Babbitt: *An American Life* (Twayne) locates the novel in the historical context of the 1920s before proceeding to a superb, wide-ranging discussion of its satire, romance, and cultural symbolism, and its significance as "a mocking, yet heroic authentication of Lewis's fanatic American-ness," which was linked to his Midwestern esteem for pioneer and frontier values. Love suggests that *Babbitt* succeeds, not because of its realism and satire, but because Lewis *failed* to make these pure, concluding that perhaps "no one can claim to understand American life in the twentieth century without having read [the book]."

A second essay by Clare Virginia Eby, "*Babbitt* as Veblenian Critique of Manliness" (*AmerS* 34, ii: 5–23), illustrated by John Lo Presti, continues her exploration of Veblen's significance to American literary realism. Eby offers an expert reading of *Babbitt* as a Veblenian critique of "the imbecile institution of white, middle class American manliness in the early decades of this century" that sheds light on the problem of the "two Babbitts" and elucidates Lewis's understanding of the damage Babbitt's "duty of being manly" causes the autonomous self. D. W. Reitinger points out that Lewis, who had an ear for modern parlance, also appreciated the richness of language and culture behind names and naming in "A Source for Tanis Judique in Sinclair Lewis's *Babbitt*" (*NConL* 23, v: 3–4), uncovering "Tanis" as an anagram of "saint," and "Judique" as an alteration of "Jude," to arrive at a modern saint for Babbitt who, as a flawed American male, is surely a "hopeless case."

v Jack London, John Dos Passos, and Upton Sinclair

The most important event in London scholarship this year is the publication of the eagerly awaited three-volume *Complete Short Stories of Jack London* (Stanford), ed. Earle Labor, Robert C. Leitz III, and I. Milo Shepard. A stunning achievement, the work contains 197 stories arranged chronologically by date of composition, including five stories never before published and 28 that appear here for the first time since their original magazine publication, appendixes including an expanded version of London's own record of his sales, a list of textual emendations, an index of story titles, and an excellent, lucid introduction that should be required reading. Another resource is Russ Kingman's *Jack London: A Definitive Chronology* (Rejl, 1992), which supplies a day-to-day account of the author's life with bibliographical information to 1992. Kingman seldom offers interpretation, but this book should prove useful. He does *not* comment on London's death. However, Charles W. Denko's fascinating "Jack London. A Modern Analysis of His Mysterious Disease" (*Journal of Rheumatology* 20: 1760–63) takes a clinician's look at London's several bouts of illness and diagnoses systemic lupus erythematosis, unknown in London's day. Using Charmain's diary, pictures of London's hands that show joint swelling, and information provided by Becky

London, Denko builds his convincing case that, ironically, London probably died from an abdominal complication of "the wolf disease."

Tony Williams traces the generally unsuccessful struggle of Hollywood to adapt London's novels for the movies in *Jack London—The Movies: An Historical Survey* (Rejl, 1992). This thoroughly researched study includes 20 stills and a list of both American and international films of his works. In a related essay, "Clarence E. Shurtleff Presents Jack London, 1919–1921" (*Wide Angle* 15, iii: 56–72), Williams shows how Shurtleff's high-quality adaptations modified London's novels so that they lacked any forceful opposition to growing consumerism and illustrates how a radical writer can become recuperated as a nonpolitical movie commodity after his death. Of tangential interest to London scholars is Pascal James Imperato and Eleanor M. Imperato's *They Married Adventure: The Wandering Lives of Martin and Osa Johnson* (Rutgers, 1992), a well-documented biography of the American filmmakers and explorers, for whom Charmain and London provided role models and friendship.

In "London Calling: The Importance of Jack London to Contemporary Cultural Studies" (*W&D* 11, ii: 27–43) Christopher Gair argues compellingly that the contradictions and discontinuities in London's writing (particularly *Martin Eden*), juxtaposed with other texts (such as Horatio Alger's), make him an ideal supplement to other histories of his era. Gair calls *The Valley of the Moon* London's treatment of race anxiety in the face of the Progressive "melting pot" in a second essay, " 'The Way Our People Came': Citizenship, Capitalism and Racial Difference in *The Valley of the Moon*" (*SNNTS* 25: 418–35), and he calls the apparent triumph of the novel's sentimental (domestic) voice "an abandonment of socialist tendencies in London's earlier fictions and an embrace of middle class culture rejected in *Martin Eden*." In a fresh reading of *The Sea-Wolf* in *Having It Both Ways* (pp. 55–78) Forrest G. Robinson blames reader resistance and the cultural expectation that women will be passive and dependent for the common view that Maud is a "twittering" female, showing how the novel indirectly reveals elements of quiet initiative and self-reliance in her behavior and finding her a "much more distinctive and sophisticated and forceful character than her fictional companions, and the critics, have recognized." Reed Whittemore critiques and excuses London's research methods for his 1903 novel, "a striking piece of reportage on the social swamp that was the East End of London," in "Rediscovering *The People of the Abyss* by Jack London" (*GaR* 47: 733–

39); and Robert C. Leitz III reprints a previously unknown rave review that heralds the discovery of London in the 19 April 1900 issue of *Town Topics* ("Jack London in 1900: Besting Norris in the Far North," *FNS* 16: 6–7).

A special issue of *Thalia* (12 [1992], i–ii) on London's humor, ed. and introduced by Jacqueline Tavernier-Courbin, demonstrates the vitality of London studies. Tavernier-Courbin's fine introduction, which reviews the variety of forms humor takes in London's work, is followed by Lawrence Berkove's discussion of Thomas Stevens's triple function: to cloak serious thought in the guise of comedy, to demonstrate the validity of evolutionary theory, and to question the aspect of evolution that identifies it with progress; Susan Gatti's analysis of the particularly dark strain of humor in Darrell Standing; Jeanne Campbell Reesman's feminist reading of *The Little Lady of the Big House,* in which London ruthlessly examines his own difficulties as a husband and lover in a painfully ironic look at the position of women in American society; and Servanne Woodward's Bergsonian reading of "The Wife of a King" that foregrounds London's desire to enlarge "the social circle of laughter *ad infinitum.*" In addition, Laurent Dauphin points out the rhetoric of the absurd that informs "Moon-Face"; Thomas R. Tietze and Gary Rield argue that London's self-described racism is actually *not* present in the ironic narrative voice of the South Sea tales; John Whalen-Bridge explains both the topical humor and the dual perspective in *The Iron Heel;* Garyn R. Roberts explicates the effect of Gorden Grant's brilliant illustrations on *The Scarlet Plague;* and Clarice Stasz pinpoints reasons for the cartoon characters, stale plot, and comic rhetoric of *Adventure.* A final note: the new *Jack London Journal,* ed. James Williams, welcomes articles that reflect on "the connections and exchanges among the social, political, and psychological worlds in which London moved."

John Dos Passos is represented by two thoughtful analyses. Thomas Strychacz's perceptive chapter in *Modernism, Mass Culture, and Professionalism* offers "a whole new configuration of Dos Passos's career" resting on the professional ethos that informs his writing. Modern readers, who share a number of discursive premises with Dos Passos, read him too easily, ignoring key structural identities that imply a complicity between modernist writer and professional reader in a "complex, multileveled engagement" with the text and that deal with the legitimation of the individual voice within a mass society. In "Dos Passos and the 'Middle-Class Liberal'" (*CRevAS* 23, ii: 149–60) David Heinimann positions Dos Passos's liberalism between the pragmatic and idealistic traditions, then expertly shows how *The Big Money* was meant to politicize the middle class that Dos Passos believed should govern the United States.

The spotlight on Upton Sinclair dimmed this year. The lone essay is Kathryne V. Lindberg's "Mass Circulation versus *The Masses:* Covering the Modern Magazine Scene" (*BoundaryII* 20, ii: 51–83), which details Sinclair's battle against "the financial appeal and corruption" of George Horace Lorimer, editor of the *Saturday Evening Post,* whose finger on the pulse of middle-class America's taste gave the *Post* and popular magazines like it a major role in determining public policy. Of interest as well is Reed Whittemore's *Six Literary Lives,* a collection of engaging essays on writers who manifest a Socratic skepticism toward the issues of their times, which includes chapters on London, Dos Passos, and Sinclair.

vi W. E. B. Du Bois, Nella Larsen, Jean Toomer, and Others

Foremost among this year's Du Bois studies is *W. E. B. Du Bois: Biography of a Race, 1868–1919* (Holt), David Levering Lewis's penetrating psychological examination of the first half of Du Bois's life. Meticulously researched, this biography is the first to use Du Bois's now unrestricted personal papers; it rewards the reader with clear prose, careful analyses of Du Bois's historical, sociological, literary, and journalistic works, and new perspectives on the workings of the newborn civil rights movement. The centrality of Du Boisian thought to African American studies is undeniable. For instance, Eric J. Sundquist divides *To Wake the Nations* into three parts: "Slavery, Revolution, Renaissance," "The Color Line," and "W. E. B. Du Bois." The final third extensively explores Du Bois's vision of "the ideological structures that both supported and became codified within dominant modes of national literature"; absorbing readings are offered of *The Souls of Black Folk* as it relates to black spirituals and the foundations of African American culture (pp. 457–539) and of *Darkwater* as a prism through which to read his developing views of Africa as a force in world and U.S. culture (pp. 540–625). A complement to Sundquist's book, *Lure and Loathing: Essays on Race, Identity, and the Ambivalence of Assimilation* (Penguin), ed. Gerald Early, collects 20 essays by black intellectuals and writers in response to Du Bois's famous statement that "one ever feels his twoness—an American, a Negro."

Two excellent intertextual studies deserve notice. In "Justifying the

Margin: The Construction of 'Soul' in Russian and African American Texts" (*SlavR* 51: 749–57) Dale E. Peterson compares *The Souls of Black Folk* with works by Turgenev and Dostoyevsky to illustrate the long, hidden subtext that links Russian and African American ethnic traditions in a confrontation with European cultural literacy. Kenneth W. Warren in *Black and White Strangers,* pp. 109–30, juxtaposes *The Souls of Black Folks* with Henry James's *The American Scene* to illustrate the complicated, often contradictory ways that notions of racial identity figure in literary critiques of America's commercial order. Du Bois's fears that black American life was in danger of endorsing Gilded Age greed is Mark David Higbee's topic in "W. E. B. Du Bois, F. B. Ransom, the Madam Walker Company, and Black Business Leadership in the 1930s" (*InMH* 89, ii: 101–24), which details the 1937–38 dispute in which Du Bois became embroiled.

Du Bois's differences with Booker T. Washington are of perennial interest. In *Discourse and Culture* (Routledge, 1992, pp. 129–47) Alan Munslow offers an evenhanded, thorough, and clear explanation of the ideological differences between Du Bois and Booker T. Washington. Munslow's analysis of "the divided consciousness" and the reasons he gives for Du Bois's ultimate failure to create a viable alternative black culture make this a superb introduction to the issues involved. Thomas E. Harris in his longer, more diffuse study, *Analysis of the Clash Over Issues Between Booker T. Washington and W. E. B. Du Bois* (Garland) shows that Du Bois examined and understood the issues more correctly, but Washington understood the audience better.

In the single essay of note on Alain Locke, "A Black Aesthete at Oxford" (*MR* 34: 411–28), Jeffrey C. Stewart follows the first black Rhodes Scholar and finds that his struggle with the first racial discrimination he had experienced turned an aggressively assimilated man into a race man. Walter Kalaidjian takes a sweeping look at the "flood tide of the Negrophile movement" in *American Culture Between the Wars* in which he covers the *Messenger*'s role in the promulgation of Locke's "New Negro," concluding that Soviet-style prolecult failed among the black community because the Cominterm "fundamentally misread the distinctive, vernacular signs of black expression." Kalaidjian also offers a thorough discussion of Carl Van Vechten's *Nigger Heaven,* its reception and impact, and points out that the vernacular recovery of black jazz, the blues, and slave songs in the works of Harlem Renaissance writers functioned "as a counterdiscourse" (which white benefactors such as

Van Vechten patronized and popularized) to the everyday white world. The 83 black-and-white photographs of distinguished African Americans, selected by Rudolph P. Byrd from the James Weldon Johnson Memorial Collection at Yale and collected in *Generations in Black and White: Photographs by Carl Van Vechten* (Georgia), are splendid. Each photograph is accompanied by a brief biographical sketch, and the collection also benefits from Byrd's introduction. Another general essay, "Masks and Masquerade: The Iconography of the Harlem Renaissance" (*MQ* 35: 49–61) by Patti Capel Swartz, perceptively examines the use of masque (carnival) and masks as the means by which the marginalized black community of the Harlem Renaissance celebrated their culture and, in a nice reversal, marginalized white spectators. Wallace Thurman's *Infants of Spring* (Northeastern, 1992), is again available. In "The Moment of Revision: A Reappraisal of Wallace Thurman's Aesthetics in *The Blacker the Berry* and *Infants of the Spring*" (*CLAJ* 37: 81–93) Renoir W. Gaither critiques Thurman's "provocative" use of the picaresque literary form to subvert bourgeois aesthetics and the social values of the New Negro.

Jessie Fauset and Dorothy West are two of 14 women included in the first definitive collection of Harlem Renaissance stories by women, *The Sleeper Wakes* (Rutgers), ed. Marcy Knopf. Nellie Y. McKay provides a graceful foreword to the 28 stories, virtually unavailable until now, that appeared first in periodicals such as *The Crisis, Fire!!,* and *Opportunity.* The book provides exciting new avenues for study. Eva Rueschmann also pairs Fauset and West to examine the "particular narrative and psychological significance of sisters in the development of a self" in *Significance of Sibling Relationships in Literature.*

Two essays and two chapters constitute the year's work on Nella Larsen. In addition to Debra B. Silverman's excellent essay (see Stein section), T. S. McMillin strenuously objects to narrow readings of Larsen's novels and argues that we must recognize and explore "the hegemonic discourses of sexuality, race, class, and gender" that he locates in "Passing Beyond: The Novels of Nella Larsen" (*WVUPP* 38: 134–46). In *Quicksand* the search for selfhood equals the struggle to define and express sexuality; in *Passing* two different discourses of women's sexuality, one repressive and one affirming, compete. *The Coupling Convention,* Ann duCille's study of the subversive use of the marriage convention by black women writers, contains two chapters pertinent to fiction from 1900 to the 1930s. The first, "Blue Notes on Black Sexuality: Sex and the

Texts of the Twenties and Thirties" (pp. 66–85), provides a historical context and lens through which to focus on the works of Fauset, Larsen, and Zora Neale Hurston in relation to classic blues and "the-so-called Harlem Renaissance." "The Bourgeois, Wedding Bell Blues of Jessie Fauset and Nella Larsen" (pp. 86–109) examines the ways in which these authors, considered anachronistically reticent by some, "wrote the female body into the literary text," critiqued the social practices and gender conventions that limit women's choices and prescribe women's roles, and depicted independent, successful, single, black professional and working-class women. In *Mules and Dragons* Mary E. Young contends that Larsen broke with the tradition of women's novels to criticize "the hypocrisy of the African-American middle-class with its imitation of Euro-American middle-class values" by creating a heroine who was a sexual being (pp. 55–59).

Three excellent books attest to Jean Toomer's increasing stature. Intrigued by the "disappearance" of Nella Larsen and Jean Toomer after the Harlem Renaissance, Charles R. Larson tracked down the facts in an awe-inspiring effort. In his innovative, intertwined dual biography, *Invisible Darkness: Jean Toomer and Nella Larsen* (Iowa) he dispels the misconception that "they vanished into the white world and lived unproductive and unrewarding lives." Besides his insights into the personalities of these two "haunted" authors and his intelligent textual analyses, Larson shows that virtually every hitherto-published fact about Larsen's life is wrong. Robert B. Jones makes a major contribution to Toomer studies with *Jean Toomer and the Prison-House of Thought* (Mass.), the first comprehensive survey of Toomer's writings. Jones frames his thorough, well-written study in terms of Kierkegaardian stages of development. The "aesthetic" encompasses Toomer's early work (1918–23), which was informed by Orientalism, symbolist idealism, and imagism; the "ethical" covers what Rudolph Byrd called "the Gurdjieff years" (see *ALS 1991,* pp. 235–36); and the "religious" considers the influence of Quaker religious philosophy on Toomer's late work (1940–55). Jones includes a comprehensive bibliography of published and unpublished works. Some previously unpublished works can be found in *A Jean Toomer Reader: Selected Unpublished Writings* (Oxford), ed. Frederik L. Rusch, which adds to Toomer studies a fertile collection of letters, sketches, short fiction, including a children's story, poems, and a play, arranged thematically with informative notes.

Cane retains the principal critical focus, at least for one more year. In

"Jean Toomer and American Racial Discourse" (*TSLL* 35: 226–50) George Hutchinson accuses both black and white critics of "discursive violence" and puts forth his convincing argument that *Cane* achieves Toomer's purpose, "to cross racial boundaries without violence, embarrassment, or perversion," by dramatizing the difficulty of speaking or writing outside the dominant discourse of race. Janet M. Whyde in her fine essay, "Mediating Forms: Narrating the Body in Jean Toomer's *Cane*" (*SLJ* 26, i: 42–53), suggests that the quest for the self-defined, unified self gets played out most vividly in *Cane* through Toomer's narrative representations of the body, the site for both oppression and repression and a problematic sign of one's race. Noting that *Cane* bears the geographical imprints of rural Georgia, Chicago, Washington, D.C., and Harpers Ferry, but *not* New York, Onita Estes-Hicks discusses the significance of D.C. to Toomer's imagination in "Jean Toomer and the Washington Roots of the Harlem Renaissance" in *Claude McKay: Centennial Studies* (Sterling, pp. 50–59), ed. A. L. McLeod. Using census, tax, and other official records, as well as seven newly discovered letters (included here) from Nathan Toomer to a friend, Kent Anderson Leslie and Willard B. Gatewood, Jr., remove some of the mystery surrounding Toomer's absent father in " 'This Father of Mine . . . A Sort of Mystery': Jean Toomer's Georgia Heritage" (*GaHR* 77: 789–809).

Of the writers in this section, only Arna Bontemps is identified with the South. Kirkland C. Jones reminds us of Bontemps's "deep abiding affection" for the region, and in "Bontemps and the Old South" (*AAR* 27: 179–85) he cites an undated letter Bontemps wrote to Toomer that reveals his fascination with the Old South as a literary theme. Marcia Gaudet's comparison of Ada Jack Carver's "The Old One," Ernest Gaines's "Just Like a Tree," and Bontemps's "A Summer Tragedy" in "Images of Old Age in Three Louisiana Short Stories" (*LaEJ* 1, i: 62–64) shows that these texts share similar characters, settings, and theme.

Breaking new ground, "James Weldon Johnson's *New York Age* Essays on *The Birth of a Nation*" (*SCRev* 10, iv: 1–17), by Lawrence J. Oliver with Terri L. Walker, represents the first separate study of the hundreds of individually titled, 2,500-word essays that Johnson wrote between 1914 and 1923 for his weekly "Views and Reviews" column in *New York Age*. Oliver provides a detailed examination of Johnson's reaction to D. W. Griffith's film in the 22 April 1915 column and suggests that all of the essays be collected and edited. In "Irony and Subversion in James

Weldon Johnson's *The Autobiography of an Ex-Coloured Man*" (*SAF* 21: 83–96) Roxanna Pisak argues that the order Johnson subverts in his novel is not just racial order, but "the entire constitutional order of American society and government, as well as the basic order of human kindness and humanity"; Pisak demonstrates the central significance of the unreliable narrator whose distorted vision soon turns out to be a common trait as readers perceive "distortion in the narrator, in his text and world, and then in ourselves and our world." Johnson's poetry collection, *Saint Peter Relates an Incident* (Penguin), is also reissued, with a fine introduction by Sondra Kathryn Wilson.

Claude McKay: Centennial Studies (Sterling, 1992), ed. A. L. McLeod, collects the papers presented at the 1990 international conference commemorating (as closely as possible) the centenary of McKay's birth. As the volume demonstrates, McKay inspires a wide variety of responses. Essays on his political stances are offered by Michael G. Cooke (pp. 41–49), H. H. Anniah Gowda (pp. 60–69), and Cary D. Wintz (pp. 172–81); Jamaica's "presence" in his work is discussed by Elaine Campbell (pp. 12–21), P. S. Chauhan (pp. 22–31), and K. Chellappan (pp. 32–40); his search for meaning is explored by Usha Shourie (pp. 135–47) and Emmanuel S. Nelson (pp. 106–13). Carl Pedersen (pp. 114–22), Joyce Hope Scott (pp. 123–34), and Nigel Thomas (pp. 160–71) discuss *Home to Harlem;* McLeod finds McKay's ideal woman in *Banana Bottom* (pp. 70–81), while Harold Barratt locates instances of male bonding in *Banjo* (pp. 1–11); Diane Harper places McKay's work next to Zora Neale Hurston's (pp. 82–93); K. T. Sunitha looks at his earliest short stories (pp. 148–59); and Edris Makward examines his influence on young French-speaking intellectuals (pp. 94–105). Apparently that influence extended even further; Mireia Aragay has found Josep Miracle's introduction to a 1931 Catalan translation of "Near-White" (*LHY* 34, ii: 48–56).

vii Immigrants, Exiles, and Western Writers

The expansion of this section reflects the growth of multicultural and ethnic studies. The most prominent of the immigrant writers is Anzia Yezierska. In "The Rebirth of Anzia Yezierska" (*Judaism* 42: 414–22) Wendy Zierler attributes the interest to feminists' discoveries of the "rich mother lode" in Yezierska's descriptions of the writer's struggles and her understanding of the elusive promise of the American dream, a theme

repeatedly treated in her fiction. The best analysis of Yezierska's achievement comes in Thomas J. Ferraro's expert reading of *The Breadgivers* as
"an inquiry into the contribution ethnicity has made to the triumphant
reformation of the middle class" (*Ethnic Passages,* pp. 53–86). Ferraro
points out that Yezierska pays particular attention to what the "varieties
of 'incorporation' within the United States" meant for immigrant daughters, and he compares Sara Smolinsky to Sister Carrie to show that Sara's
movement and desire, unlike Carrie's, attempt to ameliorate specific
forms of social oppression. Stephen Fender reads *The Bread Givers* with
Mary Antin's *The Promised Land* and Henry Roth's *Call It Sleep* as novels
that address the Old World/New World conflicts of immigrant families
(*Sea Changes,* pp. 165–68). Guy Szuberla takes a look at a variety of ethnic and racial groups found in Chicago writing in "Babel, The Crowd,
and 'The People' in Early Chicago Fiction" (*Exploring the Midwestern
Literary Imagination,* pp. 151–66) as "equivocal formulations of the melting pot myth" that prefigure ethnic divisions, racial conflicts, and mob
violence. In a related article, " 'The Genuine Article': Ethnicity, Capital
and *The Rise of David Levinsky*" (*AmLH* 5: 643–62), Philip Barrish argues
that in Abraham Cahan's novel and other immigrant stories from the
period, specific forms of self-division work as primary mechanisms in the
cultural and economic aspects of "the rise." Marian J. Morton deftly uses
Russian immigrant Emma Goldman's prolific publications—lectures,
editorials, books, essays, and her autobiography—in *Emma Goldman and
the American Left: Nowhere at Home* (Twayne) to trace "the uneasy and
sometimes unhappy evolution of her political philosophy" and the
events of her turbulent life, which ended in forced exile.

    As Annette White-Parks points out in "Journey to the Golden Moun-
tain: Chinese Immigrant Women" (*Women and the Journey,* pp. 101–17),
Chinese women often began their voyage to the United States as captives, slaves, or duped mail-order brides, essentially exiled from their
homes. White-Parks focuses on Sui Sin Far's depictions of culture shock
in Chinese brides, the reticence of merchants' wives (never to be mistaken for passivity), child theft, and prostitution to demonstrate how
Chinese women persisted in maintaining their personal and cultural
autonomy. Commending Sui Sin Far's attempts to dispel myths and
stereotypes of Chinese-Americans, Mary E. Young maintains in *Mules
and Dragons* that her individualistic and rebellious women directly
challenge the Chinese tradition that a woman has to obey. On the other
hand, Sui Sin Far's sister, Onoto Watanna, supported herself and her

children "by exploiting and possibly confirming prevalent racist and sexist stereotypes."

According to John Bodnar's "In Defense of Multiculturalism" (pp. 3–12), the first of two essays on Rölvaag in *Nordics in America: The Future of Their Past* (Norwegian-American Historical Assn.), ed. Odd S. Lovell, *Giants in the Earth* questions whether the common project of building the American nation is worth the kind of loyalty that abandons the claims of human relationships for the ideological abstractions of authority. In " 'The Psychology is the Action': Ole Rölvaag's Interpretation of Immigrant Life" (pp. 117–27) Kristoffer F. Paulson argues that Rölvaag's last two books are "a dramatic rendering of the Americanization of *Peder Victorious*," in which Rölvaag, consciously condemning Whitman's optimistic view of the future and dismissal of the past, makes a passionate appeal for the retention of cultural identity. Ingeborg R. Kôngslien explicates the double perspective that emerges in the emigrant novels of Johan Bojar, Alfred Hauge, Vilhelm, and Rölvaag in "Emigration: The Dream of Freedom and Land—And an Existential Quest" in *Fin(s) de Siècle in Scandinavian Perspective* (Camden House, pp. 203–21), ed. Faith Ingwersen and Mary Kay Norsemg. Davis S. Gross sees Per and Baret as two halves of the manic-depressive personality in his interpretation of *Giants in the Earth* as a rendition of the mystery, terror, and reality of "the dark heart of the pioneer experience" in "No Place to Hide: Gothic Naturalism in O. E. Rölvaag's *Giants in the Earth*" (*Frontier Gothic*, pp. 42–54).

Although he claims he has not set out to rehabilitate Zane Grey, Arthur G. Kimball does resuscitate him with his major study, *Ace of Hearts: The Westerns of Zane Grey* (TCU). Kimball offers fresh readings of all 56 of Grey's westerns to demonstrate Grey's use of seduction as a metaphor of unrestrained economic activity and erotic desire as an ironic source of violence, his ambiguous portrayal of law, and the disturbing and equally ambiguous presence of his Native Americans. A useful appendix lists the novels with short plot and character summaries. A flurry of Grey scholarship may come out of this provocative book. Richard A. Lutman enumerates the characteristics of Grey's appealing heroines in "A Woman to Live in Your Heart Forever" (*Journal of the West* 32, i: 62–68); feminine, rugged, and loyal, Grey's women would defend their honor and protect their lovers to the death. Forrest G. Robinson claims that Grey "favored the romance form because of its tolerance for the kinds of confusion he was prone to," and he shows how

Riders of the Purple Sage allows readers to approach matters of genuine concern without sustained challenges to their prepossessions in *Having it Both Ways* (pp. 3–11).

In his chapter on *The Virginian* (pp. 41–54) Robinson proposes that Owen Wister brings the reader face to face with a major cultural tension between male and domestic ideals, then "diminishes it to a point of virtual invisibility," thereby evading resolution of the conflict between nature and civilization for both the fictional cowboy and his audience. Madonne M. Miner argues that *The Virginian* demonstrates the cultural imperative which dooms love and friendship between men by illustrating how Wister closes off possibilities for manly love in his rendering of the Virginian's friendships with Lin McLean and Steve in "Documenting the Demise of Manly Love: *The Virginian*" (*Journal of Men's Studies* 1: 33–39).

The Autobiography of John C. Van Dyke: A Personal Narrative of American Life, 1861–1931 (Utah), ed. Peter Wild, springs a few surprises about the complex, paradoxical man who taught Americans to value the desert: he had a daughter, though he never married; he was close friends with Carnegie, whose U.S. Steel ravaged the land; and he encountered the desert in Pullman cars and first-class hotels, not as the rugged frontier horseman so dear to our national consciousness. In addition to his well-researched introduction, Wild does a splendid job of bridging gaps and identifying unknown references with explanatory notes; the book includes a foreword by Philip L. Strong, Van Dyke's "first cousin once removed," a map of Van Dyke's Southwest desert, and five pages of photographs. John P. O'Grady includes a chapter on Mary Austin's "profound awareness of the shadow side of the wild" in *Pilgrims to the Wild* (pp. 123–53). O'Grady submits that Austin never failed to personify the wild as female, a rival force with which women must contend and ultimately be reconciled, in works that blur the distinction between fiction and autobiography.

Two essays increase our understanding of the Native American female voice. In "Ella Cara Deloria and Mourning Dove: Writing for Cultures, Writing Against the Grain" (*Critique of Anthropology* 13: 335–50) Janet L. Finn finds parallels and contrasts in the two writers' works, demonstrating the creative resistance in their writings and lives as she explores their choice of the novel as a vehicle for voicing Native American women's experiences. In "Zitkala-Sä (Gertrude Simmons Bonnin): A Power(full) Literary Voice" (*SAIL* 5, iv: 3–24) Dorothea M. Susag focuses attention on Zitkala-Sä's three autobiographical essays, reading them against her two cultures to reveal a powerful feminine and ethnic voice. Zitkala-Sä's native heritage of spiritual power and story works "to overcome forces that would suppress the feminine Indian voice, to articulate her personal and tribal experience, and to indict those who had victimized her people," and she links Zitkala-Sä's work to Deloria's, particularly in their common use of the Iktomi trickster figure of Dakota mythology.

viii General Works and Additional Authors

Robert M. Crunden's conversational and frequently witty *American Salons* covers the well-known (and a great many lesser-known) modernists of Paris, London, and New York, but the most informative chapters concern those figures who lived in the "Provinces"—Philadelphia, New Orleans, Baltimore, Chicago, etc. The essays in *Women and World War I* also provide several perspectives on the period, and Dorothy Goldman's essay (pp. 188–208) deals specifically with Cather, Wharton, Atherton, and Dorothy Canfield Fisher.

Fisher's star in definitely on the rise with the formation of the Dorothy Canfield Fisher Society and the publication of her letters, *Keeping Fires Night and Day: Selected Letters of Dorothy Canfield Fisher* (Missouri), ed. Mark J. Madigan. This collection contains 189 letters selected from more than 2,500 items, Madigan's gracefully written introduction, a chronology, a bibliography, a calendar of letters, 11 photographs, and notes on "notable recipients" (including Cather, Du Bois, Albert Einstein, Robert Frost, and E. B. White). The scholarship evident in this book makes it gratifying; Fisher's voice makes it a joy. Rose Wilder Lane is another whose time seems to have come. William Holtz's *The Ghost in the Little House: A Life of Rose Wilder Lane* (Missouri), the first biography of the first biographer of Henry Ford, Charlie Chaplin, and Jack London, details the editorial help Lane gave her mother with the popular Little House books as well as her painful struggle "to free herself from the emotional bondage to her mother that burdened her for much of her life." In "Rose Wilder Lane's *Free Land:* The Political Background" (*SDR* 30 [1992], i: 46–60) Holtz contextualizes the novel and reads it as a dramatized alternative to the social philosophy of the Roosevelt administration. Suzanne Fierston begins her "Rose Wilder Lane: Restless Pioneer" (*Prologue* 25: 17–24) with Lane's 1918 story "Independence Day" and follows her career as a "bachelor girl" and journalist in Europe. Susan Glaspell's stories are reprinted under the title *Lifted Masks and*

Other Works (Michigan), ed. Eric S. Rabkin. Veronica Makowsky makes "one blow against the hydra heads of Glaspell's obscurity" with a well-written, book-length study, *Susan Glaspell's Century of American Women: A Critical Interpretation of Her Work* (Oxford).

The intriguing B. Traven maintains his hold on scholars. Richard E. Mezo takes a historical and sociological approach to Traven's work, avoiding speculation about Traven's identity in favor of close readings in *A Study of B. Traven's Fiction: The Journey to Solipaz* (Mellen). Kenneth Payne compares Traven's *Government,* set in Porifirio Díaz's Mexico, and Nawal el Saadawi's *God Dies by the Nile,* set in Anwar Sadat's Egypt, in "Representations of the Peasantry in the Rural Fiction of B. Traven and Nawal El Saadawi" (*NewComp* 13 [1992]: 127–39). Payne demonstrates that both radical novelists critique the political status quo, display the same concern for the victimized and downtrodden under authoritarian states and in repressive social situations, and manage to avoid a conventionally naturalistic interpretation by depicting the tentative stirrings of possible social change in their peasant characters. Now that we know B. Traven was Ret Marut, James Goldwasser wants to know who Ret Marut was, and to that end he has searched the Riverside archives where he found a two-page 1901 manuscript that he suspects is Traven's earliest known piece ("Ret Marut: The Early B. Traven" (*GR* 68, iii: 133–42). The stories of another mystery man are the focus of Eugene Current-Garcia's *O. Henry: A Study of the Short Fiction* (Twayne), a comprehensive survey which shows how a "three-pronged cultural background" contributes content and form to the distinctive O. Henry mix. Following the Twayne format, the book includes a selection of representative critical responses, a chronology, and a selected bibliography.

Edgar MacDonald's painstakingly researched *James Branch Cabell and Richmond-in-Virginia* (Miss.) not only explains why Cabell is claimed by fantasists as an early Tolkien, but he locates his career in the context of his contemporaries, especially Ellen Glasgow, and provides a "biography of a social cosmos"—turn-of-the-century Richmond—that forged the writer's artistic sensibility. The book contains a chronology, bibliographical notes, and 16 pages of family photographs. The James Branch Cabell Society has announced that this year's *Kalki* will be the last. For the record, that volume (37) contains Harlan L. Unamsky's "Cabell's Vision of Ettarre" (pp. 3–17), Paul Padgette's "A Visit to Richmond" (pp. 18–20) and "A Cabellesque Book" (pp. 21–23), Dorys Crow Grover's "James

Branch Cabell as Poet" (pp. 24–28), and Desmond Tarrant's "A Question of Values" (pp. 29–31).

H. P. Lovecraft maintains his hold. David Mogen builds his essay "Wilderness, Metamorphosis, and Millennium: Gothic Apocalypse from the Puritans to the Cyberpunks" (*Frontier Gothic,* pp. 94–108) around Lovecraft's definition of American gothicism, which emphasizes frontier mythology and locates indigenous sources of horror in Calvinist theology and the wilderness. Donald R. Burleson proposes that Lovecraft leaves open the question whether the unsettling of comfortable systems by casting new light on them constitutes an illumination or a plunge into darkness and whether indeed darkness is comfort or horror in "Lovecraft's 'The Colour Out of Space'" (*Expl* 52: 48–50). Will Murray imagines an ingenious panel discussion on the craft of writing, featuring Algernon Blackwood, Robert W. Chamberson, and Lovecraft himself in "Lovecraft, Blackwood, and Chamberson: A Colloquium of Ghosts" (*StWF* 13: 2–8).

In *White on Black: Contemporary Literature about Africa* (Illinois, pp. 11–13) John Cullen Gruesser contends that Edgar Rice Burroughs can be seen as a fantasy writer oblivious to the blatantly racist version of African discourse he encodes in his texts; Gruesser argues that at the same time the texts reveal "the most unconscious and best depiction of the effect that Africanist discourse has on a non-African." Burroughs may be in hot water, but Tarzan has again become a popular figure. Allen Carey-Webb shares his discovery that *Tarzan* turns out to be a useful text for thinking about Conrad's novel in "*Heart of Darkness, Tarzan,* and the 'Third World': Canons and Encounters in World Literature, English 109" (*CollL* 10, i: 121–42), pointing out remarkable similarities between the books that underscore shortcomings and "missing pieces" in Conrad's critique of British imperialism. In "Tracking the Sign of Tarzan: Trans-Media Representation of a Pop-Culture Icon" (*You Tarzan: Masculinity, Movies and Men* [St. Martin's, pp. 106–25], ed. Pat Kirkhan and Janet Thumin), Walt Morton borrows from recent theories of reception and spectatorship to examine differences among Burroughs's original novels, comic strip versions of them, and film adaptations. For those who care, *Tarzan in Color* (NBM) reproduces Harold Foster's 1931–32 Sunday comic strip adaptations.

Drew University

14 Fiction: The 1930s to the 1960s

Catherine Calloway

Seventeen writers covered in this chapter are featured in book-length studies this year. Vladimir Nabokov receives the most attention, with four critical studies, followed closely by Richard Wright, Flannery O'Connor, and Katherine Anne Porter, each of whom is the focus of three books. In addition, John Steinbeck, Peter Taylor, and Zora Neale Hurston are the subjects of essay collections. Southern writers continue to increase in popularity, with *SoQ* devoting special issues to Robert Penn Warren, Eudora Welty, and Porter. Djuna Barnes is also honored with a special issue of *RCF*. As in 1992, scholarship remains sparse on Westerners, iconoclasts, and detectives.

i Proletarians

a. John Steinbeck   Steinbeck scholars will welcome two new volumes of essays. *The Steinbeck Question: New Essays in Criticism* (Whitston), ed. Donald R. Noble, includes 17 essays on a variety of Steinbeck's works and themes. *The Grapes of Wrath* is the topic of several essays: Michael G. Barry's "Degrees of Meditation and Their Political Value in Steinbeck's *Grapes of Wrath*" (pp. 108–24); Jackson J. Benson's "John Steinbeck: The Favorite Author We Love to Hate" (pp. 8–22); Sylvia J. Cooks's "Steinbeck's Poor in Prosperity and Adversity" (pp. 125–42); and H. R. Stoneback's "Rough People . . . Are the Best Singers: Woody Guthrie, John Steinbeck, and Folksong" (pp. 143–70). *Cup of Gold* and *Tortilla Flat* are discussed in Dennis Prindle's "The Pretexts of Romance: Steinbeck's Allegorical Naturalism from *Cup of Gold* to *Tortilla Flat*"(pp. 23–36). *Burning Bright* is the subject of John Ditsky's " 'I Know It When I Hear It on Stage': Theatre and Language in Steinbeck's *Burning Bright*"(pp. 223–38). *East of Eden* as a naturalistic work is the topic of Charles L. Etheridge, Jr.'s

"Changing Attitudes Toward Steinbeck's Naturalism and the Changing Reputation of *East of Eden:* A Survey of Criticism Since 1974" (pp. 250–59). Robert S. Hughes, Jr., discusses Steinbeck's short fiction in "Steinbeck and the Art of Story Writing" (pp. 37–50), and Robert E. Morsberger examines Steinbeck's development as a major war writer in "Steinbeck's War" (pp. 183–212). John H. Timmerman in "The Shameless Magpie: John Steinbeck, Plagiarism, and the Ear of the Artist" (pp. 260–78) defends Steinbeck against charges of plagiarism in his early work.

An unusual feature of Noble's volume is its inclusion of four essays about Steinbeck's female characters. In "Steinbeck's Cloistered Women" (pp. 51–70) Charlotte Hadella examines the repressive role of women in Steinbeck's valley stories, where characters delude themselves into seeking false Edens. Paul Hintz in "The Silent Woman and the Male Voice in Steinbeck's *Cannery Row*" (pp. 71–83) notes the pivotal role of women in that book and *The Sea of Cortez* who, because of their gender, are silenced by the male voices who name them. Paradoxically, Hirtz asserts, "the process of naming estranges the mind from the thing named, at the same time that it makes knowledge of the thing possible." In "Missing Women: The Inexplicable Disparity Between Women in Steinbeck's Life and Those in His Fiction" (pp. 84–98) Mimi Reisel Gladstein notes the difference between Steinbeck's own life, where women played very active, vocal roles, and his fiction, where they are conspicuously absent. Gladstein concludes that perhaps Steinbeck's insecurity regarding women resulted from his contact with active, powerful women whom he could control only by creating passive female characters. Michael J. Meyer in "Fallen Adam: Another Look at Steinbeck's 'The Snake'" (pp. 99–107) examines the character of the mysterious dark lady who assumes the role of the temptress and provides insight into Doc, the story's main character.

Tetsumaro Hayashi's *A New Study Guide to Steinbeck's Major Works, With Critical Explications* (Scarecrow) is the third in a series of study guides of Steinbeck's most frequently taught works. Hayashi collects 11 essays, each written by a member of "a new generation of active Steinbeck teacher-scholars in the 1990s," such as Louis Owens, Charlotte Hadella, Patrick W. Shaw, Barbara Heavilin, Michael J. Meyer, and Helen Lojek. Each chapter contains sections on background, plot synopsis, critical explication, topics for research and discussion, and a selected bibliography. A brief checklist of critical sources is included.

David Cassuto in "Turning Wine into Water: Water as Privileged

Signifier in *The Grapes of Wrath*" (*PLL* 29: 67–95) notes the significance of water—both its presence and its absence—in Steinbeck's novel. According to Cassuto, the motif "represents an indictment of the American myth of the garden and its accompanying myth of the frontier," which had to be rewritten "to encompass [the] corporate capitalism" that emerged as the result of water's "symbolic power."

The Winter of Our Discontent has been popular with contributors to this year's issues of *StQ*. Robert S. Hughes, Jr., in "What Went Wrong? How a 'Vintage' Steinbeck Short Story Became the Flawed *Winter of Our Discontent*" (26: 7–12) offers an explanation as to why Steinbeck's novel does not measure up to "How Mr. Hogan Robbed a Bank," the story from which it was developed. According to Hughes, the problem lies with genre. *Winter of Our Discontent* was the first novel that Steinbeck tried to base on a short story, and his revisions in setting, theme, characterization, and point of view did not work well. In "Transforming Evil to Good: The Image Iscariot in *The Winter of Our Discontent*" (26: 101–10) Michael J. Meyer perceptively notes the many Judas/Christ parallels in the novel, clearly demonstrating how Steinbeck intended these parallels to indict contemporary society. Whereas the Judas figure should be viewed tragically, Steinbeck indicates that instead society will invert it and view it heroically. Peter Valenti's "Steinbeck's Geographical Seasons: *The Winter of Our Discontent*" (26: 111–17) applies reader-response theory to suggest that readers must read Steinbeck's last novel differently from his earlier writing.

Other Steinbeck works also elicit critical commentary in *StQ*. Barbara A. Heavilin in "Steinbeck's Exploration of Good and Evil: Structural and Thematic Unity in *East of Eden*" (26: 90–100) explores the novel's theme of good over evil. Steinbeck uses this theme to unify the novel, particularly at the close where he makes clear that good—and love—can serve as forces of triumph rather than defeat. In "The Pastures of Contested Pastoral Discourse" (26: 38–45) Kevin Hearle demonstrates the way in which "Steinbeck uses many of the central discourses of the American West—rural idyll, the cowboy individualist, and the yeoman farmer/backbone of democracy—dialogically in opposition to one another . . . to critique the pastures-in-the-sky nature of American national discourses of the West as garden."

b. James Agee and Others James Agee, Henry Roth, and Kenneth Fearing are each represented by one article this year. In " 'Practically an

American Home': James Agee's Family Solitudes" (*SLJ* 25, ii: 39–56)
George Toles demonstrates how the protagonists in Agee's works, particularly in *Let Us Now Praise Famous Men* and *A Death in the Family*, search for surrogate families and homes that endow them with a sense
of love and identity. Toles briefly compares Agee's "nostalgic vision" with
that of Thornton Wilder, for each writer wishes to "accommodate the
writer's self within an idealized family or community setting, where an
absent parent's presumed intention for one's life and the self's own
confused image of what it wants are magically reconciled."

   Elaine Orr in "On the Side of the Mother: *Yonnondio* and *Call It
Sleep*" (*SAF* 21: 209–23) examines Tillie Olsen's and Henry Roth's novels
in light of how the mother figure is viewed in the text. *Yonnondio* invites
its readers to "become textual daughters" who are closely attuned to the
maternal figure in the novel, while *Call It Sleep* "recreates masculine
readers" who enjoy "the narrator's collaboration with Oedipal matri-
cide." Often overlooked as a fiction writer, Kenneth Fearing as an artful
novelist is the subject of T. Jeff Evans's "Narratology in Kenneth Fearing's
Big Clock" (*JNT* 23: 188–200). Evans focuses on the way that Fearing in
the process of creation actively engages readers by "suturing" or "stitch-
ing" them into the text, employing such devices as self-reflexivity.

c. Richard Wright, Ralph Ellison, and James Baldwin   Wright is the
subject of three books this year. *Conversations with Richard Wright*
(Miss.), ed. Keneth Kinnamon and Michel Fabre, contains 63 interviews
from 1938 until 1961 that provide insight into Wright's personality, ideas,
responses to events, and opinions. *Richard Wright: Critical Perspectives
Past and Present* (Amistad), ed. Henry Louis Gates, Jr., and K. A. Appiah,
contains 20 brief reviews and 22 critical essays on Wright's work. In the
critical essays Keneth Kinnamon, Laura E. Tanner, Barbara Johnson,
Ross Pudaloff, Joyce Anne Joyce, and Barbara Foley write on *Native Son*.
Black Boy is the focus of essays by Robert Stepto, Janice Thaddeus,
Abdul R. Janmohamed, and Timothy Dow Adams. Carla Cappetti,
Horace A. Porter, and Herbert Leibowitz write on both *Black Boy* and
American Hunger. Dan McCall focuses on *American Hunger*, William
Burrison on *Lawd Today*, Houston A. Baker, Jr., on *12 Million Black
Voices*, Earle V. Bryant on *The Long Dream*, and Claudia C. Tate and
Mae Henderson on *The Outsider*. Edward Margolies examines Wright's
short stories, John M. Reilly discusses the nonfiction, and Valerie Smith
deals with the theme of alienation in the fiction. A chronology of

Wright's life and work and a selected bibliography close the volume. Margaret Walker's *Richard Wright: Daemonic Genius* (Amistad) serves a threefold purpose: "to define Richard Wright, to analyze and assess his work, and to show the correlation between the man and his work." Walker divides her study into five sections that cover the main periods of Wright's life: his early formative years in a primarily white and chaotic South; the rebellious Chicago years when he answered the call to become a professional writer; the New York decade; the trek to Paris in search of freedom; and the several traumatic years before his death.

In *Visible Ellison: A Study of Ralph Ellison's Fiction* (Greenwood) Edith Schor views *Invisible Man* as the culmination of themes that Ellison addressed in his earlier writing, particularly in his short fiction. Schor devotes two chapters to Ellison's short stories before turning to *Invisible Man*. She concludes with a chapter on Ellison's later fiction and a selected bibliography of works by and about him. Philip Gould in "Ralph Ellison's 'Time-Haunted' Novel" (*ArQ* 49, i: 117–40) argues that by examining other works of African American discourse, such as *The Crisis, Negro Digest,* W. E. B. Du Bois's autobiographical works, and *Phylon,* readers can clearly see the influence of other writers on Ellison, particularly in his writing of *Invisible Man.*

Michael F. Lynch in "Beyond Guilt and Innocence: Redemptive Suffering and Love in Baldwin's *Another Country*" (*Obsidian* 17, i–ii [1992]: 1–18) demonstrates how Rufus's suffering and self-destruction help, rather than destroy, the other characters' lives. Lynch reads *Another Country* affirmatively, in the process demonstrating how Baldwin believes that redemption, hope, and forgiveness are possible, even in the bleakest of circumstances. According to Terry Rowden in "A Play of Abstractions: Race, Sexuality, and Community in James Baldwin's *Another Country*" (*SoR* 29: 41–50), Rufus is alienated from his own black community, yet he manages to transcend his marginality. As a result, he matures, when other characters do not, and he gains a "self-awareness . . . as a specific self in the specific world in which Baldwin has placed him." In "The Everlasting Father: Mythic Quest and Rebellion in Baldwin's *Go Tell It on the Mountain*" (*CLAJ* 37: 156–75) Michael F. Lynch examines the quest motif as it applies to the initiation of John Grimes. Baldwin follows the traditional mythological pattern whereby the protagonist's "quest for the father" is transformed into "a quest for himself" and thus becomes an act of self-discovery. In "The Substance of Things Hoped For: Faith in *Go Tell It on the Mountain* and *Just Above My Head*"

(*Obsidian* 17, i–ii [1992]: 19–32) Nagueyalti Warren points out that in both works there is a lack of the faith that recurs so frequently in other Baldwin fictions. However, this loss does not imply an agnostic viewpoint. "Instead," Warren notes, Baldwin "affirms a God within the individual and within the collective self of Black people that is the source of all life, intelligence, and creativity."

Wright, Ellison, Baldwin, and Toni Morrison are the focus of Charles Scruggs's *Sweet Home*, which treats "the conceptual meeting of utopia and dystopia in twentieth-century Afro-American literature." Scruggs examines the thematic image of the city and the urban environment in these writers' works. According to him, "the idea of a visionary city is a durable and on-going tradition in black urban literature." Underneath "the city of brute fact" exists a "city of symbol, of community, of civilization, of home."

d. Dorothy Parker   Dorothy Parker is represented in one book, Randall Calhoun's *Dorothy Parker: A Bio-Bibliography* (Greenwood). Calhoun begins with "A Biographical Sketch" of Parker that blends familiar information with new material. Section two consists of a "Primary Bibliography" (including lists of reviews), short fiction, screenplays (including movie scripts that were coauthored), published interviews, miscellaneous work, and poems and essays from newspapers and magazines. In the third section Calhoun moves to a "Secondary Bibliography" that includes almost 200 annotated sources published from 1922 through 1992. The book concludes with essays by Richard E. Lauterbach, Wyatt Cooper, and Joseph Bryan III.

ii Southerners

a. Robert Penn Warren   "The Great Dragon Country of Robert Penn Warren" is the subject of a *SoQ* special issue. While most of it is devoted to Warren's poetry, his fiction receives some attention. In "The *Night Rider* Revisited: A Historical Perspective" (31, iv: 68–74) Thomas H. Winn briefly notes the strong historical dimension in a novel that skillfully blends fact and fiction. Warren scholars will appreciate James A. Grimshaw, Jr.'s "Biographical Trends in Warren Criticism: The 1980s" (31, iv: 51–67), which includes a brief bibliography of selected criticism, books, partial books, essays, and reviews. According to Steven T. Ryan's "*World Enough and Time*: A Refutation of Poe's History as Tragedy" (31, iv: 86–94), Warren goes beyond Poe's tragic version of the death of Colonel Solomon P. Sharp in Kentucky in 1825 by adding the grotesque, using parody to show how the historical people involved are unable "to enact a perfect vengeance," and stressing "the illusionary, solipsistic nature of the grand love of Jeremiah Beaumont and Rachael Jordon." That novel is also the subject of Michael G. Barry's "Interpretation and Justice: The Heart of *World Enough and Time*" (*SLJ* 25, ii: 57–68). Using a plethora of examples from various characters and situations, Barry demonstrates the significance of "the relationship of word to object, of language to reality, of signifier to signified." According to Barry, language, which is expressed through a multiplicity of voices, has the power to change the past and to affect the future. In "Robert Penn Warren's West" (*SLJ* 26, i: 54–63) Joseph R. Millichap contends that the West as setting and symbol was as important as the South to Warren.

Allen Tate's work generates one good article this year. John R. Strawn's "Larry Buchan as the Voice of Allen Tate's Modernist Aesthetic in *The Fathers*" (*SLJ* 26, i: 64–77) argues that Tate blends modernist techniques with the past in his writing. As a result, *The Fathers* achieves the same "aesthetic principles" that readers find in Tate's poetry and essays.

b. Flannery O'Connor, Eudora Welty, and Katherine Anne Porter
Three books and a number of critical articles attest to O'Connor's continuing popularity. Anthony Di Renzo in *American Gargoyles: Flannery O'Connor and the Medieval Grotesque* (So. Ill.) departs from earlier scholars in viewing O'Connor's use of the grotesque as "a purposeful accomplishment, deeply rooted in medieval art and satire." Di Renzo discusses O'Connor's use of a Christ figure, her emphasis on human anatomy, her "interplay between the saintly and the demonic," her interest in the carnivalesque, and the influence of medieval folk art as a source for her writing. Robert Cole's *Flannery O'Connor's South* (Georgia), first published in 1980, has been reprinted. Those who missed the earlier edition will enjoy Cole's personal accounts of O'Connor, whom he knew briefly, as well as his insights into her writing and the South that she depicted. As part of the Women's Writers Series, Frederick Asals edits *"A Good Man Is Hard to Find"* (Rutgers), a collection of essays that accompanies the short story by that title as well as a lengthy introduction by Asals (pp. 3–25), an essay by O'Connor on her own work, and a letter from O'Connor to John Hawkes. The casebook reprints 10 essays on "A Good Man Is Hard to Find" by critics J. O. Tate, Hallman B. Bryant,

W. S. Marks III, William S. Doxey, Michael O. Bellamy, William J. Scheick, Madison Jones, Carter Martin, J. Peter Dyson, and Mary Jane Schenck.

In "Revolting Fictions: Flannery O'Connor's Letter to Her Mother" (*PLL* 29: 197–214) Ann E. Reuman draws parallels between O'Connor and Franz Kafka, whose fiction contains traces of resentment toward parental figures. O'Connor's fiction changed significantly in the 1950s when she shared living quarters with her mother in Andalusia. Reuman speculates that stories such as "Revelation," "The Comforts of Home," "Good Country People," and "The Enduring Chill" may have been directed toward O'Connor's mother, with private clues hidden in the stories that would reveal O'Connor's feelings toward her parent without causing her any public humiliation. Robert Butler in "Visions of Southern Life and Religion in O'Connor's *Wise Blood* and Walker's *The Third Life of Grange Copeland*" (*CLAJ* 36: 349–70) finds comparisons between O'Connor and Alice Walker. Although the two writers may appear to be writing different types of fiction, they are similar in that, most obviously, both O'Connor and Walker are Southern writers; both feel that they belong to the South, yet are in some way alienated from it; and both rely heavily on religion and Christian beliefs. George Monteiro in "The Great American Hunt in Flannery O'Connor's 'The Turkey'" (*Expl* 51: 118–21) draws parallels between one of O'Connor's earliest and least familiar stories and Melville's *Moby-Dick* and Thomas Bangs Thorpe's "The Big Bear of Arkansas" and "Wild Turkey Hunting." Through his acquisition and loss of a turkey, O'Connor's protagonist undergoes an initiatory experience which may or may not be a "true visitation of Grace." Michael W. Crocker's and Robert C. Evans's "Faulkner's 'Barn Burning' and O'Connor's 'Everything That Rises Must Converge'" (*CLAJ* 36: 371–83) studies the undeniable influence of Faulkner. Both are stories of initiation that contain similar elements: sons who are unhappy with their current situations, domineering parental figures, circular structures, conflicts between adults, and an emphasis on family heritage. They also show the way in which the past impinges on the present. However, the two stories also differ significantly. O'Connor's protagonist is more assertive than Faulkner's in that he will not look back after he leaves home. In addition, Sarty has tried to find good in his father, he will find no joy in his having to leave, and he does not actually witness his father's death.

In "The Existential Intuition of Flannery O'Connor in *The Violent*

Bear It Away" (*NConL* 23, iv: 2–3) Raymond Benoit examines the character of the truck driver who gives Tarwater a ride in light of existentialism and Kierkegaardean philosophy. Since the truck driver exists in a vacuum, with his only destination Detroit, the reader must necessarily overlook him. Robert Donahoo's "Tarwater's March Toward the Feminine: The Role of Gender in O'Connor's *The Violent Bear It Away*" (*CEA* 56, i: 96–106) defends O'Connor's use of female characters, arguing that O'Connor deliberately "associate[s] women with absence" and places male characters in situations that demand their embrace of both male and female qualities. Short stories such as "Parker's Back" and "The Artificial Nigger" also contain plots where men are forced to rely less on the masculine and, through their vulnerability, more on the feminine. Gender is important as well in David Havird's "The Saving Rape: Flannery O'Connor and Patriarchal Religion" (*MissQ* 47: 15–26). Havird examines the female protagonists in "Greenleaf," "Revelation," and "Good Country People" who try to usurp their feminine roles by taking on masculine qualities in the hope of dominating both male and female characters. However, all the women accomplish is their transformation into "castrated versions of the male." Even worse, argues Havird, is that "the monstrous female characters become scapegoats for *Flannery* O'Connor, whose sin of authorship is greater even than their own prideful rejection of woman's conventional role as angel of the house." In "Allegorical Evil, Existentialist Choice in O'Connor, Oates, and Styron" (*MQ* 34: 383–97) Terry White finds thematic links between the women characters of O'Connor's "A Good Man Is Hard to Find," Joyce Carol Oates's "Where Are You Going, Where Have You Been?," and William Styron's *Sophie's Choice*. In each work a female character confronts a chilling, vicious, and exceptionally destructive evil, forcing the reader to note the "moral entropy where Christianity has been put into abeyance," and to acknowledge the existence of a horror that is unusually violent and macabre. In "Individuation and Religious Experience: A Jungian Approach to O'Connor's 'Revelation'" (*SLJ* 25, ii: 92–102) Rebecca K. Rowley draws numerous parallels between Jungian theory, which helps to reveal "some of the darkness and profound mystery which distinguishes O'Connor's grotesque fiction," and O'Connor's characters, whose actions reveal their "initiation [in]to the [Jungian] process of individuation." In *Deadly Musings* (pp. 194–221) Michael Kowalewski considers the metaphoric nature of O'Connor's style of writing, including her tendency toward "hypercoldness." Citing such works as *The Violent Bear It*

Away, "Greenleaf," and *Wise Blood,* Kowalewski examines the way in which O'Connor uses similes to change even a seemingly "innocent scene into one of humorous grotesquerie and impending violence."

Eudora Welty is well represented this year, including articles published in a special issue of *SoQ.* Alexandr Vaschenko's "That Which 'The Whole World Knows': Functions of Folklore in Eudora Welty's Stories" (*SoQ* 32, i: 9–15) points out the unique combinations of folklore in Welty's writing. Some stories, particularly those narrated and set in Natchez Trace, imitate the "local legends" folk genre, while others, such as those in *The Golden Apples,* where the telling of the story replaces narration, fall into the category of the "small town gossip narrative." Folklore is also commented on in "Idyllic Chronotop in *Delta Wedding*" (*SoQ* 32, i: 21–26), where Natalia Yakimenko traces the idyllic pattern of the *chronotop,* the relationship between time and space, that allows Welty's Mississippi setting the prominence of a Winesburg, Ohio, or a Yoknapatawpha County. Aleksei Zverev in *"Losing Battles* Against the Background of the Sixties" (*SoQ* 32, i: 27–30) views Welty's novel as more relevant to the 1960s than to the 1930s of the depression era that it portrays because in both cases "the mythical view of existence is in conflict with historical consciousness," a conflict that is particularly crucial to the sixties. Language is the subject of Eben E. Bass's "The Languages of *Losing Battles*" (*SAF* 21: 67–82). Through a close reading of Welty's novel, Bass illustrates the many forms that language, both oral and written, takes in *Losing Battles,* from combat rhetoric to biblical emblems to hymns to the Beecham family's oral history. The various forms of language are significant because through them "male authority is questioned . . . in an undercurrent of irony, sometimes funny, sometimes sad." Ekaterina Stetsenko in "Eudora Welty and Autobiography" (*SoQ* 32, i: 16–20) focuses on the relationship of Welty's life to her fiction. According to Stetsenko, Welty's *One Writer's Beginnings* is significant because it goes beyond the story of Welty's life to focus on the creative process so important to a writer. Gary M. Ciuba in "Time as Confluence: Self and Structure in Welty's *One Writer's Beginnings*" (*SLJ* 26, i: 78–93) also notes the interrelationships between Welt's autobiography and fiction. *One Writer's Beginnings* uses Welty's concept of *confluence,* the symbol "for both the content and flow of Welty's memories"; as a result, her short fiction "join[s] in confluence with her life story."

Other articles deal with individual stories. Marilyn Arnold in "The Edge of Adolescence in Eudora Welty's 'Moon Lake' " (*SoQ* 32, i: 49–61) reads the story as an initiation account of adolescent loss of innocence. The restrictive bonds of society reject the natural instincts and deny the "human passion" that the lake symbolizes. In "Occasional Travelers in China Grove: Welty's 'Why I Live at the P.O.' Reconsidered" (*SoQ* 32, i: 72–79) Axel Nissen offers numerous evidences that the narrator is not, as many critics have viewed her, mentally unbalanced. Instead, rather than an unreliable narrator or mentally unstable, Sister is just lonely. Deborah Wilson's "The Altering/Alterity of History in Eudora Welty's *Robber Bridegroom*" (*SoQ* 32, i: 62–71) focuses on the way in which Welty blurs the "boundaries between historical fact and imaginative fiction." Through historical revisionism, Welty brings dead Native Americans to life, reminding the reader that another side of the story exists, not merely that of the white male historian, and that all history is a blend of fact and fiction. In " 'The Treasure Most Dearly Regarded': Memory and Imagination in *Delta Wedding*" (*SLJ* 25, ii: 79–91) Suzanne Marrs compares Welty's "The Delta Cousins" with her later novel to demonstrate the significance of Waverly, a plantation that Welty visited while in college. By transforming Waverly through memory and imagination and by expanding that setting and interspersing it with other locales, Welty strengthens the setting for *Delta Wedding*, at the same time revealing the intricacies of her imaginative process. In "Images of the Depression in the Fiction of Eudora Welty" (*SoQ* 32, i: 81–91) Ruth D. Weston points out that even though Welty wrote about and photographed images of the depression, her writing and photography transcend the poverty of that era to reveal "the rich human spirit and sustaining sense of community that helped people survive." The Russian response to Welty's writing is discussed in "Eudora Welty and Southern Literature in World Perspective: A Panel Discussion" (*SoQ* 32, i: 31–39), the transcript of a forum that took place on 17 May 1991 at a conference on "The Artistic World of Eudora Welty." Moderated by Sergei Chakovsky, a Soviet researcher of world literature, the panel briefly examined the role that Welty and her Southern literary heritage play in the literature of the Soviet Union and other nations. In "Welty's *A Curtain of Green*" (*Expl* 51: 242–43) Alan Brown notes the significance of Mrs. Larkin's name in "A Curtain of Green," a name relating to both birds and flowers, two elements "of the natural world to which the protagonist returns."

Katherine Anne Porter is the subject of three books and a number of articles. In *Katherine Anne Porter's Artistic Development* (LSU) Robert H. Brinkmeyer, Jr., divides Porter's artistic output into three periods: the

Mexico years of the 1920s; the Texas years of the 1930s and 1940s, where she came to embrace her Southern heritage; and the period that lasted from World War II until the 1960s. Unlike many scholars who accept Porter's claim that her writing remained basically the same throughout her career, without shifts in perspective and values, Brinkmeyer points out the many roles that are evident in Porter's writing, noting "Porter's ongoing development as a thinker and observer" and examining how this "development affected the shape and texture of her art." The Mexican era of Porter's life and writing is the focus of Thomas F. Walsh's *Katherine Anne Porter and Mexico: The Illusion of Eden* (Texas, 1992). Walsh attempts to chronicle Porter's Mexican years as completely as possible, drawing on some previously unrelated experiences and showing how those experiences affected her Mexican and non-Mexican writing. Walsh also explores the interrelationship of theme and imagery in the variety of genres found in Porter's fiction or nonfiction writing. *"Flowering Judas": Katherine Anne Porter* (Rutgers), ed. Virginia Spencer Carr, is a useful casebook for the study of Porter's own favorite story. "Flowering Judas" is preceded by a thorough introduction to Porter's life and work by Carr (pp. 3–25), followed by three brief essays by Porter on her writing (pp. 53–62), an interview by Barbara Thompson (pp. 63–85), and seven critical essays on the story, some previously unpublished, by Ray B. West, Jr., Leon Gottfried, David Madden, Darlene Harbour Unrue, Jane Krause DeMouy, Thomas F. Walsh, and Robert H. Brinkmeyer, Jr.

Porter is also honored in a special issue of *SoQ*. In " 'The Man in the Tree': Katherine Anne Porter's Unfinished Lynching Story" (31, iii: 7–16) Jan Nordby Gretlund offers a rare but insightful glimpse into some of Porter's unpublished fiction. Gretlund examines "The Man in the Tree," which is valuable for several reasons: it contains numerous authorial annotations detailing Porter's writing process; it reveals attitudes toward race in her mythological town of Kyle, Texas; and it includes instances of comic relief not often found in her writing. Unrue in "Katherine Anne Porter, Politics, and Another Reading of 'Theft' " (*SSF* 30: 119–26) argues that political themes can be found in a number of the stories. Using "Theft" as a paradigm text, she shows how political themes are central to it. In "Reading the Endings in Katherine Anne Porter's 'Old Mortality' " (*SoQ* 31, iii: 29–44) Suzanne W. Jones demonstrates how in "Old Mortality" and "Pale Horse, Pale Rider" Porter steers away from the popular plot lines of quests and marriage. However, Porter does not succeed in providing a true feminist reading of her text, particularly in "Old

Mortality" where her "typical modernist ambiguous ending . . . runs counter to the plot's interest in creating feminist readers." Unrue's "Katherine Anne Porter and Henry James: A Study in Influence" (*SoQ* 31, iii: 17–28) focuses on Porter's well-known admiration of Henry James, who particularly influenced her writing of *Ship of Fools* and who "became for her the symbol of the primacy of art." The theories of utilitarianism and retributivism are the subject of Debra A. Moddelmog's "Concepts of Justice in the Work of Katherine Anne Porter" (*Mosaic* 26, iv: 37–52). Through an analysis of *Ship of Fools* and short stories such as "María's Concepción" and "Noon Wine," Moddelmog insightfully delves into Porter's interests in the concepts of justice and injustice, concluding that retributivism, not utilitarianism, is the most acceptable form of legal system. Janis P. Stout in " 'Something of a Reputation as a Radical': Katherine Anne Porter's Shifting Politics" (*SCRev* 10, i: 49–66) thoroughly examines Porter's changing political views, which at one time or another embraced a number of ideologies, including communism, anticommunism, and pacifism; Stout also looks into the possible origins for Porter's radicalism as well as the reasons that she turned away from some previously held beliefs.

c. Peter Taylor, Erskine Caldwell, and Thomas Wolfe Essays on Peter Taylor's work increase. *Critical Essays on Peter Taylor* (Hall), ed. Hubert H. McAlexander, contains 13 brief reviews and 17 critical essays. In his introduction (pp. 1–25) to Taylor's life and writing, McAlexander provides a helpful critical overview of Taylor scholarship. Christopher Metress (pp. 201–15) writes on *A Summons to Memphis,* James Penny Smith (pp. 98–107) on *A Woman of Means,* Robert Penn Warren (pp. 73–76) on *A Long Fourth and Other Stories,* and Ashley Brown (pp. 77–86) on both *A Woman of Means* and *A Long Fourth and Other Stories.* A number of scholars focus on individual Taylor stories: Maureen Andrews (pp. 154–61) and Roland Sodowsky and Gargi Roysircar Sodowsky (pp. 148–53) write on "Spinster's Tale"; Simone Vauthier (pp. 162–79) on "Porte Cochere" and (pp. 227–53) on "Venis, Cupid, Folly, and Time"; David M. Robinson (pp. 180–92) on "The Old Forest"; Ron Balthazor (pp. 216–26) on "In the Miro District"; and Madison Smartt Bell (pp. 254–61) on "A Wife of Nashville," "The Hand of Emmagene," and "Old Forest." Barbara Schuler (pp. 87–97), Jan Pinkerton (pp. 108–15), Jane Barnes Casey (pp. 124–35), Alan Williamson (pp. 136–47), and David H. Lynn (pp. 193–200) discuss a variety of Taylor's stories.

Bertram Wyatt-Brown in "Aging, Gender, and the Deterioration of Southern Family Values in the Stories of Peter Taylor" (*Aging and Gender in Literature*, pp. 296–313) also examines the role of age and gender in the South in such Taylor stories as "In the Miro District" and "Three Heroines." According to Wyatt-Brown, "The tales provide a striking opportunity for analyzing the difference that gender makes in understanding the relative positions of aging men and women in family life and the ruptures in connectedness that arise."

Erskine Caldwell is represented by Harvey L. Klevar's *Erskine Caldwell: A Biography* (Tennessee). The culmination of a study of Caldwell's life and works that began in the late 1970s, Klevar's biography is endorsed by both Caldwell and his wife, Virginia, who granted Klevar access to all of the Caldwell materials at four different libraries. In constructing Caldwell's biography Klevar relies on stories that Caldwell related publicly, the personal testimonies of people who knew him, and information garnered from written accounts. The last years of Caldwell's life are not recounted as fully as his earlier ones.

Two articles focus on Thomas Wolfe's short fiction. In "The Narrative Discourse of Thomas Wolfe's 'I Have a Thing to Tell You'" (*SSF* 30: 45–52) John L. Idol, Jr., explains how Wolfe used narrative devices to describe the evils of Nazism. Wolfe's metaphoric use of a train journey, while a familiar literary technique, allows him to set forth his vision for the future: that humanity will not be destroyed and that humans will unite and "travel together as brothers and sisters." Patricia Gantt's "Weaving Discourse in Thomas Wolfe's 'The Child by Tiger'" (*SoQ* 31, iii: 45–57) focuses on Wolfe's use of multiple narratives and points of view to draw the reader into the text. This year's issues of *TWN* concentrate primarily on biographical matters. Webb Salmon authors a two-part article on "Thomas Wolfe's Financial Relationship with His Family" (17, i: 1–13; ii: 1–12), and Inez G. Hollander explores Wolfe's friendship with Hamilton Basso (17, i: 14–20). Other articles deal with Wolfe as a writer. In "Metadramatic Aspects of Thomas Wolfe's Fiction" (17, ii: 27–32) Tramble T. Turner notes the influence of metadrama on Wolfe's fiction. Matthew Webb Levering in "Around the Park with Aline Bernstein and Thomas Wolfe" (17, ii: 46–54) notes how Wolfe appropriated the last chapter of Bernstein's "An Actor's Daughter" as "the main source for 'In the Park,'" achieving more "cosmic reach" than Bernstein by using her "plot to create language, which, through its complete affirmation of life, transcends time and death." The British reaction to *Look*

Homeward, Angel is examined in John S. Phillipson's "The Reception of *Look Homeward, Angel* in England: 1930 and 1958" (17, ii: 55–60). British and American reviews were similar, especially in praising Wolfe's skillful characterization.

d. Zora Neale Hurston and Arna Wendell Bontemps   Hurston scholars also have had a productive year. In "Hurston's 'Spunk' and *Hamlet*" (*SSF* 30: 397–98) David G. Hale draws parallels between Hurston's story and Shakespeare's tragedy. Margaret D. Bauer in "The Sterile New South: An Intertextual Reading of *Their Eyes Were Watching God* and *Absalom! Absalom!*" (*CLAJ* 36: 384–405) finds similarities between the characters in Hurston's and Faulkner's works. Both novels focus on the sterility that can result when people try "to build a New South on the same foundations as the old." Thomas Cassidy's "Janie's Rage: The Dog and the Storm in *Their Eyes Were Watching God*" (*CLAJ* 36: 260–69) speculates why Hurston's novel "turns its eyes away from the complexities of Janie's and Tea Cake's relationship." According to Cassidy, "Hurston wants to have it both ways. She wants to have Janie be responsible for deciding to live without Tea Cake but not responsible for any harm which she might do to him." Sharon Davie in "Free Mules, Talking Buzzards, and Cracked Plates: The Politics of Dislocation in *Their Eyes Were Watching God*" (*PMLA* 108: 446–59) argues that Hurston uses the buzzard story, bodily imagery, and the free mule tales to actively encourage "readers to question . . . the hierarchical mode itself" as well as to invert and mock traditional, normally accepted hierarchies. The multiplicity of meanings in the text serve to undermine readers' previous knowledge of hierarchy and to engage them in an open text that continually changes and evolves. In " ' . . . Ah said Ah'd save de text for you': Recontextualizing the Sermon to Tell (Her) story in Zora Neale Hurston's *Their Eyes Were Watching God*" (*AAR* 27: 167–78) Dolan Hubbard argues that Hurston intended in the novel to challenge other black authors "to accept and promote the integrity of black culture," particularly black idiom. Wendy Dutton's "The Problem of Invisibility: Voodoo and Zora Neale Hurston" (*Frontiers* 13: 131–52) is an interesting account of Hurston's study of voodoo, her difficulty in relating her research and knowledge of voodoo in her writing, and the reasons why she left much of her story of voodoo relatively untold.

Hurston is also the subject of two books. *Zora Neale Hurston: Critical Perspectives Past and Present* (Amistad), ed. Henry Louis Gates, Jr., and

K. A. Appiah, contains 20 brief reviews of Hurston's major books and 14 critical essays appraising her work. In the critical essays Gates (pp. 154–203), Cynthia Bond (pp. 204–17), and Maria Tai Wolff (pp. 218–29) discuss *Their Eyes Were Watching God*. *Mules and Men* is discussed by Barbara Johnson (pp. 130–40) and Houston A. Baker, Jr. (pp. 280–308). Deborah E. McDowell (pp. 230–40) focuses on *Moses, Man of the Mountain,* Françoise Lionnet-McCumber (pp. 241–66) on *Dust Tracks on a Road,* Eric J. Sundquist (pp. 39–66) on *Jonah's Gourd Vine,* and Lillie Howard (pp. 267–79) on *Seraph on the Suwanee*. Susan Willis (pp. 110–29) examines the themes of distance and alienation in Hurston's fiction. The editors include a chronology of Hurston's life and a selected bibliography. Hurston's influence on Alice Walker is considered in *Alice Walker and Zora Neale Hurston*. In addition to Lillie P. Howard's "Introduction: Alice and Zora—'The Call and the Response'" (pp. 3–12), which provides an overview of Hurston's and Walker's lives and literature, the book contains essays on *Their Eyes Were Watching God* and *The Color Purple* by Alice Fannin (pp. 45–56), Emma J. Waters Dawson (pp. 69–82), and Valerie Babb (pp. 83–93). JoAnne Cornwell (pp. 97–107) writes on *Their Eyes Were Watching God* and *The Third Life of Grange Copeland;* and Ayana Karanja (pp. 121–37) on *Jonah's Gourd Vine* and *The Color Purple*. Trudier Harris (pp. 31–42) compares the use of folk materials in Hurston's and Walker's works; Mary Ann Wilson (pp. 57–67) discusses both writers' use of spirituality; and Ann Folwell Stanford examines the subject of sexual ideology in a variety of their writings. Mary L. Navarro and Mary H. Sims (pp. 21–29) write on the ways in which Walker was influenced by Hurston's work, particularly *Mules and Men;* and Howard (pp. 139–46) focuses on *The Temple of My Familiar* and *Possessing the Secret of Joy*. One has to give the editor credit for undertaking the project, given that neither Walker nor Harcourt Brace Jovanovich would grant permission for passages to be quoted.

Arna Wendell Bontemps is represented in one article this year, Kirkland C. Jones's "Bontemps and the Old South" (*AAR* 27: 179–85), which discusses the influence of Louisiana and the Old South on his writing.

iii Expatriates and Émigrés

a. Vladimir Nabokov   Nabokov inspires no less than four book-length studies. In *Aerial View: Essays on Nabokov's Art and Metaphysics* (Peter Lang) Gennady Barabtarlo explores the language, the quest motif, and other structural and narrative techniques in such works as *The Enchanter, The Russian Lolita, Invitation to a Beheading,* and "Revenge." After an examination of "Nabokov's Cryptography," Barabtarlo concludes with an appendix of archival and bibliographical material. The background information and the comparisons of Nabokov's individual works are particularly useful. David Rampton's *Vladimir Nabokov* (St. Martin's) provides a critical, chronological overview of Nabokov's literary career designed for neophyte and scholar. While Nabokov's novels are examined individually, Rampton makes the necessary critical connections between works to demonstrate the evolution of his writing and ideas. Julian W. Connolly's *Nabokov's Early Fiction: Patterns of Self and Other* (Cambridge, 1992), while providing a thorough analysis of specific texts, is more limited in scope than the books by Barabtarlo and Rampton. Connolly focuses on Nabokov's earliest fiction, the stories he wrote from 1924 until 1939. Edited by Charles Nicol and Gennady Barabtarlo, *A Small Alpine Form: Studies in Nabokov's Short Fiction* (Garland) includes 16 previously unpublished essays that focus on a variety of his most neglected stories. Barabtarlo writes on "Revenge," Connolly on "Fight," D. Barton Johnson on "Terror," Natalia Tolstaia on "A Busy Man," Robert Grossmith on "Perfection," "Time and Ebb" and "A Guide to Berlin," Zoran Kuzmanovich on "A Christmas Story," Stephan Matterson on "Spring in Fialta," John Burt Foster, Jr., on "Mademoiselle O," Galina L. De Roeck on "The Visit to the Museum," Nicol on "The Assistant Producer," Leona Toker on "Signs and Symbols," Yvonne Howell on "Lance," Susan Elizabeth Sweeney on "Scenes from the Life of a Double Monster," Mikhail Epstein on "The Visit to the Museum," and Priscilla Meyer on several of the tales.

In "Nabokov in Postmodernist Land" (*Crit* 34: 247–60) Maurice Couturier questions the definition of postmodernism and debates the modernist/postmodernist issue that surrounds Nabokov's work. Couturier concludes that both Nabokov and Donald Barthelme were archetypal postmodernists whose literary works are "text oriented" rather than late modernists who were "reality oriented" like Gass, Coover, and Pynchon. Joseph Nassar in "Transformations in Exile: The Multilingual Exploits of Nabokov's Pnin and Kinbote" (*VLang* 27: 252–72) considers the "engaging multilingual subtexts" of *Pnin* and *Pale Fire.*

b. Djuna Barnes Djuna Barnes's work continues to inspire critical debate, with an entire issue of *RCF* (13, iii) devoted to it. Scholars interested in a biographical or bibliographical approach may find useful Peter Mailloux's "Djuna Barnes's Mystery in Morocco: Making the Most of Little" (pp. 141–48), Mary Lynn Broe's "'A Love from Back of the Heart': The Story Djuna Wrote for Charles Henri" (pp. 22–32), and Jamie Stevens's "Djuna Barnes: An Updated Bibliography" (pp. 201–04). More significant for the purposes of this chapter are the articles that discuss Barnes's fiction. In "*Ryder* as Contraception: Barnes v. the Reproduction of Mothering" (pp. 97–106) Sheryl Stevenson focuses on the maternal aspects of Barnes's first novel, *Ryder*, which goes beyond patriarchal issues to deal with women and their "enslavement to reproduction." Donna Gerstenberger in "Modern(Post)Modern: Djuna Barnes Among the Others" (pp. 33–40) argues that Barnes, while frequently classified as a modernist, departs from modernist techniques. Citing a variety of works, Gerstenberger distinguishes her from such modernists as T. S. Eliot and Virginia Woolf.

Nightwood continues to attract the most attention. Bonnie Kime Scott in "Barnes Being 'Beast Familiar': Representation on the Margins of Modernism" (*RCF* 13, iii: 41–52) demonstrates the important role that the bestial and the natural play in her writing. Through animal imagery, Barnes "develops a vast intermediate ground of gender, diversified by racial, homosexual, lesbian, and bisexual identifications." Karen Kaivola in "The 'Beast Turning Human': Constructions of the 'Primitive' in *Nightwood*" (*RCF* 13, iii: 172–85) examines the prevalence of the "primitive otherness" in the novel. Significantly, among these "primitive others," Barnes places blacks, lesbians, and Jews; however, lesbian difference is differentiated from African and Jewish difference, which "essentializes both black difference . . . and Jewish difference." In "Djuna Barnes's *Nightwood* and 'the Experience of America'" (*Crit* 34: 100–12) Ahmed Nimeiri disputes Leslie Fiedler's assertion in *Love and Death in the American Novel* that *Nightwood* is flawed because "it is too little concerned with the experience of America." Instead, Nimeiri argues, such experience is central: "That the novel ends with Robin and Nora in America indicates that it is more concerned with the experience of the United States during a time of crisis after the old certainties and values have been tested and proved inadequate." Carolyn Allen in "The Erotics of Nora's Narrative in Djuna Barnes's *Nightwood*" (*Signs* 19: 177–200) thoroughly investigates the "lesbian erotics" that permeate the novel and views *Nightwood* "as a theoretical fiction, or as a fiction of theory—a narrative that produces theory as well as a story" that may be "a critique of Freud's writings on homosexuality and narcissism." Cheryl Plumb's "Revising *Nightwood:* 'A Kind of Glee of Despair' " (*RCF* 13, iii: 149–59) details Barnes's extensive revision of the novel. In "A Book of Repulsive Jews?: Rereading *Nightwood*" (*RCF* 13, iii: 160–71) Meryl Altman poses more questions than answers about Barnes's portrayal of Jews and homosexuals in the novel.

c. Anaïs Nin   Nin scholars will welcome Philip K. Jason's *Anaïs Nin and Her Critics* (Camden House). Divided into six main areas—"Issues in Nin Criticism," "Bibliography, Biography and General Assessments," "Nin's Critical Prose," "Nin's Shorter Fiction," "Nin's Longer Fiction," and "Nin's Diary"—Jason's book attempts "to trace, describe, and assess the critical response to Anaïs Nin's work," which is no easy task. Jason includes a wealth of material and offers a thorough and insightful overview of the Nin canon. A summation of the varied critical responses to Nin's work and a useful primary and secondary bibliography conclude the volume.

iv   Easterners

a. Saul Bellow   Bellow receives less attention this year, although he is the subject of several worthwhile articles. In "From Poem to Cartoon: Comic Irony in Saul Bellow's *More Die of Heartbreak*" (*Crit* 34: 203–19) Elaine B. Safer examines the ironic mode of the novel, with numerous examples of the way the characters' "intellectual aspirations" and "social relationships form . . . basic incongruities." Murray Baumgarten in "Urban Rites and Civic Premises in the Fiction of Saul Bellow, Grace Paley, and Sandra Schor" (*ConL* 34: 395–424) explores the significance of the city in selected works by the three writers. Bellow scholars will also be interested in Joe W. Kraus's "Interviews with Saul Bellow" (*BB* 50: 181–87), a valuable list of interviews conducted from 1953 until 1990.

b. Bernard Malamud   Philip Hanson in "Horror and Ethnic Identity in 'The Jewbird' " (*SSF* 30: 359–66) examines parallels between Poe's "The Raven" and Malamud's story, suggesting that the concept of "fate" in Malamud's text is "defined in more historical terms" than it is in Poe's poem and that Malamud goes further than other contemporary Jewish writers in exploring the subject of Jewishness. James Beyer's "*God's Grace* and Bernard Malamud's Allusions: A Study in Art and Racial Insult"

(*SAJL* 12: 87–93) perceptively analyzes Malamud's many allusions in the novel to such texts as *Moby-Dick, Robinson Crusoe, Animal Farm,* and "A Curtain of Green," concluding that in *God's Grace* Malamud was also rewriting his own earlier novel *The Tenants.* Bonnie Lyons's "The Contrasting Visions of Malamud and O'Connor" (*SAJL* 12: 79–86) provides a thorough comparison of Malamud's and Flannery O'Connor's writings. According to Lyons, the two authors were similar in their interest in spiritual and moral issues, in their use of nature primarily for scenic background, and in their resistance to psychosexual themes. However, as a comparison of "A Good Man Is Hard to Find" and "The Magic Barrel" may indicate, O'Connor and Malamud were also vastly different writers. In "The 'Loathly Landlady,' Chagallian Unions, and Malamudian Parody: 'The Girl of My Dreams' Revisited" (*SSF* 30: 543–54) Joel Salzberg underscores the importance of a neglected story by showing how Malamud used "various levels of parodic play" in it. Through black humor, Malamud "deflate[s] the Chagallian vision of marital union through his own brand of fantasy." Elisa New in "Film and the Flattening of Jewish-American Fiction: Bernard Malamud, Woody Allen, and Spike Lee in the City" (*ConL* 34: 425–50) notes the influence of Malamud's *The Tenants* on other contemporary Jewish writers. According to New, the novel anticipated the urban setting depicted by writer-director Spike Lee in the 1989 film *Do the Right Thing.* In "An Early Version of Malamud's 'The German Refugee' and Other Early Newspaper Sketches" (*SAJL* 12: 94–108) Lawrence M. Lasher discusses some of Malamud's early news sketches as rehearsals of his fiction, particularly "The Refugee," which he revised for publication more than two decades later in "The German Refugee." Much of the article is devoted to reprinting the six early sketches.

Malamud is also represented in a book-length study. Edward A. Abramson's *Bernard Malamud Revisited* (Twayne) contends that Malamud should be grouped with such American writers as Faulkner, Hawthorne, Hemingway, and Melville. Abramson also analyzes Malamud's novels and selected short stories.

c. Shirley Jackson and Kenneth Roberts Both Shirley Jackson and Kenneth Roberts are the subjects of critical books this year. Joan Wylie Hall in *Shirley Jackson: A Study of the Short Fiction* (Twayne) comments on Jackson's work and reprints essays by Jackson and other writers, including Judy Oppenheimer, Helen E. Nebeker, Fritz Oehlschlaeger, and Peter Kosenko. The volume concludes with a selected bibliography of primary and secondary works. The "first book-length account of Roberts's life and letters," Jack Bales's *Kenneth Roberts* (Twayne) covers the writer's career chronologically in six chapters. Particularly relevant is chapter 5, which discusses Roberts's "passion for water dowsing and his three books on the subject." Bales also concludes his book with a brief selected bibliography of primary and secondary works.

v Westerners

a. Frank Waters   Edited by Vine Deloria, Jr., *Frank Waters: Man and Mystic* (Swallow) offers eight memoirs and 13 commentaries by various individuals about Waters and his work. The anthology is a fitting tribute to an accomplished regional writer whose work has only recently received long overdue acclaim.

b. Darcy McNickle   As in 1992, Darcy McNickle is the subject of an excellent article. In "Feather Boy's Promise" (*AIQ* 17: 45–67) Jay Hansford C. Vest demonstrates that *Wind from an Enemy Sky* is more than a dramatization of conflict between Anglo-American and Native American cultures. As more than five pages of explanatory endnotes indicate, Vest's argument is thoroughly grounded in Native American folklore and tradition.

vi Iconoclasts and Detectives

a. William Burroughs   Criticism is sparse again this year on the Beats and detectives. Burroughs scholars will welcome one essay and one book. In "The Long Last Goodbye: Control and Resistance in the Work of William Burroughs" (*JAmS* 27: 223–36) David Ayers argues that Burroughs's writings center on a search for both "physical and spiritual freedom from a range of repressive forces, including, finally, death itself." Barry Miles's *William Burroughs: El Hombre Invisible* (Hyperion) is an insightful addition to Burroughs scholarship. Miles examines the role that Burroughs has played as an icon of popular culture. Part biography, part literary criticism, Miles's book traces Burroughs's career from its beginnings in the Beat Generation.

b. Nathanael West and Henry Miller   West scholarship spikes up slightly this year. In "The Storyteller, the Novelist, and the Advice Columnist: Narrative and Mass Culture in *Miss Lonelyhearts*" (*Novel* 27: 40–61) Rita Barnard draws thematic parallels between *Miss Lonelyhearts* and "The Storyteller: Reflections on the Work of Nikolai Leskov," an essay by Walter Benjamin that was published three years after West's novel. Richard Keller Simon in "Between Capra and Adorno: West's *Day of the Locust* and the Movies of the 1930s" (*MLQ* 54: 513–34) argues that in *The Day of the Locust* West draws extensively on popular Hollywood motion pictures, borrowing contemporary images and characters from B movies and revising episodes from domestic and foreign films. In doing so, West parodies Hollywood productions. *Miss Lonelyhearts* is the ostensible focus of Mark Schoening's "Dr. Lonelyhearts" (*AmLH* 5: 663–85). Burdened with psychoanalytic jargon, Schoening's article is in truth more about Fitzgerald's "The Crack-Up" and *Tender is the Night* than West's text. However, Schoening concludes that both Fitzgerald's and West's novels make statements about modern love, specifically "the popular psychology of conditional love" that emerged during the 1930s.

Henry Miller figures prominently in Erica Jong's *The Devil at Large: Erica Jong on Henry Miller* (Random House), which Jong categorizes as "part memoir, part critical study, part biography, part exploration of sexual politics in our time." Jong offers a fresh look at an old subject in the hope that Miller's message will finally be heard. It was "the connection between Eros and life," Jong notes, that Miller wanted his readers to understand. Jong offers an intimate look at Miller the man and writer, interspersing her narrative with snippets of conversations and letters from Miller and people who knew him.

Arkansas State University

15 Fiction: The 1960s to the Present

Jerome Klinkowitz

What was innovation? The conceptual incongruity of this question does not prevent it from being asked, even as scholars of the last great period of fictive experimentalism look forward to what they believe will be the next. As the generation that pioneered certain styles of antirepresentation in the 1960s takes leave of the present scene, critics have begun taking longer views of their work. At the same time, key figures collect their nonfiction as a way of helping shape this perspective. And as for what comes next, this year's most thoughtful commentators are already placing bets on who will be the most studied writers as the millenium turns.

i General Studies

For a new edition of his highly respected *The Modern American Novel* (Viking) Malcolm Bradbury redrafts three chapters, totaling nearly 100 pages, that sort out the past three decades as three distinct eras in terms of literary innovation, disruption, and renovation. The 1960s were indeed transformative of society as well as of fiction; Bradbury describes the period's "spirit of avant-garde revival" and credits it as being "as behavioral as it was aesthetic." From these beginnings, writers of the 1970s turned inward to more personal concerns, narrowing the focus to their own imaginations. By the 1980s, fictive attention turned outward once again, but this time to engage realism in experimental terms. A more judgmental but equally synthesizing approach is taken by Richard Kostelanetz in his *Dictionary of the Avant-Gardes* (Chicago Review), where early successes in performance (John Barth), typography (Ray-

My thanks to Julie Huffman for help with the research toward this essay.

mond Federman), and absurdist visions of science and history (Thomas Pynchon) yield to more academically acceptable work later in each author's career. Remaining independent of universities for employment and audience is Kostelanetz's subtext, as is evident in the sustained avant-gardism of such novelists as Kenneth Gangemi and Madeline Gins.

Ever since Alan Wilde's *Middle Grounds* advocated a new style of "mid-fiction" to moderate the extremes of innovation and traditionalism (see *ALS 1987*, pp. 284–85), critics have sought useful metaphors for fiction that eschews adversarial polemics. Most successful is Arthur M. Saltzman, whose *The Novel in the Balance* (So. Car.) takes nothing away from the most radical of fictive experiments while showing how such tactics achieve a sense of the provisional so characteristic of our times. In the wake of earlier ruptures by John Hawkes, E. L. Doctorow, Robert Coover, Don DeLillo, Leslie Marmon Silko, and Ronald Sukenick, newer writers such as Marilynne Robinson, Tim O'Brien, Paul Auster, Joseph McElroy, Charles Johnson, and Stephen Dixon strive for balance and consolidation—without, of course, denying any of the valid points such necessary ruptures had established. Saltzman's greatest contribution may be in his broadened understanding of that much-maligned style of fiction called literary minimalism, which he redefines as a mode of inquiry far beyond the satirical. Yet there are still merits in a strategy of opposition, as Jay Clayton demonstrates in *The Pleasures of Babel: Contemporary American Literature and Theory* (Oxford). As opposed to those critics who believe contemporary American fiction has become realistically conservative, Clayton builds the case for "an oppositional technique" that thanks to an association with "unauthorized forms of knowledge" yields a genuinely new style of writing, found most readily in the multicultural literatures previously excluded from academic discourse.

Gay literature is one of the multicultural interests Clayton studies, and his thesis is challenged by James W. Jones's contribution to editors Timothy F. Murphy and Suzanne Poirier's *Writing AIDS: Gay Literature, Language, and Analysis* (Columbia). "Refusing the Name: The Absence of AIDS in Recent American Gay Male Fiction" (pp. 225–43) makes the case for just the pressures of "authorized language" that Clayton assumes gay literature escapes. When writers create characters who are "innocent victims" of AIDS, their act assumes that there can be someone who deserves the disease. Because AIDS itself is often not named in fiction, its linguistic absence becomes a signification in itself, which in turn may escape the grammar of marginalization. More directly outspoken was opposition to the Vietnam war, a challenge David Wyatt studies in *Out of the Sixties: Storytelling and the Vietnam Generation* (Cambridge). Being antiwar generated a sense of personal involvement with an era, creating a tension between one's self and history; this fresh approach to identity eventually converted resistance to history into a storytelling impulse evident in the works of Ann Beattie, Sue Miller, Ethan Mordden, Alice Walker, and Michael Herr, as well as in the films of George Lucas. Who speaks (and how) are issues Louise K. Barnett finds central in *Authority and Speech*. For her, Kurt Vonnegut speaks in a Twainian voice well beyond the bounds of legitimate satire; his *Breakfast of Champions* shows forces as beyond human control, and public language as meaningless or misleading. Pynchon's *The Crying of Lot 49* opposes such meaninglessness with open-ended signification, while Donald Barthelme's *Snow White* conflates speech with narrative in the fundamental materiality of culture. Finally, there is the now familiar ploy of defamiliarization; Gordon Slethaug finds it useful in *The Play of the Double in Postmodern American Fiction* (So. Ill.) for explaining Pynchon's carnivalization in *Gravity's Rainbow,* John Hawkes's demystification of accepted opinions in *The Blood Oranges,* Barth's doubling of culture and literature in *Lost in the Funhouse,* Richard Brautigan's destabilizations of artistic perception in *The Hawkline Monster,* and Federman's exploration of fictionality beyond conventional author/character distinctions in *Double or Nothing.*

The consolidation of Raymond Federman's position as a mainstream author angers Kostelanetz (for its departure from the avant-garde) and pleases Slethaug (who finds in Federman's work an apt conclusion to the innovations first undertaken by Vladimir Nabokov). Federman's own view of fiction's course is given full perspective in his *Critifiction: Postmodern Essays* (SUNY), a volume dedicated to the proposition that in creating fiction one necessarily engenders a discourse about it. If writing itself is quotation, then the fictive imagination is the only tool capable of permitting the "flagrant displacements" that can make such fiction interesting. Since the central topic of Federman's fiction—the loss of his family in the Holocaust—is unstateable, he "writes in order to cancel, or better yet, in order to absent the very story he wants to tell," thus making the issue of quotation irrelevant. Postmodern fiction, the last gasp of innovation, was thus motivated "by doubt and distrust," facing as it did the impossibility and the necessity of writing in the face of subjects equally unspeakable. Federman turns all this to his advantage by adopting a pose of self-reflexiveness, which in highly ironic fashion allows him to destroy any novel he is in the process of writing. Most instructive are Federman's admitted influences: not the overly thematic fictive treatises of Nazi atrocities, but the improvisation of jazz, the action of Abstract Expressionism, and the American publication and literary success of such authors as Beckett, Borges, and (naturally) Nabokov. A similar program of influences and responses distinguishes the commentary of Rod Padgett in *Blood Work: Selected Prose* (Bamberger), while novelist William O'Rourke's *Signs of the Literary Times* (SUNY) weaves a similar fabric from the ostensibly different threads of social and religious involvement.

One of Federman's early advocates, Larry McCaffery, finds himself in 1994 heeding Kostelanetz's dictum and looking for something new. But he also risks censure from Clayton, who feels critics such as McCaffery have given up prematurely on mainstream fiction in favor of science fiction and cyberpunk when in fact there are genuinely oppositional voices in the multiculture (opposed to the 1960s counterculture once sufficiently inclusive to number Federman as a disruptivist). For today's new world of Generation X-ers, McCaffery proposes *Avant-Pop* (Black Ice), an interactive critifiction in which he plays a hard-boiled crime-novel detective to Kathy Acker's B-movie sexuality, an approach others have regretted as the fetishization of this author important for so many other things. For *RCF* 13, ii, presented as the first of this otherwise conservative journal's "Younger Writers" issues, McCaffery guest-edits a series of responses to his choices for the future: William T. Vollman, Susan Daitch, and David Foster Wallace. The most reliable contribution, "Where an Author Might Be Standing" (pp. 39–45) by Madison Smartt Bell, measures the innovation of these authors against innovation's ultimate test: liberation. Their cause, Bell believes, is motivated by a reaction against minimalism, just as minimalism was motivated as a backlash against that most reductive style of innovative fiction, metafiction. Here Arthur G. Saltzman's rereading of what was minimalism helps close the circle and leaves scholarship free to engage truly contemporary fiction on its own and not label-makers' terms.

A reliable survey of Generation X material is provided by Elizabeth Young and Graham Caveney in *Shopping in Space: Essays on America's Blank Generation Fiction* (Atlantic Monthly). Bret Easton Ellis, Jay McInerney, Michael Chabon, Joel Rose, Tama Janowitz, Lynn Tillman, Gary Indiana, David Wojnarowicz, and Dennis Cooper are studied in chapters written alternately by Caveney and Young, but most valuable is

Young's introductory "Children of the Revolution: Fiction Takes to the Streets" (pp. 1–20), where the fiction of these younger writers is related to the innovations of Federman, Sukenick, and Steve Katz—an approach suggested but not as completely explored by Robert Siegle in *Suburban Ambush* (see *ALS 1989*, pp. 256–57).

How all of this will look a hundred or a thousand years from now is a thought that occurs to Ishmael Reed, whose *Airing Dirty Laundry* (Addison-Wesley) makes a strong case that fiction works best when liberating imaginations from the tyranny of unexamined assumptions—in other words, when deconstructing perceived reality. The virtue of Reed's critical deconstructions is that they make no distinctions between perceived friends or enemies. The joy of reading his literary essays collected here is that one finds him asking all groups to examine their relationship to the "official religions" of their group, whether it be the white middle-class bias of the critical establishment that calls "Tom Wolfe's anti-Semitic, antiblack *Bonfire of the Vanities* the 'defining work' of the 1980s" or the empire-building tactics of a professional avant-garde that capitalizes itself on funds from public universities and the National Endowment for the Arts. That self-styled punk fiction is written by young professionals trained in postgraduate MFA programs is less offensive than the fact that like minor league baseball players these young writers-to-be arrive at such institutions as the University of Iowa Writers Workshop already under contract to agents, a privilege NCAA regulations make impossible for their college athlete classmates. Throughout *Airing Dirty Laundry* Reed's sympathy is with the alienated and the marginalized, and it is among them that he finds the most persuasive contemporary fiction.

ii Women

Donald J. Greiner's *Women Without Men: Female Bonding and the American Novel of the 1980s* (So. Car.) describes an innovative canon shift whereby male characters in fiction still bond but reject the traditional mandate to leave women behind as they do so. Female bonding comes to the fore as a strategy against exploitation, Gloria Naylor being especially adept at portraying an emptiness at the center of African American masculinity. Here is where Greiner's study becomes profitably controversial by asking whether such female bonding will exclude men even as male bonding just now no longer excludes women. In Greiner's view, patriarchal texts need not be completely repudiated but can be revised to accommodate women who accept calls to quest into the wilderness; Joan Didion and Diane Johnson are his prime examples. Elsewhere, Greiner finds the "old marriage plot" still lingering, but as in the novels of Hilma Wolitzer, Meg Wolitzer, Marilynne Robinson, and others, women turn to other women for the strength that bonding provides.

What Greiner would consider an earlier, "Movement" stage in fiction with women as an issue is treated well by Katherine B. Payant in *Becoming and Bonding: Contemporary Feminism and Popular Fiction by American Women Writers* (Greenwood) and by Lorna Sage in *Women in the House of Fiction: Post-War Woman Novelists* (Routledge, 1992). Payant sees a movement in the Movement from sexual politics toward cultural feminism; her prime cases are Marge Piercy's radical feminism (as polemic), Mary Gordon's white ethnicity (as cultural), and Toni Morrison's Afra-Americanism (as a womanist ideal). Lorna Sage's range is necessarily broader, with the benefit of seeing Joyce Carol Oates react to this movement with a form of "addicted writing"—that is, fiction generated by other fiction as pastiche or parody.

Ethnicity becomes an important issue in Bonnie Winsbro's *Supernatural Forces: Belief, Difference, and Power in Contemporary Works by Ethnic Women* (Mass.). In the hands of "ethnic women" spirituality performs differently than in the older literary canon; spirit now is not so much a power over life as a tool for communication. Lee Smith's *Oral History* uses an Appalachian view of the supernatural to define subjects from the outside, showing the problematics of identity being able to emerge; Louise Erdrich writes *Tracks* to show how Native American identity is defined from both inside and outside, its power threatened by contacts with the inside; Leslie Marmon Silko's *Ceremony* considers how to survive this contact and return home. A sense of movement distinguishes Naylor's *Mama Day,* Morrison's *Beloved,* and Maxine Hong Kingston's *The Woman Warrior,* in which strength can be gained from both civilized and native sources, present selves are defined by confrontations with the past, and identities are grasped by giving life to one's ghosts. A political slant on these same issues is taken by Chikwenye Okonjo Ogunyemi in "Womanism: The Dynamics of the Contemporary Black Female Novel in English" (pp. 231–48), a contribution to editors Vèvè A. Clark, Ruth-Ellen B. Joeres, and Madelon Sprengnether's *Revising the Word and the World: Essays in Feminist Literary Criticism* (Chicago). Extraliterary determinants on novels by African Americans prompt different sexual strategies, and therefore a different style of feminism: womanism, of which resistance to sexism is just one part (together with colonial, racial, national, and economic issues).

Sisters, mothers, and female selves continue as focusing devices for critical studies. Editors JoAnna Stephens Mink and Janet Doubler Ward use *Significance of Sibling Relations in Literature* to frame Connie R. Schomburg's "To Survive Whole, To Save the Self: The Role of Sisterhood in the Novels of Toni Morrison" (pp. 149–57), in which sisterhood is redefined beyond the biological to include emotional bonding, particularly as women form a larger community; the advantage of such redefinition is the bulwark provided against the dangers of estrangement, in which wholeness and worth as an individual relate to values of more broadly defined sisterhood. That a nongendered utopian future retains the idea of motherhood is pondered by Elaine Orr in "Mothering as Good Fiction: Instances from Marge Piercy's *Woman on the Edge of Time*" (*JNT* 23: 61–79); it is the process of fictive re-visioning that necessitates this role. Deborah Kuhlmann's "Mothering Our 'Dream Children' from Gail Godwin" (*Short Story* n.s. 1, i: 61–73) identifies the need to re-create and regenerate new life from the ruins of experience as a similar act.

iii Toni Morrison and Other African Americans

A major step toward integrating mainland African American fiction with offshore developments is taken by Paul Gilroy in *The Black Atlantic: Modernity and Double Consciousness* (Harvard). Like most current scholars, Gilroy gives prominent attention to Morrison's work, reading *Beloved* for "its interest in history and social memory" as expressed "in an experimental and openly political spirit." Gilroy diverges when he argues that her success "should not be exclusively assimilated to the project of building an ethnically particular or nationalist cultural canon," because the logic of her text transcends such boundaries. In revisiting the conditions of slavery, larger confrontations are being restaged, including those between "rational, scientific, and enlightened Euro-American thought and the supposedly primitive outlook of prehistorical, cultureless, and bestial African slaves." When considered with Afro-Caribbean situations, the fiction of Morrison and other mainlanders takes shape as a "counterculture of modernity" that Gilroy calls "Black Atlantic," not so much an ethnicity as a reinvention drawing on diverse materials "sampled" (as the term from hip-hop music puts it) from hybrid cultural forms. Fiction thus produced recognizes and responds to the fact that radicalized reason is complicit with white supremacist terror; a usable black vernacular culture thus succeeds beyond the period nationalisms such supremacy would enforce. As a multicultural ideal, Gilroy's vision shares much with the accessibly deconstructive method of Ishmael Reed's *Airing Dirty Laundry* (see *i* above).

Complementing Gilroy's thesis with more specific readings is Moira Ferguson's *Colonialism and Gender from Mary Wollstonecraft to Jamaica Kincaid* (Columbia). Kincaid's *Annie John* and *A Small Place* are pertinent to gender relations and colonial rebellion in a special way because *A Small Place* intertextualizes *Annie John,* particularly as conflicts can be reexamined beyond the character's own capacity to identify; Annie John thus "has changed herself into a sign of language without voice," something that a stronger vernacular evident in *The Black Atlantic* would hope to rectify. How Clarence Major, a mainland writer drawn at times to the Caribbean experience, undertakes this task is studied profitably by Nathaniel Mackey in *Discrepant Engagement: Dissonance, Cross-Culturality, and Experimental Writing* (Cambridge); here, rational definitions are set against chaos, with a constructive emphasis on such issues as animality, "unChristianity," perceived uncleanness, and irrationality. Major's approach is to exploit technical disruptions and take iconoclastic stances in ways that question nonvernacular language's access to reality. Back home, Reed does much the same thing in his "grotesque attacks on American social, economic, and political avatars," says Kathryn Hume in "Ishmael Reed and the Problematics of Control" (*PMLA* 108: 506–18), an important essay that corrects misapprehensions of Reed's presumed idiosyncracies by associating them with the similar thematics of Pynchon, Acker, Piercy, Norman Mailer, and ultimately Burroughs—a reminder that such undertakings are part of a much larger transformation that entails the development of American literature in general.

Reed's work would change the American canon from within. Morrison's fiction undertakes a less disruptive but equally effective quest in the manner of its own composition. Two contributors to editor W. M. Verhoeven's *Rewriting the Dream: Reflections on the Changing American Literary Canon* (Rodopi, 1992) make this point, Richard Todd outlining in "Toni Morrison and Canonicity: Acceptance or Appropriation" (pp. 43–59) how *Beloved* makes special demands on its readers by turning a story of slavery's terrors into one of art by means of plotting, Kofi

Owusu finding a unity of critical theory and fictive expression that lets Morrison relate the idea of a "master narrative" to the circumstance of slavery itself ("Rethinking Canonicity: Toni Morrison and the [Non]Canonic 'Other,'" pp. 60–74). Denise Heinze turns back to W. E. B. Du Bois's thoughts about individuals living two lives as insiders to one tradition and outsiders to another as a way of explaining Morrison's two-sided use of dominant language. *The Dilemma of "Double-Consciousness" in Toni Morrison's Novels* (Georgia) thus shows how new meaning can be slipped into old linguistic forms. Each of Morrison's successive novels revoices in bolder fashion earlier concerns, including the aesthetics of needs, the way idealized beauty reduces human beings to objects, the forces against black matriarchy, and the Protestant work ethic as a catalyst of greed. The resolution to doubleness is in fantasy, Heinze believes, crediting Morrison with an ultimately spiritual response to life. How the power of narration is essentially undifferentiated from the power of creation is established by Shirley A. Stave in "Toni Morrison's *Beloved* and the Vindication of Lilith" (*SoAR* 58, i: 49–66), a reading that deconstructs "the demon mother" so that "mothers and children can interact as full human beings, free of mythologies that would limit and damage them." As for the symbolic, Jean Wyatt handles that in "Giving Body to the Word: The Maternal in Toni Morrison's *Beloved*" (*PMLA* 108: 474–88). Once recognizing herself as a subject, Sethe is able to narrate the mother-daughter story in a way that reinvents language capable of expressing "the desperation of the slave mother who killed her daughter"; yet this "enclosure of the mother in the symbolic" consigns Beloved herself to the world "outside language and therefore outside narrative memory," where her story "continues to haunt the borders of a symbolic order that excludes it."

Morrison's *Beloved* figures as a central text in Charles Scruggs's *Sweet Home*. For Scruggs, legitimization depends on a community's restoration of what to other eyes is an invisible city, a matter of transparent presences within old definitions; history can be used to make the past relevant to the future, formed as it is around the conditions of black life; what is to be admired in *Beloved* is its "escape, however ambiguous, from a hopeless repetition of action and memory." Commodity culture, of course, can quickly make such stories invisible, and Morrison's *The Bluest Eye* strives to write them before this can happen. Such is the point made by Jane Kuenz in *"The Bluest Eye:* Notes on History, Community, and Black Female Subjectivity" (*AAR* 27: 421–31).

Alice Walker's major influence is given thorough study by the contributors to *Alice Walker and Zora Neale Hurston*. Walker reacts to Hurston as a singer rather than as a member of the literati; rather than appropriate people's stories, she gave them back their own, something Walker herself would emulate. In the fiction of each, both feminine and subregional traditions are shared, with an emphasis on characters' abilities to speak of one's self, a trait enabled by the narrative generations of folklore. Today Walker's work is in turn transformed as it is marketed by film to a wider audience. Joan Digby considers these ramifications in "From Walker to Spielberg: Transformation of *The Color Purple*" (pp. 157–74), an important contribution to editor Peter Reynolds's *Novel Images: Literature in Performance* (Routledge) that suggests transformation itself is apparent as the novel's essence.

A question remains whether novels such as *The Color Purple* are Southern or Northern fiction. This issue and others are explored in several contributions to *AAR* 27, ii, including one that suggests "the encapsulation of creativity" can be as limiting as chattel slavery and colonialism. Kiarri T.-H. Cheatwood titles his essay "Fire-Casting as Eternal De-Fascination with Death: Writing About the South, and the Responsible Necessity of Reading and Knowing Black South Writing in the Quest for Afrikan World Salvation and Restitution" (pp. 301–13) and charges that "As the South is the stepchild of this illegal nation and, thus, an endless victim of poor press, Black South Writing is underknown and, thus, underrecognized in favor of Up-South or Northern Black Literature."

iv Amy Tan, Maxine Hong Kingston, and Other Asian Americans

A major, defining work joins the critical canon with the publication of Sau-ling Cynthia Wong's *Reading Asian American Literature: From Necessity to Extravagance* (Princeton). Wong's special interest is in the intertextuality of these writings, a reinforcement of patterns not readily apparent to universalistic views. For example, she makes clear how "encounters with the racial shadow" function well beyond conventional concepts of the double; universalist theories can only partly explain the psychology and physicality of violence for a radically marginalized group. It is Wong's belief that Asian-American minorities have never had the chance to define their own personalities or feel completely free to participate in what are their societies, something novels and stories by such writers as Frank Chin and Kingston strive to correct.

Asian-American work gets beneficial attention as well in *All My Relatives: Community in Contemporary Ethnic American Literatures* (Michigan) by Bonnie TuSmith. There is a bias against clinging to the past that complicates such writing, TuSmith suggests, but finds a healthy counterforce in the indigenous language of a community. Like Wong, she perceives a pressure in Asian-American affairs toward being "a model minority," something Ishmael Reed notices in *Airing Dirty Laundry* as well, given that such pressures are often used by the dominant culture as a weapon against African Americans (see *i* above). But works by Frank Chin and Kingston resist these pressures, radicalizing the notion of what constitutes success.

Amy Tan receives welcome attention in Walter Shear's "Generational Differences and the Diaspora in *The Joy Luck Club*" (*Crit* 34: 193–99). It is her novel's structure rather than its specific theme that conveys "not merely the individual psychic tragedies of those caught up" in the post-Chiang diaspora "but the enormous agony of a culture emeshed in a transforming crisis." This structure, interestingly enough, has canonical roots in the work of story cycles by Sherwood Anderson, Hemingway, and Faulkner—"books that feature distinct, individual narratives but that as a group simultaneously dramatize the panorama of a critical transition in cultural values." Kingston's *The Woman Warrior* receives fresh treatment by Thomas J. Ferraro in *Ethnic Passages,* where it is characterized as fulfilling the classic hope of ethnic literature: that one's native community can receive into its care the gift of song that has been won from outside but which, brought home, sounds a cry for the expansion of human possibility within. A similar process underscores the thesis of John J. Deeney's "Of Monkeys and Butterflies: Transformation in M. H. Kingston's *Tripmaster Monkey* and D. H. Hwang's *M. Butterfly*" (*MELUS* 18, iv: 21–39), where character transformation transcends stereotyping, at least as a strategy.

v Cynthia Ozick and Other Jewish Americans

The structures of a work of fiction are often its most compelling elements. How one author uses structures to examine her subject from a multiplicity of angles anchors Elaine M. Kauvar's analysis in *Cynthia Ozick's Fiction: Tradition and Convention* (Indiana). Ozick strives well beyond mere discoveries of self and history; for her, both Hebraism and Hellenism simultaneously inherit and betray the tradition she wishes to explicate. Pitting tradition against the creativity of art yields new appreciations of responsibility. Ozick's fiction is especially valuable in calculating and dramatizing the psychological consequences of unleashing rage, an attitude that places her beyond strictly confining definitions of the ethnic or feminist.

Gender politics would seem to be a hot subject among critics of Philip Roth. In "Ventriloquists' Conversations: The Struggle for Gender Dialogue in E. L. Doctorow and Philip Roth" (*ConL* 34: 512–37) Marshall Bruce Gentry supposes "a historical opposition between feminism and Judaism" that implies compromises with assimilation; but here Bakhtinian theoretics comes to the rescue, letting Roth's and Doctorow's otherwise gender-bound novels be read as dialogues with what socioreligious tradition would say is unspeakable. That Roth faces a similar struggle with the tradition of sports literature is entertained in my own "Philip Roth's Anti-Baseball Novel" (*WHR* 47: 30–40), in which "tapping into such ready-made signs and structures as the game and its histories provide solves a problem Roth had been wrestling with since the 1960s": that current reality outstrips the ability of a novelist to fictionalize it.

An exceptionally insightful treatment of an understudied novel is provided by Robert Merrill in "Mailer's *Tough Guys Don't Dance* and the Detective Traditions" (*Crit* 34: 232–46). The nuances of film noir are crucial to understanding Mailer's art, given its retrospective cast, just as the book itself is filled with a "stylized excess" that recalls this movie subgenre in a way that fleshes out its protagonist's problems (and in the process avoids the formal confusions that hamper *An American Dream*).

vi Walker Percy and Other Southerners

Two major but previously unpaired authors contribute to Paul Giles's thesis in *American Catholic Arts and Fictions* (Cambridge, 1992): Walker Percy, whose "analytical Catholicism" functions as the convert's choice of "one possibility among others," and Donald Barthelme, whose rebellion against institutionalized forms of reason generated a fictive response as remarkable as that previously attributed to Barthelme's revulsion against self-indulgent romantic egoism. For Giles, "Barthelme's ghostly Catholicism is no philosophical system but a lurking irrational shadow, an intimation of absence that seems to undermine the premises of quotidian life." Another innovator, Ishmael Reed, is linked with Walker Percy by Violet Harrington Bryan in *Myth of New Orleans,* a study that sees *The Moviegoer* as moving away from the romantic myth of New Orleans and beyond the retreat of suicide, while Reed embraces the city's Hoodoo as a true multicultural aesthetic, relating the jazz impulse to historical mythmaking. To complete the year's sudden impulse of relating Percy to the experimental fiction crowd so apparently distant from him, Patrick Semway, S.J., offers "Gaps and Codes: Walker Percy's 'Carnival in Gentilly'" (*Shenandoah* 43, i: 47–56), which tracks this story's history as a part of *The Moviegoer* extracted for Barthelme's journal, *Location;* the extract itself motivates the subsequently published novel as a "countersong," the parody of which allows both works to be seen in a new light.

A certain amount of revisionism characterizes work on William Styron as well. The author's *Inheritance of Night: Early Drafts of* Lie Down in Darkness (Duke) includes an introduction by James L. W. West III that draws attention to various narrative strategies besides the acknowledged Faulknerian ones; most interesting is the presence of F. Scott Fitzgerald in the handling of incest. Some of this revision comes from the hand of an attorney and former law clerk, Daniel S. Fabricant, whose "Thomas R. Gray and William Styron: Finally, A Critical Look at the 1831 *Confessions of Nat Turner*" (*American Journal of Legal History* 37: 331–61) examines the trial history of this important source for Styron's novel; his conclusion is that Gray's document was not admitted into evidence and thus "can no longer be seen as the legitimate and accurate historical record of Nat's prosecution," much less as a valid determinant of destiny.

Long-overdue attention to one of the region's most interesting authors is well paid in *Perspectives on Cormac McCarthy* (Miss.), ed. Edwin T. Arnold and Dianne C. Luce. David Paul Ragan's "Values and Structure in *The Orchard Keeper*" (pp. 15–25) finds a narrative method in this work's apparently wandering structure, while Arnold counters fears of McCarthy's nihilism by crediting the direction of resolutions (as always toward the possibility of redemption) in "Naming, Knowing and Nothingness: McCarthy's Moral Parables" (pp. 43–67). The idea of "settlement" is the author's major theme, says Thomas D. Young, Jr., in "The Imprisonment of Sensibility: *Suttree*" (pp. 95–120). Death as ritual rather than mystery informs Steven Shaviro's "'The Very Life of the Darkness': A Reading of *Blood Meridian*" (pp. 143–56). Other essays deal with McCarthy's success as a screenwriter, the gnostic centrality to his tragic vision, and the essential homeward journey evident in his work. A sound bibliography (pp. 195–210) by Luce concludes this volume, a model of its kind for the study of an important yet understudied author.

Concerns of women and African Americans intersect in editor Carol S. Manning's *Female Tradition.* "Dismantling Stereotypes: Interracial Friendships in *Meridian* and *A Mother and Two Daughters*" (pp. 140–57) allows Suzanne W. Jones to show how Alice Walker and Gail Godwin "dismantle the stereotypes of Southern womanhood produced by the patriarchy of the Old South," stereotypes that survived both abolition and desegregation. The shared experiences based on commonality of gender and class do not erase difference but see that it is "not misread or misnamed" as anything other than culturally conditioned. This same volume includes Mary Hughes Brookhart's "Spiritual Daughters of the Black American South" (pp. 125–37), which considers the South a psychological space that one can reclaim without having lived there (as Toni Morrison has done); role models and notions of authority link traditionally Southern black roles to those of modern women, Brookhart believes.

vii Leslie Marmon Silko and Other Writers of the West and Southwest

"Writing Nature: Silko and Native Americans as Nature Writers" (*MELUS* 18, ii: 47–60) is Lee Schweniger's occasion for establishing this group's contribution to the otherwise Euro-American phenomenon popularized by Thoreau, Muir, Joseph Wood Krutch, Aldo Leopold, Edward Abbey, and Annie Dillard, a contribution noteworthy for its "startling contrast" with strictly European examples. Silko, N. Scott Momaday, and others "write nature" well beyond the confines of "nature writing" as a genre and escape the tradition (dating to Linnaeus and Gilbert White) that informs the Euro-American. As a result, nature is treated in less dominant ways in their work.

Though ostensibly a Southern writer, Cormac McCarthy "has been concerned with things western (and Latin American) . . . for at least the last decade," Tom Pilkington indicates in "Fate and Free Will on the American Frontier: Cormac McCarthy's Western Fiction" (*WAL* 27: 311–22). The result has been an especially harsh realism in McCarthy's recent fiction, a result of combining his Southern influences (O'Connor and Faulkner) with the existentialism of R. G. Vliet and the passionate polemics of Edward Abbey, especially as those polemics relate to ecological survival.

A writer already discussed as a generalist and African American (see *i* and *iii* above) is treated as a Westerner by Jay Boyer in *Ishmael Reed* (BSWWS No. 110). Reed's California base provides the ethnic diversity he so values in fiction, but there are strong elements of the old-fashioned Wild West in novels as early as *Yellow Back Radio Broke Down* and as recent as *The Terrible Threes*, where the word "cowboy" serves as "an epithet for reckless behavior." Yet cowboys themselves are seen sympathetically as characters caught in a historical transition that allows no easy solution, a predicament Reed identifies with that of African Americans (where the rich tradition of "HooDoo" offers capacities denied by white culture, which when successful "puts the black beyond the boundaries of white acceptance"). In the process of struggling with these transitions Reed reinvents the novel, much as have his most innovative colleagues.

viii The Mannerists: John Updike and John Cheever

Published nearly one-third of a century ago, John Updike's second novel continues to merit study for its own sake and for what it says about his ongoing, immensely productive career. For *New Essays on* Rabbit, Run (Cambridge) editor Stanley Trachtenberg has no trouble finding four first-rate studies that explain why this very early work remains Updike's best-known fiction. Trachtenberg's own "Introduction" (pp. 1–29) is a model reputation study that draws on Updike's own reports of compositional method and intent. The author's widely noted style fascinates Philip Stevick, who in "The Full Range of Updike's Prose" (pp. 31–52) remarks how *Rabbit, Run* can be remembered for its "stylistic moments" even beyond their narrative functions; such style is certainly foregrounded more than is done by most contemporaries, but it becomes especially noteworthy in this novel because it is just one of two voices, the other being the deliberately "lumpish banality" employed to characterize Rabbit's life. A good survey of how this novel fits its times is provided by Sanford Pinsker. His "Restlessness in the 1950s: What Made Rabbit Run?" (pp. 53–76) considers how this decade of conformity so effectively generated the rebellious response Updike employs in realizing his character, Harry "Rabbit" Angstrom. How this work fascinates Europeans is explored by Erik Kielland-Lund in "The Americanness of

Rabbit, Run: A Transatlantic View" (pp. 77–94); while an exceptionally original treatment can be found in Stacey Olster's " 'Unadorned Woman, Beauty's Home Image': Updike's *Rabbit, Run*" (pp. 95–117), where hindsight gained from subsequent novels "may indicate women's imaginative limitations to an author who is devoted to a real/unreal continuum that defines God as 'the union of the actual and the ideal' and, in wedding the tangible and transcendental, conceives of all things as 'masks for God.' "

Just the opposite philosophical orientation characterizes the most typical work of John Cheever, according to Daniel T. O'Hara in *Radical Parody: American Culture and Critical Agency After Foucault* (Columbia, 1992). Drawing on the contingency theories of Bloom and Rorty, the critic finds in Cheever a convincing portrayal of the contingent imagination in America, a society in which there is no belief in universals but only adaptation to current rules of the game; such a context breeds reactive practice along the lines of 19th-century England where architecture could produce the studied "folly." The other side of Cheever, spiritual to the point of emulating Dante, is explored by Stanley J. Kozikowski, whose "Damned in a Fair Life: Cheever's 'The Swimmer' " (*SSF* 30: 367–75) traces structural parallels with the *Inferno.* David Scott Ward discovers similarly profound antecedents for an understudied story in "King Lear and Human Dignity in John Cheever's 'The Fourth Alarm' " (*Short Story* n.s. 1, ii: 64–67).

ix Realists Old and New

A candid appraisal of the writer who sought to reestablish literary realism for his time is made by John M. Howell in *Understanding John Gardner* (So. Car.). Crucial to Howell's interpretation is that Gardner lost control of his art after 1977, failing as a scholar (with Chaucer) and a critic (the debacle of *On Moral Fiction*). At his best, Gardner used characters as clowns, with consequent advantages and limitations; his cartoonist's eye captures the gothic as it inhabits the real. Against Sartre, Gardner positioned himself as a poet-priest in search of order, Howell believes, with plenty of statements from the author himself to back it up. For Robert A. Morace, the situation is perhaps more complex than even Gardner viewed it. "*Dialogues* and Dialogics" (*MLS* 23, iii: 73–90) draws on Bakhtin to show that *The Sunlight Dialogues* is anything but a novel of ideas culminating in a "moral advance." Instead, read dialogically it becomes "an openended, multidirectional sign" that succeeds as "an interdependent, unfinalizable whole," making Clumly's supposedly conclusive speech eminently conditional.

More reductively thematic is Joyce Carol Oates, if her most appreciative critics are to have their way. An underlying structure of "family, power, and resistance" compels Marilyn C. Wesley to see Oates as an especially driven writer in *Refusal and Transgression in Joyce Carol Oates' Fiction* (Greenwood). Oates challenges, questions, and eventually revolts against the authority of such structures, especially when they concern the economic power of family; she is especially adept at resisting "engendered relationships that encode that power and regulate its experiential effects." Oates proves herself to be Jay Woodruff's most articulately revealing commentator in *A Piece of Work: Five Writers Discuss Their Revisions* (Iowa). Her method, even for short stories, consists of cutting and pasting, working on discreet sections of the narrative at different times with no complete drafting through; as a result, the voice of her fiction is always changing, especially as she likes to begin with endings and revises much even after publication. Like many authors, she has thrown away her word processor in favor of retyping her work as a way of cultivating its voice. Rewarding attention to *By the North Gate* is paid by Greg Johnson in "A Barbarous Eden: Joyce Carol Oates's First Collection" (*SSF* 30: 1–14); this less frequently studied volume showcases her major influences (Nietzsche, Faulkner, and O'Connor) in a microcosmic way and demonstrates her thematic inclusiveness (more apparent here before she began experimenting with form and technique in her bolder works of the late 1960s and early 1970s).

Another resister "to every kind of oppression" is studied by Mara Faulkner in *Protest and Possibility in the Writing of Tillie Olsen* (Virginia). Olsen's choice of characters is particularly successful because she "makes silent persons writers," in the process practicing an "organic feminist criticism" that generates communal dialogue. A distinctly different style of resistance is evident in the subject of Ernest Suarez's *James Dickey and the Politics of Canon: Assessing the Savage Ideal* (Missouri), where the author's second novel, *Alnilam*, encapsulates this ideal as a combination of power and imagination. As with Oates, it is a structured bureaucracy that energizes these characters' personalities; yet for Dickey, art will not mix with politics, while poetry remains the purest catalyst for self-realization.

Joan Didion can happily be a political writer, as Sandra Hinchman establishes in "Didion's Political Tropics: *Miami* and the Basis for Community" (pp. 233–39), a contribution to editor Sharon Felton's *The Critical Response to Joan Didion* (Greenwood). Like Didion's Los Angeles, the Florida metropolis lacks a unifying narrative, allowing Didion to impose one via her bleak vision continued from *Democracy*. Complementing Hinchman's view is Laura Julier's treatment of the nonfiction, "Actual Experience, Preferred Narratives: Didion's *After Henry*" (pp. 248–58), which maps the disjunction between narrative experience and its real-life counterpart; of special note is how culturally approved stories conflict with one's own record of the events. Literary politics characterize Jaye Berman Montresor's "This Was in 1992, in Iowa City: Talking with Ann Beattie" (pp. 219–54) in Montresor's *The Critical Reaction to Ann Beattie* (Greenwood). Beattie responds to critic John W. Aldridge's disparaging of fictive minimalism, but she also reveals analytical interests in a wide range of societal activities that make her fiction anything but spare.

Well beyond charges of minimalism, false or true, is Paul Auster, whose *New York Trilogy* draws increased attention. Its first novel prompts William Lavender to reread mystery-solving as a model of the narrative act, concluding in "The Novel of Critical Engagement: Paul Auster's *City of Glass*" (*ConL* 34: 219–39) that "It is Auster's portrait of the author as a developing function," a "new authorial identity" that can survive "in an age when authority is not necessarily bound to the text by 'spontaneous attribution.'"

x Experimental Realism: Grace Paley and W. P. Kinsella

Of continued interest is representational fiction that violates the conventions of representation. The paradoxes thus raised are faced squarely by Judith Arcana in *Grace Paley's Life Stories: A Literary Biography* (Illinois). Not the least point of Arcana's genius is that she is willing to study Paley's life as well as her art; the volume's true brilliance, however, is its ability to distinguish art from propaganda without sacrificing political pertinence. Especially valuable is how Arcana contrasts Paley's innovations with those of a more inhibited metafictionist, William H. Gass, whose modernist affinities prevent him from privileging voice in the way that Paley does. "Much of what Grace Paley asserts in her stories, as in political action, is the strength and force of individual character embodied in human presence," Arcana shows; that this human presence does not depend on unstated assumptions of an uninterrogated humanism is what makes Paley's work different from so much of what has gone before. Such distinctions become evident in Murray Baumgarten's "Urban Rites and Civic Premises in the Fiction of Saul Bellow, Grace Paley, and Sandra Schor" (*ConL* 34: 395–424); rather than simply lament the demise of a certain kind of "respectable, middle-class city virtues" as does the avowedly humanistic Bellow, Paley undertakes "a clear-eyed exploration of the state of liberation of contemporary Jewish women in the decaying yet vital city," a city that "makes possible their liberation from patriarchal structures" such as Bellow would impose.

R. C. Feddersen discovers a similar phenomenological approach to structures in his "Interview with W. P. Kinsella" (*Short Story* n.s. 1, ii: 81–88). Disdaining mythic interpretations of baseball in his fiction, Kinsella laughs, insisting "It's just a game, after all," and proceeds to dismiss both moralistic and intellectualized responses; more pertinent are his affinities with Richard Brautigan, especially as the fiction of both authors works as an arena for the action of their writing rather than for the dramatization of ideas. Like Paley, Kinsella feels perfectly free to use his own life for fiction; but also like Paley, he insists that it be "elasticized" and made more supple by the imagination.

xi Innovative Fiction from Barth to Vonnegut

An overused term is criticized for its imprecision by Nicholas Birns in "Beyond Metafiction: Placing John Barth" (*ArQ* 49, ii: 113–36), an important article that follows recent trends toward recovering notions of character in otherwise nontraditional fiction. "Metafiction seems avant-garde, but it is in fact retro-idealist," Birns points out, regretting that the term proves equally useful to those who endorse such work and others who condemn it. How Barth can be referential without being a realist is the crucial issue, understandable when the author's historical and political use of Maryland is examined.

A similarly compelling argument against one key innovator's presumed emphasis of language as play is made by Michael Zeitlin, whose "Father-Murder and Father-Rescue: The Post-Freudian Allegories of Donald Barthelme" (*ConL* 34: 182–203) proposes instead that Barthelme's fictive art derives its substance from an emulation of Freudian psychoanalysis. Zeitlin objects strenuously that the author is not a fragmentist; that Barthelme's close contemporary Richard Brautigan was is suggested by the form of Michael McClure's chapter in *Lighting the Corners: On Art, Nature, and the Visionary* (New Mexico), "Ninety-One Things About Richard Brautigan" (pp. 36–68), a reproduction of "notes written at typing speed as I reread all of Richard's writings" in preparation for McClure's famous *Vanity Fair* article responding to Brautigan's suicide (see *ALS 1985*, p. 291). Of great interest is McClure's belief that Freudian analysis offers anything but an explanation of what Brautigan and his fiction were about.

Robert Coover's range through what some critics call histiographic metafiction prompts four worthwhile studies. In " 'A Parody of Martyrdom': The Rosenbergs, Cold War Theology, and Robert Coover's *The Public Burning*" (*Novel* 27: 85–101) Molly Hite establishes that Coover's motive is less to criticize American government of the 1950s than to satirize the response of such cold war intellectuals as Leslie Fiedler "who needed to maintain a sense of their own decency and tolerance while at the same time supporting an increasingly hard governmental line on the question of suppressing dissidents." Fiedler was notoriously unsympathetic to the Rosenbergs; the quotation in Hite's title is his. Coover's own lack of sympathy is examined by Robert Walsh in "Narrative Inscription, History and the Reader in Robert Coover's *The Public Burning*" (*SNNTS* 25: 332–45). Not interested in a novelistic identification with his characters, the author instead immerses himself in "the entire atmosphere of Cold War hysteria that condemned them," in which their guilt or innocence is almost fully irrelevant." Such styles of cultural thought are a narratological factor, Pierre Joris suggests, using *A Night at the Movies* to make his case in "Coover's Apoplectic Apocalypse or 'Purviews of Cunning Abstractions' " (*Crit* 34: 220–31). How Coover's experiments from the 1960s inaugurated a liberation of forms that influences even realistic fiction today is argued by the author himself in the exceptionally analytical "Interview with Robert Coover" (*Short Story* n.s. 1, ii: 89–94) conducted by Farhat Iftekharuddin, a conversation that makes a sound defense of the otherwise abused term "metafiction" as "the embrace of all fictional forms that preceded it: no narrowing dogmas, only vast new possibilities."

Corrective readings characterize recent work on William H. Gass. To those who believe that narrative lines and a dramatization of "language herself speaking" sums up the author's second novel, Michael Kaufmann points out the importance of the work's physical performance in "The Textual Body: William Gass's *Willie Masters' Lonesome Wife*" (*Crit* 35: 27–

42). Ann-Janine Morey takes pause at the androcentrism (if not outright misogyny) of the male-female dynamics in *Omensetter's Luck*. Her *Religion and Sexuality in American Literature* (Cambridge, 1992) considers the novel's "fox in the well" theme of a male spirit contained in an unexpected hollow, which when applied to concerns of language and authorship breeds a fear "that telling the story is not enough," a feeling that words, like the body, will betray us"—a situation that produces "a language of multiple containment" rather than liberation.

With research by James Park Sloan under way on the autobiographical elements of Jerzy Kosinski's fiction, the last flurry of hagiographies and personally biased accounts are being published. That Kosinski's work suffered as he became a plaything of the rich and famous is evident, though unintentionally, from Dorothea Straus's "Remembering Jerzy Kosinski" (*PR* 60: 138–42), a curiously written memoir couched in such language as "Paris is divided in two by the Seine" and slanted toward glamorizing Kosinski through sexual innuendo. How the *New York Times*'s chief editors "did not hesitate to push for favorable mention of friends in the news pages," friends that included Kosinski, is documented by Edwin Diamond in *Behind the Times* (Villard), and the embarrassment of having to do such work is detailed by reporter John Corry in a fascinating chapter, "Ideology and the Culture" (pp. 200–222), of his own memoir, *My Times: Adventures in the News Trade* (Putnam). Corry's assignment was to defend Kosinski from charges of plagiarism; his remarkably successful strategy was to describe the accusers as dupes of the international communist conspiracy. Especially valuable is his candor in admitting that "Jerzy had become incidental. The integrity of the *Times* was now at stake," and furthermore that in the newsroom "Appearance was what counted." With crucial correspondence on *The Painted Bird* now available for study at the Houghton Library, Harvard, such affairs should soon be settled to scholarly satisfaction.

In terms of publicity, Kosinski's opposite has been Thomas Pynchon, whose work nevertheless generates reams of response. Placing that fiction in a poststructuralist framework, Hanjo Berressem finds a textualization of both world and subject, a process that emancipates the signifier from the signified. *Pynchon's Poetics: Interfacing Theory and Text* (Illinois) draws heavily on French thought, including Lacan's dysfunction of thinking and being, Derrida's gap between knowledge and representation, and Baudrillard's semiotic reading of the political economy to the extent of having a simulatory society from which the referent is profitably excluded. These theories underlie Pynchon's texts and allow the author to question the autonomy of subject, creating new typographies of art and nature, text and body, and control versus self-regulation. More limited in approach but helpful in understanding is M. Keith Booker's *Literature and Domination: Sex, Knowledge, and Power in Modern Fiction* (Florida), where Pynchon is seen as portraying a "daisy chain" of victimizers whose serial victimization in human relationships asks readers to examine their own complicity.

For once, attention to Pynchon shifts away from *Gravity's Rainbow* in favor of *Vineland* and *The Crying of Lot 49*. But two important studies are offered of *V.*, by Michael Kowalewski in *Deadly Musings* and by Ronald W. Cooley in "The Hothouse or the Street: Imperialism and Narrative in Pynchon's *V.*" (*MFS* 39: 307–25). Depicting violence is the way Pynchon's writing "escapes routinization," says Kowalewski, who counsels that "Our difficulty in 'finding' that author . . . is more than just biographically important, especially in how it imaginatively shapes the forms of violence in Pynchon's fiction and how we respond to them." Preemptive impulses preempt our attention, especially when fantastic events are treated realistically, yielding "insistently noncommital narrative impulses." It is an imaginative resistance to such violence that is the basis of Pynchon's larger themes. Cooley's thesis is that *V.* succeeds as an anti-imperialistic novel because of its "relatively coherent critique of the historical fact of empire," in the process subverting "the discursive conventions that make any attempt by an authorial *I* (however disguised) to tell the story of an Other."

The Crying of Lot 49 interests critics as a detective story. For Jon Thompson, it serves as a paradigm for understanding postmodern crime fiction written by Ishmael Reed, Don DeLillo, and Gabriel García Márquez as well. Thompson's *Fiction, Crime and Empire: Clues to Modernity and Postmodernism* (Illinois) sees the difference between modern and postmodern as the postmodern's refusal to privilege high culture over low, its disinclination to refine art away from life, and its commitment to view matter semiotically rather than symbolically, all of which is evident in Pynchon's second novel. Debra A. Moddelmog reads it as an anti-detective narrative, one that subverts the customary structure of characters learning about the crime. In *Readers and Mythic Signs: The Oedipus Myth in Twentieth-Century Fiction* (So. Ill.) Moddelmog traces how

Pynchon reverses the order in his stories of the crime and its investigation, a key factor being Oedipa's losing sight of reality in favor of living without absolutes in a metaphysical void. Tensions and ambiguities within this situation are to some extent resolved by William Gleason, whose "The Postmodern Labyrinths of *Lot 49*" (*Crit* 34: 83–99) suggests that "the labyrinth can be seen as a mediating form between matriarchal and patriarchal systems of power."

For work on Pynchon's blockbuster, one must look to Robert L. McLaughlin, who contributes "IG Farben's Synthetic War Crimes and Thomas Pynchon's *Gravity's Rainbow*" (pp. 85–95) to editors M. Paul Holsinger and Mary Anne Schofield's *Visions of War: World War II in Popular Literature and Culture* (Bowling Green, 1992). Here the great German manufacturer becomes a symbolic villain, responsible for crimes against humanity and a worldview that destroys nature and dehumanizes people.

Dedicated to the dubious proposition that Thomas Pynchon's fourth (and much maligned) novel merits a book of essays is *The Vineland Papers* (Dalkey Archive), ed. Geoffrey Green, Donald J. Greiner, and Larry McCaffery. Five of the volume's 12 critical pieces are reprinted from the *Vineland* issue of *Crit* 32, i (1992); among the collection's original materials "Pynchon's Groundward Art" (pp. 89–100) by Joseph Tabbi speaks most honestly. After *Gravity's Rainbow,* almost anything would be a "falling off." That is not Tabbi's dissatisfaction. Rather, "for the reader who has been moved by complexities of form and language beyond the alienation depicted in *Gravity's Rainbow,* the return [home to America] can seem imperfectly achieved, the new optimism arbitrary, settled in advance, and sustainable only by an almost willed holding back of darker forces and paranoia that still obviously come through."

An interesting contrast between Pynchon and Ronald Sukenick is drawn by Jeffrey T. Nealon in *Double Reading: Postmodernism After Deconstruction* (Cornell). *Gravity's Rainbow* ostensibly answers the question of how to proceed after the end of the end by thematizing this dilemma; because ambiguity becomes his theme, Pynchon's work thus resists the thematic criticism that would expose its essentially referential nature. Sukenick's *The Endless Short Story,* however, moves beyond issues of representation by being endless itself; as a story without closure, it rejects the transcendental signified and instead allows its text to enact the destructuring of language and representation, thus opening the way for genuinely new creation. A similar tactic distinguishes Ishmael Reed's work, as described in Richard Hardack's "Swing to the White, Back to the Black: Writing and 'Sourcery' in Ishmael Reed's *Mumbo Jumbo*" (*ArQ* 49, iv: 117–38), where all Western History is seen as being reconfigured "as a perpetual restaging of the conflict between 'primitive,' pre-Western Black, or 'Jes Grew' beliefs . . . and repressed, Western, white, or 'Atonist' creeds."

Kurt Vonnegut's equally controversial use of aesthetics and art history prompts David Rampton to write "Into the Secret Chamber: Art and the Artist in Kurt Vonnegut's *Bluebeard*" (*Crit* 35: 16–26), a study that shows how the author "focuses the reader's attention on the nature of creative representation in a new way" by including references to debates over representational versus abstractly expressive art—in the process generating a new debate in an art world "where knowledge still counts for something."

xii   Hunter S. Thompson and Other New Journalists

"The New Journalism" refers to reporting that uses the tools of fiction writing, but in Thompson's case the borrowing involves matters of substance as well as technique. Joining Paul Perry's earlier biography of Thompson (see *ALS 1992*, p. 295) are E. Jean Carroll's *Hunter: The Strange and Savage Life of Hunter S. Thompson* (Dutton), Peter O. Whitmer's *When the Going Gets Weird: The Twisted Life and Times of Hunter S. Thompson* (Hyperion), and G. B. Trudeau's *Action Figure! The Life and Times of* Doonesbury's *Uncle Duke* (Andrews & McMeel). Although all four volumes contribute to the picture, Carroll's is the most analytical and therefore insightful. Drawing on original and reprinted bits of oral and printed history, Carroll assembles an interactive collage that speaks for Thompson's self-fictionalization, a technique seen as confusing by Whitmer (who finds the author's projection as "Raoul Duke" distracting) and one-dimensional to Trudeau (whose comic strips capture Thompson's self-conscious dramatizations but omit the creative basis for the writer's pose).

That any serious American writer could have so long a life in a popular comic strip is remarkable; the closest analogue would be *Life* magazine's fetishization of Hemingway in the 1940s and 1950s. How Thompson and his work qualify for such treatment is explained by James N. Stull in

Literary Selves: Autobiography and Contemporary American Nonfiction (Greenwood). For Stull, Thompson casts the authorial self as fugitive, using trickster motifs against the social order; this adversarial stance leads him to use a much greater amount of artifice than even feature journalism would allow, making Thompson more of a fictionist. Stull also studies Norman Mailer's *The Armies of the Night* to this effect, learning how Mailer fashions here a new provisional identity in the form of an aggressive persona that responds to misrepresentation. As opposed to the more simply extrinsic, ethnographic work of Tom Wolfe, Thompson and Mailer are the ones who push the relationship between a singular self and its world to truly fictive extremes.

xiii Science Fiction

Feminist utopias have created a separate space for women. Here alternative science and reworked myths respond to a more traditionally male-dominated style of science fiction, Robin Roberts suggests in *A New Species: Gender and Science in Science Fiction* (Illinois). But because these feminist utopias reverse the male dystopian pattern, they exist in response to a patriarchal culture rather than independent from it. Against this state of affairs Roberts projects a feminist science fiction that "rejects the essentialism and simplicity of the feminist utopian strategy" and instead includes possibilities of integration beneficial to both men and women.

More comfortable in reacting to patriarchy is Marleen S. Barr, whose *Lost in Space: Probing Feminist Science Fiction and Beyond* (No. Car.) argues that valid social structures can be created to counteract patriarchal myths. Feminist fabulation challenges the fixed definitions of hierarchies, but it also closes off certain childhood stories as "false nostalgia for a nonexistent past"; preferrable are the imaginary and theoretical texts for a new paradise that a feminist stance can generate.

During the 1980s science fiction writers perceived a loss of power over human form, Scott Bukatman says in *Terminal Identity: The Virtual Subject in Postmodern Science Fiction* (Duke). At this point the subject became a machine operating in the electronic space reserved for postmodern language. Virtual reality as thus created portrayed a subject estranged from rational control; as technology penetrates the body, all that can survive are fantasies of technological control. A realistic application for Bukatman's thesis can be found in editors George Slusser and Eric S. Rabkin's *Flights of Fancy: Armed Conflict in Science Fiction and Fantasy* (Georgia), particularly Joe Haldeman's "Vietnam and Other Alien Worlds" (pp. 92–102), a riveting account of the nature of killing and responsibility via the new devices of nontraditional war.

University of Northern Iowa

Timothy Materer

i Wallace Stevens

In the last *ALS* review of modern poetry (1990) Lee Bartlett suggested that we should recognize William Carlos Williams as well as Ezra Pound and Wallace Stevens as the chief poets of the 1900–1940 era. Although this year's scholarship confirms the importance of both Stevens and Williams, Stevens has inspired not only the greater number of works but also the more interesting ones. The two books on Williams focus on his career as a physician. The four books on Stevens include two intensive critical studies of his poetry, a collection of essays on feminist topics, and a book on Stevens and modern art which is a major contribution to scholarship. Both poets are the subjects of numerous articles, but again the work on Stevens is more exciting.

A special "Poets Reading Stevens" issue of *WSJour* contains poems and brief critical pieces on Stevens by poets from John Allman to Al Zolymas. Among the most interesting is "Stevens as Dutchman" (17: 13–15) by John Updike. Updike notes that Stevens has now eclipsed in popularity the other poets he studied in college: E. E. Cummings, Marianne Moore, Robert Frost, and even T. S. Eliot. Updike regrets that he can no longer consider Stevens a "personal discovery," and he is doubtful of critics like Harold Bloom who make Stevens, especially in his late works, a poet of the sublime. Updike values Stevens as a poet whose Dutch "earthiness . . . stubbornness and industriousness" are at the root of even his most "fanciful sublimnations." Updike might thus be suspicious (as I am) of the thesis of David Jarraway's *Wallace Stevens and the Question of Belief* (LSU) that Stevens's poems are subtle speculations on the nature of belief in an age of "postmetaphysical and post-theological thought." Of course, Stevens himself posed the issue of belief after the death of the gods, and his dialectical meditations about what is real or imagined are clearly the substance of his poetry. However, Jarraway attempts to chart a clear progression in Stevens's thought about belief as if he were a philosopher or a contemporary "a/theologian" rather than a poet. Although this comprehensive volume contains many fine close readings, the attempt to characterize Stevens's evolving thought by comparing him to other thinkers is often confusing. Ezra Pound said that his public claimed he dumped his notebooks on them, which is sometimes the effect of Jarraway's book. When he treats a philosopher such as Nietzsche at length, he is clear and informative. But the numerous relatively brief comparisons of Stevens to thinkers such as Derrida, Blanchot, and Levinas are usually bewildering. For example, when Jarraway compares the "genealogy of belief" in late Stevens to that in Heidegger's philosophy as interpreted by Robert Bernasconi (who, moreover, distinguishes Heidegger I and Heidegger II), ideas are piled on ideas until the thesis is lost. When Jarraway compares what he is saying about Stevens to what Derrida says of Focillon, one no longer knows what he is saying about Stevens. Nevertheless, the commentary on many of the poems, such as the analysis of the "idea of God" in "The Comedian as the Letter C," and the subtle and illuminating reading of "Final Soliloquy of the Interior Paramour," makes this a valuable book.

In contrast to Jarraway, Daniel Schwarz in *Narrative and Representation in the Poetry of Wallace Stevens* (St. Martin's) sees little development in Stevens; he is no Dante or Milton, and if one looks for some "grand vision" one will "find the poems redundant." This frank admission is followed by another about Stevens's irresponsiveness to history: "he is often indifferent to the external world [and] avoids or oversimplifies politics." Schwarz is thus refreshingly critical of Stevens's concept of "Major Man," which he finds "not only naive but unpleasant," a figure "who does not do anything, love anyone, interact with his community." This frankness makes Schwarz's praise of Stevens as a great modernist all the more convincing. He particularly values Stevens's creation of a dramatic context for his poetic voices and the way he uses metaphors "as a kind of Zeno's paradox . . . always bisecting his way to the moment of revelation, but never getting there." Schwarz's thesis also focuses on a paradoxical quality in Stevens that his poems' "secret codes and apparent lack of narrative distance" inspire the reader to understand the poem in terms of a narrative: "the reader is enclosed in a room from which his desire for narrative becomes the exit to understanding." This approach leads to interesting readings of the entire canon, including lesser-known poems like "The Prince of Peacocks."

A volume on *Wallace Stevens and the Feminine* (Alabama), ed. Melita Schaum, is a mixture of essays both explorative and reductionist. Jacqueline Vaught Brogan's "'Sister of the Minotaur': Sexism and Stevens" (pp. 3–22), is the reductionist kind as it chastises Stevens for the "very disturbing way" that "women in his poetry remain too obviously fixtures—empty ciphers for masculine rumination and scripting, even de-scription." Since Stevens was masculine, it is hard to imagine his ruminations as being anything else, and it is hard to imagine what is wrong with females as "figures" in a poem (it might be a problem in a novel) or with "de-scribing" (a term she does not define, though the hyphenation suggests some sort of violation). Remarkably, Brogan says she does not like "to indulge in psychological explanation" when the essay is largely given over to such speculation. One finds the same indulgence in C. Roland Wagner in "The Concealed Self" (pp. 117–39) when he speculates that "an ambivalent attachment to the nurturing pre-Oedipal mother is central to our understanding of Stevens" and that it "helps to explain his marriage [and] his religious beliefs." Mary B. Arensberg's "A Curable Separation: Stevens and the Mythology of Gender" (pp. 23–45) is a more sensitive and sensible discussion of the Freudian background of Stevens's feminine figures. In "A Woman with the Hair of a Pythoness" (pp. 46–57) Barbara M. Fisher warns that a Jungian approach to Stevens may make us miss all that is inventive and intellectually alive in him—indeed, "poiesis itself." The essay that best captures this poiesis is Paul Morrison's "The Fat Girl in Paradise: Stevens, Wordsworth, Milton and the Proper Name" (pp. 80–114). The metaphorphoses of the archetypal "fat girl" in these three poets best captures the specifically Stevensian use of the archetype, which is far more interesting and surprising than any Jungian anima. The editor herself contributes an essay on "Views of the Political in Stevens and H. D." (pp. 171–89), and Daniel T. O'Hara and Lisa M. Steinman both contribute essays on Ralph Waldo Emerson's influence on Stevens.

Stevens and the art of painting is a frequent topic of Stevens's critics, and it is intelligently discussed in Schwarz's book; but there has been nothing to compare to Glen MacLeod's definitive study, *Wallace Stevens and Modern Art* (Yale). MacLeod's describes Stevens's early friendship with Walter Arnesberg, one of the organizers of the epoch-making Armory Show of 1913, as well as his contacts with Arnesberg's friend

Marcel Duchamp and others in Arnesberg's circle. MacLeod's documentation of Stevens's fascination with modern art demonstrates the influence of Duchamp and the Dada movement on *Harmonium* as well as the influence of Picasso and the debates over abstraction and surrealism (McLeod reminds us that Picasso for many years was the leading surrealist) on *The Man with the Blue Guitar*. McLeod looks at the way painters like Picasso and Mondrian were discussed in American and French art journals in the 1930s to see how terms like "reality" and "abstraction" were used at the time Stevens was exploring them. Mondrian emerges from McLeod's analysis as a crucial figure because of the way he represented an aspect of Stevens's Dutch heritage—"the austere spirituality of Calvinist theology, the abstract tendencies of philosophical rationalism." Although Stevens had in the 1930s associated abstraction with formalist aesthetics, by the time of *Notes Toward a Supreme Fiction* he associated it with the "spiritual content of Mondrian's aesthetics." In Stevens's late poems, such as "The Auroras of Autumn," MacLeod reveals his affinity with the Abstract Expressionists as Stevens himself continued to absorb the lessons of the most advanced art and theory: "There is an obvious visual similarity between the flashing, ceaseless, wavelike movements of Stevens's title image . . . and Pollock's 'signature' abstract imagery, the serpentine tracery of his 'poured' paintings." *Stevens and Modern Art* is a work of important scholarship and sensitive interpretation.

The relationship between Stevens and Emerson is again the topic in David Michael Hertz's *Angels of Reality*. In demonstrating the significance of Emerson's concept of "nature and organism" for the three artists, Hertz shows how "the same ideological seeds generated different artistic fruit." Although there is nothing especially new in this book, despite Hertz's quarreling with Harold Bloom's theory of influence, Stevens is placed in a fascinating context. Helen Vendler's chapter on Stevens (pp. 370–94) in *Columbia History of American Poetry* is an expert survey of his Americanness, the "seductive mimicry of the thought process" in his poetry, the difficulty his metaphors may give new readers, his wordplay on Latin roots, the trochaic falling rhythms within his pentameter, and his "assertion of the immense social importance of the imagination." (It is curious that Vendler so firmly dismisses the story of Stevens's deathbed conversion to Catholicism when other critics who mention it find it possible or even likely.) Vendler also appears in *WSJour* with a lively essay entitled " 'Notes Toward a Supreme Fiction': Allegorical Personae" (17: 147–61). Essays on *Notes* by A. Walton Litz (17: 162–67) and Paul G. Italia (17: 168–79) also appear in this issue. Like Jarraway, Thomas Austenfield in "Rituals of Reading in the Poetry of Wallace Stevens" (*SoAR* 58, i: 67–83) sees the poet's conception of imaginative reading as an act of faith. A reading which creates the "interactive relationship between text and reader" parallels the way we relate imaginatively to reality in a religious ritual: "Right reading is substitute theology." The side of Stevens that Updike values, his keen sense of place, is analyzed in William Doreski's "Wallace Stevens in Connecticut" (*TCL* 39: 152–65), which takes issue with the tendency of critics like Bloom to see "transcendence" where there is instead, or at least also, "geographical actuality." Paul Bauer's "The Politics of Reticence: Wallace Stevens in the Cold War Era" (*TCL* 39: 1–31) is the best single Stevens essay of the year. Like MacLeod, Bauer carefully puts Stevens's ideas and vocabulary (political rather than artistic) into historical context. Bauer illuminates some of the same issues that Schwarz raises concerning Stevens's political insensitivity and demonstrates a complexity about these issues that historical hindsight tends to discount. Bauer's reading of "Esthétique du Mal" in relation to Marxist and New Critical theorizing is especially valuable. His description of Stevens's awareness of how a utopian nostalgia for a simpler world (for example, in Eliot or Allen Tate) could lead to authoritarian politics is a major clarification of Stevens's politics.

ii William Carlos Williams

Although the two book-length studies of Williams both concern the way the poet's medical training mesh with his literary theory, both make distinctive contributions. In *Modernism, Medicine, and Williams* (Okla.) T. Hugh Crawford holds that the development of Williams's modernism was influenced more by medical concepts of clarity, cleanliness, and the objective gaze than by contact with figures like Eliot and Stevens. Williams's belief in the "rhetoric of clarity" and the doctor's authority receives some Foucauldian criticism for its violation of the patient. As Crawford writes of a scene in *Paterson* where a woman undresses, "In Williams's texts there is a double penetration: the doctor unveils the patient for diagnosis and treatment, and at the same time, the author unveils a private scene to his readers." However, as Williams observed the development of modernism, he began "to question its authority and the cultural power of technoscientific discourses in general," which Crawford says led him to a form of postmodernism that "makes problematic all notion of appropriation and violation." The book contains excellent readings of stories like "Mind and Body," "Old Doc Rivers," and "The Use of Force" and interesting material on subjects like Thomas Eakins's portrayal of doctors and the development of modern medical technology.

In *William Carlos Williams and the Diagnostics of Culture* (Oxford) Brian A. Bremen argues that Williams's role as a doctor and his role as a poet became more congruent as he moved from the "confused romanticism of *Spring and All* to the methodological empiricism of *Paterson.*" Although Bremen's work is more ambitious than Crawford's, the breadth of its references sometimes works against the analysis. For example, within 10 lines Bremen sketches in Heinz Kohut's theory of wisdom, Jessica Benjamin's concept of "intersubjectivity," Jürgen Habermas's social theory, and D. W. Winnicott's conception of "destruction" in a paragraph which immediately precedes additional dense summaries of Hegel and Margaret Mahler. Following all these references, it takes a while to see that Bremen is simply commenting on Williams's sense of how one destroys narcissistic impulses. Like Crawford, Bremen emphasizes the way Williams's poetic language breaks up conventional thought, interrogating itself and allowing the reader to fill in the gaps creatively. But this idea is only obscured when he borrows a term from Pierre Bourdieu to claim that Williams's language influences " 'the habitus'— those 'systems of durable transposable *dispositons,* structured structures predisposed to function as structuring structures." Which simply means, as many critics have said, that Williams's poetry attempts to break up engrained, societal habits of mind. Bremen is far more cogent when he shows how Kenneth Burke's relationship with Williams, which was at times nearly an intellectual collaboration, demonstrates the importance of empiricist thought to Williams's development. The application of Burke's *Attitudes Toward History* (1937) to Williams's American sense of tradition is illuminating. However, the analysis of Williams's traditionalism is marred by a narrowly ideological attack on Eliot, which includes a personal attack on his character. But Bremen's contrast of Eliot's and Pound's concern with fitting experience into an "already existing order" and Williams's search for new forms seems valid. Like Crawford, Bremen praises Williams for forcing his readers to abandon "whatever fixed point of view we bring to the work."

Two essays on Williams develop topics related to Crawford's and

Bremen's books. Like Bremen, Jeff Poggi and Sergio Rizzo in "The Novel Poetry of *Paterson*" (*Sagetrieb* 12, i: 31–41) are interested in Williams's inclusion of prose within his poetry "in an effort at contextualizing, or historicizing, the poetic." Williams as a cultural critic is the concern of Thomas F. Bertonneau's "Consecrated in Blood/Unjustly Accused: The Ethical Paradox of William Carlos Williams' *In the American Grain*" (*Sagetrieb* 12, i: 7–30). Bertonneau's analysis of the ethical contradiction in Williams's implicit approval of blood sacrifice among the Aztecs but not among the Puritans is itself ethically clear-sighted. Williams's indifference to the fate of the victims of Aztec ritual slaughter is a kind of blindness that one does not find in *Paterson*. Instead, Williams defends all victims without exception as well as "the ethos that has struggled for more than two thousand years to bring into the light the mythic obfuscation of violence." The article is also notable for the way Bertonneau analyzes the failure of Williams's critics to see the ethical flaws in the poet's primitivism. This article reminds one that too many critics, in their eagerness to cite philosophers, sociologists, and psychoanalysts, fail to cite other literary critics. The result (as in Bremen's book) is that the reader is less able to judge if the critic is really presenting new insights or just expressing the old ones in new terminology.

The criticism of Williams's authoritarian "gaze" in Bremen and Crawford is also expressed in an ingenious analysis of some of Williams's *Spring and All* poems in Sharon Dolin's "Enjambment and the Erotics of the Gaze in Williams's Poetry" (*AI* 50: 29–53). The doctor's privilege of looking but not being seen appears in enjambed lines like "a girl with one leg / over the rail of a balcony." Dolin finds not only the need to dominate the female body in Williams but also, as in "At the ball game," a "questioning of class and gender schisms." Christopher MacGowan's piece on Williams in *Columbia History of American Poetry* (pp. 395–417) is an expert survey of his career that discusses both his Americanism and his modernism.

iii W. H. Auden

Although Stevens and Williams capture the most attention this year, the most acclaimed book is on W. H. Auden, Anthony Hecht's *The Hidden Law* (Harvard). As Peter Davison put it, this book is a "long swim in the heady liquor of poetry," though one may find it a bit too long at times. Hecht attempts to avoid any "a priori agenda, hidden or overt," and he comments on the poems chronologically—rather repetitiously asking the reader to "note" this or that aspect of a poem. Nevertheless, the discussion is generally lively. Unlike the many critics who apply rigid theoretical grids to an author, Hecht is too intelligent to be violated by ideas. His expert summaries of thinkers from St. Paul to Homer Lane always concern those who mattered to Auden himself. Hecht's knowledge of and sensitivity to painting and music inform many analyses. His attention to Auden's meters, verse forms, and punctuation keeps us aware that he is writing about a poet above all and not merely a cultural critic.

Hecht's topics include Auden's conception of art as frivolity, heroism, the relation of public events to private lives, and the centrality of language to understanding the world. Hecht's conclusion explains that he tried to avoid the kind of criticism that appears under titles like "Desublimating the Male Sublime." Yet he has to admit that he has a theme of his own, which he designates in his title. The "hidden law" concerns the fate working within human experience—a kind of poetic or divine justice. The final chapter develops this providential theme and represents Hecht at his best, digressing on Frost, Yeats, Eliot, and folk ballads. For those who admire Hecht's poetry, an added pleasure in reading the book is to find another hidden code. Like John Berryman writing on Stephen Crane or Susan Howe on Emily Dickinson, Hecht is writing about his own personal and poetic development. An important essay on Auden, especially if one still thinks of him merely as an English poet, is Claude J. Simpson's the "American Auden" in *Columbia History of American Poetry* (pp. 505–33). Simpson argues that Auden's emigration to America allowed him to put behind him the versions of romanticism and modernism of his earlier work and "to reorient himself and his place in literary tradition." Simpson's discussion of Auden's influence on poets such as Theodore Roethke, Richard Wilbur, and James Merrill also show how central to American poetry he became.

iv Robert Frost

Frost never seemed more the quintessential American poet than in George Bagby's *Robert Frost and the Book of Nature* (Tennessee). Bagby thinks that the "predominant ironist conceptions" of modern critics have underestimated his transcendental elements and the way Frost, like the American Romanticists, has his "cultural roots in seventeenth-century habits of mind." Although he travels a well-traveled road in comparing

Frost to Emerson and Thoreau, the emphasis on a more romantic Frost than critics have given us is welcome. However, his argument that Frost emerges in certain poems as "a major visionary poet in the tradition of Blake, Wordsworth, Emerson, and Thoreau" is never substantiated. There is a problem about the word "secular" in the following claim that Frost is at times "a powerful seer who not only pursues but often finds a literal, although secular, revelation in, and with the help of, the natural world." Bagby never explores what this "secular" revelation might be because his comparisons to Wordsworth and Emerson always involve a divine revelation of some kind of "Wholeness." Most of the book is taken up with his classification of Frost's poems into four categories of emblem poems: fablelike, prototypical, meditative, and heuristic. The categories overlap so much that he spends much of this time explaining his categorizing scheme rather than developing his thesis.

Other critics emphasize the problematic rather than the emblematic quality of Frost's poetry. Jay Parini's "Robert Frost and the Poetry of Survival" (*Columbia History of American Poetry*, pp. 260–83) recognizes his Wordsworthian quality, but he also stresses the masks the poet wore, and he characterizes his poetry as "curiously elusive despite its famous lucidity." This elusiveness is the subject of Richard Poirier's article on "Frost, Winnicott, Burke" in *Transitional Objects and Potential Spaces: Literary Uses of D. W. Winnicott* (Columbia), ed. Peter L. Rudnytsky. According to Winnicott, an English psychoanalyst of the object-relations school, there is a "core of personality" that never communicates with the world. Poirier believes that Frost draws on this core in developing his "extraordinary capacity for not communicating." Far from thinking that natural things can be emblematic, Frost believes with Kenneth Burke (and Emerson) that words create things, which gives still more power and ambiguity to the poet's language. Poirier notes the paradox that in his poems of deception and hiding and in his admissions that he is a trickster and deceiver, Frost is "pretending to be outrageously truthful and available. The availability, the admission of disguise, is the ultimate mask of a permanently hidden Frost."

In " 'Design of darkness to appall': Religious Terror in the Poetry of Robert Frost" (*RFR*, pp. 50–57) Edward J. Ingebretsen, S. J., writes that Frost's poem "Design" reveals "the other face of Emerson's transcendentalism, presenting a solitude and separateness as antinomian as it is mystical." Ingebretsen argues for Jonathan Edwards's influence on Frost and that the "language of Calvin permeated his thinking." In "For Once,

Then, Something; the Sublime Reality of Fictions in Robert Frost" (*RFR*, pp. 86–92) Jo-Anne Cappeluti analyzes Frost's awareness of the way fictions "both endorse and critique, set up and subvert." The very title of James R. Dawes's "Masculinity and Transgression in Robert Frost" (*AL* 65: 297–312) would presumably set Anthony Hecht's teeth on edge. The rather too subtle thesis is that, although homosexuality is not a "central focus" in Frost, an "awareness of its absence-always-threatening-to-become-presence (as the unknown of fear or desire) informs much of Frost's work." Nevertheless, the article contains fine analyses of poems such as "The Tuft of Flowers," "Paul's Wife," "The Ax-Helve" and "Mending Wall" (though he neglects to cite Norman Holland's related reading of "Mending Wall" in *The Brain of Robert Frost*). Sheldon W. Liebman's "Frost on Criticism" (*NEQ* 66: 399–415) reminds us that "no modern poet has spoken out so strongly and unequivocally against the whole critical enterprise" as Frost. Frost's critical and sometimes contemptuous attitude toward teachers and critics of poetry is reflected in the characters of "guide and initiate" in poems like "A Fountain," "The Black Cottage," and "Snow." The guide "negates and affirms, misleads and directs" because his initiates or readers will not see what there is to see unless they find their way alone. Finally, William H. Pritchard's *Frost: A Literary Life Reconsidered* (Mass.) has appeared in a second edition that contains a new preface in which Pritchard replies to his critics.

v Elizabeth Bishop and Marianne Moore

In C. K. Doreski's *Elizabeth Bishop: The Restraints of Language* (Oxford) Bishop is quoted as telling her biographer that she was "weary of always being compared to, or coupled with," Marianne Moore. Although none of her critics fail to make this well-worn point, Doreski's book spends more time comparing Bishop to William Wordsworth. Both poets organize their poems around the observation of the natural world and moments of epiphany. The difference between the two poets is found in Bishop's "ultimate distrust of epiphany." She was dissatisfied with her poem "The Fish" and preferred "The Moose" because at its end, even though the encounter with the moose may seem epiphanic, the poem "retreats into domesticity and the commonplace." It suggests the life that the observers share with the moose without "violating the poem's essential self-containment by evoking the sublime." Thus Bishop respects the "restraints of language" and reveals "the unnerving power of reticence that requires interpretation through recognition that language *is* experience." Doreski's book is a thorough analysis of Bishop's achievement in both poetry and prose. One only wishes that her references to figures like Frost, Susan Howe, and Foucault were more fully developed. For example, she invokes Foucault on the "death of the author," but does not seem to realize that Foucault's theory calls for something far more radical than Bishop's "reticence." Further analysis of the difference of the two conceptions of authority might have said more about Bishop's modernism.

Doreski says that Bishop thought poetry should appeal to the imagination rather than "the sociopsychological construct the individual presents to the ordinary world." Given that conviction and her weariness of being paired with Moore, Joanne Feit Diehl's *Elizabeth Bishop and Marianne Moore: The Psychodynamics of Creativity* (Princeton) seems just the kind of criticism Bishop might well have feared. It analyzes Bishop's supposed Oedipal struggle to find her own identity in terms of her precursor Moore. Although the thesis sounds Bloomian, Diehl says that not only Harold Bloom, but Sandra Gilbert and Susan Gubar, are too Freudian in their conception of influence. Instead of Freud, Diehl turns to Melanie Klein for "a powerful heuristic model for dealing with issues related to adult creativity." However, the key to the development of creativity is still conflict: in this case, between admiration and envy (of the mother's breast, of the forerunner's art). If a fault of Bloom's Freudian model is that it seems rather adolescent, then the pre-Oedipal model of Klein seems rather infantile. Moreover, the analysis focuses on the "oppositional tension inherent in the Kleinian view of creativity," which means it seems no different from a Freudian analysis.

This tension is seen in Bishop's memoir of Moore, "Efforts of Affection." Diehl finds throughout Bishop's memoir the pressure caused by her sense that if Moore really knew her, specifically that she was a lesbian, her friend would have repudiated her. In every anecdote Diehl finds Bishop's attempt to fight off Moore's suffocating maternal power. Diehl cites Bishop's remark about a commentator on Moore that "humor [is] a gift these critics sadly seem to lack." Bishop's comment seems appropriate to Diehl's interpretation of Bishop's account of the time Moore clipped a few hairs from a baby elephant for a bracelet: "Moore triumphs; she gets the elephant hairs; but the need to appropriate, to take something from an animal to replace what she herself has lost, and her use of Bishop to complete the act, suggests a kind of violation as well." Everything in Diehl's analysis suggests a kind of violation or an exercise of Moore's will-to-power. Fortunately, Diehl's "intertextual" reading of the two poets' works is more rewarding. Although they are similar in their clarity and powers of observation, Bishop recognizes the "subjective eros of sensation" as Moore rarely does. Diehl's fine comparison of Bishop's "The Man-Moth" and Moore's "The Pangolin" observes how vulnerable Bishop's persona is compared to Moore's. She attributes Bishop's greater psychic vulnerability and openness to her experience of her mother's insanity.

Jeredith Merrin's "Marianne Moore and Elizabeth Bishop" (*Columbia History of American Poetry,* pp. 343–69) begins with the admission that the twin subject of her article implies that Moore and Bishop are "some special subspecies of female American poet," and it ends with the assertion that "it is time that each poet had a chapter of her own." Between these framing statements, Merrin concentrates on their differences. Unlike Bishop, Moore is "always delineating virtues and vices." Both poets take the observer's stance, but in Bishop nature seems more dramatic and psychological, colored by her "deep uncertainty and spiritual restlessness." This chapter contains interesting material on the poets' use of Renaissance models and their relationship to modern art. Aside from Doreski, Moore's critics all develop the conception of the poetic muse as an archetypal mother. Similarly, Robin Riley Fast in "Moore, Bishop, and Oliver: Thinking Back, Re-Seeing the Sea" (*TCL* 39: 364–79) uses the two poets' poems about the sea (to which she adds Mary Oliver's) to suggest their sense (again, in opposition to Bloom's agonistic model of influence) of "identification and mutuality" that develops between mother and child.

Two interesting general studies devote chapters to Elizabeth Bishop, Stephen Cushman's *Fictions of Form in American Poetry* and Vernon Shetley's *After the Death of Poetry: Poet and Audience in Contemporary America* (Duke). Cushman's chapter is an extensive and welcome discussion of Ezra Pound's influence on Bishop. Focusing on Bishop's sestina "Visits to St. Elizabeths," he considers the two poets' shared concern with madness, exile, and politics as well as their meetings when Bishop was a poetry consultant and Pound a prisoner in Washington, D.C. By "fictions of form," Cushman means the terms (such as "open" and "closed") that poets use to think about the shape and rhythms of their poetic language. The Bishop chapter presents a fine analysis of her syntax, especially her use of parataxis, and of metrical forms (like the Pound-influenced sestina in "Visits"). Shetley's book addresses the problem that modern poetry, with its fabled difficulty and obscurity (two qualities he carefully distinguishes), has lost a general audience. The problem of contemporary poetry is to find a way of "embodying subjectivity in public language" and to go beyond what he sees as an "unexamined belief in the power of subjectivity to shape meaningful poetic forms often seen among the MFA mainstream." This subjectivity rings hollow in a skeptical age like our own with its doubts about an objective self. Bishop surmounts this difficulty because she writes personal lyrics in which "metaphor becomes an instrument of skepticism as the poet uses it to question the mind's appetite for analogy." Shetley would agree with Doreski that the strength of Bishop's poetry is her interrogation of her own language and her conviction that "language *is* experience." Shetley might be echoing what Poirier and Parini say of Frost when he writes of Bishop's poetry concealing its "recalcitrance and strangeness behind an appearance of openness."

vi Hart Crane and Allen Tate

The two poets in Langdon Hammer's *Hart Crane and Allen Tate: Janus-Faced Modernism* (Princeton) are far more dissimilar than Bishop and Moore. Although Tate is buried rather than praised in this account of his personal and literary relations with Crane, he is fairly treated, along with Eliot, as a representative of the new literary establishment that developed out of the modernist experiment. Hammer sees both Eliot and Tate as poets who strove to retain the prestige that literature had as the birthright of a leisure class. Though modernism began as an "adversary culture," poet-critics like Eliot and Tate developed a form of modernism that was proceeding "toward public authority and institutional power" as well as a new traditionalism that emphasized the poet as craftsman. For Tate, this view of the poet was connected to the conservative Agrarianism of his Fugitive period and led to the consolidation of his power as an academic New Critic. The crucial text in Tate's career is his "Ode to the Confederate Dead," in which one finds the "replacement of the visionary poet with the craftsman."

Hammer argues that once Tate submitted to tradition, he had to dissociate himself from Crane. This opinion is undermined, however, by the fascinating biographical details Hammer himself provides of the disruptiveness to the Tate household of Crane's manic presence, which might have been sufficient reason for Tate regarding Crane as a madman rather than a mystic. Hammer also considers Tate a victim of a "homophobic structure of literary society" in which the "naming and minoritizing of gay male writing" was a function of the dominant New Criticism. Hammer's analysis of the "architectural collapse" of *The Bridge* portrays a tragic poet whose sense of isolation as a romantic was reenforced by his isolation as a gay writer. Although he does not underestimate Crane's personal and literary faults, Hammer admires Crane as a poet who was true to the original avant-garde impulse of a "transgressive modernism": "Like a conscience, he insisted on the early, 'naive' motives of modernism—a visionary, romantic modernism."

In "Hart Crane's Difficult Passage" (*Columbia History of American Poetry*, pp. 419–51) romanticism and modernism also provide the terms of J. T. Barbarese's assessment of Crane's career. Crane's departure from the "approved rhetoric characterized by impersonality, objectivity, the variable foot, and paratactic structure" made his poetry "complex homework" for the New Critics. Barbarese would agree with Hammer that we need a wider sense of the heritage of modernism than we have yet developed to understand Crane's achievement. Finally, Crane's readers will want John Norton-Smith's useful *A Reader's Guide to Hart Crane's White Buildings* (Mellen).

vii Robert Penn Warren

Among the best essays in *Columbia History of American Poetry* is Patricia Wallace's "Warren, with Ransom and Tate" (pp. 477–505). As in Hammer's book, Tate's limitations are firmly but sensitively defined, and John Crowe Ransom's lyric gift receives its due praise. Warren is the major figure among these Fugitive poets thanks to his willingness to risk the failure of his romantic aspirations and his capacity for change throughout his career: "Ransom is, in his way, a more polished poet than Warren, and Tate perhaps labored harder to write a perfect (and perfectly difficult) poem. But both Ransom and Tate hold something back in their poetry and thus neither is what Calvin Bedient has called Warren—our poet of 'tragic joy.'" Wallace also shows how Warren is, as much perhaps as Frost, a poet of our national experience. This quality is well recognized in the special issue of *SoQ* (31, iv) devoted to "The Great Dragon Country of Robert Penn Warren." The issue's title is taken from the lead R. W. B. Lewis article (pp. 13–36) of the same title about the development of Warren's poetry, which stresses the "pivotal role" of his 1953 verse play, *Brother to Dragons*. The "dragons" represent Warren's sense of, not a principle of evil, but "the violent swerve of things, the unanticipated disruption or loss, the irreducible mystery at the heart of life." In *Brother to Dragons* Warren's narrative and imagistic gifts combine and so make possible the remarkable poetic development that began with *Promises* in 1957 and continued into the 1980s. Two more articles in this issue present important overviews of Warren's poetry. In "Wisdom on the Slant: Warren Over the Long Haul" (pp. 37–50) James H. Justus distinguishes Warren from other poets of national significance such as the Fireside Poets and Robert Frost. These poets took on public roles, became increasingly didactic, and were beloved by a wide audience. (It does not matter that Frost's didacticism and lovableness were an illusion; the public persona is what mattered.) Justus praises Warren for never indulging in "wisdom literature." Even in his late poetry the "dialectical quality" of Warren's poetry prevented the nostalgia about the past (the dragon-ridden past) that makes a poem popular or the "encapsulation" of a truth that makes a poet seem wise. L. Larry Allums's "Robert Penn Warren's Fugitive Years: A Revaluation" (pp. 75–85) focuses on the irony of Warren's early poetry to show that it pervades all of his work. His analysis of Warren's irony and the poetic principles set out in his "Pure and Impure Poetry" (1943) leads Allums to challenge Bloom's characterization of Warren as a poet of the "American Sublime." Even in his most sublime passages, such as the description of the wild geese in "Heart of Autumn," there is a quality of "self-deprecating parody." Throughout his career, Warren stood by the principle of his 1944 essay that the poet "proves his vision by submitting it to the fires of irony." Briefer essays on the theme of innocence in Warren's poetry (pp. 95–100), on his poem about the Hiroshima bombing, "New Dawn" (pp. 101–05), and a useful article on "Biographical Trends in Warren Criticism" (pp. 51–67) compete this timely survey.

viii General Studies

In addition to *After the Death of Poetry* and *Fictions of Form in American Poetry* (discussed under Bishop), two other general studies are of particular interest, Nathan R. Scott, Jr.'s *Visions of Presence in Modern American Poetry* (Hopkins) and Elisa New's brilliantly comprehensive *The Regenerate Lyric*. Both authors defend their interest in religious poetry and in poets who still have a faith in logos or glimpses of an ontological presence within the world. The poets whom New admires are driven less by the "Nietzschean will to power on which current theories rely as by what William James called 'the will to believe.' " Scott defends the intimations of "unknown modes of being" (in Wordsworth's phrase) from the strictures of critics who believe a language of signifiers can never indicate the presence of such a metaphysical signified.

To counter the prevailing poststructuralist criticism, Scott invokes Martin Heidegger's principle of "letting-be," which allows what he calls "releasement toward things." Scott calls Heidegger's principle "nothing other than an attitude of simple enthrallment before the various givens of the earth—in their dimension of *presence*." Scott emphasizes that Heidegger thought poetry rather than philosophic inquiry could best register this quality within our existence. In its own limited terms the deconstructionist view of presence as a "superstitious illusion" is irrefutable; but literature, especially poetry, offers a different and deeper testimony about the world.

Scott argues his thesis through an analysis of 10 modern and contemporary poets, including Stevens, Auden, Bishop, and Warren. In the opening Stevens chapter, his subject is much like Jarraway's; but unlike Jarraway, he finds a way to transcendence in Stevens, which he calls the "route downward." The "conventional opinion" of Stevens's critics that he believes in no God merely reveals their own inability to think of God except in terms of a figure from an archaic mythology or as a metaphysical being " 'dwelling' incorporeally beyond the world." But Stevens's sense of divine immanence within the world is "that mysterious dynamic that simply lets all the particular beings of earth be." Scott's treatment of Auden is less probing than that of Stevens, and his chapter is mostly an account of Auden's career and summaries of his poems. But its concluding pages are an eloquent praise of Auden's poetry as "untouched by any skepticism about its own capacity to handle systematic ideas" and "its chosen task of being 'witness to the truth.' "

As admittedly the "most thoroughly secular poet of her generation," Bishop would seem to be the most intractable subject for Scott's approach. Her skeptical consciousness and suspiciousness of the epiphanic seems to rule out any sense of presence. Scott acknowledges that when Bishop looks at the world, it does not seem to look back; but he nevertheless claims that "she bestows upon it and all its creatures an attention so passionate that very often the distinction between the self and the not-self seems altogether to have been dissolved." On the other hand, Warren, the author of *Incarnations* and *Being Here,* is an ideal poet for Scott's purpose. Scott too focuses on *Brother to Dragons* as a transitional volume and gives a fine account of Thomas Jefferson's role in the poem and of the theme of innocence in both this poem and *Audubon: A Vision.* Although he does see Warren as a poet of the "Romantic sublime," Scott disagrees with Bloom's characterization of him as an Emersonian. Warren himself in "Homage to Emerson" dissociated himself from the thinker who believed there was "no sin . . . not even error" and told an interviewer that he had an almost "pathological flinch from Emersonianism, from Thoreauism, from these oversimplifications." His sense of the sublime is a paradoxical feeling of "the *presence* of the *Deus absconditus.*" Although the world is "veiled and unsearchable," Warren represents it as "instressed with splendor." The world's beauty appears "tangled and hieroglyphic," yet Warren still speculates, "Can it be that the world is but the great word / That speaks the meaning of our joy?"

Elisa New identifies two traditional ways of interpreting American literature. The Roy Harvey Pearce/Hyatt Waggoner approach claimed that Emersonian concepts of linguistic power and originality are the key to the development of American poetry. In contrast, Yvor Winters's view emphasized the "ongoing influence of an experiential Calvinism" whose subject was "human isolation in a foreign universe." (By now, the reader has noticed that Bloom is the most influential critic of the day, but Winters is heavily cited.) Although New discusses both traditions, she is more interested in the anti-Emersonian one and believes Winters is right (in a judgment that also supports Bagby's reading of Frost) that the "key to Hart Crane and Emily Dickinson is not Emerson but rather the seventeenth-century devotional lyric." Her thesis is that the American poet's "native mandate" is not originality but "regeneracy." Among the modern poets analyzed by New, Stevens alone is an Emersonian. She discusses relatively little-known Stevens poems such as "Life Is Motion" ("In Oklahoma, / Bonnie and Josie, / Dressed in calico,/ Dance around a stump") to show how Stevens imagines an original world: "Stevens' gardens are places no God supervises; his America is a place no Israel discovered." She shows that the key word "savage" in Stevens is related to Emerson's desire for an "original relation" to the universe, and that Stevens and Emerson also share the limitation of having "a philosophical attitude to evil verging on chill."

Hart Crane and Frost are New's examples of "poets of a fallen temperament writing in a densely theological grain." Frost is less fully treated and is paired with Lowell as New England poets who are doubtful of what Frost called a "religion so 'material-human' as Emerson's." But the major poet of the Fall and of the longing for regeneration is Hart Crane. New is like Hammer in stressing that Crane will be underestimated if he is read, as the New Critics read him, as a romantic failure. Her survey of Crane's critics, such as Waggoner and Bloom, shows how tenacious the interpretation of Crane as a romantic or Orphic poet has been. But Crane is not, as Bloom would have it, a poet of power but of Augustinian powerlessness. Crane's subject is not a Romantic "ineffable transcendence" but the unknowable Calvinist god: "Crane's verse rediscovers that human condition whose remediation such notions as faith and covenant are addressed to: the condition of sin." In her analysis of *The Bridge* New shows that it is actually Crane's poetic strategy to show that the "moments of epiphany, of the absolute, are always brought to earth." In Crane as much as in Frost a sense of regeneration arises, not from a fresh, Adamic perception of the world, but from an intense awareness of its fallen state.

The chapters on poets of the 1900–1940 era in *Columbia History of American Poetry* have been discussed under the author categories. Important general chapters include Margaret Dickie's "Women Poets and the Emergence of Modernism" (pp. 233–59), Lynn Keller's "The Twentieth-Century Long Poem" (pp. 534–63), and Arnold Rampersad's detailed and definitive essay on "The Poetry of the Harlem Renaissance" (pp. 452–76). A second major reference work is *The New Princeton Encyclopedia of Poetry and Poetics* with its many entries of interest to readers of modern poetry, including Michael Davidson's comprehensive essay on "American Poetry" (pp. 47–65).

University of Missouri, Columbia

17 Poetry: 1940s to the Present

Lorenzo Thomas

Critical studies of postwar American poetry published in 1993 seem to have reached a consensus on two views that began to be noticed in the dissertations of the late 1980s. First, although there is no agreement on a terminal date, it is evident that many feel it is time to fill in that parenthesis in the encyclopedia heading "Modernism (1910–)." Secondly, and this seems to be accepted as gospel, modernism and its academic support system are viewed as a somewhat tyrannical "dominant discourse" that has consigned many excellent poets to the shadows of critical neglect. These poets are represented in anthologies—if at all—by one or two poems and their books are not only out of print but absent even from bins in used bookstores.

The currency of these axioms does not represent a polar shift. The magnets have not fallen to the floor, and all of our notes, of questionable urgency as always, are still attached to the refrigerator. Some, indeed, would say that the resulting collage of contradictory messages—some of them new, others fading into the nostalgia that supersedes obsolescence—is precisely what constitutes postmodernism.

Critical attention this year seems focused particularly on poets who interrogate or embody issues of race and gender, and the year also offers a wide range of work on neglected writers. In some quarters there is even the suggestion that the genre itself has suffered neglect.

i The State of the Art: General Studies

For a large segment of the literate public, contemporary poetry fell under the problematizing shadow of a Dana Gioia essay that appeared in the *Atlantic* and served as the opening chapter of his collection *Can Poetry Matter?: Essays on Poetry and American Culture* (Graywolf). Gioia's complaint is that poetry has lost any audience beyond the circle of academic critics and poets (or, more precisely, creative writing students). The aesthetic of modernism is partly responsible, but the real fault, he thinks, stems from the establishment of a closed, academically entombed professional subculture. For Gioia, universities do not nurture the genre but "imprison poetry in an intellectual ghetto." Gioia's collection also includes an interesting and solid study of Weldon Kees, one focusing on Robinson Jeffers, and short reviews of a number of contemporaries. Other essays return to his concern about poetry's popularity. Gioia finds that Robert Bly enjoys a wide audience because of his "edifying sentimentality," while Ted Kooser writes excellent and meaningful poetry in an accessible, regional mode but remains little known.

Dana Gioia's jeremiad is echoed from within the walls of academia by Vernon Shetley's erudite *After the Death of Poetry: Poet and Audience in Contemporary America* (Duke). The expectations readers bring to a text determine whether or not it is "experienced as difficult," and, for Shetley, modernist difficulty "was an effect, and not a cause, of the disappearance of the common reader." He properly identifies the role of the New Critics in preparing two generations of well-prepared modernist readers, but he also yearns for what Richard Poirier has called "aristocratic ease" in reading poetry. As his discussion proceeds, Shetley finds that Elizabeth Bishop, James Merrill, John Ashbery, the Language Poets, the "MFA mainstream," and the New Formalists have all failed the potential reading audience. In carefully organized chapters he weighs and finds each of their approaches wanting and that the academy itself has fragmented its functions between literature departments and writing programs. Without a doubt, this book will provoke strong debate. Shetley seems closer in spirit to Allan than to Harold Bloom. He claims to see no chance at all for poetry to regain a large audience and warns that "poetry's death should haunt the rest of culture; there seems something monstrous about the notion that the form of expression which through most of the history of human culture was considered the highest, most powerful, and most prestigious should have now become a sort of leisure sector of mental life, avoided by those who seek to wield genuine cultural power."

Close technical examinations of prosody might also be viewed as an increasingly neglected area of criticism. Poets may be asking "Can poetry matter?" but the common reader's frequent question "What makes this poetry?" is addressed in a highly original manner by Annie Finch in *The*

Ghost of Meter. Finch traces the presence of iambic pentameter and dactylic rhythms in poems that are advertised as "free" or, in her more precise terminology, metrically variable. Although some contemporary musicians still believe that certain rhythms reflect emotional or mental states, Finch argues that poets at the turn of the century rejected the Aristotelian idea that metrical forms have "inherent meaningful qualities," making one meter appropriate for an elegy, for example, rather than for a love lyric. The success of this early free verse movement meant that by midcentury traditional English metrics represented "an active choice—a force to add to a poem—instead of . . . a given to react against." Nevertheless, Finch thinks that a "metrical code" can be discerned in the echo or deliberate application of regular meter in free verse poems; this can be used as a critical measure to assess a poet's "attitudes toward the meter's cultural and literary connotations." Finch applies this measure to readings of Anne Sexton, Theodore Roethke, Allen Ginsberg, Charles Wright, Audre Lorde, and Judy Grahn.

Meter vanishes entirely in Lee Upton's essay "Structural Politics: The Prose Poetry of Russell Edson" (*SoAR* 58, ii: 101–15). Fully engaging the politics of form, Upton contends that Edson not only evades "predetermined form but capitalizes upon it, for the prose poem is a hybrid that resists definition." Upton sees this as an appropriate choice and reads Edson's texts as "profoundly political [because] they question forms of power as these are summoned in language." Through comedy and absurdity, Upton believes, the poet attempts to achieve "a larger liberation from convention"—social as well as literary.

The sighting of words such as "sublime" and "splendor" is rare enough in current criticism to make one wonder if their continued existence is not endangered. But readers will spot their colorful flight in the elegant prose of Nathan A. Scott, Jr.'s *Visions of Presence in Modern American Poetry* (Hopkins). Standing adamantly against "the complete abrogation of meaning that is posited by deconstructionist ideology," Scott reaches back to Wordsworth and Coleridge in offering a critical view that is also Emersonian. For Scott, the term "presence" means that "the poetic world is rooted in the concrete particularity of lived experience" and that all things in this world exist in relationship to each other. Uninterested in solipsism or in the idea that the critic is more important than the poet (or the poem), Scott's model for criticism is found in his view that "the poetic imagination is regularly captivated by things, by that which is *other than* the human mind." Nor does this lead Scott toward a sociological approach. He offers authoritative discussions of Wallace Stevens, W. H. Auden, Roethke, Elizabeth Bishop, Robert Penn Warren, Richard Wilbur, A. R. Ammons, James Wright, and Howard Nemerov. Scott acknowledges that poets are "adept in the art of supervising language," but he is most interested in what these poets have to say about how to take full advantage of our presence here and live with an alert awareness.

The poets studied by Scott also are examined in historical context in *Columbia History of American Poetry*. A major reference work, this volume includes concise and basically useful introductory surveys on Confessional poetry by Diane Wood Middlebrook, the Black Arts poets by William W. Cook, the Beats by Ann Charters, and Native American poets by Lucy Maddox. Other chapters treat John Berryman, James Merrill, John Ashbery, Philip Levine, and Charles Wright from a thematic perspective.

ii Biographical Contexts

Among the most interesting critical productions of the year are some that illuminate the lives of neglected poets. Even though she chose to be silent after the publication of her *Collected Poems* in 1938, Laura (Riding) Jackson began to exert an influence on contemporary poets and attract new attention from critics after 1980. Enigmatic and self-invented, she seemed to revise herself as continuously as she did her poems. Deborah Baker's *In Extremis: The Life of Laura Riding* (Grove) is a thoroughly researched and readable biography. Baker presents and judiciously comments on the short-lived mutual infatuation of Riding and the Fugitives, her long sojourn in Europe with Robert Graves, and encounters with Gertrude Stein and others. Much more concerned with the life than the works of the poet, writing in a popular but serious style, Baker nevertheless provides information that will enhance readings of the recently reissued *Selected Poems: In Five Sets* (Persea) and *First Awakenings: The Early Poems of Laura Riding* (Persea, 1992).

A welcome addition to biographies of poets is *Sorrow Is the Only Faithful One: The Life of Owen Dodson* (Illinois), James V. Hatch's excellent portrait of the African American poet and playwright. Dodson began writing sonnets in college and was influenced by older Harlem Renaissance poets, especially Countee Cullen. He came into his own voice during World War II and published *Powerful Long Ladder,* his first collection of poems and verse dramas, in 1946. Associated with Langston

Hughes and James Baldwin, Dodson created works in the 1950s that helped express the consciousness that forged the civil rights movement. Although he was far from receptive to some of its tenets and media posturings, Dodson himself was an influence on some of those who would constitute the membership of the 1960s Black Arts Movement. Benefiting from the subject's full cooperation, Hatch's work is thorough and unflinching in detail.

Sometimes fascinating and historically valuable is Frank Marshall Davis's *Livin' the Blues: Memoirs of a Black Journalist and Poet* (Wisconsin), which records seven decades of the author's literary experiences in Kansas, Chicago, Atlanta, and Hawaii. Based on a manuscript not entirely revised at the time of Davis's death, editor John Edgar Tidwell notes that the book is "a virtual collage, pulling together the recollections of a jazz reporter and music historian, a photographer, an editorial writer . . . and, of course, a poet." Unfortunately, rich as this life is, Davis's poetry is not the major focus of this memoir.

Moving in circles that sometimes intersected with Davis's, Edwin Rolfe was well-connected on the Left literary front in the 1930s and served with the Abraham Lincoln Brigade in the Spanish Civil War. The House Committee on Un-American Activities hearings in 1951 destroyed Rolfe's Hollywood screenwriting career, and what his editors call "the culture of paranoia" made it difficult for him even to publish poems. The appearance of *Collected Poems of Edwin Rolfe* (Illinois), ed. Cary Nelson and Jefferson Hendricks with a long biographical introduction, completes (but does not supersede) a project begun with the publication of *Edwin Rolfe: A Biographical Essay and Guide to the Rolfe Archive* (Illinois, 1990), prepared by the same team of scholars.

Rarely do collections of a poet's letters spark dinner party conversations among those who did not know them personally, but the appearance of Jenny Penberthy's *Niedecker and the Correspondence with Zukofsky, 1931–1970* (Cambridge) certainly had that effect. The letters Lorine Niedecker wrote to Louis Zukofsky cover her entire creative career, and Penberthy's meticulously documented 100-page introductory essay is really an excellent critical biography. "What can at times seem like Niedecker's excessive absorption in Zukofsky's fortunes," Penberthy warns, "is more likely a reflection of his own editorial bias" since both poets, anticipating publication of their correspondence, edited their holograph copies in their own collections carefully beginning in 1947. A relationship that began when Niedecker first read Zukofsky's poems in the Objectivist issue of *Poetry* (February 1931) grew into literary mentorship, perhaps blossomed as intimate romance, and certainly ripened into a lifelong friendship. Penberthy notes that their relationship was "far from uncomplicated," and, because their letters from 1931–41 are no longer extant, she does a fine job of reconstructing from other sources a sense of the poetic cross-influence they shared. The letters published are notable for their warmth and comfortable revelations and show Niedecker to have been as intense in her love of people as of nature.

A more conventional offering, *Talking Together: Letters of David Ignatow, 1946 to 1990* (Alabama), ed. Gary Pacernick, includes correspondence addressed to Ralph J. Mills, Jr., and Jerome Mazzaro that offer helpful glosses to Ignatow's published work. An earlier group of letters to William Carlos Williams, Langston Hughes, and others, shows the young poet beginning to establish himself in a literary universe. *Tales Out of School: Selected Interviews* (Michigan) by Robert Creeley is a volume in the "Poets on Poetry" series that contains transcripts of tape-recorded interviews with Creeley conducted by sympathetic fellow poets such as Lewis MacAdams and Michael André. Tom Clark's *Robert Creeley and the Genius of the American Common Place* (New Directions) contains Clark's biographical sketches of the poet as well as a 20-page "Autobiography" by Creeley and interesting photographs.

"The Stories of My Life," a 40-page memoir of early childhood influences and poems read in elementary school through high school, adds value to *Proses: On Poems and Poets* (Copper Canyon) by Carolyn Kizer. Self-assured in her opinions and appreciations—whether chastising Karl Shapiro, restating what she finds right about Creeley and Gary Snyder, or attempting to direct long overdue attention to the precisions of Marie Ponsot—Kizer manages to be simultaneously elegant and conversational. Adrienne Rich's essays and reviews of contemporary poets, collected in *What Is Found There: Notes on Poetry and Politics* (Norton), is not at all memoiristic but will certainly provide material for critics of Rich's own poetry. She has wise things to say, quotes poets carefully and to useful effect, and maintains a relentlessly radical feminist stance. Like Gioia, Rich also worries about the poetic state of the Union. From her point of view, however, the poet's place in contemporary American society is "interstitial living . . . more difficult, risky, and wearing than it has ever been, and this is a loss to all the arts—as much as the shrinkage of arts funding, the censorship-by-clique, the censorship by the Right, the censorship by distribution." Rich still speaks her mind, and she does not bite her tongue.

iii Major Voices: Wallace Stevens, Elizabeth Bishop

The poets who emerged in the 1950s have identified as their smooth and jagged ashlars the monumental figures of Wallace Stevens and William Carlos Williams. If Williams is claimed as precursor (and actual mentor) by the Beats and others, Stevens is clearly an influence on major figures such as James Merrill and John Ashbery. Paul Bauer's "The Politics of Reticence: Wallace Stevens in the Cold War Era" (*TCL* 39: 1–31) effectively re-creates the intellectual climate of the early 1950s, presenting Stevens as a model of the "amorphous middle ground of American culture, the 'vital center' opposed equally to extremes of both left and right." Among the younger writers who first appeared in that era and found this middle ground a difficult place to stand, the object of much recent critical attention is Elizabeth Bishop. Some of the industry devoted to Bishop is generated by the feeling that, after Robert Lowell, she is the next of that generation to truly deserve recognition as a major American poet; some is derived from her status as a heretofore neglected figure and, therefore, a suitable focus for feminist and contextual criticism.

In *Elizabeth Bishop: The Restraints of Language* (Oxford) C. K. Doreski contends that the poet's carefully modulated "restraint" should be reconsidered. "Rather than an escape from emotion," says Doreski, "this represented its liberation not only from bathos but from the high ironies of modernism, which had become as perfunctory as Victorian sentiment." By means of intelligent close readings of Bishop's published poems, Doreski examines the poet's formal choices and interest in literary tradition (particularly the genre of travel narratives). These exercises in form, she feels, transcend sociological or gender issues. Taking a very different starting point, Victoria Harrison in *Elizabeth Bishop's Poetics of Intimacy* (Cambridge) offers a feminist reading of Bishop's work based on a clear biographical discussion. Harrison's close attention to the poet's process of invention and revision (reproduced in typographic facsimile) is quite impressive and helps her to construct a convincing argument for Bishop's desire to understand "relationships of power, possession, and love" through the medium of literature. Harrison

offers an excellent chapter that investigates Bishop's place in the politi-
cized intellectual milieu of the 1930s and 1940s. She claims—despite
some of Bishop's own public disclaimers—that Bishop's later poems
often show her "locating the 'significant, illustrative, American, etc.'
center precisely in the voices of the traditionally marginalized." Some
readers, however, may find this political stance more clearly articulated
by the critic than by Bishop.

Gender is the focus of Lorrie Goldensohn's *Elizabeth Bishop: The Biography of a Poetry* (Columbia). Based on Bishop's unpublished materials,
the book reconstructs the poet's long period in Brazil with her companion Lota de Macedo Soares and provides a reading of Bishop's work
informed by an examination of her emotional life. Goldensohn, Harrison, Bonnie Costello, Brett Candlish Millier, Thomas Travisano, and
other leading Bishop scholars are represented with thought-provoking
essays in *Elizabeth Bishop: The Geography of Gender* (Virginia), ed. Marilyn May Lombardi. These feminist interpretations constitute an impressive symposium notable for clarity and accessibility.

iv Charles Olson, Paul Blackburn, Denise Levertov, John Ashbery

In *The Grounding of American Poetry: Charles Olson and the Emersonian
Tradition* (Cambridge), a study that curiously lacks the rhetorical energy
of either poet, Stephen Fredman examines Olson's attempt to realize the
long-sought goal of creating an intrinsically American poetry. In a
culture that begins in estrangement from Europe, one that peculiarly
belongs to a modernity that—according to Fredman—is "in opposition
to tradition," the American poet has had to resolve questions of ancestry,
self-authorization, definition of community, and relation to geographical
place. Carefully argued and documented, this monograph shows how
Olson drew on Williams, Thoreau, and Emerson to formulate a set of
provisional answers that were formulated in 1950 as the theory of "projective verse." The poetic practice that followed the theory involved
the Black Mountain group that included Robert Creeley, Robert Duncan, Denise Levertov, Ed Dorn, Paul Blackburn, Joel Oppenheimer,
and others. Fredman does not extend his discussion to the musicians
and visual artists (e.g., John Cage and Josef Albers) who also participated
and influenced Olson's circle. He does, however, offer fine discussions of
specific poems, the relationship between Duncan's thought and Emer-

son's, and a useful guide to understanding the disjunctive grammatical structure of Olson's "projectivist" poems.

Peter Baker employs Derrida as a lens to examine "the poem as gift" in the works of Paul Blackburn in "Blackburn's Gift" (*Sagetrieb* 12, i: 43–54). Noting that "prevailing orthodoxy is rarely an effective measure of any poet's worth," Baker attempts to refute charges of Blackburn's sexism and suggests that poems composed of casual remarks in the vernacular may actually be read (and may have been intended) as Marxian critiques of the status quo. Such poems, he adds, might also be seen as self-discovery exercises that recall Emily Dickinson's practice. In his explication of several Blackburn poems Baker presents a consistent critical metaphor: "Blackburn's gift requires nothing in return. There is no receipt marked for possible exchange or return. The work itself is unremunerated, by an artist who is unselfconsciously, disinterestedly presenting something for contemplation."

Opening on the premise that "the artist and her art are indivisible," Audrey T. Rogers in *Denise Levertov: The Poetry of Engagement* (Fairleigh Dickinson) presents a reading of Levertov as politically engaged throughout her career. Levertov is one of those writers whose "political and social consciences [are] the centerpiece of their art." Rogers discusses all of Levertov's work through 1988, including her World War II poems and those that offered strident protest during the Vietnam War. The book effectively relates Levertov to her contemporaries and to what Rogers calls the "revolutionary" tradition of the Romantics—"explaining the world of visible things." In a different direction, the growing body of criticism concerning John Ashbery is joined by Frank J. Lepkowski's "John Ashbery's Revision of the Post-Romantic Quest: Meaning, Evasion, and Allusion in 'Grand Galop'" (*TCL* 39: 251–65). Avoiding one realm of politics, Lepkowski finds this poem "a dance of the intellect of a most energetic tempo" and laments that it has been overshadowed by Ashbery's "Self-Portrait in a Convex Mirror."

v Thematic Criticism: Black Arts Movement, Vietnam War

A poem, Frank O'Hara famously said, "should be at least as interesting as the movies." Laurence Goldstein tests the social implications of that statement in "'Mama How Come Black Men Don't Get to Be Heroes?': Black Poets and the Movies" (*IowaR* 23, iii: 110–31). Goldstein's discussion focuses on Wanda Coleman and includes mention of Welton Smith,

Robert Hayden, Thylias Moss, and Ishmael Reed. The article examines stereotyped images of African Americans in Hollywood movies and in poems that critique the negative effects of such images. The work discussed follows a pattern that first achieved popular attention with the direct-action political poetry of the 1960s Black Arts Movement. Just as it is said that Milton gave Satan all the best lines, however, this particular essay appears to be more interested in the movies than in the poems.

Violet Harrington Bryan offers an important contribution to the history of the Black Arts Movement in the final chapter of *Myth of New Orleans*. Spearheaded by Amiri Baraka, Larry Neal, and Askia Muhammad Touré in New York in the early 1960s, the Black Arts Movement soon developed a nationwide network of poets, musicians, visual artists, and community theater groups. There were energetic centers in San Francisco, Chicago, Detroit, and other large cities. More extensive in geographic scope than the Harlem Renaissance of the 1920s, the work produced was primarily addressed to African American audiences. Bryan focuses on the contributions to the movement that emanated from New Orleans, especially through the efforts of Tom Dent. Bryan concisely reports Dent's organizational activities with the Free Southern Theatre and the literary journal *Nkombo,* and she offers close readings of his poems. She discusses the influence of Dent's New Orleans group on Ishmael Reed and presents excellent discussions of the poetry of Brenda Marie Osbey, author of three highly regarded collections, and Sybil Kein, who writes in both English and the Afro-French Creole language of Louisiana that first appeared in literary form in Armand Lanusse's 1845 anthology *Les Cenelles.* Bryan suggests that all of these writers, while contributing to contemporary African American literature, also continue a significant and unique regional heritage.

Lasting for more than 20 years—much of that time hidden from the American public's attention—the war in Vietnam did not yield the immediate poetic eloquence of Karl Shapiro's *V-Letter* (1944) or the tortured later re-creation of James Dickey that help to fix World War II in our literary history. There were some considerably powerful poetic Vietnam documents from Michael Casey, Walter McDonald, and others; and Yusef Komunyakaa's continuing recollections of his tour as a medic are part of the work that earned him the 1994 Pulitzer Prize. Critics such as Don Ringnalda think that "the Vietnam War *should* have resulted in a body of honest, extremely disconcerting poetry" and in a special issue of *JACult* (16, iii), a group of these critics review some of the poets of the Vietnam War and attempt to assess the poetic rather than directly political value of the work. The issue includes essays on Casey, Bruce Weigl, Robert Bly, and others. Lorrie Smith contributes "The Subject Makes a Difference: Poetry by Women Veterans of the Vietnam War" (pp. 71–80). Don Ringnalda in "Rejecting 'Sweet Geometry': Komunyakaa's *Duende*" (pp. 21–28) compares Komunyakaa's work on a thematic level to Federico García Lorca and to World War I poets such as Robert Graves. An important reading of Allen Ginsberg's antiwar "Wichita Vortex Sutra" is offered by David Jarraway's "Standing by His Word: The Politics of Allen Ginsberg's Vietnam 'Vortex' " (pp. 81–88). Jarraway proposes the televised Vietnam War as an example of postmodernism *avant le lettre*. Without considering the possible influence of similar ideas proposed by Amiri Baraka during the period, Jarraway analyzes Ginsberg's direct-action activism and interests in "Black Magic language and formulas for reality." While most discussions of the Vietnam War poetry written by soldiers is thematic—concerned with the events and the poet's subjectivity—Vince Gotera's "The Fragging of Language: D. F. Brown's Vietnam-War Poetry" (pp. 39–45) takes a different approach. "Brown's fragmentation," Gotera writes, "is closely related to the avant-gardism of Language Poetry" and "may have a greater ideological impetus than those poets whose only subject is language itself." Gotera efficiently explicates Brown's poems and places the work in the context not only of the poet's affiliation with the L=A=N-=G=U=A=G=E group but also Brown's relationship to the earlier concerns of George Orwell and Thomas Merton regarding "the disinformative tautology of official language" and the possibility that poetry can counter or at least effectively expose such linguistic distortions of reality.

vi Contextual Criticism: Robert Duncan, Jack Spicer, Bob Kaufman, and James Dickey

In some ways, critics also aspire to the function that Thomas Merton sought for poetry. Many of the critical issues of the current moment concern the relationship of criticism to "official language" or the fear that criticism may sometimes behave as if it were such a language. These concerns can be seen in the work of such outstanding emerging critics as Maria Damon and Ernest Suarez.

Although there is a growing body of critical discussion of Robert Duncan, he is included in Damon's fine study *The Dark End of the Street:*

Margins in American Vanguard Poetry (Minnesota) because she is concerned with the poet's marginality as a gay man in San Francisco in the early 1950s. Damon's chapter on Duncan and Jack Spicer offers a detailed picture of the bohemian milieu that preceded both the San Francisco Renaissance of the late 1950s and the "Summer of Love" that created the post-Beat Generation hippie life-style. Damon's readings of Spicer and Duncan are not, however, a matter of viewing their work through a "life-style" lens that may be of questionable relevance. She is interested in language, and she shows, for example, that the idiosyncratic Spicer created works intended for a male homosexual audience and written in the 1950s jargon of that subculture. Nevertheless, Damon carefully avoids adopting "a perspective of the late 1960s and 1970s when the 'ethnicization' of gay culture and its alliance with other 'target groups' became an important strategy in gay power politics." Instead, she shows how these poets encoded and expressed the subculture's values and thereby contributed to the later articulation of political strategies. Damon is particularly effective in arguing the philosophical influence of Walt Whitman's view of Plato as a precursor for the poetics of Duncan, Spicer, and Robin Blaser. While she is familiar with Derrida, and with Deleuze and Guattari, Damon prefers primary sources and is an excellent explicator. She matches this skill with a historically grounded grasp of American popular culture to produce a wide-ranging but focused discussion.

These qualities are fully employed in the book's best chapter—a useful and insightful study of Bob Kaufman, the African American surrealist who is credited as a major figure in the early development of Beat poetry. In this most thorough recent reading of Kaufman, Damon offers biographical details that support his role as mentor to Ginsberg and others, while she also traces the African American cultural elements that Kaufman—socially deracinated though he may have been—never abandoned in his poems. While Damon's wide-ranging American Studies approach allows her to raise interesting questions regarding the limitations of articulate language, aleatory compositional techniques, and the dimensions of the surrealist image, she does not employ a structure that allows extensive discussion of these matters. Her careful and tantalizingly opinionated textual notes, however, will direct interested readers to sources that will enable them to pursue their own investigations.

The approach exemplified by Damon's study is precisely what Ernest Suarez feels requires his riposte to what many critics seem to think our age demands. In *James Dickey and the Politics of Canon: Assessing the Savage Ideal* (Missouri) Suarez combines close readings of many poems with a skillful exposition of the poet's career and intellectual development. With commendable clarity, Suarez succeeds in demonstrating that Dickey deserves more serious critical consideration beyond the appreciation of a regional coterie. Drawing on previously unpublished correspondence, Suarez interprets Dickey's early influences from other poets such as Pound and Frost as a sort of Oedipal drama—a search for a poetic father—that also, calculatedly, helped to further Dickey's emerging career as a poet. The early interest in Pound also aided Dickey's development of "the narrative image," the term Suarez applies to the poet's personal adaptation of modernist techniques. Also discussed is Dickey's relationship to Robert Lowell and Robert Bly. A good argument shows how Dickey's best-selling novels proceed from his poetic concerns and reconfigure the theme of primitivistic pantheism as a force of spiritual regeneration and reintegration of the fragmented modern self. Dickey's "Slave Quarters," denounced by Bly as "repulsive," is—in Suarez's terms—a "representation of a racist's consciousness" that, because of the poet's skill, is ultimately redemptive. Suarez, however, seems innocent of any knowledge of the complexities of racial representation or recent work in the area by scholars such as Michael Rogin, Eric Lott, or even Robert Toll. This will possibly be the most controversial aspect of his work.

The true polemic, however, appears in Suarez's charge that Dickey has fallen victim to "political correctness." His career and literary reputation represent "a battleground between the advocates of criticism that directly foregrounds political and social issues and those who favor aesthetic criticism that indirectly affirms humanistic values." Consequently, says Suarez, Dickey is praised by an "unlikely combination of elitist New Critics and the popular media" while being neglected by those who are responsible for the formation of the postmodern canon. It can be said that Suarez does a fine job of petitioning for Dickey's reentry into the arena of serious critical attention.

University of Houston–Downtown

18   Drama

James J. Martine

During the last decade or so, the very matter of what scholarship does—
or should do—has been subject to scrutiny in a number of radical ways,
and the nature of the study of literature has been questiond. The last
time this essay was written, however, Peter A. Davis suggested that
theater scholarship operates largely in isolation, unaware of most new
theories in complementary fields (see *ALS 1991*, p. 335). Several books
published in the past two years begin by wondering whatever happened
to American drama. Why have literary theorists so little to say about
American theater? The news is that the fabulous invalid once again has
risen from the grave's edge and brought back her attendant scholars and
the professoriate with her. She is alive and well and so is American drama
scholarship. There is no publication drought. The pervasiveness of
Foucault, Derrida, and Lacan notwithstanding, it has been said that the
study of American drama lags far behind trends and fads in history and
what now passes as study in what used to be called literature. If drama
study in America does not exist in isolation, it is the least affected (nice
word that) of the genres of American literary study. I am not sure that is a
bad thing. It is as though the scholars and critics in this field have taken
Emerson at his word and realized as truth that if American scholars plant
themselves indomitably on their instincts, and there abide, the huge
world will come round to them.

While much of the above may be so, even as we acknowledge the very
real and significant contributions of feminists and other scholars examining the works of writers of color, after reading what follows, let us agree
at least that a moratorium be declared for the next year on the use of the
word "marginalized." The compulsively politically correct will note that
I have not made distinctions on the basis of gender or race. I have done
this fully aware of their disapprobation. I choose, as an ideal, to integrate

rather than segregate all authors. There is, to be sure, a continued vitality to feminist writing, but the period of self-definition and theoretical exploration draws to a close, and the time has come for all writers regardless of gender or color to take their proper place in the ranks of American drama. I am old-fashioned enough to make distinctions in the final two sections of this chapter on one basis only. Differences in gender and race pale in the face of death, the true equalizer.

i Reference Works and Anthologies

In *ALS 1991,* Davis correctly reported that the crop of dramatic reference texts had leveled off as the field became saturated; similar conditions still exist. There are, however, two items worthy of note. The second edition of Gerald Bordman's *The Oxford Companion to American Theatre* (Oxford, 1992) covers the field from Alex Aarons to *Zoo Story* and like its predecessor eight years before it is arranged in two-column pages for easy access; moreover, this standard reference source now contains more than 3,000 entries on playwrights, plays, actors, directors, producers, songwriters, dramatic movements, and entities from the Abbey Theatre company to famous playhouses like the Ziegfeld Theatre in Manhattan. The smart reader will also want to save room on the shelf next to the *Oxford Companion* for the *Cambridge Guide to American Theatre.* Davis in this space (see *ALS 1991,* p. 336) called Don B. Wilmeth the consummate American theater bibliographer, and Wilmeth includes 2,300 entries—alphabetically arranged—written by more than 80 contributors including dependable experts and scholars like Philip Kolin, Brenda Murphy, and Bruce McConachie. No less a scholarly light than Stanley Weintraub, for example, is represented by the entry on Shaw and the American theater. Davis provides the entries on Walter Murry and Thomas Kean, long associated with one of the first professional touring groups in this country. Wilmeth himself and C. Lee Jenner supply the reliable 21-page introduction; and Walter J. Meserve writes the entries on 18th-century playwright and politician Robert Munford, 19th-century figures such as William "Billy" Mitchell, Samuel Benjamin Judah, George Henry Miles, Danforth Marble, and Josephine Preston Peabody Marks, as well as essays on Arthur Laurents and Sidney Kingsley. The accuracy of the entries is assured by the scholarly reputations of the contributors, although entries on specific plays necessarily cannot provide detailed plot synopses or textual analyses. The *Cambridge Guide* is a useful reference tool for concise, carefully selected, and authoritative information on American drama, including numerous topics that are generally placed outside the realm of what was once considered legitimate theater such as circus, magic, vaudeville, and burlesque. Its entries comment on academic theater, AIDS in the American theater, ethnic theater, female-male impersonation, and feminist theater as well as theatrical societies and associations, Yiddish theater, and the Borscht belt. There are also entries on gay and lesbian theater, Asian-American theater, and African American theater.

Although it is organized alphabetically, Thomas S. Hischak's *Stage It with Music: An Encyclopedic Guide to the American Musical Theater* (Greenwood) will not be confused with the volumes noted above. Hischak describes more than 300 individual musical shows from *The Black Crook* of 1866 to 1992's *Jelly's Last Jam*. The author provides additional entries on performers, composers, and the like, and the entries are packed with anecdotes and subjective commentary as well as brief raw data. It is a pleasant enough volume, but do not be deceived by the word "encyclopedic" in its subtitle. It is not as comprehensive as works by Gerald Bordman and Stanley Green, which are listed in Hischak's selected bibliography. The book rewards casual browsing, however. No previous mention has been made in *ALS* of L. Terry Oggel's *Edwin Booth: A Bio-Bibliography* (Greenwood, 1992), a meticulous and exceptionally thorough compilation of materials by and about Booth, arguably the greatest actor of the 19th century. With this volume Greenwood maintains its position as a leading publisher of theatrical reference books. Perhaps the quality of this Oggel work will send readers back to *The Letters and Notebooks of Mary Devlin Booth* (Greenwood, 1987), ed. Oggel, a remarkable collection of materials by and about a woman who performed with Joseph Jefferson and Edwin Forrest, was a favorite of Julia Ward Howe, and was married to Booth from 1860 until her death in 1863 at age 23.

Few anthologies of note were published this year, continuing a steady decline since the turn of the decade. Significantly, the new books have little to do with the mainstream, except perhaps as the mainstream broadens. The first of these is *Crosswinds: An Anthology of Black Dramatists in the Diaspora* (Indiana), ed. William B. Branch, an impressive volume which contains ten plays by writers from Black Africa and of Black African descent. It includes familiar fare like Amiri Baraka's *Slave Ship* and August Wilson's *Joe Turner's Come and Gone,* but these are overshadowed by the works of two Nobel laureates, Wole Soyinka's *Death and the King's Horseman* and Derek Walcott's *Pantomime*. While only four of the writers—Baraka, Wilson, Branch, and Richard Wesley— were born in the continental United States and are thus "American," Branch's introduction deals with the matters of nationality, consciousness based on Black African descent, and the pan-African cultural system as well as the relation of African American theater to world drama. Few black dramatists provide diversionary entertainments. These playwrights have axes to grind, evils to expose, and sermons to preach. The anthology also includes *Woza Albert!*, the collaborative work of Percy Mtwa and Mbongeni Ngema; Edgar White's *Lament for Rastafari;* Abdias do Nascimento's *Sortilege II: Zumbi Returns;* Branch's own *In Splendid Error;* Wesley's *The Talented Tenth;* and Efua Sutherland's *Edufa.*

If Sutherland's is the only female voice in Branch's volume, *The Politics of Life: Four Plays by Asian American Women* (Temple), ed. Velina Hasu Houston, is exclusively devoted to examining the politics of women of color in an inamicable American society. Included are two plays by Wakako Yamauchi. *The Chairman's Wife* examines the life of Madame Mao through her reign as the most powerful woman in China to her end in a prison hospital, suffering from throat cancer, and in *12-1-A* Yamauchi draws from her personal history to center on a Japanese-American family sent to an incarceration camp in Arizona. Genny Lim focuses on the socioeconomic exploitation of immigrant Chinese on sugar cane plantations in *Bitter Cane,* and Houston concludes the volume with her own *Asa Ga Kimashita* (*Morning Has Broken*), about a Japanese patriarch who loses his estate because of regulations imposed by the United States after World War II. Houston's lengthy introduction (pp. 1–31) on feminine experience as political experience and her challenges to the erosive elements of racism, sexism, and antifeminism make a significant essay. A blend of artistic voice and academic vigor shapes her introduction and this anthology.

ii Theater History

James H. McTeague in *Before Stanislavsky: American Professional Acting Schools and Acting Theory 1875–1925* (Scarecrow) seeks to demonstrate that many persons and agencies were involved in training actors in the United States before Konstantin Stanislavsky and the Moscow Art Theater arrived here in 1923. In support of this thesis, McTeague supplies a

50-year history of U.S. acting schools from Steele MacKaye's Lyceum Theatre School, through the establishment of the American Academy of Dramatic Arts (the oldest and longest-lasting professional acting school) in 1892, to the National Dramatic Conservatory founded by F. F. Mackay, the foremost proponent of the intellectual, or "anti-feeling," method of acting. McTeague's book focuses on particular schools and chronicles not only American contributions to the principles of acting but the concern with the fundamental place of theater in society. A highly specialized, not to say esoteric, item is Ramon Gutiérrez's "The Politics of Theater in Colonial New Mexico: Drama and the Rhetoric of Conquest," in *Reconstructing a Chicano/a Literary Heritage* (Arizona, pp. 49–67), ed. María Herrera-Sobek, which focuses on a single facet of the Spanish ideological enterprise in North America: how the Spaniards used theater to indoctrinate the Pueblo Indians. The piece is noteworthy because of the current interest in ethnic identity and culture that may lead to the discovery of what the volume editor perceives to be a direct connection between colonial literary writings and contemporary Chicano literature.

The traditions of Western Marxism provide the framework and the foundational metaphors for Bruce A. McConachie's *Melodramatic Formations: American Theatre and Society, 1820–1870* (Iowa, 1992). Certain that the relevant issue for theater historians is not the relative artistic merit of the period's melodramas, McConachie uses the plays to investigate the ways in which contextual social realities shaped 19th-century American theater. While British melodramas outnumbered American plays of the time perhaps 5-to-1, and more than double that for social comedies, the volume examines American plays almost exclusively. Tracing the decline of one kind of cultural dominance and the gradual rise of another, the book is organized chronologically into three major parts: the waning of a paternalistic theater for the elite, which covers the first fifteen years of the study; the theater of yeoman independence for the Jacksonians (1830–55); and the respectable business-class theater (1845–70), just before the Panic of 1873 destroyed American stock companies. Copiously annotated, McConachie's book is moderate in its position, intelligent in relating early American drama to social and intellectual history, and most interesting in its analyses of theatrical performance practices relating what happened onstage to the sociocultural aspects of what was happening in the theaters and among their audiences. McConachie is not alone this year in his examination of melodrama. The genre is the subject of inquiry in Jeffrey D. Mason's *Melodrama and the Myth of America* (Indiana). While Mason does not identify himself with any of the current methodologies, he does borrow from deconstruction, semiotics, and feminism. He appropriates most especially Marxist critical techniques because he believes they best elucidate the functioning of a capitalist social system. Mason's book is unusual in that he focuses on only five plays—*Metamora* (1829), *The Drunkard* (1844), *Uncle Tom's Cabin* (1852), *My Partner* (1879), and *Shenandoah* (1889)—to comment on, in turn, the cultural treatment of the Native American, melodrama and the antebellum temperance movement, the politics of race, and the ways in which melodrama can reconstruct myth. Mason presents an especially original treatment of the postbellum South. He concludes that Americans base their worldview on the melodramatic conceptions of binary oppositions, yet our most successful melodramas offer new ways of understanding our national myths.

Like McConachie's volume, James S. Moy's *Marginal Sights: Staging the Chinese in America* (Iowa) is part of Iowa's Studies in Theatre History and Culture Series. Noting that the dominant cultures in the Western tradition in drama have always represented marginal or foreign racial groups as "othered," Moy suggests that the need to demean these othered people serves to maintain an advantage for the dominant culture. Because Asians and other people of color lived as beings without a real presence, they could not argue against their marginalization. Othered initially by European xenophobia, Asian-Americans have found it especially difficult to displace 19th-century stereotypes. Moy's extended essay consists of ten readings, each of which considers strategies in the staging of the Chinese in American drama. Of special interest are the chapters on O'Neill's positive if not realistic portrayal of the Chinese in *Marco Millions* and the racism growing into pornography apparent in other presentations. Moy argues that the stereotypical representations of Asians were not dispelled until David Henry Hwang's *M. Butterfly* and Philip Kan Gotanda's *Yankee Dawg You Die,* both in 1988. Each receives modest explication. While Moy's focus is on the Chinese, the implications are clear for the staging of marginalized people in general.

Since *ALS 1991,* a handful of outstanding theatrical histories have appeared. The first of these, *The American Stage: Social and Economic Issues From The Colonial Period To The Present* (Cambridge), ed. Ron Engle and Tice L. Miller, is an exceptional collection of 19 essays which describe how social and economic forces shaped the 250-year history of theater in America. Largely written by eminent theater historians, among them the late Charles Shattuck, the essays are nicely arranged chronologically and are augmented by Oscar G. Brockett's fine introduction and a summary checklist of selected books from 1960–90 compiled by Don B. Wilmeth. Space limitations make it impossible to comment on all the gold that glitters in this volume, but special applause is in order for Walter J. Meserve's "Social Awareness on Stage: Tensions Mounting, 1850–1859" (pp. 81–100), Marvin Carlson's considerations on the development of the American theater playbill (pp. 101–14), Felicia Hardison Londré's informative piece on women playwrights from 1890 to 1929 (pp. 131–40), Ronald H. Wainscott's instructive article on 1920s theater (pp. 175–89), and Barry B. Witham's data-enriched essay on the economics of the Federal Theatre Project (pp. 200–214). The volume also treats such topics as the theater's response to slavery, prostitution, alcoholism, and women's rights.

Four other volumes deserve a place on the reference shelf as well as a general audience. Gerald M. Berkowitz's *American Drama of the Twentieth Century* (Longman, 1992) introduces American drama in a historical and cultural context. It is literary history with a plot that presents the outline of 20th-century American drama as a clearly discernible arc, and it proposes that the dominant and most fertile style is realistic, contemporary, middle-class domestic melodrama. The volume demonstrates that domestic realism maintained its position as the native and natural style for American drama. Berkowitz's volume is a study of drama rather than theater, his focus always on the literature rather than production history. Divided chronologically by historical or theatrical turning points, each chapter covers roughly 15 years. One small problem: a reader interested in a single writer may have to look in more than one place; Arthur Miller, for instance, turns up in both chapters 4 and 6. This is a small inconvenience in a volume otherwise so good. Nothing exceptional marks Berkowitz's commentary or brief play synopses, but his observations are measured, his perspective sound, and his account accurate. All major dramatists are included: O'Neill, Shepard, Rabe, Williams, Mamet, both Wilsons, even Neil Simon. The sections on women dramatists (pp. 198–203), such as Wasserstein, Henley, and Marsha Norman, and minority voices (pp. 203–06) will seem too slight for some, but Berkowitz insists on the enduring merit of those works and writers included in this outstanding introduction to the meat-and-potatoes history of 20th-century American drama. The volume includes a graphic chronology of drama 1890–1991 (pp. 210–68).

Readers expecting greater depth of insight and development will find it in two volumes of Twayne's Critical History of American Drama. Gary A. Richardson's *American Drama From the Colonial Period Through World War I: A Critical History* is published two years after but covers the historical period before Jordan Y. Miller and Winifred L. Frazer's *American Drama Between the Wars: A Critical History* (1991). Richardson's volume seeks to rectify the attitude that the first 150 years of American drama were more fun than intelligent. He argues for the need to reexamine neglected works with a more contemporary critical perspective, which results in a greater understanding of the earliest dramatists' achievements, although he chooses "plays that are, in the main, fairly well known and readily accessible to students of early American drama." The book is divided into three general sections: the first discusses the period between the foundation of the English colonies and the early 19th century; the second points to tensions between elite and populist dramatic culture; and the third covers the more complex drama after the Civil War and explores, like McConachie and Mason, melodrama as the later 19th century's dominant form. Richardson's final chapter examines plays which deal with issues of gender from 1900 to 1920. A brief chronology of major plays concludes the volume. Miller and Frazer's volume on the drama *l'entre deux guerres* chronicles the coming of age of modern American drama, and the authors precisely recount the impact of the new spirit of vital and uncompromising American modernism. O'Neill is the dividing line, yet contributions by Glaspell, Elmer Rice, Clifford Odets, George S. Kaufman, Lillian Hellman—even Orson Welles—which changed the form of American drama are also examined. The little theater movement as well as the lasting contributions of the Provincetown Players, the Neighborhood Playhouse, the Group Theatre, and the Federal Theatre Project receive due comment. The stories recounted are wonderful; for instance, the now-legendary tale of the opening of Marc Blitzstein's *The Cradle Will Rock* is as dramatic as the radical labor musical itself. With valid and dependable judgments, this is one of the two most important books published on American drama since *ALS 1991*.

The other signal volume is also the product of scholarly experience and a first-rate mind. Over the past few years C. W. E. Bigsby has produced numerous critical analyses of major American plays. His three-volume critical introduction to 20th-century American drama and his study of the period 1959–66 with its focus on political and social dramatists like Miller and Albee remain highly regarded. In *Modern American Drama, 1945–1990* (Cambridge, 1992) Bigsby attempts to cover the post-World War II period. Since the author is on familiar ground in individual chapters on O'Neill, Williams, Miller, and Albee, there are, he concedes, bound to be some echoes; still, this guide retains his authority. Bigsby strikingly explores the relation of the Open Theatre, the Living Theater, and the Performance Group to performance theater in which artists become living sculptures, deprived of narrative role, psychological depth, or social relationship. Robert Wilson's name does not appear with Lanford's or August's in any other history of American drama. Nor do the names Richard Foreman and Lee Breuer. While even Bigsby's volume is long on August Wilson and short on Lanford Wilson, it devotes more space to Robert Wilson than to the other two Wilsons combined. The chapter on the "performing self" is significant scholarship and should be required reading. His final chapter on politics, race, and gender is adequate, treating mostly household names. Although Bigsby's book does not pretend to be comprehensive, it unfortunately omits even a mention of Tony Kushner, Mart Crowley, John Guare, Terrance McNally (all of whom seem major players to me), and although *Torch Song Trilogy* is once mentioned parenthetically, I am still waiting for someone—anyone—to give Harvey Fierstein the serious consideration his work merits.

To remain au courant, a wise reader will ultimately seek out Gerald Weales's "American Theater Watch, 1992–1993" (*GaR* 47: 563–73). This updating by a highly respected scholar *does* comment on Kushner, then goes on to Wendy Wasserstein, Mamet, and Paul Rudnick, all of whom had plays in New York during the 1992–93 season. Weales devotes a gentle paragraph to *The Last Yankee,* a minor Arthur Miller play, but he saves a little room, as does Ron Jenkins (of whom, more shortly), for an appreciation of the Pickle Family Circus. Four other studies in this area are of interest. John W. Frick in " 'He Drank From the Poisoned Cup': Theatre, Culture, and Temperance in Antebellum America" (*JADT* 4, ii: 21–41) deals with the strictly 19th-century phenomenon of temperance entertainment and the appropriation of domestic melodrama for the advancement of the temperance cause in dramas such as T. P. Taylor's *The Bottle,* J. B. Johnstone's *The Drunkard's Daughter,* and Charles W.

Taylor's *Little Katy, or the Hot Corn Girl*, one of the most successful plays of the 1850s. Richard Wattenberg's "Challenging the Frontier Myth: Contemporary Women's Plays About Women Pioneers" (*JADT* 4, iii: 42–61) is a gendered analysis of the frontier myth in plays of the 1980s. This essay is especially good on Beth Henley's *Abundance* and Darrah Cloud's adaptation of Willa Cather's novel *O Pioneers!* Jack Hrkach in "Drama Along the Turnpikes: The Earliest Theatrical Activity in the Villages of Central and Western New York" (*JADT* 4, iii: 76–92) restricts his commentary to a specific geographic area and the period from 1790 until 1817. Contemporary New York theater is the locus of John V. Antush's "Roberto Rodriguez Suarez: Transcultural Catalyst of Puerto Rican Drama" (*JADT* 4, ii: 42–53), an encomium to Suarez and a good introduction to Hispanic theater.

iii   Criticism and Theory

While technically only Marybeth Hamilton's " 'I'm the Queen of the Bitches': Female Impersonation and Mae West's *Pleasure Man*" (pp. 107–19) and Elizabeth Drorbaugh's "Sliding Scales: Notes on Stormé DeLarverié and the Jewel Box Revue" (pp. 120–43) in *Crossing the Stage: Controversies on Cross-Dressing* (Routledge), ed. Lesley Ferris, deal with matters American, the thorough bibliography (pp. 171–90) is a useful entrée to theoretical and pedagogical scholarship on the politics and discourse of gender in theatrical performance. Because it is chock-full of charts and graphs, Bernard Rosenberg and Ernest Harburg's *The Broadway Musical: Collaboration in Commerce and Art* (NYU) might have been listed with reference works. Because its focus is on the socioeconomic realities of the business of the theater and is so carefully and informatively developed, it might have settled comfortably in the group of theater histories. At heart, however, this volume about the relationship of business to the musical theater supports a position that this linkage is built into Western civilization and its development as a large-scale capitalist industrial economy; the authors demonstrate that the business of American musical theater is as collaborative (and often as creative) as the art of creating musicals. Rosenberg and Harburg make even the financing of Broadway theater fascinating. The précis of the 38 interviews they conducted are delightful if often grim reading—drawing on some of American drama's most celebrated artists. The appendixes include charts on productions of new musicals since 1899, prime city box-

office totals, and leading road show moneymakers. Also listed are musical productions with their opening and closing dates since 1945–46. The
authors have created a readable, interesting, and useful book.

Observing that the avant-garde has become an important part of the
major theater tradition in many European countries while Anglo-
American theater has resisted alteration, Marvin Carlson in *Deathtraps:
The Postmodern Comedy Thriller* (Indiana) posits that in New York and
London the thriller or comedy of suspense has eroded the conventions of
realism with postmodern playfulness. The modern mystery thriller has
succeeded on American commercial stages where nonrealistic dramatists
such as Strindberg, Brecht, or Beckett never established themselves.
While much of the book is devoted to writers like Agatha Christie, Tom
Stoppard, and Anthony Shaffer, the patient Americanist will be rewarded with observations on Ira Levin's *Deathtrap* and Larry Gelbart's
book for *City of Angels*. Carlson concludes that the games played by
comedy-thriller authors suggest the deepest concerns and fears of contemporary culture. Although there are copious scholarly apparatuses and
a lengthy bibliography, Eric Lott's *Love and Theft* may stretch a bit thin
its premise that minstrelsy is an index of popular white racial feeling in
the United States. One of the book's arguments, that in blackface
minstrelsy's audience contradictory racial impulses were at work, may be
tenable, but the assertion that blackface minstrelsy "arose from a white
obsession with black (male) bodies which underlies white racial dread to
our own day" reduces the subject to the level of a bad Mel Brooks film
joke. Moreover, viewing Melville's "Benito Cereno" as a version of
minstrel show seems strained. Yet much of Lott's commentary on race,
working-class culture, and class formation in the 1840s is instructive. The
"love and theft" of the title loosely articulates the simultaneous drawing
and crossing of racial boundaries in minstrel shows, an interesting part of
Lott's proposition, and the volume itself is a product of its political times
in investigating the ironies of cultural and racial reaction. However it
might be told, it is a gnarled history from about 1830 to the various
versions of *Uncle Tom's Cabin* in the mid-1850s as the nation edged
toward civil war.

Jeannie Marlin Woods's *Theatre to Change Men's Souls: The Artistry of
Adrian Hall* (Delaware) studies the theory and practice of a stage director
who has been a major force in the development of American regional
theater. Hall's reputation rests on his having established the Trinity
Repertory Company and serving as its artistic director from 1964 until

1989, while assuming the same role at the Dallas Theater Center in 1983. For six years, as artistic director of both major regional theaters, he presented 34 American and world premieres, including works by Sam Shepard, and he adapted for the stage such novels as *Billy Budd* and *All the King's Men*. According to Woods, Hall's chief contribution has been the bold theatricality of his spectacular stagings, which have been described as an eminently American style. Also worth noting is Ron Jenkins's *Acrobats of the Soul: Comedy and Virtuosity in Contemporary American Theatre* (Theatre Communications). The author was a clown trained at the Ringling Brothers Clown College, and his observations are on a broad style of comedy that taps into deeply ingrained American values of self-reliance. His gathering is an eclectic group, from Le Cirque du Soleil to Bill Irwin, the Flying Karamazov Brothers to Penn and Teller. Readers should find the chapter on Spalding Gray especially interesting. While the choices for Jenkins's study may seem unusual, the resulting book is extraordinary.

iv Eugene O'Neill

The giant of American drama still casts the longest shadow and causes the most ink to be spilt. Because of the dedication, patience, and good humor of Fred Wilkins and the vitality of the *Eugene O'Neill Review* as well as the plethora of scholarly material on America's premier playwright, the need for me to be selective is paramount. That having been said, our discussion begins elsewhere—in China—with *Eugene O'Neill in China: An International Centenary Celebration* (Greenwood, 1992), ed. Haiping Liu and Lowell Swortzell, a product of the 1988 O'Neill centennial celebration at Nanjing. Delayed by the student uprising in June 1989, this volume contains 30 scholarly papers, some of which have been published elsewhere. Notable contributors include theater historian Felicia Hardison Londré and O'Neill scholars Virginia Floyd, Paul Voelker, Jean Chothia, and Egil Tornqvist. Floyd provides the keynote address, and her "Eugene O'Neill's *Tao Te Ching:* The Spiritual Evolution of a Mystic" (pp. 3–12) explores the dramatist's adolescent Catholicism, Irish mysticism, and early discovery of Taoism. Voelker's "Eugene O'Neill, World Playwright: The Beginnings" (pp. 99–109) turns its attention to O'Neill's earliest dramas with a foreign setting, the one-act plays *The Movie Man* and *The Sniper*. Chothia examines the use of stage language and speech in "Register and Idiolect in *The Iceman Cometh* and

Long Day's Journey into Night" (pp. 157–63); Londré's contribution is "Dramatic Tension Between Expressionistic Design and Naturalistic Acting in *The Emperor Jones*" (pp. 183–97), which sees that play in its 1920 premiere as shaped by the influence on O'Neill of the German expressionists and the casting of Charles Gilpin in the title role. A reader especially interested in Gilpin and the play will want to read David Krasner's "Charles S. Gilpin: The Actor Before the Emperor" (*JADT* 4, iii: 62–75). Swortzell provides an overview of *"The Emperor Jones* as a Source of Theatrical Experimentation, 1920s–1980s" (pp. 200–209); and Tornqvist in "Ingmar Bergman and *Long Day's Journey into Night"* (pp. 241–48) provides a suggestive reaction to Bergman's 1988 production at the Royal Dramatic Theatre in Stockholm. The volume also provides a forum to lesser-known O'Neill scholars.

The focus of *The Critical Response to Eugene O'Neill* (Greenwood), ed. John H. Houchin, is basically historical, reprinting representative critical reviews of productions in addition to scholarly articles. The volume is user-friendly, with reviews and essays arranged chronologically by play beginning with Heywood Broun's 1917 review of *Bound East for Cardiff* through Judith E. Barlow's cogent 1988 indictment of the narrow limits of the conventional male view in "O'Neill's Many Mothers: Mary Tyrone, Josie Hogan, and Their Antecedents" (pp. 283–90). This format allows the student-scholar interested in a particular play to compare the attitudes of initial reviewers with the considered evaluations of academicians. Thus Alexander Woollcott, Ludwig Lewisohn, Stark Young, Brooks Atkinson, George Jean Nathan, Robert Benchley, Walter Kerr, and Clive Barnes stand cheek by jowl with established scholarly evaluations, such as Doris M. Alexander's *"Strange Interlude* and Schopenhauer" (pp. 105–17), John Henry Raleigh's "Communal, Familial, and Personal Memories in O'Neill's *Long Day's Journey into Night"* (pp. 203–12), and Laurin Porter's *"A Touch of the Poet:* Memory and the Creative Imagination" (pp. 238–50). A convenient and worthwhile gathering of reprints.

The most recently published numbers of *EONR* maintain the same level of quality as earlier issues. The Spring 1992 (16, i) volume features Gloria Cahill's "Mothers and Whores: The Process of Integration in O'Neill's Plays," Michael Basile's "Semiotic Transformability in *All God's Chillun Got Wings,"* Robert Cooperman's "Unacknowledged Familiarity: Jean Toomer and Eugene O'Neill," Wayne Narey's "Eugene O'Neill's Attic Spirit: *Desire Under the Elms,"* Tornqvist's "To Speak the

Unspoken: Audible Thinking in O'Neill's Plays," Madeline C. Smith and Richard Eaton's first-rate handling of previously unpublished material on the censorship controversy and ultimate success of *Strange Interlude* in middle America in their highly readable "Everything's Up to Date in Kansas City," Brenda Murphy's nice intertextual study "Fetishizing the Dynamo: Henry Adams and Eugene O'Neill," and Barbara Voglino's " 'Games' the Tyrones Play." The Fall 1992 (16, ii) issue includes Edward L. Shaughnessy's "Ella O'Neill and the Imprint of Faith" (pp. 29–43), a nicely illustrated, interesting piece about the playwright's mother in her youth; the prolific Frank R. Cunningham's adventure in pedagogy, "Eugene O'Neill in Our Time: Overcoming Student Resistance" (pp. 45–55); Stephen A. Black's "Reality and Its Vicissitudes: The Problem of Understanding in *Long Day's Journey Into Night*" (pp. 57–72); David Aaron Murray's "O'Neill's Transvaluation of Pessimism in *The Iceman Cometh*" (pp. 73–79); and Yvonne Shafer's "A Berlin Diary: The Iceman Cometh" (pp. 81–103). Of special interest is "Greed of the Meek," O'Neill's scenario for act one of the first play in his projected eight-play cycle (pp. 5–11), ed. and introduced by Donald Gallup; and Smith and Eaton return with "The O'Neill-Komroff Connection: Thirteen Letters from Eugene O'Neill" (pp. 13–28), in which O'Neill's 1925–36 letters to Manuel Komroff are annotated with reference to Komroff's "A Story Teller's World."

Comment on the 1992 issues of *EONR* occurs here because as happy subscribers to the journal know (and accept) publication can sometimes run just a tiny bit behind; it is worth the wait. A single "double" issue for 1993 is promised before the next *ALS*. Several other items were published that O'Neillians will want to see. Ralph A. Ciancio's "Richard Wright, Eugene O'Neill, and the Beast in the Skull" (*MLS* 23, iii: 45–59) supplies a comparative study of *The Hairy Ape* and Wright's *Native Son*. S. Georgia Nugent's provocative "Masking Becomes Electra: O'Neill, Freud, and the Feminine" (*CompD* 22: 37–55) has been reprinted twice this year, in *Drama and the Classical Heritage: Comparative and Critical Essays* (AMS Press), ed. Clifford Davidson et al. (pp. 254–72), and in Houchin's *Critical Response to O'Neill* (pp. 134–48). Nugent charges that O'Neill used Freud not to reveal but to mask "the dark continent" of feminine sexuality, and her article marks out a new way to read *Mourning Becomes Electra*. Another work that offers feminist psychoanalytic techniques is Ann C. Hall's *"A Kind of Alaska": Women in the Plays of O'Neill, Pinter, and Shepard* (So. Ill.), which argues that through the female characters, these authors' plays expose the process by which patriarchy attempts to oppress women; yet often their characters resist and thereby encourage the dramatic male counterparts and the audience alike to recognize the oppression of women. Hall's introduction is remarkable and—even better—understandable on her use of the work of Jacques Lacan and Luce Irigaray to examine women's resistance to "a kind of Alaska," a metaphor appropriated from Pinter to characterize the "objectified placement of women within patriarchal constructs." In other words, women resist being "iced over" by male expectations. No matter where readers are on a scale of consciousness-raising, they will find Hall's commentaries on *The Iceman Cometh, Long Day's Journey into Night,* and *A Moon for the Misbegotten* fresh and compelling.

v Sam Shepard

If O'Neill remains America's most written about dramaturgist, Shepard's works have seen the greatest increase in scholarly activity. From two brief mentions two years ago, a cottage industry has begun to grow around this dramatist *cum* musician who has an impressive second career as a film actor. Once Ann C. Hall gets her torch going, she runs from O'Neill straight across *"A Kind of Alaska"* (see above) to illuminate the work of Shepard in her chapter "Fire in the Snow" (pp. 91–116). Shepard has been characterized as the theater's version of Clint Eastwood's high plains drifter, perpetuating his lone cowboy role. However, Hall's original readings identify Shepard's female saviors in *Buried Child,* Shepard's Pulitzer Prize winner, which Hall identifies as another "long day's journey into night," *True West,* and *A Lie of the Mind.* Hall's feminist perspective offers important new insights into Shepard's plays. Jim McGhee assumes another perspective in *True Lies: The Architecture of the Fantastic in the Plays of Sam Shepard* (Peter Lang), which suggests that Shepard's dramas exist in a world of the fantastic, which future theater historians will characterize as neorealist or ultrarealistic. McGhee defines a major characteristic of the fantastic in Shepard's dramas as an unexpected event, a direct 180-degree reversal of accepted ground rules. The author then analyzes act structures, characters, themes, and staging to support his thesis before concluding with further evidence for it from Shepard's personal life and biography, that memories of formative experiences reappear in his characters in play after play.

Rereading Shepard: Contemporary Critical Essays on the Plays of Sam

Shepard (St. Martin's), ed. Leonard Wilcox, collects 13 original essays of varying merit and interest. The senior scholars comport themselves nobly. Gerald Weales's opening essay, "Artifacts: The Early Plays Reconsidered" (pp. 8–21), provides the sort of work we have come to expect during his distinguished career; Charles R. Lyons characterizes Shepard's family plays as "pseudo-realism" in "Shepard's Family Trilogy and the Conventions of Modern Realism" (pp. 115–30); and the prolific Felicia Hardison Londré concludes the volume with "A Motel of the Mind: *Fool for Love* and *A Lie of the Mind*" (pp. 215–24), a coda to the discussion of the family plays that sees the motel as a "fantasy arena" which signifies both self-invention and entrapment. Other essays seem more interested in theoretical approaches than in Shepard. Dennis Carroll's "Potential Performance Texts for *The Rock Garden* and *4-H Club*" (pp. 22–41) is a contemporary critical analysis augmented by charts and tables of the "polyphony of emission" of sign systems. I have already expressed an appreciation of Hall's work, and her "Speaking Without Words: The Myth of Masculine Autonomy in Sam Shepard's *Fool for Love*" (pp. 150–67) suggests she has seen nothing to change her mind. David J. DeRose in "A Kind of Cavorting: Superpresence and Shepard's Family Dramas" (pp. 131–49) disagrees with Weales; Susan Bennett, "When a Woman Looks: The 'Other' Audience of Shepard's Plays" (pp. 168–79) disagrees with Hall. And so it goes. Jane Ann Crum in " 'I Smash the Tools of My Captivity': The Feminine in Sam Shepard's *A Lie of the Mind*" (pp. 196–214) concludes the debate on Shepard's family drama by underscoring differing feminine reactions to male oppression. Other essays are by Wilcox, Gerry McCarthy, Sheila Rabillard, Ann Wilson, and Sherrill Grace.

Modern Drama's annual special issue is devoted to Shepard (36, i) and includes Carol Rosen's " 'Emotional Territory': An Interview with Sam Shepard," Henry I. Schvey's "A Worm in the Wood: The Father-Son Relationship in the Plays of Sam Shepard," Gregory W. Lanier's "The Killer's Ancient Mask: Unity and Dualism in Shepard's *The Tooth of Crime*," Leonard Wilcox's "West's *The Day of the Locust* and Shepard's *Angel City:* Refiguring L.A. *Noir*," Jeffrey D. Hoeper's "Cain, Canaanites, and Philistines in Sam Shepard's *True West*," Gary Grant's "Shifting the Paradigm: Shepard, Myth, and the Transformation of Consciousness," Steven Putzel's "An American Cowboy on the English Fringe: Sam Shepard's London Audience," and Susanne Willadt's "States of War in Sam Shepard's *States of Shock*." Despite Jim McGhee's speculation that theater historians of the next century will find Shepard among a handful of dramatists whose plays will survive, only time will tell if this year's burst of scholarly enthusiasm is short-term or enduring.

vi Tennessee Williams and Arthur Miller

Because Williams was brutally frank about his years of drug and alcohol addiction and candid about his promiscuous homosexuality, while he considered his writing process to be private, Ronald Hayman's *Tennessee Williams: Everyone Else Is an Audience* (Yale) has been much anticipated, and the book will be interesting to those new to Williams's biography. Hayman, who has written biographies of Bertolt Brecht, Franz Kafka, and Marcel Proust, avoids gossip generally and highlights the dramatist's twin fears—of failure and of death; he also elaborates on Williams's confidential relationships with women. Much of Hayman's material draws on other published sources, and he offers summary rather than analysis of the plays. While the book provides interesting insight into Williams's restlessness and bears witness to his craftsmanship, Mel Gussow's review in the *New York Times* suggests we still await a better life study.

Meanwhile, scholarship on Williams thrives. If work on Shepard is a cottage industry, a Williams condominium was raised this year, almost single-handedly the effort of Philip C. Kolin, who has emerged as a major figure in Williams studies. Kolin this year alone published a half-dozen articles. Among them: "An Interview with Wolf Ruvinskis: The First Mexican Stanley Kowalski" (*LATR* 26, ii: 159–65), "Tennessee Williams Sends His Autobiography to Mexico" (*MissQ* 46, ii: 255–56), "The Existential Nightmare in Tennessee Williams's The Chalky White Substance" (*NConL* 23, i: 8–11), and "Cleopatra of the Nile and Blanche DuBois of the French Quarter" (*ShakB* 11, i: 25–27). Kolin also edited the year's major volume of Williams scholarship, *Confronting Tennessee Williams's* A Streetcar Named Desire: *Essays in Critical Pluralism* (Greenwood), the first collection of original essays devoted exclusively to that play. The volume contains two more essays by Kolin, an outstanding introduction (pp. 1–17) and "Eunice Hubbel and the Feminist Thematics of *A Streetcar Named Desire*" (pp. 105–20), in addition to 13 other articles, including Herbert Blau's reflective and evocative "Readymade Desire" (pp. 19–25); Calvin Bedient's "There Are Lives that Desire Does Not Sustain: *A Streetcar Named Desire*" (pp. 45–58), which sees the action of the play as a masculinist rout of female abjection, Blanche as a divided woman, part fluttery surface and part inner crypt of an impossibly retained empowering mother, and the play itself as a powerful contribution to the modern literature of grief; June Schlueter's outstanding examination of *Streetcar's* competing narratives, " 'We've had this date with each other from the beginning': Reading Toward Closure in *A Streetcar Named Desire*" (pp. 71–81); and Mark Royden Winchell's appraisal of the play's appeal to the popular imagination, "The Myth Is the Message, or Why *Streetcar* Keeps Running" (pp. 133–45). Those with a special interest in *Streetcar* will want to read the other generally fine essays by William Kleb, Laura Morrow and Edward Morrow, Laurilyn J. Harris, Lionel Kelly, W. Kenneth Holditch, Bert Cardullo, Robert Bray, Jurgen C. Wolter, and Gene D. Phillips, S.J.

A special number devoted to Williams was published by *SAD* (8, ii), ed. Colby H. Kullman and Kolin. The volume contains John L. Gronbeck-Tedesco's "Absence and the Actor's Body: Marlon Brando's Performance in *A Streetcar Named Desire* on Stage and in Film" (pp. 115–26), which reads the play as an allegory of postwar America. Laura Morrow and Edward Morrow apply Chaos and AntiChaos theory to "Humpty-Dumpty Lives! Complexity Theory as an Alternative to the Omelet Scenario in *The Glass Menagerie*" (pp. 127–39). Laurilyn J. Harris's "*Menagerie* in Manila and Other Cross-Cultural Affinities: The Relevance of the Plays of Tennessee Williams on the Filipino Stage" (pp. 163–74) is a carefully documented assessment of *The Glass Menagerie* interpreted by and adapted to Filipino society. And Kolin offers an initial multicultural reading in "Sleeping with Caliban: The Politics of Race in Tennessee Williams's *Kingdom of Earth*" (pp. 140–62).

There are some Williams items this year that Kolin has not written or edited. Kaarina Kailo, "Blanche Dubois and Salomé as New Women: Old Lunatics in Modern Drama" (pp. 119–36) in *Madness in Drama* (Cambridge), ed. James Redmond, challenges the stereotypes of gender-appropriate behavior in a comparison of the classic lunatic women of modern drama, contrasting the assertive verbal force of Oscar Wilde's Salomé with the muteness of Blanche's self and voice. Nicholas O. Pagan's "Tennessee Williams's Theater as Body" (*PQ* 72: 97–115) takes its keys from the antilinguistic tendency of Antonin Artaud and reads Williams, allowing that theater cannot free itself from language, in terms of a presumed affinity between theater and body. Pagan concludes that Williams's theater is at its best when the homosexual body is absent because "the body of the gay male which is absent invests Williams's theater with an extremely pervasive erotic presence." In " 'Through Soundproof Glass': The Prison of Self-Consciousness in *The Glass Menagerie*" (*MD* 36: 529–37) Eric P. Levy argues that the self-consciousness of the characters is more fundamental to the play than nostalgia.

Perhaps the most politically correct volume of the past two years is David Savran's *Communists, Cowboys, and Queers: The Politics of Masculinity In The Work of Arthur Miller and Tennessee Williams* (Minnesota, 1992), the work of "a seditious academic eager to valorize and reclaim the promises of the New Left, the women's movement, and gay and lesbian liberation." Once he completes his agenda in a revisionist introduction with the expected villains—Joe McCarthy, Harry Truman, the Truman Doctrine, and the Marshall Plan—(although there are some surprises: Richard Nixon and Nikita Khrushchev are virtually interchangeable because, as near as one can figure, both are masculine heterosexuals), Savran gets around to Miller who "seems to personify masculine playwriting" and Williams who represents "the other, a feminine, or even vaguely aberrant, theater." Having thus established his straw persons, Savran attempts to take apart these gendered character sketches and replace them with more nuanced and incisive portraits. But the task does not yield a balanced book: Miller occupies a 55-page section while Williams earns 98 pages. Conceding that "Miller and Williams make strange bedfellows," Williams rises from this one ahead. Allowing for his decided list to port, Savran is not bad on the historical and social background against which to see Miller, is adequate on *Death of a Salesman*, dismisses *The Crucible* with a single sentence, burdens *A View from the Bridge* by making it a general statement about the "structure of Cold War masculinity," and concludes with a mapping of gender in *The Misfits*, before dismissing *After the Fall* "as a self-serving construction designed . . . to quell the gossip." The remainder of Miller's writing is ganged in five pages. Williams makes out better qualitatively. Savran is interesting on Williams as political radical from *The Glass Menagerie* and *Streetcar* to *Cat on a Hot Tin Roof* (including a nice sidebar on Miller's sustained critique of that play); the volume's third part takes up Williams's fiction. Savran asserts that Williams's "most conspicuous failure as a revolutionary lies in the fact that his writing remains far more attentive to the utopean potential of masculine than feminine eroticism." He concludes overall that "in the gloom of the present historical moment, marked by an emphatic turn to the right in the First World . . . and the tightening of the First World's neocolonial grip . . . the need for sites of resistance—such as the revolutionary theatre—is arguably even more urgent." If only this book could have fulfilled the promise of its wonderful title in which Savran (as Allen Tate says of Emily Dickinson) inextricably fuses a heterogeneous series in a single order of perception.

As is the case ordinarily in Miller studies, *Death of a Salesman* this year draws the largest number of responses. Anne Stavney in "Reverence and Repugnance: Willy Loman's Sentiments Toward His Son Biff" (*JADT* 4, ii: 54–62) writes about that play's most often discussed relationship, although she takes a different spin by observing what she takes to be Willy's ambivalence toward Biff within René Girard's framework of triangular desire. Granger Babcock's " 'What's the Secret?': Willy Loman as Desiring Machine" (*AmDram* 2, i: 59–81) suggests that Willy is more machine than man and cannot see that success or status is largely determined by extrinsic influences. In Babcock's scheme Willy's brother, Ben, represents the brutality of American imperialism, and all the men in the play are models of what he calls the masculine unconscious; the critic further claims that in Miller's view "masculine desire is an instrument used by the publicity apparatus of American capital to organize and to regulate social relations and the economy." One of the bright and most active young Miller scholars, Steven R. Centola, in "Family Values in *Death of a Salesman*" (*CLAJ* 37: 29–41) resists Babcock's political reading, while conceding Miller's oft-noted attack on the false values of a venal American society, and observes that the play ultimately captures the audience's attention not because of a neo-Marxist attack on social injustice but because of its powerful story of a man, nearing death, who wants to justify his life. Donald P. Costello in "Arthur Miller's Circles of Responsibility: *A View from the Bridge* and Beyond" (*MD* 36: 443–53) reflects on the interconnections among ever-widening circles of responsibility: to self, family, society, the universe. While Costello looks briefly at works from *All My Sons* to *The Archbishop's Ceiling*, exploring the significance of Miller's concern about the outside world and its relatedness to the self, the real merit of his article is his focus on *A View from the Bridge*, one of Miller's great plays that has been largely neglected.

A single book-length study of Miller was published this year, and that devoted to a single play. My own The Crucible: *Politics, Property and Pretense* (Twayne) is similar in format to other volumes in the Masterwork Studies Series, containing a chronology of Miller's life and works, a section on literary and historical context, ten chapters devoted to a reading of the play, and an annotated bibliography. Robert A. Martin, one of the most knowledgeable and respected Miller scholars, says in *The Heath Anthology of American Literature* that this "is one of the most complete and comprehensive studies of *The Crucible* to date" and that the "critical judgment is astute." Let me hear an amen.

vii Edward Albee and David Mamet

Some of the most creative scholarship of the year has been devoted to these two writers. Albee, as always, is much in the public eye; his dramas remain popular abroad from Spain to Eastern Europe, and this year American scholars have renewed their interest. A special issue of *AmDram* (2, ii) devoted to Albee includes a half-dozen articles by academics. Deborah R. Geis in "Staging Hypereloquence: Edward Albee and the Monologic Voice" (pp. 1–11) suggests that the ability of some of Albee's principal characters to manipulate language presents the audience with what is essentially a monologue, and the unfulfilled striving for dialogue places his works far beyond Williams and Miller into postmodernist fragmentation and refusal of coherence. Andrew B. Harris in "*All Over:* Defeating the Expectations of the 'Well-Made' Play" (pp. 12–31) focuses a fresh eye on the resounding 1971 defeat of the ill-fated *All Over*. Robert M. Post in "Salvation or Damnation?: Death in the Plays of Edward Albee" (pp. 32–49) distinguishes between literal and figurative—physical and psychological—deaths which permeate the dramas. The suggestive "Albee's *Who's Afraid of Virginia Woolf?:* The Issue of Originality" (pp. 50–75) by Jerre Collins and Raymond J. Wilson III explores how Albee's most famous play maintains its originality despite intertextual cues that amount to "virtual instructions to read the play intertextually"; Collins and Wilson suggest that the most original aspects of this drama are dispersed into its sources. In "Crafting Script into Performance: Edward Albee in Rehearsal" (pp. 76–99) Rakesh H. Solomon, using the 1978 revival rehearsals for *Fam and Yam* and *Sandbox,* follows Albee as director as he makes a script become effective theater. Solomon continues his ongoing decade-long dialogue with Albee in "Text, Subtext, and Performance: Edward Albee on Directing *Who's Afraid of Virginia Woolf?*" (*ThS* 34: 94–110), an interview recorded at Houston's Alley Theatre on 6 January 1990. The *AmDram* special number concludes with its playwright's forum, Edward Albee's "The Hamlet Machine," a short scene from a new play, *Fragments.*

Walter Meserve once observed that Albee in conversation could be "arrogant, arch, friendly, fatuous, intelligent, and superficial" (see *ALS 1988*, p. 388). Those planning to read Albee's "On Alan Schneider and Playwriting" (*AmDram* 1, ii: 77–84), in a text provided by Robert Skloot, ed. Norma Jenckes, are advised that there is a demitasse on Schneider, a hearty bowl of Albee on Albee, and that little else has changed. Somewhat like Collins and Wilson, John Ditsky in "Steinbeck and Albee: Affection, Admiration, Affinity" (*StQ* 26: 13–23) proposes sources, here in the work of the Nobel Prize-winning novelist. A dedicated Albee scholar, Jeane Luere, in "A Turn at the Top: Valid or Invalid Alteration of Script in Albee's Direction of Beckett?" (*SoAR* 58, iv: 85–100) comments on Albee—known for his refusals to allow alterations of *his* texts—his staging of *Krapp's Last Tape,* and his bizarre casting and apparently capricious tampering with Beckett's less familiar *Ohio Impromptu* at the Alley Theatre in 1991.

While David Mamet has yet to receive similar scholarly attention, his position as a major dramatist seems secure. In "The Critical Eye: Sexual Perversity in Viragos" (*Theater* 24: 111–13) Daniel Mufson provides a fairly objective roundup of critical reaction to Mamet's controversial *Oleanna* before Mufson's political correctness sprays vitriol at Mamet's purported misogyny. *Oleanna's* provocativeness inspired heated arguments; Mufson pours fuel on the fire. Tony J. Stafford in "*Speed-the-Plow* and *Speed the Plough:* The Work of the Earth" (*MD* 36: 38–47) begins with a survey of the scholarship, this time on *Speed-the-Plow,* before inventively using the play's curious title as a clue to decode its meaning and comparing it to Thomas Morton's drama originally performed in 1800 London. David Skeele in "The Devil and David Mamet: *Sexual Perversity in Chicago* as Homiletic Tragedy" (*MD* 36: 512–18) sees Mamet as a moralist presenting visions of the spiritual emptiness of America and the play as a sermon appropriating the homiletic quality of a 16th-century subgenre of a medieval morality play.

viii The Dead Playwrights Society

There are writers whose canons are necessarily closed but in whose works some interest remains. Using Michel Foucault and Simone de Beauvoir as guides, Joan T. Hamilton in "Visible Power and Invisible Men in Clare Booth's [*sic*] *The Women*" (*AmDram* 3, i: 31–53) takes a revisionist look at Boothe's play, which earlier critics saw as antifeminine. Two important new books this year may be the long-awaited harbinger of a just assessment of Susan Glaspell, hidden for too long in the shadow of Eugene O'Neill. Mary E. Papke's *Susan Glaspell: A Research and Production Sourcebook* (Greenwood), intended to serve a wide variety of scholarly investigators from the undergraduate to the theater historian, is the sort of dream piece with which scholars like to begin their research. Papke includes a brief chronology and a nice introductory essay. The most valuable feature, however, is a chronological overview of Glaspell's dramatic works from *Suppressed Desires* (1915) and *Trifles* (1916) to *Alison's House* (1930). Each entry presents a plot summary, a production history, and a record of the play's critical reception—except for "Springs Eternal" (written in 1945), which exists only in typescript and has not been produced. Papke's bibliography of primary sources includes Glaspell's short stories, novels, plays, poems, and essays. The bibliography of reviews and other secondary sources is thoroughly annotated, presented in chronological order, and amply illustrates the rise and fall and rise once more of Glaspell's critical reputation. For the scholarly-impaired, the volume is cross-indexed throughout. A valuable book. Because they were published contemporaneously, Veronica Makowsky in *Susan Glaspell's Century of American Women: A Critical Interpretation of Her Work* (Oxford) did not have the advantage of Papke's annotated bibliographies, but her work does not suffer. This book, as well, should play a role in the recovery and reinterpretation of Glaspell's oeuvre. Makowsky places the dramatist in the context of Anglo-American feminism and the female literary tradition, but she focuses primarily on Glaspell's fiction with special attention to the depiction of women. Also providing a biographical context, Makowsky's book is of particular interest for the years from 1915 through 1928, the time of Glaspell's involvement with the Provincetown Players when she did not publish any novels, and Makowsky is intelligent in her evaluation of dramas like *Trifles, The People, Woman's Honor, Bernice, Inheritors,* and *The Verge.* Since Glaspell's work has been "restored" and "reinterpreted" in the contexts of feminism and "the female literary tradition," it is time to see how easily her drama may be "mainstreamed"—both for scholars and in production. Glaspell has long been characterized as one of the greatest women playwrights. Along with this necessary task of acknowledging her gender-specific contributions to drama, it is now appropriate to consider in her works those issues beyond gender. While next year's *ALS* may not have a section titled *O'Neill-Glaspell,* neither should it sweep this important dramatist into a gender-centric amalgam of "feminist theater."

Before analyzing the dramatist's last play, John Gruesser in "Lies That Kill: Lorraine Hansberry's Answer to *Heart of Darkness* in *Les Blancs*" (*AmDram* 1, ii: 1–14) carefully traces Hansberry's knowledge about and interest in Africa, then proposes that she reverses established tradition by employing African focus, emphasis, and methods to tell an African story. Gruesser concludes that *Les Blancs* explodes the usual distorted Euro-American image of that continent. In "Hansberry's *A Raisin in the Sun*" (*Expl* 52: 59–61) David D. Cooper focuses sharply on that play's penultimate scene as reflecting Hansberry's belief that social idealism is tied to individual moral obligation. William E. H. Meyer, Jr., in *"Bus Stop*: American Eye vs. Small-Town Ear" (*JACult* 16, i: 35–38) sees William Inge's play as a portrait of the Emersonian "transparent eyeball" and a dramatization of the evolution of small-town hyperverbality into American hypervisuality before surmising that *Bus Stop* indicates that unless American hypervision unites men and women in a manner in which *both* feel power and worth, the result must be loneliness.

Other essays examine writers whose reputations are not primarily associated with drama. Especially interesting is Keith Newlin's "Melodramatist of the Middle Border: Hamlin Garland's Early Work Reconsidered" (*SAF* 21: 153–69), an informative article which demonstrates that Garland was no mere dabbler but a serious dramatist who wrote at least 17 plays, four of which were produced. Tony J. Stafford's " 'Gray Eyes Is Glass': Image and Theme in *The Member of the Wedding*" (*AmDram* 3, i: 54–66) centers on Carson McCullers's play adaptation of her novel. Following the evolution of what was initially an original television drama through to its posthumous productions for the commercial stage, Mark Royden Winchell is informed and informative on "Rod Serling's *Requiem for a Heavyweight:* A Drama for Its Time" (*SAD* 8: 13–20) in his attempt to account for the play's failure on Broadway. Neale Reinitz's "Edmund Wilson: Playwrights, Farewell!" (*MD* 36: 454–66) is a wonderfully well-written reminder that Wilson published nine plays, two of which were staged professionally; Reinitz presents an honest evaluation.

ix The Quick, in Alphabetical Order

A number of contemporary playwrights also attracted significant scholarly attention this year. Using *Am I Blue, Crimes of the Heart, The Wake of Jamey Foster,* and *The Miss Firecracker Contest* as evidence, Colby H.

Kullman in "Beth Henley's Marginalized Heroines" (*SAD* 8: 21–28) points out that Henley's protagonists are heroic because of their continuing quest for meaning, dignity, and selfhood confronting the ultimate futility and absurdity of life. Noting recurring imagery of homicide and suicide in Henley's scripts, Alan Clarke Shepard in "Aborted Rage in Beth Henley's Women" (*MD* 36: 96–108) suggests that her Southern heroines retreat from a violence bred by rage in a pattern of surrender in which they seek to preserve their lives within the system they have inherited, not able to actuate fully the feminist awakenings that stir in their consciousness. Janet V. Haedicke's " 'A Population [and Theater] at Risk': Battered Women in Henley's *Crimes of the Heart* and Shepard's *A Lie of the Mind"* (*MD* 36: 83–95) engages the weighty matter of domestic violence against women and comes to an ironic conclusion. Kenneth E. Johnson in "Tina Howe and Feminine Discourse" (*AmDram* 1, ii: 15–25) posits in Howe's unique dramaturgy a discourse that works within but against the phallocratic nature of language which subordinates one set of beliefs to another. Rosette C. Lamont publishes two pieces on Howe. She follows "Tina Howe's Secret Surrealism: Walking a Tightrope" (*MD* 36: 27–37), a pleasant narrative which links the comedy of manners of Howe's later plays to Howe's own idol, Eugene Ionesco, with "After Ionesco: The Surrealist Comedy of Tina Howe" (*Theater Week* 3 May 1993, pp. 19–20), another disarmingly unpretentious but informed commentary, this one accompanied by an interview.

The interview has become an increasingly popular form of scholarly endeavor, and an even more recent development is the photo essay. Philip C. Kolin in "The Adrienne Kennedy Festival at Great Lakes Theater Festival: A Photo Essay" (*SAD* 8: 85–94) concludes his brief comments on Kennedy's *The Ohio State Murders* with a selection of a dozen photographs taken at the initial festival. Elin Diamond in "Rethinking Identification: Kennedy, Freud, Brecht" (*KR* 15, ii: 86–99) traces Freud's texts and the Brechtian insights most relevant to Kennedy's plays. Also of interest is John Williams's review, "Intersecting Boundaries: The Surrealist Theatre of Poet/Playwright Adrienne Kennedy" (*AAR* 27: 495–500).

The extravagant hoopla surrounding *Angels in America* has brought much attention to Tony Kushner, but it is still too early in his career to know if his work is special or specious. For the present, however, Gordon Rogoff in "Angels in America, Devils in the Wings" (*Theater* 24, ii: 21–29) presents an insightful essay which includes a suggestive comparison of the New York and London productions and a brief account of the genesis of *Perestroika,* Part II of *Angels.* In "Dramatizing AIDS" (*HudR* 46: 189–94) Richard Hornby explains why he finds *Angels* to be compelling drama; the final portion (pp. 193–94) of Hornby's article is a subjective but entertaining response to David Mamet's *Oleanna.* Harry Haun provides two popular articles of interest to scholars on Kushner in "Of Angst and Angels" (*Playbill* 11, ix: 8, 10, 14–15) and "The Great Work Continues" (*Playbill* 12, i: 12, 16, 20–21).

In "An Interview with Karen Malpede" (*SAD* 8: 45–60) Richard E. Kramer converses with a feminist dramatist about her view of theater as a political force. Louis Botto in "The Loman Family Picnic" (*Playbill* 12, iii: 42, 45–46) examines the relation of Donald Margulies's play of that name to Miller's *Death of a Salesman.* June Schlueter's "Ways of Seeing in Donald Margulies' *Sight Unseen*" (*SAD* 8: 3–11) is the first scholarly study of this Obie Award-winning playwright. Scholarship has not been so kind, at least in quantity, to the once promising, now underappreciated Terrence McNally, certainly a major dramatist. Benilde Montgomery in "*Lips Together, Teeth Apart:* Another Version of Pastoral" (*MD* 36: 547–55) places McNally's work, far from the yuppie realism which it has been accused of being, in the ancient pastoral literary tradition. Another noteworthy conversation is "An Interview with Mark Medoff" (*SAD* 8: 61–83), in which Mimi Gladstein questions the author of *When You Comin Back, Red Ryder?* and *Children of a Lesser God.* William W. Demastes in "Jessie and Thelma Revisited: Marsha Norman's Conceptual Challenge in *'night, Mother*" (*MD* 36: 109–19) surveys the debate about the realist format and the feminist dialectic as it applies to Norman's drama before concluding that the play is universal because it transcends gender-specific considerations even as it addresses gender-specific issues, using the realist form to present a radical vision. The 1984 play often offered as evidence of the unfulfilled promise of David Rabe is the subject of two new reevaluations: Tony J. Stafford's "The Metaphysics of Rabe's *Hurlyburly:* 'Staring into the Eyes of Providence'" (*AmDram* 1, ii: 61–76) and David Radavich's "Collapsing Male Myths: Rabe's Tragicomic *Hurlyburly*" (*AmDram* 3, i: 1–16).

If some stars seem subject to eclipse or stasis, the ascendancy of others can be spectacular. Such is the case of Anna Deavere Smith, whose one-woman shows have brought her enormous critical success. Richard Schechner's "Anna Deavere Smith: Acting as Incorporation" (*TDR* 37, iv: 63–64) sees her art as more that of African, Native American, and Asian ritualists than the work of conventional Euro-Americans. Since Smith surely has expanded the limits of a new documentary theater and is poised before high expectations for her future work, it is important to see her clearly. Recommended are two interviews: Carol Martin's "Anna Deavere Smith: The Word Becomes You" (*TDR* 37, iv: 45–62) and Barbara Lewis's "The Circle of Confusion: A Conversation with Anna Deavere Smith" (*KR* 15, iv: 54–64).

Jean-Claude van Itallie is the subject of Gene A. Plunka's "McLuhan, Perfect People, and the Media Plays of Jean-Claude van Itallie" (*AmDram* 3, i: 67–86), which points out the dramatist's 20-year preoccupation with the stultifying power of the contemporary media on American society. Van Itallie, a practitioner of Tibetan Buddhism, speculates on why the truly serious is simultaneously humorous and why we can laugh through tears in "On Laughter" (*AmDram* 3, i: 87–89). "Serious Laughter" (*Playbill* 11, vi: 8, 12, 14), on the other hand, is Mervyn Rothstein's deft look at Wendy Wasserstein's *The Sisters Rosensweig*.

Mark William Rocha's "Black Madness in August Wilson's 'Down the Line' Cycle," in *Madness in Drama* (Cambridge, pp. 191–201), ed. James Redmond, proposes that Wilson is now America's preeminent playwright, placing him in the company of O'Neill, Miller, and Williams because Wilson supplies a unique aspect to American theater, an American history which is the product of an African rather than a European sensibility; Rocha centers on what Wilson's black communities do when a madman is within their midst. Sandra G. Shannon in "Blues, History, and Dramaturgy: An Interview with August Wilson" (*AAR* 27: 539–59) questions Wilson at length about the cultural and political agendas underlying his plays and his role as a black writer. This is followed by Jay Plum's "Blues, History, and the Dramaturgy of August Wilson" (*AAR* 27: 561–67), which examines Wilson's contention that the black community may flounder because it has failed to turn to its history for guidance. Plum finds the blues aesthetic the connective force that links past and present. Michael Riedel's "The Man from Missouri: Lanford Wilson on *Redwood Curtain*, Writing, and Pain" (*Theater Week* 3 May 1993, pp. 21–26) contains a brief overview and an interview with the more neglected Wilson, although I suspect that scholarship on him will burgeon shortly. And so it goes.

St. Bonaventure University

19 Themes, Topics, Criticism

Gary Lee Stonum

This chapter, like American literary scholarship itself, periodically reinvents itself as scholars pursue changing interests. The most important recent change seems to be the reborn attention to history, which has arrived about the same time as a mainstreaming of poststructuralist theory. These developments close a gap between the mainly historical themes and topics studied by Americanists and the understanding of criticism and critical theory held by many Americanists, and they also lessen the need for this chapter to survey the year's work in theory. As a result, I concentrate instead on broad claims made this year about American literary history, about American identities and their textual construction, about the forms and genres of American writing, and about the critics and critical methods associated specifically with American literature. Within all these categories special attention is paid to scholarship in African American literature, because claims made on its behalf have far-reaching consequences.

i Literary History

The year's general historical studies divide roughly between those concerned with method and those concerned more strictly with rewriting aspects of American literary history. An example of the first category, *Readers in History,* gathers a dozen essays seeking to historicize reader-response criticism and to recommend such criticism as a means of understanding history. In his introduction and in "Historical Hermeneutics and Antebellum Fiction: Gender, Response Theory, and Interpretive Contexts" (pp. 54–84) James L. Machor describes the twofold

Thanks once again to Sarah Turner for help with the research for this chapter.

challenge addressed by the book: first, of locating historical evidence for specific acts of reading and, second, mitigating the reader-response critic's own inevitable historical situatedness. To meet the first, Machor cites the example of Nina Baym's work to argue that in the antebellum United States published reviews provide the best data about reader response. To meet the second, he sermonizes fearlessly on behalf of the metacritical awareness derided by Stanley Fish as "theory-hope." Most of the volume's essays practice a rhetorical hermeneutics of the sort Steven Mailloux has for some time advocated. Mailloux's own "Misreading as a Historical Act: Cultural Rhetoric, Bible Politics, and Fuller's 1845 Review of Douglass's *Narrative*" (pp. 3–31) is a fine application of the method in its attention to the representational contexts of Fuller's review. Another, broader application is Raymond Hedin's "Probable Readers, Possible Stories: The Limits of Nineteenth-Century Black Narrative" (pp. 180–205), which studies how black voices are conditioned in anticipation of a white audience's response. Hedin also strikingly takes up the second challenge Machor notes. He pointedly compares the situation of 19th-century black authors to that of contemporary white critics of black literature, who are likewise tempted to seek authentication through the voice of the racial other. As examples of historical method, none of these often interesting essays does anything that would sharply distinguish a concern for readers from one for authors and texts. Indeed, most seem content to view the history of reading as a history of published representations. Such publications are seen as one author's re-presentations of the signs, texts, or discourses of others, either directly as in the case of book reviews, or indirectly as with responses to a style or a generic model.

By contrast Eric Lott's *Love and Theft* both provides a much denser historical context for its subject and probes more deeply into its complicated appeal. In addition to his more orthodox sources in the new social history, Lott uses psychoanalytic film theory to speculate persuasively about why audiences thronged to the minstrel shows and how they consciously or unconsciously understood them. I do not have the competence to evaluate Lott's specific historical claims, but if these are at all credible his book will stand as a landmark of the new cultural studies. Unlike some examples of such work, *Love and Theft* is genuinely and profitably interdisciplinary in combining political theory (to ponder the relation of race and class), social history (to understand in detail the production and circulation of minstrel shows in antebellum New York), and semiotics (to read the complex, often contradictory meanings put into play by blackface entertainments). Lott argues that, contrary to simplifying claims on either side of the question, minstrelsy had both black and white roots. More strikingly, he shows that it regularly signified both racialist and progressive attitudes about slavery, the abolitionist movement, and black Americans. Indeed, he argues that as part of its appeal to urban artisans the minstrel show provided a language in which different, sometimes conflicting attitudes could find expression. "At every turn [in its development from the 1830s up to the Civil War] blackface minstrelsy has seemed a form in which transgression and containment coexisted, in which improbably threatening or startling sympathetic racial meanings were simultaneously produced and dissolved."

The year's most ambitious reflection on historical method is William C. Spengemann's "Early American Literature and the Project of Literary History" (*AmLH* 5: 512–41). After surveying the founding of early American literature as an object of study, Spengemann points out, as trenchantly as anyone has yet done, that its corpus is neither early (except with respect to claims at once suspiciously teleological and conspicuously question-begging), nor American (if that be defined as pertaining to the as yet unborn United States), nor literary (at least not apart from a dubious relation to later practices and studies and to an even more suspect theory of literary history). Partly reiterating his case against the separation of "American" from "English" literature and partly allowing nevertheless for an ingenious version of literary exceptionalism, Spengemann proposes basing American literary history on language. His model is the European ideal of national literary history as the history of texts written in a single language, no matter where the authors are born or where they live, which he argues is the only basis for a discipline that is both literary and historical. According to this model literary history as such arises from the interplay of *langue* with *parole,* that is of English or any other language understood as a whole system with the specific texts that are written in the language and that continuously modify its character. More specifically, Spengemann proposes defining early American literature according to the vicissitudes of the English language in response to the discovery of the New World and the events taking place thereafter on that soil. Attention to the English language as used in London, Philadelphia, Halifax, and Nassau would then allow early American literature to live up to its name. It would be early with respect to the continuing development of the language system already in place, it would be American in a directly or more often indirectly referential sense, and it would qualify as literary to the precise extent that the works in question live to condition the language in later days.

Inadvertent corroboration of Spengemann's argument comes from Marc Shell's "Babel in America, or the Politics of Language Diversity in the United States" (*CritI* 20: 103–27), a rambling survey of U.S. language policies and practices. Shell's point seems to be that our laudable attention to ethnic and cultural diversity comports oddly with silence about the hegemony of the English language.

Another perspective on American language can be found in William E. H. Meyer's luridly if inaccurately titled "The Irony of American Metaphor: An Essay in the Brutality of Aesthetics" (*LangQ* 31: 103–20). Meyers briskly surveys American literature for metaphors of seeing, which he thinks is a distinctively American trope. So rhapsodic is Meyer's national focus that he mistakenly naturalizes John Marcher of "The Beast in the Jungle" as an "American Pilgrim."

In the "Introduction" and "Afterword" to their collection *Oratorical Culture in Nineteenth-Century America* (pp. 1–26, 247–50) Gregory Clark and S. Michael Halloran sketch a three-phase history of American rhetoric. The neoclassical rhetorical culture of the early Republic understood moral authority to lie in the public consensus of citizens. As this communitarian model increasingly lost ground to individualism, the older rhetoric of public argument was overtaken by a rhetoric of identification, in which listeners were invited to identify with the representative selfhood projected by the speaker. This passage from, say, John Adams to Andrew Jackson and from Edwards to Emerson was then itself surpassed after the Civil War by a rhetoric of professional expertise, which claimed a meritocratic and scientific authority for its pronouncements. Of the primarily biographical essays in the collection that fill out or supplement Clark and Halloran's narrative, the most provocative is Nicole Tonkovich's "Rhetorical Power in the Victorian Parlor: *Godey's Lady's Book* and the Gendering of Nineteenth-Century Rhetoric" (pp. 158–83), which uses the career of Sarah Josepha Hale to indicate the conflicting attitudes women could have about the rise of professionalism and the attendant redrawing of boundaries between public and private.

Of the methodologically more orthodox exercises in literary history, Jerome Loving's *Lost in the Customhouse* is at once the boldest and the least revisionist. Individually examining a dozen writers from Irving and Hawthorne to Chopin and Dreiser, and also promoting a general thesis about the distinctive character of 19th-century American literature, Loving bids to join the classic line of synoptic studies headed by F. O. Matthiessen and D. H. Lawrence. Loving genially reasserts the cold war consensus, namely, that America's best writers are those who adhere to modernist aesthetic values. With few exceptions, he agrees that these are the writers canonized primarily by scholars associated with academic American Studies or (more loosely) with the New Criticism. Loving's purpose is restorative or even, technically speaking, reactionary, but he is less concerned to argue against current methods (New Historicism, ideological critique, feminism, queer theory) than to borrow selectively from them and use the results to defend an updated thesis about American authorship. His version of American exceptionalism, antinomianism, and anticipatory modernism argues that American writers typically look back to a time before innocence was lost and seek a new beginning that will recapture that time. Irving's Rip Van Winkle and Melville's Ahab are thus exemplary protagonists in a revamped Emersonianism, both seeking recuperation of an unfallen identity. More originally, Loving extends the argument into what he calls the second phase of the American Renaissance, postbellum literature from Whitman to Dreiser and Chopin. He sees these later writers as still searching for a reborn selfhood but doing so within everyday circumstances rather than in escape from them. An important consequence is that, in male writers as well as female, an American Eve assumes the place reserved before the Civil War for Adam. Loving's is an obviously ambitious and, I think, significant work, as much for its catholic tone as for its specific readings and arguments. It seeks, frankly, to make the academic world safe again for dead white American men (and women), and it does so according to an appealing, classic strategy by which the specifically literary is sifted out from its biographical, social, and political contexts. Unexamined, however, is the once secure but now challengable assumption that such a sifting gets at what one most wants out of the writings of the past. In other words, Loving never addresses what I take to be the severest challenge of the race, class, and gender school, namely, that American literature comprehensively represents the entirety of American experience.

Susan Howe's *The Birth-Mark* also treats established writers (Dickinson, Melville, the Puritans) and an old consensus, the New England-centered views of Perry Miller and F. O. Matthiessen, but she does so in the manner of a feminist Charles Olson. Here is the personal, even private, viewpoint of a poet examining her regional and national past. Howe gathers and meditates upon what she takes to be voices of alterity or discourses that do not quite fit expectations, especially the utterances of women, but I do not see that she proposes anything new about them. She does, however, link this alterity to another, more striking theme, the misjudgment of editors and textual scholars who eliminate or regularize the spacing, marginalia, and other such material obiter scripta in hand-written manuscripts. Originating as a claim about Dickinson's distinctive and presumably intentional authorship, Howe's brief on behalf of the handwritten object is less persuasive when applied to arguably less deliberate compositions.

Although primarily a study of particular authors and texts, Eric Sundquist's *To Wake the Nations* deserves notice here for redefining the American Renaissance to "include the most daring rebirth of all—the rebirth of African American resistance to slavery and the rebirth of unbiased principles of liberty that had been wrenchingly betrayed in the flawed revolution of the founders." In other words, Sundquist frankly and directly makes ideological rectitude a criterion of value and hence of membership in the literary canon. However, he is sufficiently preoccupied with local readings of Martin Delany, Charles Chesnutt, and others that he barely addresses the consequences his claims would have for a more synoptic view of American literature.

Nicholas K. Bromell's *By the Sweat of the Brow* proposes to heal a widely acknowledged division in *American Renaissance,* between Matthiessen's literary and social allegiances. Bromell's idea is to examine how work is represented in the period and to ponder how or whether writing is a kind of work. The intention is intriguing, and some of the local readings are good, but Bromell himself laments that the era's thinking never surpasses familiar contrasts between mental and physical labor and so the era's writers never resolve the problem he puts to them. The shortfall in results points up the arbitrariness of Bromell's historical (and national) focus. Because antebellum America neither invented nor very interestingly deployed the understanding of labor within which it lived, it does not seem to provide an appropriate period for investigating the issues Bromell wants to pursue.

Russ Castronovo's "Radical Configurations of History in the Era of American Slavery" (*AL* 65: 523–47) inconclusively examines a series of mid-19th-century texts which reflect on a heroic vision of the American past and which variously question this vision, sometimes without apparently intending to do so. A notable problem with the essay is that it makes no attempt to substantiate its historical claims. Castronovo posits as firmly established in antebellum culture, and already even moss-covered, a "monumental" version of American history as the unsullied story of liberty's triumph. One could, of course, debate whether or when such a version ever got secured, but Castronovo strangely does not bother to support his thesis. Instead, he blithely assumes the factuality of monumentalism and then goes on to examine how various writers more or less unwittingly challenge it.

Especially by comparison to the burgeoning interest in the 19th century, the pace of work on American literary modernism and post-modernism seems to have slackened considerably. The one book that seeks to be more than a series of close readings is Walter Kalaidjian's disappointing *American Culture Between the Wars,* which proposes to revive the literary and visual agitprop of the 1920s and 1930s and to link such work to postmodern art and poetry. Unlike Cary Nelson's similar project of recovering forgotten leftist poetry, however, Kalaidjian's histo-riography suffers from shapelessness and superficiality. For example, Kalaidjian reports but regularly trivializes significant ideological quar-rels, as when he blandly endorses both sides of the debate between communists and black cultural nationalists. In addition, he does more amassing of names, events, and works than analysis of their value and significance. This shallowness in turn vitiates his most original claim, namely, that left-wing art between the wars shares important similarities with such more recent movements as language poetry and the art of AIDS activists. On the other hand, the book does offer a valuable archive of images and voices sometimes thought to have been eclipsed by canonical high modernism.

In "Postmodernism/*Fin de Siècle:* The Prospects for Openness in a Decade of Closure" (*Criticism* 35: 161–91) Marjorie Perloff calls attention to the gulf between two versions of postmodernism, one first proclaimed in the late 1960s and the other triumphing in the early 1990s. The first is epitomized for Perloff by David Antin's performance poetry, and the second by Fredric Jameson's theoretical speculations. In addition to a difference in genre between literature and theory, we get what Perloff calls the hardening of a term that both postmodernisms centrally honor. Through the 1970s "difference" is understood by poet and theorist alike as allied with playfulness and openness; by the current decade the word has come to denote somber, pre-cut and comparatively inviolable distinctions, such as those said to obtain between races and genders. Perloff is unhappy with the change, which she sees as part of an unhealthy drive toward totalization. Among other faults, theory-driven postmodernism regularly commits what she calls the Synechdochic Fallacy, the facile reading of some single phenomenon as epitomizing the age. The problem is not epitomes or synecdoches per se (Perloff uses them also) but the often surreptitious or question-begging assumptions by which an example is singled out as representative.

ii Genres

Genre studies are not necessarily distinct from historical ones. For example, as a way of reasserting the ubiquity of conversion as a phenomenological and psychological model in American autobiography, Peter A. Dorsey's *Sacred Estrangement* retraces the history of conversion rhetoric from Augustine to William James. He notes that anticipations, reversals, and witting evasions of the model can be found even in a number of texts that are sometimes thought to have spurned religious conversion as an ineluctably white male pattern. Dorsey seems most interested in theoretical questions (is conversion at bottom a textual or an extratextual phenomenon?) and interpretive ones (how should we read particular autobiographies by Henry James, Henry Adams, Edith Wharton, Ellen Glasgow, Zora Neale Hurston, and Richard Wright?), but he succeeds more fully in sketching a unitary history of the genre. According to his narrative, American life writing moves from the sacred conversion narratives of Puritan testimonial through a secularization process in the 19th century and then onto various attempts to transform or transcend the model in the writings of women and blacks.

In Andrew Levy's *Culture and Commerce* the short story finds its Pierre Bourdieu. Writing as a literary scholar who is also the product of a prestigious MFA program, Levy focuses on the social and institutional contexts in which stories are written and read, thus defining the genre not as a textual form but as a social contract. More specifically and at his best, Levy studies not short stories but the discourse about them: the claims made by critics and authors from Poe to Bobbie Ann Mason; the arguments of editors, anthologizers, and writers of handbooks; and the lore passed on by contemporary creative writing programs. These claims circulate about two seemingly contradictory propositions, both traceable to Poe: that the short story is easy to read and write (especially by comparison to the novel) and that, at least for the writer, it requires the utmost discipline and craft. Levy has a remarkable ability to see similar beliefs and purposes where others have seen only differences. He argues, for example, that Poe's variously thwarted schemes to establish a magazine propose a marketing strategy much like that eventually successful for the *New Yorker*. More searchingly, he notes that the relentlessly middlebrow handbooks for would-be writers that flourished from 1910 to 1935 codified and popularized most of the ideas that are still retailed as inside advice by university-level writing workshops. The similarity is no wonder, he suggests, since those two seemingly different literary worlds are both constituted by similarly booming economies, the earlier a marketplace for short stories in commercial magazines, and the later a marketplace for the cultural capital of teaching appointments, publication in prestigious literary magazines, and other currencies of status and authority.

Studying Dickinson, Whitman, Stephen Crane, Eliot, and a few others, Annie Finch in *The Ghost of Meter* proposes the existence in American poetry of a metrical code, one in which prosody can have a fairly specific semantic role. In particular, she claims that iambic pentameter can function thematically and not just rhythmically in those poets who normally avoid it. Their use of the meter or, in some circumstances, their marked departure from it variously signifies rigidity, tradition, female sentimentality, and patriarchal authority, depending on context. Finch's is an important, innovative argument if valid, but I find it vitiated by two problems. One, endemic to prosody, is that although readers and listeners frequently disagree about poetic scansion, the discourse of prosody hypostasizes metrical terms as if they denoted reliable, verifiable, or even indubitably factual phenomenon. Producing such discourse thus always risks building a castle out of sand. The other problem is that, at least with the poets I know best, Whitman and Dickinson, Finch ignores some major difficulties of textual scholarship. Dickinson she quotes from the Johnson edition, which has for a number of years been under attack precisely for its decisions about lineation and metrics. Whitman she quotes exclusively from the deathbed edition, ignoring all earlier and often metrically quite different versions. This matters a great deal to her argument. The single most telling example of her claim that Dickinson associates pentameter with patriarchy, for instance, is poem 1677, but that text is extant only in a transcript by her sister-in-law. Similarly, although Finch rightly takes "I celebrate myself and sing myself" as conspicuously iambic pentameter, from which "Song of Myself" then departs, that line appears only in later editions. In the earlier and (many argue) the better and stylistically more characteristic versions, the line reads only "I celebrate myself."

Stephen Tatum in "Literature Out-of-Doors" (*AmLH* 5: 294–313) revises Jane Tompkins's contention that the literature of the American West arises as a masculinist antithesis to the domestic novel. Tatum argues instead that the mythic westerns of Owen Wister and his contemporaries extend the otherwise woman-centered tradition of sentimental fiction, importing a redemptive, sometimes homosocial domesticity into a landscape deemed as now more hospitable to sentimental values than the East. The difference is that the West is not so directly threatened by the New Woman, who on the Atlantic seaboard is noisily abandoning her appointed sphere. Linking the western generically to the domestic novel (which Tompkins also largely does) allows Tatum to see a continuity between earlier and contemporary Western writing, which can otherwise be strikingly different in ideological bent and ethnic provenance. Even though recent work by Hispanic and Native American writers (Rudolfo Anaya and Leslie Silko, for example) challenges Wister's programmatic racism and sexism, it shares a similar faith in the uniquely redemptive power of Western terrain.

Several other studies this year more directly examine the intersection of genre and race. Noting the centrality of love and marriage to the novel as a genre, Ann duCille in *The Coupling Convention* seeks to identify what one might call a specifically African American domesticity. To do this she must challenge the belief of some critics that black literature is hostile or indifferent to the bourgeois understanding of romance and marriage found in white fiction. However, because she deals mainly with plot and overt theme rather than with form or with generic conventions and because she shies away from judgments about quality, duCille has difficulty confronting the more serious form of this belief, namely, that the earlier African American writers who do address love and marriage (Pauline Hopkins, Frances Harper, and Jesse Fauset, for instance) do it badly or in bad faith. DuCille rightly contests glib or polemical claims about what should count as genuinely black culture—the dirty blues of a Bessie Smith as in principle more authentic than the coifed and polished fiction of a Nella Larsen—but she does much less well in making a persuasive case about the merits of such middlebrow writing.

In "The 'Complex Fate' of Being an American: The African-American Essayist and the Quest for Identity" (*CLAJ* 37: 64–80) Andrew J. Angyal raises very important questions about how and why a number of African American writers have turned to the personal essay, but he seems innocent of previous scholarship on the essay as a genre and his article thus turns instead into a sophomore-level introduction to Du Bois, Ellison, and Baldwin.

In "White Slaves: The Mulatto Hero in Antebellum Fiction" (*AL* 65: 501–22), Nancy Bentley offers an ingenious argument about generic constraints on the portrayal of biracial men. By contrast to biracial women, white women, or black men with appropriately dark skin, neither white men nor biracial men get portrayed before the Civil War as suffering passively and thus redemptively. By contrast to dark-skinned figures of Christian martyrdom (Uncle Tom, most importantly), mulattos such as Stowe's George Harris or Frederick Douglass in his battle with Covey adopt instead the "white" role of a Byronic or Dumasian avenger when their bodies are in peril. Later, as African American writers sought to articulate new forms of heroism, they did create such black men of action as Douglass's Madison Washington, but in so doing they conspicuously avoided mulatto heroes. William Wells Brown offers the most striking confirmation of this claim, for having changed the skin color and the identity of his hero between the 1853 and 1864 editions of *Clotel*.

iii Identities

One of the few pieces this year to link gender and national character, Carroll Smith-Rosenberg's disappointing "Subject Female: Authorizing American Identity" (*AmLH* 5: 481–511) sets out to examine female agency and female subjectivity in the construction of the American identity during the early days of the Republic. What we get instead, however, are readings of Charles Brockden Brown and Susanna Rowson that depend heavily on plot summary and dubiously reductive historical claims. Elizabeth S. Prioleau's "The Minister and the Seductress in American Fiction: The Adamic Myth Redux" (*JACult* 16, iv: 1–6) surveys six novels in which a male Protestant minister is seduced by a woman. Prioleau argues that this is a distinctively American story and notes that its moral grandeur declines continually from Hawthorne to Updike.

Ronald A. T. Judy's dazzling, dense *(Dis)Forming the American Canon* mobilizes linguistic resources worthy of a Spitzer or a Curtius in order to trouble the phenomenological philology of which they were otherwise the last masters. Judy moves from critiquing the widely accepted claim that slave narratives found African American literature (and ground its place in American studies) to unpacking Kant's conspicuously arbitrary exclusion of African peoples from Reason and then to explicating a 19th-century manuscript written in Arabic by an American slave. Holding together this seemingly unlikely range of materials is a persistent but somewhat shadowy claim, namely, that early African American writings reveal a textual indeterminacy capable of putting in question the hegemony of reason and hence of the social institutions which, so Enlightenment rationalists believed, are, or ought to be, based in reason. In other words, African American writing can deconstruct Western modes of thought and behavior. In particular, because the manuscript known as *Ben Ali's Diary* is structurally and even grammatologically alien to Western philosophy's account of itself and yet also is in some sense manifestly legible and rational, it undoes philosophy's claim to be universal and hence its warrant to legislate for all mankind.

Judy's conclusions are nearly the opposite of those in another study of the relation between black culture and European thought, Paul Gilroy's *The Black Atlantic: Modernity and Double Consciousness* (Harvard). Gilroy insists on the importance of Enlightenment notions of reason to black intellectuals and more generally of Europe's hospitality to such figures as Du Bois and Richard Wright. Much of *The Black Atlantic* is devoted to studying the European sojourns of African American writers and artists and, as the title would suggest, to arguing for a common bond between black people in the United States and Europe. Against a background of controversies over Afrocentrism, however, its sharpest, albeit sketchiest claims are that black thought has a home within Enlightenment universalism and that it makes an essential contribution to Western modernism.

The issue between Gilroy and Judy, part of a general debate about the heritage of the Enlightenment, is as important a one as exists today in the humanities. However, the two critics argue on fundamentally different planes and so never fully engage one another. Gilroy's book presents itself as an essay in cultural studies, and as in his earlier work he is especially interested in relations between high and popular culture. By contrast, Judy's more austere work resembles Paul Bové's, politically engaged but fiercely abstract and stereotypically Germanic speculation of the kind in which a conflict of the faculties is more telling than any conflict in the streets.

iv Critics and Methods

The Critics Who Made Us: Essays from Sewanee Review (Missouri), ed. George Core, gathers two dozen essays on critics who flourished in the 1930s, 1940s, and 1950s. Most of these are genial appreciations without much more than sentimental interest, but Wendell Harris's "Kenneth Burke" (pp. 139–53) provides as clear and succinct an introduction to Burke's key ideas as I have encountered.

Two essays take on the New Historicism from the perspective of older methods and beliefs that are threatened by such work. Gregory Jay in "Ideology and the New Historicism" (*ArQ* 49, i: 141–56) attacks Howard Horwitz (and through him the entire "Berkeley school" of neopragmatists) for reducing cultural criticism to the politically disingenuous reading of representations and rhetorical practices. Such work openly abandons the notion of ideology, replacing it by a monolithic cultural logic and thereby denying any possibility of a standpoint from which one might criticize the culture. Expanding directly on Fredric Jameson's similarly neo-Marxian critique of Walter Benn Michaels, Jay also deplores the tendency of New Historicism to flatten psychic and literary particularities.

Writing on behalf of deconstruction rather than Marxism, Tim Dean in "Wanting Paul de Man: A Critique of the 'Logic' of New Historicism in American Studies" (*TSLL* 35: 251–77) attacks the work of Walter Benn Michaels (and behind him, the influence of Foucault) for occulting the category of the subject. Without ever quite arguing the point, New Historicism transforms the poststructuralist subject into a bundle of conflicting but determined and determinable interests and beliefs. Dean, following Lacan and many others, insists that any notion of the subject must make room for the unconscious and therefore must be understood as constitutively split. Dean's subtle critique founders a bit, however, when this silent or even surreptitious redefining of the subject is allegorized as the repression of deconstruction in general and the charismatic authority of de Man in particular. A low point is reached when Dean calls Michaels a de Man wanna-be.

In *Psychological Politics of the American Dream: The Commodification of Subjectivity in Twentieth-Century American Literature* (Ohio State) Lois Tyson proposes a criticism that can close the divide between proponents of the psyche and of social determinism, which is in a very rough sense the dispute between Dean and Michaels. Her method, examining the psychology of commodity relations, is not especially novel, however, and indeed she uses it mainly as a frame for providing able but familiar readings of five novels and plays. In other words, despite the claims she makes for it, her work only marginally engages the basic theoretical issues.

Finally, several essays reflect on aspects of a trend toward (or, from one American Studies perspective, back to) cultural studies. Both substantive and conceptually the best of these is Susan Willis's "Hardcore: Subculture American Style" (*CritI* 19: 365–83). The essay combines a shrewd, journalistic account of teen culture circa 1990 (just before MTV discovered the Seattle rock bands) with an impassioned, if familiar plea about method in cultural criticism, namely, that the critic should not forget or forgo class analysis in the enthusiasm of describing how subcultures produce new cultural meanings and styles. Mark Hulsether's "Evolving Approaches to U.S. Culture in the American Studies Movement, Consensus, Pluralism, and Contestation to Cultural Hegemony" (*CRevAS* 23, ii: 1–55) divides the history of American Studies into the four phases listed in his subtitle. His intention is to legitimize Gramscian ideas by showing how they answer to established historiographical questions. Charles Bernstein's "What's Art Got to Do with It? The Status of the Subject of the Humanities in the Age of Cultural Studies" (*AmLH* 5: 597–615) might most charitably be described as poet's prose: one writer's casual and deeply self-centered view of current literary and cultural theory. Were it not written by a distinguished author and published in a major journal, it would attract no attention.

Case Western Reserve University

i French Contributions: Daniel Royot

Although French scholarship has remained unrecorded in *ALS* for the last three years, a comprehensive retrospect is beyond the scope of this contribution. Mostly book-length studies and significant articles published as far back as 1991 will be mentioned. This panorama of American literary studies bears witness to the wide range of interest among French scholars. Past and present are equally represented, and the current canon seems to be well-entrenched. Any onslaught on dead white male writers would certainly find it impossible to storm such strongholds as Poe and Faulkner studies.

a. 18th-Century Literature Several publications commemorated the bicentennial of Benjamin Franklin's death, among them Jean Robert Rougé's special issue of *Frontières* on 18th-century culture; Daniel Royot's "Espace, frontière et peuplement dans la pensée franklinienne" (*EA* 45 [1992]: 324–33); *Benjamin Franklin des Lumières à nos jours* (Didier Erudition, 1991), ed. Gérard Hugues and Daniel Royot, and Christian Lerat's *Benjamin Franklin, quand l'Amérique s'émancipait* (PUB, 1992). Lerat sheds new light on the personality of Franklin and relates how the self-taught apprentice became a dedicated educator, exploiting the potentialities and ambiguities nurtured from Enlightenment philosophy. A selective anthology illustrates the career of the American citizen whom Marie Antoinette called "l'ambassadeur électrique."

b. 19th-Century Literature A spectacular revival of criticism on major 19th-century writers has emphasized Melville, Thoreau, Poe, and Whitman. Michel Granger's steady research gained full recognition with the publication of *Henry D. Thoreau, Narcisse à Walden* (PUL, 1991). His finely structured discussion follows Thoreau's quest of autonomous wisdom at Walden Pond until he achieves a "mastery of inner violence." It evaluates Thoreau's far-reaching experience, rendered through a new paradoxical discourse opening on the unknown. In *Caliban* (29 [1992]: 49–59) Alain Suberchicot analyzes "the vital surge" toward the transcendentalist sublime in Thoreau's *Journal.* Referring to the dual connotations of the word sublime ("limen" as threshold and "limus" as oblique), Suberchicot quotes Harold Bloom's *Ruin the Sacred Truths* to support his own thesis that Thoreau's spiritual experience misses its mark, eludes control, and leads back to "the human" as reflected in the literary text. Also probing into New England literature, Renaud Zuppinger sees an "anamnestic process" in the shift from European to Western culture in a Hawthorne tale ("Vanitas Vanitatis ou la gemme mal aimée: 'The Great Carbuncle,'" *EA* 46: 10–20).

A seminal study of Poe was published by Henri Justin in 1991 under the title *Poe dans le champ du vertige* (Klincksiek). Justin enlists structuralist theories to visualize the concentric forces at work in Poe's textual space, with reference to such concepts as vertigo, attraction, repulsion, coherence and paradox, contradiction and tension. Justin's sophisticated dialectics link the "psycho-cosmic element" to the artist's acute consciousness in configuring his imaginary space, as also illustrated in "Le Vortex: raison et vertige" (*Les Cahiers du Cerli* 2: 69–77).

The Melville harvest is especially rewarding thanks to two major publications. Viola Sachs edited *L'imaginaire-Melville* (PUV, 1992) and Philippe Jaworski the special Melville issue of *Profils américains* (vol. 5), with interesting contributions by Michel Imbert on paper money and Scriptures in *The Confidence-Man* and on the primitive masquerade in *Typee*. Dominique Marçais, another dedicated Melville scholar, contributed "Revolution and Identity in *White-Jacket* and *Israel Potter*" to *L'imaginaire* (pp. 52–54). The centenary of Walt Whitman's death was commemorated in a 1992 issue of *EA* ed. Roger Asselineau, who proposes a new way of reading *Leaves of Grass* based on Gaston Bachelard's books on "material imagination" and the role played by the four elements in the creation of poetry. In addition to contributions by four American scholars, Jeanine Belgodère explains that the contrasted dynamics and recurrent patterns in *Leaves of Grass* herald the new dance aesthetics ("Le motif de la danse dans *Leaves of Grass*," 45: 299–310). For Claudette Fillard, Whitman's annexes to *Leaves of Grass* exemplify the vital need of keeping up the "motions" of writing ("Le vannier de Camden: vieillesse, poésie et les annexes de *Leaves of Grass*," 45: 311–24).

In the field of cultural studies, volumes 14–15 of *Voix et Langages aux États-Unis,* published by GRENA (Université de Provence), a prolific research center in American studies, assesses the subversive power of language in a broad perspective. In "Emancipation et parole poétique dans l'oeuvre de Walt Whitman" (14: 43–52) Annick Duperray mobilizes Bakhtin's problematic views of the relationships between language and myth to show that the power of words may deflect the fatality of experience. In *"Adventures of Huckleberry Finn:* le langage en question" (15: 33–60) Michèle Bonnet reveals Twain's reinterpretations of the dividing line between fiction and reality, truth and lie.

Duperray's *Echec et écriture, essai sur les nouvelles de Henry James* (Publications de l'Université de Provence) is a monumental interpretation of James's short fiction. Duperray contends that James's stories enlarge on the confrontation between nature and culture and the function of symbolic death to emancipate the ego from narcissistic fascination through the intersubjective experience of "the other's alienation." Duperray's study is indebted to René Girard, Jacques Lacan, Paul Valadier, and Jean-Paul Sartre. It recognizes James as a "counterrealist" who gives up the need for a truth beyond human limits, within a universe having lost the sense of the sacred. *Polysèmes,* published by the University of Sorbonne Nouvelle, devotes its fourth issue to comparative studies of art and literature. In terms of tone, representation, and point of view, Evelyne Labbé examines the functions and drifts of the pictorial code in James's fiction ("Henry James, l'in[dé]fini du tableau," pp. 77–100). In *Profils américains* (3 [1992]: 67–77) Georges-Michel Sarotte considers *The Bostonians* as the fictional allegory of James's psychic predicament, torn as he was between his regional origins and his imaginary domain. A specialist on Eudora Welty, Danièle Pitavy-Souques turns to fruitful comparative studies by considering women's voices in "De G. Flaubert à K. Chopin, du paraître à l'être: notes sur Emma Bovary, Thérèse Lafirme, Edna Pontellier dans *The Awakening*" (*EA* 46: 477–86). The divided mother figure is portrayed in " 'Désirée's Baby' de Kate Chopin: portrait d'une mère vestale" by Catherine Morgan-Proux (*Alizés-Trade Winds,* October 1992).

c. 20th-Century Fiction to World War II   As an overture, homage is naturally paid to Pierre-Yves Pétillon's *Histoire de la littérature américaine* (Paris: Fayard, 1992), an impressive volume of biographies and minute analyses of individual works extending over half a century (1939–89). An interesting appraisal of *The Education of Henry Adams* is to be found in Annick Duperray's "Henry Adams and the Reader's Education" in *L'éducation aux États-Unis, mythes et réalités* (Publications de l'Université de Provence, 1992, pp. 11–21). Duperray gathers that Adams outlined the peculiar form of radicalism now described as "soft ideology," founded on the pragmatic interplay of complementary or contradictory doctrines. In "Finding a voice for Sexual Experience in *Sister Carrie* and *Jennie Gerhardt*" (*Voix et Langages* 1: 53–66) Charles Holdefer elucidates the interplay between knowing and not-knowing in the light of Paul de Man's judgments on the process of literary history, thereby showing how Dreiser's fiction is still attractive "under the scrutiny of new expectations." In "Ordre et Désordre dans *McTeague,* le rêve et la fêlure" (*Idéologies dans le monde anglo-saxon* 6:133–48) André Muraire resorts to Darwinian philosophy to substantiate his view of the rift between the construction of the American dream and "the chaos of reality" in Frank Norris's fiction.

In *Les États-Unis à l'épreuve de la modernité* (Presses de la Sorbonne Nouvelle), ed. Daniel Royot, Warren French returns to the cultural values of the Lost Generation by confronting a tradition of joy as exemplified in the westering spirit, with the nation's tastemaking psyches of our century ("The Lostness of a Joyless Generation," pp. 67–89). Martine Chard-Hutchinson and Christine Raguet-Bouvart underscore the notion of corporeity in "L'évolution de la problématique de la corporéité dans *The Great Gatsby* and *Tender is the Night*" (*RFEA* 55: 83–93). They judge that corporeal fragmentation mirrors the gap between appearance and being, foreshadowing "the atomization of the individual bereft of his social and personal identity." By reasserting the superiority of time—the absolute master of human destiny—Daisy, not Tom, precipitates the fall of Gatsby, according to Alain Geoffroy in "Daisy Buchanan, the Heart of *The Great Gatsby*" (*Alizés-Trade Winds,* October 1992, pp. 83–94).

Patricia Bleu-Schwenninger crowns her research on the author of the *U.S.A.* trilogy with the publication of *John Dos Passos, l'écriture miroir* (Grenoble: Ellug). By focusing the camera eye on the world and himself,

Bleu-Schwenninger writes, Dos Passos transcribed his "autobiographical space" into the language of the people and portrayed a civilization meaningless under the weight of its illusions. In "L'orchestration de la modernité dans *The Big Money*" (*EA* 46: 420–26) Bleu-Schwenninger also shows that of the novels in the trilogy, only *The Big Money* exhibits carefully controlled construction. Dos Passos thus invites the reader to decipher the text by taking into account a diversity of heterogeneous elements as well as his own experience of modernity.

In "The Uses of Language in *Babbitt*" (*Voix et Langages* 1: 67–86) Barbara Lemeunier considers that through Sinclair Lewis's satiric mode the characters' discourse is not one of creation but of closure that restates and reinforces accepted values. In "The Ideology of Passive Acceptance in the Works of Henry Miller" (*Voix et Langages* 2: 61–78) Charles Holdefer acknowledges Miller's anticipation of postmodernist techniques. Marie Christine Lemardeley-Cunci's case study of *Of Mice and Men, Des Souris et des Hommes de John Steinbeck* (Paris: Gallimard, 1992), deserves special mention for its rich intertextuality and extensive thematic treatment. Deliberately cosmopolitan is Robert Sayre's article on the commitments of American writers in the 1930s ("La Guerre d'Espagne: écrivains et écriture aux États-Unis," *RFEA* 55: 43–55).

Faulkner remains a monument among French critics as proved by an issue of *Europe* (1992), which would be worthy of a full-length article, considering the outstanding quality of the contributors. Alain Geoffroy finely organizes in book form his "psycho-temporal analysis" of Faulkner (*Le Ressac de l'enfance chez William Faulkner,* Didier Erudition, 1991) around the metaphor of nature, vegetation, and the garden, "peopled with insular beings besieged by the surge of time." In Geoffroy's literary landscape, Faulkner's earth owes its survival to an unrelenting resistance to the onslaught of waters. Attentive to Faulkner's short fiction, Robert Sayre sees the stories as a strategy of resistance to modernity through form and content ("Romanticism and the Faulknerian Short Story of the Early 1930s," *JSSE* 20: 65–80).

Jewish-American fiction is still heartily welcomed by general readers and duly reviewed by such scholars as Rachel Ertel, Martine Chard-Hutchinson, and Claude Lévy. Meanwhile, fellow workers have emerged. Paule Lévy published "La vitre, le miroir et le masque: ébauche d'une étude sur l'altérité dans *Herzog*" in *L'altérité dans le monde anglophone* (PUM, pp. 199–207), and "Words, Words, Words: rhétorique de la satire dans le roman *Mr. Sammler's Planet* de Saul Bellow" ("Configurations critiques de l'ethnicité aux États-Unis," in *Les Cahiers de Charles V,* 15: 121–41).

d. Literature and the Performing Arts   Interdisciplinary research on theater, film, and literature has increased. Following a conference at the University of Rennes on Arthur Miller, an issue of *Coup de Théatre* (11 [1991]) presented an attractive sampling of articles, among which Georges-Michel Sarotte's "De Frank Wagner à 'Miss Francis,' heur et malheur de la virilité: père et fils dans *Death of a Salesman*" (pp. 83–92) stresses the virile, homoerotic, and androgynous elements in American literature. In "Le théatre de Tennessee Williams à l'écran: tactiques et stratégies" (*RFEA* 56: 175–84) Sarotte examines the various ways in which screenwriters and directors transformed Williams's Broadway plays into movies intended for the general public—ranging from moderately faithful renditions of the theater plays to more cinematic, "opened-up" versions. The article also analyzes the consequences of the deletion or addition of scenes, characters, and dialogue, and of censorship or self-censorship. Sarotte turns to "self-censorship as self-inflicted torture" in "Censure et auto-censure dans l'oeuvre de William Inge" (*Cycnos* 9: 61–70).

Several contributions bear on the American literary scene in *La Littérature anglo-américaine à l'écran* (Didier Erudition), ed. Gérard Hugues and Daniel Royot. Christine Raguet-Bouvart detects shortcomings throughout the adaptation of James's fiction in *"The Europeans:* la traduction cinématographique de James Ivory" (pp. 91–101). "Sur la piste des Pères fondateurs" by Gérard Hugues is a perceptive study of law and order in Walter Van Tilburg Clark's *The Ox-Bow Incident* (pp. 81–90). Jacqueline Simon compares Dreiser's novel with George Stevens's film in *"A Place in the Sun:* de *An American Tragedy* à une tragédie hollywoodienne" (pp. 103–18). Leonard Frey evaluates the avatars of the bildungsroman in "Baseball's and Mark Harris's Fiction and Cinema Projections in *Bang the Drum Slowly*" (pp. 119–24).

e. Contemporary Literature   Marc Chénetier edited the issue of *RFEA* (54 [1992]) devoted to "the voice in contemporary American fiction." In "Repères pour l'étude d'une voix fantôme, ou petit concert, en guise d'introduction à un autre" (pp. 319–32) Chénetier's richly problematic views introduce the debate on "the voice of the literary text" in relation to the physical voice. In Jean-Jacques Lecercle's interpretation of Barthelme's short story "Sentence," the analysis of the voice in/of the sentence draws on the critical resources of enunciation linguistics, the theory of the relationship between language and death put forward by Giorgio Agamben, Bakhtinian dialogism, and Walter Benjamin's theology of language. The personified sentence is seen to be a modern incarnation of Scheherazade ("La voix dans 'Sentence' de Donald Barthelme," pp. 332–51). Hervé Laurens's "La voix du narrateur dans *Overnight to Many Distant Cities*" (pp. 353–64) attempts to reveal how Barthelme succeeds in asserting the power of technique and structure over the raw material of words with a view to achieving meaning. In Anne Battesti's interpretation of Pynchon, impersonated or contaminated voices point to a haunting dispossession, inflicted on the shifting addressees as well as on the reader ("Pynchon: voix, lieux communs," pp. 365–76). "Sous l'invocation du Sud: la Voix dans la fiction sudiste et l'oeuvre de Shelby Foote" (pp. 377–84) by Paul Carmignani reveals that in Foote's fiction initiation into the realm of the written word often takes place only after the protagonist, a would-be novelist, immerses himself in some sort of *flumen verborum* or exposes himself to an oracular voice echoing myths and legends, while "voice however ephemeral is the unsubstantial fabric literature is made of." Commenting on Don DeLillo's *End Zone*, François Happe recognizes the failure of two voices trying to assert their authority: the voice of the narrator whose control is challenged by a parasitic authorial voice and the voice of the single-minded coach, "a landlocked Ahab," embarked on the doomed pursuit of the original univocality of the Word ("Voix et autorité dans *End Zone* de Don DeLillo," pp. 385–93).

In *La Mort de Méduse: l'art de la nouvelle chez Eudora Welty* (PUL, 1992) Danièle Pitavy-Souques examines Welty's mythmaking. The space inscribing the characters is studied in "the shield of Perseus," the thematic structure then examined in the part devoted to Medusa and fascination. The components of Welty's creative imagination and narrative strategy are dealt with in the final chapter. While powerfully synthetic, the volume is also rich in minutiae. Two other views of Eudora Welty deserve attention. In "Arrêt sur image et temporalité dans *One Writer's Beginnings* de Eudora Welty" (*Polysèmes* 4: 101–27) Géraldine Chouard concentrates on the use of time in pictorial representation. Claudine Verley explores fragmented, chaotic narrative in "Les métamorphoses du texte et les avatars de la circularité dans *The Whole World*

Knows" (*RFEA* 56: 193–204). Verley makes clear that myth denies both history and the story of Maidee's suicide. The text repeats the dialectics of circle and center, opening and closure, static circularity and dynamic cycle at work in the whole of *The Golden Apples*.

This year saw a bonanza of Nabokov studies. In "Nabokoviana" (*RFEA* 58: 411–20) Maurice Couturier surveys current biographies and critical works devoted to the author of *Lolita*. Noting the scarcity of current narratological analyses, he points to several revisionist interpretations based on the author's ethical and metaphysical approaches. Couturier sees a sophisticated form of censorship in a new-fashioned tendency to discard Nabokov's flamboyant eroticism. In *Nabokov ou la tyrannie de l'auteur* (Paris: Seuil) Couturier brilliantly demonstrates that Humbert appeals to the judgment of the good reader, thus substituting poetic mirage for the erotic pleasure of the first part of *Lolita*. Therefore, Nabokov constantly retains his authorial control by testing our moral capacity to withstand his libertine strategies. A special issue of *Cycnos* publishes the proceedings of an international conference on Nabokov held at the University of Nice in 1992. In this volume Couturier delineates the terms of the challenge in "The Distinguished Writer vs. the Child" (10: 47–54); Raguet-Bouvart discusses "Textual Regeneration and the Author's Progress" (10: 91–97); Suzanne Fraysse traces the construction of an autobiography through the reader-writer relationship ("Look at the Harlequins!" 10: 143–49). In 1992, Raguet-Bouvart published "Sens et essence du texte de Vladimir Nabokov in 'Ecriture moderne'" (*Les années trente* 15: 43–55), in which "art toying with meaning" as well as "the joy of creation" are shown to reflect the sense of modernity.

Brautigan sauvé du vent (Paris: L'Incertain, 1992) by Marc Chénetier is a revised edition of a book published by Methuen in 1983. Avoiding the pitfalls of hagiography and often delving into virgin ground, Chénetier's textual and narratological inroads allow him to shed light on Brautigan's cheerful despair, his obsession with the danger of reified language, and his irreverent art.

In *William Styron: le désir foudroyé* (PUN) Patrick Badonnel conducts a psychoanalytical investigation of Styron's fiction. The psychogenesis of the characters' morbid crises is brought out through an Oedipial structure. As Badonnel finely argues, Styron transcends the pathological to reach a humanistic vision of God, freedom, and truth, the hero thus becoming a literary archetype.

Several articles in *Voix et Langages* treat American topics. In " 'Bringing the Corners Forward': Voices and Language in *Rabbit at Rest*" (2: 99–126) Barbara Lemeunier examines how Updike paradoxically demonstrates the impoverishment of language and myth. Annick Cizel's "La voix de l'Afrique dans *The Coup* de John Updike" sees the novel as a castigation of materialistic American society in relation to African culture (2: 79–98). Sylvie Mathé explores Holocaust fiction in "Voix de l'émotion, voix de l'indicible: *The Shawl* de Cynthia Ozick" (1: 11–42) and turns to the work of another contemporary novelist in "Voix de la solitude, voix de la mémoire: la leçon de ténèbres de Paul Auster dans *The Invention of Solitude*" (2: 127–54). In *La littérature anglo-américaine à l'écran* Mark Niemeyer assesses Kurt Vonnegut's fiction on film in "Editing Out the Narrator: George Roy Hill's Adaptation of *Slaughterhouse-Five*" (pp. 135–44). Ron Kovic's *Born on the Fourth of July* is likewise compared with its film version in "Narration des idéologies et idéologie de la narration" (pp. 165–77) by André Muraire. Claire Maniez has two remarkable articles on William Gass: "On Talking to Oneself: 'Icicles' de William Gass" (*QWERTY* 1 [1991]: 223–31) and "The World Within the Words of William H. Gass's 'In the Heart of the Heart of the Country' " (*EA* 45 [1992]). Her close examination of "Heart" shows that it is above all a piece of metafiction that explores, through the portrait of a solipsistic narrator, the problems of representation of the real. Writing is for the narrator a way to recover himself, however imperfectly, through the country and the people he tries to describe. Also valuable is the issue of *Profils américains* on Raymond Carver, with articles by Claudine Verley ("Raymond Carver: Voir l'insolite" [4: 43–47]) and Annick Duperray ("De l'onde à la parole ou le langage des rêves dans l'oeuvre de Raymond Carver" [4: 29–41]).

f. Ethnic Literature   *Ecritures hispaniques aux États-Unis, mémoire et mutations* (Publications de l'Université de Provence, 1990), coauthored by Yves-Charles Grandjeat, Elyette Andouard-Labarthe, Christian Lerat, and Serge Ricard, was a breakthrough in the study of contemporary Hispanic literature in the United States. The tensions generated by the efforts to establish a Chicano or Nuyorican identity are described in terms of memory and mutation, interdependence and ambiguity, ideology and commitment. Other subjects include transitive, polyphonous or eclectic space, semantic resistance, and narrative interventions in "the linguistic arena."

Under the guidance of Jean Béranger, the Centre de recherches sur l'Amérique anglophone (CRAA) of Université Michel Montaigne in Bordeaux published in 1992 *Le Je dans tous ses éclats* (n.s. 17) with articles on Hispanic, Indian, Greek-American and Jewish-American literatures. Mention should be made of the major contributors: Elyette Andouard-Labarthe ("L'individu hors de soi d'Omar Salinas ou la quête d'un subjectum," pp. 25–43), Nicole Bensoussan ("Little World, Hello! de Jimmy Savo," pp. 45–50), Elisabeth Béranger ("Une femme faite d'histoires: la construction du sujet dans *Storyteller*," pp. 61–70), Marcienne Rocard ("Le moi sans frontières d'Alma Villanueva dans *Bloodroot*," pp. 71–80), Suzanne Durruty (*"Bread Givers* ou l'éternel émigrant," pp. 81–90), Jean Béranger ("Les mises en scène du JE: le moi inachevé et le moi reconstruit d'Emmanuel Carnevali," pp. 91–108), Bernadette Rigal-Cellard ("Les problèmes de l'autobiographie indienne: les cas de Black Elk et de Refugio Savala," pp. 127–44), Jean Cazemajou ("Désirs, musique et nostalgie dans *The Mambo Kings Play Songs of Love* d'Oscar Hijuelos," pp. 145–56), Ginette Castro (*"The Woman Who Lived in a Prologue:* une Ariane Juive-américaine dans le labyrinthe de son moi," pp. 165–76), Nicole Ollier ("Roi ou sujet? Je e(s)t tous les autres, Je suis lion d'après *Lion at My Heart* de Harry Mark Petrakis," pp. 177–98), and Christian Lerat ("De la thérapie du vagabondage au soi et hors de soi dans *The Autobiography of a Brown Buffalo* d'Oscar Zeta Acosta," pp. 203–24).

Ecrire la différence (n.s. 18), also published by the CRAA in Bordeaux, consists of the proceedings of an international conference on interculturalism and the writing of difference; it involves numerous French scholars, among them Nicole Bensoussan (*"Golden Wedding* ou la mise en scène de la différence," pp. 87–94), Robert Rougé ("Le ressourcement du moi dans le roman italo-américain," pp. 109–18), Suzanne Durruty (*"Tell Me a Riddle* de Tillie Olsen," pp. 131–38), Bernadette Rigal-Cellard ("Analyse de deux mises en scène interculturelles du sujet: les pactes autobiographiques de Momaday dans *The Names* et de Vizenor dans *Interior Landscapes*," pp. 161–74), Elisabeth Béranger ("Joy Harjo: au delà de la ligne de partage," pp. 175–86), Daniel Royot ("Perspectives transculturelles sur la chasse à l'homme: *The Ox-Bow Incident* et *The Ballad of Gregorio Cortez*," pp. 203–10), Marcienne Rocard ("Du Bon usage de la différence: *Borders* de Pat Mora," pp. 279–88), Jean Cazemajou (*"Migrant Souls* d'Arturo Islas: les Chicanos sur le divan, mémoire, différ[a]nce et écriture," pp. 289–302), Elyette Benjamin-Labarthe ("Un effet induit de l'idéologie: de Chicano à Chicana et vice-versa, ou une réconciliation littéraire inattendue," pp. 303–12), and Yves-Charles Grandjeat ("Doxy and Heterodoxy in the Emerging Chicano Critical Discourse: Metacritical Notes on *Criticism in the Borderlands*," pp. 313–24).

In *Voix et Langages,* Joelle Bonnevin sees a double narrative structure coupled with a dual language in Louise Erdrich's *Track* as expressions of ethnic survival ("Voix et langages des Indiens Chippewa dans *Tracks* de Louise Erdrich" (2: 211–28). In the same volume Wolfgang Binder also examines Ed Vega's portrait of the Puerto-Rican community, especially the author's use of "the map of Manhattan to a Latin beat" as a foil and a text for acts of "multiple reciprocate acculturation" ("A Hispanic Voice of Satire: Ed Vega's Portrait of the Puerto-Rican Community," 1: 229–44). In "Rites et célébrations dans deux oeuvres de Paule Marshall" (*RFEA* 51 [1992]: 36–43) Françoise Charras shows how Marshall explores primal myths and creates a new ritualistic experience through her representation of personal and communal rites ("pagan, Christian, African or American"). In *Les États-Unis à l'épreuve de la modernité,* Mathieu Compaoré suggests that W. E. B. Du Bois's prophetic voice defined a new African American dream, deviating from the views held by Harlem Renaissance writers ("W. E. B. Du Bois et la condition des Africains Américains au lendemain de la première guerre mondiale," pp. 155–66); Aloyse Eyang assesses the cultural impact of jazz and blues as expressed through Langston Hughes's poetic evocations ("Langston Hughes, Jazzonia et la Renaissance de Harlem," pp. 181–204). According to John F. Callahan ("History and the Crisis of Feeling: Observations on American Culture in the 1920s," pp. 167–80), Sterling Brown and Hughes recognized that the predicament of feeling, though it might be briefly transcended by individuals, could not be overcome except by their generation's mingling tradition with individual talent. The crisis of feeling thus expressed a crisis of survival for society at the most immediate physical and spiritual level of experience. In *Alizés-Trade Winds* for November 1992, Françoise Clary's "Race et valeurs religieuses acculturées dans *Invisible Man* de Ralph Ellison" (pp. 75–88) is an evaluation of *Invisible Man,* elaborating on the protagonist's sense of freedom and capacity to survive. The basic thesis is derived from a quotation from Ellison's book ("humanity is won by continuing to play in the face of certain defeat"). Corinne Duboin's "Segregation and the Representation of Urban Space in Richard Wright's *Native Son*" (pp. 105–14) develops Wright's naturalistic approach in the treatment of fictional space.

The interest in Toni Morrison's fiction continues this year, exemplified

in *Beloved, She's Mine* (Paris: CETANLA), ed. Geneviève Fabre and
Claudine Raynaud. In "Beloved, Arbre de chair, arbre de vie" (*EA* 46:
440–46) Anne Marie Paquet sees the narrative grow like a powerful tree,
all images of the tree eventually coming together in the parable of the
biblical Tree of Jesse and the Tree of Life. The black woman's identity and
representation also constitute the central theme in Claude Le Fustec's
"Quête de femme: la question de l'image de la femme noire américaine à
travers trois romans de Toni Morrison: *The Bluest Eye, Sula* et *Beloved*"
(*Alizes-Trade Winds*, October 1992).

g. Poetry   Last to be considered is the revival of interest in poetic studies.
Current-day critics generally avoid neoscholastic approaches and concentrate on textual analysis with a variety of methodological stances.
Based on Carl Bode's edition of *The Collected Poems of Henry Thoreau*,
Alain Suberchicot's "L'oeuvre poétique de Thoreau" (*EA* 44 [1991]) sees
the foreshadowing of modern American poetry in Thoreau's aesthetic
play with words, arbitrary association of images, and deep-rooted individualism. Christine Savinel's *Emily Dickinson et la grammaire du secret*
(PUL) is a landmark in French scholarship. With intense critical acumen,
the author reads "the cryptic space" appropriated by the word seen as text,
place, and representation. Elliptic forms create a vacuum, eliminating
referential functions and giving access to "the ineffable." Different from
the riddle, the "fundamental secret" retains its mysteries, as substantiated
by the absence of echo in unpublished poems and the sense of negative-
ness shown along the "Calvary of life." Meanwhile, the burning auto-da-
fé metaphorically translates "the poetic law of secret." Savinel's felicitous
rhetorical developments constantly adorn Lacan's elaborate phraseology.
Like Dickinson, she could grow blazing stars on Puritan granite. Savinel
also develops her critical views in "La reine du Calvaire, le tableau in-
connu dans l'oeuvre d'Emily Dickinson" (*Polysèmes* 4: 47–75).

In "La morphologie du lieu dans les premiers poèmes de Wallace Stevens" (*Ecriture poétique moderne* 2: 115–24) Suberchicot suggests that "the
geometric morphology of place" is at odds with the reflexive, egotistic
process of the poet's intellect. Paule Lévy renews our view of Frost
(" 'Home Burial' de Robert Frost: poème de la déchirure et de l'absence")
in *L'absence dans les pays de langue anglaise* (PUR, pp. 97–111). Taking
a short leave from Whitman in a concise essay, Roger Asselineau defines W. D. Snodgrass's poetry as preapocalyptic or instantaneous. Thus
"Snodgrass walking through the universe" is fully assertive, while "his

job is to celebrate: what IS, away from theories and trends" ("Poésie et peinture dans l'oeuvre de W. D. Snodgrass," *EA* 46: 199–201).

A special issue of *Interspace* titled "Censure et anti-censure dans la poésie américaine," jointly ed. Jacqueline Ollier and Alain Suberchicot, is devoted to censorship in American poetry. Covering both past and present and bearing on a great variety of subjects, there are articles by Asselineau (*"Leaves of Grass:* censure et auto-censure," 7: 3–12); Elyette Benjamin-Labarthe ("Femmes et censure: la poésie chicana," 7: 13–28); Antoine Cazé ("Ezra Pound/Guy Davenport: l'impossible lieu de la modernité," 7: 29–38); Jeanne Houghton ("La censure dans l'écriture féminine de H.D.: Le cas de *Helen in Egypt*" 7: 39–50); Taffy Martin ("Censure et féminité dans l'oeuvre poétique de Diane Wakoski," 7: 51–60); Nicole Moulinoux ("Wallace Stevens et Picasso: d'une censure à l'autre," 7: 61–70); Jacqueline Ollier ("Censorship and Auto-Censorship in Twentieth-Century Poetry: Eliot, Pound, Williams," 7: 71–82); William Sharpe ("Unspeakable New York: Censorship and the City," 7: 83–92); Suberchicot ("Censure et statut de la création poétique chez Ralph Waldo Emerson," 7: 93–106); and Michèle Merzoug-Garnier ("William Carlos Williams: pour une poétique de l'autocensure," 7: 107–24). *Alizés-Trade Winds* (January 1993) published two articles on Robert Lowell: "Amphibious Creatures: Images of Transcendence in Robert Lowell's Poetry" by Jacky Martin (pp. 11–22) and "La mort et l'eau: obsessions et contrastes dans l'oeuvre poétique de Robert Lowell" by Françoise Clary (pp. 23–32). Both critiques deal with the poetic mind in relation to existential commitments. Suberchicot stresses Lowell's distrust of the lyrical ego and affirmation of cultural claims in "Robert Lowell et l'élaboration d'une conscience de soi dans 'The Drinker'" (*QWERTY* 2 [1992]: 193–98). In *Polysèmes,* Marie-Christine Lemardeley-Cunci establishes connections between a painting by Edwin Romanzo Elmer and Adrienne Rich's poem ("Le deuil de l'image dans *Mourning Picture*" 10: 129–47). Elyette Benjamin-Labarthe, who specializes in Chicano studies, has extended her field of research with an original anthology, *Vous avez dit Chicano: anthologie thématique de poésie chicana* (Talence: Maison des sciences de l'homme d'Aquitaine).

ii Italian Contributions: Algerina Neri

Specific studies and careful translations with introductions or afterwords are features of Italian scholarship this year. While Melville, James, and

Pound have received the usual attention, Edith Wharton and 20th-century poetry take center stage this year. Critics have been less fasci-nated by ethnic studies, a major topic in recent years, but they have displayed a growing interest in women writers. Wharton, Alcott, Cho-pin, Stein, Barnes, Cather, H.D., Bishop, and Paley have been lovingly investigated, mainly by women scholars.

a. General Work, Criticism, Bibliography   The exploration of cultural links between Italy and the United States after World War II is the topic of *Immaginari a confronto: I rapporti culturali tra Italia e Stati Uniti: la percezione della realtà tra stereotipo e mito* (Marsilio), ed. Carlo Chiarenza and William L. Vance. The contributions explore the mechanisms, more or less in evidence, that control the individual and collective imagina-tion. In "Il mito americano di tre generazioni antiamericane" (pp. 15–28) Umberto Eco examines the myth of America from Cesare Pavese's time onward to conclude that the Italian idea of America has always been pure invention; it has not become even an alternative ideology, but the end of ideology in our contemporary generation. In " 'A Place of Brightness': la controcultura americana nella geremiade transatlantica" (pp. 113–26) Alessandro Portelli investigates the same theme. Not only is America "the gigantic theater where everyman's drama is enacted with greater freshness than everywhere else," as Pavese said, but it is the only theater. As in the Puritan jeremiad, criticism against America only gives back more America. The qualities that make Isabel Archer "noble" but also bring her to ruin—"a fixed determination to regard the world as a place of brightness, of free expansion, of irresistible action"—are those same features that fascinate and scare us about America, like light, which enlightens but also burns and blinds. Literature, however, seems to record and underline conventional truths, repetitive stereotypes. Postwar American novels about Italy and Italians try to show the uselessness of comparisons, as William L. Vance argues in "Stereotipi, differenze e verità nel romanzo e nel racconto americano sull'Italia" (pp. 29–48) through reference to works by John Horne Burns, John Cheever, Ber-nard Malamud, and Helen Barolini. In "Oleografia: scrittura al fem-minile negli Stati Uniti e in Italia" (pp. 99–112) Mary Russo points out how American feminism is much more aware of French than Italian feminist thought. She then sensitively discusses the critical position of *Viaggio e scrittura: le straniere nell'Italia dell'Ottocento* (Florence: Libreria delle donne, 1988). Cultural links and exchanges between Italy and the United States are becoming steadily more varied and enriching. The impressive exposition "American Art 1930–1970" at Turin in 1992 attracted a large public, and a useful review by Michele Bottalico appeared in "Tra due e più culture: arte americana 1930–1970" (*Tempi Moderni* 2: 18–19). The exploration of American literature by Italian cultural circles needs further attention. In "'Un respiro del mare': Luigi Berti e la Letteratura Angloamericana" (*Paragone* 30 [1991]: 68–76) Ornella De Zordo considers the sympathetic work that Luigi Berti devoted to American contemporary authors as translator, critic, and journalist. A pyrotechnic contribution comes from Matteo Sanfilippo's *Il Medioevo secondo Walt Disney* (Rome: Castelvecchi), which ranges through literature, cinema, music, and comics. After an agile discussion of the uses of the Middle Ages made by American culture and literature, Sanfilippo underlines the power of American mass production, which has led the elite culture to formulate new images and myths. This process has been so thorough that nowadays it is difficult to imagine the Middle Ages as different from the picture that comes from American comics and movies. A general and informative work about 20th-century prose and poetry is Tommaso Pisanti's *"Spoon River" e altro Novecento* (Naples: Liguori).

Italian academics have always appreciated Northrop Frye's work, so his *Double Vision* was promptly translated into Italian as *La Duplice Visione* (Marsilio). As Agostino Lombardo emphasizes in his perceptive introduction, the book's strength comes from its aim: "the comprehension of the structures of life, the individuation of its rhythm, the attempt to comprehend the difficult world where man is bound to live through literary criticism." In "Prospettive storiche, critiche e politiche del 'Discorso teoretico' postmoderno" (*Allegoria* 11 [1992]: 77–90) Margherita Ganeri interviews Fredric Jameson, and in the same issue (pp. 100–09) she discusses his 1991 book on postmodernism. In "La città postmoderna in Fredric Jameson" (*L'asino d'oro* 4, vii: 134–44) Ganeri examines the feelings of bewilderment caused by the postmodern architecture of buildings and commercial centers, which mirror the decadence of contemporary society. An essential working tool for Americanists appeared this year, *Repertorio Bibliografico della Letteratura Americana in Italia, Vol. V–VI, 1965–1974* (Rome: Centro Studi Americani), under the supervision of Biancamaria Tedeschini Lalli and the careful coordination of Alessandra Pinto Surdi.

b. Literature to 1800   An intriguing picture of colonial literature emerges from a useful study, *La letteratura americana dell'età coloniale* (Rome: La Nuova Italia Scientifica), ed. Paola Cabibbo. The essays present the genesis and first appearances of those literary and cultural archetypes found in 18th-century writings that remain a constant feature of the American imagination. Paola Cabibbo discusses John Smith and the invention of Pocahontas and Indian captivity narratives. Donatella Izzo focuses on William Bradford; Mario Corona presents Puritan sermons, diaries, and journals; while Alessandra Contenti examines Puritan poetry. Laura Coltelli explains Quakerism and John Woolman, Paola Russo follows the dynamics of the witches' trials in Salem, and Giorgio Mariani both investigates the role of Indians in Puritan historiography and traces the frontier's place in American culture. Paola Castellucci devotes a lengthy study to Southern culture and literature, while Luca Briasco enlightens the reader about the figures of Cotton Mather and Jonathan Edwards. Anna Secco discusses Benjamin Franklin's *Autobiography*.

The theme of autobiography is continued in Itala Vivan's "Functions of Autobiography in the Empire of the Puritan Imagination" (*Culture* 7: 23–29). Puritan autobiography, Vivan argues, is the matrix of the creative tension of American culture: optimism toward history meant as mission, and therefore toward man as an elected and privileged executor of such history and mission, and "the antithetic and pessimistic vision of a real enemy who threatens God's plot, a perennial presence hidden behind masks forever changing." That there is no biography, only history, is affirmed by Larzer Ziff in *Benjamin Franklin: An American Genius,* ed. Gianfranca Balestra and Luigi Sanpietro (Bulzoni). Franklin's astonishing range of interests and activities emerges from the book's various essays, which originated in a conference at the University of Milan. Though his Italian connections were varied and rich, Franklin never visited Italy. Thomas Jefferson too would have liked to travel in Italy, but he had to make do with the letters his secretary, William Short, wrote during Short's 1788–89 trip to investigate the Italian economic situation. Alessandra Pinto Surdi translates some of those letters about Rome in her "Voyage autour de ma . . . Rome: il viaggio immaginario di Jefferson attraverso le lettere di William Short" (*l'Astrolabio* 5, xii: 47–50).

c. 19th-Century Literature   The 1992 Columbus celebrations have left their mark on this year's output as well. The papers by Italian and foreign scholars included in a special Columbus issue of *Letterature d'America* were originally presented at a workshop coordinated by Biancamaria Tedeschini Lalli. The University of Venice also organized a conference whose proceedings have been published as *L'immaginario americano e Colombo* (Bulzoni). Rosella Mamoli Zorzi translated Irving's book on Columbus (see *ALS* 1991, p. 436); in "The Life and Voyages of Christopher Columbus di Washington Irving e la pittura americana dell'Ottocento" (pp. 45–61) she traces the book's influence among American painters, especially John Vanderlyn, and she points out the European painters whom Irving admired during his European years. In "Voyage Among the Vanquished: Washington Irving's Companions of Columbus" (*LAmer* 44: 5–30) Cristina Giocelli closely examines Irving's work, which reveals the writer's anxiety about the significance of the Conquest. He soothes his mixed feelings by keeping the balance between two sets of losers: the kind but savage Indians, and the enduring but reckless discoverers. Emma Marras in "Rediscovering America: The Biography of Christopher Columbus by Washington Irving" (*Quaderni di Gaia*, pp. 59–71) finds Irving's biography both truthful and accurate, while it also succeeds in bringing to life a complex, mythic figure. Marina Camboni focuses her attention on Whitman's "Prayer of Columbus" to explore Columbus's role in the poet's whole work in "Columbus on Stage: The Representation of Whitman's Personal and American Drama" (*LAmer* 44: 90–110). A reassuring and conservative idea of America as "otro mundo," the model offered by Columbus in opposition to the more revolutionary Vespucci's "new land," is adopted by Phillis Wheatley in her poems in order to make others accept her being black and female. In her perceptive essay, "Paesaggi eroici e figure neoclassiche: la Columbia e la Clorinda di Phillis Wheatley" (*L'immaginario americano e Colombo*, pp. 67–81), Francesca Bisutti presents the signs of liberation from the accepted code in the figures of Wheatley's poetry. In the same volume Sergio Perosa shows how Pocahontas is at the origin of the metaphor or myth of the carnal union with America. He follows this idea through the works of W. C. Williams, Michel Tournier, and John Barth in his lively essay "Possesso, congressi carnali, metafore" (pp. 27–39).

No books have been published on Poe this year, but five fine essays pay homage to him. In "La narrativa di Edgar Allan Poe," in *Percorsi: Studi dedicati ad Angela Giannitrapani* (Viterbo: BetaGamma), ed. Mirella Billi and Massimo Ferrari Zumbini, Poe's reputation for extraordinary technique and morbid sensitivity are scrutinized by Agostino Lombardo, who finds a common theme in Poe's works: the exploration of the precarious human condition and the ambiguity and deceptiveness of reality. The lucidity and technical consciousness of the artist is the only way to oppose violence and chaos, and in this way the artist's work has a moral quality. In "Modernità di un classico: Strategie narrative nella scrittura di E. A. Poe" (*Ling&L* 17 [1991]: 63–70) Ornella De Zordo shows how the more exact Poe's writing style becomes, the more chaotic is the reality it portrays. The aesthetic theories of Poe's "Poetic Principle" are applied by Michele Stanco to the "Oval Portrait" in "Teorie estetiche 'narrate': 'The Oval Portrait' di E. A. Poe" (*L'asino d'oro* 3, v [1992]: 147–59). In "Poe's Raven and the Defilement of Pallas" (*Igitur* 1 [1992]: 81–87) Gordon Poole finds a comic element in the poem. The raven, a symbol of romantic gothicism, perches on the bust of Pallas, the symbol of classicism, and leaves it "nevermore." "Sheer physiological necessity will cause the unstirring bird to defile the bust of Pallas, and the poor, classical scholar will have quite a time keeping it clean." In "Orfeo Romantico: Edgar Allan Poe" (*Il Lettore di Provincia* 86: 53–58) Maria Fara Scalas also finds Poe's art a combination of the radiant enlightenment of Apollo and the subterranean knowledge of Dionysus. A stimulating essay by Gian Carlo Belletti is "Veleni e profumi: su 'Rappaccini's Daughter' di Nathaniel Hawthorne" in *Indiscrete presenze: Forme dell'orrore soprannaturale in letteratura* (Alessandria: Edizioni dell'Orso), ed. Maria Rita Cifarelli and Roberto De Pol. Belletti points out that Hawthorne does not want to affirm the importance of reality as opposed to narrative fiction, but to transcend the contradictions of both realms to convince the reader to find truth in himself.

Thoreau had to face reality and the intrusiveness and menace of the modern world. In *Treni di carta* (Genoa: Marietti) Remo Ceserani investigates the slow process that Western literature had to undergo to make this hurtful experience of modernity familiar. In "Thoreau e il fischio lacerante del mostro d'acciaio" (pp. 85–92) Ceserani looks at Thoreau's critical reaction to the train and its whistle, which represents modernity with its greed and rudeness among the otherwise human sounds of Nature. Einaudi reprints *Leaves of Grass* under the title *Foglie d'Erba* with Enzo Giachino's fine introduction and a new presentation by Franco Buffoni. To understand Whitman's poetry fully, Buffoni points out the importance of his self-censorship, which made him distort sexual elements in his poems in his desire to be perceived by posterity as the American bard, healthy and vigorous, ready to conquer, produce, and reproduce. In "The Marks of Time in the Editions of *Leaves of Grass:* A Proposal for Interpretation" (pp. 51–60) in *Walt Whitman Centennial International Symposium* (Granada: Universidad de Granada, 1992), ed. Manuel Villar Raso et al., Marina Camboni analyzes "Prayer of Columbus" by way of a preliminary interpretive study on the evolution of *Leaves of Grass.* She shows how the text evolved from an initial blending with its author's life to a progressive detachment and final autonomy. In the same volume Biancamaria Tedeschini Lalli subtly investigates "Whitman and Rhetoric" (pp. 225–36). She demonstrates the deep relationship that links Whitman and the Transcendentalists to modern theories of discourse. Language not based on rules, but on usage, is at the center of Whitman's mythopoesis. He strongly believed that both American language and poetry partake of the ideological tension between the Transcendentalists' diachronic element of construction and idealistic organicism to synchronically capture change, growth, mutation.

Ruggero Bianchi has published a completely new translation of *Moby-Dick* (Turin: Mursia). From the point of view of language and interpretation, Pavese's 1933 translation remains, inevitably, the model to be confronted. After analyzing its merits and defects, Bianchi concludes that Pavese's translation is a "betrayal because he is too faithful to the text and to himself." Bianchi devotes 80 pages of introduction to his interpretation of Melville's masterpiece. In "Il Bianco Oggetto del Desiderio" he expands on Melville's process of writing and his attitude toward his work once finished; he then maintains that *Moby-Dick* ends with the whale as an object of love and desire rather than of hate and revenge. A sound and scholarly contribution on *Moby-Dick* comes from Luca Briasco's *La ricerca di Ishmael: Moby-Dick come avventura dell'interpretazione* (Bulzoni). Briasco divides *Moby-Dick* into four parts to investigate Ishmael's hermeneutic mechanisms as character/narrator/artist while pointing out the problematic knots of the text. In the first three parts Ishmael deconstructs Western thought, and in the last chapters he confronts the world that has been restored to its enigmatic character as an infinite whole of incompatible interpretations. Ishmael's itinerary ends with acceptance of a world that has lost its transparency and turned into a labyrinth. Melville's ever-enchanting works have always challenged the best Italian poets to translate him in an effort to approach his elusive universe, and in *"Billy Budd,* Gabbiere di parrocchetto: Assaggi sul tradurre in prosa montaliano" (*Ling&L* 10 [1992]: 145–49) Silvia Zangrande dwells on Eugenio Montale's translation of the novel and his effort to be faithful more to the original's musicality and narrative dimension than to its construction and syntax. Gordon Poole discusses a neglected work in "Herman Melville's 'The House of the Tragic Poet'" (*Quaderni del Dipartimento di Linguistica, Univ. Calabria* 8: 137–48). In "L'Angelo della palude: Melville e la guerra totale" (*Giano* 14: 120–27) Poole points out how Melville perceived the Civil War as a new type of warfare: total conflict with wholesale destruction of lives. Poole discussed the same topic more generally in "Le origini americane dei concetti di 'guerra di annientamento' e di 'popolo nemico'" (*Giano* 9 [1991]: 121–32). Giorgio Mariani presents an able and comprehensive study of the history and strategies of Melville criticism in *Allegorie impossibili* (Bulzoni), which covers both the United States and Europe. The book, which could have been merely a useful academic treatise, tells a weighty, dramatic story that aims not at evaluating the thoroughness of single interpretations but at building a context. Mariani believes that criticism as well as literature reflect a nation's cultural, social, and civil history. As Lombardo writes in his afterword, Mariani's work "has been not only an exercise of literary criticism, but a larger cognitive research, the strenuous attempt to trace the face and meaning of America and the world through Melville's work." Gianfranca Balestra investigates Lewis Mumford's work on Melville in "Lewis Mumford e la letteratura: lo studio su Melville e altri scritti" (pp. 99–112) in *Lewis Mumford nella storia e nella critica* (Brescia: Grafo, 1992), ed. Rossella Cominotti and Giuliano Della Pergola. Balestra also comments on Mumford's literary output. This contribution is included in a more general book that attempts to assess Mumford's cultural importance.

In the introduction to the first Italian translation of *N. 44: The Mysterious Stranger, N. 44: Lo straniero misterioso* (Einaudi) Guido Carboni points out the many facets of this fable, which balances between impotence and omnipotence, freedom and cruelty, nostalgic escape into the fantastic and a grasp of contemporary contradictions. In Twain's prose, Carboni feels the old narrator's effort to recapture his adolescent voice. Daniela Daniele dwells on the American domestic novel in "Il potere della modestia: Louisa May Alcott, *Little Women* e il romanzo domestico americano" (*Quaderni del Dipartimento di Linguistica, Univ. Calabria* 8: 11–26), underlining Alcott's dissociated relation between domestic writings and the romanticism of gothic novels.

This year Henry James's letters, autobiography, and essays have received much more attention than his novels. Sergio Perosa has published

Un Bambino e gli Altri (Vicenza: Neri Pozza). In the foreword, "L'immaginazione coltivata," he compares James's and Yeats's autobiographies, both of which are fragmented, occasional memoirs and rememberings without narrative plan; the past is disclosed as an indulgence in a continuous flow of images, impressions, and experiences. Just as in *W. W. Story and His Friends*, James pushed the protagonist aside, turning the book into the story of his generation told through personal recollections, so in the autobiography he records the birth and the evolution of that "strange monster" of his aims and of the "act of Life" in which he is stubbornly engaged. Rosella Mamoli Zorzi presents a fine bilingual edition of James's published and unpublished letters to Jessie Allen, *Lettere a Miss Allen 1899–1915* (Milan: Rosellina Archinto). They belong to the same period as *A Small Boy and Others* and record James's and Allen's friendship, which started at Palazzo Barbaro in Venice. A common and amusing interest in their acquaintances' stories and solidarity in difficult moments are transformed by James's linguistic whim into a refined verbal game. Giovanna Mochi gathered James's essays on French novelists in *La lezione dei maestri: Il romanzo francese dell'Ottocento* (Einaudi). Through an analysis of French writers' fascinating stories and their great, exclusive passion, James reveals his concerns. His envy of their skill in conveying impressions and his resentment and aspiration toward the quantity of experiences they could cope with turned into uneasiness with a sexual and physical life from which he believed himself excluded. Yet while he feared the impact that reality could have on creativity, he had a dread of losing or being unable to come into contact with that reality. Christopher Newman feels the same uneasiness toward French society in *L'americano* (Newton Compton), which has been newly translated. In the lively foreword, "Una vettura come un'altra," Guido Fink discusses Newman's attitude toward Europe. He has come to Paris to buy (ugly) paintings and the best possible wife, but his Wall Street mentality causes him to lose the game, although perhaps he did not intend to win it, as James comes to believe in the preface to the New York Edition of the novel. In "L'Euro-America di H. James: Pandora e la vertigine del Tra" (pp. 171–91) in *Sulla Soglia* (Rome: il Calamo), ed. Paola Cabibbo. Antonella Piazza Coppola examines "Pandora" as a moment of balance in the process of transformation of James's international theme. In "L'ambiguità di *What Maisie Knew*" (*Ling&L* 9: 57–70) Chiara Cillerai maintains that the text's gaps of meaning can be ascribed to James's intention to produce a situation in which the reader must fill in the hiatus. In "'Awkward Ages' in *The Awkward Age*" (*Il lettore di provincia* 88: 75–90) Cillerai again reads the novel not only as Nanda's ritual passage into womanhood but as an investigation of a historical moment when grown-ups, realizing that they have lost the identity they thought they had acquired, are no longer sure about the code of principles that guaranteed them a specific role in society.

The ambiguous construction of the text and of its heroine are the hints Mario Materassi puts forward in his perceptive introduction to the bilingual translation of Kate Chopin's *Il risveglio* (Marsilio). He presents Chopin's masterpiece as a work of irresistible seduction, which, like human experience, defies any attempt to find a single answer. The power of the imagination is tested in the delicate story by Thomas B. Aldrich, *Marjorie Daw* (Pavia: Ibis), carefully translated by Piero Pignatta. Alessandra Contenti also translates *Chita: L'ultima isola* (Milan: Tranchida Editori). She underlines Lafcadio Hearn's poetic prose, rich in rhythmic elements and stylistic refinements.

d. 20th-Century Prose   Because of the success of director Martin Scorsese's film *The Age of Innocence* (1993), Edith Wharton has become popular in Italy. Gaetano Prampolini presents six short stories with an Italian background in *Pienezza di vita: Racconti italiani* (Florence: Passigli). He also explores Wharton's fortunes in Italy in his "Edith Wharton in Italy" (*EWhR* 9, i [1992]: 24). In the same magazine Gianfranca Balestra argues that Wharton's *The Valley of Decision,* like her *Italian Backgrounds,* focuses on Italy and its history rather than on the protagonists. In her foreword "Censura del desiderio e linguaggio della passione" to *La Scogliera* (Milan: La Tartaruga) Balestra thinks the novel the most autobiographical and Jamesian she wrote. Here the heroine's individual research is inseparable from the social customs against which she fights but which ultimately defeat her. Balestra has also published a scholarly contribution on Wharton, *I fantasmi di Edith Wharton* (Bulzoni). Balestra's aim is to show the thematic, stylistic, and technical development of Wharton's fantastic short stories. After a discussion of the "genre," Balestra underlines how the imagination allows dangerous and suppressed wishes to surface. These processes are followed through three different periods into which Wharton's literary career is divided. "Exorcism," an unpublished short story, is included. Willa Cather's *Il mio mortale nemico* (Milan: Anabasi) appears in a fine translation with an afterword by Barbara Lanati. In her "Ritratto d'artista come una signora qualunque" Lanati finds the novel formally perfect, a work in which it is difficult to detect the "mortal enemy." Myra could be her own enemy as she obstinately keeps dreaming the American dream. Gertrude Stein's portraits are discussed by Lanati in an introduction to "Gertrude Stein, *Autobiografia di Alice B. Toklas:* ciò che la 'fotografia sa,'" in *Il testo autobiografico nel Novecento* (Milan: Guerini Studio), ed. Reimar Klein and Rossana Bonadei. Another portrait by Stein, lovingly edited by Liana Borghi, is *Portrait of Mabel Dodge at the Villa Curonia* (Florence: Estro), a work that Dodge had printed in 1912 and distributed among her friends. Bound in assorted Florentine wallpapers, the copies "show us a strong contrast between the simplicity of the floral motif on the covers and the inpenetrability of the text contained between them," as Simona Capelli points out in an afterword. Paola Zaccaria explores the position of women in "La parola meteca di Djuna Barnes" (*Il piccolo Hans* 77: 92–114). The spatial and linguistic dislocation of Barnes's characters make them "beings in transformation," expatriates, refugees, outlaws.

Mario Materassi published two fine contributions on William Faulkner. In the foreword and afterword of *Pensando a casa: Lettere alla madre e al padre* (Milan: Rosellina Archinto) he finds that Faulkner's letters to his parents differ according to the mask he wears. However, as Materassi asserts, the letters should be read as a testimony of specific interests, a mirror of cultural idiosyncracies, an intimate space that must be protected; they offer subtle, unusual emotions as well as a biographical curiosity. Materassi proposes eight short stories that he thinks comparable to Faulkner's best work in *Otto storie della Contea di Yoknapatawpha* (Milan: Garzanti). In his subtle, well-balanced introduction he suggests that each story has its own code that provokes the search for an interpretive key. Certainly, the short stories are unique pieces, tesserae of a vast frescoe. In 1991 Italian Americanists celebrated the centenary of Herman Melville's death and Henry Miller's birth. The times when we tried to hide Miller's books in newspapers or plastic covers are past, as Materassi points out in his "Henry Miller, Il limite dell'esplicito" (*Il Ponte* 49, iii: 358–70). The Mondadori publishing house consecrates Miller by issuing his works in the prestigious series "I Meridiani," *Opere* (Milan: Mondadori, 1992), ed. Guido Almansi. Materassi finds it reductive to associate Miller only with sexual liberation, and he insists on Miller's eclecticism. The trilogy testifies to an extraordinary intellectual curiosity uncommon to any other work of the first half of the 20th century, he claims. Paul Bowles is another American writer who has been suddenly discovered by the Italian public because of director Bernardo Bertolucci's movie *The Sheltering Sky* (1990). Italian publishers have printed all of Bowles's works as well as his wife's over the past few years. In "La rinomata ditta Bowles & Bowles" (*Il Ponte* 49, x: 1155–65) Materassi shows how Bowles is at his best when he represents the clash between Western culture and the North African Arab world, a theme unusual in American narrative. Daniela Daniele explores postmodern narrative techniques in her fine "A proposito di arte multimediale: note sull'eredità delle avanguardie nel racconto postmoderno americano" (*Le Voci della Poesia* 1 [1992]: 64–67). The postmodern revival of a pervasive irony entering the text at multiple levels deconstructs narrative, according to Daniele, questioning and undermining the legitimacy of any rhetoric of power as well as the narrator's individual identity. Daniele discusses this issue again in "Kierkegaard Unfair to Schlegel: l'ironia endemica nel racconto postmoderno di Donald Barthelme" (*Igitur*, 4, ii [1992]: 25–40). In "Myth and Carnival in Robert Coover's *The Public Burning*" (*RSAJ* 3 [1992]: 5–22) Roberto Dainotto describes Coover's idea that fictions are social rituals instituting a sense of reality. In *The Public Burning* reality as recorded in the official documents of the Rosenberg trial amounts to nothing more than the fiction created by the novel's first-person narrator, Nixon. Richard Ford's narrative is presented by Eraldo Affinati in "Richard Ford: il mistero, l'amore e l'Harley David-son" (*Nuovi Argomenti* 44 [1992]: 118–22). Franco Minganti comments on the new translation of *V.* in "Il ritorno di *V.:* Thomas Pynchon l'esploratore" (*Linea d'Ombra* 81: 26–27). Stefano Rosso translates chapter 10 of Vonnegut's autobiography (*Il piccolo Hans* 74 [1992]: 149–65). In the same issue Giuseppina Restivo interprets Vonnegut's use of history in "Da Dresda alle Galapagos: il 'lavoro della storia' in Kurt Vonnegut" (pp. 166–85). She suggests that Vonnegut's works confirm a typical narrative trend in the American tradition, a historical-anthropological engagement that has privileged romance and in recent years surrealism and science fiction. Carlo Pagetti's long involvement with science fiction is described in his stimulating volume *I sogni della scienza: Storia della science fiction* (Rome: Editori Riuniti). Contrary to what might be expected, it is not a handbook but a series of considerations on the encounter of literary tradition and technological imagination from Swift to Cyberpunk. A strong point is Pagetti's analysis of Philip K. Dick; he not only knows the California writer well but shows an emotional involvement in his work. The passion of Italian scholars in this field is indicated by the theme chosen by the Italian Association for American Studies at its 1993 conference on "Imagination and Technology: An Ongoing Challenge."

Short stories, poems, and interviews with American writers have been published in "Per le strade degli U.S.A." (*Linea d'Ombra* 85: 26–75), an issue mainly dedicated to contemporary American literature. Martino Marazzi reviews recent collections of essays and emphasizes the liveliness of American essay production and the publishing opportunities that American writers have in "Nella selva del saggio americano" (*Belfagor* 48: 710–16). "Literary Creativity and the Publishing Industry" is the title of a roundtable discussion organized by Mario Materassi in New York in November 1992, during which authors and editors had a lively, idiosyncratic exchange about the impact of market considerations on the writer, the influential role of the *New York Review of Books* and the *New York Times Book Review,* the structural changes undergone by the publishing industry, the phenomenon of small publishing houses, and related topics. A transcript was published in *RSAJ* (3 [1992]: 73–112). In the same issue Roberta Kalechofsky publishes a story, *Myra Is Dying* (pp. 113–30). Two other contributions deal with Native American literature. In "Transactions in a Native Land: Mixed-blood Identity and Indian Legacy in Louise Erdrich's Fiction" (pp. 43–58) Daniela Daniele explores Erdrich's mixed-blood version of the colonialist theme of ethnic intermarriage. Anna Secco's "The Search for Origins Through Storytelling in Native American Literature: Momaday, Silko, Erdrich" (pp. 59–71) discusses the writers' search for their cultural and historical identity in their storytelling through which they affirm and "make new" the everlasting value of their ancestral past.

The position of Native American writers is explored by Giorgio Mariani's fine essay, "Doppia liminalità: Note sulla letteratura degli Indiani d'America" in *Sulla Soglia: Questioni di liminalità in letteratura* (Rome: Il Calamo), ed. Paolo Cabibbo, pp. 261–82. Native literature is born on the borderline of two cultural, literary, and often antithetical traditions; it tries not so much to achieve a perfect synthesis of these two worlds but an acceptable compromise. Native American writers, on the other hand, are aware that the inescapable and enriching confrontation with Western culture and American society cannot become a constant wandering in search of identity. Gaetano Prampolini presents four bilingual "sequences" by N. Scott Momaday in *La strana e verace storia della mia vita con Billy the Kid (e altre storie)* (Rome: Salerno Editrice). In his afterword Prampolini discusses Momaday's works and suggests that their varieties of form (poetry, lyric prose, prose) reflect the author's idea that the more perfect and various we are in our language, the more conscious we are of ourselves and our existence. Laura Coltelli presents four Native American women, Paula Gunn Allen, Joy Harjo, Linda Hogan, and Leslie Marmon Silko, in *Garland Directory of Minority Women: Native American Women* (Garland), ed. Gretchen M. Baccaile.

At last, a 20th-century American classic has been translated into Italian, and the wait has been well rewarded. *Cane* has been skillfully translated by Daniela Fink and presented in a bilingual version as *Canne* (Marsilio), with a scholarly introduction by Werner Sollors. Paola Zaccaria writes "Zami, armata della sua pelle bianca" (*Legendaria* 3–4: 11) to commemorate Audre Lorde and discuss her work. The publication of Mario Maffi's *Nel mosaico della città* (see *ALS 1992*, p. 338) prompted Daniela Daniele to write "Il prisma delle identità: memoria etnica e sottoculture nell'East Village di New York" (*Nuova Corrente* 111: 173–93), a survey of the recent social and cultural history of New York's Lower East Side. In his social and cultural exploration of the United States this year Maffi has examined the Chinese migration to Angel Island (in San Francisco Bay) in "I fantasmi di Angel Island" (*Leggere* 54: 51–55), whereas Sergio D'Amaro's "Joseph Tusiani, autobiografia del Bronx" (*Il Ponte* 49: 919–22) is dedicated to Italian migration to New York City.

e. 20th-Century Poetry and Drama The year's yield of Pound studies was more than usually plentiful. To mark the 20th anniversary of the poet's death in Venice, Luca Gallesi has edited a 600-page volume, *Ezra Pound 1972–1992* (Milan: Greco & Greco, 1992), to which nearly 40 writers contributed memoirs, essays, and poems. Giano Accame writes on Pound's reputation as an economist (pp. 17–45), Anna Lo Giudice and Massimo Pesaresi on classic and Greek elements in the criticism and poetry. However, most of the scholarly contributions deal with Pound's Italian connections and writings. Massimo Bacigalupo has discovered that after Cantos 72–73, written in Italian in 1944–45, Pound drafted two further Italian Cantos, 74–75, which he later discarded but partially used in the Pisan Cantos. These Italian drafts, and many earlier fragments in English, are quoted and discussed in Bacigalupo's "Palinsesti dei Canti pisani" (pp. 63–118). This must be the fullest account so far published of the genesis of Pound's "paradiso." Stefano Maria Casella (pp. 155–98) considers the preparation of Pound's 1932 edition of Guido

Cavalcanti, reconstructing in detail his visits to Verona (where his slips with notes have been preserved in some of the codices he consulted). This is fascinating detective work among old letters, hotel bills, and jottings. Luca Cesari devotes attention to Pound's colorful friend Everardo Marchetti, proprietor of the Palace Hotel in Rimini (pp. 211–23). Marchetti actively helped Pound in the 1920s while Pound researched his Malatesta Cantos, and Marchetti is the source of some of the stories about the Romagna region in *The Cantos*. Marchetti also communicated to Pound his enthusiasm for Mussolini, another Romagnolo, as Canto 41 records. He volunteered in 1940, at 50, for the Duce's disastrous Greek campaign, and he died a broken man soon after it ended. Caterina Ricciardi (pp. 495–517) believes that in some passages of the Pisan Cantos, Pound is thinking of Piero della Francesca's *Resurrection*, a fresco in Borgo Sansepolcro. This careful scholar returns to the subject in a long article, "Piero della Francesca nella poesia di Ezra Pound," pp. 41–59 in *Piero della Francesca nella cultura europea e americana* (Città di Castello: Edimond), ed. Attilio Brilli, where she also analyzes passages from "Mauberley," Canto 8, and Canto 45. A final contribution to *Ezra Pound, 1972–1992* is Claudia Salaris's interesting discussion of Pound and Marinetti (pp. 519–39), which proposes a direct influence of Marinetti's last poem, "Quarto d'ora di poesia della X Mas," on Canto 72, Pound's elegy (in Italian) for his Futurist colleague and friend. Salaris, an expert on Futurism, has uncovered a 1915 interview by Pound in the Russian Futurist journal *The Archer*, reprinted here in an appendix (pp. 587–91). A Neo-Futurist reading of Pound can also be found in the year's most unusual Poundian essay, "Vita di Pound," presented in colorful vignettes with comic-strip lettering by Pablo Echaurren and published as a poster (Milan: Libridamuro Guaraldi). Echaurren, a prominent radical artist, recounts Pound's life in epic fashion, with gusto, and presents him as the fighter against all orthodoxies, usury above all.

Pound's links to Italy are likewise explored by Luca Cesari in a sumptuous edition of Pound's early translation of Saint Francis's "Cantico di Frate Sole," *Most High Lord* (Verrucchio and Rimini: Pazzini). This large-format book is really an experiment in typography and interpretation, an artifact in which Cesari expresses his love for the tradition of stone and light to which he believes both Saint Francis and Pound were committed. More traditional scholarship is served by Stefano Verdino in *Storia delle riviste genovesi: da Morasso a Pound* (Genoa: La Quercia). Verdino, an Italianist, discusses two magazines to which Pound contributed, *L'Indice* (Genoa) and *Il Mare* (Rapallo), and offers a sympathetic account of Pound's solitary campaigns and of his later paradoxical status as practically "the only real writer of Mussolini's republic, the only poet of that tragedy from the other side." An international Pound conference was held in Rapallo in July, drawing some 60 scholars, most of them Americans. Massimo Bacigalupo, one of the organizers, detailed the presence of Rapallo in Pound's poetry in articles for *Secolo XIX* (11 July) and *La Stampa* (10 July). A sensitive account of the conference, "Rapallo: Discussing Ezra," was offered by a participant from New Zealand, C. K. Stead, in *London Magazine* (April–May 1994, pp. 100–04). An intimate portrait of Pound by his Italian doctor and friend is included in Giuseppe Bacigalupo's *Ieri a Rapallo* (Udine: Campanotto, pp. 75–89). It seems noteworthy that the cantankerous poet was able to retain the affection and admiration of so many friends in Italy and abroad; he surely continues to provoke interest and debate in his adopted country. Newton Compton brought out in its popular "1000 Lire" series, i.e., 100-page booklets selling for about 50 cents, a selection of Pound's *Aforismi e detti memorabili,* ed. G. Singh, an amusing collection of Poundian nuggets of wisdom and folly, with a short introduction, a biography, and a useful bibliography. Another curiosity is the publication of a trilingual edition of *Cathay,* called *Antiche poesie cinesi* (Einaudi), ed. Alessandra C. Lavagnino and Maria Rita Masci. The Chinese and English texts are placed on facing pages, and Italian translations of both are given at the bottom of the page. This is a model edition, whose example American and English publishers might imitate. The only heretofore untranslated poem by Pound to appear this year was the lively "Redondilla" of 1911, which Massimo Bacigalupo presents in *Poesia* (vol. 62) with a preface. In the same issue Paolo Valesio translates and discusses Pound's unpublished polemical essay about cultural foundations; a toned-down version appeared as "Where Is American Culture?" in the *Nation,* 18 April 1928.

Renzo Crivelli has written the useful *Introduzione a T. S. Eliot* (Bari: Laterza). Franco Buffoni presents some of Eliot's poems comparing different translations and interpretations by Sanesi, Tonelli, and Praz in "Terra Guasta o terra Desolata?" (*Testo a Fronte* 3, iv [1991]: 113–21). Remo Ceserani is intrigued by Robert Frost's "Stopping by Woods on a Snowy Evening," a poem rich in meaning and internal tension, and he discusses it in "La Musa commentata: Robert Frost" (*L'Indice* 10: 8). Wallace Stevens is still one of the most appreciated American poets among Italian scholars. *Il piccolo Hans* includes four good contributions in its 1992 number. In "Stevens e la visibilità dell'aria" (pp. 69–87) Ermanno Krumm underlines Stevens's attention to atmosphere; Nadia Fusini translates and comments on some of Stevens's poems (pp. 88–108); Alan Bass explains "The Snow Man" in relation to Freud's concept of fetishism in "Feticismo, realtà e 'The Snow Man'" (pp. 109–47); and in "Wallace Stevens tardo romantico" (pp. 148–58) Baldo Meo stresses Stevens's greater closeness to poets such as Ashbery and Ammons than to writers of his own generation such as Pound and Eliot because of his need to formulate the poetic self in less dramatic tones. Meo also points out how Stevens, like the Romantic poets, believes in the power of the imagination. The same Romantic roots are explored by Carla Pomarè in *La visione e la voce: Percorsi paralleli dai romantici ai moderni* (Alessandria: Edizioni dell'Orso). Pomarè's starting point was her interest in what she considers to be Stevens's main theme: the relationship between imagination and reality and its metaphoric transposition into poetry. She sketches out two typologies through which to read the complex relationships which bind the 19th and 20th centuries: the representation of poetic activity as vision and voice; poetry as revelation through a glance or a song becomes the guideline for analyzing the ways through which romantic and modern poets confront the significance of their artistic experience. W. C. Williams also received careful attention this year. Cristina Giorcelli and Maria Anita Stefanelli edited *The Rhetoric of Love in* The Collected Poems of William Carlos Williams (Rome: Edizioni Associate). The book emphasizes *rhetoric* as "the persuasive argument which is hermeneutically developed by the artist to affect and elicit responses" and *love,* which is a "central concern in Williams' mythopoesis." The essays by American and European scholars are divided into three sections: the first examines Williams's rhetoric of love from a theoretical perspective, the other two his "sacred" vision of love. Among the most noteworthy contributions: Caterina Ricciardi's "Between Sacred and Profane: Rain as a Figure of Love" (pp. 131–52), Mario Domenichelli's "W.C.W.: Triumphs of Love" (pp. 153–70), Cristina Giorcelli's "The King's Whore: Debasement and Transcendence of Woman in Williams' Late Poetry" (pp. 249–73), and Maria Anita Stefanelli's "Pathology and Seductiveness in Williams' Language of Love" (pp. 273–96). Stefanelli also published *Figure ambigue: Disgiunzione e congiunzione nella poesia di W. C. Williams* (Bulzoni). Through various figures, the poet expresses tensions between classical and modern forms, the English

language, and American idiom. This year Andrea Mariani devotes atten-
tion to James Merrill's allusions to Yeats in "Yeats in Merrill: maschera e
figura," in *Yeats Oggi* (Rome: Dipartimento di letterature comparate
della Terza Universita degli studi di Roma, pp. 89–105), ed. Carla de
Petris. John Ashbery's poetry is discussed in several magazines. Massimo
Bacigalupo interviewed Ashbery while he was at the University of Genoa
(*RSAJ* 3 [1992]: 23–32), and Nicola Gardini presents him in "John
Ashbery: Il presente della poesia" (*Poesia* 65: 2–11). In the same issue
Bacigalupo publishes "Ashbery, o l'inafferrabile dell'esistenza" (pp. 11–
12). In "Leo Romero: un poeta dalla parte della luna" (*RSAJ* 3 [1992]: 33–
42) Franca Bacchiega highlights Ashbery's indebtedness to his land and
culture, as well as the originality of his delicate portrayal of an American
tradition.

The emblematic title of *Voci e silenzi: La re-visione al femminile nella
poesia di lingua inglese* (Urbino: QuattroVenti), after describing the
variety of tonalities of feminine poetic voices, also shows how the
strategy of silence becomes a way to express inner divisions and ambiguities. In "Voices of the Tradition," the common aim of the essayists is to
point out the significance of gender in the poetry of Emily Dickinson
(Nadia Fusini's "Poesia sposa del tremendo," pp. 27–38), H.D. (Marina
Camboni's "Le parole sono farfalle: Mitopoiesi verbale nella poesia di
H.D.," pp. 65–80), Marianne Moore and Elizabeth Bishop (Bianca
Tarozzi's "Il genere occultato: Marianne Moore e Elizabeth Bishop,"
pp. 81–92) and Sylvia Plath (Gabriella Morisco's "Sylvia Plath e il suo
'Jargon yet unspoken,'" pp. 93–114). The second part, "Silenzi etnici,"
includes Fedora Giordano's "Wendy Rose: le parole dell'assenza" (see
ALS 1991, p. 443). Two sound and scholarly contributions on H.D.'s
trilogy and an anthology of poems by Elizabeth Bishop have been
published in "Esperidi," an American poetry series ed. Marina Camboni.
Camboni carefully translates, presents, and comments on H.D.'s *Trilogia*
(Caltanisetta: Salvatore Sciascia Editore). She briefly introduces the
reader to H.D.'s world, offers a bilingual translation, and ends with her
perceptive interpretation of H.D.'s effort through myth and poetry to
plunge into history to build a universe free from war. The same pattern
of presentation is adopted in *Dai libri di geografia* by Bianca Tarozzi, who
dwells on Bishop's pictorial vocation. In 1977, Octavio Paz described
Bishop's poetry as "fresh, clear, drinkable." In "Fresca, chiara, potabile:
La poesia di Elizabeth Bishop" (*Ling&L* 10 [1992]: 63–72) Maria Abram
supports his description against other critical judgments. Raffaella Bac-

colini offers two stimulating contributions on H.D.: "Remembering and Rewriting Shakespeare: H.D.'s *By Avon River*" (pp. 247–60) in *Shakespeare e la sua eredità* (Parma: Edizioni Zara), ed. Grazia Caliumi, and "What's in the Name? Language and Self-creation in Women's Writing" (pp. 44–64) in *The Representation of the Self in Women's Autobiography* (Bologna), ed. Vita Fortunati and Gabriella Morisco, where Baccolini contends that women such as H.D. reclaim a new identity that is no longer impersonal but unconventional and renamed through language and its deliberate deconstruction. Daniela Daniele presents and translates a selection of poems by Grace Paley, *In Autobus* (Rome: Empiria), in which she stresses Paley's attention to women hidden from history. Masolino d'Amico translates Arthur Miller's *La discesa da Mount Morgan* (Einaudi) and David Mamet's *Oleanna* (Genoa: Costa & Nolan).

University of Pisa

iii Japanese Contributions: Keiko Beppu

Japanese scholarship on American literature for 1993 illustrates T. S. Eliot's notion in "Tradition and the Individual Talent" that "No poet, no artist of any art, has his complete meaning alone." Indeed, no significant scholarship on American literature in Japan today can enjoy the autonomy of exclusively aesthetic or formalist criticism. The predominance of feminist criticism is one such indication, led by Kazuko Watanabe's *Feminism Shosetsu Ron: Joseisakka no Jibun Sagashi* [A Study of the Feminist Novel: Women Writers in Search of Self] (Takushoku shobo) and Yoshiko Tomishima's *Onna ga Utsuru* [Woman Losing Her Mind: A Study of Hysteria] (Keiso shobo). Tomishima's book in particular is an ambitious scholarly attempt to relate the symptoms of "hysteria" to Anglo-American culture. Tomishima's critical concern goes beyond literary appreciation and embraces a great many nonliterary texts.

Another significant publication is *Bungaku America Shihonshugi* [Literature/America/Capitalism] (Nan'undo), ed. Masashi Orishima et al., which features 16 original "dialogues" with "American literature and capitalism." In his introduction Orishima challenges Japanese Americanists with a question: "What can/should literary criticism do in a postmodern society in the age of late capitalism?" With this question in mind, reassessments of the interdependence between ideology and literature and criticism become the litmus test for all "honest," meaningful criticism.

Except for critical biographies of Hamlin Garland and William Faulkner, this year registered no significant book-length studies of individual writers. Noteworthy is the collaboration of scholarly researchers resulting in such ambitious publications as *America Bunka no Genten to Dento* [American Culture: The Roots and the Tradition] (Sairyusha), compiled by the Sophia University Center for American-Canadian Studies.

As is the custom in this section, articles surveyed are restricted, with a few exceptions, to those published in the academic journals *SALit, SETLit,* and *EigoS*. Unless otherwise indicated, all books have been published in Tokyo.

a. General Studies and Literary Criticism   Scholarly works surveyed in this section deal with specific themes and/or critical theories in historical context; hence, they read as variant literary histories of the United States. *Literature/America/Capitalism* deserves first mention. Its contributors explore, from their diverse methodological and political perspectives, the indivisible relation between the United States and capitalism as represented in literature. The chapters are organized into (1) The Symbol; (2) Criticism; (3) Observation. Authors discussed range from Benjamin Franklin to such postmodernists as Thomas Pynchon, Sam Shepard, Richard Powers, Steve Erickson, and Don DeLillo, to traditionally canonical authors such as Melville, James, Dreiser, Faulkner, Salinger, Fitzgerald, and Bellow. Naturally, extraliterary texts—the literature of biology, genetics, and psychoanalysis—are brought into the critical arena. A variety of stimulating discussions are offered. Most convincing (to me) is Takao Tomiyama's chapter on Faulkner and genetics, entitled "Who Is Popeye?" Tomiyama's observation of the criminal and the feebleminded in Faulkner's works is well-supported by relevant scholarship in criminology and genetics and by Tomiyama's reading of political and historical documents. That Faulkner is not only a great American novelist but a powerful, if read rightly, voice on contemporary social issues is a provocative judgment.

Yoshiko Tomishima's *Woman Losing Her Mind* collects Tomishima's previously published articles and marginalia; yet it deserves some comment here for two reasons: (1) the book is a fully articulated feminist manifesto; (2) it is a serious study, free from ideological bias, of the cultural and intellectual history of Anglo-American society on both sides of the Atlantic from the 19th century to the present. Tomishima's diagnosis of the heroine's *hysteria* in Charlotte Perkins Gilman's "The Yellow

Wall-paper" is extended to that of frequently diagnosed illnesses in Victorian England. Furthermore, her clinical survey includes the *hypochondria* that plagued such eminent 18th-century English authors as Richardson, Smollett, Johnson, and Boswell.

Kazuko Watanabe's *A Study of the Feminist Novel,* a collection of previously published articles, is important because of the author's comprehensive historical and cross-genre perspective. The writers and genres examined include (1) woman's bildungsroman—Elizabeth Phelps, Sarah Orne Jewett, Willa Cather; (2) woman's autobiography—Mary McCarthy, Maya Angelou, Maxine Hong Kingston; (3) women and sexuality—Kate Chopin, Erica Jong, Rita Mae Brown; (4) the feminist utopia novel—Charlotte Perkins Gilman, Ursula Le Guin, Marge Piercy, Joanna Russ; (5) mother-daughter relations—Amy Tan, Sue Miller, and Alice Walker. Although the book may be a handy guide to students interested in women's literature, it fails to define the "feminist novel."

A special number of *Review of American Literature,* published by the Tsukuba American Literary Society, collects original essays on Poe, Whitman, Melville, James, Faulkner, Hemingway, and Nabokov. The contributors attempt a new approach to using "the autobiographical mode as a critical apparatus." In her introduction Kazuko Takemura argues that one can trace the subtle strategies by which personal discourses are latently textualized and then appropriated by the society's power structure, a critical stance shared by the editors of *Literature/ America/Capitalism.* A selected bibliography is comprehensive.

b. 19th-Century Fiction and Poetry   No monograph was published this year on any of the established 19th-century writers. Collections of essays include *Melville and Melville Studies in Japan* and *Lafcadio Hearn Saiko: Hyakunengo no Kumamoto Kara* [Lafcadio Hearn Revisited: After a Hundred Years in Kumamoto] (Kobunsha), prepared by Saikichi Nakashima et al. The Melville volume is a scholarly achievement in its plan and execution; the essays by Japanese Melvillians cover the writer's full career: "The Literary Interaction Between Hawthorne and Melville After *Moby-Dick*" by Ginsaku Sugiura (pp. 21–40); "A Bird in an Out-of-Joint Time: Captain Ahab in *Moby-Dick*" by Arimichi Makino (pp. 41–67) "*Moby-Dick* as a Mosaic" by Toshio Yagi (pp. 69–97); "Melville's 'Transcendentalism' in the Context of His Time" by Masayuki Sakamoto (pp. 99–121); "*Israel Potter* and Its Ideological Contamination" by Kazuko Fukuoka (pp. 123–40); "A Sweet Charity for Melville the Confidence Man" by Keiko Beppu (pp. 141–56); "The Imagination of Death: An Essay on *Clarel*" by Shizuo Suyama (pp. 157–68); "Beyond 'the Talismanic Secret': Some Aspects of Melville's Later Poetry" by Kiyotoshi Murakami (pp. 169–93); "Dynamism in *Billy Budd*" by Kiyofumi Tsubaki (pp. 195–219). Of special interest to Melville scholars abroad are Ohashi's introductory chapter, "Melville in Japan: Reception Among Writers and Critics" (pp. 3–20), and Masao Tsunematsu's "Bibliographical Essay" (pp. 221–43).

Lafcadio Hearn Revisited, featuring many invaluable illustrations, is an anthology of 13 original essays written to celebrate the centenary of the writer's residence in Kumamoto City in Kyushu. Focusing on Hearn's three-year residency, the book portrays in detail the master reteller of Japanese folk tales in English. Among the essays dealing with Hearn's life and work in the United States, Shigemi Satomi's "Hearn the Writer and America" (pp. 43–54) makes a good case for Hearn's critical insight by citing his reviews of such American writers as Poe, Hawthorne, and James. Satomi observes that Hearn was an early appreciator of Henry James's story "The Last of the Valerii," an evaluation that is proof of his critical acumen. But the anthology's greatest virtue lies in its cross-cultural explorations in both American and Japanese culture and society, offering rich materials for prospective scholars.

Zenichiro Oshitani's *Hamlin Garland no Jinsei to Bungaku* [Hamlin Garland: The Man and His Work] (Osaka: Osaka Kyoikutosho) is the first book-length study of the writer in this country. It is a readable critical biography of "a son of the Middle Border," quite personal in tone and approach. Garland's relation to his parents, his commitment to Henry George's "single-tax" reform, his personal encounters with Howells, Twain, Whitman, and James, all receive judicious treatment and are well-woven into the narrative. The book reflects critical trends here and abroad, but Oshitani's discussion of *Rose of Dutcher's Coolly* as a feminist fiction is too facile. The bibliography is well-informed and informative. More than anything else, *Hamlin Garland* relates a sympathetic story in plain prose, which is yet another account of the westering experience.

Articles on other 19th-century writers demonstrate steady and continued interest in the period. Ritsumei Fukuda's "E. A. Poe in Scotland" (*EigoS* 139: 118–19) discusses a possible link between places in Scotland and the surrealistic landscapes in Poe's stories. Another interesting discussion is Takayuki Tatsumi's article, "A New Americanist's Reading

of the Businessman" (*Review of American Literature*, pp. 11–23). Tatsumi argues, with critical authority, that Poe's story shares the popular
(pseudo-)scientific discourse of the Jacksonian republic. Poe's phreno-
logical parody of the Franklinesque "self-made man" reads as "a crypto-
autobiography of a literary businessman."

In "Analysis of Miriam's Sin in *The Marble Faun*" (*SALit* 30: 1–17)
Motoko Suzuki observes that, like her namesake in the Old Testament,
Hawthorne's heroine sins against the sovereignty of God. Arimichi
Makino's chapter on Melville, " 'Providence' and 'Mammonism' " in
Literature/America/Capitalism (pp. 178–95), makes a strong case for
Melville the staunch prosecutor of American capitalism. Similarly, ref-
erence should be made to Kenzaburo Ohashi's discussion of James's
The Golden Bowl, "Mind, Love, and Money" in the same book (pp. 213–
28), even though Ohashi offers no radically new reading of the novel.
Chikako Tanimoto's "Swimming into the 'Semiotic' Chora: A French
Feminist Reading of Kate Chopin's *The Awakening*" (*SALit* 30: 19–39)
successfully applies Julia Kristeva's *ecriture feminine*, but nothing more.

In " 'Existence with a wall': Emily Dickinson's Prison Imagery" (*SELit*
[1994]: 65–80), Hiroyuki Koguchi in a close analysis argues that this
imagery functions as an incubator of extraordinary emotion and imagination and that while Dickinson's prison poems repeat the clichés—
walls, cages, bars, spiders, beams, darkness, and windows—the images
show the genuine struggle between confinement and liberation, the
conflict that generates the lyrical tension in her poetry.

c. 20th-Century Fiction   Book-length studies on individual 20th-cen-
tury writers this year are even slighter than those on the 19th-century.
The sole exception is *Faulkner—America Bungaku, Gendai no Shinwa*
[William Faulkner—American Literature, a Myth of Our Time] (Chu-
okoron sha) by Kenzaburo Ohashi, the foremost Japanese Faulkner
scholar. A conscientious critical biography, the monograph is intended
for the general Japanese reading public, and its clear, plain, elegant prose
make it accessible to anyone interested in Faulkner's works. Ohashi's
introduction boldly profiles the author in our time, showing how vibrant
Faulkner's fictional world is to our contemporary ethos and how feasible
a reflection that world is of our ethos. Great emphasis on earlier master-
pieces leaves Ohashi little room for Faulkner's Snopes trilogy. His intention to include much in a limited space also results in a curtailed

discussion of other important works. (No thorough textual assessment, of course, can be expected of a book of this kind.) Still, there is no better indication of Faulkner's Japanese reputation than its publication.

Several articles on Faulkner also testify to his critical popularity among Japanese scholars. Fumiko Hayashi's essay in *Literature/America/Capitalism,* "The Dynamism of Desire: Capitalism in *Pylon* and *Absalom, Absalom!"* (pp. 249–64), applies the capitalist demand/supply paradigm to his reading of the two literary texts. Toshiro Kuwabara's "The Overall Narrative Movement of *Go Down, Moses* and the Use of Popular Narrative in 'Pantaloon in Black'" (*SALit* 30: 57–74) astutely analyzes the structure of one of Faulkner's experiments in narratology.

Mikako Takeuchi's *"Barren Ground* and Ellen Glasgow's Pastoral" (*SALit* 30: 41–56) is an indispensable footnote to Watanabe's *A Study of the Feminist Novel.* Takeuchi presents Glasgow's heroine as "a forceful pioneer" who makes the barren land yield a rich harvest.

Other articles worthy of mention are Shinichi Nakashima's "Hemingway and the Spanish Civil War: *For Whom the Bell Tolls* as a Political Autobiography" (*Review of American Literature,* pp. 62–72); Yoko Nakagawa's "Why was she crying 'like an old woman?'—The Mirror and Elisa in 'The Chrysanthemums'" (*SALit* 30: 75–87) on Steinbeck's story; Kiyohiko Murayama's "Dreiser Criticism and Capitalism: Walter Benn Michaels on *Sister Carrie*" (*Literature/America/Capitalism,* pp. 196–212); and Takaki Hiraishi's "Gender Is the Night: Capitalism/Schizophrenia/Gender in *Tender is the Night*" (*Literature/America/Capitalism,* pp. 281–94).

d. Contemporary Fiction, Poetry, and Drama   Few book-length studies on contemporary American literature appeared this year. Even so, a great number of articles were published on contemporary novelists, poets, and playwrights.

The first of these, Takayuki Tatsumi's *Metafiction no Boryaku* [Metafiction as Ideology] (Chikumashobo), is a collection of previously published articles and essays, written with journalistic flourish; in its entirety the book reads like a sly apologia for metafiction. Tatsumi offers plausible readings of the contemporary sociocultural landscape on both sides of the Pacific. An insightful cross-cultural study of both American and Japanese society in the postmodern/late capitalist age, it examines the writings of Pynchon, Barth, Federman, Rudy Rucker, Yasutaka Tsutsui, and other postmodernists in relation to a "theory of metafiction." Tatsumi's chapter on Yasutaka Tsutsui, the Japanese champion of metafiction, is a full-fledged discussion of the Japanese author and the theoretics of metafiction (pp. 59–96). Tatsumi's book should be read together with two chapters in *Literature/America/Capitalism:* Motoyuki Shibata's discussion of Richard Powers's "The Counterfeit Money and the Photo: *Three Farmers on Their Way to a Dance*" (pp. 23–38); and Nobuo Kamioka's "American Literature in the Age of Electronics: Fear of Death and *White Noise*" (pp. 54–67).

Contemporary American poets also received critical attention this year. Tadao Kunishiro's "Two Sisters of Sylvia Plath" (*SALit* 30: 107–31) and Yumiko Sakata Koizumi's "The Unspeakable Mother: Sylvia Plath's 'Medusa'" (*SALit* 30: 133–47) are excellent feminist readings. In "Gary Snyder's 'Bioregionalism'" (*EigoS* 139: 106–10), Katsumi Yamasato expounds on and endorses the environmental insights in the poet's works. Tomoyuki Iino discusses the role of geography in John Ashbery's poetry in "John Ashbery's Geography and Poetry: *Rivers and Mountains*" (*EigoS* 139: 326–30).

American drama is a neglected field in Japan, but two stimulating articles appeared this year. Mitsunori Nagata's "The Mamet Syndrome and Feminism: Mamet, Kopit, and Korder" (*EigoS* 139: 170–72) is a provocative commentary on how feminism affects male-oriented writers for the American stage today. Tadashi Uchino's "The Age of Sam Shepard: From Self-expression to Representation and Then?" (*Literature/America/Capitalism,* pp. 39–53) concerns itself with the representation of the decentralized self in postmodernist society.

e. American Studies Koji Oi's *Howaito Shitii no Genei: Chicago Bankokuhaku to America teki Sozoryoku* [The White City Unmasked: The Chicago World Exposition and American Writers] (Kenkyusha) is a collection of previously published articles, but it deserves a brief comment because Oi's expertise is much valued among Americanists in Japan. Here, his apt observations on responses to the World Exposition by Adams, Howells, and Dreiser provide an interesting reading of the American 1890s.

American Culture: The Roots and the Tradition, mentioned earlier, is one of the outstanding scholarly accomplishments this year. A collection of 12 original essays by scholars in diverse disciplines, it presents a valuable assessment of American culture examined in historical contexts. The discussions of various American experiences—for example, King

Philip's War, the Salem witch trials, McCarthyism, the response to Catholicism in the WASP community, African Americans in white America, F. O. Matthiessen's suicide—constitute a kaleidoscopic picture.

Kobe College

iv Scandinavian Contributions: Jan Nordby Gretlund, Elisabeth Herion-Sarafidis, and Hans Skei

The emphasis of Scandinavian work on American literature at present is on contemporary fiction and criticism. As usual, some attention is given to Dickinson, Whitman, Hawthorne, and James, but the focus of these studies is narrow: Hawthorne and James on Rome; Whitman's sexuality, etc. The broad focus is on 19th-century writers only when they can be seen in relation to contemporary developments: Twain and David Lynch; Poe and Stephen King; Poe and psychoanalysis, etc. Southern literature gets a great deal of attention in Scandinavia. Besides an interest in Poe and Twain, there are studies of antebellum general literary history in the South and on women diarists. And in our century Faulkner, Porter, O'Connor, Lee Smith, and Alice Walker figure most prominently. Aside from Walker, however, surprisingly little interest was shown in other African American writers. Hemingway, Malamud, Updike, and Arthur Miller still survive in the Scandinavian mind as classics. But fortunately there is also the slightly disturbing presence of Henry Miller, Paul Auster, and Bret Easton Ellis. The most pleasing development is the interest in recent or contemporary American poetry with analyses, interviews, introductions, and translations. Laura Riding, Adrienne Rich, Susan Griffin, Beverly Dahlen, William Stafford, Michael Palmer, and Julie Kalendek have all received some attention, as has Wallace Stevens. Another obvious development in Denmark, Norway, and Sweden is in the number of studies on critical theory, mostly on narrative technique and on literature and context.

a. 19th-Century Poetry   In a brief article, "Dickinson's 'This is my letter to the world'" (*Expl* 51: 165–67), Domhnall Mitchell presents a reading of a poem that resists the tendency to identify the speaker of the poem with the writer herself. Mitchell finds it more reasonable to perceive the speaker as a representation of Dickinson's view of her own situation as a poet, but this reveals a conflict in the text. A wish to communicate is articulated, but the substance of that communication is withheld. All in all, Mitchell finds the poem to be a "tease, inviting intimacy while maintaining a proper distance."

Walt Whitman's homosexuality and his poetic vision of the love of comrades as an ideal of American and democratic masculinity are considered important for Danish gay history between 1869 and 1912, according to Wilhelm von Rosen's *Månens Kulør* [The Color of the Moon] (Copenhagen: Rhodos, pp. 545–69). In his treatment von Rosen makes it clear that although *Democratic Vistas* had been translated into Danish as early as 1871, it was primarily through Johannes V. Jensen's translations from *Leaves of Grass* that Whitman came to influence a generation of poets in Denmark. Jensen wrote a novel, *Hjulet* (1905), in which a homosexual character, who is a murderer and a hypocritical revivalist, quotes long passages from Whitman's poetry. Von Rosen argues that it would be unreasonable to try to sever Whitman's sexual orientation from the political, social, cosmic, and mysterious whole of his poetry and prophecy. And it is pointed out as "striking" that Whitman in his Calamus poems does not see an opposition between homosexuality and heterosexuality. Von Rosen describes how Whitman's unmistakable poetic eroticizing of male relationships influenced John Addington Symonds and Edward Carpenter in the homosexual emancipation in England in the 1870s and 1880s. In Denmark, Whitman's sexuality was described as "feminine." And it was made clear by several critics in this century's early years that their fascination with his poetry was an aesthetic enthusiasm that did not originate in "degenerate thinking."

b. 19th-Century Prose   Jan Nordby Gretlund's "1835: The First *Annus Mirabilis* of Southern Fiction" was published in *Rewriting the South* (pp. 121–30). Gretlund claims that before 1936 no other year rivals 1835 in the productivity and excellence of Southern letters. It is the literary achievement of 1835 that justifies use of the term "renaissance" in the expression the Southern Literary Renaissance. When nothing in politics seemed urgent enough to prevent them from devoting their full energy to their art, such figures as Thomas Holley Chivers, John Pendleton Kennedy, William Gilmore Simms, Augustus Baldwin Longstreet, and Nathaniel Beverley Tucker benefited from the rare moment in antebellum history and published some of their best work. It is also argued that 1835 was the last year in the 19th century in which writers in the South wrote *American* literature, "since from that year until the 1930s its writers became increasingly *Southern* in their outlook." This first flowering of literary accomplishment was brief. Pressures on the writers to become more politically oriented increased dramatically, and Southern literature became "hag-ridden" by political rhetoric.

In the same volume (pp. 131–40) Clara Juncker's "Southern Sojourn: Frances Anne Kemble" is an essay on Kemble's *Journal of a Residence on a Georgian Plantation,* which was written in 1838–39 (1863) seen as "an example of feminine historiography and autobiography." Juncker calls it "a partially suppressed tale of marital grief and disappointment." But it is pointed out that in Kemble's Christian mind her moral outrage over the treatment of the 600 slaves on the Georgia sea island plantation often came to overshadow her story of marital disenchantment and dissatisfaction with the patriarchal forces defining her. The book is in epistolary form, occupying "a feminine space between the private and the public, and between fact and fiction," Juncker claims. Kemble's choice of metaphors reveals her protest against slavery. Her bodily metaphors of maimed and suffering bodies on the plantation come to suggest the collapse of human dignity and humanity in the social body.

In his "Filosofien, den sublime terror og den kvindelige krop" [Philosophy, Sublime Horror, and the Female Body] (*Hug* 13: 44–49) Claus Bratt Østergaard writes on Freud, de Sade, and the terrifying, with references to Poe's "The Oval Portrait" and "Berenice" and with an emphasis on Poe's ideas about beauty and death. Østergaard returns to this subject in his "Den gotiske—en saer form" [Gothicism—A Strange Dimension] (*Ny Poetik* 1: 7–21). The essay, which contains a section on Poe and perversion, considers him to be the first writer to give gothicism a psychological perspective. The perverse element in Poe's fiction is supposedly created through repetition, and repetition is associated with death and attempted returns to life. Østergaard argues that the perversion becomes an ironic metaperversion when a narrator, who is also the subject of his tale, reflects on it.

In *Poe, King, and Other Contemporaries* J. Lasley Dameron shows convincingly how Poe influenced three modern-day novelists: Thomas Harris, Arthur C. Clarke, and Stephen King. Dameron claims that "it is difficult to imagine the existence of these writers if Poe had not lived." Although Poe's influence on them is mostly "indirect," it is nevertheless "substantial," especially in adopted motifs, style, and subject matter. Dameron details the parallels between Harris's *Red Dragon* and *The Silence of the Lambs* and Poe's detective stories. He then shows persuasively that King, although he "does not acknowledge Poe as one of his favorite writers," includes verbal echoes in *The Shining* of Poe's "The Masque of the Red Death" and "The Fall of the House of Usher." And King echoes "The Raven" in *Gerald's Game* and "William Wilson" in *The Dark Half.* Finally, King draws on *Pym* in *The Stand,* especially in the novel's conclusion. Clarke's three odyssey novels draw on Poe's science fiction. *2010: Odyssey Two* relies on Poe's "The Balloon Hoax" and *Pym.* Dameron concludes that often "it is Poe who first provided the essential blueprint."

Lene Østermark-Johansen's "The Decline and Fall of the American Artist: The Fatal Encounter with Rome in Hawthorne, Story and James" (*Analecta Romana* 21: 273–96) pursues the relationship between the city of Rome and the American artist in the 19th century. Østermark-Johansen has selected Hawthorne, William Wetmore Story, and Henry James as prominent representatives of changing American attitudes to the city. Rome's main attraction to them was its power to negate the native scene in their art, but this seems to have been the only idea the writers shared fully. The essay tries to establish why the American representation of the city changed so obviously in the course of the century. The political identification of American artists tended to be with the Rome of the past, whereas Italy of the 19th century was watched "with the advanced country's sympathy for a slightly backward ally." Hawthorne's notebook entries reveal the contrast between poetic Italy and prosaic America as well as his ambivalent attitude toward the city. It remains for him "a questionable and troublesome enjoyment." The essay is, however, mostly about James's changing attitude to Rome. It is argued that "in the assessment of his predecessors James also assesses himself"— that is, in relation to Hawthorne and Story and Rome. In his biography of Story, James "paints a picture of Italy as the femme fatale who mercilessly overwhelms the susceptible Story." In this way James supports the idea of Rome as a dangerous place that lures innocent Americans abroad, gives them a lesson in the ways of the Old World, and returns them disillusioned to their own country. In his final period James considered enjoyment of the Eternal City incompatible with the American artist's integrity.

In Christen Kold Thomsen's "Psykoanalytiske billeder i melodramatisk regi: Tom Sawyer og Blue Velvet" [Psychoanalytic Images in a Melodramatic Setting: Tom Sawyer and Blue Velvet] in *At se teksten* (Odense, pp. 115–25), ed. A. S. Sørensen, B. H. Jørgensen, and L. O. Sauerberg, it is claimed that in fiction and film the classic stories of psychoanalysis no longer serve as authoritative frames for interpretation. Instead, the Oedipus story, for example, has now in popular genres become a world of images colored by melodrama. The psychoanalytic motifs in the work of Stephen King and film director David Lynch are simply invoked as atmosphere-creating references. Thomsen goes on to show that in American literature this use of psychoanalytic thoughts was also employed by Mark Twain. The effect is often the sensational change of individuals, who live boring lives, into "heroic" characters who mobilize traditional moral values in order to survive a melodramatic and often irrational struggle between good and evil.

c. 20th-Century Prose Orm Øverland's "Augsburg Publishing House: The Penultimate Chapter of Norwegian-American Literature," in *Norwegian-American Essays* (Oslo: NAHA, pp. 11–27), ed. Djupedal et al., gives detailed information about the Augsburg Publishing House, which was run by the Norwegian Lutheran church. Øverland maintains that the history of Norwegian-American literature cannot be separated from its institutions, although he presents no theoretical models for this view; his discussion focuses on the significance of one press for the advancement of literature in Norwegian from about 1912 to the mid-1920s. Much of Augsburg's importance can be attributed to Anders M. Sundheim, who felt forced to retire because of demands from the church to concentrate on religious literature. Under Sundheim's leadership, Augsburg became the leading publisher of literary works in Norwegian, having Ole E. Rölvaag as one of its authors. The regular publication of the Christmas annual, *Jul i Vesterheimen* (which was discontinued only in 1957), contributed significantly to the upholding of a Norwegian-language culture in the United States. Sundheim's wish to publish books of "a religious and of a purely literary character" was of course debatable, but it clearly gave Augsburg the position Øverland claims for it. It contributed significantly to the "penultimate chapter" of the history of Norwegian-American literature, whereas the last chapter was to be written in the publishing capitals of the two nations: Oslo and New York, where Aschehoug and Harper became the important publishers. The irony, of course, is that when the best literature produced by the Norwegian culture in the United States was written, there was no longer a culture (or a public) to sustain it.

In "Den hårdkokta stilen: Hemingway och svenska författare" [The

Hard-boiled Style: Hemingway and Swedish Writers] (*Tvärsnitt* 2: 44–54) Rolf Lundén continues his work on Hemingway (see *ALS 1992*, pp. 357–58). While tracing the ebbs and crests of Hemingway's literary career in Sweden, Lundén identifies echoes of his style in a number of Swedish writers—suggesting that Hemingway's fiction for many of them has functioned as a kind of point zero, a measuring rod of precision and simplicity.

Finn Jensen's *Englen fra Brooklyn* [The Angel from Brooklyn] (Gyldendal) is subtitled "a journey through Henry Miller's universe." In reaction to the many Miller biographies, Jensen wants to break the silence on his fiction. He attempts to demonstrate that Miller's development as a writer can be seen as one continuous self-interpretation. He argues that Miller's texts represent a complicated mirror mechanism of their own creation. According to Jensen, Miller was the last of the romantic poets or the first of the Beats. Jensen admits that Miller never devised a unified cosmology, but he argues that it is obvious from what we have that Miller thought the Apollonian show was over and the Dionysian dance about to begin. Miller felt that being would once again become more important than doing. The book is a chronological study of Miller's fiction, and it is structured on his movements between New York and Paris, his friendships with Anaïs Nin and Lawrence Durrell, the notable excursion to Greece, and the final years in California. A good part (perhaps too large a part) of the book consists of quotations from Miller's fiction. Jensen claims that Miller's thoughts on culture, which were mainly a rejection of a capitalistic world order, grew out of a clash between European and American values. Miller foresaw the dangers of technology. The study is given coherence through its concentration on Miller's changing literary heroes from Strindberg, D. H. Lawrence, Balzac, and Rimbaud to Gogol. The masters are seen only through their importance for Miller. The more focused chapters on the trilogy of "The Rosy Crucifixion," *Sexus, Nexus,* and *Plexus,* are the best part of the study. In his discussion of these novels Jensen concentrates on such topics as women, suffering, passion, degradation, redemption, and the search for a Jewish identity; and he adds that Miller found that he could not realize himself simply through carnal lust. In the late fiction, sex is used primarily to illustrate the brutality, the perversion, and the callousness of life in the big city. Jensen argues that Miller always was somewhat removed from his fiction; and he concludes that Miller knew that he could not be one with his own vision if he wanted to live and communicate his message. Jensen sees Miller's fiction as the last words in Western literature before emptiness and silence.

Erik Nielsen in "Om død og tid" [On Death and Time] (*K&K* 20: 105–16), an essay on Faulkner's "A Rose for Emily," considers the story "a very generous description of Yoknapatawpha's ideological and mental profile." In the story Faulkner employs a binding motif, it is argued. Miss Emily is bound to the town and forced to embody the stable integrity of the golden antebellum years. Her life is bound psychologically by region, class, and time, and these ties make it impossible for her to live her own life. Nielsen focuses on Faulkner's use of static time and concludes surprisingly that in this story the past itself is dead. He goes on to postulate that this became Faulkner's main theme in his major novels. But Faulkner's idea of time is much more dynamic than indicated in this essay. Whatever else he wrote about the past, Faulkner never proclaimed it dead. On the contrary, he demonstrated again and again in his fiction that the present is not only what is but also what was, now remembered.

Jan Nordby Gretlund's "'The Man in the Tree': Katherine Anne Porter's Unfinished Lynching Story" (*SoQ* 31, iii: 7–16) deals with an unpublished and yet substantial manuscript. The manuscript, also tentatively titled "The Southern Story," is important primarily for the strong antiracist opinions that Porter expresses, but also for the new information it offers on white and black lives known from Porter's Miranda stories. The plot is primarily an account of a lynching and its aftermath, and the focus is on pride and shame within one household. Gretlund speculates that as pages not directly connected to the main plot began to pile up, Porter may have come to think that she was really writing a novel, and he argues that this may have been one reason she never finished it as a short story. The essay makes clear that this is not a publishable text. As it is, not even the basic structure can be determined with any certainty. But, Gretlund maintains, the manuscript contains many wonderful passages that deserve to be published, and in this essay some of them are.

Karl-Heinz Westarp's *Flannery O'Connor: The Growing Craft* (Summa) is a synoptic variorum edition of four short stories: "The Geranium" (1946), "An Exile in the East" (1954), "Getting Home" (1964), and "Judgement Day" (1964). The book attempts to give readers access to O'Connor's workshop by showing her writing on what remained basically the same material from the beginning to the end of her career.

Westarp illustrates O'Connor's habit of art in her daily routine. He details the artistic development in her fiction, from the heavy-handed use of symbolism in her first story to her growing social awareness in the 1950s and a deepening eschatological emphasis in the stories of her final year. Finally, Westarp states, O'Connor's concept of "home" is no longer "an idealized South but a symbol of a safe haven to be reached after death." By synoptically aligning the four versions of the same narrative material on facing pages, the book clarifies O'Connor's way of changing structural and compositional elements. The biggest challenge in this effort seems to have been to establish the probable sequencing of the last pages of "Getting Home" and "Judgement Day," but Westarp does so convincingly.

Lee Smith is a Southern writer whose work has begun to attract interest in Scandinavia, as evidenced by the translation into Swedish of her novel *Fair and Tender Ladies* a few years ago. In " 'Tell Me a Story. . . . I Am Starved for Stories': Storytelling, Voice, and Self-Development in Lee Smith's *Fair and Tender Ladies*" (*AmerSS* 25: 106–19) Elisabeth Herion-Sarafidis argues that in this epistolary narrative, the act of storytelling is assigned truly life-giving properties. In this discussion of Smith's strategy of telling a story through voice alone, *Fair and Tender Ladies* is seen as a text about a woman's quest for inner equilibrium; it is a book, ultimately, about self-creation. The emerging sense of self of Ivy Rowe, the sole sender of a lifetime's worth of letters, is reflected through the vitally important act of writing.

Karl-Heinz Westarp's essay "Conscience of a Decade: Arthur Miller," in *Cracking the Ike Age,* ed. Dale Carter (Aarhus, pp. 124–31), tries to show how Miller managed to live through the most turbulent years of his life by taking a stand for sincerity and personal dignity. Miller came to see the fulfillment of his social duty as a part of his self-realization. With the autobiographical *Timebends* as his point of departure, Westarp outlines "the most prominent arguments" Miller used in his defense of "the freedom of literature" against the monolithic philosophy and political intolerance of the McCarthy period. The essay also explains why Miller chose to present his truth about society through realism, although he was tempted to change to the mode of the absurd. *The Crucible* is seen as Miller's appeal for personal freedom and responsibility in the face of centralized state manipulation.

Pointing to the thematic consistency of Malamud's work, Bo R. Holmberg's "Bernard Malamuds kvarlåtenskap" [The Literary Remains of Bernard Malamud] (*Horisont* 40: 66–70) deals briefly with *The People and Uncollected Stories* from 1989, which includes the unfinished, posthumously published novel *The People* and 16 short stories. Holmberg identifies the theme of moral and spiritual change as central in Malamud's narratives—that is, a "change of heart" which signifies man's ability to learn and to assume responsibility for his fellowman.

Erik Kielland-Lund's "The Americanness of *Rabbit, Run*," in *New Essays on* Rabbit, Run (Cambridge, pp. 77–94) focuses in great detail on "the image of the United States" in Updike's novel, showing that the book in one sense shows "how we live now, in the U.S." But there is more to the novel, and most of the myths about America and the very Americanness of *Rabbit, Run* are undercut and questioned by the text itself. Kielland-Lund discusses at some length the European fascination with America, and he maintains that Updike's work relies on some of this fascination because it conveys deeper thematic and mythical structures under the surface appearance of events and actions. Perhaps, then, Kielland-Lund suggests, *Rabbit, Run* has remained popular because its America of the 1950s reflects enduring concerns of a social, psychological, and very American character. The special Americanness of *Rabbit, Run* is found in Harry Angstrom's obsession with sports and in his constant use of sports metaphors when he is thinking about sex or religion. Harry feels—in part on the basis of his basketball performances in high school—that he is cut out for something larger than the ordinary life he leads. Kielland-Lund points to this theme as the most pervasive one in the novel, and he analyzes its implications at length. "In these inchoate longings for a more satisfactory life beyond the norms of ordinary society," he writes, "Harry Angstrom is repeating one of the most pervasive themes in American literary history, as well as acting out many of the ideals of Emersonian transcendentalism." When Harry flees from what he sees as his imprisonment, the novel in a concrete way becomes even more American. His flight is down the highways of America, and the text becomes a web of American names, ways, and phenomena. Kielland-Lund concludes that it is "the open-minded quest for answers to fundamental questions which is really the most significant American tradition" that the novel upholds. The detailed analyses of the text itself, however, indicate that the Americanness of *Rabbit, Run* is found in the specific, the local, and the personal rather than the abstract and general.

Birgit Olsen's "Et amerikansk mareridt" [An American Nightmare] (*K&K* 20: 117–34) discusses the reception of Bret Easton Ellis's *American*

Psycho. Olsen summarizes the novel's publishing history, mentions its negative critical reviews, and speculates about the continued attention being paid to it. She rejects the notion that the novel is simple speculation on images of violence. Instead, she claims that it has a permanent disturbing effect as an image of the United States in the 1980s. The real reason it has caused such an uproar, Olsen claims, is that *American Psycho* strikes a nerve in America's image of itself; it is an unwelcome portrait of a country in which everything is falling apart. Olsen's essay is rewarding reading as a counterbalance to the usual interpretations. As in his two previous novels, Ellis depicts a world from which all individuality has disappeared. There is no historical continuity in this world, and the novel has no coherent progression. Its language is superficial and cliché-ridden because the characters have no emotions or individual characteristics. The structure of traditional values and norms has broken down, and only meaningless exterior signs still exist. The same is true of the novel's structure, which is superficially imposed. The main character is unable to distinguish between this ersatz reality and his hallucinations. That is, the novel offers no positive or redeeming counterweight to the modern world. According to Olsen, the book's shocking effect has little to do with its devotion to scenes of pure violence; much more likely, that effect results from treating all norms and values as obvious illusions.

Hans Skei analyzes modern American crime fiction in "Er heltene trette" [Are the Heroes Tired?] (*Samtiden* 2). Heroic fiction in general is discussed, and that discussion is applied to such hard-boiled male writers as Hammett and Chandler. Skei speculates on the fact that female writers dominated the who-done-it genre for so long, whereas male writers had the whole field of tough crime fiction to themselves. Sara Paretsky and Sue Grafton, among others, are treated, with emphasis on their heroines to show how women writers have entered this once exclusively male field.

Brita L. Seyersted's "The Image of Europe in Writings by African-American Women" (*ArAA* 18: 37–52) deals with the image of the Old World and with the use of Europe as literary material in the writings of African American women in the 19th and 20th centuries. Seyersted's interesting approach is planned as part of a book-length study. In "Signifying Difference: Alice Walker's Black Feminine Aesthetics," pp. 199–208 in *Multiculturalism and the Canon of American Culture* (Amsterdam: VU University Press), ed. Hans Bak, Clara Juncker sees Walker's *Temple of My Familiar* as rooted in the oral tradition of African American narrative, a modern version of "front-porch storytelling." According to Juncker, the presence of the orality of black feminine writing comforts some and disturbs others. The chorus of alternating voices in the novel comes to represent a black communality, which explodes Anglo-American discourses with laughter, song, and body. Walker's women insist on interruption and repetition in their stories and construct their own rites and temples. A useful bibliography of contemporary "African-American Women's Studies" is supplied.

d. 20th-Century Poetry Alan Shima's *Skirting the Subject: Pursuing Language in the Works of Adrienne Rich, Susan Griffin, and Beverly Dahlen* (Almqvist and Wiksell) might be considered a Swedish contribution to a growing academic interest in the work of experimental poets in the United States. Intrigued by "women's language," Shima pursues feminist interest in the relationship between language and reality as manifested in the works of three poets involved in writing intellectual, didactic poetry and in challenging masculine modes of representation and power. Arguing that "women's language" is a blend of "hypothetical speculations, political intentions, interpretive practices, and ethical convictions," Shima explains that his skirting of the subject is a "critical strategy which implements exploratory readings." This allows him to proceed indirectly in examining the critical assumptions and textual strategies of Rich, a prominent figure in the feminist movement, and the less well-known Griffin and Dahlen. While Dahlen's work is aesthetically related to process-oriented "language" poetry, Rich and Griffin both focus on the codes and structures of language from a feminist perspective. All three are committed to the politics of feminism, but their textual strategies differ. Out of Rich's involvement with what she deems a necessary revision of the history of women spring texts that seek to bare the complex relationship between women's experience and the conceptual modes by which that experience is represented. Her poetic project is described by Shima as one "of recovery and *documentation.*" Focusing his discussion on her essay "When We Dead Awaken" and poems from the collection *The Dream of a Common Language,* he charts Rich's "gynocentric search for female identity." Rich calls for a "new language which articulates past silences," and she finds in the credibility of women's actual experiences a guarantee of authentic expression. Shima considers Griffin a successor to Rich in her concern with the connections between social structures and their sustaining, patriarchal discourses. He points to a resemblance in the way "women's language" is manifested in their texts. Griffin also raises the question of how "women's language" can occur in a thoroughly patriarchal society in her book *Woman and Nature: The Roaring Inside Her.* As ordinary genre distinctions are dissolved, the "dialogical elements of the text suggest a reuniting of women to the physical and spiritual being within themselves and to the primal forces of nature." While Shima's angle on Griffin's text is to treat it as a "*dramatization* of gender-marked discourses," when it comes to Dahlen's writing, especially her later work *A Reading,* he views it as a project of invention, where the poet seeks to textualize "repressed, non-translatable forces and impulses of subjectivity" (see *ALS 1991,* p. 467). Differing, then, from the documentary modes of Rich and from the dramatizations of Griffin, Dahlen's work shows a minimum of narrative and historical continuity as it "warps the traditional distinctions between fact and fiction, between intention and chance." It is Shima's contention that the emerging feminist paradigm reconstructs "woman" conceptually and offers a challenge to the dominant modes of discourse. Focusing his study on the homogeneous consensus of "women's language," he yet identifies its heterogeneous manifestations in these three poets' work.

Thomas E. Kennedy interviews William Stafford for *APR* (22, iii: 49–55). Stafford suggests that for him tradition "is not the tradition of literature but of human discourse." He does not believe it makes sense to tag a poet with being subjective, as "objective things are convergences of a lot of subjectives." He also does not believe in creating an audience or doing something to please it. He strongly opposed the Gulf War, which demonstrated a "failure of imagination," and the "new kind of orthodoxy" that makes "every oppressed person a hero and a martyr." He does not care whether or not poetry is experimental, though he has "more respect for current prose writers than current poets." Stafford considers himself "a-language-that-I-meet-when-I-talk-to-the-mailman kind of poet." In general, he compares himself to an oyster in that "the oyster takes what the tide brings in."

Poul Borum has been very active in translating American poetry into Danish, including Wallace Stevens's "Adagia" for *Den Blå Port* (25–26: 141–43). And for the same periodical (27–28: 157–70) he has translated and introduced 10 poems by Laura Riding. Borum considers her one of the great lyricists of our century. Her combination of rational analysis and musical diction is unique, he claims. Borum is also a herald of new American talent. He has translated Michael Palmer's *An Alphabet Under-*

ground, which has been published as a dual-language edition (Ringkøbing: After Hand), and he has introduced and translated poems by Julie Kalendek (*Information* 24 Sept., p. 9).

e. Theory and Criticism   Frits Andersen's " 'Waste' og 'Value' i fortaellingens økonomi" [Waste and Value in the Economy of the Narrative], *EST V: Fortellingens teori* (Oslo: NAVF, 1992, pp. 7–22), ed. Karin Gundersen et al., is primarily about Thomas Pynchon's *The Crying of Lot 49.* Pynchon shows us, according to Andersen, that narrative theory has a tendency to overlook anything that resists the story's progression. The realism of the novel rests on a unified presentation of both the plot and its obvious opponents such as waste, description, and noise. But Pynchon (like Brautigan) questions our notions of value and waste by demonstrating that what we usually consider junk, superfluous rubbish, and irritatingly disturbing trash may be the most important elements in a novel's creation. Waste is valuable in its ability to release new energies and resources. To the same volume (pp. 71–84) Morten Kynderup contributes "En invitation: fri adgang til utilgaengeligheden" [In Invitation: Free Access to Inaccessibility], an essay on Paul Auster's New York Trilogy, particularly *The Locked Room.* The novel seems to have a straightforward, traditional plot with a happy ending. But the plot contains in itself, Kynderup claims, the idea that the truth is never simple and the promised solution never comes. The novel is finally about itself. And a close reading reveals that in many places the text undercuts its narrative authority by declaring its own impossibility. In another essay in the same volume, "På leksikalske lekeplasser [On Lexical Playgrounds]: Paul Auster, the New York Trilogy" (pp. 165–78), Hans Skei discusses the intertextual and metafictional strategies used by Auster in creating this strange, postmodern trilogy, with particular emphasis on the uses to which Poe, Melville, and Hawthorne are put.

Auster's work is also the subject of Peter Kirkegaard's "Cities, Signs, and Meaning in Walter Benjamin and Paul Auster" (*OL* 48: 161–79). No thorough examination of Auster's work is attempted, but the essay serves well as a catalog of the novelist's themes and techniques. Kirkegaard writes on Benjamin's theories of big-city life, allegory, and language and exemplifies them with passages from Auster's work. Kirkegaard's purpose is to discuss Benjamin's proper position in relation to more recent theories of signification. It is not argued that the novelist has studied Benjamin's work. What is found interesting is that so many of Benjamin's ideas, concepts, and interests prove themselves "fully operational" in Auster's novels.

In the field of critical theory there is evidence of a growing concern that the study of literature should not be separated from the study of the historical, social, and political dimensions of culture. This is the context of Øyunn Hestetun's criticism. "Text, Context, and Culture in Literary Studies" (*AmerSS* 25: 27–37) is a purely theoretical essay in which she presents a conflict between "textualizing and contextualizing approaches to the study of literature." Maintaining that this opposition is overcome by critics who have understood that "the text is an inscription of culture," she discusses this "third way" by referring primarily to Gilbert and Gubar's *The Madwoman in the Attic* and Jameson's *The Political Unconscious,* both of which overcome the dichotomy between formalist approaches and those relying on the extraliterary. Hestetun's assertion that the type of analysis written by contemporary feminist or Marxist critics has been done before is even more interesting. She finds that Henry Nash Smith's *Virgin Land* represents a negotiation between textual and contextual analysis. Hestetun's essay is closely related to her concerns in *A Prison-House of Myth? Symptomal Readings in* Virgin Land, The Madwoman in the Attic, *and* The Political Unconscious (Almqvist and Wiksell). Willing "to affirm nothing but fragmentation, negation, and the deferral of meaning," postmodernism, Hestetun suggests, leaves us locked in passivity and paralysis. She proposes that a "hermeneutic of affirmation in combination with a hermeneutic of suspicion will at least create a space for agency, for the possibility of critical intervention and the continued revision of meaning." She begins with a strategic maneuver (which is definitely a simplification) that enables her to distinguish between "intrinsic" approaches and the "contextual" study of literature. She then settles for the contextual. Arguing for deep structural relationships between texts usually considered to advocate disparate approaches, Hestetun's own work is an interesting illustration of her proposed strategy. She believes that despite "obvious differences in terms of theoretical framework terminology, motivation, aims, and expressed politics," Smith's "myth and symbol school" approach, the feminist criticism of Gilbert and Gubar, and Jameson's Marxist hermeneutic exhibit similarities in critical assumptions and interpretive strategy. Her rationale for selecting these texts is their sharing of what she calls a dual hermeneutic—"a discourse of demystification coupled with a discourse of affirmation"—and their refusal of deconstructive methods. While it is true that all three texts focus on the cultural production of meaning, performing critical analyses that can be described as cultural critique, some obvious problems of comparison exist. For instance, Smith focuses mainly on aspects of popular culture in the United States, while Gilbert and Gubar foreground manifestations of high culture produced by women, dealing with both Britain and the United States. The lack of consensus concerning the concept of culture among these texts might also be considered problematic. But while Hestetun recognizes the clear gap between Smith's cultural holism and Gilbert and Gubar's overt politicizing of "the issue of sociocultural hegemony in terms of gender or class," she argues that her concern is with continuities and similarities. In her attempt to escape the conflict between different trends in contemporary approaches to the study of literature, between textualizing and contextualizing critical strategies, she proposes a third, intermediary way of reading. By "symptomal reading" she means a strategy for opening the text to different layers of embedded meaning, seeking to situate the text in a cultural context and, in the effort to get at cultural specifics, to move beyond the text proper. On the lookout for connections, symptomal reading does not shy away from either affirmative statement or generalizing gesture. Turning away from what she deems a discourse of negation, Hestetun suggests that critical theory should be prepared to talk about a remythologizing, "in the mode of a hermeneutic of affirmation, in recognition not only of the permanence of ideology, but also in recognition of our need for a defining center in line with an ideology of hope."

The Political Unconscious is about to be published in a Swedish translation. A shortened version of the introduction to this translation appeared in the Swedish journal *Res Publica*. This issue also contains a long interview with Jameson conducted in October 1993 by Sara Danius and Stefan Jonsson, and a new essay on *The Political Unconscious* by Jameson himself, "*Eftertankar om* Det politiska omedvetna" [Afterthoughts Concerning *The Political Unconscious*]. In "Historisera alltid! Fredric Jameson's kartläggning av samtidskulturen" [Always Historicize! Jameson's Mapping of Contemporary Culture] (*Res Publica* 24: 3–19) Danius characterizes Jameson's critical project, his ongoing investigation of contemporary culture, as one of totalization, "an operation which does not proceed from a totality but instead from the idea that the totality has become invisible and has vanished from the horizon of lived experience." Considering a text to be a symbolic act in the sense that the writer/text seeks unconsciously to "solve or neutralize social contradictions in a symbolic manner," Jameson attempts, instead of determining the meaning of a text or describing its structure, to bare the circumstances under which a (particular) text acquires meaning. His critical model, writes Danius, consists of double elements, containing simultaneously a hermeneutic of suspicion and a hermeneutic of sympathy.

Odense, Uppsala, Oslo Universities

21 General Reference Works

Gary Scharnhorst

Budget cuts suffered in recent years by academic and research libraries have taken their toll by discouraging the publication of new reference works, to judge from the ebb tide of new titles this year. Of all the chapters in *ALS 1993,* this survey of reference tools is virtually the only one to register a net reduction in scholarly productivity. For whatever reason, moreover, the general reference market is increasingly a niche filled by new releases from the presses of Garland, Gale, Greenwood, and G. K. Hall. Mirroring the broader trends in literary studies, most of these new volumes, however modest in number, are devoted to women's writings, ethnic and regional literatures, and popular fiction.

Perhaps the single most significant new reference publication this year is *Columbia History of American Poetry.* Unlike *The Columbia History of the American Novel* a couple of years ago, this volume by its editorial practice does not presume to interrogate the very premises of literary history. Rather, the 31 chapters of *CHAP,* most of which contain proper names in their titles, divide the topic in a manner that is more familiar than faddish. However traditional its organization, the *CHAP* is hardly revanchist in purpose. Largely bereft of jargon and scholarly apparatus, the essays without exception are written by distinguished poets and critics. Among the contributions that warrant special mention are those by John McWilliams on "The Epic in the Nineteenth Century" (pp. 33–63), Lawrence Buell on "The Transcendentalist Poets" (pp. 97–120), Cynthia Griffin Wolff on Dickinson (pp. 121–47), Donald Pease on Whitman (pp. 148–71), Jeffrey Meyers on Poe (pp. 172–202), Helen Vendler on Stevens (pp. 370–94), and Arnold Rampersad on "The Poetry of the Harlem Renaissance" (pp. 452–76). Several essays are discussed in more detail in earlier chapters of *ALS 1993.*

Thomas M. F. Gerry's *Contemporary Canadian and U.S. Women of*

Letters: An Annotated Bibliography (Garland) is the sort of hybridized project that illustrates some of the hazards faced by bibliographers in the present climate of literary studies. Gerry lists the writings of 16 North American women "who have written both poetry and/or fiction, and literary criticism and/or theory," among them Carolyn Heilbrun and Sandra Gilbert. (He inexplicably omits Gilbert's chapter on "Poetry: The 1940s to the Present" for *ALS 1979*.) That is, Gerry crosses the borders of gender to compile lists of writers across geographical boundaries who have transgressed the margins of genre. In his introduction he nods in the direction of the theoretically minded feminist critics for whom he is presumably writing, acknowledging the "gaps" in his coverage and the "arbitrariness" in his system, even apologizing as a male for his "complicity with the enemy" and his "inability to escape to any great degree [his] upbringing and education in patriarchal society." The larger question in my mind, however, is one of audience. I would not bet my next royalty check that there are many readers for such a book. It seems designed for library sales almost exclusively, and who will check it from the shelves is anyone's guess.

Much as Gerry's theoretical assumptions seem to complicate his bibliographical task, Susanne Carter's assumptions seemingly shape the parameters of her research and the type of evidence she uncovers. In *Mothers and Daughters in American Short Fiction: An Annotated Bibliography of Twentieth-Century Women's Literature* (Greenwood) Carter lists 242 stories by 192 women which explore the mother-daughter relationship, divides them thematically into seven chapters (e.g., "Abuse and Neglect," "Death"), and summarizes their plots. Carter's compilation is selective, however, focused mostly on stories published within the past two decades. Significantly, some omissions (e.g., Charlotte Perkins Gilman's "Martha's Mother" in the April 1910 issue of *The Forerunner*) tend to undermine Adrienne Rich's claim, which Carter echoes, that the subject of mothers and daughters has been "silenced" until recently.

More satisfactory on all counts is *Contemporary Lesbian Writers of the United States: A Bio-Bibliographical Sourcebook* (Greenwood), ed. Sandra Pollock and Denise D. Knight. Each of the 100 entries in this volume, on such figures as Rita Mae Brown, Audre Lorde, and May Sarton, contains a biographical sketch, discussion of the writer's major work, an overview of critical responses, and a primary and secondary bibliography. Pollock and Knight's preface is substantive, theoretically informed, and mercifully free of hand-wringing and tortured intellectual posturing. Editors

Joseph M. Flora and Robert Bain continue their series of reference guides to Southern writers in *Contemporary Fiction Writers of the South: A Bio-Bibliographical Sourcebook* (Greenwood), with 49 entries by 47 contributors in the familiar five-part Greenwood format. Unlike their earlier volume *Fifty Southern Writers After 1900* (see *ALS 1987*, p. 497), which focused on the mostly white male authors of the Southern Renaissance, Flora and Bain's new sourcebook describes a more diverse group of regional writers, including Brown, Gayl Jones, Cormac McCarthy, Pat Conroy, Gail Godwin, and John Kennedy Toole. This guide will shortly be followed by Flora and Bain's companion volume on contemporary Southern dramatists, essayists, and poets.

Casper LeRoy Jordan's monumental *Bibliographical Guide to African-American Women Writers* (Greenwood) should also serve to bolster scholarship on such established or newly canonized writers as Toni Morrison, Alice Walker, and Zora Neale Hurston, as well as help to reclaim from the margins such neglected figures as Mary E. P. T. Lambert, who published a novel and a collection of poems in 1867 and who, to date, has yet to attract any significant critical attention. Apart from a few specialists, moreover, who would have guessed that Hurston discussed Robert Taft's candidacy for president in the *Saturday Evening Post* in 1951? Or that Walker interviewed Eudora Welty for the *Harvard Advocate* in 1973? In all, Jordan lists publications by and about more than 900 figures, beginning with Lucy Terry in 1746. Although he lists selected secondary sources without comment or annotation, his compilation of primary texts is a model of its kind—detailed, accurate, and exhaustive.

Hall issues two new volumes in its Reader's Guide to Mystery Novels series this year. Both are apparently pitched at the mystery buff market. In *A Reader's Guide to the Private Eye Novel*, Gary Warren Niebuhr identifies about a thousand titles by 90 writers in the subgenre that, originating in the *Black Mask* serials of the 1920s, includes the hard-boiled detective stories of Dashiell Hammett, Raymond Chandler, Mickey Spillane, and Robert B. Parker. In *A Reader's Guide to the American Novel of Detection*, Marvin Lachman identifies more than 1,300 additional works featuring amateur detectives by 166 writers such as Erle Stanley Gardner, Gore Vidal ("Edgar Box"), and Carolyn Heilbrun ("Amanda Cross"). Their lists of pseudonyms, settings, and recommended texts notwithstanding, Niebuhr's and Lachman's plot synopses are thin gruel indeed. The series is also afflicted with a stubborn case of neat distinctions. Neither of these sourcebooks lists the works of John D.

MacDonald, whose Travis McGee novels and others presumably will be included in a forthcoming series volume on "suspense" stories, or the Joe Leaphorn/Jim Chee novels of Tony Hillerman, which presumably will be included in the volume on "police procedurals." Of related interest: *The Fatal Art of Entertainment* (Hall), Rosemary Herbert's interviews with 13 mystery writers, among them Hillerman and Sue Grafton.

Popular fiction of a different stripe is surveyed in *Science Fiction and Fantasy Book Review Annual 1991* (Greenwood), ed. Robert A. Collins and Robert Latham, a mammoth survey-review of new writing which, despite its title, covers calendar year 1990. Some 550 of the 880 pages are devoted to a total of 670 critical notices, although the range of books reviewed—everything from Thomas Pynchon's *Vineland* and reprints of Poe to cyberpunk and the screenplay of *Abbott and Costello Meet Frankenstein*—is a bit too catholic for my taste. Each of the other gerrymandered sections—science fiction, fantasy, horror, young adult fiction, and children's literature—sports an overview of the year's events and a recommended reading list, with occasional supplemental essays (e.g., Michael A. Morrison and Stefan Dziemianowicz's "The Legacy of Howard Phillips Lovecraft," pp. 117–29), profiles of such authors as Greg Bear, and an annual index of award-winning formula stories.

Would but Thomas E. Kennedy's *Index to American Short Story Award Collections, 1970–1990* (Hall) have been appended to a more substantial critical study. Overpriced at $40, this 116-page hardcover simply lists the several hundred tales in the dozens of anthologies awarded the Pushcart Prize, the AWP Short Fiction Award, the Drue Heinz Literature Prize, the Flannery O'Connor Award, the Iowa School of Letters Award, or published over the years in the University of Illinois Short Fiction series. At the very least, such an index should have been more inclusive. As Kennedy allows, several other fine series, including the Milkweed National Fiction Award and the Triquarterly Award series, are omitted.

In contrast, Robert L. Gale's *Cultural Encyclopedia of the 1850s in America* (Greenwood) should prove a handy reference for generalists and specialists. A project similar in design and purpose to Gale's cultural dictionary of the 1890s, published last year (see *ALS 1992*, p. 209), this volume contains about 450 entries from the predictable (Melville, *The Scarlet Letter*) to the arcane (Gadsden Purchase, Adah Isaacs Menken). Gale's snapshots of the decade are by no means skewed in favor of Brahmin culture; as he notes in his preface, the "efforts of women writers" were "wrongly undervalued in the 1850s. *Ruth Hall* is worth a hundred songs of Hiawatha."

Similarly ambitious in its reach and thorough in its grasp of detail is the voluminous *Cambridge Guide to American Theatre.* With nearly 2,500 cross-listed entries, many of them illustrated, on playwrights, performers, composers, set designers, producers, theaters, plays, repertory companies, and theatrical themes and topics, this tool is one of the most engaging works of scholarship I have ever encountered. A compendium of useful information, it deserves a wide audience among American theatrical historians and cultural critics.

Finally, as David Nordloh noted last year in this space (see *ALS 1992,* p. 368), the Dictionary of Literary Biography series (Gale), a project of superencyclopaedic breadth with well over 130 volumes in print, "appears to be slowing a bit" as it exhausts "the list of eligible authors, genres, and periods." No doubt this barrel has been tapped so long and been drawn so low there is little left but foam—excepting only Robert Gale's forthcoming volume on Western American writers. Still, this year occasions the publication of three new volumes in the series germane to this chapter: *American Proletarian Culture: The Twenties and the Thirties,* ed. Jon Christian Suggs; *American Newspaper Publishers, 1950–1990,* ed. Perry J. Ashley; and *American Short Story Writers Since World War II,* ed. Patrick Meanor. Ashley's volume includes entries on 54 figures born between 1870 and 1941, including S. I. Newhouse, Arthur Hays Sulzberger, William Randolph Hearst, Jr., and Rupert Murdoch. Meanor's volume includes entries on 40 fiction writers born between 1909 and 1961, most of them frequent contributors to little magazines and academic reviews, including Paul Goodman and the unjustly neglected John Fante.

University of New Mexico

Author Index

Subject Index